GEORGIA INTESTATE RECORDS

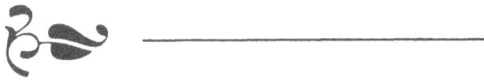

GEORGIA INTESTATE RECORDS

By *Jeannette Holland Austin*

CLEARFIELD

Reprinted for
Clearfield Company, Inc. by
Genealogical Publishing Co., Inc.
Baltimore, Maryland
2005

Foreword

his work contains abstracts of the earliest intestate records of Georgia, or, more precisely, abstracts of the intestate records of fifty-seven Georgia counties formed before the 1832 Land Lottery. Basically, it is a finger-tip guide to the estate records of those who died intestate (without making a will), extracted from such records as letters of administration, guardianship bonds, administrators' bonds, minutes of the Inferior Court, loose and original papers, minutes of the Court of Ordinary, Superior Court minutes, writs, and miscellaneous estate papers.

Since it would have been almost impossible to abstract *all* Georgia estate records, I selected the first extant record book (containing the earliest records) of most of those counties formed before the 1832 Land Lottery, as well as Fulton (1853), White (1857), Dawson (1857), and Webster (1853). I abstracted all relevant genealogical information therein, but of course additional information might be found in later record books.

Besides the name of the deceased and the dates of the various estate records, information given in the abstracts includes some or all of the following: names of administrators, guardians, and sureties (often relatives of the deceased), names of surviving spouse and children, names of orphan children and heirs, and, where a will is recorded, the names of legatees. In addition, each entry contains a reference to the county and a specific source citation to assist the genealogist in further research.

Jeannette Holland Austin

TABLE OF SOURCES

Baldwin, L/A (1832-1852)
Bibb, Administrators and Guardians Bonds (1828-1851), AB, GB
Bryan, Court Records, Writs, Bk B (1810-1815), CR
Bryan, Minutes of Inferior Court, (1794-1811), MIC
Bryan, Minutes of Superior Court, (1794-1797), MSC
Bryan, Superior Court Writs (1805-1809), Writs
Bulloch, Minutes of Inferior Court, Bk X (1815-1843), MIC
Bulloch, Wills and Miscellaneous, Bk B (1816-1836), Misc
Bulloch, Wills and Miscellaneous, Bk B, 3-A (1816-1836), Misc
Butts, Administrators and Guardians Bonds (1828-1851), AB, GB
Butts, Equity Records (1826-1841), ER
Butts, Equity Records (1837-1845), ER
Camden, Minutes Superior Court (1797-1843) (1802-1852), MSC
Chatham, Administrations (1783-1791), Adms
Cherokee, Minutes of Court of Ordinary (1833-1841), OM
Cherokee, Wills and Bonds, Vol. B (1848-1860), WB
Clarke, Administrators Bonds, Bk A, (1801-1827), AB
Clarke, Loose Papers, LP
Cobb, Bond Bk A (1855-1857)
Cobb, Index to Estates (1865-1900), A-C only
Cobb, Minutes of Interior Court, Civil Proceedings (1865-1877), MIC
Columbia, Estates (1788-1798), Ests
Dawson, Wills and Bonds (1857-1862), WB
DeKalb, Administrators Bonds, Vol. 2 (1852-1863), AB
Dooly, Inventories & Apprs., Bks A, E, I, N (1838-1847), I&A
Dooly, Ordinary's Docket, (1847-1901), OD
Effingham, Minutes of Court of Ordinary, Bk 3 (1827-1850), OM
Effingham, Miscellaneous Estates, Bk B (1791-1802), Misc
Elbert, Adms and Guardians Bonds, Will Bk (1809-1812), AB, GB
Elbert, Adms and Guardians Papers, Will Bk (1803-1806), AB, GB
Elbert, Adms, Guardians Returns, Bk A, B, C, E-F (1804-1809), AB, GB
Emanuel, Appraisements of Estates (1812-1841), A
Emanuel, Guardians and Administrators Bonds (1812-1849), AB, GB
Fayette, Adms and Guardians Bonds, Returns (1829-1854), AB, GB
Franklin, Inventories, Minutes, Wills (1804-1807), IMW
Franklin, Ordinary Minutes (1786-1813), OM
Fulton, L/A, L/G (1854-1856)
Fulton, L/A, L/T, L/G (1856-1868)
Gilmer, Ordinary's Miscellaneous Records (1836-1845), Misc
Glynn, Minutes of Inferior Court (1817-1828), MIC
Greene, Estates, Bk A (1791-1803), Vol. 5 (1821-1826), Ests
Greene, Misc Wills, Inventories, Apprs, Bk A (1787-1801), Misc
Gwinnett, Administrators Bonds, Bk E (1871-1876), AB
Habersham, Minutes of Inferior Court, Bk 4A (1824-1836), MIC
Hall, L/A, L/T, L/G Guardianship (1829-1856)
Hancock, Wills and Ests, AA, P. 1-175, (1794-1815), AA
Hancock, Wills and Ests, AAA, P. 1-76, (1794-1815), AAA
Hancock, Wills and Ests, AAAA, P. 2-191 (1794-1815), AAAA
Harris, General Index to Estates (1828-1865)
Harris, Wills, Bonds, Bk A (1833-1849) (1828-1865), AB, GB
Houston, Guardians Bonds (1852-1855), GB
Jackson, Remnants of Minutes of Court of Ordinary, (1812-1824), OM
Jasper, Minutes of Court of Ordinary and Wills, Vol. I, OM
Jasper, Returns, Vol. 5 (1821-1823), P. 1-47, AR
Jasper, Wills, Inventories, Apprs, Returns, Bk A (1807-1817), WAR
Jasper, Wills, Inventories, Apprs, Returns, Bk A (1808-1821), WAR
Jefferson, Wills, Apprs, etc., Bks 1, 3 (1796-1827)
Jones, Guardians and Admrs Bonds (1811-1815), AB, GB
Jones, Minutes of Court of Ordinary (1816), OM

Laurens, Admrs and Guardians Bonds, Vol. A (1808-1823)
Lee, L/A (1857-1860)
Lee, Minutes of Superior Court (1853-1855), MSC
Liberty, Docket of Estates (1783-1793), Ests
Liberty, Minutes of Inferior Court (1805-1819), MIC
Lincoln, Guardians Bonds (1821-1839), GB
Lumpkin, Admrs and Guardians Bonds (1850-1852), AB, GB
Montgomery, Admrs and Guardians Bonds (1830-1840), AB, GB
Morgan, Administrators and Guardians Bonds (1816-1827), AB, GB
Morgan, Superior Court Writs (1809-1811), SCW
Oglethorpe, Minutes of Inferior Court (1794-1802), MIC
Oglethorpe, Minutes of Inferior Court (1800-1805), MIC
Paulding L/A, L/T, L/G (1856-1860)
Paulding, L/A, L/T, L/G (1856-1866)
Pike, Minutes of Inferior Court, Bk A1 (1823-1829), MIC
Putnam, Administrators and Guardians Bonds (1809-1814), AB, GB
Randolph (now Jasper) Wills, Sales, Invs (1835-1840)
Randolph-Jasper (now Jasper), Miscellaneous Estates (1810-1814), OM
Richmond, Adms and Guardians Bonds, Divisions (1777-1830), AB, GB
Screven, Minutes Court of Ordinary, Bk I (1811-1829), Index only, OM
Stewart, Minutes of Inferior Court (1834-1844), MIC
Tattnall, Inventories & Apprs (Wills, Bonds, Sales) (1837-1840), I&A
Tattnall, Minutes of Inferior Court 1805-1816), MIC
Troup, Guardians Bonds (1848-1849), GB
Twiggs, Miscellaneous Deeds, Wills, Estates (1809-1900), Misc
Warren, Admrs Bonds (1811-1835), AB
Warren, Admrs Bonds, Bk A, Deed Bk A, (1811-1835), AB
Warren, Minutes of Inferior Court (1794-1807) (1807-1814), MIC
Washington, L/A, Vol. B (1829-1843)
Webster, Court of Ordinary Docket (1854-1875), OD
White, Admrs and Guardians Bonds, Bk I (1858-1870), AB, GB
Wilkes, Admrs and Guardians Returns, Bk I (1809-1816), Retns
Wilkes, Mixed Records (1781-1783), MxR
Wilkes, Mixed Records, Wills, Admns, Deeds (1777-1778), MxR
Wilkes, Original Records (1777-1830), OR

                    Explanation of Abbreviations:

A= Appraisement
ADMS= Administrations
AR = Annual Return
AB = Administrator´s Bond
Ests = Estates
ER = Equity Records
GB = Guardian´s Bond
I&A = Inventories and Appraisements
IMW = Inventories, Minutes, Wills
L/A = Letters of Administration
L/D = Letters of Dismission
L/G = Letters of Guardianship
LP = Loose Papers
L/T = Letters of Testamentary
MIC = Minutes of Inferior Court
Misc = Miscellaneous
MSC = Minutes of Superior Court
MxR = Mixed Records
OD = Ordinary´s Docket
OM = Ordinary´s Minutes
OP = Original Papers
secs = securities
surs = sureties
WAR = Wills, Inventories, Appraisements
WB = Will Book

GEORGIA
INTESTATE
RECORDS

AARONS, Zachariah, decd, John J. Dickerson, admr, James L. D. Harbin, sur, 7/4/1854, Cherokee, AB
ABBOTT, Armstead F., orph of John, decd, Prudence S. Abbott, gdn, Thomas D. Perkinson, Wm Perkinson, sur, 5/9/1859, Cherokee, GB
ABBOTT, Docie, decd, William Henderson, admr, 1889, Cobb
ABBOTT, Elijah, decd, Holland McTyeire, admr 2/12/1829, John McTyre, sec, Richmond, AB
ABBOTT, Elijah N., orph of John, decd, Prudence S. Abbott, gdn, Thomas D. Perkinson, Wm Perkinson, sur, 5/9/1859, Cherokee, GB
ABBOTT, John, decd, William R. Abbott, admr, Thomas D. Perkinson, sur, 10/11/1858, Cherokee, AB
ABBOTT, Levi, decd, William Henderson, admr, 1888, Cobb
ABBOTT, Theodora F., orph of John, decd, Prudence S. Abbott, gdn, Thomas D. Perkinson, Wm Perkinson, sur, 5/9/1859, Cherokee, GB
ABBOTT, Thomas D. P., orph of John, decd, Prudence S. Abbott, apptd gdn, Thomas D. Perkinson, William Perkinson, surs, 5/9/1859, Cherokee, GB
ABERCROMBIE, James, decd, William Sitton issued L/A 2/2/1841, Eli W. Narramore, Jesse D. Hardage, secs, Hall, AB
ABERCROMBIE, Robert, decd, Mrs. Nancy Abercrombie caveats application for leave to sell lands of decd 3/1/1813, Warren, MIC
ABERCROMBIE, Robert (Colonel), decd, Nancy Abercrombie, William Jones, Aaron Smith apptd temp admrs, 5/4/1812, Warren, MIC
ABERCROMBIE, Robert, decd, Mrs. Nancy Abercrombie, wid, William Jones, Aaron Smith, temp admrs, Ezekiel Smith of Hancock Co, Solomon Lockett, sur, 5/4/1812, Warren, AB, MIC
ABERCROMBIE, Robert, decd, Nancy Abercrombie, William Jones, Aaron Smith, admrs, 5/4/1812, AB, Warren
ABERCROMBIE, William C., decd, Robert Abercrombie, admr, 2/8/1802, William Flournoy, M. Hubert, surs, 11/2/1801 L/D gtd 1/3/1806, Warren, AB, MIC
ABERNATHY, Caleb, decd, John G. Thurmond issued L/A 4/3/1815, Laurens, AB
ABLE, A. R., decd, late of Edgefield Dist, S. C., LWT pvd 9/5/1859, J. L. Able, exr, Paulding
ABRAHAMS, Jacob, decd, 6/23/1836 appraisal, Richmond
ACCORD, John, decd, Rudolph Strawbaker apptd admr, 5/19/1784, Chatham, Adms
ACHORD, Lewis D., decd, Edmund Womack, admr, 1836, Bulloch, MIC
ACORD, Nathaniel, John M. Wade, gdn, p. 156, Screven, OM
ACREDGE, John, decd, John Curry issued L/A 11/4/1839, Washington
ADAIR, Bozeman, decd, J. B. Adair, admr, J. H. Craton, B. H. Adair, sur, 3/5/1866, Paulding, AB
ADAM, Francis, decd, LWT pvd 3/7/1842, Micajah Bland was apptd exr, Washington
ADAMS, Alsey, orph of Israel E., decd, Hiram Dobbs, gdn, John W. Dobbs, sur, 1/7/1856, Cherokee, GB
ADAMS, Ann Porter, youngest ch of Florida Virginia Adams (wife of Habersham J. Adams of Putnam Co.), decd, 1885, age 25 on 4/25/1890; heirs of Florida V.---Carro J. White, Mamie Lampkin (wife of Cobb Lampkin), Nettie J. (Henrietta) Adams, Clarke, LP
ADAMS, Benjamin T., decd, Nancy Adams issued L/A 10/1863; Nancy and W. D. E. Adams issued L/A 1/1866, Webster, OD
ADAMS, C., decd, Henry Lasseter issued L/A 1/1864, Webster, OD
ADAMS, David, decd, 1796 retns, recpt of Booker B. Easter and wife, Moneyca, being late widow of decd, for her share of sd est; 1796-1801 pd Elizabeth & Sally Aken & George Alexander, T. Aken, Fleming Aken, Mary Barden, Elbert, AR
ADAMS, David J., decd, Robt Adams Eldon, issued L/A 11/19/1851, Harris. AB
ADAMS, Elizabeth, orph of Israel E., decd, Hiram Dobbs, gdn, John W. Dobbs, sur, 1/7/1856, Cherokee, GB

1

ADAMS, F. W., H. J. Adams, trustee, 1878, Cobb
ADAMS, Gardner, decd, Milton A. Candler, admr, issued temp L/A
11/12/1860, permanent L/A 1/14/1861, C. Murphey, sur, DeKalb, AB
ADAMS, Hiram, orph of Israel E., decd, Hiram Dobbs, gdn, John W.
Dobbs, sur, 1/7/1856, Cherokee, GB
ADAMS, H. M., decd, Alice and John Q. Adams, exrs, 1897, Cobb
ADAMS, H. S., minor, 1872, Cobb
ADAMS, Israel E., decd, James M. Fielder, admr, George W. Rainey,
sur, 2/7/1853, Cherokee, AB
ADAMS, James, decd, David Adams applied for L/A 1/29/1791; James
Tuttle, Sr., Thomas Burk, John Wever, Sr., apprs, Elbert, AR
ADAMS, James, decd, LWT dtd 12/5/1829 pvd 5/4/1829 by Robert
Norris names wife, Nancy, "my children", Habersham, MIC
ADAMS, James, decd, acct of est by Jon Adams, acting exr
1/10/1799, pd Wm Allen, Jean McGaughey, legatees, Robert Harper,
Robt Chambers, Esther Mills, Hancock, AA
ADAMS, James, Shirley Sledge, gdn, Cullin Sledge, Robert Adams,
Wilkin Jackson, John Dean, 11/2/1812, Jones, GB
ADAMS, James C., decd, Samuel G. Castleberry issued L/A 5/3/1865,
Wesley McAllister, W. B. West, secs, White, AB
ADAMS, Jesse, decd, John M. Adams, admr, Samuel Adams, sur,
11/9/1857, Cherokee, AB
ADAMS, John, decd, LWT pvd 5/6/1816, John Cowan, admr, makes retn
1/6/1817, Jackson, OM
ADAMS, John, decd, div 1835 to heirs: Oliver M. Porter, in rt of
wife, Alphia T., Judith Adams Jacksons, Hezekiah D. Adams,
Clarke, LP
ADAMS, John F., decd, Rufus R. R. Asbury issued temp L/A
4/21/1866, A. J. Comer, sec, White, AB
ADAMS, John Maxie, minor, Rebecca Adams, gdn, 1877, Clarke, LP
ADAMS, John, Sr., decd, James S. Elliott, admr, 11/3/1856, John
L. Evins, sur, DeKalb, AB
ADAMS, John W., decd, Littleton Mathis issued L/A 7/2/1839,
Washington
ADAMS, Mary, decd, 1877 heirs-Mary, Max, Dora, ch of Flournoy
Adams, decd, Herbert Parker, Henry Walker, Wiley Adams, ch of
Julia Adams, decd, Habersham Adams, Anna Stiles, Margaret
Clements, F. Lampkin, Mary Jackson, Robt Adams, Clarke, LP
ADAMS, May E., minor, R. E. Cason, gdn, 1875, Cobb
ADAMS, Melissa, decd, W. P. Clay, J. T. Adams, admrs, 1900, Cobb
ADAMS, Nolie G., minor, Rebecca Adams, gdn, 1877, Clarke, LP
ADAMS, Salathael, decd, James Spruill, admr, 9/1/1862, W. E.
Spruill, Stephen Martin, surs, DeKalb, AB
ADAMS, Sarah F., minor, Joseph F. Adams, gdn, 1/27/1863, Harris
ADAMS, Seth K., decd, Oliver H. P. McClendon, admr, Asa Buttrill,
Hiram H. Doss, surs, 10/7/1845, Chatham, Adms
ADAMS, Seth K., decd, Oliver H. P. McClendon, admr, John Andrews,
Joseph Little, surs, 11/17/1845, Butts, AB
ADAMS, Sylvania, James Jowers issued L/G 1/1861, Webster, OD
ADAMS, William, James Jowers issued L/G 1/1861, Webster, OD
ADAMS, William, decd, L/A issued A. A. Adams 10/1873, Webster, OD
ADAMS, William C., decd, Hezekiah W. Scovill, admr, 1/26/1826
bond, William Manly, sur, Clarke, AB
ADAMS, Wilson, orph of Israel E., decd, Hiram Dobbs, gdn, John W.
Dobbs, sur, 1/7/1856, Cherokee, GB
ADAMSON, Dorothy, decd, LWT dtd 11/12/1794 pvd 1/5/1801 by Peter
Boyle, dau, Mary; Anner, Elizabeth, Alexander & Charles James
McDonald, ch of my dau, Mary & Charles McDonald, Hancock, AAA
ADARE, (also sp ADAIR, Susanna, orph of John, decd, Bozeman Adare
(also sp Adair) apptd gdn 3/3/1806, Jackson, OM
ADCOCK, John, decd, John A. Adcock, admr, 11/6/1837; Lydia
Adcock, gdn, Harris

2

ADCOCKS, William, LWT presented, Mary Ann Adcock, extrx, 9/5/1856, Paulding
ADKINS, Joseph, decd, John Drew, Judah Drew, admrs, 8/3/1818, Emanuel, AB
ADKINS, Joseph, decd, John Drew, admr, 9/12/1818, Emanuel, A
ADKINS, Joseph, orph of Joseph, decd, William Fountain, Hardy Anderson, gdns, 3/1/1819, Emanuel, GB
ADKINSON, Joseph A., decd, Jesse H. Goss issued L/A 11/3/1823, Morgan, AB
AGERET, Fanny, a free woman of color, applied to ct for appointment of Samuel Clarke as her gdn 6/2/1818, Camden, MIC, GB
AGERETT, George, "free child of color" Belton A. Copp, gdn applied for order directing Thos H. Miller, exr of Agerett est to pay est funds on hand since 1/1/1820 (George & Rosaline only heirs), 1/6/1823, Camden, MIC
AGERETT, George, colored child of John, Belton A. Copp, gdn, required to give bond, 6/3/1823, Camden, MIC
AGERETT, John, decd, Thomas H. Miller qualified exr, 10/6/1817, Camden, MIC
AGERETT, Rosaline, Belton A. Copp, gdn, applied for order directing Thos H. Miller, exr of Agerett est to pay est funds on hand since 1/1/1820 (George & Rosaline only heirs), 1/6/1823, Camden, MIC
AGERETT, Rosaline, colored child of John, Belton A. Copp, gdn, required to give bond, 6/3/1823, Camden, MIC
AGERTON, Sabrey, decd, B. F. Porter issued L/A 3/5/1855, Allen Blake, sec, Hall, AB
AIKEN, sisters--Betsey decd 1853, Frances decd 1845, Polly decd 1845, Rhoda decd 1857 and Tabitha decd 1858, Clarke, LP
AIKEN, John, decd, William Byron and William Aikens qualified exrs of LWT 5/2/1814, Warren, MIC
AKEN Joseph, decd, Sally and Thomas Aken apply for L/A, 4/5/1796; apprs: James Tait, George Darden, Cornelius Sale; purchasers at sale: Thomas, William and Sally Aken, Elbert, AR
AKERS, William, decd, Nancy Akers, Thomas Terry, admrs, 9/6/1858, Thomas Mathews, Tarlton Carter, surs, DeKalb, AB
AKIN, Elizabeth, decd, Benjamin Kemp issued permanent L/A w/LWT annexed 1/1867; W. L. Akin to sell lands 9/1867, Webster, OD
AKIN, Henry M., decd, d. 2/29/1876, his wife, Susan S. d. 3/5/1876; Leonard Schemenell, gdn of minor ch: Lucy Cage, age 12 and Aldia T., age 3, Clarke, LP
AKIN, Jacob C., decd, Elizabeth Akin apptd admx 11/1854; William L. Akin issued L/A 7/1856; William P. Cato applies for L/A 9/1856, Webster, OD
AKIN, James, decd, Elihu Atwater was apptd admr, 6/9/1802, Camden, MIC
AKIN, John, decd, LWT pvd 5/2/1814, Warren, MIc
AKIN, Nancy, decd, Peter Alexander, exr, 3/24/1809, Elbert, AB
AKIN, Samuel bound to James E. White as an apprentice to learn blacksmith trade 1/6/1812, Elbert, GB
AKIN, Samuel, decd, James Akin applies for admn 5/6/1816, Jackson, OM
AKINS, John, decd, John Akins, admr be donis non w/LWT annexted 1/5/1824, Benjamin Hurt, sur, Warren, AB
AKINS, William, decd, Joseph D. McFarland, James Bailey, admrs, 1/5/1824, Nelson Gunn, Benjamin Crenshaw, secs, Warren, AB
AKRIDGE, Calvin Walker, over age 14, son of Virgil W. Akridge, decd, John Calvin Johnson, gdn, 5/16/1860, Clarke, LP
AKRIDGE, Simeon A., decd, John T. Akridge issued L/A 9/3/1860, Fulton

AKRIDGE, Virgil W., decd, Thaddius B., Calvin W., Louisa M. and
Lavenia W., orphs, 1850, Clarke, LP
ALBRITTON, John, decd, Richard and Henry Albritton issued L/A
12/4/1815; Jethro Weaver, apptd admr de bonis non 7/2/1821,
Laurens, AB
ALDEN, Hannibal, decd, Horatio Alden, admr 1/6/1821, Saml Hale,
sec; heirs recpts: David T. & Almeda Child, Jabez W. & Lydia
Giddings, Josiah & Martha Converse, Clarissa Ellsworth, Zephaniah
Alden, Horatio & Joseph Alden, Jr., Richmond, AR
ALDRICH, Job, decd, Riley Sprague, admr, Andrew J. Miller, sec,
3/5/1832, Richmond, AB
ALDRIDGE, Ellenor, Nancy Aldridge, gdn, 1880, Cobb
ALEXANDER, Adam, decd, Mrs. Louisa F. Alexander, admx, gtd leave
to sell 200 acres, "High House" tract, 130 acres in Sunbury,
2/3/1817; and admx gtd leave to sell Sunbury lots 11/11/1817,
Liberty, MIC
ALEXANDER, Elijah A., natural gdn of his ch: Jane Louisa,
Lawrence Melvin, William Rufus and Thomas Jefferson Alexander,
minors, William A. Alexander, sec, White, GB
ALEXANDER, Elizabeth, dau of Robert of North Carolina, Robert
Collins, one of legatees, in rt of wife, applies to partitition
personal est 1/7/1822, Jasper, OM
ALEXANDER, Elizabeth Adair, now wife of Robert Collier, dau of
Robert J. Alexander of Lincoln Co., N. C., John Moore apptd gdn,
5/7/1821, Jasper, OM
ALEXANDER, George, decd, Mary and William Alexander apply for
L/A, 9/4/1809, note to Wm Pickings signed by Nancy Alexander and
Peter Alexander, exrs 10/31/1806; purchasers at sale: Mary,
Polly, Lucy, Mourning and Wm Alexander, Elbert, AB
ALEXANDER, George, decd, William and Mary Alexander, admrs, 1810
retns; heirs recpts: R. Taliaferro Gains, William Alexander, John
F. Cook and John Hulme 2/25/1811, Elbert, AR
ALEXANDER, James, decd, pvd 10/7/1791, wife Tabitha, ch: Bethiah;
bro. John Lister Alexander, Greene, Misc
ALEXANDER, J. B., decd, J. Y. Alexander, admr, 1890, Cobb
ALEXANDER, John, decd, Moses Alexander apptd admr, 1/1/1838,
Randolph, OM
ALEXANDER, John, decd, W. R. Montgomery, admr, 1881, Cobb
ALEXANDER, John, orph of John, decd, Smith Alexander, gdn,
1/8/1833, Clarke, LP
ALEXANDER, John H., tr for mother, Nancy, wid of Smith Alexander
& her ch-Jno H., Sarah Gann, Henry's wf, Mary Gann, Seaborn's wf,
Elizabeth Stephens, Nathan's wf, David, Wm, Nancy, Henry, Elijah,
Thos, Eliza, all Cobb Co., 1862, Clarke, LP
ALEXANDER, Mary, Milley S. Alexander, gdn, 1882, Cobb
ALEXANDER, Mary, dau of Robert J. Alexander of Lincoln Co., N.
C., John Moore apptd gdn 5/7/1821, Jasper, OM
ALEXANDER, Mary E., decd, E. X. Lester, gdn of minor orphs: Nelly
and Ida, 3/5/1894, Clarke, LP
ALEXANDER, Matthew, decd, L/A issued William B. Wofford 4/6/1835,
Habersham, MIC
ALEXANDER, Nathan, decd, J. R. Alexander, admr, 1881, Cobb
ALEXANDER, Nathaniel, decd, Mary Alexander applied for L/A
5/10/1790 on her husband, Greene, Misc
ALEXANDER, P. W., decd, Theresa Alexander, extrx, 1886, Cobb
ALEXANDER, R. G., decd, J. Y. Alexander, exr, 1870, Cobb
ALEXANDER, Robert, decd, Samuel Tate, exr, makes retn 7/1843;
John P. Alexander, gdn of minor heirs: Margaret Ann, Narcissa
Ann, released 9/18/1843, Gilmer
ALEXANDER, Robert, son of Robert J. Alexander of Lincoln Co., N.
C., John Moore apptd gdn 5/7/1821, Jasper, OM

4

ALEXANDER, Samuel, decd, Moses Alexander, admr, Joseph Hill, sec, 9/10/1822, Warren, AB
ALEXANDER, Samuel D., orph of John, decd, Bedford Landferd, gdn, 1/4/1841, Clarke, LP
ALEXANDER, W. C., Josie Alexander, gdn, 1892, Cobb
ALEXANDER, William, decd, John N. Alexander issued L/A 3/7/1853, James Roberts, Benjamin J. Rice, Wm A. Fowler, James Black, secs, Hall, AB
ALEXANDER, William, decd, recpts of Ezza Alexander & Standley Jones for their share dtd 8/29/1809; Peter & Nancy Alexander, exrs; recpt of Nathl Allen, the gdn of James Head, to settle bond given to heirs of James Head; recpt of William Page for his share, Elbert, AR
ALEXANDER, W. S., (Dr.), decd, W. H. Fuller apptd gdn of: Anna (age 18), Sallie (age 12), Charley (age 8), ch of sd decd who recently died in Ga.´s lunatic asylum, 3/19/1890, Clarke, LP
ALEYWINE Lena, John Dunn, gdn, 1889, Cobb
ALEYWINE, Salley, John Dunn, gdn, 1889, Cobb
ALEYWINE, Zacharia, decd, Irene Aleywine, wid, 1889, Cobb
ALFORD, Benjamin, decd, John T. Alford, admr, 9/6/1852, James Pierce, sur, DeKalb, AB
ALFORD, Bynum, decd, Elijau Stewart, admr, 1/12/1852, Paul A. Harilson, Wm Goldsmith, surs, DeKalb, AB
ALFORD, Zadock, decd, Ludowick Alford issued L/A 5/3/1824, John M. Butler, William Cole, secs, Morgan, AB
ALFORD, Zadock, decd, Ludowick Alford, gdn of orphs: James Floyd, David Sherrod and S. Warren (?) 3/15/1826, William O. Copeland, sec, Morgan, GB
ALFRED, Eliza, orph of Haywood, decd, Matilda Alfred, gdn, 9/3/1849, Cherokee, GB
ALFRED, James, orph of Haywood, decd, Matilda Alfred, gdn, 9/3/1849, Cherokee, GB
ALFRED, Mary G., orph of Haywood, decd, Matilda Alfred, gdn, 9/3/1849, Cherokee, GB
ALFRED, Nancy, orph of Haywood, decd, Matilda Alfred, gdn, 9/3/1849, Cherokee, GB
ALFRED, Sarah, orph of Haywood, decd, Matilda Alfred, gdn, 9/3/1849, Cherokee, GB
ALFRED, William C., orph of Haywood, decd, Matilda Alfred, gdn, 9/3/1849, Cherokee, GB
ALGER, James, decd, Sarah Alger, wid and admx, Bryan, Writs
ALLBRIGHT, Catharine, decd, Holder Hudgins issued L/A 11/5/1838, Zaccheus and Beverly Hudgins, secs, Hall, AB
ALLEN, Absalom, minor of James and Nancy, Daniel Ramey, gdn 1/16/1817, Joseph Brown, sur, Clarke, GB
ALLEN, Barbery, orph of George, chose James Robertson her gdn, George Famer, sec, 3/2/1807, Oglethorpe, OM
ALLEN, Betsy, minor of James and Nancy, Daniel Ramey, gdn 1/16/1817, Joseph Brown, sur, Clarke, Gb
ALLEN, Clarisy W., minor orph of George Allen, Fanny Allen, gdn, Mary Bullock, sec, 3/2/1807, Oglethorpe, OM
ALLEN, Charles C., decd, W. P. McClatchey, admr, 1894, Cobb
ALLEN, Drury, decd, LWT 1826 wife-Elizabeth, grch-Pleasant, Young D, Barbara, Robt, Polly (Josiah´s ch), Susannah, Drury, Lewis, Chas, Elizabeth, Josiah, Nancy, Martha Pyron; Nancy, Clement´s wid; Stokes Allen, Young D. Allen, Nancy Yarborough, Pike, MIC
ALLEN, Elisha, decd, George T. Allen, admr, 11/8/1824, Abel Funderburk, George Kellum, Benjamin Allen, surs, Warren, AB
ALLEN, Elizabeth, decd, Robert Allen, admr, retn 1/2/1808, Richmond, AR

5

ALLEN, Fanney, minor orph of George Allen, decd, chose Wyatt
Bullock her gdn, Winfrey Lockett, Stephen Allen, sec, 3/2/1807,
Oglethorpe, OM
ALLEN, George, decd, Mary Allen, gdn of orphs: Whitmell and
Elizabeth, 5/3/1819, Morgan, GB
ALLEN, George, decd, Mary L. and John R. Allen, admrs 5/29/1822,
Anderson Watkins, sec., Richmond, AB
ALLEN, George, decd, Stephen Allen, Absalom Ramey, admrs, 9/1806,
Oglethorpe, OM
ALLEN, Henry, minor son of George, decd, chose Stephen Allen gdn,
Wyatt Bullock, Alexander Davis, secs, 9/5/1809, Oglethorpe, OM
ALLEN, James apptd gdn of his minor children: Absalom, Betsy and
Nancy (or Naomey) 12/6/1819, Absalom Ramey, David Shay, surs,
Clarke, GB
ALLEN, James, apptd gdn of his ch (and wife, Nancy)--Absalom,
Betsey and Naomey, minors, 12/6/1819, Daniel Ramey apptd gdn
1/16/1817, Clarke, LP
ALLEN, James, decd, Payton R. Jenkins, gdn of orphs: Nathaniel
N., Henry J., James N. and Eliza C., 2/6/1816, William Jenkins,
George Washington Jenkins, secs, Morgan, GB
ALLEN, Jane, orph of William F., decd, Sarah Allen apptd gdn
11/5/1849, Benjamin Cleveland, Willis Darden, secs, Troup, GB
ALLEN, John, decd, Bryan Allen, gdn of Susanna Johns, commonly
called Susanna Allen, minor, reputed dau of decd 5/2/1814,
Laurens, GB
ALLEN, John, decd, John McDade, Jr., admr 1/6/1842, Jesse Kent,
sec, Richmond, AB
ALLEN, John, decd, Mary Allen dismissed as admx 11/7/1836,
Bulloch, MIC
ALLEN, John, decd, inv and appr by Alexander Brannen, William
Brannen, Jesse Moore, 3/30/1835, Bulloch, Misc
ALLEN, John, orph of John, decd, Bryan Allen, gdn, Laurens, GB
ALLEN, Lula E., Thomas M. Allen issued L/A 11/1857, Webster, OD
ALLEN, Mary T., orph, is bound 8 yrs. to W. T. Leonard,
5/11/1858, White, GB
ALLEN, Matilda, Abner Camp, testamentary gdn of, apprs apptd
12/1853, Fayette, AB
ALLEN, Naomi, minor of James and Nancy, Daniel Ramey, gdn
1/16/1817, Joseph Brown, sur, Clarke, GB
ALLEN, Nathaniel B., minor orph of George Allen, Fanny Allen,
gdn, Mary Bullock, sec, 3/2/1807, Oglethorpe, OM
ALLEN, Nemeses L., minor orph of George Allen, Fanny Allen, gdn,
Mary Bullock, sec, 3/2/1807, Oglethorpe, OM
ALLEN, Polley H., orph and minor of George Allen. Fanny Allen,
gdn, Mary Bullock, sec, 3/2/1807, Oglethorpe, OM
ALLEN, R. A., decd, J. O. Allen, admr, 1900, Cobb
ALLEN, R. A., decd, Susan A. Allen, extrx, 1878, Cobb
ALLEN, Robert, decd of Savannah, William Clark, Matthew Clark,
Solomon Shace, exrs of LWT 1/17/1791, Chatham, Adms
ALLEN, Robert, decd, Elizabeth & Robt Allen, admrs 8/3/1801;
purchasers: Elizabeth, Drury & Robt Allen, Lewis Collins; pd
Elizabeth West, Drury, Jesse, Robt, Young & Wm Allen, Stephen
Williams, Stephen Norris, Levin Collins, Richmond, AB
ALLEN, Samuel, decd, Alexander M. Allen, admr 3/2/1840, Etheldred
Tarver, Christopher C. Averett, sec, Richmond, AB
ALLEN, Samuel, decd, Francis Allen applied for L/A 1/18/1796,
Greene, Misc
ALLEN, Samuel, decd, Sherwood Allen, admr, Gideon Allen, Benjamin
Allen, secs, 3/3/1823, Warren, AB
ALLEN, Sarah Frances, orph of William F., decd, Sarah Allen was
apptd gdn 11/5/1849, Benjamin Cleveland, Willis Darden, secs,
Troup, GB

6

ALLEN, Sherwood, decd, Sarah Armstrong, widow, admx 9/19/1800, Fanny Forsuth, sec, Richmond, AB
ALLEN, Susannah B., minor orph of George, decd, Fanny Allen, gdn, Mary Bullock, sec, 3/2/1807, Oglethorpe, OM
ALLEN, Temperance Ann, orph of William F., decd, Velvan Thomason apptd gdn 11/5/1849, Richard F. Thomason and John Goram, secs, Troup, GB
ALLEN, Valentine Brazell applied for Peyton Skipwith to be apptd as his gdn 4/14/1807, Camden, MIC, GB
ALLEN, Washington, decd, John F. Espy, admr, Wyatt Wilson, sur, 6/5/1876, Gwinnett, AB
ALLEN, William bound to Fulton Kemp, p. 131, Screven, OM
ALLEN, William, decd, Hugh Montgomery, exr, made retns 8/7/1815; Robert Allen and William Allen, legatees, ask for division 8/7/1815, Jackson, OM
ALLEN, William, decd, John M. Hawkins, admr, R. M. Brown, sur, DeKalb, AB
ALLEN, William, decd, LWT pvd 1/13/1795 names wife, Margaret, and Jince McConel Finney and William Allen, Greene, Misc
ALLEN, William, decd, LWT pvd 10/6/1806, Jackson, OM
ALLEN, William F., decd, Churchill Allen apptd gdn of orphs: Sarah Frances and Jane, Benjamin Cleveland and Willis Darden, secs, 11/5/1849, Troup, GB
ALLGOOD, John W., decd, John E. Allgood and Francis Allgood, exrs, 1897, Cobb
ALLISON, Alexander, decd, shopkeeper, Sarah Allison, admx, 9/17/1787, Chatham, Adms
ALLISON, John R., decd, John A. Beard, admr, 9/21/1825, William E. Jackson, sec, Richmond, AB
ALLISON, Margaret, decd, non-cupative LWT witnessed by Rebecca Walker, Mary Huskey, Elizabeth Juskey, and William Berry, John Allison, surs, 1/4/1808; William B. Allison, admr, dismissed 7/6/1812, Warren, MIC
ALLISON, Robert W., decd, Matthew T. Barber, admr, Thomas J. McMichael and James R. McCord, surs, 1/13/1815, Butts, AB
ALLISTON, Charles, orph of Charles W., decd, William H. Hester, apptd gdn, 1/8/1866; sd orph is under age 14 and the son of the present wife of W. H. Hester; inheritance due Charles from LWT of Bryant Walters, decd, Clarke, LP
ALLMAN, Phillip, decd, Thomas Palmer of Savannah, Ga., carpenter, admr, to make inventory 3/27/1783, Chatham, Adms
ALLWELL, Hugh, decd, appraisers report 6/1796; Matthias Maher, Charles Tubman and David Reid, apprs, Richmond
ALMOND, Augustus W., decd, L/A issued Talitha F. Almond 7/2/1866, Fulton
ALSABROOK, Martha A. L., minor orph of Anderson, decd, Alexander D. Wimberly, gdn, 4/1/1861, Fulton, GB
ALSABROOK, Martin A. L., orph, Alexander D. Wimberly apptd gdn 4/1/1861, dismissed 6/23/1866, Fulton, GB
ALSABROOK, Sarah A. R., minor orph of Anderson, decd, Alexander D. Wimberly, gdn, 4/1/1861, Fulton, GB
ALSTON, Philip H., decd, Sarah D. Alston, widow, presents LWT for lawful probate 7/1832, Habersham, MIC
AMASON, Uriah, decd, Edward L. Langman issued L/A 11/4/1840, Washington
AMBROSE, David, decd, Gracy Ambrose and Henry T. Morgan apply for L/A 11/12/1832, Effingham, MIC
AMOSS, C. M., decd, B. B. Amoss issued L/A 2/2/1863, Fulton

ANCAUX, Lidia, decd, John M. Berrien apptd admr 1/7/1839, Bulloch, MIC
ANCIAUX, Lydia, decd, inv and appr by Jonathan Griner, Jason Floyd, John Mikel, John Waters, General E. Mikell, 2/1/1839, Bulloch, Misc
ANDERS, William, decd, John Timberlin and Ann Anders issued L/A 1/1/1810, Laurens, AB
ANDERSON, Abram, decd, Susannah and William Anderson issued L/A 10/1/1866, Thomas J. Sears, sec, White, AB
ANDERSON, Adolphus, minor, William Smith, admr, 1/10/1859, Harris
ANDERSON, Albert Elmers, orph of Edward R., decd, Mary A. M. Anderson, gdn, 1/13/1854, Clarke, LP
ANDERSON, Ally, decd, Hezekiah Anderson, exr, p. 116, Screven, OM
ANDERSON, Brazar Cook, decd, Mrs. Sarah Anderson issued L/A, Greene, Misc
ANDERSON, Carolous, decd, Owen Fountain, admr, appraisal 10/31/1829, Emanuel, A
ANDERSON, Charles E. H., orph of Edward R., decd, Mary A. M. Anderson, gdn, 11/25/1851, Clarke, LP
ANDERSON, David, decd, John Anderson, Mrs. Mary Anderson, Andrew Walthour, qualified exrs, dismd 12/28/1784, Liberty, Ests
ANDERSON, David, decd, Micagee White and Mourning Anderson issued L/A 5/2/1814, Putnam, AB
ANDERSON, Eli, decd, Robert J. Cowart, admr, George Hoye, sur, 9/2/1850, Cherokee, AB
ANDERSON, Elizabeth, minor, retn to Mary Anderson, gdn, 1840, Butts, ER
ANDERSON, Elizabeth, orph of James, Mary Anderson, gdn, Nathaniel Anderson, sec, 12/16/1837, Butts, GB
ANDERSON, Emery F., orph of James C., decd, Nancy C. Anderson, gdn, 11/23/1843, Clarke, LP
ANDERSON, Henry, Ella Anderson, gdn, 1891, Cobb
ANDERSON, Henry N., D. N. Anderson, gdn, 1893, Cobb
ANDERSON, H. S., decd, D. N. Anderson, admr, 1891, Cobb
ANDERSON, J. A. G., John Anderson, gdn, 1855, Cobb, BB
ANDERSON, James, decd, David Kimbell, John Anderson, admrs, 12/1838 pd Mary Anderson, gdn for James, Elizabeth, Martha & Mary; David Anderson, heir, pd sh; also David Kimbell, John, Nathan & Isham Anderson, their sh 5/21/1840, Butts, ER
ANDERSON, James, decd, David Kimbell, John Anderson, admrs, Nathaniel Anderson, Robert B. Saunders, sec, 2/15/1836, Butts, AB
ANDERSON, James, decd, list of property, 1836, Butts, ER
ANDERSON, James, orph of James, Mary Anderson, gdn, David Anderson, sec, 12/16/1837, Butts, GB
ANDERSON, John, decd, Honour Anderson apptd admx 2/15/1784, Wilkes, MxR
ANDERSON, John, decd, Robert W. Wilson, james Wilson, Andrew Walthour, qualified exrs 11/4/1789, Liberty, ests
ANDERSON, Leila, Leila H. Anderson, gdn, 1894, Cobb
ANDERSON, Martha, minor, retn on est with Mary Anderson, gdn, 1840, Butts, ER
ANDERSON, Martha, orph of James, Mary Anderson, gdn, John Anderson, sec, 12/16/1837, Butts, GB
ANDERSON, Nathan, decd, Richard Anderson issued L/A 10/28/1805; 9/2/1806 Charlotte, Nelson and Jackson, minor orphs, are destitute and Sylvester Nelson apptd gdn, Jackson, OM
ANDERSON, Thomas, decd, Mrs. Susannah Anderson, admx 11/5/1790, Chatham, Adms
ANDERSON, William, decd, David Hall was apptd admr, 6/1/1812, Camden, MIC
ANDERSON, William P., decd, Saxon Anderson, admr, 1896, Cobb

ANDERSON, William W., orph of James C., decd, James W. Anderson, gdn, 11/6/1843, Clarke, LP
ANDERSON, W. P., decd, Catherine Anderson, admx, 1885, Cobb
ANDERSON, Zadock, decd, Sarah E. Anderson issued L/A 5/4/1863, Abijah Williams, sec, White, AB
ANDREWS, C. C., decd, Julia Andrews, wid, admx, 1878, Cobb
ANDREWS, David, decd, J. B. Andrews, admr, James W. Andrews, sur, 2/6/1876, Gwinnett, AB
ANDREWS, Edwin R., Philip H. Lundy, James A. Wooten, gdn, 12/10/1838, Harris
ANDREWS, Elbert P., decd, John Moore, admr, 5/5/1834, Petery Cody, Sion Hill, Joseph Ford, surs, Warren, AB
ANDREWS, Emma, Julia E. Andrews and M. P. Appling, apptd gdns, 1878, Cobb
ANDREWS, Garnett, decd, Jane (Genney) Andrews, apptd admr, 3/1807, Oglethorpe, OM
ANDREWS, Isham, decd, John and Sarah Corneliuson, qualified admrs, 11/21/1788, Liberty, Ests
ANDREWS, John, bound to William Pickron, p. 68, Screven, OM
ANDREWS, Martha, orph of Robert, John Andrews, gdn, William Jarrell, John Goodman, James R. McCord, 12/7/1839, Butts, GB
ANDREWS, Micajah, decd, William Harvey and wife, Elizabeth, admrs, Lewis Gardner, Daniel Marshall, secs; appraisers: Daniel Marshall, Ambrose Jones, Jeremiah Lampkin and John Peake, Richmond, AB
ANDREWS, Nancy, orph of Robert, John Andrews, gdn, William Jarrell, John Goodman, James R. McCord, sec, 12/7/1839, Butts, GB
ANDREWS, Robert, decd, John and Walter S. Andrews, admrs, 1841 retn; div 4/7/1841 to heirs: Sarah Andrews, wid, J. B. Carmichael, John Andrews, Thomas H. Connel, W. J. Woodward, Martha, William, Sarah and Walter S. Andrews, Butts, ER
ANDREWS, Robert, decd, Walter S. Andrews, admr, John Andrews, Willis Jarral, David L. Duffey, David J. Bailey, Stephen Bailey, Thomas Folds, sec, 7/8/1839, Butts, ER
ANDREWS, Robert, decd, sale 11/27/1839; Thos H. Connell, Margaret Connell (formerly Andrews), John B. & Mary Carmichael (formerly Mary Andrews), Walter S., John, Wm, Nancy, Martha & Sarah Andrews, ch, div prop 3/5/1840, Butts, ER
ANDREWS, Sarah, orph of Robert, John Andrews, gdn, William Jarrell, John Goodman, James R. McCord, sec, 12/7/1839, Butts, GB
ANDREWS, Thomas, bound to Elijah Lipsese, p. 68, Screven, OM
ANDREWS, Warren, decd, Payton Baker, admr, Jeremiah Beall, James Pace, secs, 3/23/1818, Warren, AB
ANDREWS, William, decd, David Andrews, gdn of orphs: Howell, Polly, James, Micajah, Caty, 12/7/1812, Lauresn, GB
ANDREWS, William, orph of Robert, John Andrews, gdn, William Jarrell, John Goodman, James R. McCord, sec, 12/7/1839, Butts, GB
ANESLEY, Madison, orph of John H., decd, James Barber, gdn, 3/1/1841, Clarke, LP
ANGEL, Ann, decd, Bartlett Johns, exr, failed to qualify 7/7/1812, Jackson, OM
ANGLIN, James, decd, LWT pvd 4/17/1778, ch: John, David, William, Henry, Catherine, Wilkes, MxR
ANSLEY, Benjamin, decd, tailor, d. intestate, William Ray apptd admr 6/5/1783, Chatham, Adms
ANSLEY, Benjamin, decd, William Ray of Savannah, bricklayer, admr, apptd admr 8/20/1784, Chatham, Adms
ANSLEY, Epsy, William Ansley apptd gdn of his dau, 5/3/1813, Warren, MIC
ANSLEY, Thomas, decd, LWT pvd, Abel, Samuel, Thomas and Joseph Ansley qualified exrs 3/6/1809, Warren, MIC

ANTHONY, Cicero H. apptd gdn of his minor ch: John D. F., Uler E.
N. and Rosa R., all under age 14, est of their grparents, John S.
and Elizabeth O. K. Freeman, decd, 1875, Clarke, LP
ANTHONY, William A., orph of Joseph C., decd, Mark Anthony, gdn
11/7/1825, Samuel C. Cole, sec, Lincoln, GB
APPLEBY, William, decd, James Appleby issued L/A 9/4/1809,
Jackson, OM
APPLETON, Samuel, decd, John Finn, admr, 1826 retn; John Finn
apptd gdn 1/16/1820 of Sarah Jane, minor orph (Sarah Jane died
8/23/1837), Richmond, AR
APPLEWHITE, James J., decd, 4/1844, David C. Sears, exr, apprs:
William Sessions, John Little, Robert Bell; purchasers at sale:
James J., Jesse, G. W. and John Applewhite, G. W. and R. A. Bell,
C. A. Beall, etc., Stewart, Adms
APPLEWHITE, Robert, decd, 3/1840, Robert and Jesse Applewhite,
admrs; apprs: Joseph Wood, John Sampson, Sampson Bell, David C.
Sears; purchasers at sale: Elizabeth, G. W., John and Robert
Applewhite, Jr, etc., Stewart, Adms
APPLEWHITE, Thomas B., decd, J. E. S. Wilson issued L/A 6/1857,
Webster, OD
APPLING, Daniel, decd, John Appling, admr 9/1/1786, George Hunt,
Nathan Bush, secs; apprs: James Simms, Wm Wright, Peter Farrar,
Richmond, AB
APPLING, John, decd, L/A gtd Hamilton Wynn 1/1827, Habersham, MIC
APPLING, Otho A., orph of William A., decd, John Brown, gdn,
1/1/1816, Clarke, LP
APPLING, Otho H., decd, LWt pvd 1/7/1822, Jasper, OM
APPLING, Otho H., orph of William, decd, John Brown, gdn,
1/1/1816, Reubin Hill, sur, Clarke, GB
APPLING, Otho Harmong of Jasper Co., decd, LWT dtd 11/30/1821,
Columbia Co., exrs-Jane W. Appling, wife, friends, Jno Brown, Jno
R. Golding, Wm Appling; dau, Cornelia Ann, wit-Walter A. Appling,
E. D. Appling, Penelope Appling, Jasper, Ests
APPLING, Walter A. apptd gdn of his ch: Thomas K., Walter A.,
Jr., Mary, Otho A., Edmund J., Henrietta A. J., Martha R.
(Rebecca M.), 3/6/1843, Clarke, LP
APPLING, Walter A., Sr., Walter A. Appling, admr, 1868; citation
for admr to appear Oct. term, 9/9/1869, Cobb, MIC
APPLING, William, orph of William, decd, John Nunnally, gdn,
11/2/1818, Clarke, LP
APPLING, William, orph of William, decd, John Nunnally, gdn,
11/2/1818, George W. Moore, Thomas Wells, surs, Clarke, GB
ARCHER, Amariah W., orph of James K., decd, Josiah J. Everett,
gdn, 11/4/1839, Tattnall, GB
ARCHER, Daniel A., minor of James K., decd, retn of Josiah J.
Everett, gdn, 12/31/1837, Tattnall, I&A
ARCHER, James K., decd, 5/20/1836 apprs: William Todd, Nathan
Brewton, Sr., Benjamin Brewton, Tattnall, I&A
ARCHER, James, decd, Mary Ennis, admx, p. 59, Screven, OM
ARCHER, James, decd, William Cavnah, exr, p. 100, Screven, OM
ARCHER, John, decd, Penelope Archer, gdn, files retn for Labinch?
and Mary Ann, orphs 4/27/1836, Tattnall, I&A
ARENDALL, Laughlin, decd, LWT exhibited 8/2/1866, John L.
Arendall, exr, Fulton
ARLINE, John, decd, Henry Pullen, Lewis Sanders, Phereby Arline
issued L/A 9/7/1812, Laurens, AB
ARMER, James, decd, William Armer and Joseph Cowden issued L/A
3/3/1806, Jackson, OM
ARMOR, James, decd, LWT pvd by James King and Wm Hitchcock, L/T
issued Wm Armor, 5/1816, Jasper, OM

ARMOR, William, in rt of his wife on est of James McMichael, decd, applied to sell pt of lot 131 in 12th dist of Jasper Co., 1/1819, Jasper, OM

ARMOUR, Robert, decd, William Armour issued temp L/A 4/2/1855, W. S., R. E. S., R. L. and John Armour, secs, Hall, AB

ARMSTRONG, Hugh, decd, Sherman Armstrong, admr 3/1/1824, Jesse Armstrong, Edward Kinsey, Samuel S. Hillman, surs, Warren, AB

ARMSTRONG, James, decd, Sarah Armstrong, wid, temp admr 9/19/1800, Fanny Forsyth, sec, Richmond, AB

ARMSTRONG, Jesse, decd, LWT pvd 1/13/1840, Jesse B. and William Armstrong, exrs, Washington

ARMSTRONG, John, decd, LWT names wife, Ann and her ch: James, John, Nancy Hickman, Mary Nobles, Susannah Powell, pvd 7/1810, Jasper, OM

ARMSTRONG, John, Sr., decd, John and Ann Armstrong, exrs, apply for L/D 11/1814, Jasper, OM

ARMSTRONG, Peggy W., orph and minor of Thomas, decd, William Thompson apptd gdn 11/27/1796, Robert Thompson, sur; David Partreek apptd gdn 6/18/1805, John Tanner, John McCarthy, surs, Oglethorpe, MIC

ARMSTRONG, William, decd, J. O. Allen, admr, 1881, Cobb

ARNETT, Annis, William Arnett, gdn, p. 150, Screven, OM

ARNETT, Dicey and Peter, Robert Arnett, admr, p. 127, Screven, OM

ARNETT, Edmond, decd, Catharine Arnett, admx, 1811 refn, pd William Arnett $127, pd Wm Hunt, tuition, Wilkes, Retns

ARNETT, Robert, gdu acct appvd, p. 195, Screven, OM

ARNOLD, John (Reverend), decd, James Smith, exr, filed schedule of est, 4/1/1805, Camden, MIC

ARNOLD, Moses, decd, 1810-11 retns, Stephen Arnold, exr, recpt of Stephen Arnold, Jr. for legacy, except his pt of slave, the property of John Favor during life of his wife, who is wid of Moses Arnold, decd, Wilkes, Retns

ARNOW, Columbus J., decd, George J. Arnow apptd admr 3/1/1852, Camden, MIC, AB

ARNSTORFF, Gothief, decd, Cletus Rahn, admr, applied for L/D 7/5/1847, Effingham, MIC

ARNSTORFF, Israel, decd, Lewis Weitman applies for L/A 2/23/1839, Effingham, MIC

ARONES, George, decd, John Clifton, admr, 9/23/1815, appr, Emanuel, A

ARRINGTON, Henry, decd, Edward Rowel, Lud Williams and Mrs. Arrington's retns 1793-5, admrs; apprs: Robert Walton, Ambrose Gordon, Hugh McGee 7/17/1793, Richmond, AR

ARRINGTON, Henry, minor orph of Henry, decd, Elizabeth Arrington named; Valentine Walker apptd gdn, 6/6/1808, John Murray, Anderson Watkins, secs, Richmond, GB

ARWOOD, Barbay A., decd, A. C. Edwards, gdn, 1870, Cobb

ASH, (ASHBOCKER), George & John, minors of Geo Adam Ash, caveat 10/22/1801 by Wm & Susannah Burnside, nep of Matthias Ash; Hannah Ash & David Gugel, admrs of sd Matthias Ash; Gugel not kin; they are natural gdns of minors, Effingham, Misc

ASH (ASHBOCKER), Matthias, decd, Mrs. Hannah Ash, relict, applies for admn, 7/20/1801, Effingham, Misc

ASHFIELD, Dorothy, decd, appr by Stephen Parker, Francis Poythers 10/4/1787; recpts of Jane Parker, George Mills, Frederic Ashfield, John Johnston, Greene, Misc

ASHFORD, William H., decd, orphs: Alexander W., Clement, 12/19/1871, Clarke, LP

ASHLEY, Charles Edgar, son of William, decd, William Ashley, gdn, 3/3/1834, Peter Lamar, Hardy Leveret, secs, Lincoln, GB

ASHLEY, Nathaniel, decd, George Cook, admr, p. 59, Screven, OM

11

ASHLEY, Tabitha, Mrs., decd, LWT pvd; William T. Hopkins, George Lang qualified exrs 4/2/1844, Camden, MIC
ASHLEY, William, LWT produced by Isaac Bailey, Ludowick Ashley, John Bailey, exrs, 1/7/1834, Camden, MIC
ASHMORE, Strong, decd, John Evans, qualified admr, dismd 3/20/1785, Liberty, Ests
ATCHISON, James, decd, Winnifred Atchison apptd temp admr, George Hargraves, sur, 1/1/1807, Warren, MIC, AB
ATKINS, Asa, decd, Morgan Co., 2/20/1811 recpt of Jeremiah Atkins for his pt of his father's est, being in hands of John Billingslea, gdn, since turned over to Jeremiah Miles, gdn, Wilkes, Retns
ATKINS, Everest B., decd, J. H. Atkins, exr, 1897, Cobb
ATKINS James H., James M. Atkins, gdn, 1889, Cobb
ATKINS, Thomas K., decd, Sarah E. Atkins L/A 4/6/1863, Fulton
ATKINSON, Alexander, decd, Edmund Atkinson apptd admr, 9/7/1840, Camden, AB, MIC
ATKINSON, Ann, minor, John Atkinson apptd gdn of his minor sister, 6/2/1818, Camden, MIC, GB
ATKINSON, Arthur C., decd, Thomas P. Atkinson, exr, 1834 retn, (business in Clerke, Oglethorpe, Wilkes, Taliaferro, Appling Co.'s), 9/11/1835, Butts, ER
ATKINSON, Arthur C., decd, of Clarke Co., LWT, wife, Elizabeth, ch: Thomas P., Washington G., Susannah Garrett, Sarah Glass, Mary B. Hancock, Winniford A. Fletcher; named Joseph H. Atkinson, Amos McKee pvd 10/6/1828, Butts, ER
ATKINSON, Edmund, minor, Alexander Atkinson apptd gdn of his minor bro, 6/2/1818, Camden, MIC, GB
ATKINSON, John, decd, Alexander Atkinson for self and as gdn for E. Atkinson, Richard Land and his wife, Mary, William Lang and Nancy, his wife, heirs of est, apply for division 1/5/1825, Camden, MIC
ATKINSON, John, decd, Alexander Atkinson, gtd dism as admr, 1/3/1826, Camden, MIC
ATKINSON, Letitia J., decd, Israel Geer apptd admr, 1/4/1841, dismissed 1/13/1845, Camden, MIC
ATKINSON, Nathan, decd, LWT pvd, John Atkinson and Alexander Atkinson, exrs, 6/3/1817, Camden, MIC
ATKINSON, Ransom, decd, Stephen Swain, admr, 6/12/1824, appr, Emanuel, A
ATKINSON, Tillman J., decd, Sophronia Atkinson, admx, 1882, Cobb
ATKISSON, Martha, child of Cornelius, Cornelius Atkisson, gdn, 1/10/1838, Butts, GB
ATKISSON, Patrick, child of Cornelius, Cornelius Atkisson, gdn, 1/10/1828, Butts, GB
ATKISSON, Susan, now Susan McKeown, child of Cornelius, Cornelius Atkisson, gdn, 1/10/1828, Butts, GB
ATWATER, Elihu, decd, Alfred Doolittle apptd admr w/LWT annexed 6/7/1831, Camden, MIC
ATWELL, John, decd, James Atwell apptd gdn of minor orphs: John and Reuben 11/7/1825, James Atwell, Redden Atwell, James Tennison, secs, Richmond, GB
ATWOOD, Alfred, decd, William Savage, admr 1/8/1823, Arba Washburn, sec, Richmond, AB
ATWOOD, Isaac, decd, John Course, admr 8/16/1791, Abraham Jones, William Glascock, secs, all of sd co.; appraisors: William Glascock, Thomas Glascock, Thomas. Watkins, George Handley, Benjamin Harris, John Green, Richmond, AB
AUBREY, Chandler, decd, Martha Aubrey apptd admx 12/30/1786, William Cureton, Elisha Roberts, secs, Richmond, AB
AUBURY, (AUBERRY?) Philip, decd, LWT pvd by James Hambleton and Johnson Frost 7/3/1809, Jackson, OM

AUSTIN, Davis, decd, Mrs. Mary Ann Austin, qualified admx 10/15/1788, Liberty, Ests
AUSTIN, Henry, decd, John Cubbedge, exr, 5/10/1820, Bryan, CR
AUSTIN, Isaac, orph abt 16 yrs old, was bound to Thomas Kelly, blacksmith 6/6/1824, Habersham, MIC
AUSTIN, Isaac, poor orph, bound to Joseph Weldeon for 14 yrs, 11/6/1832, Habersham, MIC
AUSTIN, John, decd, Thomas F. Austin, admr, 12/6/1852, T. F. Austin, W. E. Sprewell, surs, DeKalb, AB
AUSTIN, John, orph abt 9 yrs old, bound to Thomas Kelly, blacksmith 6/6/1824, Habersham, MIC
AUSTIN, Thomas, decd, John C. Austin, admr w/LWT annexed, 4/5/1852, William A. Austin, N. H. Austin, Joel Adkins, Joseph Walker, surs, DeKalb, AB
AUSTIN, William A., decd, Lucinda Austin, extrx, 1882, Cobb
AUTRY, Simon, decd, Thomas Bankston was apptd admr 9/20/1783, Wilkes, MxR
AVERA, Willis A., decd, James A. Avera applies for L/A 7/20/1858, Joshua F. Sikes and Kinchen Taylor, surs, Lee
AVERAT, Albright, decd, appr 1/6/1801; purchasers at sale: Archibald Averat, Patty Griffin, John Averat, Wm Worthen, Wm Averat, Jr., Benjamin Averat, John Averat, Jr., David Averat, Thomas Dixon, etc., Hancock, AAAA
AVERELL, Thomas, decd, Philip H. Mantz, apptd admr 1/8/1840, Harriet L. Averell, Jno W. Houghton, secs; 4/5/1841 recpt of Harriett Averell for her share; 4/5/1841 Harriet L. Averell apptd gdn of: Clara, Thomas, Alfred & George, minors, Richmond, AB
AVERITT, Abner, decd, Green H. Chairs was issued L/A 11/5/1821, Laurens, AB
AVERY, Holmes M., decd, Mary B. Avery, wid, admx, 1893, Cobb
AVERY, Lucinda, decd, Benjamin Bullard, exr, 1866, Cobb
AVERY, Sara E., decd, M. M. Sessions, admr, 1883, Cobb
AVRET, Jesse, decd, Charles E. Clarke and Nancy Avret apptd admrs 10/20/1835, Jesse P. Green, James McNear, William B. Green, Thomas Lambeth, Edmund Palmer, secs, Richmond, AB
AWTREY, Merrill C., decd, Orlando Awtrey, exr, 1890, Cobb
AWTREY, Sarah, decd, S. H. Alexander, exr, 1891, Cobb
AYCOCK, James, decd, of Chatham Dist, Ga. ceded lands, LWT pvd 7/15/1777 names ch: Agnes Groce, William, Richard, James, John, and Sherod; 1/1/1778 debtors--Jno Bradford to Wm Aycock, Dr. for horse lent in Va. about 1745; Henry Pope to Wm Aycock ca 1757, Wilkes, MxR
AYCOCK, William, decd, Thomas Woolridge, admr, filed 1807 retn, Elbert, AR
AYCOCK, William, orph of Jesse, decd, chose Benjamin Aycock for his gdn 7/6/1840, Bulloch, MIC
AYCOCK, William, decd, Thomas Napier was apptd gdn of orphs--- James, Richard, Milton, Juda, Tabitha, minor heirs; 1810 retn of Thomas Wooldridge, admr, includes board for ch & expense for drawing in the land lottery, also Jacob Lindsay's recpt for his legacy, Elbert, AR
AYERS, Gadwell, decd, Benjamin Dunagan was issued L/A 7/6/1835, Fulton
AYERS, Jincy, John Ayers apptd gdn 7/5/1813, Franklin, OM
AYERS, Mary A., decd, Martin O. Thompson issued temporary L/A 9/23/1856, Amos W. Hammond, sur, DeKalb, AB
AYERS, Nimrod, decd, John M. Born apptd admr, 3/23/1857, James H. Born, sur, DeKalb, AB

BABB, Charles, decd, Thomas McCoy issued L/A 11/1/1826, Thomas McCoy, William Johnston, secs, Morgan, AB
BABBITT, Benjamin, decd, Elihu Lyman, qualified admr 11/24/1787, Liberty, MIC
BABCOCK, James, decd, order to sell property, p. 2, Screven, OM
BACHLOTT, John, decd, Alexander Bachlott, admr, LWT annexed, dismissed, 6/2/1840; caveat filed by Francis Rudolph (overruled). An appeal to jury was entered by Rudolph in rt of his wife, Mary 6/3/1837, Camden, MIC
BACHLOTT, John, decd, LWT pvd, Lewis Bachlott qualified as exr 7/1/1833, Camden, MIC
BACHLOTT, Joseph, decd, Richard A. Hill, admr, to sell assets of est to support minor child, Mary, 6/3/1833, Camden, MIC
BACHLOTT, Joseph, decd, Richard A. Hill and wife, Mary, apptd admrs, 4/2/1827, dismissed 6/3/1837, Camden, MIC
BACHLOTT, Lewis, Emily Rudolph (late Bachlott) dismissed as extrx, 1/5/1836, Camden, MIC
BACHLOTT, Lewis, decd, LWT probated, 1/6/1835, Camden, MIC
BACHLOTT, Mary, decd, Robt Bessant, exec LWT, pvd by M. H. Hebbard, 1/3/1837, Camden, MIC
BACKLEY, Barbara gives deed of gift to her two grch: Josiah and Hannah Margaret Backley, ch of her son, Christian Backley, 3/22/1802, Effingham, Misc
BACKLEY, Frederick, decd, Mrs. Louisa M. K. Backley, wid, applied for L/A 9/10/1846, Effingham, MIC
BACKLEY, Jonathan, decd, John Charlton, admr, produces accts 7/6/1829, Effingham, MIC
BACKLEY, Lukey, minor orph of Jonathan, decd, Mary Backley apptd gdn 9/7/1829, Effingham, MIC
BACON, Edmond and Sarah, decd, late of Laurens and Liberty Co. s, Daniel Barnard issued L/A de bonis non 1/4/1841, Tattnall, AB
BACON, John, decd, Elizabeth Bacon, wid, admx 7/13/1812, Isham Malone, Nicholas Ware, secs; 1812-1823 retns retns of Eliza R. Bacon, 1818 tuition pd for William and John Bacon, Richmond, AR
BACON, John, decd, Edward Sumner, qualified admr 12/12/1785, Liberty, MIC
BACON, John, decd, Obedience Bacon, admx 1785, Robt Dixon, Jno Appling, secs; 2/1/1786 Jos Pannill of Wilkes Co & Jas Fox, admrs, Richmond, AB
BACON, John, decd, Thomas Bacon, Peter Winn, Jos. Quarterman, qualified exrs 12/20/1786, Liberty, MIC
BACON, John, Jr., decd, James Girardeau, qualified admr 7/21/1790, Liberty, MIC
BACON, John, Sr., decd, John Bacon, admr 12/15/1797, Nicholas and Matthew Fox, secs, Richmond, AB
BACON, Jonathan, decd, Wm Bacon, Edward Sumner, Peter Goulding, admrs, 3/14/1785, Liberty, MIC
BACON, Josiah, decd, Palmer Goulding, Wm Thompson, admrs, gtd leave to sell prop, 1/25/1813, Liberty, MIC
BACON, Rebecca, decd, Peter and Palmer Goulding, qualified admrs 3/7/1789, Liberty, MIC
BACON, Rebecca, decd, Thomas Goulding, qualified admr 3/8/1786, Liberty, MIC
BACON, Thomas, decd, Thomas Bacon, Jr., exr, gtd leave to sell prop., 8/1815, Liberty, MIC
BACON, Thomas, Jr., decd, Wm. Girardeau, qualified admr 5/23/1786, Liberty, MIC
BACON, William, decd, Lazarus Mallard qualified admr 12/25/1788, Liberty, MIC
BACON, William, decd, Agnes Bacon, admx 1/3/1793, Thomas Carr, Habakkuk Wright, secs, Richmond, AB

BADGER, Glancus R., minor orph of J. B., decd, John R. Wallace, gdn, 10/8/1861, Fulton, GB
BADGER, J. B., decd, Cyruse issued L/A 8/1/1859; John R. Wallace, admr de bonis non, LWT annexed, 3/4/1861, Fulton
BADGER, Martha Caroline, decd, LWT pvd, Badger, admr, 7/3/1865, Fulton
BADGER, Oranio Rinaldi, minor orph of J. B., decd, John R. Wallace, gdn, 10/8/1861, Fulton, GB
BADGER, Viola R., minor orph of J. B., decd, John R. Wallace, gdn, 10/8/1861, Fulton, GB
BADGER, Zuleika, minor orph of J. B., decd, John R. Wallace, gdn, 10/8/1861, Fulton, GB
BAGBY, Benjamin, decd, Sarah M. Bagby, admx, W. T. Bagby, B. C. Bagby and H. H. Bagby, surs, 9/4/1876, Gwinnett, AB
BAGBY, Thomas M., decd, Edmund Bagby, John P. Bagby, admrs, Samuel Harvis, James H. Chambers and James M. Hutson, secs, 2/3/1848, Cherokee, AB
BAGGETT, Burton, decd, A. Reynolds, exr, 1870, Cobb
BAGGETT, John, decd, William Otwell issued L/A 7/22/1805, Jackson, OM
BAGLEY, Alfred, minor of Thomas M., decd, John R. Bagley and William J. Linch, gdns, 3/3/1851, Cherokee, GB
BAGLEY, Martha, minor of Thomas M., decd, John R. Bagley and William J. Linch, gdns, 3/3/1851, Cherokee, GB
BAGLEY, Martin, minor of Thomas M., decd, John R. Bagley and William J. Linch, gdns, 3/3/1851, Cherokee, GB
BAGLEY, Thomas, minor of Thomas M., decd, John R. Bagley and William J. Linch, gdns, 3/3/1851, Cherokee, GB
BAGWELL, Bryant, decd, G. L. Chatham, admr, 1893, Cobb
BAGWELL, Parthenia, Sara Bagwell, gdn, 1874, Cobb
BAILEY, Amelia, illegitimate child of Elizabeth, William Gaar, gdn, John Daniel and George Gaar, secs, 9/7/1812, Elbert, GB
BAILEY, Charles, decd, L/A gtd John Donaldson, with John Baldwin as sec, 9/1821, Jasper, OM
BAILEY, Charles, decd, Thomas J. Bailey, admr, David J. Bailey and Stephen Bailey, surs, 6/18/1851, Butts, AB
BAILEY, David, decd, Elizabeth Bailey apptd admx 1/8/1805, Camden, MIC
BAILEY, David, decd, Sarah Bailey apptd admx 1/7/1840, dismissed 6/7/1841, Camden, MIC
BAILEY, Dickson, minor under age 14, David Dickson, gdn, 5/4/1812, Jackson, OM
BAILEY, Elizabeth, dau of Jane, widow of Caleb, decd, Jonathan Lane, gdn, I. Collier, James Wills, surs, 1/1809, Oglethorpe, OM
BAILEY, James, decd, Jane Bailey, admx, 4/9/1855, Cherokee, AB
BAILEY, James, decd, L/A issued William Bailey 5/7/1832, Washington
BAILEY, Jane, decd, Morton Bedsole apptd admr, Samuel Nutt, sec, 7/3/1830, Butts, AB
BAILEY, Jesse, decd, William Bailey, admr, 1802, Wilkes, OP
BAILEY, John, George W. Thomas and Robert Lang, admrs, pay house rent for family and ask to buy home in St. Mary's, Ga., 1/5/1842, Camden, MIC
BAILEY, John, Robert Lang and David Bailey apptd admrs 1/1846, Robert Lang, admr, dismissed 3/4/1850; David Bailey dismissed as admr 1/5/1852, Camden, MIC
BAILEY, John, decd, Robert Lang and George W. Thomas apptd admrs 9/2/1839, Camden, MIC

15

BAILEY, John, decd, Guy Smith and Mary Bailey issued L/A
9/5/1821; William Robinson and Pleasant Watts issued L/A
11/8/1821; William Robinson, James Holmes L/A 1/8/1822; William
Robinson, gdn of orphs---William, Jeremiah, Emma and Robert
1/15/1822, Asa Edwards gdn, Morgan, AB, GB
BAILEY, John, decd, Thomas Hudspeth, Russell Bailey, admrs,
receipts of Rachel and Fanny Bailey, Jesse Russell, Moses
Holtzclaw, heirs, 1816-1817, Wilkes, OP
BAILEY, John, decd, William and Zachariah Bailey, exrs,
dismissed, 6/16/1825, Camden, MIC
BAILEY, John, decd, admrs authorized to sell 99 shares of stock
in Bank of St. Marys, 3/1/1842, Camden, MIC
BAILEY, John, decd (Clerk of Court), Robert Brown apptd in his
place, 7/10/1839, Camden, MIC
BAILEY, John Barneby, decd, John Blanton, admr 8/25/1792, Samuel
Jack, William Longstreet, secs, Richmond, AB
BAILEY, John, decd, James Baker, admr, 5/5/1823, Benjamin
Crenshaw, Hartwell Battle, surs, Warren, AB
BAILEY, John (Dr.), decd, 4/1842 inv, apprs: John S. Rice, James
W. Woodward, Samuel Hadden, Stewart, Adms
BAILEY, John T., decd, Hudspeth R. Bailey, admr, 1816 Retn,
heirs: Fanny and Dorcas Bailey, William Cornealson, J. Robinson,
Jesse Russell, Wilkes
BAILEY, Martha Susan, decd, Stephen Bailey, admr, Rufus McCune,
sur, 1/19/1850, Butts, AB
BAILEY, Pierce, decd, James Bailey, admr, 11/1/1812, Warren, MIC
BAILEY, Pierce, decd, Jennie Bailey, admx, 11/1/1813, Elisha
Allen, Joseph Johnston, Benjamin Crenshaw, surs, Warren, AB
BAILEY, Ransford, decd, Mariner, Isaac N. Chappelle, admr,
4/2/1832, Camden, MIC
BAILEY, Rebecca, age over 14, orph of Wesley C., decd, chose
Elisha M. Thompson her gdn (no date), Clarke, LP
BAILEY, Robert, decd, temporary L/A issued Joseph T. Camp
2/3/1826, William Beall, sec; permanent L/A issued 3/15/1826,
James C. Cook, sec, Morgan, AB
BAILEY, Thomas, decd, late of Morgan Co., Benjamin Fuller, exr
7/4/1814, in rt of wife, Mary Fuller, formerly Bailey, produced
cy of proceedings in Morgan Co., Jackson, OM
BAILEY, Thorogood, decd, Morton Bedsole, admr, A. Bailey, sec,
12/12/1830, Butts, AB
BAILEY, Wesley E., decd, Elisha M. Thompson apptd gdn of orphs:
John S. and Robert W., 6/26/1873, Clarke, LP
BAILEY, William, decd, Alexander B. Hawkins apptd gdn of orphs:
Margaret F., Mary E., Lewis and William of Leon Co., Fla.
2/14/1872; Robert G. Taylor apptd gdn of orphs: Maggie, Minna and
Wm of Jefferson Co., Fla., 8/7/1882, Clarke, LP
BAILEY, William J., minor, selects William W. Seals for his gdn,
11/24/1827, Camden, MIC
BAILLIE, Robert, decd, George Baillie, qualified admr 12/5/1785,
Liberty, MIC
BAILLIE, Robert, decd, Ann Alexander, John Baillie, General
Lachlan McIntosh and Alexander Forrester, exrs 10/22/1791,
Liberty, MIC
BAILLIE, Robert Carribe, decd, Phillip Low, John Irvine, admrs,
10/16/1783 (dism 1793), Liberty, MIC
BAILY, Sarah, deaf and dumb, of age, Ishmael Dunn, gdn, C. C.
Bowen, sur, 5/1850, Fayette, GB
BAIN, Archibald, decd, William Gibson apptd admr, 9/7/1812; Sarah
Stewart apptd admx 9/13/1815, Camden, MIC
BAIN, Arthur, decd, Sarah Bain, admx, inv and appr 4/27/1827;
apprs: James Rawls, Aaron Cone, Robert Cone, William Wright, A.
Richardson, Bulloch, Misc

BAINS, John L., minor orph of Lawrence, decd, John Spears apptd gdn 1/7/1817, Jasper, OM
BAIRD, Frances Elizabeth of Autauga Co., Ala., formerly Frances Elizabeth Daniel of Ga. who m. Charles Baird who d. in Texas intestate, distributee of uncle, Thomas Daniel, apptds Burrell Rogers, atty, 7/13/1837, Wilkes, OP
Baird, James, decd, Margaret Baird was apptd admx, 9/13/1815, Camden, MIC
BAIRD, Jane, decd, LWT pvd by Claborn Castleberry and James Barr, 9/5/1808, Jackson, OM
BAIRD, Mary, asks that M. H. Hibbard be apptd her gdn, 3/8/1825, Camden, MIC
BAKER, A., decd, W. A. Wilson, admr, 1876, Cobb
BAKER, Allen, Nicholas Hobson, gdn, 6/28/1797, William Bailey, John Stiles, William Clift, surs, Oglethorpe, MIC
BAKER, Artemus, decd, Wm. J. Baker qualified exr 1/12/---, Liberty, MIC
BAKER, Beal, decd, E. M. Johnson issued L/A 9/4/1848, William Tedder, Josiah Pricket, secs, Hall, AB
BAKER, Beal, decd, Elias and Joseph Baker issued L/A w/LWT annexed, Joseph D. and James G. Baker, secs, (no date) Hall, AB
BAKER, Benjamin, decd, Wm. Baker, Nathaniel Baker, qualified admrs, 5/13/1786, Liberty, MIC
BAKER, Blake, decd, Daniel Hutchinson, Idey Baker, admrs, 5/5/1823, William Harbuck, Benjamin Sandiford, surs, Warren, AB
BAKER, Charles, decd, Priscilla Baker, admx, 10/15/1794, Willis Perry, James Thomas, surs, Warren, AB
BAKER, Charles, decd, Adam Jones and Priscilla, his wife, admx, 9/5/1808, Warren, MIC
BAKER, Charlotte (Mrs.) and children, John W. Baker, trustee, 1866, Cobb
BAKER, Christopher, Nicholas Hobson, gdn 6/28/1797, William Bailey, John Stiles, William Clift, surs, Oglethorpe, MIC
BAKER, Edwin, decd, Nancy Baker, John Harris, admrs, 11/5/1832, Archibald Seals, Jethro Darden, surs, Warren, AB
BAKER, Elisha, decd, James Pace, admr, 12/1841; apprs: David Hillhouse, Samuel Goode, Franklin Cowan; purchasers at sale: Frances Baker, Francces Boykin, M. M. Britt, Dock Armstrong, John Fitzgerald, George L. Miller, etc., Stewart, Adms
BAKER, Frances, Nicholas Hobson, gdn, 6/28/1797, William Bailey, John Stiles, William Clift, surs, Oglethorpe, MIC
BAKER, Francis, decd, R. B. Baker, exr, 1880, Cobb
BAKER, John, Nicholas Hobson, gdn 6/28/1797, William Bailey, John Stiles, William Clift, surs, Oglethorpe, MIC
BAKER, John, decd, Nicholas Baker and John Roach issued L/A 3/1/1819, Laurens, AB
BAKER, John B., decd, Thomas Stevens, Wm Baker, Sr. qualified admrs 4/20/1790, Liberty, MIC
BAKER, John T., decd, ltr dtd 1850 of John S. Dobbins, Ala. to uncle Aaron F. mentions sisters Elisa (John Baker's wife) & Sarah; decd recd rt of wf from est of Moses W. Dobbins of Walton Co., the bro. of Elisa, Sarah & John S., Clarke, LP
BAKER, John V., decd, Margaret M. Baker, wid, extrx, 1886, Cobb
BAKER, Jonathan, decd, Jonathan Baker, James Cone issued L/A 3/1/1841, Washington
BAKER, Joshua, decd, Mary Baker issued L/G 11/1/1847 of: Theresa Frances and Augustus Cicero, orphs, Henry Parks, sec, Hall, GB
BAKER, Margaret, decd, Frank Eddleman issued L/A 9/3/1866, Fulton
BAKER, Mathew, Nicholas Hobson, gdn 6/28/1797, William Bailey, John Stiles, William Clift, surs, Oglethorpe, MIC
BAKER, Nicholas, Nicholas Hobson, gdn 6/28/1797, William Bailey, John Stiles, William Clift, surs, Oglethorpe, MIC

17

BAKER, Polly, Nicholas Hobson, gdn, 6/28/1797, William Bailey, John Stiles, William Clift, surs, Oglethorpe, MIC
BAKER, Sarah, decd, Sellaway Green, admx, p. 74, Screven, OM
BAKER, Techener, Nicholas Hobson, gdn 6/28/1797, William Bailey, John Stiles, William Clift, surs, Oglethorpe, MIC
BAKER, Thomas, decd, Thomas Stevens, Wm Baker, Sr., Samuel Spencer, qualified exrs 1/12/1790, Liberty, MIC
BAKER, Thomas E., orph of Thomas, Jr., decd of Liberty Co., John E. McCall apptd gdn 5/5/1823, Bulloch, MIC
BAKER, William, decd, A. Baker, admr, 1871, Cobb
BAKER, William (Major), Artemus Baker, qualified exr 2/14/1785, Liberty, MIC
BAKER, William R., decd, Mary Baker, Lazarus Mallard, Joseph Way, qualified admrs 5/11/1789, Liberty, MIC
BAKER, William Sanford, illegitimate orph of Sarah, decd, John G. Williams, gdn, 9/20/1836, Hall, GB
BALDREE, Isaac K., decd, inv 9/4/1837, apprs: Thomas Green, Stephen Findley, Arthur Moore, Tattnall, I&A
BALDWIN, Augustus, decd, Rebecca T. Baldwin & Wm J. Hobby, admrs 2/7/1809, Jno Bacon, Thos Barrett, secs; sale 4/22/1809, Rebecca T. Baldwin, admx & 11/6/1809 apptd gdn of: Louisa R. T., Augustus C. and Abraham W. H., Richmond, AB
BALDWIN, Henry H., decd, Sarah Baldwin, wid, admx, 1894, Cobb
BALDWIN, J. J. d. 1/20/1844, Clarke, LP
BALDWIN, John F., decd, Vina Baldwin, admx, 1884, Cobb
BALDWIN, Joseph, decd, Ezekiel Bryan, Jr., gdn of orphs---Adaline, Baldwin, James P., Rebecca, Alexander and Lucy E., 5/12/1842, Randolph, GB
BALDWIN, Sylvanus, decd, J. F. Baldwin, admr, 1877, Cobb
BALDWIN, Sylvanus, decd, Willis Roberts, admr, 1855, Cobb, BB
BALDWIN, T. D., Martha Gulliver, gdn, 1887, Cobb
BALDWIN, William D., decd, Christopher S. Baldwin, admr, 2/1842; apprs: William Porter, John Irvin, William David; purchasers at sale: Widow, G. A. and Augustus Baldwin, T. G. Barfield, J. J. Burks, Neil Culpepper, etc., Stewart, Adms
BALDWIN, William W., decd, Joseph Baldwin, admr, E. S. Rogers, sur, 9/19/1851, Bibb, AB
BALL, Isaac, decd, Hardy Pitts and Archalaus Butt, admrs, 9/17/1819, James Loyless, sur, Warren, AB
BALL, Jesse, late of Jasper Co., Thomas Lacy, admr, Robert Mapp, Simon H. Saunders, sur, 5/2/1842, Butts, AB
BALL, Jesse, idiot, Thomas Lacy, gdn, Samuel Wilkinson, Simon H. Saunders, sur, 11/17/1845, Butts, GB
BALL, John, decd, James M. Parker, admr, C. Wilder, A. J. Dickson, sur, 1/12/1852, Bibb, AB
BALL, Wade H., decd, (owner of mercantile business in Lumpkin), G. B. and J. F. Ball, admrs; apprs: Erasmus T. Beall, Hollis Boynton, Nathan Clifton, Warren A. May, Stewart, Adms
BALLARD, Fenton B., orph of William of Jones Co., decd, 9/1830, Sarah Ballard, gdn, James Freeman, sur, Stewart, L/G
BALLARD, Frederick F., decd, John G. Shown, admr, p. 104, Screven, OM
BALLARD, Irvin A., orph of William of Jones Co., decd, 9/1830, Sarah Ballard, gdn, James Freeman, sur, Stewart, L/G
BALLARD, James, decd, Robert Chivers made gdn of orphs, 1808 Retn pd tuition for Louisa, Evey, Lucy, Matilda and Sophia, Wilkes, GR
BALLARD, James, decd, Thomas Grant, admr, pd Daniel Owen, gdn of Lucy Ballard, now Lucy Hill, Sophia and Matilda Ballard, 1817, Wilkes, AR
BALLARD, James, decd, Thomas Grant, admr de bonis non, 1817 Retns, Wilkes, AR
BALLARD, John H., orph of William of Jones Co., decd, 9/1830,

Sarah Ballard, gdn, James Freeman, sur, Stewart, L/G
BALLARD, Joseph W., orph of William of Jones Co., decd, 9/1830,
Sarah Ballard, gdn, James Freeman, sur, Stewart, L/G
BALLARD, Lavina P., orph of William of Jones Co., decd, 9/1830,
Sarah Ballard, gdn, James Freeman, sur, Stewart, L/G
BALLARD, Louisa, orph of James, decd, Robert Chivers, gdn, 1811-
1812 Retns, Wilkes, OP
BALLARD, Lucy, orph of James, decd, Robert Chivers, gdn, 1811-
1812 Retns, Wilkes, OP
BALLARD, Milton J., orph of William of Jones Co., decd, 9/1830,
Sarah Ballard, gdn, James Freeman, sur, Stewart, L/G
BALLARD, Nathan, decd, John Dyson, exr, receipt of Charles Duke
for Mary and Nancy Ballard's part 1/18/1806; Charles Duke in rt
of his wife, Mary. Edny, James and John Ballard, legatees,
Wilkes, OP
BALLARD, Sophia, orph of James, decd, Robert Chivers, gdn, 1811-
1812 Retns, Wilkes, OP
BALLARD, William Leroy, orph of William of Jones Co., decd,
9/1830, Sarah Ballard, gdn, James Freeman, sur, Stewart, L/G
BALLENGER, Sarah A., decd, James A. Pate issued L/A 9/4/1865, Fulton
BALLINGER, Mary E., E. E. Ballinger, gdn, 1863, Cobb
BANCHSTON, Abner, decd, Elizabeth Banchston, Isaac Parker, John
Reaves, John W. Fletcher, Benjamin Bridges, admrs, Harris
BANDY, James, decd, William R. Scott, exr, 1819, Bryan, CR
BANDY, James, decd, Laney Bandy apptd admx, 9/8/1812, Camden, MIC
BANISTER, James, Sr., decd, LWT pvd 9/2/1862, wife, Martha; ch:
Salina Phillips, wife of William L.; Powell, Deverex, James, Jr.,
Elizabeth, Jarrett Banister, and Martha Stewart, wife of Clark,
Dawson, WB
BANK, Thomas, decd, John Frazer, gdn for orphs: Mark A., Anna,
Elizabeth, 11/7/1831, Mark Bank, sec; Anna Bank, gdn for
Margarette 11/6/1831, John Thank, sec, Lincoln, GB
BANKS, Elizabeth, decd, Josiah Serman, 1/6/1817, Bulloch, MIC
BANKS, W. P., decd, J. Z. Foster, admr, 1888, Cobb
BANKS, W. R., decd, Mrs. G. W. Banks, admr, 1870, Cobb
BANKSON, John, decd, R. M. Brown, admr, 10/3/1853, DeKalb, AB
BANKSTON, Abner, decd, John Goodman, James R. McCord, admrs,
James H. Stark, John Andrews, John W. McCord, surs, 6/4/1844,
Butts, AB
BANKSTON, Abner, decd, Thomas J. Saunders issued temporary L/A,
Simon H. Saunders, Richard Barlow, sur, 4/22/1844, Butts, AB
BANKSTON, Abner, decd, Elizabeth Bankston, Isaac A. Parker, John
Reeves, gdn or orphs, 12/12/1836, Harris, GB
BANKSTON, Abner, decd, John Fletcher, Samuel Dobbs, gdn of
orphs, 7/22/1836, Harris, GB
BANKSTON, Harry, orph of Henry, decd, Sarah Bankston, gdn, James
Langford, sur, 12/2/1816, Clarke, GB
BANKSTON, Henry, decd, Sarah Bankston apptd gdn of ch: Peggy,
Nancy, Judy, Mary, John and Henry, 12/2/1816, Clarke, LP
BANKSTON, Henry, decd, Sarah Bankston, James Langford, admrs, A.
Parker, S. Elder, Wm George, sur, 2/24/1812, Clarke, AB
Henry Parks issued L/A 1/5/1835, Isaac Dorsey, Nathan G. Newton,
secs, Hall, AB
BANKSTON, James E., decd, William R. Bankston, admr, Reason
Blisset, sur, 5/7/1844, Butts, AB
BANKSTON, John, illegitimate, age 1 yr, Robert McMahan apptd gdn
for 20 yrs, Parham Lindsey, sur, 9/6/1841, Butts, GB
BANKSTON, John, orph of Henry, decd, Sarah Bankston, gdn, James
Langford, sur, 12/2/1816, Clarke, GB
BANKSTON, Judy, orph of Henry, decd, Sarah Bankston, gdn, James
Langford, sur, 12/2/1816, Clarke, GB
BANKSTON, Mary, orph of Henry, decd, Sarah Bankston, gdn, James

Langford, sur, 12/2/1816, Clarke, GB
BANKSTON, Nancy, orph of Henry, decd, Sarah Bankston, gdn, James
Langford, sur, 12/2/1816, Clarke, GB
BANKSTON, Olive, orph of Abner, decd, Chas F. Newton, gdn, Wm H.
C. Mickelberry, Richard Barlow, sur, 11/8/1847, Butts, GB
BANKSTON, Peggy, orph of Henry, decd, Sarah Bankston, gdn, James
Langford, sur, 12/2/1816, Clarke, GB
BANKSTON, Peter, decd, 1804 heirs: Lawrence Bankston, Priscilla
Bankston (wid of Peter), Wm Browning, Nimrod Taylor, Andrew
Bankston, Thomas Davis, Hiram Bankston, Wm Bankston, Shadrack
Carpenter, Clarke, LP
BANKSTON, William, decd, Sarah Bankston, admr, Jacob Bankston,
Joseph Cowling, sur, 7/2/1811, Clarke, AB
BANKSTON, Willie Ann, orph of Abner, decd, Charles F. Newton,
gdn, William H. C. Mickelberry, Richard Barlow, sur, 11/8/1847,
Butts, GB
BARANTINE, Sarah E., decd, Jesse Barantine, admr, Wm H. Blalock,
sur, 3/1855, Fayette, AB
BARBER, Greensby W., decd, est 1883, wife, Mary T., ch: G., W.
L., William John W. Barber, S. A. Bowling, formerly Barber) and
Julia K. Brown, formerly Barber, Clarke, LP
BARBER, Israel, decd, George W. Thomas, admr, gtd leave to sell
5/4/1835, Camden, MIC
BARBER, Israel, decd, Isaac Bailey, admr, George W. Thomas later
apptd, 1/6/1835; Thomas dismissed 3/7/1836, Camden, MIC
BARBER, James, decd, est 1847, wife, Penelope, Clarke, LP
BARBER, J. N., decd, Mrs. E. A. Barber, admx, 1896, Cobb
BARBER, J. O., decd, C. C. Barber issued L/A 3/1865, Webster, OD
BARBER, John, orph of Holden, decd, David Hall issued L/G
9/24/1839, Washington
BARBER, Lucinda, orph of Holden, decd, David Hall issued L/G
9/24/1839, Washington
BARBER, Rachel, Sarah and William Barber, gdns, 1876, Cobb
BARBER, R. V., Sarah J. Barber, gdn, 1888, Cobb
BARBER, Sarah, decd, wid of Robert, decd, LWT names: Greensby W.
Barber, Elizabeth Ann Archer (grdau of Harvey Archer), Sarah
Barber (grdau, wife of Green W. Barber and dau of Saml Bryant),
Clarke, LP
BARBER, William, decd, Sarah J. Barber, admx, 1876, Cobb
BARBER, William, orph of Presley, decd, Wyly White, gdn,
11/7/1825, George B. White, Alexander McAlphin, secs, Morgan, GB
BARBER, Y. C., decd, Clk Superior Ct applies for L/A on est
12/1864, Webster, OD
BARCLAY, Alexander, decd, Elizabeth Barclay, admx 10/5/1786,
Chatham, Adms
BARDEN, Austin, orph of C. Arthur, decd, Green Walden, gdn,
3/1/1853, Houston, GB
BARDIN, William, decd, Mary Burdin, extrx of LWT, 10/17/1803,
Warren, MIC
BARFIELD, Alexander, decd, D. D. Barfield, admr, 1885, Cobb
BARFIELD, D. D., decd, Martha and S. C. Barfield, admrs, 1894,
Cobb
BARFIELD, Jeremiah, decd, exr, Lloyd Barfield 1/13/1851; heirs:
Solomon and G. W. Barfield, Clarke, LP
BARFIELD, Solomon, decd, LWT dtd 11/14/1837 pvd 11/20/1837 names
wife, Jemima and ch: Coleman, Frederick, Solomon, Samson, Guily,
now Mrs. Roach, Abi, now Mrs. McCoy, Milly; exr, sons, Frederick,
Coleman and wife, Jemima, Randolph
BARFIELD, William, decd, LWT exhibited 5/3/1830, L/A issued James
Jones and Jesse Barfield, Washington

BARGE, Charles, a lunatic son of Abraham, Hannah Barge issued L/G 5/3/1841, Washington
BARKER, Darky Ann, Hopson Milner apptd gdn 9/1821, Jasper, OM
BARKER, Gray, decd, Thomas Hightower apptd admr, 6/14/1858, Cherokee, AB
BARKER, Thomas R., decd, William A. Elder, admr, Richard Barlow, sur, 7/7/1845, Butts, AB
BARKLEY, Elizabeth, orph of John, decd, Jane Barkley, gdn, Saml Nutt, Morton Bledsole, sur, 3/4/1833, Butts, GB
BARKLEY, Elizabeth Ann, orph of John, decd, Jane Barkley, gdn, 3/4/1833, Samuel Nutt, Morton Bedsole, secs, 3/4/1833, Butts, GB
BARKLEY, Jane A., orph of John, decd, Jane Barkley, gdn, Saml Nutt, Morton Bledsole, sec, 3/4/1833, Butts, GB
BARKLEY, Jane Arbeline, orph of John, decd, pd Jane Barkley for clothing, 1830, Butts, GB
BARKLEY, Jennet A., orph of John, decd, 1830, Butts, ER
BARKLEY, John, decd, Jane Barkley, admx, 9/20/1828, Butts, AB
BARKLEY, John, decd, ann retn of Jane Barkley, gdn for minors, pd Samuel Snoddy, 1838, taxes, 4/4/1840, Butts, ER
BARKLEY, John, decd, inventory, purchasers at sale: Jane Barkley, R. J. D. Barkley, Luke Robinson, William B. Nutt, Clark Hammel, William Messer, etc., 3/1/1839; Samuel R. Nutt, admr, pd: James Weakley vs. John Barkley (Henry Co. case), 3/25/1830, Butts, ER
BARKLEY, John, decd, retn by Samuel R. Nutt, admr, 1835, Jane Barkley recd fifi on George W. Martin, 7/8/1835, Butts, ER
BARKLEY, John N., orph of John, decd, Jane Barkley, gdn, Saml Nutt, Morton Bledsole, sur, 3/4/1833, Butts, GB
BARKLEY, Nancy G., orph of John, decd, Jane Barkley, gdn, Saml Nutt, Morton Bledsole, sur, 3/4/1833, Butts, GB
BARKSDALE, Horatio, decd, Mrs. Mary Barksdale, admx, 1/13/1845, Baldwin, AB
BARKSDALE, John, decd, Samuel Barksdale, Pinkney Harvey, Stephen Burnley, admrs, Michael Harvey, Josiah Beall, surs, 10/22/1803, Warren, MIC
BARKSDALE, Thomas, decd, Jeremiah Walker apptd admr 10/8/1784, Wilkes, MxR
BARKSDALE, William, decd, Mary Barksdale, admx, 7/2/1821, Ebenezer Bird, Zachariah Darden, surs, Warren, AB
BARLEY, Bates, gdn acct appvd, p. 19, Screven, OM
BARLOW, Rebecca, minor orph, Allen H. Curry, gdn, 3/4/1833, James Hogan, sec, Lincoln, GB
BARLOW, Thomas, decd, Mary and John Barlow issued L/A 1/10/1814, Laurens, AB
BARMORE, Wiley, decd, Sarah A. Barmore, wid, admx, 1867
BARNADY, Margaret, minor, Robt Stafford apptd gdn, or James H. Downs, 1/6/1851, Camden, MIC
BARNADY, Peter, decd, Peter Korb, gdn of Margaret Barnady & Mrs. Catherine Lane, ask for division 11/13/1843, Camden, MIC
BARNARD, Frances Elizabeth, Timothy J. Barnard apptd tr for his mother and her children, viz: Charles D., Timothy J., Annie Lizzie, Marrie, replacing Nathl L. Barnard, former tr, Clarke, LP
BARNARD, James, decd, John Barnard of Island of Wilmington, admr, gives six mos to get est appraised 11/20/1783, Chatham, Adms
BARNARD, John, decd, planter, John Barnard apptd admr, 11/23/1783, Chatham, Admns
BARNARD, Nathaniel L. apptd trustee for his wife, Frances E., formerly Dougherty, and her children 3/24/1869, Clarke, LP
BARNES, Alfred, orph of Nathan, decd, Lewis Bundy, gdn, 11/1/1824, Absalom Barnes, sec, Morgan, GB
BARNES, Amanda, W. S. Brown, gdn, Cobb
BARNES, Blanch, H. A. Barnes, gdn, 1897, Cobb

BARNES, Catherine, minor orph of George, decd, John Murray apptd gdn 11/22/1805, Will Kennedy, James Murren, secs, Richmond, GB

BARNES, Cordal, decd, Priscilla Barnes bt all household effects at sale 9/3/1808, Henry Kinnebrew made oath that decd left no Will, applied for L/A, Elbert, AB

BARNES, Elizabeth, W. S. Brown, gdn, Cobb

BARNES, George, decd, Henry Crossle issued L/A 12/4/1797, Alex R. Murray, sec, Richmond, AB

BARNES, Hannah, decd, Robert M. Williamson, etc., admrs, p. 20, Screven, OM

BARNES, Henry, decd, Archibald Stewart, gdn of orphs: Leonard, Gillod, Leander, Davis and Permelia 9/7/1818, Edward Williams, James Morrow, secs, Morgan, GB

BARNES, James, decd, Isaac Barnes, admr, Elijah Barnes, Joseph Donaldson, Phillip Evans, sur, 3/4/1850, Cherokee, AB

BARNES, James J., decd, J. W. and J. J. Barnes, admrs, 1884, Cobb

BARNES, John, minor orph of George, decd, John Murray apptd gdn 11/22/1805, Will Kennedy, James Murren, secs, Richmond, GB

BARNES, John, orph of Nathan, decd, Lewis Bundy, gdn, 11/4/1824, Absalom Barnes, sec, Morgan, GB

BARNES, John H., decd, William Brown and William L. Barnes, admrs, 6/15/1857, Cobb, BB

BARNES, John J., William L. Barnes, gdn, 1855, Cobb, BB

BARNES, Joseph Y., decd, Gay Upchurch, admr, J. H. Johnson, I. Whaley, surs, 3/1842, 1846 retn, Fayette, AB

BARNES, Julian, orph of James, decd, Benjamin Sherrod, Jesse Scarborough, gdn, 7/16/1829, Emanuel, GB

BARNES, Linwood, John E. Moseley, gdn, 1895, Cobb

BARNES, Martha Ann, orph of Nathan, decd, Absalom Barnes, gdn, 11/1/1824, Lewis Bundy, sec, Morgan, GB

BARNES, Matilda, orph of Nathan, decd, Absalom Barnes, gdn, 11/1/1824, Lewis Bundy, sec, Morgan, GB

BARNES, Mattie, John W. Barnes, gdn, 1885, Cobb

BARNES, Nancy C., William L. Barnes, gdn, 1855, Cobb, BB

BARNES, Sally, decd, Ransom Barnes issued L/A 1/5/1847 of wife's est, Thomas and John Barnes, secs, Hall, AB

BARNET, Abraham, decd, Mary and Samuel Barnet, Robert McAlphin, admrs, 11/10/1792, Greene, Misc

BARNET, Cordelia, poor orph, Nathan Word, gdn, 11/1830, Habersham, MIC

BARNETT, Arrabella, orph of William, decd, James Calhoun issued L/G 7/3/183; L/G issued John N. Calhoun 1/13/1840, Washington

BARNETT, Isabella, Churchwell Gibson, gdn in place of Isaiah Tucker, 5/7/1810, Warren, MIC

BARNETT, Jane A., orph, Samuel Barnett, gdn, 1/7/1828, Wilkes, OP

BARNETT, Jesse of Richmond Co, decd, Eleanor Barnett, admx, 5/12/1789, Columbia, AB

BARNETT, Jesse, decd, Eleanor Barnett, admx 5/12/1789, Randolph and John Ramsey, secs; apprs: 7/9/1789, John Smith, John Ramsey, Michael McNeill, Richmond, AB

BARNETT, John, decd, John Franklin Burnett, admr, James Turner, Benjamin McCree, sur, 5/2/1814, Clarke, AB

BARNETT, Joseph R., decd, Joroyal Barnett issued L/A 1/3/1843, Ransom Barnes, Robert Lawrence, secs, Hall, AB

BARNETT, Margrate, Churchwell Gibson, gdn in place of Isaiah Tucker, 5/7/1810, Warren, MIC

BARNETT, Nathan, decd, Leonard Barnett, admr, Wm J. Barnett, sur, 10/12/1822, Clarke, AB

BARNETT, Nathan, decd, Nathan Barnett, admr, receipt of Jesse Evans, gdn of Elizabeth, Nancy and John Barnett, legatees, 2/17/1801, Wilkes, OP

BARNETT, Richard, decd, Jesse Lee apptd admr with LWT, 1/4/1803, Camden, MIC
BARNETT, William, decd, William Barnett, admr 3/10/1788, Solomon Ellis, Beverly Lowe, secs; apprs: 3/10/1788, Solomon Ellis, Joel Crawford, Beverly Lowe, James McNeill, Richmond, AB
BARNETT, William, Churchwell Gibson, gdn in place of Isaiah Tucker, 5/7/1810, Warren, MIC
BARNETT, William J., orph, Samuel Barnett, gdn, 1/7/1828, Wilkes, OP
BARNETT, Zilla A., dau of Wm H., decd, late of Chambers Co., Ala., Thomas W. Sheats apptd gdn in place of Flournoy W. Adams 1/16/1861; Zilla m. John W. Warren before 3/13/1863; Flournoy W. Adams apptd gdn 3/6/1858, Clarke, LP
BARNS, John, decd, Davis M. House issued L/A 4/2/1860, Samuel S. House, W. L. Sumter, secs, White, AB
BARNWELL, Robert, decd, Samuel K. McCutchen and William Barnwell issued L/A, James Law, James Ryles, Josiah H. Gill, Paul Furr, secs, Hall, AB
BARNWELL, Robert, decd, W. R. Montgomery, admr, 1881, Cobb
BARR, Alfred A., decd, John Jangsletter, admr, Julius Peek, sur, 12/21/1848, Bibb, AB
BARRATT, Benjamin H., decd, Joseph Maddox, admr, Wm Maddox, sur, 11/7/1825, Clarke, AB
BARREN, Josiah Jackson, Isaac H. Moreland, gdn, 2/2/1852, Houston, GB
BARRENTINE, Jacob, decd, LWT pvd by Josiah H. Carter 3/1856, Webster, OD
BARRENTINE, John W., decd, L/A issued Zach Goss 10/1862; M. H. Busb issued L/A de bonis non 1/7/1864, Webster, OD
BARRET, Ninian, decd, LWT presented 5/4/1807, Franklin, IMW
BARRETT, Charles, decd, D. A. Barrett, exr, 1870, Cobb
BARRETT, Elihu, decd, W. W. Barrett issued L/A 10/18/1826, William Porter, sec, Morgan, AB
BARRETT, Eliza, orph, John Barrett, gdn, 12/6/1826, Thomas O. Horne, William Wood, Morgan, GB
BARRETT, George, decd, Juda Barrett, wid, 1892, Cobb
BARRETT, Isaac, decd, LWT names wife, Mary and ch: Isaac, Elizabeth Roberson, Poley Kid, Kezziah Whitney, Ninion Barrett (son), Polly Barrett, Harriett Barrett, dtd 12/20/1806, exrs: Isaac Barrett and Ninion Barrett, Jr., Franklin, IMW
BARRETT, James S., decd, Dora Barrett, wid, admx, 1896, Cobb
BARRETT, J. D., decd, Dora Barrett, wid, admx, 1896, Cobb
BARRETT, John, decd, Annie Barrett, extrx, 1890, Cobb
BARRETT, Joseph S., gdn of his ch: Nancy, John H. and James M., 5/7/1827, Joseph Morrow, Creed M. Jennings, secs, Morgan, GB
BARRETT, Lewis, Sr., decd, Lewis, Erasmus, Milley, Pamela, Robert, Parmelia, Nancy and Benjamin Barrett, heirs, Wilkes, OP
BARRETT, Margaret Ann, minor child of Nathan C., Mary Crawford apptd gdn 9/5/1836; Joseph F. Morton gdn 9/3/1849, Clarke, LP
BARRETT, Mary, decd, wife of Lewis, John Spearman, Robert Toombs, gdns (1814) of Robert, Lewis, Erasmus, Benjamin, Nancy Parmelia, Wilkes, GR
BARRETT, Nancy W., now age 21, asks for div of mother's est, Mary Barrett, decd, sd Mary entitled by LWT of her father, Gabriel Toombs 8/3/1813, Wilkes, OP
BARRETT, Ninian, LWT dtd 12/20/1806 names wife, Mary and ch: Isaac, Nancy Howard, Elizabeth Robinson, Patsy Kidd, Keziah Whitney, Ninian, Delilah, Polly, and Harriet, pvd 5/4/1807, Franklin, OM
BARRETT, Reuben, decd, A. M. Barrett, admr, William Kelley, William Anderson, surs on bond 1/14/1861, Dawson, WB

23

BARRETT, William G. apptd gdn of his minor ch: Martha, Mary L., William L. P., Edward B., Jane A. H., John J., James L. P. and Anna M. D. Barrett 12/6/1852 because of inheritance from the est of Samuel Pedsian late of Lumpkin District, South Carolina, Clarke, LP
BARRINGER, Daniel, decd, John L. Barringer, admr, 7/7/1834, Baldwin, AB
BARRINGTON, Ceball, decd, 1/1841, Thomas N. Gardner, admr; John Fitzgerald, E. H. Baker, James Adams, James P. Orr, Francis E. Boykin, Stewart, Adms
BARRINGTON, Willis, decd, 1/1838, James S. Lunsford, admr, apprs: Moses Ramsey, William Garrett, Wayne W. Eilands; purchasers at sale: Celia Barrington (wid), Samuel Adams, Mathew Averett, M. Barrington, etc., Stewart, Adms
BARRON, George W., orph of Joseph, decd, Gillum Scogin, gdn, sur, Wm Hopson, Noel Pace, 1/10/1848, Troup, GB
BARRON, Isaac N., orph of Joseph, decd, Gillum Scogin, gdn, Wm Hopson, Noel Pace, sur, 1/10/1848, Troup, GB
BARRON, James, decd, Osborn Miller, gdn of orphs: Amanda E., Sarah A., William J. and Margaret E., 1/9/1854, Houston, GB
BARRON, Jane, orph of Joseph, decd, Gillum Scogin, gdn, Wm Hopson, Noel Pace, sur, 1/10/1848, Troup, GB
BARRON, John, decd, Smith Barron, admr, inventory 11/26/1830, purchasers at sale: Morton Bledsoe, Smith, Susan, Henry, Wm, and Joseph Barron, etc., Butts, ER
BARRON, Joseph A., orph of Joseph, decd, Gillum Scogin, gdn, Wm Hopson, Noel Pace, sur, 1/10/1848, Troup, GB
BARRON, Nancy A., orph of Joseph, decd, Gillum Scogin, gdn, Wm Hopson, Noel Pace, sur, 1/10/1848, Troup, GB
BARRON, Samuel, decd, appr 3/5/1802; purchasers at sale: Jane Barron, Linzy Thornton, Jesse M. Pope, John Barron, etc., Hancock, AAAA
BARROW, James, decd, Reuben Barrow, admr, 6/8/1801, Hugh Reese, David Nusom, surs, Warren, AB
BARROW, John, 11/1/1830, recd of Jacob Mincy and John C. Everett, exrs of LWT of Philip Mincy of Bulloch Co., decd, $360 in full for a legal bequest from LWT, Cullin Barrow, atty, Bulloch, Misc
BARROW, John Sr., decd, Stephen W. Burnley, exr of LWT, pvd same 3/5/1810, Warren, MIC
BARROW, Reubin, decd, his LWT pvd by Benjamin Bledsoe and William Brannen, wits., 11/2/1812, Warren, MIC
BARRY, Andrew, devd, Armisted Barry and Keziah Barry issued L/A 3/1802, Franklin, OM
BARRY, John, decd, Smith Barry, admr, 10/12/1831, Butts, AB
BARTLES, Sarah H., J. N. Bartles, gdn, 1885, Cobb
BARTLETT, Jonathan, decd, David Braston, admr, 11/5/1790, Chatham, Adms
BARTLETT, Myron, decd, Thomas M. Griffith, admr, Thomas Dell, sur, 9/4/1848, Bibb, AB
BARTLETT, Reuben, decd, Elizabeth Bartlett, admx, 1/9/1854, Thomas Cook, sur, DeKalb, AB
BARTON, Arthur, decd, 9/26/1842; apprs: John Green, William McDaniel, John M. Bottoms; purchasers at sale: Robert B. Davies, Hugh Walden, Ben. Bridges, Thomas Fails, Sam Robison, James Gamble, John Bullard, Susan Cutts, Dooly, I&A
BARTON, Benjamin, decd, Robert Barton applies for dismission 11/5/1827, Effingham, MIC
BARTON, Bethenia, orph of Presley, decd, Elizabeth Barton, gdn, 3/18/1826, Morgan, GB
BARTON, Elias, orph of Presley, decd, John Barton, gdn, 3/15/1826, Morgan, GB

BARTON, Gincy, orph of William, decd, Thomas Hester, gdn, 11/1/1830, Clarke, LP
BARTON, Henry A., decd, Sarah and Robert applied for L/A 11/1830, Effingham, MIC
BARTON, James, decd, John Barton issued L/A 11/6/1820, Henry Casey, sec, Morgan, AB
BARTON, John, decd, Ann Barton, admx 12/11/1804, William McTyeire, sec; apprs: Dread Dawson, James Leatherlin, Edward Burch, John Prescott, Richmond, AB
BARTON, Joseph, orph of Presley, decd, John Barton, gdn, 3/15/1826, Morgan, GB
BARTON, Robert, Jr., decd, William Barton, admr 9/7/1818, Robert Barton, Nathan Marsh, surs, Warren, AB
BARTON, Simeon, decd, Charles A., Robert and Benjamin Barton, Clem Powers and Zaza Powers apptd trustees of property 1/2/1832, Effingham, MIC
BARTON, Thomas, decd, Henry Casey was issued L/A 5/15/1823, Morgan, AB
BARTON, Willoughby, decd, James Barton and Benjamin Nowland, admrs 10/5/1807, Hugh Magee, Bird Booker Tindall, secs; appraisers: Edward Rowell, Joseph Ware, Archibald Hatcher, Hugh Magee, Richmond, AB
BARTOW, Warren W., decd, Littleberry Jackson issued L/A 11/4/1867, Fulton 11/4/1867, Fulton
BARWICK, Stancil, decd, d. 6/7/1890; heirs---wife, Mrs. E. Barwick, ch--Mrs. Callie Council and Mrs. Ruth Ansley, both of Sumter Co., Ga.; Mrs. Laura Smith of Oconee Co., Ga.; Jno Addison Barwick over age of 14, Joseph W., Mary E., Thomas, Clara E., William and Howell Cobb Barwick, Clarke, LP
BASEMORE, Reddick B., decd, Kinard Taylor, admr, 4/8/1863, Harris, AB
BASFORD, Estell, Laura Bassford, gdn, (no date) Cobb
BASKINS, Robert W. was apptd gdn of his minor ch: Charity J., Sarah M., Susan E., Ellener A. and Mildred M. Baskins, 12/5/1853, Houston, GB
BASS, Alexander, orph of Martha, decd, Daniel Zachry apptd gdn, Harris, GB
BASS, Allen, decd, L/A gtd to John Sturdivant and Elizabeth Bass, with John Martin, Martin Towns, Alexander Flewellen, secs, 7/1813, Jasper, OM
BASS, Allen, decd, admr asks for distribution of est by John Martin, Neilly McCoy, John Townes, H. Bass, Alexander Flewellin, 11/1820, Jasper, OM
BASS, Allen, orph of Allen, decd, Elizabeth Bass, gdn, Wm Mason, John Martin, sec, 1/3/1814, Jasper, OM
BASS, Ann O., orph of William T., decd, Mary A. E. Bass apptd gdn of her minor dau, (no date) Clarke, LP
BASS, Batson, decd, Zadock Bass, admr, 3/9/1819, John Fontaine, Jeremiah Butt, Nathan Boddle, surs, Warren, AB
BASS, Edward, decd, Hilliard I. Hightower, Daniel Hightower, Alexander Bass, William Anderson, gdns of orphs 9/4/1837, Harris
BASS, Elizabeth apptd gdn of Maria, William, Allen, and Juana, orphs and minors of Allen, decd, 1/3/1814, Jasper, OM
BASS, Henry, decd, temp L/A issued Creed M. Jennings, 2/5/1826, Joseph T. Camp, sec; permanent L/A to sd Creed M. Jennings and John J. Barrett 5/1/1826, William Wood, sec, Morgan, AB
BASS, Henry C. orph of William T., decd, Mary A. E. Bass apptd gdn of her minor son, (no date) Clarke, LP
BASS, Herrard L., orph of William T., Mary A. E. Bass apptd gdn of her minor son, (no date) Clarke, LP

BASS, Juana?, orph of Allen, decd, Elizabeth Bass, gdn, William Mason, John Martin, sec, 1/3/1814, Jasper, OM
BASS, Lemuel, decd, Cullen Bass, admr, 11/4/1862, Harris, AB
BASS, Maria, orph of Allen, decd, Elizabeth Bass apptd gdn, William Mason, John Martin, secs, 1/3/1814, Jasper, OM
BASS, Martha, decd, LWT pvd 11/1/1847, Harris
BASS, William, orph of Allen, decd, Elizabeth Bass, gdn, William Mason, John Martin, sec, 1/3/1814, Jasper, OM
BASS, William A., decd, John Sturdivant apptd admr 12/23/1820, Jasper, OM
BASS, William T., died 7/5/1863, Clarke, LP
BASS, Wyatt J., orph of William T., decd, Mary A. E. Bass apptd gdn of her minor son, (no date) Clarke, LP
BASSEAR, John, decd, Lewis Lassear, admr, dismissed, 6/3/1828, Camden, MIC
BASSETT, Richard, decd, LWT pvd 11/12/1840, Kibly Bassett and Spencer Morris qualified as exrs, Harris
BASWELL, John C., decd, 1887, Cobb
BASWELL, W. P., decd, Cordelia Baswell, extrx, 1898, Cobb
BATES, John, decd, Fleming Bates, admr, 1803-1804 inventory, Wilkes, OP
BATES, Mathias, decd, Russell J. Bates and Charles Nix, exrs, 1883, Cobb
BATES, Stephen, decd, LWT dtd 7/4/1851 pvd 9/1851 names wife-Sary & ch: William T. & George V.; the heirs agree to divide property 11/5/1851, all of full age, signed John R. Bates, Jarrell Ellison, Phillip Abernathy and Polly Ann King, Cherokee
BATON, William, decd, 1/1837, Eady Baton (widow), admx; apprs: John Rusing, James S. and John Lee, Thomas Justice; purchasers at sale: Eady Baton, Bivin Justice, John Lunsford, John Rousseau, Stewart, Adms
BATTLE, J., decd, James W. Cato, William Griggs and W. C. Osborne, apptd admrs 6/6/1835, Harris, AB
BATTLE, John, decd, John L. Martin, admr, 3/1/1824, Hartwell Battle, sur, Warren, AB
BATTLE, John, decd, Rhoda Battle and Colonel Samuel Alexander issued L/A 2/13/1804, Robert Abercrombie, Micajah Little, surs, Warren, AB, MIC
BATTLE, John, decd, Noah Kelsey, gdn of orphs ordered to come into ct by next term and give his bond 7/1/1811, Warren, MIC
BATTLE, John, decd, Rhoda Battle, admx, 11/4/1811, Warren, MIC
BATTLE, John, decd, Rhoda Battle appeared before the court and made her choice of 1/3rd of estate 1/4/1808, Warren, MIC
BATTLE, Nancy, Thomas W. Scott, gdn of Nancy (formerly Nancy Right), has settled her gdnship and asks to be dismissed, 9/1806, Oglethorpe, OM
BATTLE, Rhoda, decd, Hartwell Battle and James Langdon apptd admrs 5/7/1821, Elisha Allen and William Darden, surs, Warren, AB
BATTON, Sarah, William B. Batton of Jasper Co. was apptd trustee for his wife, the dau of Henry Jennings, decd, of Clarke Co. 2/3/1863, Clarke, LP
BATTS, George, decd, Jesse Batts issued L/G 11/6/1840, (orphs not named) Washington
BATTS, Joel, decd, John Batts qualified as exr of LWT pvd 12/9/1854, Lee, MSC
BATTS, Nathan, decd, Jesse Batts issued L/A 11/6/1840, Washington

BAUGH, David, decd, inv dtd 5/24/1808 by John Baugh, Jesse
Blackwell, John Walraven 7/4/1808, Franklin, OM
BAUGH, Robert, decd, William Baugh L/A 9/7/1812, Putnam, AB
BAW, David, decd, Jonathan Baw issued L/A 5/2/1808, Franklin, OM
BAXLEY, Radin, decd, Gilley Baxley, admx, 9/5/1814, Laurens, AB
BAXTER, Eli L., decd, Mrs. Mary W. Baxter apptd admx 9/1862,
Quitman, Wood Co., Tx; marr lic of Ambrose Fitzgerald and Mrs.
Mary W. Baxter 1862, Wood Co., Tx, Clarke, LP
BAXTER, Eli L., son of Thomas W. Baxter, Clarke, LP
BAXTER, James, decd, David Chestnut, admr, 1/14/1855, Robert
Baxter, sur, DeKalb, AB
BAXTER, Mary (Mrs.), she d. 3/29/1869, Clarke, LP
BAXTER, Susannah, decd, inventory 12/11/1789, Wilkes, OP
BAXTER, William B., decd, Mrs. S. C. Baxter, wid, admx 1871, Cobb
BAYES, Joseph, decd, John Bush, Zachariah Bayes, exrs, 1/12/1795,
Wilkes, OP
BAYNARD, Ephraim, decd, of S. C., est 7/19/1866, Clarke, LP
BEACH, James, decd, L/A issued Sanders Vann and Catherine Beach,
3/2/1818, Jasper, OM
BEACHAM, Elijah, decd, John S. Drew, Abraham Coward, John G.
Olliver, admrs, 1/8/1822, Emanuel, AB
BEACHAM, Elijah, decd, of Montgomery Co., Ga., Gideon Hays, admr,
4/27/1812 appr, Emanuel, A
BEACHAMP, William, decd, Martha Beachamp issued temporary L/A
3/4/1853, Isaiah Parker, sur, DeKalb, AB
BEAL, Helena, decd, wid, LWT pvd, Ulric Nobles, sole exr,
1/6/1791, Chatham, Adms
BEAL, Jacob, Hezekiah, gdn, 1802-5 retns, Richmond, GR
BEAL, Nathaniel, decd, Henry Beal admr 1/6/1829, Camden, MIC
BEAL, Richard K., decd, George Granberry, exr, 1/1845, Harris
BEAL, Verlinda R., orph of Wm B., Nathan Beal, gdn, J. A. Groves,
Zephaniah Beal, sur, 9/5/1825, Clarke, GB
BEAL, Zephaniah, decd, Elizabeth W. Beal issued L/A 3/2/1801,
Littleberry Bostick, Hezekiah Beal, secs, Richmond, AB
BEALL, A. R., decd, John Q. Alford, P. O. Beall, admrs, Almen
Stratten, James F. Johnson, surs, 11/1838, 1847 retn, Fayette, AB
BEALL, Asa, decd, Francis F. Fleming, gdn for orphs: Benjamin and
Harriet, 1/2/1837, Shadrack Turner, Stephen Stovall, Wm B.
Cantalaw, secs, Lincoln, GB
BEALL, Benjamin B., decd, Robert A. Beall, admr, 12/5/1814, A.
Moncrief, Chappell Heath, secs, Warren, AB
BEALL, Elizabeth, decd, Elijah Jones, admr, 2/1/1825, John
Veazey, John McCrary, surs, Warren, AB
BEALL, Howard, decd, L/A gtd Elias and Thomas Beall 1/7/1822,
Elias Beall to have leave to remove admn to Oglethorpe Co.
1/7/1822, Jasper, OM
BEALL, Josiah, decd, Thaddeus & Elias Beall, admrs, Thaddeus
Beall, Sr., sur, 10/11/1806; admrs gtd leave to sell 3 slaves
3/7/1808, Warren, MIC
BEALL, Mannan, decd, Elijah Jones, John McCrary, admrs, 5/5/1823,
Samuel Hall, Henley Jones, surs, Warren, AB
BEALL, Thaddeus, decd, Jeremiah & Thomas Beall, admrs, Thos.
Pennington, sur, 7/4/1808; Emelia Beall, decd's relict, chose her
1/3rd pt of est 1/2/1808, Warren, AB, MIC
BEAM, Henry M., orph of Albert, decd, Julia H. E. Dixson, gdn,
9/3/1849, Cherokee, GB
BEAM, Jesse W., orph of Albert, decd, Julia H. E. Dixson, gdn,
9/3/1849, Cherokee, GB
BEAM, John B., orph of Albert, decd, Julia H. E. Dixson, gdn,
9/3/1849, Cherokee, GB
BEAM, Julia A., orph of Albert, decd, Julia H. E. Dixson, gdn,
9/3/1849, Cherokee, GB

BEAM, Julius A., orph of Albert, decd, Julia H. E. Dixson, gdn, 9/3/1849, Cherokee, GB
BEAM, Katherine F., orph of Albert, decd, Julia H. E. Dixson, gdn, 9/3/1849, Cherokee, GB
BEAM, Thomas, orph of Albert, decd, Julia H. E. Dixson, gdn, 9/3/1849, Cherokee, GB
BEARD, Adam, decd, 10/1809 Thomas Peacock, surviving partner of decd vs. Thomas Mann, Bruan, Writs
BEARD, Jane, decd, William Beard, one of exrs, makes retn 9/2/1811, Jackson, OM
BEARD, Matthew, decd, George Beard, admr, 8/3/1784, Liberty, MIC
BEARD, William, decd, William S. Wilson, gdn of orphs: John and Elizabeth, 1/3/1837, Randolph, GB
BEARDEN, Asa J., orph of Edward, decd, Wm H. Blalock, gdn, Wm J. Russell, Z. Blalock, surs, 8/1852, 1853-1854 retns, Fayette, GB
BEARDEN, Edward, decd, Jeptha Landrum, Sr., admr, Thomas J. Head, W. W. Bearden, Walter J. and Thomas E. Campbell, surs, 11/1848, 1851-1854 retns, Fayette, AB
BEARDEN, Jefferson, orph of Edward, decd, Wm H. Blalock, gdn, Wm J. Russell, Z. Blalock, surs, 8/1852, 1853-4 retns, Fayette, GB
BEARDEN, Larkin, orph of Edward, decd, Wm H. Blalock, gdn, Wm J. Russell, Z. Blalock, surs, 8/1852, 1853-1854 retns, Fayette, GB
BEARDEN, Pertheney, orph of Edward, decd, Wm H. Blalock, gdn, Wm J. Russell, Z. Blalock, surs, 8/1852, 1853-4 retns, Fayette, GB
BEARDEN, Polly, orph, age 14, bound to John S. Rushten, 3/1813, Jackson, OM
BEARDEN, Quiller, orph of Edward, decd, Wm H. Blalock, gdn, Wm J. Russell, Z. Blalock, surs, 8/1852, 1853-4 retns, Fayette, GB
BEARDEN, Sarah Ann, orph of Edward, decd, Wm H. Blalock, gdn, Wm J. Russell, Z. Blalock, surs, 8/1852, 1853-4 retns, Fayette, GB
BEARDEN, Vicey, orph of Edward, decd, William W. Bearden, gdn, Wm Watson, Jeptha Landrum, Sr., surs, 3/1850, 1851-1854 retns, Fayette, GB
BEART, Henry, orph ca age 9 (his father not being fit to care for him), bound to Elijah Cowan 11/7/1808, Jackson, OM
BEASLEY, Alexander W., orph of Write M. Beasley, decd, B. L. W. Smith, Nathan Barwick, gdns, 3/5/1849, Emanuel, GB
BEASLEY, Ambrose, decd, Royland Beasley, admr, 1814-1815 Retn, Wilkes, AR
BEASLEY, Berry W., decd, Cyrus McLee L/A 9/1856, Webster, OD
BEASLEY, Elizabeth, orph of Write M., decd, B. L. W. Smith, Nathan Barwick, gdns, 3/5/1849, Emanuel, GB
BEASLEY, Fereby, orph of William, Henry Durden, gdn, 3/6/1837, Emanuel, GB
BEASLEY, Henry, decd, LWT dtd 9/11/1852, pvd 11/1852, names wife, Martha and ch: Warren and Savannah; John Martin apptd admr, Daniel H. Bird, sur, 9/23/1853, Cherokee, GB
BEASLEY, James, decd, Richd Beasley, Wm Earnest, exrs of LWT, pvd by Wm Howard, James Beasley, 6/3/1799, Warren, MIC
BEASLEY, James, orph of Write M. Beasley, decd, B. L. W. Smith, Nathan Barwick, gdns, 3/5/1849, Emanuel, GB
BEASLEY, James, decd, of Chattooga Co., Ga., Frances Brown apptd James Beasley her atty to handle her share of est 8/6/1855, Clarke, LP
BEASLEY, James M., decd, William G. Beasley, admr, J. C. Cobb, sur, 10/23/1847, Bibb, AB
BEASLEY, J. F., decd, B. H. Curmerson, admr, 1893, Cobb
BEASLEY, John R., orph of Write M., decd, B. L. W. Smith, Nathan Barwick, gdns, 3/5/1849 Emanuel, GB
BEASLEY, Margaret, dau of Chapman, decd, James Beasley apptd gdn 11/13/1856, Clarke, LP

BEASLEY, Mary Ann, orph of William, Henry Durden, gdn, 3/6/1837, Emanuel, GB
BEASLEY, Morris, decd, Jasper L. Keith, admr, James Ramsey, Daniel Bird, sur, 6/9/1856, Cherokee, AB
BEASLEY, Richard, decd, Nathan Holtzclaw, admr, heirs: Royland and Jincy Beasley, wid, Nancy Rucker, Jense Holtzclaw, 3/2/1818, Wilkes, MxR
BEASLEY, Richard, decd, Margaret and Robert Beasley, admrs, James Gray, sur, 12/11/1804, Warren, MIC
BEASLEY, Robert, decd, William Beasley, gdn of orphs: Robison, Polly, Saymore, Elizabeth and Robert, 3/4/1816, William Gill, Nathan Hackney, secs, Morgan, GB
BEASLEY, Thomas George, decd, Margaret F. Beasley issued L/A 10/5/1863, Fulton
BEASLEY, William, decd, Elizabeth Beasley, admx, 3/6/1837; Henry Durden, gdn of orphs: Mary Ann and Fereby, Emanuel, GB
BEASLEY, Write M., decd, B. L. W. Smith, Nathan Barwick, gdns of Alexander W., James, Write M. and John R., orphs of decd, 3/5/1849, Emanuel, GB
BEASLEY, Write M., orph of Write M., decd, B. L. W. Smith, Nathan Barwick, gdns, 3/5/1849, Emanuel, GB
BEASON, Isaiah, ordered that Sampson Lane be apptd gdn 7/4/1808, Franklin, OM
BEATY, James, decd, John Guyton and Elender Beaty issued L/A 7/3/1820, Laurens, AB
BEATY, Samuel, decd, Thomas and James Beaty, Jr. issued L/A 7/6/1818; John Thomas, admr de bonis non 7/3/1820, Laurens, AB
BEATY, William, decd, Mary Beaty and Joseph Blackshear issued L/A 5/5/1817, Laurens, AB
BEAVERS, Amanda H., orph of Silas M. of Morgan Co, S. Higgins, gdn, S. Sanders, T. Douglass, sur, 1/14/1840; Edmund McDaniel, gdn, 1/25/1845, Butts, GB
BEAVERS, Eliza L., orph of Silas M., of Morgan Co., S. Higgins, gdn, S. Sanders, T. Douglass, sur, 1/14/1840; Edmund McDaniel, gdn, 1/25/1845, Butts, GB
BEAVERS, Nancy, decd, Francis M. Beavers, admr, J. M. Gresham, sur, 2/2/1874, Gwinnett, AB
BEAVERS, Robert, decd, LWT pvd by William Headen and Solomon Strickland, (probably 1804), Jackson, OM
BEAVERS, Sarah E., orph of Silas M., of Morgan Co., S. Higgins, gdn, S. Sanders, T. Douglas, sur, 1/14/1840, Butts, GB
BEAVERS, Sarah E. (now Sarah E. Higgins, wife of John Higgins), a minor, orph of Silas M. Beavers of Morgan Co., Edmund McDaniel, gdn, 1/25/1845, Butts, GB
BEAVERS, Silas M., decd, Edmund McDaniel, admr de bonis non, Martin R. McDaniel, John B. Thurman, sur, 1/5/1845, Butts, AB
BEAVERS, Silas M., late of Morgan Co., decd, Sterling T. Higgins, gdn of orphs: Amanda H., Eliza L. and Sarah E., Simon H. Sanders, Thomas Douglas, secs, 1/14/1840, Butts, GB
BEAVERS, William, decd, Joseph McConnell, admr w/LWT annexed, Dolphus E. Wiley, William Beavers, sur, 11/1/1858, Cherokee, AB
BECK, John, decd, Ann Beck, admx, petitions to ratify proceedings of a division of all property which has taken place in South Carolina, 5/5/1828, Effingham, MIC
BECKHAM, Demery, decd, Simeon, admr, gtd leave to sell perishable property of est, 1/5/1821, Glynn, MIC
BECKHAM, John S., decd, Elliott Loudermilk, A. B. Griffin, admrs, 9/4/1837, Harris
BECKLEY, Orren, decd, John Adams presented authority from heirs & admr to settle affairs of estate, 12/7/1816, Camden, MIC
BECKLEY, Orren, died in St. Marys 10/19/1815, w/o known heirs, 11/4/1815, Camden, MIC

BECKTLY, Christian, decd, Mrs. Elizabeth Becktly, relict, admx, 7/20/1801, Effingham, Misc
BECKWITH, John, decd, William Beckwith, admr, 7/2/1819, Benjamin Crenshaw, sur, Warren, AB
BEDDINGFIELD, Charles, of Richmond Co., Ga., decd, William Wallace, admr, 8/4/1789, Columbia, AB
BEDDINGFIELD, John H., decd, Martha A. Beddingfield issued L/A 1/27/1834, Washington
BEDELL, Absolom, LWT pvd 1/12/1846, R. H. Dixon, exr, Harris
BEDELL, Charles, decd, William Johnson, J. M. Ramey, exrs, LWT pvd 11/5/1844, Harris
BEDELL, Christopher C., decd, George C. Bedell, George Osborne, admrs, 12/14/1835, Harris, AB
BEDELL, John, minor, George Osburn, gdn, Toliver Wells, petitioner, 11/3/1845, Harris, GB
BEDELL, Pendleton, decd, heirs: L. P. Thomas, in rt of wife, Edward Bedell, Pendleton Bedell, Robert Bedell, 11/30/1842, Clarke, LP
BEDELL, Robert, son of Pendleton, decd, Lovic P. Thomas apptd gdn 1/10/1848, Clarke, LP
BEDES, Matthias, decd, David Williford, Wm Cook apptd admrs, 6/4/1805, Camden, MIC
BEDGOOD, Henry, illegitimate child of Lydia Bedgood, Drury Jackson issued L/G 5/7/1832; Josiah T. King issued L/G 3/1/1842, Washington
BEDINGFIELD, Charles, decd, William Wallace issued L/A 7/22/1789; slaves assigned to Charles, Martha, Mary and John Bedingfield, Richmond, AB
BEGEL, John Valentine, aged abt 11 yrs, bound out to David Reisser until age 21 to learn shoemaker's trade and be educated 7/20/1801, Effingham, Misc
BELCHER, Samuel, decd, John Belcher issued L/A 12/23/1823, Matthew Belcher, sec, Morgan, AB
BELCHER, William, decd, James Belcher of Savannah, Merchant, admr, 2/18/1785, Chatham, Adms
BELDING, William, allowed $60, p. 62, Screven, OM
BELL, Abby, B. F. Bishop, John H. Marlon, gdns, 1878, Cobb
BELL, Alfred C. and his wife, Susan P. Bell, formerly Snelling, L/G to Sampson Bell 11/1856, Webster, OD
BELL, Allen J., orph of John, decd, Richard Banks, gdn 11/4/1850, William R. Bell, sec, Hall, GB
BELL, Anderson W., orph of John, decd, William R. Bell, gdn, Richard Banks, sec, 11/4/1850, Hall, GB
BELL, Arlemisia Tabitha, decd, Benjamin Payne issued L/A 7/25/1811, Obediah Crawford, Gabriel Clarke, secs, Richmond, AB
BELL, G. C., Allen J. Bell, gdn, 1877, Cobb
BELL, Guilford E., orph of Hiram, decd, Frederick Bell gtd L/G 1/1857, Webster, OD
BELL, James, decd, Aaron Bell, gdn of Narciss and Harriett, orphs, 11/4/1850, John Deavours, sec, Hall, GB
BELL, J. C., decd, Lucy M. Bell, wid, admx, 1881, Cobb
BELL, Jeremiah, decd, Milly and William Bell, admrs, 3/5/1838, Randolph, AB
BELL, John, decd, Narcissa and William R. Bell issued temp L/A 3/5/1850 and perm L/A 5/6/1850, William A. Bell, Richard Banks, secs, Hall, AB
BELL, John L., orph of William, decd, Benjamin F. Porter, gdn, Raymond Sandford, sec, 10/4/1852, Hall, GB
BELL, Joseph, decd, Catherine Bell, Benjamin Warnick, admrs, 9/2/1822, Emanuel, AB
BELL, Joseph, decd, George W. Evans, gdn of orphs: Susannah and Margaret 3/6/1837, Jesse Higgs, Wm C. Phillips, Montgomery, GB

BELL, Joseph, decd, Mary H. Bell, wid. asks for dower, Bowling W. Stark, Mary Bell, admrs, 10/5/1829, Wilkes, OP
BELL, Julia H., D. A. Bell, gdn, 1878, Cobb
BELL, Lewis, decd, James M. Bell, gdn of orphs, produced exemplification from Stewart Co., 6/1854, Webster, OD
BELL, Madison, orph of John, decd, Isaac Rylee, gdn, James Rylee, sec, 1/13/1851, Hall, GB
BELL, Mamie A., B. A. Bell, gdn, 1892, Cobb
BELL, Margaret, decd, Fannie L. Bell, admr, 1892, Cobb
BELL, Margaret J., Margaret Bell, gdn, 1888, Cobb
BELL, Narcissa, J. C. Bell, gdn, 1878, Cobb
BELL, Robert, decd, Peter Winn qualified as admr 1/25/1791, Liberty, MIC
BELL, Sampson, decd, LWT pvd 3/1875, Webster, OD
BELL, W. A., Allen J. Bell, gdn, 1877, Cobb
BELL, William, decd, Benjamin F. Porter, gdn of orphs: James L., Daniel C., Sarah E. and Eliza A., 9/7/1852, Raymond Sandford, sec, Hall, GB
BELL, William, decd, William M. Bell issued L/A 5/3/1847, James Law, B. F. Porter, secs, Hall, AB
BELL, William, decd, William M. Bell, admr, Philip J. Evans, sur, 10/4/1852, Cherokee, AB
BELL, W. R., decd, Margaret Bell, admx, 1876, Cobb
BELL, Zachariah, decd, Green B. Hide issued L/A de bonis non w/LWT attached 1/10/1853, H. Jarratt, sec, Richmond, AB
BELLAH, Hiram, illegitimate son of Hannah, Samuel Bellah, gdn, Calvary F. Knight, sur, 1/5/1835, Butts, GB
BELLENGER, John, decd, Albert C. and John F. Ballenger qualified as exrs, 1866, Cobb
BELLENGER, John M., minor orph of John N., decd, James A. Pate, gdn, 8/23/1867, Fulton, GB
BELLENGER, Mary F., J. B. and E. E. Ballenger, gdns, 1866, Cobb
BEMELAUSs?, Henry, decd, LWT exhibited 7/1/1863, Emile Von Gordtsnoven?, exr, Fulton
BENDER, John, decd, L/A gtd Mary and Griffin Bender 7/7/1814, Jasper, OM
BENHAM, Lyman, decd, William King L/A 11/3/1822, Morgan, AB
BENNETT, Anthony, decd, Benjamin Lane, John Kirkland, admrs, 9/4/1826, Emanuel, AB
BENNETT, D. A., decd, I. N. Scott, admr, 1895, Cobb
BENNETT, Francis, I. N. Scott, gdn, 1896, Cobb
BENNETT, Hugh, decd, William Fleming, exr of LWT, gtd leave to sell undivided 1/1 interest in 2 tracts in Liberty Co. land 11/20/1809, Libery, MIC
BENNETT, Hugh, decd, Rebecca Bennett, Jas McCulloch, Jno Osgood qualified exrs 1/21/1791, Liberty, MIC
BENNETT, J. B., decd, Ida Bennett, extrx, 1895, Cobb
BENNETT, Joel, decd, Elijah Bennett issued L/A 11/1/1852, William Bennett, sec, Hall, AB
BENNETT, John, decd, John Peacock, Jr., admr, authorized to give deed to Morgan Mara, 1/31/1806, Liberty, MIC
BENNETT, Julian Barnes, illegitimate son of Benjamin Bennett, John Bennett, Bennett Bennett, gdns, 9/6/1842, Emanuel, GB
BENNETT, Matthew, decd, James House & wife, Mary, admx, gtd leave to sell prop in Sumter, S. C., 1/26/1807, Liberty, MIC
BENNETT, Reuben, decd, LWT dtd 1/1807 names wife, Elizabeth, ch: Winston, Elizabeth Evans, Ann Strozier, Jinney, William, Hannah, Richard, Asenah, Reuben, Polly; grch: Salley Powers, Bennett Powers; son-in-law, William Powers, Morgan, SCW
BENNETT, Reuben, decd, Stephen Evans, admr, 1810 Retn pd Elizabeth, gdn of Reuben Polly and Winston Bennett, Wilkes, AR

BENNETT, Reuben, decd, Case by Stephen Evans, admr, Anderson
Dabney, John Strozier, William Powers, all legatees vs.
Elizabeth, Winston and William Bennett, exrs; file caveat in rt
of wives; LWT refused for probate 2/15/1809, Morgan, SCW
BENNETT, Smith W., decd, John W. Bennett, admr, George M. Lowe,
sur, 7/12/1847, Bibb, AB
BENNETT, Thomas, decd, Thomas Hyde and Cornelius McCarty issued
L/A 7/2/1810, Jackson, OM
BENNETT, Willison, decd, Elizabeth Bennett, qualified admx
2/6/1791, Liberty, MIC
BENNING, Pleasant M., decd, Richard E. Benning, Ed. Benning,
admrs 4/1853, Harris
BENSON, Andrew M., decd, R. M. Benson and L. W. Fowler, admrs,
1878, Cobb
BENTLEY, Frances and minor child apply for year's support,
8/31/1869, Cobb, MIC
BENTLEY, Jeremiah, decd, heirs: Abi Bentley, wid, Mary and Jesse
Norman, Joseph, Sally, Alexander, Betsy, Jeremiah, William,
Cynthia and James Bentley, William and Patsy Nunnally, Osman and
Ada Nunnally, 12/29/1817, Wilkes, AR
BENTLEY, Jeremiah, decd, petition of Abi Bentley, wid, for div to
heirs: Willis Nunnally, William A. Bentley, Elizabeth Bentley,
Anderson T. Nunnally, Jesse Norman, 6/24/1818, Wilkes, OP
BENTLEY, Sam, decd, W. J. Hudson, admr, 1869, Cobb
BENTLEY, Samuel, decd, citation for admn of est to be heard Oct.
term, 8/27/1869, Cobb, MIC
BENTLEY, William, decd, Jane Bentley, Peter Smith, Benjamin
Ballard, exrs, 1802, Wilkes, OP
BENTON, Aaron, decd, Winnifred Benton, admx, Leroy Mims, Johnston
Wright, sur, 5/24/1805, Warren, MIC
BENTON, Archibald, orph of Mordecai, decd, Priscilla Benton, gdn,
Lillian Williamson, Hillery Pratt, sur, 9/2/1811, Jones, GB
BENTON, Casandra, orph of Mordecai, decd, Priscilla Benton, gdn,
Lillian Williamson, Hillery Pratt, sur, 9/2/1811, Jones, GB
BENTON, Francis, decd, Thomas Myhand, admr 5/3/1813, William
Myhand, sur, Warren, AB
BENTON, John, decd, 12/1836, appraisers: D. Sylvester, H. R.
Skelton, Benjamin Hill; purchasers at sale: Mrs. John Benton, J.
Davis, R. B. Goare, etc., Stewart, Adms
BENTON, John, decd, Winnifred Benton, admx, 8/14/1805, Leroy
Mims, Johnson Wright, surs, Warren, MIC
BENTON, John, orph of Mordecai, decd, Priscilla Benton, gdn,
Lillian Williamson, Hillery Pratt, sur, 9/2/1811, Jones, GB
BENTON, Josiah, decd, John Kelly, Amos Benton, admrs, Thomas P.
Stubbs, William Collins, surs, 12/9/1851, Bibb, AB
BENTON, Lucinda, orph of Mordecai, decd, Priscilla Benton, gdn,
Lillian Williamson and Hillery Pratt, surs, 9/2/1811, Jones, GB
BENTON, Lucy Jane, minor, Philip Williams, gdn, Harris, GB
BENTON, Martha, George C. Benton, gdn, Harris, GB
BENTON, Mary, Phillip Williams, gdn, Harris, GB
BENTON, Priscilla, orph of Mordecai, decd, Priscilla Benton, gdn,
Lillian Williamson, Hillery Pratt, sur, 9/2/1811, Jones, GB
BENTON, Susannah, dau of Mordecai, decd, chose James Pittman,
gdn, 10/2/1815, Jackson, OM
BENTON, Susannah, orph of Mordecai, decd, Priscilla Benton, gdn,
Lillian Williamson, Hillery Pratt, sur, 9/2/1811, Jones, GB
BENTON, Thomas H., decd, William Johnson, admr, Harris
BERGMAN, C. F., decd, Mary C. Bergman and Lewis Weitman apply for
L/A 9/7/1832, Effingham, MIC
BERNADY, Peter, decd, Catherine Bernady, as admx, 6/4/1827,
Camden, MIC

32

BERNADY, Peter, decd, Catherine Lane, admx, gtd leave to sell prop in Lee Co, 1/6/1835, Camden, MIC
BERNELL, Daniel, decd, 12/10/1824 appraisal of estate, Emanuel, A
BERNHARD, Pollie, minor over age 14, requests W. R. Bernhard for her gdn to replace William Porter of Nashville, Tennessee, 1/1/1883, Clarke, LP
BERNICE, John, decd, late of 4th Georgia Battalion, Oliver Lewis, admr 4/9/1784, Chatham, Adms
BERRAN, Henry, decd, 12/1839, J. P. Harvey, admr; apprs: J. B. Brown, L. C. Morgan, Charles H. Warren, Stewart, Adms
BERRIAN, Martha P., orph of Richard, decd, James J. Taylor apptd gdn 7/2/1838, Clarke, LP
BERRIE, Martha Elizabeth, of Jacksonville, Florida--LWT pvd 1/1/1850 by Henry Holland's ch-Marshall Berrie S, Elizabeth B, Jane A; Exrs-H. D. Holland & bro Wm A. Berrie; Cod, DuVal Co, Fla, Holland ch born after LWT were: Louisa, Selma, Mary & Henry, Glynn, MIC
BERRIE, William, decd, Mrs. Catherine A. Berrie qualified admx, 6/7/1842, Camden, MIC
BERRY, Green, decd, Jesse Coleman issued temporary L/A 2/24/1814, Putnam, AB
BERRY, James W. G., decd, James H. Bell, admr, William C. Dial, Frederick Freeman, sur, 4/9/1855, Cherokee, AB
BERRY, John apptd gdn of his minor ch: William B. and Augustus 5/1/1837, Clarke, LP
BERRY, John, decd, orphs, Robt (to age 71), Mary & Elizabeth (to age 18) bound to Stephen Brooks (ca 1804); Benjamin Camp's report of decd's prop & apptd gdn of Joshua, Robt, Polly, Betsy & Wm 9/2/1811; Eli Whaley gdn 3/2/1812, Jackson, OM
BERRY, John J. D., son of John, decd, David Berry, gdn, Thomas M. Harkness, sur, 5/8/1843, Butts, GB
BERRY, Joshua, orph of John, decd, age 7 last Sept. 28, bound to William Cates until age 21, 10/28/1805,
BERRY, Nicholas, Robert Arnett, gdn, p. 161, Screven, OM
BERRY, Obadiah, the accts of John B. Berry, gdn, 3/3/1828, Effingham, MIC
BERRY, Obadiah, decd, John B. Berry to have leave to sell negro named Adam 5/7/1838, Effingham, MIC
BERRY, Richard M., decd, James H. Bell, admr, Benjamin F. Freeman, Thomas D. Evans, sur, 12/12/1854, Cherokee, AB
BERRY, Robert, orph of John, decd, age 7 on next Feb. 10th, is bound to Joshua Betts 10/28/1805, Jackson, OM
BERRY, William, orph of John, decd, age 2 the 16th of June last, is bound to William Cates until age 21, 10/28/1805, Jackson, OM
BERRY, William, decd, Susannah & Tolever Berry, admrs, Geo Philips, Hezekiah Luckie and Samuel Brightwell, secs, 1/1809, Oglethorpe, OM
BERRYHILL, Samuel, decd, Robert Berryhill issued L/A 9/28/1795, Wm Boyd, Reuben Harrison, secs, Richmond, AB
BESS, Christopher, orph of Harris, decd, George W. Adcock, gdn, Simon J. Tidwell, sur, 6/6/1859, Paulding, GB
BESS, Harris, orph of Harris, decd, George W. Adcock, gdn, Simon J. Tidwell, sur, 6/6/1859, Paulding, GB
BESS, Littleton, orph of Harris, decd, George W. Adcock, gdn, Simon J. Tidwell, sur, 6/6/1859, Paulding, GB
BESS, Sarah, orph of Harris, decd, George W. Adcock, gdn, Simon J. Tidwell, sur, 6/6/1859, Paulding, GB
BESS, Sion, orph of Harris, decd, George W. Adcock, gdn, Simon J. Tidwell, sur, 6/6/1859, Paulding, GB

BESSANT, Abraham, decd, Isaac Crews, John Bessant, admrs, 11/7/1814; Mrs. Ann Bessant apptd gdn of her minor ch: Abraham, Robert, Alexis and Adeline; James and Peter G., her sons over age of 14 chose her as their gdn 4/3/1820; Ann Bessant, admx, gtd leave to sell lot in St. Marys, 6/2/1835, and leave to sell lot in Jefferson and St. Mary's, sd co., 10/10/1836, Camden, MIC

BESSANT, Abraham (Judge), decd, Justice of court, John Bessant, Isaac Crews apptd temp admrs, 10/3/1814, Camden, MIC

BESSANT, Alexis, decd, Mrs. Mary Bessant qualified extrx of LWT, 1/4/1847, Camden, MIC

BESSANT, John, decd, Mary Bessant appointed admx, 11/6/1815, Camden, MIC

BESSANT, Robert, decd, Willis Lang, admr, gtd leave to sell, 6/2/1840, Camden, MIC

BEST, Tarlton B., Thomas B. and William D. Camed, gdns, p. 96; Thomas B. Campbell, admr, p. 118, Screven, OM

BEST, William (Reverend), decd, Samuel Best apptd admr, 9/18/1815, Camden, MIC

BETTERTON, J. B., decd, E. Faw, exr, 1870, Cobb

BETTIS, John, decd, Matthew Bettis, atty for Stephen Bettis, admr, 4/15/1796, Frederick Swearingen, George Miller, secs, Richmond, AB

BEVIL, Claiburn and James, James Dampier, gdn, p. 111, p. 196, Screven, OM

BEVIL, Delia and Paul, gtd leave to sell real estate, p. 44, 70, Screven, OM

bBEVIL, Eliza W., Paul R. Bevil, gdn, p. 115, Screven, OM

BEVIL, James, decd, Joseph Ball, etc., apprs, p. 93, Paul Bevil, etc., apprs, p. 34, Screven, OM

BEVIL, Paul, decd, James Boston, etc. divided est, p. 118, Screven, OM

BEVIL, Paul Sr. and Martha, James Bevil, admr, p. 93, Screven, OM

BEVIL, Paul, Sr. and Eliza, Paul Bevil, Jr., admr, p. 93, Screven, OM

BEVIL, Stephen and John G., Paul Bevil, Sr., gdn, p. 114, Screven, OM

BEVILL, Paul, decd, LWT admitted to record 3/4/1834; W. H. Scruggs gtd leave to sell prop 3/4/1834, Effingham, MIC

BEVILLE, McLin, bastard son of Frances Lunday, bond dtd 6/29/1793 by Frances Lunday, Robert Beville and Nathaniel Lunday, sur, Effingham, Misc

BEYERS, Lawrence, decd, Elisha Moreley, one of securities of Jesse Champion, admr on est of decd, wishes to be dischd, 11/3/1817, Jasper, OM

BIBBS, Jesse of Adams Co., Mississippi, power of atty to Joshua Glass formerly of Oglethorpe Co., Ga. to recover from John Landrum a legacy left Bibbs by LWT of William Harper 8/24/1807, Wilkes, OP

BICE, M., decd, Lavonia Swetman, wid, admx, 1893, Cobb

BICKERSTAFF, Ripley, orph of Robert, decd, Creed T. Wise, gdn, Andrew R. Bickerstaff, sec, 11/6/1837, Butts, GB

BICKERSTAFF, Ripley H., minor or Robert, decd, retn for ward by Creed T. Wise, 1/21/1840, Butts, ER

BICKERSTAFF, Robert, decd, A. R. Bickerstaff, admr, 1/1839 pd legatees: Wm R. Head, Alsey Durham, Hugh Wise, Jos. W. Slaughter, Henry P. Slaughter, Creed T. Wise, Pollard B. Bickerstaff, & self as gdn for Robert, Butts, ER

BICKERSTAFF, Robert, decd, late of Alabama, Anderson R. Bickerstaff, admr, Parham Lindsey, Creed T. Wise, secs, 7/20/1836, Butts, AB

BICKERSTAFF, William J., orph of Robert, decd, Creed T. Wise, gdn, Andrew B. Bickerstaff, sec, 11/6/1837, 1838 retn, Butts, GB

34

BIDDENBACH, Mary (Miss), decd, Christian Biddenbach, admr, 11/14/1793, Effingham, Misc
BIDDENBACH, Mathias, decd, Trustees, Ebenezer Congregation, admrs, 9/21/1793, Effingham, Misc
BIDDLE, Pendleton T., decd, Lovick P. Thomas gdn of orphs: Pendleton J., William E. and Robert J., 5/7/1838, Clarke, LP
BIGGS, James P., minor, 9/12/1863 heirs: mother, Eliza Biggs, sisters; Ann S. Maxey (wid of Henry recently killed in battle), Mary Mourning Biggs, Peninah F. Biggs, Martha Elizabeth Biggs, bros, John F., William, and W. L. Biggs, Clarke, LP
BIGGS, Willis J., decd, heirs 10/6/1862: Eliza, James P., Martha Elizabeth, John F., Wilson L., William and Mary Mourning Biggs, Ann S. Mazey, Jesse Maxey, Peninah Biggs, Clarke, LP
BIGGS, Willis L., decd, J. Landrum gdn of Martha Elizabeth, Mary Mourning, Wm 1861; Wm J. Landrum gdn of James P. 3/8/1860; Milledge Durham, gdn of Penington F. 1863; Jno Osborn, gdn of Willis J.; James McRee, gdn of Jno F. 1861, Clarke, LP
BILBO, James, L/D, Nathaniel Lunday, p. 111, Screven, OM
BILBO, John, decd, Nathaniel Lunday, admr, 1797, retns 1782-1795, tuition pd for James Bilbo, son of decd, Effingham, Misc
BILLINGSLEA, Clem, orph, James Billingslea, gdn, 1800-1809 Retns, Wilkes, OP
BILLINGSLEA, Clement, one of legatees of James Lane, in right of his wife, Sarah A. Billingslea, formerly Sarah A. Lane, to Micajah A. Lane, also heir of said James, 2/13/1821, Wilkes, OP
BILLINGSLEA, Francis, decd, Samuel and James Billingslea, exrs, 1805 Retns, receipts of John, Walter, James, Francis and Cyrus BILLINGSLEA Howell, orph, James Billingslea, gdn, 1800-1809 Retns, Wilkes, OP
BILLINGSLEA, John, decd, James Billingslea, Asa Atkins, admrs, 1807 Retns, Wilkes, OP
BILLINGSLEA, Samuel, decd, Cyrus Billingslea, admr, recpts of Francis & Matthew Billingslea, Charity, John, Polly & Winston Billingslea, heirs, Wilkes, OP
BILLINGSLEA, Samuel, orph of John, decd, John Farmington, gdn, 9/1/1817, Morgan, GB
BILLINGSLEA, Thomas Norris, in right of his wife, Sarah, 2/25/1804, Wilkes, OP
BILLUPS, Edward P., son of Robert, decd, Asa M. Jackson, gdn, 2/6/1843; Shubale Tenney apptd 12/1/1840 and Steven Thomas apptd 1/3/1842, Clarke, LP
BILLUPS, Lucy Jane, dau of Robert R., decd, James D. Thomas apptd gdn 12/1/1840, Clarke, LP
BILLUPS, Robert R., decd, Elizabeth W. Billups, extrx 9/16/1836; Walter A. Appling for wife, Judith; Jas D. Thomas for wife; Jas D. Thomas, gdn of Lucy J. Billups, Shubale Tenny, gdn of E. S. Billups, Walter A. Appling for wife, Clarke, LP
BINGHAM, S. A., decd, W. F. Bingham, exr, 1888, Cobb
BINGHAM, S. A., Mrs. E. C. Bingham, gdn, 1889, Cobb
BINNS, Burrell, decd, Joseph Anthony, admr, Elizabeth Binns 1818 pd bd for Betsy, Sally, Ann, Burrell Binns. Recpt of Asa Pye in rt of wife, Catharine, Wilkes, OP
BINNS, Burrell, decd, Joseph Anthony, admr, 1815-6 Retns pd dower to Betsy Binns 1817 and tuition for Kitty and Sally Binns, Wilkes, AR
BINNS, Christopher, decd, Dudley Stinson, Sally Binns, wid, admrs, inventory 12/30/1818, Wilkes, OP
BINNS, Christopher, minor of Christopher, decd, Dudley Stinson, gdn, 9/3/1821, Wilkes, OP
BINNS, David, minor of Christopher, decd, Dudley Stinson, gdn, 9/3/1821, Wilkes, OP

35

BINNS, George, minor of Christopher, decd, Dudley Stinson, gdn, 9/3/1821, Wilkes, OP
BINNS, Phoebe, minor of Christopher, decd, Dudley Stinson, gdn, 9/3/1821, Wilkes, OP
BINNS, Sarah, decd, 12/14/1853, Wilkes, OP
BINNS, Susannah, minor of Christopher, decd, Dudley Stinson, gdn, 9/3/1821, Wilkes, OP
BINNS, William, decd, John B. Leonard, exr 1813 Retn, inventory 1/19/1814, Wilkes, AR, OP
BIRCH, John, decd, Mrs. Elizabeth Ann & James I. Gray of Chatham Co., admrs, 12/31/1801, Effingham, Misc
BIRD, Abraham, decd, Wm Bird, Mrs. Margaret Bird, admrs, 8/11/1800, Effingham, Misc
BIRD, Comfort, decd, Paul Chase was apptd admr, 11/7/1814, Camden, MIC
BIRD, James, decd, Sarah Bird, widow, survivor of Gotlieb Smith (her father), extrx of James Bird vs. Raymond P. Demere 5/10/1820, Bryan, Writs
BIRD, John G., decd, LWT dtd 10/21/1852, pvd 3/1/1853, names wife, Nancy and dau, Mary, Cherokee
BIRD, Penelope, decd, LWT 5/1835 names mother, Jane Bird, David Bird and M. B. Haley, Stewart, MIC
BIRD, Wiley, decd, sale of prop 7/10/1845 by Hezekiah J. Parrish and Jackson Bird, admrs, Bulloch, Misc
BIRD, William, decd, Wilson Bird, exr of LWT dtd 3/1/1813, Warren, MIC
BIRD, William (Colonel), Mrs. Catherine Bird, wid. gives notice of claim for dowry, 2/7/1814, Warren, MIC
BIRD, William, Sr., decd, LWT admitted to record 1/12/1846, Effingham, MIC
BIRDSONG, C. W., decd, Lafayette F. Birdsong issued L/G of minor orphs of decd 11/1857, Webster, OD
BIRDSONG, P. F., decd, J. D. Stapleton and C. Birdsong issued L/A 3/1863, Webster, OD
BISHOP, Amanda, orph of M. T., decd, James Graves, gdn, 3/1838, 1845 retn, Fayette, GB
BISHOP, Elbert, decd, Jesse Hubbard, admr, John O. Dickson, sur, 11/1852, 1852-1854 retns, Fayette, AB
BISHOP, Elijah, decd, John P. Marbut, admr, 2/3/1863, Jacob Chupp, sur, DeKalb, AB
BISHOP, James, decd, Samuel Cooper, admr, 2/15/1803, Joel Heath, Thomas Hutchinson, surs, Warren, AB
BISHOP, James, decd, Jno Bishop, Samuel Cooper, admrs, Joel Heath, Thos Hutchins, sur, 11/25/1802, Warren, AB, MIC
BISHOP, John, decd, Sarah Bishop and Robert Henderson issued L/A 12/2/1805, John Turman, Frizell McTyeire, secs, Richmond, AB
BISHOP, John T., decd, John M. Hawkins, admr, 8/4/1862, E. L. Morton, sur, DeKalb, AB
BISHOP, Joseph E., decd, W. H. Braswell, James H. Born issued temporary L/A 3/6/1857, G. M. Born, David Chupp, surs, DeKalb, AB
BISHOP, Nancy, orph of M. T., decd, Jesse Ward, gdn, Eli Edmondson, William Sparkman, surs, 9/1847, 1851-1854 retns, Fayette, GB
BISHOP, Peter, decd, Mrs. Jane Bishop qualified admx 9/10/1790, Liberty, MIC
BISHOP, S. E., L. A. Bishop, gdn, 1892, Cobb
BISHOP, Stephen, orph of James, chose Hinton A. Hill, gdn, 3/1828, Habersham, MIC
BISHOP, William W., decd, late of Montgomery, Alabama, William Malone, admr, C. L. Westmoreland, sur, 7/1852, Fayette, AB
BITTER, William, decd, Robert Skelton issued L/A 11/5/1821, Laurens, AB

BIXBY, James, decd, Joseph and Mariah F. Bixby qualified as exrs of LWT, 3/16/1819; Mariah F. Bixby relieved of being extrx, she having recd no prop or assets of est, applies for dismission 6/3/1823, Camden, MIC
BIXBY, John, decd, Belton A. Copp, admr, 10/17/1825, Camden, MIC
BIXBY, Joseph, decd, Belton A. Copp, apptd admr, 3/7/1825, Camden, MIC
BIXBY, Joseph, decd, Mortimer D. Millikin, admr, LWT annexed from S. C., 7/1/1833, Camden, MIC
BLACK, Edward, decd, Returns of John W. Butler, exr, 1816, Wilkes, AR
BLACK, Edward, decd, Edward Butler, exr, receipt of John Black for boarding 5 children, 1797, Wilkes, OP
BLACK, Elmira M. E., minor child of John, Kinchen Womble gtd L/G 1/9/1843, Washington
BLACK, James, decd, David M. Black issued L/A 9/5/1853, James Roberts, Richard Wilson, Joseph A. Fraser, secs; again issued L/A 2/6/1854 with John T. and Temperance Black, secs, Hall, AB
BLACK, John, decd, John Butt, Sr. and George Black issued L/A 2/8/1831, Habersham, MIC
BLACK, John, decd, pet of Thomas J. Rusk 7/12/1831 that decd made bond to John Butt for title to Lot 119, 9th Dist, Carroll Co., Habersham, MIC
BLACK, Nancy Ann apptd gdn of her dau, Emma Dora Bention 1/1890, Clarke, LP
BLACK, Peter, lunatic, Willis J. Whatley, gdn, Joshua W. White, Benj. P. White, sur, 9/4/1848, Troup, GB
BLACK, William, decd, John Wallace L/A 3/2/1814, Putnam, AB
BLACK, William, decd, Thomas Tumblin, admr, p. 8, Screven, OM
BLACKBURN, Jesse, decd, John and Martha Blackburn, admrs, John Groves, in right of his wife, Mary Ann Blackburn, Martha Blackburn, wid, 7/1/1842, Wilkes, OP
BLACKBURN, Lewis, decd, LWT dtd 10/1/1852, pvd 1/1853, names ch: Catharine Nichols, Frances H. Hutson, Elizabeth Scudder, Mary Tapler, Louisa Rodgers, Emily M. Oliver, Jackson Rogers, trustee for Sarah Rogers, Cherokee
BLACKMAN, James G., decd, John W. Laney, admr, 12/7/1863, Harris
BLACKMON, Gatsey, decd, John W. Laney, admr, 11/6/1863, Harris
BLACKMON, Homer, decd, Joseph R. Wood, admr, John H. Mecaslin, William Barnes, secs, 9/10/1860, Fulton, AB
BLACKMON, James, Elijah R. Young, gdn, p. 86, Screven, OM
BLACKMON, Joel, decd, Hollis Blackmon, John C. Blackmon, exrs, 11/3/1845; John C., Hollis and James R. Blackmon, admrs 5/1848, Harris, AB
BLACKMON, Martha, decd, Thomas G. Horne, James R. Blackmon, admrs, 1/1854, Harris, AB
BLACKMON, Miranda, minor, Francis Hudspeth, gdn, 1/1/1860, Harris, GB
BLACKSHEAR, William, E. P. Blackshear L/G 2/1865, Webster, OD
BLACKWELL, Ambrose, decd, Nancy Blackwell issued L/A 5/2/1814; admx, makes retn 9/2/1816, Jackson, OM
BLACKWELL, Elizabeth, decd, J. Y. Alexander, admr, 1895, Cobb
BLACKWELL, J. B., decd, G. B. Waddell, admr, 1894, Cobb
BLACKWELL, Joseph, decd, Dunston Blackwell, admr, 1809 recpts of R. Blackwell, Betsy C. Williamson, Banks, Joseph and Parke Blackwell, legatees, Elbert, AR
BLACKWELL, Randolph, decd, T. Shinholster, admr w/LWT annexed, S. Stephens, M. Thompson, surs, 3/17/1851, Bibb, AB
BLAIR, Alexander, decd, Felix McKinne, John McKinne, Barma McKinne, Elizabeth Blair issued L/A 10/10/1804, Richmond, AB

BOARDMAN, Daniel, decd, Jonathan Meigs, admr, 1811, Bryan, MSC
BOATRIGHT, Charles, orph of Daniel, decd, Margaret Boatright,
gdn, Sion Kirkham, Edward Surrency, surs, 9/3/1821, Emanuel, GB
BOAIRIGHT, Daniel, decd, James Waters, admr, L. Thigpen, John
Saffer, surs, 9/7/1812; James Wales apptd admr 10/17/1818,
Emanuel, AB, A
BOATRIGHT, Nancy, orph of Daniel, decd, Margaret Boatright, Sion
Kirkham and Edward Surrency, gdns, 9/3/1821; Benjamin Sherrod,
gdn, George Dekle, sec, 9/4/1826, Emanuel, GB
BOATRIGHT, Rolly gtd L/G of his minor ch: McEarly and Zelphia
Boatright 5/3/1841, Washington
BOBO, Lewis, decd, bond of Mary Bobo, extrx; inventory 10/1/1798;
James Young sd Lewis Bobo gave bond during his lifetime to land
and died without giving title thereto, 3/1802, Franklin, OM
BODENS, John K., decd, Harbut Bodens, admr, Samuel Ray, sec,
3/6/1847, Bibb, AB
BOGER, Peter C., decd, Daniel C. Boger, John H. Boger, admrs,
8/1/1853, Cherokee, AB
BOGER, Peter F., orph of Peter C., decd, Paul C. Boger, gdn, John
H. Boger, sur, 3/10/1856, Cherokee, GB
BOGGS, John M., decd, late of Arkansas, William M. Boggs apptd
admr 5/2/1853; land in Gordon, Cobb and Lumpkin Co.'s, Clarke, LP
BOGGS, John R., decd, John M. Odell and Jane Bogg issued L/A
6/4/1860, White, AB
BOHANNON, Duncan, orph of William, decd, William Spinks apptd gdn
5/4/1818, Clarke, LP
BOHANNON, Isaac W., orph of William, decd, Henry Carleton, gdn,
Edmund Hanning, sur, 5/6/1815, Clarke, GB
BOHANNON, Isaiah W. D., orph of William, decd, Henry Cartlow
apptd gdn 5/6/1816, Clarke, LP
BOHANNON, J. W. D., decd, C. W. McGinnis, admr, 2/8/1853, E. A.
Davis, Robert Webb and J. W. Kirkpatrick, surs, DeKalb, AB
BOHANNON, Wiley, Jeremiah Robertson apptd gdn of Wiley s minor
ch: Tabitha and William F., 10/23/1838; father apptd their gdn
2/12/1839, Clarke, LP
BOHANNON, William, orph of William, decd, Thomas Bell apptd gdn
11/5/1821, Clarke, LP
BOHANNON, William, decd, Barbara Bohannon, James McCord and
William Moore, admrs, W. Rossiter and R. Fullwood, surs,
3/6/1815, Clarke, AB
BOHLER, George, orph of William, decd, Absolom Bohler, gdn of
orphs 10/8/1839, F. F. Fleming, Peter Lamar, secs, Lincoln, GB
BOLDEN, William, John V. Steele apptd gdn, 1881, Cobb
BOLER, Christopher, decd, Robert Searls, gdn for orphs: John,
Katy, William and Moses 9/1/1823, William Reynolds and John
Fleming, secs, Lincoln, GB
BOLER, Moses, rph of Christopher, decd, John Eady, gdn, 5/4/1829,
James Jennings, sec, Lincoln, GB
BOLES, Jesse, decd, John Bailey, exr of his LWT 9/1806,
Oglethorpe, OM
BOLING, William, decd, Absolom Holcomb and William Boling, admrs
1/15/1828; apprs: James Allen, Hamilton Wynn, Joseph Holcomb,
William B. Wofford, Charles Baker, Habersham, MIC
BOLTON, Isaac, decd, Manoah Bolton, exr, 1820 retns, Wilkes, OP
BOMAR, WIlliam, decd, John Bailey and William Hutchinson, admrs,
8/181/1792, Greene, Misc
BOND, John, decd, Drewry W. Pace issued temporary L/A 5/6/1858,
Jane Bond, sur, DeKalb, AB
BOND, Lewis, decd, Joseph Bond filed for L/A as admr of estate
3/1854, Lee, MSC

BOND, Thomas, decd, Mark Bond, gdn for orphs: Mark, Anna and
Elizabeth 11/4/1833, John H. Sybert and Charles Hughuley, secs,
Lincoln, GB
BOND, Thomas, decd, Thomas Formby, exr, Edward Bond caveat,
3/1/1813, Wilkes, OP
BOND, Thomas, T. B. Bond, gdn, 1896, Cobb
BONDURAND, Mary J. (Mrs.), decd, she d. 5/10/1897, heirs were
children: E. J. Bondurant and F. W. Bondurant, Clarke, LP
BONE, Bailey, decd, Henry Bone, John Bone, admrs, James Coel, B.
M. C. Matthews, John Denson, W. D. Harris, sur, 5/3/1859,
Paulding, AB
BONNELL, Arthur, petition to be relieved from bond, p. 41,
Screven, OM
BONNELL, Daniel, decd, Benjamin Lane, David Cowart, admrs,
11/9/1824, Emanuel, AB
BONNER, Allen, decd, heirs: wife, Lucy, minor ch: Lucy Ann,
Frances Emily and Allen, Jerusha Bonner, Wm A. Drake, John
Morrow, Richd L. Simms, H. L. Ruse and Mahala Hill, no date,
Clarke, LP
BONNER, Allen, orph of Allen, decd, Henry Green, gdn, in rt of
his wife, Frances Emily Bonner, 1835, Clarke, LP
BONNER, Bedford, Lenorah, Matilda, William S., Mary J., Whitmell
Jr. Bonner, orphs, Colonel John Selmers apptd gdn, 1/1821,
Jasper, OM
BONNER, Claborn, decd, John Alexander, exr, 1876, Cobb
BONNER, Lucy Ann, orph of Allen, decd, Lucy Bonner, gdn, 1830,
Clarke, LP
BONNER, Rebecca, decd, William Bonner, Joseph Watson, admrs,
Archibald Simpson, sec, Wilkes, OP
BONNFR, Robert, decd, Sherwood Bugg, admr, 1/15/1791,
Columbia, AB
BONNER, Thomas, decd, 1804 heirs: Jordan, Zadock, Thomas,
Whitmele and Alden Bonner, Edmond Duke, R. Vandenford, Clarke, LP
BONNER, Whitnell, decd, L/A gtd Alley Bonner and Jonathan Bonner,
3/1819; Alley Bonner, wid, chooses 1/3 pt of est,
Jasper, OM
BONNER, William, decd, Ruth Bonner, admx, 12/5/1784, Wilkes, OP
BONNER, (or BONER) William, decd, Ruth Boner, wid, appd admx
11/4/1783, Wilkes, MxR
BONNER, William A., decd, Richard H. Waters issued L/A 9/4/1854,
J. S. Harman, sec, Richmond, AB
BONNER, Wyatt, decd,; Nancy Bonner apptd as admx 7/3/1810; James
& Nancy Bonner, admrs, gtd leave to sell negro slave, 11/4/1811;
Lewis Parham pets for order directing James Bonner, admr, in rt
of his wife & Nancy Conner, admx, to give title to 100 acres in
compliance with Bond for Title made Parham in the lifetime of
decd, 11/4/1811; admrs of est directed to make title to Lewis
Parham as per his petition, 2/3/1812; James Bonner, admr,
9/4/1815, William Brown, David Sallis, secs, Warren, MIC, AB
BOOG, Isabella, decd, LWT pvd by Archibald Clark 1/16/1843;
Mary E. King, gdn of orphs, leave to sell slave, 10/10/1836,
Camden, MIC Camden, MIC
BOOG, Isabella, orph of John & Isabella K. Boog, decd, Wm Rose of
Savannah, mercht, gdn, 2/7/1826, Camden, MIC
BOOG, James Augustus, orph of John & Isabella K. Boog, decd, Wm
Rose of Savannah, mercht, gdn, 2/7/1826, Camden, MIC
BOOG, Julia Ross, orph of John & Isabella K. Boog, decd, Wm Rose
of Savannah, mercht, gdn, 2/7/1826, Camden, MIC
BOOG, Margaret, orph of John & Isabella R. Boog, decd, Wm Rose of
Savannah, mercht, gdn, 2/7/1826, Camden, MIC
BOOG, Modina, orph of John & Isabella R. Boog, decd, Wm Rose of
Savannah, mercht, gdn, 2/7/1826, Camden, MIC

BOOKER, Wiley apptd gdn of Sarah A. D. and Eliza A. Booker 2/2/1852, Houston, GB
BOOKER, William F., decd, Charles R. Carter, admr, pd William M. Booker, Nancy H., M. A., and Thomas F. Booker, 1809, Wilkes, AR
BOON, Green, decd, Glazier and Robert Milton, admrs, William McDowell, Isaac McClendon, sec, 3/6/1814, Jasper, OM
BOON, Martha, minor orph of Lewis, decd, Harris Co., Ulyses M. Neil apptd gdn 1/3/1835; John Roe apptd gdn 11/8/1836, Randolph
BOON, Ratliff, decd, LWt pvd 2/1875, Webster, OD
BOON, Thomas, decd, Joseph and James Boon, admrs, 5/19/1794, Elisha Puritt, John Hill, surs, Warren, AB
BOOTH, Archable, decd, Zachariah Petty, admr, A. McBride, William Herring, sur, 3/1840, 1842 retn, Fayette, AB
BOOTH, Richard, decd, William Meriwether, admr, James Hendon, Robt Ligon, sur, 7/7/1823, Clarke, AB
BOOTH, Walton H., orph of Benjamin h., decd, Robert L. harris apptd gdn 1/7/1839, Clarke, LP
BOOTHE, John, decd, inv and sale 2/24/1808, David S. Booth, admr, 1811 retn, apptd gdn of orphs: Prudence W., Thomas W. and Martha 5/4/1812, Elbert, AR
BOOTY, Nicholas, decd, Warren & Richard Barrow, wit. to his LWT, 1/1/1810, Warren, MIC
BORAN, Jesse, decd, 9/8/1803 apprs-Andr. Baxter, Eli Harris, Jon Adams; purchasers-Nancy Boran, Eli Harris, Peyton Sledge, Stephen Durdan, Jno Hearn, Robt Mills, Saml Ferguson, Abram Laurence, Jas Adams; Abraham Lawrence, admr, Hancock, AAA
BORDER, Michael, decd, LWT pvd 1/6/1807; John Borders´ retn of 4 yrs 7/4/1814; pet of Martin & Malachi Cleck that admrs give title to 25 acres where decd lived in Greene Co., bond for title made 9/23/1794 in Elbert Co., 1/2/1809 Jackson, OM
BORDERS, Stephen, decd, William W. Bruce, admr 2/1864, Harris
BOREN, Benjamin, decd, Peggy Boren, wid, asks for dower,7/10/1822, Wilkes, OP
BOREN, David, orph of James, decd, William Boren, gdn, 3/4/1811, Wilkes, OP
BOREN, James, decd, William C. Boren, exr, 1810 Retn, Annis Boren mentioned, Wilkes, AR
BOREN, James, gdn, 1811 receipts of David and Hannah Boren, pd John Boren his legacy, Wilkes, GR
BOREN, Joseph, orph of James, decd, Hannah Boren, gdn, 3/4/1811, Wilkes, OP
BOREN, Nancy, orph, William C. Boren, gdn, 1810 Retn, Wilkes, GR
BOREN, Nancy, orph of James, decd, William Boren, gdn, 3/4/1811, Wilkes, OP
BOREN, Polly, orph of James, decd, Hannah Boren, gdn, 3/4/1811, Wilkes, OP
BOREN, Sally, orph of James, decd, Hannah Boren, gdn, 3/4/1811, Wilkes, OP
BORIN, D. S. M., decd, Nathan Turner, admr, 11/5/1855, E. A. Turner, James C. Avary, James Philips, surs, DeKalb, AB
BORING, Eliza N., Thomas Boring, gdn, David Croft, sur, 4/9/1855, Cherokee, GB
BORING, John J., son of Thomas, Thomas Boring apptd gdn, Isaac Boring, Sarah Boring, sur, 9/6/1852, Cherokee, GB
BORING, Mary M., John P. Boring, gdn, 1890, Cobb
BORLANE, Abraham, decd, Michael J. Kenan, admr, 11/15/1847, Baldwin, AB
BOSTICK, Samuel, planter, gift deed to sons: John Graves Bostick, William Bostick & Littleberry Bostick of Richland Co., South Carolina 8/14/1799; deed 3/7/1799 to dau, Sarah Porter of Effingham Co., 50 acres on Big Tuckaseeking Cr, Effingham, Misc

40

BOSTON, Margaret K., George Boston applied for gdnshp of his child 7/7/1845, Effingham, MIC
BOSTON, William K., George Boston applied for gdnshp of his child 7/7/1845, Effingham, MIC
BOSTWICK, C. C., decd, Andrew J. Hansel, admr, 1873, Cobb
BOSWELL, George, decd, Sarah Boswell, admx, 1825 Retns, minors: Elizabeth, Sarah, Johnson, James H. and Frances C., Wilkes, OP
BOSWORTH, Thomas C., orph of James, decd, Josiah R. Bosworth, gdn, Jeptha Landrum, George Ward, surs, 1/1841, Fayette, GB
BOTHWELL, James, John G. Vernon, gdn, John R. Golt, Ira R. Foster, sur, 12/11/1854, Cherokee, GB
BOUGH, Daniel Thomas, orph, bound to W. T. Leonard for 5 yrs, Nathan Evit, sec, 5/11/1858, White, GB
BOURQUOIS, Robert H., decd, Moselle Bourquois, wid, applied for L/A 7/3/1847, Effingham, MIC
BOUTINOU, Roswell, decd, Levi Gregory issued L/A 8/15/1805, Asa Shaw, Sylvester Porter, secs, Richmond, AB
BOWEN, Amariah W., Josiah J. Everett, gdn, 11/4/1839, GB
BOWEN, Elisha, decd, LWT pvd 4/23/1827, names wife, Penny; son-in-law, Bazzel Jones; exrs, wife, Penny and Seth Williams, Bulloch, Misc
BOWEN, Elizabeth, decd, her LWT probated, 1/5/1836 Henry Bacon, admr, dismissed, 6/3/1837; Dr. Henry Bacon, admr, J. Pottle, Jno Bessant, Alexis Bessant, etc div. est, 1/3/1837; Eli Ratcliffe pvd in Catahoula Par La. m. Charlotte Hollingsworth, heir, 1/2/1838; Samuel Thompson, minor son of Caroline Hollingsworth, decd, also co-heir, 1/2/1838 Camden, MIC
BOWEN, Jabez, decd, Charity Bowen, relict, sale of est 4/1784, Wilkes, OP
BOWEN, Jane, (Mrs.) decd, (also Samuel Bowen, decd), Joseph William Spencer and Dr. Beecroft gtd L/A 5/20/1783, Chatham, Adms
BOWEN, Jeremiah, decd, Elizabeth Bowen apptd admx, to sell schooner "Betsy Maria", 1/6/1829; admx dismissed 6/3/1833, Camden, MIC
BOWEN, Jobe, decd, inv 10/1/1783, apprs: Edward McGary, Thomas Gray, Nat Beddingfield, Wilkes, MxR
BOWEN, John, gdn for Seaborn and Mary J. Bowen makes retn 11/4/1839, Tattnall, I&A
BOWEN, John, decd, Christopher Clark, Jr., John Matthews, admrs, 12/6/1790, Wilkes, OP
BOWEN, John, decd, appraisal 3/8/1838; apprs: Nicholas Reddick, Elijah Wade, James Cox, Joel Mock; purchasers at sale: Elizabeth, Sparkman & Richard Bowen, Redding Bowen, Thos W. Pettee, Wm M. Hart, Jonathan Platt, James Trent, etc, Dooly, I&A
BOWEN, John C., decd, wife, Martha B. Bowen, LWT pvd 9/14/1836, Allen Green, Saml Huey, Saml Howell, James Huff, admrs, Harris, AB
BOWEN, Jonathan, decd, inv by Malaki Jones, admr 8/9/1796, Franklin, OM
BOWEN, Levi, decd, John Bowen, admr, makes retn 5/7/1838, Tattnall, I&A
BOWEN, Mary Jane, minor orph of Levi, decd, John Little, gdn, 11/4/1839, Tattnall, GB
BOWEN, Mahala, bound to Samuel W. Allen, p. 57, Screven, OM
BOWEN, Malachi, decd, John H. Newton issued L/A 1/9/1837, Washington
BOWEN, Mark, decd, inv of est 6/2/1836, Tattnall, I&A
BOWEN, Mary Jane, orph of Uriah N., decd, William B. Elliott apptd gdn 11/5/1844, Clarke, LP
BOWEN, Samuel, decd, (also Mrs. Jane Bowen) Joseph William Spencer and Dr. Beecroft gtd L/A 5/20/1783, Chatham, Adms
BOWEN, Seaborn, minor orph of Levi, decd, John Little, gdn, 11/4/1839, Tattnall, GB

BOWEN, Stephen, gdn of his minor son, Francis M., John D. Williard, William C. Parker, secs, 6/2/1862, Fulton, GB
BOWEN, Uriah N., decd, est 5/7/1838, Clarke, LP
BOWEN, William, decd, William H. Torrence, admr 9/7/1835; Samuel Rockwell, admr, 7/2/1838; William Y. Howell, admr 1/2/1843, Baldwin, AB
BOWEN, William, decd, Samuel Rockwell, admr, 7/2/1838, Baldwin, AR
BOWER, Benjamin, decd, Lud Harris and Mary Bowers issued L/A 11/27/1797, Benjamin Harris, John de Vampert, secs, Richmond, AB
BOWERS, Jobe, decd, Charity Bowers, wid, apptd admx 7/10/1783, Wilkes, MxR
BOWINGS (or BOINGS), Ephraim, decd, LWT dtd 1/29/1800, wife, Mary; mother, Elizabeth Bowings, Hancock, AA
BOWLES, Martin B., lunatic, Gustavus Hendrick, gdn, Abner Nolen, sec, 1/17/1834 G. Hendrick, gdn, 1840, Butts, GB
BOWLING, Harriet, orph of Thos, Jno Dean, gdn, R. Nichols, C. Garlington, sur, 1/3/1825, Clarke, GB
BOWLING, John, orph of Thos, Jno Dean, gdn, Reubin Nichols, Christopher Garlington, sur, Clarke, GB
BOWLS, Thomas, orph of Turner, decd, Wm Hubbard apptd gdn 7/7/1841, Clarke, LP
BOWMAN, A. K., decd, Ambrose Kennedy issued L/A 6/1/1852, John Miller, Vincent Sears, secs, Hall, AB
BOWMAN, Henrietta, minor of Henry G., Samuel G. Bowman apptd gdn 1/11/1847, Effingham, MIC
BOWMAN, Henry G., decd, Matthew Heidt applies for L/A 8/24/1840, Effingham, MIC
BOWMAN, June Elizabeth, minor of Henry G., Samuel G. Bowman apptd gdn 1/11/1847, Effingham, MIC
BOWMAN, Robert, decd, Robert Schley applied for L/A 7/8/1847, Effingham, MIC
BOX, Philip, decd, Merchant, Elizabeth Box, admx, 10/15/1784, Chatham, Adms
BOX, Richard, decd, James M. Stewart qualified exr 7/20/1791, Liberty, MIC
BOYD, Clancy C., ordered that Clancy O. and Nancy Boyd be apptd gdn, Fred Beasley, Alexander Oden, secs, 9/1813, Jasper, OM
BOYD, David, decd, Levina Boyd, extrx, 1877, Cobb
BOYD, Eliza, dau of Susannah Boyd, William Ashley apptd gdn, 1/11/1813, Camden, MIC
BOYD, Elizabeth M., decd, Joseph F. Glass, admr, 8/13/1863, Harris, AB
BOYD, Israel P., decd, H. M. Hammett, admr, 1867; admr applies for leave to sell lands of decd 9/10/1869, Cobb, MIC
BOYD, James, decd, John Brock, etc., div est, p. 15, Screven, OM
BOYD, John, decd, Andrew Boyd, admr, 4/7/1857, Berry Ragsdale, sur, DeKalb, AB
BOYD, J. R., decd, John Boyd issued L/A 12/1861, Webster, OD
BOYD, Keziah, decd, Hugh M. Boyd, admr, 10/6/1856, Thomas C. Howard, sur, DeKalb, AB
BOYD, Robert M., decd, Mary A. Boyd, extrx, 1865, Cobb
BOYD, Seth, Sabrey Boyd, gdn, p. 16, Screven, OM
BOYD, William, Sr., decd, William Boyd issued L/A 9/12/1811, Peter Donaldson, Charley McCollough, secs, Richmond, AB
BOYET, James, decd, Sabra Boyet, admx, p. 20, Screven, OM
BOYKIN, Francis, decd, LWT pvd by Bartlet Brown, William H. Pearson, William Williams, John T. Boykin, exrs, 11/4/1822, Jasper, OM
BOYKIN, John, decd, Sarah and Lodwick Boykin, exrs, p. 86, Screven, OM
BOYKIN, Lodwick, gdn, leave to sell cattle, p. 63, Screven, OM
BOYLE, Peter, decd, LWT pvd 1814, Jackson, OM

BRACEWELL, Richard, decd, James Bracewell issued L/A 1/4/1819, Laurens, AB
BRADBERRY, Christopher C., decd, 12/8/1868 est, Clarke, LP
BRADBERRY, Spencer apptd gdn for his wife, Rutha, for legacy bequeathed in tr for her to Dr. Henry Hull, bequest made by Jarrus Rhodes 2/8/1860, Clarke, LP
BRADEN, Joseph S., decd, late of Texas, but at death res of Fulton Co., LWT pvd 2/2/1863, A. Q. Braden, exr, Fulton
BRADFORD, Anne L., imbecile dau of Mary, decd, V. Bradford apptd gdn 1/31/1876, Anne L. Bradford d. 5/1882, Clarke, LP
BRADFORD, George, decd, William Bradford, admr, 1/2/1815, Jackson, OM
BRADLEY, Elijah, decd, Thomas Knapen issued L/A 7/6/1808, Ralph Ketchum, Anderson Watkins, secs, Richmond, AB
BRAILSFORD, Elizabeth (Mrs.), decd, wid of Samuel of Charleston, 1807, Bryan, CR
BRAMON, Russell, decd, Thomas Crawford, Jr., gdn of orphs: Susan and Elizabeth 5/12/1817, Joseph Reed, sec, Morgan, GB
BRANCH, Martha, orph of William, decd, McGilvary Overstreet, gdn, makes retn of property 5/28/1836, Tattnall, I&A
BRAND, Malaciah, orph of Thomas, decd, William Brand apptd gdn 1/7/1811, Clarke, LP
BRANDON, George, decd, Franklin Hayden issued L/A 4/1/1867, Fulton
BRANT, Levina, orph age 6, 2/14th last, bound to David Owens 3/1813, Jackson, OM
BRANTLEY, Jeremiah, decd, John Brantley issued L/A 3/5/1821, Laurens, AB
BRANTLEY, Joseph B., decd, William Ezzard issued L/A 11/10/1866, Fulton
BRASON, H. C., LWT produced by John D. Stapleton and F. F. Birdsong 1/1857, Webster, OD
BRASWELL, Benjamin, decd, William Talbot issued L/A, Guy Smith, sec, 9/10/1817, Morgan, AB
BRASWELL, Benjamin, decd, William Talbot, Thomas Swift, Green Talbot issued L/A 9/1/1825; James and John Malcomb issued L/A 9/15/1826, Morgan, AB
BRASWELL, John, bound to John Smith, p. 61, Screven, OM
BRASWELL, J. W., Alfred James, gdn, 1883, Cobb
BRASWELL, Turner, allowed $196.87 1/2, p. 82, Screven, OM
BRAWNER, J. M., decd, LWT, wife, Elizabeth and son, John A. Brawner, exrs, 1/23/1847, Harris
BRAWTON, Jesse, decd, Mary Brawton, wid, apptd admx 8/17/1778; Williby Brawton, father, apptd admr 12/12/1778, Wilkes, MxR
BRAY, Benjamin A., decd, T. Lord apptd gdn of orphs: Benjamin B., Martha, Nancy and Dora, not dtd, Clarke, LP
BRAY, Thomas, decd, Sarah Bray issued L/A 7/25/1799, Thomas Sandwich, Robert Cresswell, sec, Richmond, AB
BRAZDAL, John, decd, John Gill applied for L/A 5/26/1794, caveat filed 6/2/1794, Mary Brazdal vs. John Gill, Elbert, AR
BRAZEAL, Elijah William, decd, Eason Allen issued L/A 12/3/1821, Laurens, AB
BRAZEAL, Elizabeth Eason, orph of Willis, decd, Green Wood, gdn, 3/3/1817, Laurens, GB
BRAZEAL, Willis, decd, Nancy Brazeal and Green Wood issued L/A 7/2/1810, Laurens, AB
BRAZEL, Matthew D., decd, Stephen McCall apptd admr 6/7/1842, Camden, MIC
BRAZEL, M. D., decd, Stephen McCall, admr, dismissed, 6/3/1844, Camden, MIC
BRAZEL, Wiley, decd, Lemuel Taylor, now of age, asks his share of est be partititioned him, 4/3/1844, Camden, MIC

43

BRAZEL, Wiley, decd, R. P. Burton apptd admr, caveat filed by
heir, Mrs. Sarah Taylor, 9/5/1842; R. P. Burton dismissed
1/4/1847; heirs---Robert and William Taylor, David Tanner, in rt
of wife, Sarah, 1/16/1843; Sarah Brazel Taylor, wid and gdn of
minor ch of Laban Taylor, decd, 1/16/1843, John L. Taylor, heirs
of Laban Taylor, decd, 6/5/1842; div or est to-John L., Robert,
Wm, Lemuel, Jeremiah, Lavina A., M. J., L. L., David Tanner,
6/5/1842, Camden, MIC
BRAZEL, Wiley, idiot, Sarah Taylor, gdn, dismissed, 1/5/1842,
Camden, MIC
BRAZELL, Robert, decd, Sarah Brazell, Laban Taylor apptd admrs
8/7/1826; Mrs. Sarah Brazell declines as admx, Laban Taylor to
serve, 2/7/1827, Laban Taylor, admr, applied for div of est,
1/6/1829, dismissed 6/3/1833; Mrs. Sarah Brazell, wid, Wiley
Brazell, recd div of est, 6/1/1829 Camden, MIC
BRAZELL, Wiley, unsound mind, Laban Taylor apptd gdn, Mrs. Sarah
Tucker, present gdn, consents, 6/5/1832, Camden, MIC
Brazelton, Reuben, decd, Elizabeth Brazelton issued L/A 1/2/1844,
John A. Brazelton, R. A. Davis, secs, Hall, AB
BRAZIEL, William L., decd, George Headen issued L/A 9/4/1809,
Jackson, OM
BRAZIL, John, decd, 3/1808 James Glover, admr, ordered to give
clear titles to Benjamin Hubbard, Elbert, AR
BRAZILL, Benjamin, decd, Hesekiah Stephens issued L/A 1/1827,
Habersham, MIC
BREEDLOVE, Matilda, dau of Henry Jennings, decd, John H.
Breedlove of alton Co. apptd tr for his wife and her children
2/3/1863, Clarke, LP
BREEDLOVE, Sarah J., decd (Miss), John A. Breedlove, admr,
3/3/1845, Baldwin, AB
BRETON, Bagley Rogers, decd, Mary E. Breton, wid, admx,
10/2/1784, Chatham, Adms
BREWER, Benjamin, decd, inv retd 7/10/1807 by Charles Ingram,
John Lane, Jr., Robert Williamson, apprs, Franklin, IMW
BREWER, Benjamin, decd, est owes John Brewer for keeping a female
idiot child for 3 yrs, sworn by John Brewer, gdn, 1/1812,
Franklin, OM
BREWER, Bledsoe, orph and son of Burwell, decd, Woody Jackson
apptd master of to learn his art of mustery, William M. Stokes,
sur, 6/24/1803, Oglethorpe, MIC
BREWER, Burwell, decd, Thomas Espy issued L/A 1/6/1823, Thomas
Wyatt, sec, Morgan, AB
BREWER, Caleb, decd, Powell and Polly Stamper, admrs, 2/1/1808,
Wilkes, OP
BREWER, Edmond, decd, inv 1793, slaves, Edmond Taylor Note;
3/25/1794 sale-Elisha Towns, John, Elisha, Horatio G., Wm B. &
Sarah Brewer (wid), purchasers; 1800 pd Sarah More for Elisha
Brewer, Wm H. & James Brewer, Sr., Elbert, AR
BREWER, Elisha, decd, John and Elisha Brewer apptd admrs
11/9/1793, James Tait, Mat J. Williams and Zimri Tate, apprs,
Elbert, AR
BREWER, James, decd, Edmond Brewer, admr, 1806 retns, Elbert, AR
BREWER, James, decd, Jacob Turman apptd admr, George Turman, sec,
1/7/1811, Elbert, AB
BREWER, John, minor son of Burwell, decd, William Stone apptd gdn
6/18/1800, Joshua Grass, George Phillips, surs, Oglethorpe, MIC
BREWER, John, Sr., decd, list of accts 9/21/1798; appr
11/15/1799; money pd to heirs 4/12/1799, pd John Brewer, Jr.,
Hancock, AA
BREWER, John, orph of William, William Brewer, gdn, Thomas
Doggett, sur, 1/1/1821, Clarke, GB

BREWER, John, orph of William, decd, Thomas Doggett, gdn, Oliver Higginbotham, sur, Clarke, 1/5/1818, GB
BREWER, Sally, orph of William, decd, Thomas Doggett, gdn, Oliver Higginbotham, sur, Clarke, 1/5/1818, GB
BREWER, Thomas H., decd, LWT pvd 9/1/1845, Effingham, MIC
BREWER, William, decd, Thomas Doggett apptd gdn of Sally and John 1/5/1818, Clarke, LP
BREWSTER, Harriet J., orph of John, decd, Louisa Brewster, natural gdn, John H. Wood, sec, 5/1/1848; 12/6/1852 Louisa Brewster and Patrick H. Brewster, gdns, Samuel M. W. McConnell and John H. Wood, surs, 12/6/1852, Cherokee, GB
BREWSTER, Louisa, decd, Samuel M. W. McConnell, admr, John R. Galt, sur, Cherokee, AB
BREWSTER, Lydia, orph of John, decd, Louisa Brewster, natural gdn, John H. Wood, sec, 5/1/1848, Cherokee, GB
BREWSTER, Lydia J., orph of John, decd, Louisa Brewster and Patrick H. Brewster, gdns, Samuel M. W. McConnell and John H. Wood, surs, 12/6/1852, Cherokee, GB
BREWSTER, Orren H., orph of John, decd, Louisa Brewster, natural gdn, John H. Wood, sec, 5/1/1848, Cherokee, GB
BREWSTER, Patrick H., orph of John, decd, Louisa Brewster, natural gdn, John H. Wood, sec, 5/1/1848, Cherokee, GB
BREWSTER, Tomlinson F., orph of John, decd, Louisa Brewster, natural gdn, John H. Wood, sec, 5/1/1848, Cherokee, GB
BREWTON, James, decd, William Terrell issued L/A 6/1826, Habersham, MIC
BRIDGEMAN, Boswell, decd, Ann Bridgeman, admx, 4/5/1790 (Ann m. Thomas Loyd), Wilkes, OP
BRIDGES, David, decd, Nathaniel Bridges, admr, James Bridges, Drury Cade, sec, recpts of Berry T., Bayns, Merrell, Nancy and Jesse Bridges, heirs, 1/26/1790, Wilkes, OP
BRIDGES, Jonathan F., decd, Johnson Lawless, Sarah Bridges, admrs, 1/1844, apprs: John Williford, F. B. Applewhite, George Banks and James Perkins, Stewart, Adms
BRIDGES, Nathaniel, decd, LWT pvd by John Luckie 1/1809, Oglethorpe, OM
BRIDGES, Silas, decd, LWT pvd 1/13/1840, Asa P. Peacock, exr, Washington
BRIDGES, Thomas, decd, Susannah Bridges, admx, Wiseman Bridges and Jonathan Bridges, secs, 3/4/1790, Wilkes, O{
BRIDWELL, Johnson W., decd, Harriett and Martin Bridwell issued L/A 9/3/1866, Fulton
BRIERS, Lamance, decd, Elizabeth Briers issued L/A 3/4/1816, Elisha Mosely, Morgan, AB
BRIERS, William K., decd, Henry H. Briers issued L/A 7/20/1866, Fulton
BRIGHAM, Sidney, decd, LWT pvd 6/7/1840, Harris
BRIGHTWELL, Andrew, orph of John, decd, Isaac D. Read apptd gdn 11/2/1835, Clarke, LP
BRIGHTWELL, John, decd, 11/14/1842 heirs: William Waygood and Alsn Moon, Clarke, LP
BRIGHTWELL, John M., orph of John, decd, William Collins apptd gdn 11/7/1842, Clarke, LP
BRINCEFIELD, B. B., decd, S. M. Sellars, Mary Brincefield and Lucius Norwood, admrs, 11/2/1863, Harris, AB
BRINKLEY, E. F. (Mrs.), decd, J. F. Brinkley, exr, 1896, Cobb
BRINSON, Alexander, orph of Noah, decd, Benjamin E. Benson, Chesley B. McLemore, gdns, B. Knight, sec, 7/16/1843, Emanuel, GB

BRISCO, John, decd, John F. Barnett apptd gdn of orphs: Philip, Elizabeth L. and Mary V. 5/6/1822, Clarke, LP

BRISCOE, Eliza S., orph of John, decd, John T. Burnett, gdn, West Harris, sur, 5/6/1822, Clarke, GB

BRISCOE, Mary V., orph of John, decd, John T. Burnett, gdn, West Harris, sur, 5/6/1822, Clarke, GB

BRISCOE, Phillip, orph of John, decd, John T. Burnett, gdn, West Harris, sur, 5/6/1822; William Davis, gdn 5/3/1824, John F. Barnett, sur, Clarke, GB

BRITT, Agnes, apptd gdn of her minor ch: Sabra J. and William Lawson Britt 5/1/1837, Clarke, LP

BRITT, Reubin, decd, Thomas Carr caveats to appt Turner Parsons admr (not next of kin); sd Carr admr in Columbia Co. where decd died; Parsons sd to be authorized by persons in Conn. claiming heirship but not heirs, 5/2/1808, Warren, MIC

BRITT, William, decd, Timothy Matthews apptd admr 3/5/1810, Warren, MIC

BRITTAIN, Thomas, decd, est 6/1/1810, Clarke, LP

BRITTON, John, decd, George and John Britton, and Jane, in rt of her husband, Sanford Britton, decd, et al, Mary Britton, wife of John, decd, et al, 10/8/1838; Isaac Low, James Britton, admrs, Your Malone, Emanuel Britton, secs, 10/8/1838, Butts, AB

BROACH, Aquilla, orph of James, decd, Charles Broach, gdn, 9/6/1813, Samuel B. Hutchinson, Wm Copeland, surs, Clarke, GB

BROACH, Jones (or James) decd, est 4/3/1809; Charles Broach apptd gdn of orph: Avirilla, 9/2/1813, Clarke, LP

BROADNAX, William, decd, John Morton apptd gdn of orphs 6/1833, Clarke, LP

BROCK, Harriet, orph of Walker, decd, Isaac B. Payne, gdn, 9/7/1835, Hall, GB

BROCK, James, decd, Thomas Storey and John Chalmers issued L/A 3/5/1810, Franklin, OM

BROCK, Moses, decd, LWT pvd 7/4/1831 wife, Rebecca, ch-Rebecca, Hannah, Isaac, John, James, Reuben; frds-Thos & Geo Brock, exrs; Wright Ferguson, Archer W. Dorsey, James Quillian, John Higgins, Joshua Dorsey, apprs 5/2/1831, Habersham, MIC

BROCK, William, decd, appr by Hustus S. Moore, Joshua F. Hodges, Joseph Olliff 10/19/1841, Bulloch, Misc

BROCKMAN, George M. T., orph of James, of Oglethorpe Co., Morton Bledsoe, gdn, S. Nutt, J. Harkness, sec., 1/7/1833, Butts, GB

BROCKMAN, Henry, decd, and Ruthy Ann Brockman issued L/G 6/2/1856 of orphs: James P., Elizabeth J., Francis A. and Mary Ann S., Fulton

BROCKMAN, John B., decd, J. A. Johnson, exr, 1880, Cobb

BROGDON, Harrison R., decd, Joseph H. Brogdon, E. W. Strickland, admrs, R. S. Brown, sur, 8/18/1873, Gwinnet, AB

BROGDON, Hope J., decd, R. C. Montgomery, G. G. Brogdon, admrs, William P. Moore, sur, 4/6/1873, Gwinnett, AB

BROOK, Jervey, decd, Peter Brook, admr, 7/25/1791, Jeremiah Dicken, sec., Wilkes, OP

BROOK, John T., decd, Elizabeth Brook, admx, Felix Moss, sec, 3/6/1848, Cherokee, AB

BROOKER, John G., minor, apprenticed to John Harris until age 21, 6/8/1821, Glynn, MIC

BROOKS, Amanda, orph of John, decd, Wm H. Mixson, gdn, Wiley H. Sims, Jno B. Culbertson, sur, 9/3/1849, Troup, GB

BROOKS, Edward, decd, Fenlow McCowen, gdn of orphs: Lucy, Polley, Betsy, Nancy & Patsey 9/26/1818, James Fletcher, sec, Morgan, GB

BROOKS, Edward, decd, Martha Ann Brooks, gdn of orphs: Mary Virginia, Wiley B. and Frances Louisa, 12/11/1854, Houston, GB

BROOKS, Elbert J., decd, Britton Buttrell, admr, Asa Buttrell, sur, 11/9/1848, Butts, AB

BROOKS, George F., Mary L. Brooks, gdn, 1894, Cobb

46

BROOKS, Henry, decd, Charles Brooks, admr, 6/6/1814; dismissed 9/6/1814, Warren, MIC
BROOKS, Joab, decd, LWT pvd, and his widow and William Brooks qualified as exrs 9/6/1804, Warren, MIC
BROOKS, John, decd, Edward Shirley, Richard Shirley, Thomas Shirley, admrs, 10/15/1811, Jones, AB
BROOKS, John, decd, LWT pvd 9/8/1782, ch: Rosannah, Elizabeth, Joel, Job, Providence, Dafner?, Stephen, Roger, Ann; wife Lydia and friend, Wm Downs, exrs, Wilkes, MxR
BROOKS, John F., decd, William C. Brooks, admr de bonis non 5/5/1851, John P. Brooks, sur, Cherokee, AB
BROOKS, Josephine, B. Holleman, gdn, 1886, Cobb
BROOKS, Missouri, orph of John, decd, Wm H. Mixon, gdn, Wiley H. Sims, Jno B. Culbertson, sur, 9/3/1849, Troup, GB
BROOKS, M. J., decd, Charles A. Brooks, Mrs. M. L. Brooks, admrs, 1892, Cobb
BROOKS, Moess, free person of colour, John E. Brown, gdn, 5/4/1846, Hall, GB
BROOKS, Moses, decd, Hezekiah F. Goss, gdn of Posey P., Lultany G., Moses and Aaron Brooks, orphs, 1/1/1821, Morgan, GB
BROOKS, Moses, orph of Moses, decd, Posey P. Brooks, gdn, James Hodge, James C. Lawrence, secs, 5/25/1827, Morgan, GB
BROOKS, William, decd, James Brooks L/A 3/7/1814, Putnam, AB
BROUGHTON, Betitha, decd, LWT pvd by Hackey Walker, James Ellis, Samuel Hawill, warrant appr gtd William, Charles, Annanias, Belitha Broughton, exrs, 5/2/1814, Jasper, OM
BROUGHTON, Salley, minor of Nancy, Josiah Jordan, gdn, 1792, Wilkes, OP
BROWN, A. C., decd, William S. Brown, admr, 1866, Cobb
BROWN, Allen, decd, 3/7/1788 apprs: Robert Dixon, James Fox, Moody Burt, two tracts of 287 1/2 acres in Franklin Co. listed, Richmond
BROWN, Andrew, decd, James Morrow, gdn of orphs: Frances and Joseph 12/22/1817, Lewis Brantley, sec, Morgan, GB
BROWN, Bedford (Colonel), decd, 5/10/1820 heir-Peter Mosley in rt of his wife, Sally Brown Mosley, extrx, Clarke, LP
BROWN, Betsy Ann, decd, est 7/1/1811, Clarke, LP
BROWN, Betsy Ann, minor, Henry Saddler apptd gdn 6/7/1824, Camden, MIC
BROWN, Burrell, decd, John Matthews, exr of LWT, pvd by Leroy Minis 3/4/1798, Warren, MIC
BROWN, Clayborn, decd, J. Y. Alexander, exr, 1875, Cobb
BROWN, Cyrena, decd, Charles F. Newton, admr, Robert Mayo, sur, 5/5/1843, Butts, AB
BROWN, Edward, decd, William T. Pike, issued L/A admr 1/10/1832, Baldwin, AB
BROWN, Edward, decd, John C. Royals, admr, 4/26/1844, apprs: Wm Posey, John H. Eubanks, Axiom Webb, John Hodges, Henry Goodman; purchasers at sale: Clarissa, Butler, John, Henry and Ann Matilda Brown, J. J. Wallace, etc., Dooly, I&A
BROWN, Elizabeth, orph of Little Berry, decd, James Denmark apptd gdn 9/1/1823, Bulloch, MIC
BROWN, Eula, Louise N. Brown, gdn, 1867, Cobb
BROWN, E. W., Luddie Brown, gdn, 1887, Cobb
BROWN, Gary, decd, Jarrel Beasley of Randolph Co. apptd gdn of orphs: Elizabeth and Polly, ca 1812 (Randolph Co.), Clarke, LP
BROWN, Herod, decd, LWT pvd 11/6/1843, John B. Wright, exr, Washington
BROWN, Hiram, decd, John D. Perkinson, admr, 1890, Cobb
BROWN, Hiram, decd, William L. Brown, admr, 1867; admr applies for dismissal, 2/21/1870, Cobb, MIC
BROWN, Hugh, decd, W. G., admr, 3/1/1852, Camden, MIC

47

BROWN, Hugh, decd, final L/A gtd to James Brown 7/8/1801, Franklin, O
BROWN, Hugh, Sr., decd, Mrs. Sarah Brown, Hugh Brown apptd admrs, 9/8/1812, Camden, MIC
BROWN, James, decd, 1879, Cobb
BROWN, James, decd, Elizabeth Mitchell testified as to LWT 3/7/1820, Jasper, OM
BROWN, James H., decd, LWT names brothers Samuel & John S. of North Carolina, Sarah Greenlee (sister), Edwin P., Edward, Mary & Charles L. Williams, Henry H. Conly & Nancy, Sarah Dobbin, Robert & Martha Gage, George W., Williamm & Martha Murphy, Jamess & Matilda Conly, Samuel Brown, heirs of William Brown, decd, Jas & Elizabeth Avery, Albert G. & Elizabeth Wms, Fletcher & Hanah Starr, dtd 2/3/1857, White
BROWN, James H., M. A. E. Brown, gdn, 1883, Cobb
BROWN, James H., decd, of Habersham Co., Henry H. Conly in rt. of wife, Nancy and Ephraim Greenlee in rt of wife, Sarah, also sister of decd, James Avery in rt of wife, Elizabeth, sister of decd, caveat LWT 7/1859, White
BROWN, James R., James W. McFall, gdn, 1891, Cobb
BROWN, James, Sr. and Jr., decd, William Ross and Thomas Gardner issued L/A 9/19/1811, John McKinne, Adam Hutcheon, secs, Richmond, AB
BROWN, James W., decd, W. H. Nutting, R. E. Brown, exrs, Cobb
BROWN, Jeremiah, decd, Morel Beasley apptd gdn of ch: Betsy and Polley 6/27/1809, Clarke, LP
BROWN, Jeremiah, decd, Thomas, Elijah and Sarah Brown, temporary admrs, 12/12/1805; Thomas Brown, Elijah Brown, Sarah Brown, admrs, William Hobbs, J. Runnels, sur, 12/5/1805; inventory given Clarke Co. by Joshua Elder, John Waddle, Alexander Hall, James Turner 12/20/1805, Clarke, LP
BROWN, Jeremiah, decd, Jarrel Beasley, gdn of orphs, 1812 pd tuit of Betsey Brown, Clarke Co Retn, 9/7/1813, 1815-6 Return for orphans, Elizabeth and Mary Brown, Jasper, AR
BROWN, Jesse, decd, Uriah T. Brown issued L/A 1/5/1841, H. Jarrett, sec, Hall, AB
BROWN, Jesse, Sr., acct of sale of est 6/7/1842; John Brown, admr, sold prop, land in Bulloch Co. sold to Jesse Brown, land in Early Co. sold to Mitchell Brown, 3/15/1843; Mitchell Brown signed as having recd of John Brown, admr of est of Jesse Brown, decd, his legacy in full 4/6/1844, Bulloch, Misc
BROWN, Joel, decd, George Brown issued L/A 5/6/1866, Fulton
BROWN, John, Catharine Brown, gdn, 1804-1808 retns, est of Robert Brown, debtor, Elbert, GR
BROWN, John, decd, John J. Long and Sarah M. Brown issued L/A 7/2/1839, Washington
BROWN, John, W. C. Crews, admr with LWT, 3/4/1850, Camden, MIC
BROWN, John, decd, Mrs. Sarah Brown, wid & admx, Robert & David Brown, heirs pet ct to div est. Alexander Atkinson, Joseph Hull, Thomas E. Hardee apptd to make div 9/3/1827; David Brown, admr, applies for dismission 1/7/1834, Camden, MIC
BROWN, John, decd, Samuel M. Smith apptd exr of LWT, 3/4/1805, Warren, MIC
BROWN, John, decd, Sarah Brown apptd admx, 6/16/1825, leave to sell 8/7/1826; div. est, Sarah Brown, wid, Geo W., Jno C., Robt, David, Saml W. Brown, sons, 2/5/1828, Camden, MIC
BROWN, John B. J., orphj of I., decd, John Morebley apptd gdn 3/5/1855, Clarke, LP
BROWN, John C., W. L. Brown, gdn, 1882, Cobb
BROWN, Jones, decd, of Savannah, Mrs. Ann Brown, admx, 11/20/1789, Chatham, Adms
BROWN, Joseph, decd, inv made by Shrewsberry Payne, Joel Crain, Evans Todhunter 8/25/1801, Franklin, OM

BROWN, Josiah, decd, Sterling E. Brown, W. A. Hazling, admrs, W.
E. Brown, sur, 4/6/1874, Gwinnett, AB
BROWN, Marcus, minor orph, James F. Alexander qualified as gdn
2/17/1853, dismissed 2/7/1859, Fulton
BROWN, Matilda, James and Ludie Brown, gdns, 1880, Cobb
BROWN, M. L., M. L. Brown, gdn, 1882, Cobb
BROWN, Morgan, decd, L/A issued Richard Warthen 3/1/1841,
Washington
BROWN, O. W., decd, Green J. Blake, admr, James H. Bishop, sec,
2/19/1848, Bibb, AB
BROWN, P. A., M. L. Brown, gdn, 1882, Cobb
BROWN, P. E., decd, A. E. Brown, admr, 1893, Cobb
BROWN, Robert, decd, David Brown, admr, dismissed, 1/7/1834, Camden, MI
BROWN, Robert, minor, David Brown apptd gdn, 2/5/1828, Camden, MIC
BROWN, Robert, E. J. Brown, gdn, 1890, Cobb
BROWN, Robert, decd, 9/13/1802 est appraised by Barnabas Pace,
James Shields, Absolom Stinchcomb; Caty and Absolom Brown, admrs;
4/4/1803 purchasers at sale: Caty, Abraham, Polly, Peggy, Betsy
and Peter Brown, Elbert, AR
BROWN, Robert, decd, Halcott Alford, gdn of Robert, orph
2/4/1819, William Patrick, Ludowick Alford, secs, Morgan, GB
BROWN, Robert, decd, Richard D. Winn, admr, T. K. Mitchell, sur,
11/3/1873, Gwinnett, AB
BROWN, Robert, decd, Robert Sharp issued L/A w/LWT annexed
1/6/1817, Isham Fannin, sec, Morgan, AB
BROWN, Robert, decd, Susan Brown, wid, admx, 1867, Cobb
BROWN, Robert, decd, 1808 retn pvd by oath of Abraham Brown,
admr, 1810 retn, receipts from Silas White for pt of his wife's
father's est, and Peggy Brown for her pt of her father's est,
Elbert, AR
BROWN, Robert C., decd, Stephen Brown, gdn of orphs: Martha A.
and Amanda 3/4/1850, Ambrose Kennedy, sec, Hall, GB
BROWN, Robert S., decd, A. G. Harris, admr, J. H. Brogdon, sur,
Gwinnett, AB
BROWN, Samuel, admr in rt of wife, Martha, who was admx of est of
Beatty W. Kigny, decd, 7/2/1821, Clarke, LP
BROWN, Samuel, decd, Elizar L. Newton issued L/A 7/1/1839,
Richard Banks, sec, Hall, AB
BROWN, Sarah, decd, appr 4/23/1802; purchasers at sale: Isaac
Fann, Isaac Evans, Richard Huckeby, Hancock, AAAA
BROWN, Sarah A. E., Edmond Turner, gdn, Dooly, OD
BROWN, Silas, decd, Robert A. Brown, exr, 1869, Cobb
BROWN, S. M., decd, E. J. Brown, admr, 1890, Cobb
BROWN, Solomon, decd, Emanuel Brown issued L/A 5/1/1837,
Washington
BROWN, Thomas, decd, Elijah Brown and Betsy Ann Brown, exrs,
9/10/1807; Samuel Brown, exr, 5/25/1805; heirs: Thomas C. and
Lorenzo Brown, not dtd, Clarke, LP
BROWN, Thursdy, decd, appr 3/6/1802; legatees: Milley Brown,
Aaron Brown, Moses Brown, Hancock, AAAA
BROWN, William, decd, Edward Horn issued L/A 5/4/1818, Samuel
Pearman, sec, Morgan, AB
BROWN, William, decd, Jeremiah Davis and Benjamin Brown issued
L/A 8/5/1817, Charles Smith, Douglas W. Porter, William Gill,
secs, Morgan, AB
BROWN, William, orph of Little Berry, decd, James Denmark apptd
gdn 9/1/1823, Bulloch, MIC
BROWN, William G., decd, J. J. Eubanks, admr, 1890, Cobb
BROWN, William H., decd, Mary D. Brown issued L/A 11/1/1824,
Benjamin Tilman, Absolom Barnes, sec, Morgan, AB
BROWN, Winnie, William F. Brown, gdn, 1891, Cobb
BROWN, W. M., Hiram Brown, gdn, 1895, Cobb

BROWN, W. S., Luddie Brown, gdn, 1887, Cobb
BROWN, W. S., decd, W. R. Montgomery, admr, 1879, Cobb
BROWNFIELD, Jincey, Joseph Lane, her gdn, brought suit in Superior Court concerning release of her property 1/6/1806, Clarke, LP
BROWNFIELD, John, decd, 11/29/1810 est, heirs: Benjamin Thurman, William Shields and Micajah Thurman, Clarke, LP
BROWNFIELD, John, decd, John King, Sarah Brownfield, admrs, inv 3/10/1786, Wilkes, OP
BROWNING, John, decd, Josiah Browning apptd gdn of orphs: James A., Lucy Ann and Francis 2/4/1839, Clarke, LP
BROWNING, John, decd, est 8/13/1838, Clarke, LP
BROWNING, Joshua, decd, 6/6/1807, wife, Margaret & sons, Joshua & Wm apptd exrs; Margaret and Joshua qualified (Wm is decd), Joshua, the younger, has left Ga., Margaret declared incompetent and Aaron Parker apptd admr, not dtd, Clarke, LP
BROWNING, Joshua, decd, 1/2/1882 heirs-Marcellus D., Mrs. Nancy and Miss Bunnie Browning, Mrs. J. C. Hunter, Clarke, LP
BROWNING, Lucy Ann Susan, orph of John, decd, Marlin T. Crow apptd gdn 4/5/1841, Clarke, LP
BROWNING, Margaret, Aaron Parker apptd gdn in consequence of her alienation of mind 12/4/1844, Clarke, LP
BROWNING, Margaret, decd, 1842 ltrs-Jas McKissack, Russell Co, Ala. for shs Margaret & Joshua Browning´s ests, hrs of Thos & Mary McKissack of Ala. & Jno, J. T. & R. B. McKissack, Meriwether Co, Howell Hodges & Hastings Maddux, Clarke, LP
BROWNSON, Galen, decd, Charles Jones issued L/A 4/2/1804, Holland McTyeire, John Cashin, secs, Richmond, AB
BRUCE, Daniel, decd, John Bruce issued L/A 2/20/1795, Abimleck Hawkins, sec, Richmond, AB
BRUCE, James, decd, Christopher Meaders issued L/A 1/17/1863, David M. Horton, sec, White, AB
BRUCKNER, Charles F., decd, J. O. Bruckner issued L/A 1/11/1864, Fulton
BRUCE, Jonathan, decd, F. G. Underwood, admr, A. F. Underwood, sur, 5/11/1857, Cherokee, AB
BRUMBALOW, Jackson, decd, H. M. Hammett, admr, 1868; H. M. Hammett applies for leave to sell land (wid and minor heirs taking advantage of homestead), 8/24/1869, Cobb, MIC
BRUMBY, Ephraim R. apptd gdn of his minor ch: Alice B., Campbell W., Mary B. and McPherson W., heirs of their mother, Mary Brunby, decd, 2/26/1884, Clarke, LP
BRUMBY, McPherson W. apptd gdn of his minor ch: Mary Harris, Hardman, Annie and Wallis, heirs at law of Mary W. Nesbitt 8/30/1887, Clarke, LP
BRUMBY, T. M., decd, Mary D. Heyward, admx, 1900, Cobb
BRUN, William, decd, of Bay of Honduras, Merchant, Thomas Sikes, admr, 4/24/1790, Chatham, Adms
BRUNETT, Reme, decd, B. A. Copp, admr, forfeited his res., adm revoked, Robt Day apptd, 1/6/1835, Camden, MIC
BRUNETTE, Oliver, decd, LWT dtd 1/10/1859, names A. G. and O. F. Brunett, exrs, Paulding
BRUNETTE, Reme, decd, B. A. Copp, admr w/LWT proved on testimony taken East Florida where LWT also probated 1/5/1830, Camden, MIC
BRUNETTE, Remey, minor, Archibald Clarke apptd gdn 9/8/1812, Camden, MIC
BRUNSON, Comfort, decd, Josiah Brunson issued L/A 5/5/1808, John McKinne and Thomas Lowry, secs, Richmond, AB
BRUSTER, Henry, decd, Lovicy Bruster, widow, apptd admx 1/13/1782, Wilkes, MxR

BRYAN, Benjamin Sr., decd, Benjamin Bryan, Jr. issued L/A 9/4/1854, Jonathan Martin, sec, Hall, AB
BRYAN, Elizabeth R., orph of Hardy B., decd, Sarah E. Bryan, gdn, 5/10/1852, Houston, GB
BRYAN, Henry, John Bryan, gdn, p. 79, Screven, OM
BRYAN, James, decd, LWT admitted to record 7/1/1833; Catherine Bryan named as extrx 7/1/1833, Effingham, MIC
BRYAN, J. Clements, decd, LWT pvd 5/1839, wife Edith, ch--- Loverd, David C., Needham, Mary S. Raines, Sarah L. Evans, Margarette S. Wyche (husband, George), Charity L. Cheatham, Edith Brown, Ann Bryan, Grizzelly R. Watts, Emeline Watts, Randolph
BRYAN, John H., John Bryan, Sr., relieved as gdn, and Solomon Bryan, gdn, p. 105, Screven, OM
BRYAN, John, Jr., decd, John and Martha Bryan gtd L/A, p. 1, Screven, OM
BRYAN, Jonathan, decd, William Bruan, James Bryan, Mary Wylly and John Honetorgn, exrs of LWT 3/17/1788, Chatham, Adms
BRYAN, Julia, orph of Eli, decd, was bound to Joseph Chandler 1/3/1813, Franklin, OM
BRYAN, Latha is bound to Elias Burgess during her minority 7/5/1813, Franklin, OM
BRYAN, Robert, decd, LWT dtd 4/12/1799 pvd 1/16/1800 by Samuel Hart and Solomon Stapp, names wife, Sarah, mentions children, Hancock, AA
BRYAN, Russell, orph of Eli, decd, was bound to Joseph Chandler 1/3/1813, Franklin, OM
BRYAN, Thomas, decd, Winifred Bryan and Stephen Mills, admrs, 1/24/1839, Randolph
BRYANT, Absalom, decd, Mary Bryant, extrx, gtd leave to sell perishable prop, 1/2/1815, Glynn, MIC
BRYANT, James, decd, of Muscogee Co., Moses Padgett, Washington Glover, admrs, Harris, AB
BRYANT, Jesse P., decd, William Kilpatrick, Mary N. Bryant, William G. Kilpatrick, admrs, 7/5/1848, Bibb, AB
BRYANT, Langley, decd, Thomas E. Hardee apptd admr, 8/3/1835; Mrs. Mary Bryant qualified extrx of LWT, 9/2/1811; Thomas E. Hardee dismissed as admr 1/5/1836, Camden, MIC
BRYANT, R. R., decd, Susan Bryant, admx, 1874, Cobb
BRYANT, T. J., decd, P. O. Allgood, admr, 1877, Cobb
BRYDIE, David, decd, physick, LWT apptd Henry Keall (dead) exr; Wm Stephens, Adam Alexander, exrs; Henry Keall filed est under British usurptation; LWT carried away when British Troops evacuated Savannah, 9/26/1783; 9/21/1783, Chatham, Adms
BUCHANAN, Benjamin, LWT pvd, George T. Buchanan, Benjamin B. Buchanan, exrs, issued warrant of appr 9/1820, Jasper, OM
BUCHANAN, Elijah, decd, Gideon Hays, admr, James Watson, Eli Whidden, sur, Emanuel, AB
BUCHANAN, Green B., decd, Theodocious F. Furk, admx de bonis non, 1/12/1852, Baldwin, AB
BUCHANAN, James, decd, Edmund Buchanan issued L/A 3/3/1806, Jasper, OM
BUCHANAN, John, decd, Priscilla Buchanan, apptd admx, 1/5/1818, Jasper, OM
BUCHANNAN, Charles J., decd, Elizabeth Buchannan, widow, admx, 9/11/1866, Clarke, LP
BUCHANNAN, John, decd, L/A gtd Priscilla and Joseph Buchannan, 11/3/1817, Jasper, OM
BUCHANNAN, Mary H., decd, Wilkerson Sparks, admr, 3/1857, Harris
BUCHANNON, Frances E., decd, Horace L. Cranford, admr, 12/27/1877, Clarke, LP
BUCK, Dorothy Ann E., minor of Seaborn W., William Buck issued L/G 7/5/1842, Washington

BUCKHANNON, Robert P., decd, Joseph Lane issued L/A 1/3/1825, John Sandifer, sec, Morgan, AB
BUCKANNON, William F., decd, Burnet M. Ware issued L/A w/LWT annexed 7/3/1826, Morgan, AB
BUCKLES, John, orph of John, decd, Edward Megar, gdn, Thomas Drew, Benjamin Sherrard, sur, 7/6/1835, Emanuel, GB
BUCKNER, William, decd, LWT dtd 3/12/1799, wife, Tabitha, my children; exrs, bro., Joel Buckner and uncle, John Brown, pvd 10/7/1799, Hancock, AA
BUFFINGTON, Eliza, decd, Reuben Cash issued L/A 3/26/1836, Habersham, MIC
BUFFINGTON, John, decd, Edward Hogans, admr 1/15/1784, Wilkes, MxR
BUFFINGTON, Peter, decd, Edward Hogans, issued L/A 1/15/1784, Wilkes, MxR
BUFFINGTON, Samuel, Sr., decd, Samuel Buffington, Jr., George D. Case, admrs, 1/14/1850, Baldwin, AB
BUFFINGTON, William, decd, Josephus A. Tolleson issued L/A 5/1/1854, Charles D. Phillips, L. G. Pirkle, secs, Hall, AB
BUFFINTON, John, decd, Edward Hogans, admr 1/15/1784, Wilkes, MxR
BUFORD, Henry, order to pay $59.03, p. 29, Screven, OM
BUFORD, John, petitions court to be relieved from bond, p. 28, Screven, OM
BUICE, Archable, decd, Mathew Buice, admr, Abram L. Kirkland, sur, 5/15/1849, Emanuel, AB
BUICE, James D., decd, Minnie L. Buice, admx, 1889, Cobb
BUIS, Caswell, orph, John Buis apptd gdn, John Buis, Thomas Merrett, sec, 5/1/1815, Jasper, OM
BUIS, Elbert, orph, John Buis apptd gdn, John Buis, Thomas Merrett, sec, 5/1/1815, Jasper, OM
BUIS, Eliza, orph, John Buis apptd gdn, John Buis, Thomas Merrett, sec, 5/1/1815, Jasper, OM
BUIS, John, decd, Robt Richardson Retn pd tuit-Caswell, Elbert, Eliza Buis, heirs-Zachariah, Jno Buis-1815, Jasper, AR
BUIS, John, decd, LWT, wife, Nancy, ch: Sally Patterson, Zachariah, John, Caswell, Elbert, Eliza, "all my father's est to come at my mother's death, 5/1810, Jasper, OM
BULFINCH, John, decd, Isaac R. Youngblood issued L/A 3/6/1837, Washington
BULKLEY, Ichabod, decd, 1804 retn by admr; William Gibson, admr, dismissed, 2/5/1811, Camden, MIC
BULL, Eli, decd, Jacob Bull, admr, 2/9/1802, Mark Hardin, Jesse Bull, surs, Warren, AB, MIC
BULL, Jacob, decd, Jesse Bull, admr, 3/6/1799, Columbia, AB
Bull, Sarah Barnwell,div 7700 ac 10/1807, Camden, MIC
BULL, Stephen, Ann, wid, daus--Mary Barnwell, widow, Nathaniel, Charlotte Bull, Sarah Barnwell, division 7700 acres 10/1807, Camden, MIC
BULLARD, Elias, decd, 9/16/1840, apprs: James Knight, Willis Durham, William Smith; purchasers at sale: Elizabeth Bullard, Wm M. Hart, William G. Hammell, Wiley Mitchell, Britton Wilkes, (admr), etc, Dooly, I&A
BULLARD, Jesse, orph of William, decd, of age of 14 chose James Bullard as his gdn 9/1821, Jasper, OM
BULLARD, Jesse, Retn 1809-1811, William Bullard, gdn, 5/7/1810, Jasper, Misc Ests
BULLARD, Jesse, minor, James Bullard, gdn, 9 mos tuition 1820/1822 Hillsboro Academy, 3/3/1823, Jasper, GR
BULLARD, John, decd, inv of est 3/29/1795, Franklin, OM
BULLARD, Mahala, illegitimate child of Nancy, Shadrack Bullard, gdn, 11/1828; 9/1829 motion of gdn to sell Lot 145, 3rd Dist, formerly Troup, now Meriwether Co., Habersham, MIC
BULLARD, Micajah, decd, A. D. McEwen, admr, 1866, Cobb

BULLARD, Robert, decd, Margaret Bullard, extrx, 1845, Cobb
BULLARD, Ruby, James Powell, gdn, 1897, Cobb
BULLARD, Thomas, decd, of Elbert Co., 1/3/1826 est, Pike, MIC
BULLARD, Wilie, decd, application for leave to sell real estate
7/5/1819, Jasper, OM
BULLARD, William, decd, James Bullard, Richard Head, admrs, Moses
Perkins, Thomas Jackson, secs, 11/1814; Temperance Bullard chose
1/3rd pt of husband's est and was ordered to take plantation and
raise children 7/3/1815, Jasper, OM
BULLIN, Bela, decd, Elizabeth Bullin apptd admx 6/9/1802,
dismissed 1/6/1808, Camden, MIC
BULLIN, Bert, minor of John, decd, John Beasley apptd gdn, Seth
Ward, John Gresham, surs, 6/18/1800, Oglethorpe, MIC
BULLOCH, James, decd, of Wormslow, James Bulloch apptd admr
7/31/1788, Chatham, Adms
BULLOCK, Anna, minor dau of Nathaniel, decd, Mary Bullock apptd
gdn, Alexander Gordon and Harris Gresham, surs, 6/1802,
Oglethorpe, MIC
BULLOCK, Johnson, decd, Polley Bullock issued L/A 7/1/1811,
Putnam, AB
BULLOCK, Wyatt, minor son of Nathaniel, decd, John Bullock, gdn,
Aleander Gordon, Harris Gresham, surs, 6/1802, Oglethorpe, MIC
BUNCH, Pouncy, decd, David Bunch, admr, recpt of John A. Bunch,
admr, Gideon B. and Hannah C. Bunch, one under 14, one over 14,
choose James Boatright, gdn, Wilkes, OP
BUNKLEY, Britain, decd, Britain R. Bunkley produced LWT pvd by
Edmund Atkinson 2/7/1826, Camden, MIC
BUNLAN, Seaborn, natural son and orph of Nancy, bound to James
Elmore, 1809, Jackson, OM
BUNN, Jeremiah W., a lunatic, Jane Elizabeth Bunn and Isaac H.
Moreland, gdns, 7/3/1854, Houston, GB
BUNN, M. H., decd, Catherine Bunn, extrx, 1884, Cobb
BUNTZ, Henry L., decd, Simon Buntz applies for admn 5/2/1833;
Mary C. Bergman made her choice of child's pt of est 7/1/1833,
Effingham, MIC
BUNTZ, Henry Lewis, decd, Mrs. Judith Buntz, admx 6/6/1796,
Effingham, Misc
BURAH, Michael, decd, John Nicholson, etc. to divide estate, p.
26, Screven, OM
BURCH, Michael, decd, L/A to Charles Burch 3/5/1821, Laurens, AB
BURCH, Richard, decd, Jenkins D. Williams, James W. Cato, admrs,
Harris, AB
BURCKSTEINER, Catharine, decd, LWT admitted to record 7/4/1846,
Effingham, MIC
BURCKSTEINER, Jeremiah chose Frederick I. Nease as his gdn
11/4/1839, Effingham, MIC
BURCKSTEINER, Samuel, decd, Ann Catharine Burcksteiner and James
Rahn apply for admn 10/25/1837, Effingham, MIC
BURDETT, John, decd, Deborah and James Burdett, exrs, 6/5/1832,
tuition for Benajah and Rese Burdett, John H. Dyson, gdn of J. D.
Burdett, 1847 retn pd Malindy Burdett, 3/24/1837, Wilkes, OP
BURDETT, John C., decd, 11/1836 Nancy Burdett and Samuel Quarles,
admrs; appraisers: James Hilliard, John Fitzgerald, E. H. Baker,
James Burdett; purchasers at sale: John C. and N. A. Burdett, S.
Carrington, Timothy Carrington, etc., Stewart, Adms
BURDINE, Clark, orph of John, decd, Shaler Hillyer, gdn, division
to heirs, John Stroud in rt of his wife, Jones, OM
BURGER, Daniel N. apptd gdn of his minor ch---Malinda and Lindsey
8/17/1853, Clarke, LP
BURGER, John A., decd, widow, Elizabeth 7/13/1863, claim vs. govt
of Confederate States for services as soldier, Clarke, LP

BURGESS, Linton S., son of Jonathan, decd, of DeKalb Co., James
D. Burgess of Greene Co. apptd gdn 10/7/1861; Henry H. Burgess of
DeKalb Co., gdn, 3/5/1860, Clarke, LP
BURGESS, Nathan apptd gdn of his minor ch---Richard, Sarah,
James, William, Martha and Jonathan 1/7/1839, Clarke, LP
BURKE, Theophilus, decd, estate 1823, Clarke, LP
BURKE, Thomas A., decd, Eliza Battey Burke, widow, apptd gdn of
her ch---Sallie, age 15 and Thomas, age 12, 3/16/1880, Clarke, LP
BURNAM, Elizabeth, orph of Lewis W., decd, William W. Russell,
gdn, 11/7/1853, Houston, GB
BURNAM, William made gdn of his four minor ch---Mary C., Martha
C., Elizabeth D., Penny E., 1/10/1853, Houston, GB
BURNETT, Littleberry, decd, William Hamilton issued L/A
7/15/1835, Habersham, MIC
BURNETT, Margaret Ann, daughter of Nathan C., Joseph F. Merton
requests dismission from gdnshp (apptd 9/3/1849) 2/7/1853,
Clarke, LP
BURRESS, Mary bound to David Emanuel, p. 45, Screven, OM
BURROUGHS, Mary bound to John Price, p. 90, Screven, OM
BURT, William, decd, James J. and R. T. Burt issued L/A 7/5/1852,
Joseph Hill, Jasper Smith, secs, Lumpkin, AB
BURUS, Jonah, Thomas Burns, gdn, p. 70, John Rawls, gdn, p. 42,
Screven, OM
BURUS, Martha, John Rawls, gdn, p. 4, Screven, OM
BURUS, Thomas, decd, admr of ordered to settle est, p. 32, pd
$1475 to John Bryan, p. 40, Screven, OM
BURUS, Thomas, decd, retn by John Conyers, p. 5, Screven, OM
BUSH, Eli, orph of William, decd, above age of 14, John Napier,
gdn, 3/7/1814, Laurens, GB
BUSSEY, Nathan, decd, Robert Ware, gdn for orphs---Hezekiah, Anny
and Nathan 1/24/1829, William Paschal and Peter Lamar, secs,
Lincoln, GB
BUSSEY, William, orph of Nathan, decd, William Paschal, gdn,
1/6/1829, Robert Ware, sec, Lincoln, GB
BUSWELL, Daniel, decd, Jeremiah Jarrard issued L/A 1/4/1841,
Tattnall, I&A
BUTLER, Charles, decd, Joseph Butler, admr, p. 39, John McWade,
etc., appraisers, p. 67, Screven, OM
BUTLER, Cynthia A., daughter of Henry Jennings, James J. Jennings
apptd trustee of her and her children 2/16/1863, Clarke, LP
BUTLER, Jesse B., decd, Jonathan Day issued L/A 5/2/1825, William
Day, sec, Morgan, AB
BUTTS, Adam, decd, William Coxe issued L/A 7/11/1814, Putnam, AB
BUTTS, Anthony, decd, Salley Butts and John Butts issued L/A
1/1/1811, Putnam, AB
BYNUM, Alfred, decd, of State of Texas, Alban Chase, admr,
5/14/1839, Clarke, LP
BYRNES, Laughlin, decd, J. D. Riodan applies for L/A 6/9/1854,
Lee, MSC
CABBELL, Robert J., decd, est 7/7/1823, Clarke, LP
CABBELL, Robert W., orph of Robert J., decd, William W. Cabbell
apptd gdn 2/1/1836, Clarke, LP
CADE, John, decd, John Read applied L/A 6/13/1787, Richmond, AB
CADE, Thomas, decd, John Read applies for L/A 7/13/1787,
Richmond, AB
CAFFIN, Patience, decd, est 6/30/1866, Clarke, LP
CAHOON, John, decd, Axion Cahoon issued L/A 7/7/1817, Laurens, AB
CAIN, Joseph, decd, Samuel H. Cain issued L/A 11/7/1853, H. L.
McCormack, Charles W. Wood, secs, Hall, AB
CALHOUN, Albert, decd, William H. Calhoun, admr w/LWT annexed, W.
L. Hughes, Levi Calhoun, Samuel Cox, surs, 10/5/1847; Seth Cason,
admr de bonis non 5/14/1848, Bibb, AB

CALHOUN, James, decd, John Gillis and Stringer Calhoun issued L/A
w/LWT annexed 6/6/1836, Mark Phillips, sec, Montgomery, AB
CALHOUN, James, decd, John Gillis, gdn of minor orphs: Demares,
John H. T., Rosana and George W., 8/7/1837, Norman Gillis, sec;
Stringer Calhoun, gdn to: Betsy S. and Rebecca Jane 8/7/1837,
Montgomery, GB
CALL, Richard, decd, Alethea Call and Thomas Glascock issued L/A
8/15/1794, John Bacon, sec, Richmond, AB
CAMAK, Annie T., orph of Thomas, decd, Dr. James Camak apptd gdn
9/8/1874, Clarke, LP
CAMAK, James, decd, heirs: wife, Helen and children-Dr. James,
Thomas and Margaret Ann Camak, 1850, Clarke, LP
CAMAK, James (Dr.), decd, d. 8/13/1893, heirs: James W., Mary and
Louis Camak, Clarke, LP
CAMAK, Margaret Ann, orph of James, decd, Helen T. Camak apptd
gdn 3/4/1850, Clarke, LP
CAMAK, Mary W. apptd gdn of her minor so, Louis Camak 1893,
Clarke, LP
CAMAK, Thomas, orph of James, decd, James Camak apptd gdn
3/4/1850, Clarke, LP
CAMERON, Archibald, minor orph of John, decd, John Cameron, gdn
3/10/1819, David Langston, John Taylor, secs, Richmond, GB
CAMP, William, decd, William Dunn, admr, 8/13/1839, Randolph
CAMPBELL, Charles A., orph of Charles, decd, Charles Allen, gdn,
8/27/1821, Morgan, GB
CAMPBELL, Charles D., decd, of Texas, Andrew J. Cobb, admr,
8/11/1892, Clarke, LP
CAMPBELL, David, decd, Levin Collins issued L/A 11/21/1793, John
Rivers, George Collins, secs, Richmond, AB
CAMPBELL, Duncan, decd, John Hobson L/A 4/4/1808, Jackson, OM
CAMPBELL, Duncan G., decd, of Wilkes Co., James Meriwether, admr,
5/3/1830, Clarke, LP
CAMPBELL, Elias, decd, Clark Howell and Robert Campbell issued
L/A 2/4/1861, Fulton
CAMPBELL, James, decd, John Campbell, Thomas Kelly issued L/A
9/25/1802, John Cormick, James Walker, secs, 1809-22 retns shows
John Campbell, surviving admr, Richmond, AB
CAMPBELL, John, Jr., 1822 retns of John Campbell as gdn; 1827
retns state that John, Jr. has arrived at age of majority,
Richmond, GB
CAMPBELL, John M., orph of Robert, decd, Roderick Leonard, gdn,
5/7/1827, James H. Campbell, Hugh Means, secs, Morgan, GB
CAMPBELL, John W. C., orph of Robert C., decd, James H. Campbell,
gdn, 3/11/1823, Levi Wellborn, Reuben Massey, secs, Morgan, GB
CAMPBELL, Martin, decd, McCartain Campbell issued L/A 2/2/1793,
William Bugg, Samuel Bugg, Henry Turknett, apprs, Richmond, AB
CAMPBELL, Robert, decd, Samuel Henderson, admr, asks to make good
titles to land 4/6/1802; Robert Ellison dismissed as sec on admn
of est 2/10/1803; Samuel Campbell <sks to be dismissed as admr
7/25/1803, Campbell, OM
CAMPBELL, Robert C., decd, Hugh Means and James H. Campbell
issued L/A 11/5/1821, Morgan, AB
CAMPBELL, Robert C., decd, L. A. McAfee, gdn to---Samuel A.,
Martha, Robert, Nancy M. and Rosanna, orphs, Jonathan Martin,
sec, Hall, GB
CAMRON, John, Jr., decd, John Cameron, admr, 2/5/1816, Clarke, LP
CAMRON, Mary, orph, John Burge, gdn until she is age 18, Creed
T. Wise, sec, 11/6/1837, Butts, GB
CANDLER, William, decd, Elizabeth and Henry Candler issued L/A
11/1/1784, Richmond, AB
CANDLER, William, Jr., decd, Ignatius Few issued L/A 2/10/1790,
Richmond, AB

CANNON, Richard, decd, James Adams issued L/A w/LWT annexed 9/1831; Kinchen Carr, James Adams, Wadsworth Clandy were present when he died 7/12/1831 and said he left all his real est to wife, Elizabeth, 10/4/1831, Habersham, MIC

CANNON, William, decd, one of distributees brought suit against last surviving exr, Preston Russell, in rt of his wife, Daisy, no date, Clarke, LP

CANTELOU, Louis, decd, late of Edgefield Dist., S. C., Louis C. and Lemuel Cantelou issued L/A 3/4/1819, Walter Leigh, John Phinizy, secs, Richmond, AB

CANTERBURY, Phillip, decd, Robt Ligon, admr 7/7/1834, Clarke, LP

CANTRELL, Mary A., minor over age 14, A. F. Underwood, gdn, H. Cantrell, sec, 7/7/1866, White, GB

CANTRELL, S. M., decd, F. Cantrell, exr, 12/1867, Webster, OD

CAPPS, S., decd, Mrs. Capps issued temp L/A 2/1865, Webster, OD

CAPPS, Samuel, decd, Matilda Capps L/A 11/1866, Webster, OD

CARITHERS, Edy H. (Mrs.), decd, 8/1881 heirs: Mary McMillian, Mrs. Ellender J. Aaron, Mrs. M. S. McDonald, Johnney L. Carithers, Matilda C. Herring, H. A. Dale and Frances E. Carithers, Clarke, LP

CARITHERS, Johnny T., orph of Edy H., decd, Robert L. Bloomfield apptd gdn 9/30/1881, Clarke, LP

CARLETON, Smith, orph of Susannah, Edward Butler, gdn, 7/2/1821, Morgan, GB

CARLETON, Susannah, decd, Edward Butler issued L/A 10/3/1819; inv /7/1820, Morgan, AB

CARLISLE, Edward, decd, Thomas Curry, gdn for orphs: Charles and Edward, 3/1/1824, William Curry and Peyton Haws, secs, Lincoln, GB

CARNES, Thomas Peters, decd, Wm Carnes, admr 7/1/1822, Clarke, LP

CARR, Susannah, decd, William H. Wade to appraise est, p. 140, Screven, OM

CARRAMORE, Moses, decd, late of Pendleton Dist., S. C., Zedekiah Anderson, gdn of orphs: Malinda, Abraham B., Elvira, Michael T., 1/15/1828, Habersham, MIC

CARRAWAY, Thomas, decd, Samuel Steven, gdn of orphs, 1838 retn, Randolph

CARREL, Fanny, a bastard child, Battle Mayfield ordered to make retn as gdn 3/4/1816, Jackson, OM

CARROLL, Robert, decd, George Willkie issued L/A 3/4/1833, Hall

CARRUTHERS, James, decd, John Carruthers issued L/A 1/12/1821, Adam Hutchinson, William Mackie, secs, Richmond, AB

CARSEY, Richard, orph of Richard, decd, Thomas Carsey, E. H. Callaway, gdns, 9/3/1821, Emanuel, GB

CARSON, Andrew M., decd, Samuel Carson issued L/A 10/7/1816, Laurens, AB

CARSON, John, decd, Rachel Carson issued L/A 3/20/1790, John McManus, Joseph Burch, secs, Richmond, AB

CARSON, Joseph, decd, Samuel Patton prays that Jane Carson be apptd admr 9/2/1806, Jackson, OM

CARSON, Thomas (Doctor), decd, Joseph J. Scott issued L/A 3/7/1808, Jackson, OM

CARTER, Abraham R., decd, John T. Carter issued L/A 1/11/1831; 2/8/1831 James Forsyth sd decd in life together with John T. Carter on 3/13/1830 gave bond to Lot 152, 19th dist., drawn by decd in land lottery, wants title, Habersham, MIC

CARTER, David, decd, Phebe Carter and William Law, admrs, of Liberty Co., Bryan, CR

CARTER, Ellmore, decd, George Dame issued L/A 6/8/1836, William R. Ryals, David Cauley, secs, Montgomery, AB

CARTER, James, decd, Isaac Carter, admr, 11/8/1836, Randolph

CARTER, John, decd, Dr. John and James M. Carter L/A 12/7/1820, Augustine Slaughter, Alex. McKenzie, secs, Richmond, AB

CARTER, John, decd, Martha Carter, Robert McCoombs, Angus Martin issued L/A 10/10/1808; 1810 retn, board for 5 children; two oldest ch: Eliza and Nancy; Angus Martin, gdn for Nancy, John, Joseph, Henry and Stephen, Richmond, AB, GB
CARTER, Rhoda, decd, Asmon R. Almand issued L/A w/LWT annexed 9/7/1857, Fulton
CARTER, Solomon, decd, L/A gtd Solomon Carter 4/26/1806; James Moore made joint admr 7/25/1803; Wm Carter dismissed as sec on adm; Solomon Carter, Jr. is abt to remove from State 10/29/1803, Jackson, OM
CARTER, Thomas, decd, 10/7/1807 inv, 12/21/1807 purchasers at sale: Charles, Thomas S. and James Carter; Charles and Thomas S. Carter, admrs, Elbert, AR
CARTER, Thomas, decd, Thomas S. and Charles Carter, admrs, 1809 retns, expense of getting out of Jones Co., Ga. land grant, Elbert, AR
CARTER, Thomas Paine, James Carter, gdn, 1811 retns, Elbert, AR
CARY, Orlando, decd, John Cary, admr, 11/4/1816, Clarke, LP
CARY, Orlando, decd, John Cary, admr, 11/4/1816, Clarke, LP
CASE, Elizabeth Ann, decd, Telph Case issued L/A 7/6/1835, Baldwin, AB
CASH, Allison, minor orph of George W., decd, William Cannon, gdn, 9/1/1862, Fulton, GB
CASH, George R., minor orph of George W., decd, Polly Hudson, gdn, 9/1/1862, Fulton, GB
CASHAN, John, decd, Martin Hendrick, gdn of orphs: John, Sarah, James and Jones, 10/1/1855, Houston, GB
CASHIN, John, decd, 1827 retns of extrx, 1821 acct of Oswell Cashin, minor and J. Cashin, minor, Richmond
CASON, William, orph of Elizabeth, decd, James M. Gill, gdn, 9/7/1835, Tilman Alba and Covington Searls, secs, Lincoln, GB
CASTLEBERRY, B. F., minor son of Elisha, decd, Jane Castleberry apptd gdn 5/5/1852, Samuel G. Castleberry, sec, Lumpkin, GB
CASTLEBERRY, Henry, decd, 7/4/1807, exr Joseph East; heirs: Samuel Johnson, William East, William Howard for Milley East, Joseph East, Clarke, LP
CATCHINGS, Letha, decd, (wife of Meredith C. Catchings) Wm Peyton issued L/A 7/3/1815, Jackson, OM
CATLETT, John, decd, Lindsey Coleman, John Scott issued L/A 3/7/1811, Richmond, AB
CATO, Amanda J., L. R. Redding issued L/G 1/1857, Webster, OD
CATO, James W. R., L. R. Redding issued L/G 1/1857, Webster, OD
CAUSEY, John, decd, L. B. Causey issued L/A 1/1862, Webster, OD
CAUSEY, Levin, decd, Simon F. Stephens, admr de bonis non w/LWT annexed, J. S. Osborne, T. Sims, surs, 7/13/1851, Bibb, AB
CAVENDER, Clemmeth, decd, John Abercrombie issued L/A 4/5/1852, Charles and Isaac Heads, Ransom Barnes, secs, Hall, AB
CAVER, Jacob A., orph of Jacob, decd, Nancy Caver, gdn, 11/4/1839, Wm Bohler, sec, Lincoln, GB
CAVER, James, decd, Jacob Robinson L/A 11/3/1817, Laurens, AB
CAVIN, Forgey, decd, William Shockley, admr, makes retn 1809, Jackson, OM
CAVIN, James H., orph of Jacob, decd, Thomas Florence, gdn, 1/7/1839, Hardy Leverette and Wiley Jeter, secs, Lincoln, GB
CAVNAH, William, decd, James Archer, admr, p. 172, Screven, OM
CENTER, George W., decd, 6/17/1876 heirs: Wm Center of Bern Co., Ark. and Benton Co., Ark; unable to contact B. H. Martin of either Miss or Ark, Clarke, LP
CESSNA, Samuel C., orph of Samuel, decd, John Dawson, gdn, 3/4/1816, David McIntosh, sec, Morgan, GB
CHAFFIN, Charlotte, illegitimate child, Amos Chaffin, gdn, 9/8/1828, Habersham, MIC

CHAFFIN, Lemuel, decd, Richard Dillard apptd gdn of orphs: John
T. and Cynthia E., 7/6/1846 and 11/2/1846; John G. Mayes apptd
gdn of orphs: Antionett A., Francis A., John T. and Cynthia E.,
5/7/1838, Clarke, LP
CHAIRS, Joseph, decd, Benjamin and Green H. Chairs issued L/A
2/12/1816, Laurens, AB
CHAMBERLIN, W. S., decd, E. P. and Catherine Chamberlin issued
L/A 6/1864, Webster, OD
CHAMBERS, Matilda, orph of Applin T., decd, Miles Sanders, gdn,
8/7/1854, Houston, GB
CHAMBLISS, Rachel, decd, Andrew D. Chambliss, admr, H. H.
Solomon, William H. Chambliss, sur, 7/3/1848, Bibb, AB
CHAMPION, Micajah, decd, M. Champion issued L/A 2/28/1875,
Twiggs, Misc
CHANCE, Isaac, decd, Willoughby Barton, gdn of orphs: Thomas,
Elizabeth, John and Nancy, minors, Richmond, GB
CHANCEY, John, decd, 3/4/1861 heirs: Bettie, Calvin and Ollie
Chancey, Wm Spencer (who owns Ann Chancey's pt and Richard
Chancey's pt), grch: Wm R. Chancey, son of dau, Ann, 9/29/1859,
Clarke, LP
CHANCY, John apptd gdn of his minor ch: Sarah E., William L.,
John, Thomas and Stephen 4/4/1853, Houston, GB
CHANDLER, Bailey, decd, Abraham Chandler issued L/A 7/3/1809,
Jackson, OM
CHAPMAN, Alfred W., decd, Nancy Darby issued L/A 1/14/1861,
Fulton
CHAPMAN, George, decd, Marian G. Chapman, admx w/LWT annexed
5/7/1849, James M. Chapman, Valentine Whelchel, John Clark, secs,
Hall, AB
CHAPMAN, John, decd, Debra Chapman, extrx of LWT pvd by Benjamin
Chapman 12/14/1798, Warren, MIC
CHAPMAN, John, decd, William Auberry and Thomas Auberry issued
L/A 9/4/1818, Pleasant Watts, sec, Morgan, AB
CHAPPELL, Robert, decd, he d. 7/1898, Clarke, LP
CHASTAIN, Benjamin, idiot, Madison C. Chastain, gdn 5/6/1850, J.
W. Gober, sec, Hall, GB
CHASTAIN, Elias E., decd, Harriet E. issued L/A 5/3/1847, J. W.
McCrary, sec, Hall, AB
CHASTAIN, Francis, orph of James, decd, John H. Hose, gdn,
4/2/1855, Houston, GB
CHASTAIN, Sarah Ann, orph of E. E., decd, Nathaniel Smith, gdn,
Robert W. Brown, sec, 8/2/1852, Hall, GB
CHASTAIN, William, decd, William Chastin and John W. Gober issued
temp L/A 10/18/1849, Madison C. Chastain, James Jackson, secs,
Hall, AB
CHASTAIN, William, decd, late of Lee Co., James Laramore, admr,
Jane Chastain, admx, 5/27/1854, Lee, MSC
CHATFIELD, Hial, decd, William Micou issued L/A 3/16/1810, Thomas
Barrett, John Savage, secs, Richmond, AB
CHAVES, Philip, decd, 9/20/1796 inv, Thomas Tate, Martain Sims,
Job Hammond, apprs, 1/23/1797 sales to Harry, Gilbert and
Charlotte Chaves, Robert Martain, Martain Sims, Elbert, AR
CHEATHAM, Anthony R., decd, W. Cheatham, admr 2/10/1833; John L.,
minor son; William Nabors, admr 5/3/1841 after death of W.
Cheatham; heirs: James, Sarah, Adaline, Elizabeth, Jane and John,
Clarke, LP
CHEATHAM, John S., orph of Mary W., John J. Cheatham apptd gdn
9/7/1840, Clarke, LP
CHEATHAM, Laura L., orph of Obadiah, decd, John W. Nicholson,
gdn, 7/20/1853, Clarke, LP
CHEATHAM, Mary W., Wm Nabors apptd admr 8/3/1841, Clarke, LP

CHENAULT, Abram, orph of John N., decd, John Hardy, gdn, 3/1/1830, Shadrack Turner, sec, Lincoln, GB
CHENEY, Franklin W., d. 10/6/1892, Clarke, LP
CHENEY, Mary Louisa, decd, ch-Franklin W, Daisy, age 12-Floyd Co, Alvin D-Chattooga Co, Lilly, Winslow, Judson, Walter, Paul, Gill & stpsn Dr Dudley Cheney, Martha Carver 4/1885; bury Myrtle Hill Cemetery, beside husb, F. W., Clarke, Co., LP
CHENEY, Paul, decd (son of F. W. & Mary Louise Cheney), LWT pvd 5/4/1887 Randolph Co., d. 7/14/1886 Calhoun Co.; heirs: wife, Anna, sis-in-law, Colee Cheney, wife of W. D.; all bros, sisters & half-bro, cousin, Mrs. Carry Thomas, Clarke, LP
CHERRY, William, decd, est 11/2/1846, Clarke, LP
CHEWNING, William, decd, Permelia Chewing, James McGiboney, gdns of orphs of decd 3/3/1834, Harris
CHILDS, Nathan, decd, Littleton Johnson, admr, 5/1/1807 settlement to Thos Head, John, Nathan & Jane Childs, James Satterwhite, in rt of wife, Franky, John Wynn, gdn of Ann Wilson Childs, heirs, Elbert, AR
CHILDS, Richard, decd, John Childs, admrs bond, Mat J. Williams and James Morrison, sec, Elbert, AB
CHISHOLM, Robert J., decd, E. N. Calhoun issued L/A 2/2/1863, Fulton
CHISHOLM, William A., decd, Mrs. Rebecca and Willis L. Chisholm, admrs, George W. Adair, John J. Thrasher, Robert M. Clark, secs, 7/8/1862, Fulton, AB
CHISOLM, Marvin, orph, Henry Whatley, gdn, 7/8/1838, Butts, GB
CHISSOM, Appleton, son of William, James G. Mastin apptd gdn 9/3/1832, Clarke, LP
CHITWOOD, Caty, illegitimate child of Phoebe, given into the custody of Caleb Griffin, Sr., the reputed father, 3/26/1836, Habersham, MIC
CHRISTE, N. B., decd, H. J. Perry issued L/A 12/1873, Webster, OD
CHRISTER, Henry, decd, 1801-1803 retns, Joseph Christler, admr, Elbert, AR
CHRISTY, John H., decd, wife, Anna; ch-Eldridge J., John R., Mary L., William D., Sallie A., Walter S., Henry P., Thomas J. and Julia H., 3/7/1877, Clarke, LP
CHURCH, Alonzo (Rev. Dr.), decd, heirs---Wm L. Church (minor), Mrs. E. A. Lee, George A. Croom, John R. Church, B. S. Whitner, Anna P. Whitner, E. A. See, 12/27/1861, Clarke, LP
CHURCH, Gabriel B., decd, LWT exhibited 6/11/1866, Sarah Church, extrx, Fulton
CHURCHWELL, James, decd, Elizabeth Churchwell issued L/A 9/2/1822, Robert Jones, John Knight, secs, Richmond, AB
CLAIBORNE, William, decd, formerly of New Kent Co., Va., lately of City of Richmond in sd State, Gustavus Gaines issued L/A 2/3/1816, Eleazar Early, B. Picquet, secs, Richmond, AB
CLARK, Elizabeth, decd, William R. Ryals issued temp L/A 4/21/1836 & perm L/A 6/6/1836, Robert Partin, sec, Montgomery, AB
CLARK, F., decd, Z. S. Parker issued L/A 12/1865, Webster, OD
CLARK, Francis, decd, 1807 retn, Zachariah Smith, admr, 1809 retn pd Lewis Clark and Z. Smith, exrs for expenses; receipt of Tolliver Hall for wife, Sally's pt of est; receipt of J. V. Harris for having Z. Smith apptd gdn of orphs, Elbert, AR
CLARK, Gilbert, decd, Mildred Clark issued L/A 7/11/1789, Jeremiah Lampkin Edward Clark, secs, Richmond, AB
CLARK, John, decd, John Clark issued L/A 9/2/1806, Jackson, OM
CLARK, John M., decd, Isaac M. Penney issued L/A 8/15/1855, Clarke, LP
CLARK, Johnson, decd, LWT pvd 3/3/1806; David McCurdy, one of exrs, makes retn 7/9/1806, Jackson, OM

CLARK, John William, orph of James, decd, John H. Hose, gdn, 6/5/1855, Houston, GB
CLARK, Joseph, decd, Nimrod Clark issued L/A w/LWT annexed 3/2/1838, William and John B. Ryals, secs, Montgomery, AB
CLARK, Joseph, orph, Joseph Herron was apptd gdn 5/2/1831, Habersham, MIC
CLARK, Larkin, decd, Thomas Wright issued L/A 12/6/1826, Joseph Heard, Joseph Howard,ecs, Morgan, AB
CLARK, Patsy, minor orph of John, decd, James Clark apptd gdn 5/4/1807, Jackson, OM
CLARK, Ruth, insane, John Clarke, gdn, 11/21/1851, Hall, GB
CLARK, Zachariah, decd, bond of Abigail P. Clark and James Morrison, admrs, 3/4/1811, AB
CLARKE, Albert J., decd, Mrs. Mary H. Clarke issued L/A 1/13/1862, Fulton
CLARKE, Charles, decd, 9/30/1793 est apprd by John Shackleford, Joseph Fargeson, John Collier, Richmond
CLARKE, Columbus C., orph of David, decd, Barney E. Whiteheard, gdn, 12/5/1853, Houston, GB
CLARKE, David, decd, Lucretia Clarke, gdn of orphs: George F. and Mary Louisa 12/5/1853, Houston, GB
CLARKE, George F., orph of David, decd, John D. Clarke, gdn, 1/8/1855, Houston, GB
CLARKE, Timothy, decd, Charles Clarke issued L/A 3/17/1819, Gabriel Clarke, William Tutt, secs, Richmond, AB
CLAYTON, Augustin S., decd, William W. Clayton, exr, 8/14/1839, Clarke, LP
CLEARWATER, Eleanor, decd, Thomas Stephens L/A 8/1/1853, Hall, AB
CLEGHORN, James, decd, Avington and Nancy Cleghorn, admrs, William Spruce, Joseph Wigley, surs, 3/5/1832, Hall, AB
CLEMENT, John, decd, est 10/7/1816, Clarke, LP
CLEMENTS, Austin, decd, Lemue Chaffin and Mary Clements issued L/A 3/11/1823; Lemuel Chaffin issued L/A 5/5/1823, Morgan, AB
CLEMENTS, Isham, decd, L/A issued Thomas J. Clements 12/1868; Mrs. Mary A. Clements issued L/A 2/1869, Webster, OD
CLEMENTS, John, decd, William Boyd, Mary A. Clements, Benjamin Henry, John Murphy, admrs 6/8/1835, Harris
CLEMENTS, Louisa E. L., minor under age 14, Margaret O. Clements, gdn, 1/2/1815, Laurens, GB
CLEYTON, Austin, minor son of Edmond, decd, Gideon Tanner, gdn, James Brooks, sec, 3/24/1834, Butts, GB
CLIFTON, George, decd, est 7/22/1840, Clarke, LP
CLIFTON, Lewis, decd, inv 5/2/1840 apprs: Archibald and Daniel McNabb, Isaiah Harden, John McDonald, Tattnall, I&A
CLINCE, Thomas, decd, Susan Clince issued L/A 5/19/1866, Fulton
CLINCH, Robert Thomas, minor of Charles J. and Batavia Ella of N. Y. (living in France), John J. Thomas apptd gdn 1/7/1884; George Thomas gdn 6/3/1889, Clarke, LP
CLOWER, David, orph of John, decd, Jane Clower, gdn, 1/8/1817, William Foil, sec, Morgan, GB
CLOWER, Joseph F. apptd gdn of H. T. D. and T. F. J. Clower 6/2/1890, Clarke, LP
CLOWERS, John, decd, Jesse and George Clowsers issued L/A 3/19/1816, David Love, sec, Morgan, AB
CLUNG, George, decd, L/A to John G. Mason 9/5/1808, Putnam, AB
COATS, James, planter, decd, Thomas Watson issued L/A 11/15/1783, Joseph McCormick, sec, Richmond, AB
COATS, John G., decd, estate, no date, Clarke, LP
COATS, Josiah, decd, L/A to Robert Coats 3/2/1818, Laurens, AB

COATS, Lesley, decd, 1809-10 retns, Drusilla & Jno Coats, admrs;
Benjamin Sherod, gdn of Lesley & Frances; pd Jas Corbett for
Fanny & Sally, Peter Harris his sh, Wm & Felix Gilbert for Sally
Barron, S. Barron his sh, 1/7/1817, Wilkes, Retns
COBB, Daniel, decd, Benjamin Cobb, Lemonx Box, admrs, 9/20/1839,
Baldwin, AB
COBB, Howell, decd, d. 8/19/1909, wid, Mary McKinley Cobb; sole
heir, wife, Clarke, LP
COBB, Howell Cobb apptd gdn of his minor ch: Zack L. (age 20),
Sarah S. (age 18), Caroline E. (age 15), and Carlisle (age 13),
9/19/1884, Clarke, LP
COBB, Japhet, decd, Mrs. Harriet Cobb qualified as admx
3/20/1788, Liberty, Ests
COBB, Lucy Barrow, decd, children: Howell, Sarah Passe, John
Addison, Lucy Middleton, Mary Ann Lamar; husband, John A. Cobb,
6/5/1880, Clarke, LP
COBB, Marion Thomas, orph of Thomas R. R., decd, Augustus L. Hull
apptd gdn 11/1/1871, Clarke, LP
COBB, Mary, decd, wife of Samuel B. Cobb, Alexander Cobb apptd
gdn of their minor son, Larey Cobb, Samuel B. Cobb, sec,
11/6/1848, Troup, GB
COBB, Mary Ann, John A. Cobb apptd trustee 8/15/1869; Mary An d.
11/27/1889; heirs-Andrew J. Cobb, Lamar Cobb, Alex T. Erwin, tr
of M. A. L. Erwin, Howell Cobb, Sarah Ruckers, John A. Cobb, exr
for Lucy B. Cobb, decd, Clarke, LP
COBB, Thomas, decd, of Augusta, Catherine Cobb & Peyton Bibb
issued L/A 2/17/1816, Alex McKenzie, Wm Wright, secs; 11/13/1816
prop in Columbia Co. appd by Austin Woolfolk; 2/7/1816 Catherine
Cobb, gdn of Wm A. Cobb, minor orph, Richmond, AB
COBB, Thomas R. R., decd, d. 1/1/1880, Clarke, LP
COBBISON, John, decd, Anne Cobbison issued L/A 3/17/1797, George
Walton, Henry Osborne, secs, Richmond, AB
COBBS, John, decd, LWT pvd 5/20/1797, Thomas Cobbs, William
Beckham and Howell Cobbs, exrs, to make inv, Columbia, Ests
COCHRAHAM, David, decd, Hannah Cochraham issued L/A 7/25/1799,
George Weisinger, Robert McTyeire, secs, Richmond, AB
COCHRAN, James (Major), decd, div his prop betwn wife, Mary
Cochran, Judith Winn, Ann Key & Jane Thurmond 9/1838, Jackson, OM
COCHRAN, John, decd, apprs: Thos Colbert, John Sturdivant,
Benjamin Lassiter, 11/30/1809, Jasper, OM
COCHRAN, John, orph of Benjamin, decd, Banister Cochran, gdn,
11/4/1816, Robert Brooks, Samuel Paschal, secs, Morgan, GB
COCHRAN, Martin, decd, John L. Cochran, Washington C. Cleveland,
Joseph Weldon, admrs 9/14/1835, Harris
COCHRAN, Martin, decd, John T. Cooper gdn; J. W. Cooper, J. W.
Cato, Marion Cochran, admr, 5/6/1839, Harris
COCHRAN, Martin, decd, Marian Cochran, gdn of the orphs
11/21/1837, Harris, GB
COCKE, Jack F., decd, Gabriel Moffitt apptd gdn of minor ch: Wm
S., David P., Jack F. and Woodson, 4/1/1816, Clarke, LP
COCKE, William (Dr.), decd, late of Chatham Co., Rebecca Cocke
issued L/A 7/24/1812, Lindsey Coleman, John McKinne, secs;
11/4/1816 Rebecca Cocke, gdn of Nathl, minor orph, John McKinne,
Gilbert Longstreet, secs, Richmond, AB
CODY, David, decd, Lucretia Cody (now Sherman), releases
Churchill Gibson, Peter Cody, from bond, 10/4/1825, Warren, AB
CODY, David, decd, Lucretia Cody, admx, 11/17/1823, Churchill
Gibson, Wm B. Hundley, Peter Cody, surs, Warren, AB
CODY, Michael, decd, Rebecca Cody, admx, 1/8/1833, Thomas
Lockett, Elias Wilson, surs, Warren, AB
CODY, Richard, decd, Elizabeth Cody and Nathaniel Hutchinson
apptd admrs 1/1/1810, Warren, MIC, AB

CODY, Winder H., decd, Eliza Cody, admx 1/1835; appraisers:
William Cooper, John Harrell, Laban Morgan, Stewart, Adms
COFFEE, Elizabeth, minor of Ira, decd, Mariah Jane Coffee, gdn,
5/14/1860, Cherokee, GB
COFFEE, Frederick, minor of Ira, decd, Mariah Jane Coffee, gdn,
5/14/1860, Cherokee, GB
COFFEE, Joseph, minor of Ira, decd, Mariah Jane Coffee, gdn,
5/14/1860, Cherokee, GB
COFFEE, Sarah Jane, minor of Ira, decd, Mariah Jane Coffee, gdn,
5/14/1860, Cherokee, GB
COFFEE, Whitman, minor of Ira, decd, Mariah Jane Coffee, gdn,
5/14/1860, Cherokee, GB
COGBURN, Archibald, decd, LWT dtd 5/11/1852, pvd 6/1853, July
Cogburn and Lawson Fields, exrs, ch: Sythy fields, James F.
Cogburn, Sarah Bridwell, Francis Fowler, Mary Blalock, wife of
Hansford W. Blalock, Cherokee
COGBURN, Henry, decd, N. Cogburn issued temp L/A, Lewis Taylor,
sur, 2/27/1866, Paulding, AB
COGGINS, Harris, decd, Elijah Puckett issued temp L/A 3/23/1849,
James Roberts, sec, Hall, AB
COHEN, Philip Jacob, decd, Savannah Merchant, LWT, only qualified
exr, Adam Vann 11/18/1790, Chatham, Adms
COILE, N., decd, William W. Coile apptd gdn of orphs (his bros):
Frank Gibson and J. Gibson, 1883, Clarke, LP
COKER, Abraham, decd, Janet Handley, qualified as extrx, 9/1841,
1842 retn, Fayette
COKER, Daniel, decd, L/A to David Solomon 3/4/1833, Washington
COLBERT, Ella C. apptd gdn of her minor ch: Susie A., Alice S.
and Augusta L., orphs of William C., decd; paternal grfather,
Lindsey G. Colbert of Madison Co., Clarke, LP
COLBERT, Letty, decd, William B. Colbert L/A 7/4/1842, Baldwin
COLCLOUGH, Sarah F. was apptd gdn of her minor daus, Laura and
Sarah, 2/3/1869, the heirs of their grandfather, Thomas
Colclough, Clarke, LP
COLE, Alice, decd, Japhet Cobb, qualified as exr 6/26/1787,
Liberty, Ests
COLE, Emeline, (Miss) decd, W. D. Cole was apptd admr, 1/13/1845,
estate divided (5 slaves) betwn: William D. Cole, C. J. Cole,
Richard Cole, Christiana Cole, James M. Smith, James M. Smith as
gdn, and Richard Cole, a minor, and Ann E. Cole, 9/7/1846,
Camden, MIC
COLE, E. M. (Miss), decd, W. D. Cole, admr, dismissed, 1/4/1847,
Camden, MIC
COLE, John, decd, Peter C. Thibeau was issued L/A 3/1825,
Habersham, MIC
COLE, Josiah, decd, heirs: James D. Cole 12/17/1829, Clarke, LP
COLE, Rene, decd, William Cole issued L/A 9/2/1816; Jane Cole,
widow, states est not being managed in beneficial way, 1/7/1817,
Jasper, OM
COLE, Richard, decd, of Charleston, South Carolina, Stephen West
Moore, admr, makes final retn and dismissed 4/1/1805, Camden, MIC
COLE, Richard, orph of James J., late of S. C., decd, W. D. Cole
apptd gdn, 1/4/1847, Camden, MIC
COLE, Sally, orph of Rene, decd, Jane Cole, widow, apptd gdn
1/5/1818, Jasper, OM
COLE, Sarah, decd, estate 1/12/1857, Clarke, LP
COLE, Sarah, orph of Duke, decd, Lindsey Durham, gdn, 2/7/1825,
William Clark, Sr., Etheldred Sorrell, surs, Clarke, GB
COLE, W. D., decd, J. M. Cole issued temporary L/A 9/1866,
Webster, OD
COLE, William, decd, orph of Rene, decd, Jane Cole, widow, apptd
gdn 1/5/1818, jasper, OM

COLEMAN, Ann, orph of David, decd, Alfred Brewer gave bond as gdn in Newton Co. 5/11/1839, Butts, ER
COLEMAN, Caleb, decd, Anna Coleman issued L/A 8/21/1789, Reuben Coleman, Charles Simmons, secs, Richmond, AB
COLEMAN, Clementine, illegitimate, Jonathan Hardigree apptd gdn 11/12/1838, Clarke, LP
COLEMAN, David, decd, Alfred Brewer, gdn of orphs: David Lewis, Dorothy and Francis Harris, Francis Douglass, sec, 5/6/1839, Butts, GB
COLEMAN, David, orph of David, decd, Alfred Brewer gave bond as gdn in Newton Co., 5/11/1839, Butts, ER
COLEMAN, David Lewis, orph of David, decd, Alfred Brewer gave bond as gdn, 5/11/1839 in Newton Co., Butts, ER
COLEMAN, Dorothy, orph of David, decd, Alfred Brewer gave bond as gdn in Newton Co., 5/11/1839, Butts, ER
COLEMAN, Elijah to be bound to John Clark during his minority 5/3/1813, Franklin, OM
COLEMAN, Elliot, minor son of Caleb, decd, John and James Scott, gdns, 1/3/1803, Richmond, GB
COLEMAN, Francis H., decd, LWT exhibited 8/5/1861, Edward E. Rawson and Sarah E. Coleman, exrs, Fulton
COLEMAN, Frances Harris, orph of David, decd, Alfred Brewer gave bond as gdn, 5/11/1839 in Newton Co., Butts, ER
COLEMAN, Henry, decd, Stephen V. Gay, admr, 7/16/1855, Lee, MSC
COLEMAN, Henry, decd, est represented 7/1/1854, Lee, MSC
COLEMAN, James M., decd, H. S. Coleman L/A 1/14/1861, Fulton
COLEMAN, John, decd, LWT dtd 10/22/1778, wife, Susannah; ch: James, John, Thomas, Susannah, Charlotte, Elizabeth, Wilkes, MxR
COLEMAN, Lindsey, decd, Benja. H. Warren L/A 11/7/1821, 1/9/1822 & gdn of orphs-Clarissa & James L.; div of slaves to-Sarah, Clarissa, James L. Coleman, Green B. Marshall, (Frances' husband), Benjamin H. Warren, (Mary's husb), Richmond, AB
COLEMAN, Reuben, decd, Lucy Coleman and Thomas B. Scott issued L/A 12/29/1795, Richmond, AB
COLEMAN, Theophilus, decd, Jonathan Coleman, admr, w/LWT annexed 7/1/1816, Nancy Coleman gdn of orphs: James and John 8/5/1816, Jonathan and Josey Coleman, secs, Laurens, GB
COLLEHARD, John, decd, Malcom Currie issued L/A 3/7/1830, David Colley, sec, Montgomery, AB
COLLEY, Betsey, minor orph of Thomas, decd, Isham Smith apptd gdn, Isham Rainey, Welcome Parks, sec, 9/1806, Oglethorpe, OM, GB
COLLEY, John, decd, Francis Colley, extrx, 1816 retns pd Spain Colley, Wilkes, Retns
COLLEY, Thomas, minor orph of Thomas, decd, Isham Smith apptd gdn, Isham Rainey, Welcome Parks, sec, 9/1806, Oglethorpe, OM, GB
COLLIER, Elbert, decd, Toliver Jones, John W. Mays, admrs, 3/6/1837, Harris
COLLIER, Elizabeth, decd, William Ezzard, admr, 6/7/1859, Robert Hollingsworth, sur, DeKalb, AB
COLLIER, Henry, decd, 11/5/1840; children relinquish all rts to Esther Collier for minor heirs' benefit-William Collier, Dorcas Collier (for husb), James V. Collier, Piety Cruise (for husb), Dempsey Cruise, William McLendon, Henry Collier, Dooly, I&A
COLLIER, John, decd, John Wereat, admr, 9/5/1784, Chatham, Adms
COLLIER, Meredith, decd, LWT pvd 4/6/1863, John Collier, exr, Fulton
COLLIER, Thomas, decd, est 12/12/1860, Clarke, LP
COLLIER, William, orph of William, decd, Franklin Collier apptd gdn 3/5/1849, Clarke, LP
COLLINS, Cornelius, decd, John Collins qualified as admr 2/8/1792, Liberty, Ests

COLLINS, Eli, decd, Purnell Collins, J. W. Cots, James Ramsey, admr, 1/6/1840, Harris
COLLINS, Elizabeth, John A. F. Hankins, gdn, 6/1854, J. J. and S. T. Whitaker, surs, Fayette, GB
COLLINS, Emily C., John A. Hankins, gdn, 6/1854, John T. and S. T. Whitaker, surs, Fayette, GB
COLLINS, George W., decd, Hiram Mathis, Vincent P. Johnston, admrs, Clark F. Howell, sur, 9/2/1867, Gwinnett, AB
COLLINS, George W., orph of John G., decd, Emmaline Collins issued L/G 11/1/1841, Washington
COLLINS, Henry, decd, 9/20/1845, William Collins, admr; purchasers at sale: William, J. J. and Elizabeth Collins, Blake B. Rutland, John B. Lewis, William Slade, John Eubanks, James Culpepper, "the widow", Dooly, I&A
COLLINS, Henry, decd, George W. Collins makes retn 1/6/1840; inv by Lewis Cobb, M. Collins, Stephen Heniday, William Holland, apprs, 9/15/1838, Tattnall, I&A
COLLINS, Henry, decd, William Collins, admr, 9/20/1845, Dooly, OD
COLLINS, Hiram gave receipt to John Green, gdn, as receiving his legacy from est of James Collins, decd, 10/19/1838, Bulloch, Misc
Collins, James A., John A. Hankins, gdn, 6/1854, John T. and S. T. Whitaker, surs, Fayette, GB
COLLINS, James, alias Baker, bound to Andrew McBride, 11/3/1817, Jasper, OM
COLLINS, James, decd, John Green recd from Frances Collins, admx, the pt of Mikell Collins, orph, 2/11/1841, Bulloch, Misc
COLLINS, James, decd, Simeon L. Holiday, admr; Sarah E. Holliday, admx de bonis non, Dooly, OD
COLLINS, James, decd, inv and appr by James Hollaway, Riley Mercer, Elisha Summerlin 5/1/1835, Bulloch, Misc
COLLINS, James, decd, Mrs. Frances Collins retn as gdn of minors 9/6/1841; Ansel Parrish dischgd as sec of heirs' gdnship, John Collins recd instead 3/2/1840; div among 12 heirs, Frances and Josiah Collins named 5/4/1837, Bulloch, MIC, Misc
COLLINS, John, minor child of Thomas J., Thomas Warthen issued L/G 1/20/1842, Washington
COLLINS, John G., decd, John Curry issued L/A 11/4/1839, Washington
COLLINS, John G., orph of John G., decd, Emmaline Collins issued L/G 11/1/1841, Washington
COLLINS, John S., decd, John G. and George W. Collins issued L/A 11/4/1833, Washington
COLLINS, Joshua, decd, Thomas Warthen issued L/A 3/1/1841, Washington
COLLINS, Josiah, decd, Nancy Collins issued L/A 1/1/1810, Joel Williams, Willie Horn, secs, Laurens, AB
COLLINS, Lafayette, orph of Joshua, decd, Mary G. Collins issued L/G 1/5/1842, Washington
COLLINS, Levin, decd, Caty Collins issued L/A 3/4/1807, Wm M. Cowles, John Collins, sec; purchasers-Lewis, Moses, Sarah and James Collins, signed "in rt of wife, formerly Mrs. Collins, R. Wright." Caty Wright, formerly Collins, Richmond, AB
COLLINS, Lewis, decd, Benjamin Rowland, Robert Allen L/A 9/8/1818; ch-Martha, Mary, Kitty, Amelia, Sarah Jane; heirs-Benjamin Rowland, Geo. W. & Jesse Collins (rt of wf), Jas Palmer (rt of wf), Catherine, Amelia, Jane & Lewis (decd), Richmond, AB
COLLINS, Lucy, minor child of Thomas J., Thomas Warthen issued L/G 1/20/1842, Washington
COLLINS, Lucy J., orph of John G., decd, Emmaline Collins issued L/G 11/1/1841, Washington

COLLINS, Ludwell E., decd, Catharine Ragin issued L/A 11/23/1823
& applied for leave to sell real est; ltr from James Bryan, one
of heirs, 11/71826, Pike, MIC
COLLINS, Margaret, orph of Joshua, decd, Mary G. Collins issued
L/G 1/5/1842, Washington
COLLINS, Martha, orph of Joshua, decd, Mary G. Collins issued L/G
1/5/1842, Washington
COLLINS, Martin, John A. F. Hankins, gdn, 6/1854, J. J. and S. T.
Whitaker, surs, Fayette, GB
COLLINS, Mary, minor orph of Harasha, decd, Griffin Mercer, gdn,
Ira T. McLemore, sec, 7/4/1842, Emanuel, GR
COLLINS, Michael gave receipt to John Green, gdn, as receiving
legacy from est of James Collins, decd, 10/19/1838, Bulloch, Misc
COLLINS, Michael, orph of James, decd, John Green apptd gdn
1/4/1841, Bulloch, MIC
COLLINS, Michael A. E., John A. F. Hankins, gdn, 6/1854, John T.
and S. T. Whitaker, surs, Fayette, GB
COLLINS, Nelson L., minor child of Thomas J., Thomas Warthen
issued L/G 1/20/1842, Washington
COLLINS, Paschal, John A. F. Hankins, gdn, 6/1854, J. J. and S.
T. Whitaker, surs, Fayette, GB
COLLINS, Paschal E., decd, C. C. Bowen, admr, 11/1850, John
Bowen, admr, Fayette, AB
COLLINS, Peter, decd, Margaret Kennady apptd admx 11/12/1784,
Wilkes, MxR
COLLINS, Romalus D., John A. F. Hankins, gdn, 6/1854, John T. and
S. T. Whitaker, surs, Fayette, GB
COLLINS, Sarah A., orph of John G., decd, Emmaline Collins issued
L/G 11/1/1841, Washington
COLLINS, Seaborn, orph of John G., decd, Emmaline Collins issued
L/G 11/1/1841, Washington
COLLINS, William, orph of Joshua, decd, Mary G. Collins issued
L/G 1/5/1842, Washington
COLLINS, William L., orph of John G., decd, Emmaline Collins
issued L/G 11/1/1841, Washington
COLLY, Jacob apptd gdn of his minor son, George W., heir to est
of his grmother, Harriet Carothers, Clarke, LP
COLLY, John, decd, wid, Martha E. and one child, 9/27/1848,
Clarke, LP
COLQUHOUN, Winnefred, gdn of Thomas B., Mary F. and Edith, ch of
Angus and Winneford 1/7/1833, W. B. Ryals, sec, Montgomery, GB
COLSON, Jacob, decd, LWT pvd 2/5/1778, ch: Abram, Nancy; heirs of
wives Sarah and Milby, except prop to Milby the day of her
marriage, to be provided for during widowhood, Wilkes, MxR
COLSON, Mathew, decd, Chloe and Henry Colson, admrs, p. 71,
Screven, OM
COLT, John H., decd, records transferred from Jackson Co. 1881,
Clarke, LP
COLWELL, William, decd, James Archer, appr, p. 95, Screven, OM
COMER, A. F. apptd gdn of his minor ch: Alexander, Leah, Mary L.,
Deleney Renlie, Austin F., Jr. and Brantley C. of Madison Co.,
heirs of Charles W. Arnold, son of Mrs. Letitia Comer, decd,
Clarke, LP
COMPTON, James L., decd, Pleasant A. Compton, admr, Robert C.
Mays, Jordan Compton, secs, 1/14/1840; apprs: Robert Mays, James
B. Brown, J. R. McCord, John Hendrick, 4/9/1840, admr makes 1841
retn, Butts, AB, ER
COMPTON, John, Sr., decd, L/A issued Pleasant and John W.
Compton, 3/5/1821, Jasper, OM
COMPTON, Micajah, Mary, decd, Micajah Compton issued L/A
11/4/1850, Julius C. Hendrix, sec, Hall, AB

65

COMPTON, Thomas M. apptd gdn of his minor dau, Lora H., 1885; Thomas d. 3/19/1889, Clarke, LP
COMPTON, William, decd, John Compton issued L/A 11/2/1840, Martin Pugh, Nathan Compton, secs, Hall, AB
CONALLY, John, decd, L/A issued Sesley Conally, William Christian, David Morgan 7/6/1807, Franklin, IMW
CONANT, Garrison, decd, John Gilliam, William Hood, gdns of orph of decd 1/8/1838, Harris, GB
CONE, Aaron, decd, LWT pvd 3/13/1835, names ch: Peter, James, Robert, Barber, Aaron, Sarah Goodman; grch: John Goodman, Joseph and William Cone; daus: Ann Jones, Kizzeah Sheffield, Frances and Susannah Cone; wife Hannah; 5/9/1835 heirs receipts: Seaborn Jones, Sarah Goodman, Simeon Shuffield, Joseph C. Edwards, Aaron Cone, Hannah Cone, Peter Cone, Robert Cone, Barber Cone, Aaron Cone; James Cone, Allen Jones, exrs, Bulloch, Misc
CONE, John, Sr., 9/26/1842, apprs: Jacob Watson, Vincent McNeese, James R. Hooks; purchasers at sale: William B. Cone, Thomas Cone, Nathan Youngblood, A. Shiver, Dooly, I&A
CONE, Joseph, orph of Aaron, decd, Peter Cone made 1839 retn, 3/2/1840, Bulloch, MIC
CONE, Joseph, orph of Aaron, decd, retn by James Cone, exr 10/13/1836, left for use of family of decd until Joseph Cone becomes age 21, Bulloch, Misc
CONE, Reuben, decd, Julius A. Hayden, admr, 6/7/1852, L. Cone, John Glen, surs, DeKalb, AB
CONE, Tabitha, decd, Peter Cone apptd admr 9/1/1839, Bulloch, MIC
CONE, William, decd, Peter Cone apptd admr 9/1/1839, Bulloch, MIC
CONE, William, decd, inv and appr by Samuel Davis, William Burnsides, William Bragg, 3/4/1823; sale 2/16/1824, Peter Cone, Clerk, Bulloch, Misc
CONEY, Charley C., decd, James E. Coney applies for L/A 6/15/1857, Thomas Whitsett, Ezekiel Coney, sur, Lee
CONGER, Abijah, decd, est 9/30/1866, Clarke, LP
CONGER, Hedges T., decd, est 1/6/1836, Clarke, LP
CONKLING, David, decd, Samuel S. Lockhart issued L/A 9/2/1822, Bulloch, MIC
CONN, John, decd, Codicil to LWT names ch: Simon, John, Thomas, Isaac, Cary Martin, Peggy Murphy, Jane, Mary, Agnes; wife, Elizabeth, Franklin, OM
CONNALLEE, Peter, decd, John B. Vanover applies for L/A 6/23/1854, Lee, MSC
CONNALLY, Charles, decd, inv made 8/28/1807, Franklin, OM
CONNALLY, Charles C., orph of Cornelius, decd, Henry Bankston qualified as gdn 11/5/1855, dismissed 1/7/1867, Fulton
CONNALLY, David H., orph of C. M., decd, Thomas W. Connally qualified as gdn 11/5/1855, dismissed 2/1/1859, Fulton
CONNALLY, John, decd, Lesley Connally, William Christian and David Morgan issued L/A 9/7/1807, Franklin, OM
CONNALLY, John, decd, Thomas Connally apptd gdn for Polly, Charles and Angelica, Caswell Co., North Carolina, 11/1809, Franklin, OM
CONNALLY, Margaret F., minor orph of Christopher, Mrs. Elizabeth Connally qualified as gdn 11/1/1852, dismissed 6/3/1861, Fulton
CONNALLY, Mary N., orph of C. M., decd, Thomas W. Connally apptd gdn 11/5/1855, dismissed 4/4/1859, Fulton
CONNALLY, Price, decd, Thomas A. Kennedy issued L/A 5/6/1861, Fulton
CONNALLY, Price, minor orph of Christopher, decd, Elizabeth Connally qualified as gdn 11/1/1852, dismissed 10/3/1859, Fulton
CONNALLY, Sytha A. E., orph of C. M., decd, Thomas W. Connally apptd gdn 11/5/1855, dismissed 4/4/1859, Fulton

CONNALLY, William, minor orph of Christopher, Mrs. Elizabeth
Connally, gdn, pets to be dismissed 7/6/1866, Fulton
CONNALLY, William C., orph of Charles M., decd, Thomas W.
Connally qualified 11/5/1855, dismissed 1/7/1867, Fulton
CONNELLS, George Alexander, decd, Neil Cleveland issued L/A
9/5/1803, Frizzell McTyeire, George Conn, secs; 5/7/1804 Jane
Cleveland was issued L/A, John Savage, George Conn, secs,
Richmond, AB
CONNELL, Thomas, decd of Richmond Co., LWT pvd 6/1/1789, James
Gardner, exr, Columbia, Ests
CONNELLY, John, order tp pay $12.00, p. 47, Screven, OM
CONNER, John, decd, p/a to Edward Hagin of Wilkes Co. to sell 300
acres in Richmond Co., 9/28/1781, Wilkes, MxR
CONNER, Susannah (Mrs.), decd, Simon Conner, admr, 10/1/1790,
Chatham, Adms
CONNOR, John, decd, Mary Conner, admx 2/11/1859, A. J. Covington,
James L. D. Harbin, sur, Cherokee, AB
CONYERS, John, decd, 5/3/1801 inventory; Mrs. Conyers purchaser
at sale, Wm Jamison, admr, Elbert, AR
CONYERS, John, decd, John Brannon, etc. divided est, p. 34,
Screven, OM
COOK, Allen, decd, John Ship and John Pennington ask to be
relieved as security for Nancy Cook, admx 9/3/1810, Jackson, OM
COOK, Benjamin apptd gdn of his ch: Thomas, Delilah and Sarah,
12/1825, Samuel W. Jackson, sec, Pike, MIC
COOK, Benjamin, decd, 8/30/1800 inventory includes slaves; apprs:
Thomas Cosby, James Cosby, M. Woods, Elbert, AR
COOK, Celethy, orph of Isaac, decd, Jonathan Hagerty, gdn,
7/18/1799, Warren, GB, MIC
COOK, Charles, decd, Mary Lankester of Savannah, admx, 7/30/1784,
Chatham, Adms
COOK, Cordell, decd, William S. Cook, gdn of orphs, gtd leave to
sell land lot 6, 33rd dist. Lee Co., 6/2/1835, Camden, MIC
COOK, Edward, decd, Asa L. Cook issued L/A 2/6/1816, Laurens, AB
COOK, Elizabeth, decd, Samuel Cook, admr, Joseph Cook, sur,
1/25/1850, Cherokee, AB
COOK, Frederic, decd, Mary Cook and Richard Bracewell issued L/A
3/3/1817, Laurens, AB
COOK, George, decd, late of Fla., R. P. Burton apptd admr,
1/4/1841, Camden, MIC
COOK, Harbard, decd, Elizabeth and William N. Cook, exrs, 6/1854
retn, Fayette
COOK, Hartwell, decd, heirs were: Abby E. Booth, etc., 1873,
Clarke, LP
COOK, Isaac, decd, Eric Cook, admr, Jacob Lithner, G. Erlick,
secs, 1/13/1851, Bibb, AB
COOK, Isaac, decd, Jonathan Hagarty, admr, 7/18/1799, Edward
Hill, sur, Warren, AB
COOK, Isaac, decd, Pheriby Cook, Jonathan Hagery, admrs,
4/24/1799, Warren, MIC
COOK, Jack F., decd, Gabriel A. Moffett, gdn of William S., David
P., Jack F. and Woodson, 8/5/1816, Thomas Moore, sur, Clarke, GB
COOK, James B., orph of William, decd, John Cook, gdn, Thomas
Cook, sur, 11/3/1851, Butts, GB
COOK, James W., decd, ch: Albert H., Evie H., James J., N. E.
12/25/1869; Evie m. John M. Bostick, Clarke, LP
COOK, James W., decd, children: Henry J. and William M.,
4/5/1858, Clarke, LP
COOK, Jeremiah, decd, of Edgefield Dist, South Carolina, LWT dtd
12/3/1853, pvd 1/1858, names wife, Mary, John H. Cook, exr,
Cherokee

COOK, John, decd, David Hubert applies for adm 3/1/1801, Joseph Bower, Abner Fluwellin, sur, Warren, MIC, AB
COOK, John, tailor, decd, Fanny Cook, Lyddell Bacon issued L/A 7/25/1799, Jeremiah Wood, Conrad Leverman, secs, Richmond, AB
COOK, John J., decd, James McCoy, Jr. issued temporary L/A 9/23/1852, David H. Bird, John Martin, sur, Cherokee, AB
COOK, John, Sr., decd, appr of est 7/6/1798; apprs: John Harbirt, John Cook, Jr., Phillip Cook, admrs, Hancock, AA
COOK, John W., decd, est 7/23/1857, Clarke, LP
COOK, Jonathan, decd, Elizabeth Cook and James Clark issued L/A 4/4/1808, Jackson, OM
COOK, Joseph, decd, L/A gtd William Cook 7/5/1819, Jasper, OM
COOK, Lewis 9/19/1829 signed receipt as having recd from General Lee his pt of the est of Henry Cook, Bulloch, Misc
COOK, Lydia, decd, LWT was admitted to record 1/2/1837, Effingham, MIC
COOK, Margaret, decd, Amos Cook applies for L/A 11/18/1830, Effingham, MIC
COOK, Mary P., orph of William, decd, John Cook, gdn, Thomas Cook, sur, 11/3/1851, Butts, GB
COOK, Milo, decd, Harriett B. Cook issued L/A 6/5/1821, William J. Hobby, sec, Richmond, AB
COOK, Parmelia E., orph of William, decd, Joh Cook, gdn, Thomas Cook, sur, 11/3/1851, Butts, GB
COOK, Pheriby, orph of Isaac, decd, Jonathan Hagerty, gdn, 7/18/1799, Warren, GB, MIC
COOK, Richmond N., orph of William, decd, John Cook, gdn, Thomas Cook. sur, 11/3/1851, Butts, GB
COOK, Simeon J., decd, Jasper L. Keith, admr, Robert J. Cowart, Allen Keith, sur, 9/4/1853, Cherokee, AB
COOK, Tandy W., orph of William, decd, John Cook, gdn, Thomas Cook, sur, 11/3/1851, Butts, GB
COOK, William, decd, John W. McCord, admr, James R. McCord, sur, 9/1/1851, Butts, AB
COOK, William S. apptd gdn of his sisters--Mary S. Cook and Celia S. Cook and his bro., Reuben S. Cook 1/6/1825, Camden, MIC
COOKE, James, decd, James Watson Cooke applied for L/A 8/14/1792; apprs: John Sigmon, John Keys, Reuben Cooke, Elbert, AR
COOKERY, Henry, illegitimate, Lettice Daugharty to take charge of and maintain 8/5/1811, Tattnall, MIC
COOMBS, Mary L., decd, Hannah N. Myers, admr w/LWT annexed 11/3/1862, Fulton
COOPER, Ananias, decd, Seaborn Jones issued L/A 11/7/1808, Thomas Cumming, David Reid, secs, Richmond, AB
COOPER, Columbus, orph of Eli, decd, James Hogan, gdn, H. G. Brintle, Jesse Cooper, Moses Cooper, sur, 2/6/1860, Paulding, GB
COOPER, Cornelius, decd, inv of est, 2/29/1807; LWT names wife, Rebeccah, dtd 3/24/1808, Franklin, OM
COOPER, Eliza J., orph of Eli, decd, James Hogan, gdn, H. G. Brintle, Jesse Cooper, Moses Cooper, sur, 2/6/1860, Paulding, GB
COOPER, Elizabeth V., orph of Eli, decd, James Hogan, gdn, H. G. Brintle, Jesse Cooper, Moses Cooper, sur, 2/6/1860, Paulding, GB
COOPER, Frederick, decd, James English applied for L/A 5/20/1805, gtd 3/3/1806, Tattnall, MIC
COOPER, George, LWT pvd by James Fillingim 5/3/1802, Warren, MIC
COOPER, James, decd, Mary Cooper, admx, Harmon Wilkinson, Peter Castleberry, surs, 4/13/1798, Warren, MIC
COOPER, James A. apptd trustee for his wife, Amelia and her children in place of Hellman Jackson and Drewry W. Jackson (apptd by her father, Hartwell Jackson, Sr., late of Clarke Co.) 2/24/1860, Clarke, LP

68

COOPER, James M., decd, David Jenkins, Thomas DeLoach, George H. Bryan, gdn of orphs of decd, 7/6/1840, Harris
COOPER, John B., decd, Anderson Hunt issued L/A 11/5/1821, Laurens, AB
COOPER, Mildred, a girl abt 14, orph, bound to John Watterson for 4 yrs, 5/4/1807, Jackson, OM
COOPER, Oliver H. P., orph of Eli, decd, James Hogan, gdn, H. G. Brintle, Jesse Cooper, Moses Cooper, sur, 2/6/1860, Paulding, GB
COOPER, Richard, decd, Richard and John Cooper qualified as admrs 10/26/1789, Liberty, Ests
COOPER, Roseanna M., orph of Eli, decd, James Hogan, gdn, H. G. Brintle, Jesse Cooper, Moses Cooper, sur, 2/6/1860, Paulding, GB
COOPER, Stacy, decd, Jesse Cooper, apptd admr, Charles D. Jenkins, B. F. Wright, Moses Cooper, G. H. Spinks, surs, 4/5/1858, Paulding, AB
COOPER, Thomas, orph of Peter, decd, Wright R. Coleman, gdn, 3/3/1823, Laurens, GB
COOPER, Thomas, decd, Patsey Cooper, Obadiah Richardson, admrs; vous: James Nesbits (heir), H. Holt, Jas Cooper, gdn for Micajah, Wm Stith, Augustin Thomas, Jos. Stovall, attys for John Waller, Ellit Wood, 1/7/1799, Hancock, AA
COOPER, Thomas H., decd, Joseph M., Lloyd S. and John Cooper, admrs, 11/18/1834; James Cooper, John Cooper, exrs 1/5/1835, Harris
COOPER, Thomas L., decd, George G. Hull, admr, L. E. Bleckley, John W. Duncan, secs, 5/6/1862, dismissed 2/5/1866, Fulton, AB
COOPER, Thomas P., orph of Eli, decd, James Hogan, gdn, H. G. Brintle, Jesse Cooper, Moses Cooper, sur, 2/6/1860, Paulding, GB
COOPER, Warren H., decd, Jeptha Landrum, admr, John Huie, sur, no date, Fayette, AB
COPE, Christian, decd, div of est 11/1/1830, Effingham, MIC
COPE, Elizabeth, decd, LWT admitted to record 9/5/1831, Effingham, MIC
COPE, George Washington Cope, minor, at his own request was bound out to John D. Young for 6 yrs 1/5/1820, Camden, MIC
COPE, John, Sr., minor heir of Christian, decd, John Helvenston apptd gdn 5/4/1829, Effingham, MIC
COPE, Lewis, butcher, decd, Rosannah and John Cope, admrs, 6/14/1788, Chatham, Adms
COPE, Maria, minor heir of Christian, decd, John Helvenston apptd gdn 5/4/1829, Effingham, MIC
COPELAND, Peter, decd, LWT pvd 9/6/1847, John T. Copeland and wife, Mary, exrs, Harris
COPP, Daniel, decd, B. A. Copp apptd admr, 6/4/1827, Camden, MIC
COPP, John, decd of Savannah, Miss Esther Sabnry, James Brown, exrs of LWT 9/1/1789, Chatham, Adms
COPP, Rosaline, Lewis Bachlott apptd gdn and George Agerett in lieu of Bentley A. Copp, resigned gdn, 6/4/1832, Camden, MIC
COPPAGE, Eliza I., decd, Nottley Maddox, John I. Rowe, admrs, 9/7/1840, Harris, AB
COPPINGER, Penelope, decd, Peter Day issued temp L/A 11/10/1813; 11/17/1814 perm admr, Richmond, AB
CORBETT, James, decd, 1816 retns of Joseph W. Robinson, extr, Wilkes, Retns
CORBIN, Alexander, decd, Caswell L. Corbin issued temp L/A 4/7/1853, M. H. West, sur; perm L/A 2/6/1854, Cherokee, AB
CORBIN, John, decd, LWT dtd 1/26/1853, pvd 4/5/1853 by James Jordan names wife, Delilah, 5 sons: Joseph, Benjamin, Reubin, Jasper, Newton; five daus: Polly, Rachel, Abigail, Susan, Delilah, Cherokee

CORDLE, Martha, decd, late of Brunswick Co., Virginia., Samuel
Lark issued L/A 5/1/1820, Edmund Bugg, Edmund Smith, secs,
Richmond, AB
CORLEY, Elizabeth M., John H. Hanson, gdn, 1/3/1837, Hall, GB
CORNETT, Eli, decd, LWT, John Murphy, exr, pvd 5/19/1834, Harris
CORNWELL, Charner W., decd, Augustus A. Wilson issued L/A
3/5/1860, Fulton
CORRY, Joseph S., decd, John Glen issued L/A 8/19/1868, Fulton
CORTELYOU, John, decd, George S. Houston issued L/A 11/3/1806,
Nathaniel P. Beach, Frederick Story, secs, Richmond, AB
COSBY, James R., decd, Earain C. Cosby apptd gdn of orphs: Mary
J. and Samuel D., minors, 1/22/1867, Clarke, LP
COSBY, Nancy, decd, Mordecai John, admr, 1/7/1828, Howell Hight,
Seaborn Dozier, surs, Warren, AB
COSBY, Richmond T., decd, James Alston, admr, files retns 1808,
Elbert, AR
COSTNER, Sarah, decd, James W. Biggers, admr, 2/6/1865, Harris
COTNEY, James, decd, Edwin Adams, John Howard, gdn of orphs of
decd 6/8/1835, Harris. GB
COTNEY, James, decd, Susannah Cotney, Joel Culpepper, Seth
Cotney, gdn of orphs of decd 1/8/1838, Harris, GB
COTNEY, James, decd, William Cotney, Edwin Adams, exrs,
2/24/1835; Susannah Cotney, Seth Cotney, Joel Culpepper, admrs
1/8/1838, Harris, AB
COTNEY, James, minor, William Johnson and Susan Cotney, gdns,
4/18/1853, Harris
COTTON, John, decd, Joseph Harper, gdn of orphs: Martha E., John
L., Mary C., James B. and Sarah A., 8/1/1853, Houston, GB
COTTON, William, decd, LWT pvd 1/7/1840, wife, Nancy, ch---Seth,
Sarah (wife of James Smith); grson, Andrew Jackson Cotton (Samuel
Carter to be his gdn), Randolph
COUEY, Lizzie A., decd, Elihu Couey apptd gdn of: Ida S., Lucian
A., Oscar N., Minnie Lee and Ada L., 4/28/1890, transferred from
Morgan Co., Clarke, LP
COUKLING, David, decd, inv and appr by John Dell, Ezekiel Selph,
Frederick Smith, Benjamin Jones, Samuel Lockhart, 9/11/1822,
Bulloch, Misc
COULTER, Matilda E., decd, Alfred B. Coulter issued temp L/A
12/27/1853, D. H. Bird, sur; A. B. Coulter, admr, Riley J.
Johnson, Miles W. Johnson, sur, 3/4/1854, Cherokee, AB
COUNCIL, Willis, decd, Benjamin King was issued L/A 7/4/1811,
Putnam, AB
COURSE, Daniel, decd, of Chatham Co., Ga., John Course apptd gdn
of Caroline, minor, William White, William McLean, secs,
Richmond, GB
COURSEY, William, decd, Loyd Coursey issued L/A 11/8/1865, Fulton
COUSONS, John, decd, est 6/2/1857, Clarke, LP
COUSSONS, Thomas, decd, est 4/31/1882, Clarke, LP
COVINGTON, Emaline M., orph of Thomas, decd, Philip M. Byrd, gdn,
George Chapman, sec, 1/4/1842, Hall, GB
COVINGTON, Ninbal?, decd, Thursey Covington, gdn for orphs:
William and Julian 1/2/1837, Absolom Boler, sec, Lincoln, GB
COVINGTON, Thomas, orph of Thomas, decd, Marshall Covington, gdn,
10/11/1824, John Walton, sec, Lincoln, GB
Covington, Henry, decd, d. 1897, Clarke, LP
COWAN, John W., decd, Robert Coats was issued L/A 11/5/1821,
Laurens, AB
COWAN, Stephen, orph of Elijah, decd, under age 14, Benjamin
Stovall apptd gdn 1/3/1814, Jackson, OM

COWART, Abraham, decd, James Scarborough, admr, 4/17/1835, appr, Emanuel, A

COWART, Abraham, decd, Cullen and John H. Cowart, admrs, Josiah Drew, John R. Daniell, surs, 3/2/1835, Emanuel, AB

COWEDRY, Eliza, John Anderson, gdn, makes retn 3/4/1835, Tattnall, I&A

COWEN, Edward, decd, Davis Whelchel, Jr. issued L/A 3/7/1840, E. A. Cowen, William Cowen, R. Waters, John Clark, secs, Hall, AB

COWEN, Edward, orph of Elijah, decd, chose his brother, William Cowen as his gdn 8/1/1814, Jackson, OM

COWEN, Edward, orph son of Elijah, decd, chose his uncle, John Stovall, gdn, 1/3/1814, Jackson, OM

COWEN, Elijah, decd, LWT was pvd 7/6/1812 by Edward Adams, Jackson, OM

COWEN, Elizabeth, orph of Edward, decd, John Clark, gdn, 6/19/1840, Sevier Clark, sec, Hall, GB

COWEN, John, decd, L/A issued Clemmond Quillian 3/1825, Habersham, MIC

COWEN, Oliver P., decd, John Clark issued L/A 12/4/1854, John E. Brown, sec, Hall, AB

COWEN, Prudence, Edward Adams, gdn, notified that William Cowen will ask the estate to be divided, 9/5/1814, Jackson, OM

COWEN, Stephen, orph of Elijah, decd, chose his brother, William Cowen as his gdn 8/1/1814, Jackson, OM

COWEN, Stephen D., orph of Edward, decd, John Clark, gdn 5/3/1841, D. Whelchel, Elijah A. Cowen, secs, Hall, GB

COWEN, Thomas, decd, George W. Moore, admr, prays to sell perishable property 1/1/1810, Jackson, OM

COWEN, William, decd, James G. issued L/A 1/13/1846, John Clark, D. Whelchel, secs, Hall, AB

COWEN, William, now age 21, asks that the estate left to his father, Elijah Cowen, be turned over to him and that he be apptd gdn of his brother, Edward, 9/5/1814, Jackson, OM

COWZENS, Samuel, decd, John Chevalier apptd admr, 11/6/1815, Camden, MIC

COX, Abraham, Kinsel, Asa and Jesse, commonly called by name of Pipkin, minors, Amos Love, gdn, shall furnish sufficient clothing, board, etc., 1/7/1812, Laurens, GB

COX, Alfred D. D., decd, Nathaniel Smith issued L/A 1/10/1848, Jorryal Blackwell, sec, Hall, AB

COX, Asa, decd, William and Elizabeth Cox issued L/A 7/4/1825, Habersham, MIC

COX, Cary T., decd, L/A issued to George W. Laney 4/1856, Webster, OD

COX, Catharine, orph of Asa, decd, William Case, Jr. to have orph bound to him 7/1829, Habersham, MIC

COX, Chappell, decd, G. W. Laney and J. T. Cox issued L/A 3/1864, Webster, OD

COX, C. F., decd, G. W. Laney and John M. Cox issued L/A 1/1864; G. W. Laney, admr, ordered to receive certification of amts due est, 10/1863, Webster, OD

COX, Delany, illegitimate, L/G issued David Cox 1830, Washington

COX, Elijah, decd, Jonathan Vasser, Samuel M. Smith, L. Coleman, P. Donaldson issued temp L/A 12/9/1807; 4/30/1808, Mary Cox, perm admx, Richmond, AB

COX, Elisha, orph of John, decd, Jasper L. Keith, gdn, McAnderson Keith, sur, 1/8/1855, Cherokee, GB

COX, Elizabeth M., decd, Mrs. Francina E. Greer, admx (who was m. to George W. King by 6/6/1862), 4/11/1860, Clarke, LP

COX, Franklin B. chose Jesse Davis as his gdn 3/7/1836, Effingham, MIC

COX, George, decd, William P. Cox, apptd admr, 3/1843, Harris, AB

COX, Henry M., orph of Asa, decd, William Case, Jr. to have orph bound to him 7/1829, Habersham, MIC
COX, James, decd, 60 days after application was made to Ordinary, leave to sell 500 acres in Jefferson Co. gtd, John W. Jourdan, admr, 6/23/1854, Lee, MSC
COX, Jasper, decd, Spence Cox and William DuPree apply for adm 9/14/1797; he declining to serve and Henry Rowell served 10/16/1797, Effingham, Misc
COX, John Augustus, Martha Ann gtd L/G of her son 1/1857, Webster, OD
COX, John M., decd, LWT pvd 5/1851: wife, Irena, names ch-Sarah Jane Cox, Elisha Cox, Malissa Cox, Elizabeth Ann Pyron, Mary Martha Banks and John W. Cox; L/A issued to Irena Cox, Daniel H. Bird, Allen Lawhon, surs, 7/7/1851; Jasper L. Keith apptd admr 8/1/1853, Cherokee
COX, J. A., John D. Stapleton, gdn, 3/1864, Webster, OD
COX, John M., decd, Jasper L. Keith, admr de bonis non, William P. Hammond, M. A. Keith, surs, 8/2/1852, Cherokee, AB
COX, Jonathan, decd, Mary Cox issued L/A 3/9/1808, John Cashin, William Lyon, Peter Donaldson, secs, Richmond, AB
COX, Joseph, decd, Walter Leigh apptd gdn of daus 1/7/1811; 1812 retns pd Martha Cox, for self and sisters; 1/3/1814 retn pd Mrs. Keziah Cox, Richmond, GB
COX, Malissa, orph of John, decd, Jasper L. Keith, gdn, McAnderson Keith, sur, 1/8/1855, Cherokee, GB
COX, Richard, decd, est 5/1/1837, Clarke, LP
COX, Richard, decd, est 9/6/1863, Clarke, LP
COX, Samuel, decd, Sophia Cox and Ezekiel Cloud issued L/A 1/6/1812, Putnam, AB
COX, Sarah Ann, orph of John, decd, Jasper L. Keith, gdn, McAnderson Keith, sur, 1/8/1855, Cherokee, GB
COX, Zachariah, decd, Ewing Morrow was issued L/A 11/16/1820, Morgan, AB
COZART, Hubbard W., decd, William A. Bass and Ann M. Cozart qualified as admrs 9/4/1865, Fulton
COTTON, William, decd, LWT pvd 1/7/1840, wife, Nancy, ch-Seth, Sarah, wife of James Smith; grson, Andrew Jackson Cotton (Saml Carter to be his gdn), Randolph
CRAFT, George, orph of W. H., decd, E. W. Holland, gdn, 1/12/1863, Fulton, GB
CRAFT, Louisa, minor orph of William H., decd, William H. Harvill, gdn, 3/5/1860; E. W. Holland, gdn 11/3/1862, Fulton, GB
CRANFORD, William, decd, Philip Cranford issued temp L/A 3/22/1814, Putnam, AB
CRAVEN, Sarah, minor orph of sd co., Charles L. Williams, gdn, 1/2/1869, White, GB
CRAVEN, John H., decd, William H. Logan issued L/A 5/2/1865, F. Logan, R. R. Asbury, secs, White, AB
CRAVEN, Mary A., minor orph of sd co., Charles L. Williams, gdn, 1/2/1869, White, GB
CRAWFORD, Archibald, decd, Augustin D. Cicaty issued L/A 2/3/1818, Laurens, AB
CRAWFORD, Francis Ann Dunklin, illegitimate child of Polly, Isham Hendon, gdn, 2/7/1820, David Shay, sur, Clarke, GB
CRAWFORD, James J., decd, Mrs. Harriet R. Crawford issued L/A 7/5/1858, Fulton
CRAWFORD, John, petition to make title gtd, p. 88, Screven, OM
CRAWFORD, John, decd, inv 12/29/1777, Thomas Barnett Sr., William Barnett, Sr., William Germany, apprs, Richmond, AB
CRAWFORD, Nelson, decd, Peter Crawford issued L/A 3/7/1808, Angus Martin, William Wilkins, secs, Richmond, AB
CRAWFORD, Samuel, decd, Archibald Beall issued L/A 12/29/1797,

John McManus, Joseph Burch, secs, Richmond, AB
CRAY, Scott, decd, R. Collins, admr, T. P. Stubbs, A. C. Ross, surs, 11/4/1850, Bibb, AB
CREAMER, Alvins, illegitimate child of Frances Creamer, now Frances Blalock, Hardy Leverett, gdn, 3/2/1840, Eliel Lockhart, sec, Lincoln, GB
CRENSHAW, Maybourn, decd, Henry Rose applied for L/A 10/1/1792; 10/6/1794, Thomas Napier, caveat, vs. David, decd, Phebe Carter and William Law, admrs, of Liberty Co., Bryan, CR
CRESSWELL, David, decd, John T. Cresswell apptd admr 9/2/1816, Jackson, OM
CRESSWELL, Robert, decd, 7/11/1823 final div of est; heirs-John Phinizy in rt of wife, Martha, Gregory B. Lamar in rt of wife, Jane, William Sims, in rt of wife, Ann, John, Samuel and Mary Cresswell, minors, Richmond, AB
CREW, James R., decd, Mrs. J. L. Crew issued L/A 2/6/1866, Fulton
CRITCHER, Edwin, minor orph of Thomas, decd, Anderson Watkins, gdn, 9/4/1818, Freeman Walker, sec, Richmond, GB
CROCKER, Lemuel, decd, Isaac Ferguson, exr of LWT, Henry Pullen, James Hicks, secs, 9/29/1824, Emanuel, AB
CROCKET, Samuel, decd, Robert Crocket apptd admr 5/20/1793, inv includes 287-1/2 acres in Franklin Co.; apprs: Wm Banks, Wm McKenzie, Solomon McAlpin; admr's expenses pd to York Co., S. C. and Elbert Co., Ga. 4/18/1803, Elbert, AR
CROCKETT, Laura C. C., decd, LWT exhibited 7/2/1866, Ralph B. Badger apptd admr, Fulton, AB
CROCKETT, Robert, decd, Sarah Crockett issued L/A 1786, George Wyche, Robert Jones, James Harris, Andrew Atkinson, apprs, Richmond, AB
CROOK, Jonathan, decd, Jonathan Lyon issued temp L/A 12/2/1818, Thomas Griffin, Robert Denny, secs; 1/11/1819 sd Lyon made perm admr w/LWT annexed, Richmond, AB
CROOKSHANKS, Patrick, decd, Charity Coleman issued L/A 11/15/1815, Peter Donaldson, George Adams, secs, Richmond, AB
CROSS, Unise, illegitimate child under age 21, bound to Jesse Ponder 3/1/1830, Habersham, MIC
CROSSLE, Henry (Capt.), decd, Abraham Jones issued L/A 12/1/1800, William Poe, sec, Richmond, AB
CROSSLE, Mary, idiot, Daniel McMurphy, gdn, 1/6/1819, Abraham McKenzie, Samuel Lark, secs, Richmond, GB
CROW, Jacob, Jr., orph of Jacob, decd, chooses Isaac Reed, gdn, 2/1/1808, Jackson, OM
CROW, Lewis, orph of Jacob, decd, chooses Isaac Reed, gdn, 2/1/1808, Jackson, OM
CRUM, David, decd, 1820 heirs: James, Henry, Mary & Eliza Crum and Ann Powers, John Davis, exr of Joseph Davis; John Davis of Chatham Co., admr of Joseph Davis vs. Abraham Crum, exr of David Crum, 1819, Bryan, CR, Writs
CRUMLY, L. F., decd, H. W. Jackson ssued temp L/A 4/13/1863, William Jackson, sec, White, AB
CRUMP, Reason, decd, John C. Crump, admr, Robert Higdon, A. L. Kirkland, surs, 6/7/1830, Emanuel, AB
CUBBEDGE, John, decd, George Cubbedge and Richard Cooper qualfied as admrs 11/6/1785, Liberty, Ests
CUBBEDGE, John and Sarah's children (Stephen J. M., John A. W. and Barbara C.) vs. Alexander W. Stephens in re: plantation "Lincoln" deed to George M. Waters in tr for wife and children of John Cubbedge, 12/20/1827, Bryan, Writs
CUDWORTH, Thomas H., decd, inv by William Clifton Sr. and Jr., Shadrack Handcock, apprs, 4/3/1836, Tattnall, I&A

CULBERTSON, David, decd, Clarey Culbertson & Wm Browning applied
for L/A 3/19/1796; inv shows land in Pendleton Co., S. C., 126
acres, 400 acres in Franklin Co., Ga. 6/4/1796, Greene, Misc
CULBREATH, John, decd, Robert and Mary Graves issued L/A
7/3/1783, John Germany, sec, Richmond, AB
CULBREATH, Lewis, decd, O. M. Culbreath, exr, LWT pvd 5/1/1837;
William L., James M. and Joel Culpepper, admrs 1/8/1838, Harris
CULBREATH, Nancy, decd, James Caldwell qualified as admr,
1/2/1879, Clarke, LP
CULBREATH, Obediah, decd, William L., James M. and Joel
Culpepper, admrs 1/8/1838, Harris, AB
CULBREATH, Peter, decd, LWT pvd 4/3/1793, names daus, Sarah
Culbreath and Catherine Carr sole extrxs. James Culbreath, son of
decd, applies for L/A 3/10/1794, Columbia, Ests
CULLEN, Richard F., alien, decd, 7/18/1822, est appraised,
Richmond, AB
CULLEN, Robert H., decd, Ross Cullen, gdn of orphs: Aaron W.,
John R. and Robert H., Benjamin Jester, sec, 5/17/1838, Butts, GB
CULLEN, William, decd, James Wood issued L/A 1/3/1832, Washington
CULP, Henry T., son of Leonidas, Rebecca Culp apptd gdn of her
minor son, 4/21/1882; later gdn, Mrs. Mattie P. Jarratt nee
Mattie P. Dotson 8/1901, Clarke, LP
CULP, Peter, decd, d. 10/3/1892, exrs: B. F. Culp, H. Culp and
Mattie Parr Dotson Jarrell, Clarke, LP
CULPEPPER, E. B., decd, Mrs. R. Culpepper, extrx, 2/1862,
Webster, OD
CULPEPPER, Henry, decd, Davis Smith issued L/A 5/6/1822, John
Thomas, Jonathan Parker, secs, Laurens, AB
CULPEPPER, Joel, decd, John McMercer, James C. Bradley, admrs,
Dooly, OD
CULPEPPER, John, decd, Benjamin Kemp produced exemplification
from Stewart Co., 6/1854, Webster, OD
CULPEPPER, John L., decd, Charles Powell, Temperance Culpepper,
admrs, Dooly, OD
CULPEPPER, Joseph, decd, LWT pvd 5/6/1816, Jackson, OM
CULPEPPER, Joseph, decd, Malicah issued L/A 1/6/1823, Lewis
Brantley, sec, Morgan, AB
CULPEPPER, Nathan, decd, Sampson R. Culpepper, admr, 3/4/1833,
Jesse Beall, Elijah Jones, surs, Warren, AB
CULPEPPER, Reubin T., decd, Benjamin Kemp applies for permanent
L/A 11/1857, Webster, OD
CULPEPPER, William, decd, Daniel Culpepper offered LWT for
probate, he was apptd exr, 3/7/1808, Warren, MIC
CULPEPPER, William, decd, Richard Heath, admr, 3/21/1828, Lewis
Jackson, Thomas Seals, surs, Warren, AB
CUMMING, Elizabeth Reid, Theophilus S. Stewart of Cobb Co. apptd
trustee of her and her children in place of Wallace Cumming,
under LWT of Robert Alexander Reid, late of Richmond Co.,
9/25/1878, Clarke, LP
CUMMINS, Isabella, decd, David Cummins issued L/A 5/6/1839,
Washington
CUNNINGHAM, Charles, decd, late of Jefferson Co., Ann P.
Cunningham issued L/A 9/9/1818, Oswell Even, Anderson Watkins,
John Carmichael, secs; heirs-Ann P., wid, Robert E., Charles and
Margaret Cunningham, Richmond, AB
CUNNINGHAM, William, decd, 5/11/1801 retn pd David and Martha
Cunningham, Elbert, AR
CURETON, William, decd, LWT pvd 7/2/1810 by John and Hannah
Wallace and Wm McKey, Hugh Montgomery, exr, Jackson, OM
CURRY, Daniel, late of Troup Co., decd, Matthew Gaston, admr in
rt of wife, James R. McCord, sec, 9/7/1840, Butts, AB

74

CURRY, David, decd, David Curry issued L/A 3/5/1838, Washington
CURRY, Eli F., minor child of John, Kinchen Womble issued L/G 1/9/1843, Washington
CURRY, George, decd, David Walker issued L/A 1/7/1839, Washington
CURRY, Harriet Ann, orph of Daniel, late of Troup Co., Matthew Gaston, gdn, William Curry, sur, 1/6/1840, Butts, GB
CURRY, John L., decd, John S. Curry, Johnson Powell, gdn of orphs of decd 9/5/1836, Harris
CUTHBERT, Catherine (Mrs.), decd, decd, Mary Eustace, admx, 1/2/1789, Chatham, Adms
CUTHBERT, John, decd, Mary Cuthbert and Joseph Clay, jr., admrs, 5/13/1789, Chatham, Adms
CUTHBERT, Joseph, decd, George Cuthbert, admr, 11/4/1786, Chatham, Adms
CUTLEAU, Charles, gdn, leave to sell property, p. 75, acct appvd, p. 86, Screven, OM
CUTLIPP, John, decd, Dickerson Holiday, gdn for orphs: Mary Ann and John 1/2/1826, Travis Gideon and Wm L. Walker, secs, Lincoln,
D'ANTIGNAC, John, decd, William M. D'Antignac issued L/A 11/1827, William H. Turpin, sec, Richmond, AB
DABNEY, Anderson, decd, Tyre G. and Nannah Dabney apptd admrs w/LWT annexed 1/7/1822, Jasper, OM
DADEN, Lewis H., decd, Joseph Marechal, gdn for orphs: Victoria, Mary, Louis H. and Alexander, 7/7/1856, Fulton
DAIBER, John, decd, Dionus Fechter issued L/A 6/13/1868, Fulton
DAILEY, Ann, decd, Ephraim Whittingham issued L/A 12/8/1827, George P. Turpin, sec, Richmond, AB
DAILEY, Mary, decd, William Skinner issued L/A 7/2/1830, William McGar, James Primrose, sec; retns 3/14/1833, adm in S. C., Richmond, AB, AR
DAILEY, Joseph, decd, Mary Dailey & Arthur Foster, temp L/A 2/18/1820; 7/13/1826 Mary Dailey, wid (no issue), Dicey McCuller, decd's sister, Elijah Rogers, her tr, Saml McCuller, Dicey's husb & Wm Dailey, decd's bro, div est; William Skinner, admr 3/14/1833 retns, pd Dilcy McCullers, William Dailey, Nancy Baron and Mary Dailey, Richmond, AB, AR
DALLAS, Angus, decd, Thomas Gardner, Wm Kenada, George Barnes, Charles Tubman, Wm Petty, apprs 2/1795, Richmond
DALLIS, Thomas, decd, Isaiah Collars, gdn of orphs: George, Rebecca, Cornelous and Thomas 11/4/1839, Wiley G. Tatom, Mathew Collars, secs, Lincoln, GB
DALLIS, Thomas, decd, Thomas Dallis, gdn of minor ch: Littleton, Payton, Hulbert and Wm, 11/4/1839, William M. Lampkin, sec, Lincoln, GB
DALLAS, William, decd, William Jones apptd admr with LWT annexed 1/4/1803, Camden, MIC
DALTON, Henry, decd, Winifred Dalton and Sampson Lampkin issued L/A 11/3/1806, Thomas Dalton, sec, Richmond, AB
DALTON, Sarah, decd, William McCain issued L/A 4/22/1826, John Lampkin, George A. P. Whitfield, secs, Richmond, AB
DALTON, Thomas, decd, Sarah Dalton issued L/A 3/10/1821, Daniel Meigs, sec, Richmond, AB
DAMPUR, Daniel, decd, LWT pvd 7/5/1847, Effingham, MIC
DANBY, John, decd, Philip H. Mantz issued L/A 11/2/1830, John Morrison, sec, Richmond, AB
DANBY, John, decd, Thomas J. Wray issued L/A 9/1/1834, William C. Micou, sec, Richmond, AB
DANFORTH, Abraham, decd, Andrew J. Miller issued L/A 3/2/1840, John M. Adams, sec, 1840 retns cash for support of Mrs. Danforth and children, Richmond, AB
DALLAS, Angus, decd, Thomas Gardner, Wm Kenada, George Barnes, Charles Tubman, Wm petty, apprs 2/1795, Richmond

DALLIS, Thomas, decd, Isaiah Collars, gdn of orphs: George, Rebecca, Cornelious and Thomas 11/4/1839, Wiley G. Tatom, Mathew Collars, secs, Lincoln, GB

DALLIS, Thomas, decd, Thomas Dallis, gdn of minor ch: Littleton, Payton, Hulbert and Wm, 11/4/1839, William M. Lampkin, sec, Lincoln, GB

DALLAS, William, decd, William Jones apptd admr with LWT annexed 1/4/1803, Camden, MIC

DALTON, Henry, decd, Winifred Dalton and Sampson Lampkin issued L/A 11/3/1806, Thomas Dalton, sec, Richmond, AB

DALTON, Sarah, decd, William McCain issued L/A 4/22/1826, John Lampkin, George A. P. Whitfield, secs, Richmond, AB

DALTON, Thomas, decd, Sarah Dalton issued L/A 3/10/1821, Daniel Meigs, sec, Richmond, AB

DAMPUR, Daniel, decd, LWT pvd 7/5/1847, Effingham, MIC

DANBY, John, decd, Philip H. Mantz issued L/A 11/2/1830, John Morrison, sec, Richmond, AB

DANBY, John, decd, Thomas J. Wray issued L/A 9/1/1834, William C. Micou, sec, Richmond, AB

DANFORTH, Abraham, decd, Andrew J. Miller issued L/A 3/2/1840, John M. Adams, sec, 1840 retns cash for support of Mrs. Danforth and children, Richmond, AB

DANFORTH, James K., decd, Thomas Glascock issued L/A 5/1/1837, Henry Dalby, sec, Richmond, AB

DANFORTH, Thomas L., decd, Joshua Danforth issued L/A 10/1/1830, John W. Danforth, sec, Richmond, AB

DANIEL, Aaron, decd, Benjamin Brewton, admr, makes retn 11/14/1835, Tattnall, I&A

DANIEL, Ann T., dau of Egbert P., decd, Egbert P. Daniel, gdn, William H. C. Mickelberry, sur, 11/10/1849, Butts, GB

DANIEL, Biddy, dau of Egbert P., decd, Egbert P. Daniel, gdn, William H. C. Mickelberry, sur, 11/10/1849, Butts, GB

DANIEL, Duke A. apptd gdn of his minor ch: Marion, Giles, George and Emery 1/1/1894, Clarke, LP

DANIEL, Elias, decd, Elizabeth Daniel, admx, presented her accts 5/3/1813, Tattnall, MIC

DANIEL, Elisha, minor child of Moses, Moses apptd gdn 1/4/1841, 1841 retn, cash recd from est of Elisha Applewhite, which amt was left to his mother, Dorothy Daniel for lifetime, to go to Elisha Daniel, Richmond, GB

DANIEL, Henrietta (Mrs.), wid of William and dau of Henry Jennings, Jeremiah M. Daniell apptd trustee for her and her children 1/1862, Clarke, LP

DANIEL, James, decd, Martha Daniel gdn of orphs: Leroy S., Mary E. and James, 3/6/1843, Randolph

DANIEL, James, decd, William Templeton, Bryant Daniel issued L/A 5/17/1832, Richmond, AB

DANIEL, Nathan, decd, Sarah and Amos Daniel issued L/A 11/6/1809, Putnam, AB

DANIELL, Asa B., decd, est 5/4/1840, Clarke, LP

DANIELL, Francis M., decd, est 11/6/1865, Clarke, LP

DANIELL, James, decd, William Hardwick, Jr., exr, recd 25 negroes, stock, etc., and all my legacy that was willed by decd, signed, Levi Daniell 1/3/1799, Hancock, AA

DANIELL, Josiah, decd, est 11/21/1870, Clarke, LP

DANIELL, Josiah, orph of Josiah, decd, Lewis Lester apptd gdn 9/25/1845, Clarke, LP

DANIELL, John R., decd., Wm. B. Daniell, John R. Daniell, admrs., 7/7/1829, Emanuel

DANIELL, Levi, decd, LWT dtd 12/8/1800 pvd 1/5/1801, wife, Martha; stepmother, Nancy Daniell; children-James, Catherine and Juliett; my father, James Daniell, decd, Hancock, AAA

DANIELL, N. C., decd., H. G. Daniell, John R. Daniell, admrs., 9/2/1833, Emanuel, AB
DANIELL, Sarah A., dau of George W. Malum, Atlas A. Daniell apptd trustee for his wife and her children in place of Wm Malum 2/10/1868, Clarke, LP
DANIELL, Thomas M., decd, est 5/16/1876, Clarke, LP
DANIELL, William, decd, Jordan Flanders, admr, 9/5/1833, appr, Emanuel, A
DANIELL, William B., Josiah Daniell apptd trustee 2/6/1864, Clarke, LP
DANIELLY, Arthur, decd., Wm. E. Boren, admr., 11/4/1823, Baldwin
DANIELLY, Elizabeth (Mrs.), decd, est 7/5/1850, Clarke, LP
DANIELLY, William J., decd., Ann Eliza Danielly, admx., Robert Collins, Marmaduke J. Blady, sec., 1/10/1832, Bibb
DANIELS, Isaac, decd, Robert Johnson and Hannah Daniels, admrs, Dooly, OD
DANNELLY (DANIELLY), Francis, decd, appr 4/11/1801, Arthur Dannelly, George Stephens, admrs; purchasers: Elizabeth Dannelly, James McKissack, Jas McCormack, Jesse Clements, Jane Dannelly, Elizabeth Dannelly, Jr., Hancock, AAAA
DANSLER, Philip, decd, accts of Christian H. Dasher, exr 1/5/1829, Effingham, MIC
DANSLEY, William D., minor son of William F., decd, William F. Dansley apptd gdn, Stephen W. Beasley, Robert D. A. Tharp, sec, 3/6/1848, Troup, GB
DARBY, James W., decd, est 8/9/1820; Polly Darby apptd gdn of orphs: Wm, Julius, John, Samuel, Betsy, Orry and James, 3/5/1821, Clarke, LP
DARBY, Julius G., decd, 10/19/1903 ltr from R. K. Kelley, atty, Kansas City, Mo. that Julius G. d. intestate 6/10/1855 leaving no widow; bounty land warrant filed by F. O. Darby of Walton Co., son, Clarke, LP
DARCEY, William, decd, Andrew Hampton and David M. Daniels issued L/A 1/5/1808, Benjamin B. Darcey, sec, Laurens, AB
DARCEY, William, decd, Benjamin Darcey, Jr. shall furnish sufficient clothing board, etc., to orphs: Phereby, Caty, Joel and Willis, 2/6/1810, Laurens, AB
DARDEN, Ann, decd, Jethro Darden, admr, 3/2/1829, Septimus Torrence, James Bailey, surs, Warren, AB
DARDEN, Edmund B., over age 14, child of John, decd, chose Bedford H. Darden as gdn 1/7/1819, Jasper, OM
DARDEN, Elizabeth, Bedford H. Darden apptd gdn 1/1820, Jasper, OM
DARDEN, George W., over age 14, child of John, decd, chose Bedford H. Darden as gdn 1/7/1819, Jasper, OM
DARDEN, John, decd, Wm Head, Isaac McClendon, John Martin, Jeremiah Pearson and Allen McClendon div est, 1/1820, Jasper, OM
DARDEN, Jonathan, decd, William Stone, admr, 11/3/1834, Solomon Lockett, Septimus Torrence, surs, Warren, AB
DARDEN, Moses, orph of Stephen, decd, over age 14, Ann Darden, gdn, 5/3/1813, Warren, MIC
DARDEN, Nicholas, orph of Stephen, decd, over age 14, Ann Darden, gdn, 5/3/1813, Warren, MIC
DARDEN, Stephen, decd, Nancy and Jethro Darden, admrs, 5/4/1807, Jacob Darden, William Darden, surs, Warren, AB
DARDEN, Stephen, decd, John Baker, Solomon Lockett, Aaron Greer apptd to div pers prop 3/1/1813, Warren, MIC
DARDEN, Stephen, decd, Mrs. Anna, wid, chooses her 1/3 or est, 5/7/1810, Warren, MIC
DARDEN, Stephen, decd, Nancy Darden apptd temp admx 3/30/1807; Jethro Darden and Nancy Darden, perm admrs 5/4/1807, sur, Jacob Darden, Jethro Darden, William Darden, Warren, AB, MIC

77

DARDEN, Stephen, decd, report of partitioners to div pers est 2/7/1814, Warren, MIC
DARDEN, William, decd, Jethro Darden, admr, 11/17/1823, Solomon Lockett, sur, Warren, AB
DARLING, Benjamin, decd, Polly Darling and Nathaniel C. Snead issued L/A 7/25/1814, Robert Fraser, Zachariah Bell, secs, Richmond, AB
DARLING, Joseph, decd, 3/3/1845 div of slaves to heirs: Thomas J., Joseph, Jr., Mrs. Mary Darling, Jeremiah Nute; Joseph Darling, Jr. and Jeremiah Nute, admrs, Richmond, AB
DARNELL, Dixon W., orph of Jeremiah W., decd, Joseph Darnell, gdn, 11/7/1825, John Harris, Reuben Mann, secs, Morgan, GB
DARNELL, Richard H., decd, Thomas B. Burford, Alexander Osborn, admrs, Samuel P. Burford, James Brady, sur, 9/29/1843, Butts, AB
DARRACOTT, Francis, gdn for Elizabeth Cummings, 1815 retns pd Sylvester Johnson, husb of sd Elizabeth, one slave, Wilkes, Retns
DARROW, Lyman, decd, Joseph Thomas, admr, 1/7/1840, Camden, MIC
DART, Cyrus, LWT, Ann Dart, extrx, 12/5/1818, gtd leave to sell real estate, Glynn, MIC
DASHER, Alexander, decd, LWT presented and objections heard, sd LWT inadmissible since sd decd was minor at time of execution, 5/3/1813, Tattnall, MIC
DASHER, Christian, decd, LWT pvd 11/14/1842, Effingham, MIC
DASHER, Elizabeth S. chose William B. Dasher as her gdn 11/14/1842, Effingham, MIC
DAUGAS, John, decd, late of Charleston, South Carolina, Sebastian C. Dortie issued L/A 1/10/1823, Richmond, AB
DAUGHERTY, John, decd, John Daugherty apptd admr, 2/8/1794, Columbia, L/A
DAUGHERTY, Nancy, John Bellflower, gdn, Dooly, OD
DAUGHTRY, Thomas, Joseph Daughtry, gdn, p. 181, 143, Screven, OM
DAVENPORT, F. L. applies for L/G of her own children, 4/6/1870, Cobb, MIC
DAVENPORT, Mary P., minor of Moses H., decd, Wm P. Hinton, gdn, 12/3/1866, Clarke, LP
DAVENPORT, Seaborn L. apptd trustee for his wife, Nancy, dau of Henry Jennings and her children 4/20/1863, Clarke, LP
DAVID, Thomas B., decd, L/A to James J. Norman 10/1/1860, Fulton
DAVIDSON, Frederick, decd, James Quillian and Elijah Starr, exrs of LWT dtd 6/17/1831 pvd 11/1832 names wife, Rhody and ch: Abraham Bundine, Elisha Stephens, Peggy Jackson, John Bailey, Rhody Emily, Frederick Allan, and Azel Washington, Habersham, MIC
DAVIDSON, George H., decd, Arthur Moncrief, admr, 10/5/1818, John Butt, sur, Warren, AB
DAVIDSON, Isaac, decd, John S. Davidson issued L/A 10/14/1840, Thomas G. Hall, sec, Richmond, AB
DAVIDSON, James, decd, appr 5/8/1802, Aquila Davidson, Loyd Kelley, admrs; purchasers at sale: Aquilla Davidson, Lemuel Davidson, Isaac Evans, etc., Hancock, AAAA
DAVIS, Alexander, decd, Archibald Clark, admr, reports he has recd no assets, 6/3/1823, Camden, MIC
DAVIS, Allen, minor orph of Levi, decd, James Cone qualified as gdn 7/5/1841, Bulloch, MIC
DAVIS, Amos G., order to pay $15.00, p. 52, L/D as admr gtd, p. 78, Screven, OM
DAVIS, Angeline, decd, wife of James P., est 2/4/1884, Clarke, LP
DAVIS, Baldwin, minor orph of Thomas, decd, Hannah Davis apptd gdn 5/12/1820, Jasper, OM
DAVIS, Benjamin, decd, Ann Barton issued L/A 4/7/1806, William Lyon, sec, Richmond, AB
DAVIS, David, decd, LWT pvd by Robert Moses, Isaac Burson applies for L/A 2/10/1800, Warren, MIC

DAVIS, David P., orph of David, decd, Thomas Folds, gdn, Willis Jarrell, David Evans, sur, 1/2/1838, Butts, GB

DAVIS, Davis, Mrs. Elizabeth, decd, Joshua Loper and Joseph Davis apptd admrs 1/27/1794, LWT annexed, dtd 6/2/1792, pvd 1/27/1794, names ch: Elizabeth, George, Ann and Walter Davis, Effingham, Misc

DAVIS, Dioclecian, decd, LWT pvd 7/5/1830, John Davis, exr, Washington

DAVIS, Elizabeth, decd, LWT pvd 11/27/1846, Harris

DAVIS, Elizabeth, orph of Thomas, decd, 5/4/1835, Harris

DAVIS, Emmie, orph of Middleton P., decd, Hewell C. Davis, gdn, 6/5/1878, Clarke, LP

DAVIS, Fanny, decd, Benjamin F. Bomar issued L/A 9/3/1860, Fulton

DAVIS, Frederick, decd, L. H. Davis, T. M. Robinson, admrs, 7/3/1837, Harris, AB

DAVIS, Gahazi, decd, alias Shockley, LWT pvd by Peter Hodo, Reubin McGee qualified exr 11/9/1795, Warren, MIC

DAVIS, Gazhazi, decd, Reubin McGee, exr of LWT applies for L/D 8/11/1800, Warren, MIC

DAVIS, George W., minor orph of Thomas, decd, Hannah Davis apptd gdn 5/12/1820, Jasper, OM

DAVIS, Gideon, decd, 8/10/1801 inventory includes slaves and acct of Absolom Davis for #5 N. C. money; Jacob Higginbotham, Robert Pulliam, Roland Brown, apprs, Elbert, AR

DAVIS, Henry signed as having recd from James Cone, his gdn 7/3/1844, Bulloch, Misc

DAVIS, Henry, minor orph of Levi, decd, James Cone qualified as gdn 7/5/1841, Bulloch, MIC

DAVIS, Henry G., decd, James Moore, admr 6/5/1842, Camden, MIC

DAVIS, Hester, minor orph of Levi, decd, James Cone qualified as gdn 7/5/1841, Bulloch, MIC

DAVIS, James, decd, Jane and David Davis, James Smith, Robert Grier applied for L/A 10/30/1797, Greene, Misc

DAVIS, James M., minor orph of Thomas, decd, Hannah Davis apptd gdn 5/12/1820, Jasper, OM

DAVIS, James P. apptd gdn of his minor dau, Emma Mitt, under age 14, 7/6/885; inheritance from her mother, Angeline Davis, decd, Clarke, LP

DAVIS, Jenkin, decd, John G. Neidlinger, admr, Ann Retn 12/14/1793, Effingham, Misc

DAVIS, Jesse, son of Permelia, aged 4, bound to William E. Davis, gdn until age 18 yrs, James Law, sec, Hall, GB

DAVIS, John, decd, Henry Type, admr, to execute title of lots in Randolph Co., 7/27/1809, Oglethorpe, OM

DAVIS, John, decd, John Patterson, exr, qualified 6/23/1783, Liberty, Ests

DAVIS, John, decd, LWT dtd 5/30/1793 pvd by Wm & Joseph Davis, 12/5/1793, non-cupative LWT, names wife, Elizabeth, ch: Joseph, John, James, William, Samuel, George, and Walter, Nancy, Effingham, Misc

DAVIS, John C., minor orph of Levi, decd, James Cone qualified as gdn 7/5/1841, Bulloch, MIC

DAVIS, John Edward, decd, Mrs. Catharine M. Davis, gdn of her son, Marion Tracy Davis, 1/12/1885, Clarke, LP

DAVIS, John L., decd, Gary Davis, admr, Malachi Pickett, sur, 8/24/1859; Malinda P. Davis, admx, Harris C. Jackson, John B. Adair, sur, 10/3/1859, Paulding, AB

DAVIS, Joseph A., decd, L/A to David P. Hill 12/14/1867, Fulton

DAVIS, Joseph, decd, John Davis of Chatham Co., admr, 1819, Bryan, Writs

DAVIS, Juletta, orph of Thomas, decd, Needham Noccer apptd gdn 11/1820, Jasper, OM

DAVIS, J. W., decd, L/A issued Francis Davis 9/1862, Webster, OD
DAVIS, Lemuel, decd, Delila Davis, gdn of orphs: Samuel and Clinton 3/4/1839, John Guice, sec, Lincoln, GB
DAVIS, Levi, decd, G. R. Davis, admr, Caleb B. Pool, L. L. Davis, sur, 11/1/1875, Gwinnett, AB
DAVIS, Levi, decd, William Cogdell apptd admr 2/3/1840; ordered that Susan Davis sell 500 acres, 200 acres, 300 acres in Bulloch 5/6/1839, Bulloch, MIC
DAVIS, Lewis, decd, John Ferrell applied for L/A 7/27/1791; apprs: John Pollard, Absolom Davis, Stephen Westbrook, Elbert, AR
DAVIS, Luis, decd, apprs: Zachr Glass, Edward Woodham 12/18/1798, Greene, Misc
DAVIS, Mahala A., illegitimate dau of Elizabeth, Daniel Moore apptd gdn 1/7/1839, B. Dunagan, D. M. McCleskey, secs, Hall, GB
DAVIS, Malinda, decd, LWT pvd 11/27/1846, Harris
DAVIS, Martha, minor orph of Levi, decd, James Cone qualified as gdn 7/5/1841, Bulloch, MIC
DAVIS, Martha, alias Martha Thompson, George Davis, gdn, Peyton H. White, sur, 6/16/1834, Butts, AB
DAVIS, Maryanna, minor orph of Levi, decd, James Cone qualified as gdn 7/5/1841, Bulloch, MIC
DAVIS, Meredith, decd, Nehemiah Wade issued LA 2/28/1786, John and Nathaniel Wade, secs, Richmond, AB
DAVIS, Milley Ann, decd, distributees 9/19/1878: Sarah G. Davis and Martha J. Nations, Clarke, LP
DAVIS, Nancy A., dau of Nathan B., formerly Nancy A. Puryear, Lucy A. Puryear apptd gdn 9/23/1872 of her dau, Clarke, LP
DAVIS, Nathan, decd, Reubin McGee and Ephraim McGee apply for adm w/LWT annexed, Peter Buckles and Joseph White, sur, 9/7/1807, Warren, MIC
DAVIS, Owen, decd, Martha apptd gdn of Sally E., Martha, Richard C., Gardiner K., and Benjamin H. Davis, minor orphs, 9/1813, Jasper, OM
DAVIS, Prior L., decd, he d. 6/1890, Clarke, LP
DAVIS, Richard, decd, LWT pvd by James Montgomery, 2/12/1803, LWT names wife, Elizabeth, Joshua McConnel and wife, Elizabeth, exrs, dtd 2/23/1803, Franklin, OM
DAVIS, Sally, Absolom Davis, gdn, 1809 retns, Elbert, GR
DAVIS, Samuel, decd, James Guice, gdn for orphs: John and Joseph 3/7/1835, Meredith Wright, sec, Lincoln, GB
DAVIS, Samuel J. signed as having recd from Patrick Lanier as gdn for S. Slater, 11/30/1841, Bulloch, Misc
DAVIS, Sarah, decd, Jeremiah Davis issued L/A 5/6/1822, W. Perkins, sec, Morgan, AB
DAVIS, Silas P., decd, Samuel Douglas and William Johnson issued L/A 11/1/1824; Richard and Nicholas Smith and Nicholas Davis, admrs de bonis non 11/7/1825, Morgan, AB
DAVIS, Theophilus, decd, Wm Johnston issued L/A 12/10/1789, John Morris, Arthur Jenkins, sec, Richmond, AB
DAVIS, Thomas, decd, LWT pvd 5/2/1842, wife, Rachel, ch: Toliver, Finch, Thomas, John, heirs of Elihu Davis, Almyra Sophrona Davis, Elizabeth Brook, Melissa Smith, Parmela Sanders, and issue of decd's dau, Mary Booth, Randolph
DAVIS, Thomas Clowers, orph of Thomas, decd, 5/4/1835, Harris
DAVIS, Thomas Jefferson, orph of Thomas, decd, Jeremiah Davis issued L/A 11/6/1815, Morgan, GB
DAVIS, Thomas W., Erastus Waters filed retn as gdn for 1840, 5/8/1841, Bulloch, MIC
DAVIS, Westbury, minor orph of Levi, decd, James Cone qualified as gdn 7/4/1841, Bulloch, MIC

DAVIS, William, decd, L/A issued Elizabeth M. Davis 12/1864, Webster, OD
DAVIS, William, decd, est 4/4/1853, Clarke, LP
DAVIS, William, decd, planter, George Jones of Savannah, admr, 9/9/1783, Chatham, Adms
DAWDLE, Joseph, devd, appr, Hancock, AAAA
DAWSON, Brittain, decd, Mrs. Sarah Dawson and Elizabeth Howell issued L/A 5/25/1795, Lewis Harris, sec; apprs: Dread Dawson, Sarah Dawson, John Harwood, Wm Woodrough, Saml Bowdry 12/9/1795, Richmond, AB
DAWSON, David, decd, Dread and Sarah Dawson, John Harwood issued L/A 12/9/1795, Richmond, AB
DAWSON, Francis, William Dawson, gdn, Dooly, OD
DAWSON, George M., decd, 3/8/1853 distributees: Mary D. and Sarah D. Dawson, Clarke, LP
DAWSON, John E., decd, Richard A. Blount, gdn of: Annabella, Nancy, John, Mary and Burwell, 7/1/1816, Morgan, GB
DAWSON, Lucien W., decd, 3/14/1866, wid, Eliza W. Dawson, admx, Clarke, LP
DAWSON, Mary, decd, Mary Hatcher Dawson and Richard Dawson exrs of LWT, 6/1/1786, Chatham, Adms
DAWSON, Sarah D. J., orph of G. M., Mary D. Dawson, gdn, 3/6/1854, Clarke, LP
DAWSON, William, decd, Nathaniel Bacon qualified as admr 2/15/1785, Liberty, Ests
DAY, Francis, decd, Jenanc Day apptd admx 3/5/1867, Fulton
DAY, Sarah M., decd, wid of Major Joseph, LWT 7/6/1795 leaves everything to her mother, Elizabeth Box (LWT filed in Chatham Co.), Bryan, CR
DEAKLE, John C., decd., George Deakle, admr., James Hancock, sur., 5/3/1828, Emanuel
DEAKLE, John C., Sr., decd., "an old and infirm man",George Deakle, gdn. 2/6/1826, Emanuel
DEAL, Joseph J., minor of William, decd, Lot Rowden apptd gdn 1/7/1822, Jasper, OM
DEAL, Susan, decd., James Deal, admr., Silas Scarborough, Wm. Deal, sur., 11/7/1837, Emanuel
DEAL, Thurza, orph of William, decd, Lot Rowden apptd gdn 11/4/1822, Jasper, OM
DEAL, William, decd, Rachel Deal, admx, makes retn 2/6/1816, Jackson, OM
DEAL, William, decd, Lewis Deal apptd gdn of orphs: Eleanor, Nancy and Stephen 10/28/1805, Jackson, OM
DEAL, William, decd, Rachel Deal apptd admx 9/4/1815, Jackson, OM
DEAN, Elizabeth, minor under age 21, William Cook apptd gdn 11/1/1819, Jasper, OM
DEAN, John, decd, est 2/13/1868, Clarke, LP
DEAN, Mary, minor under age 21, William Cook apptd gdn 11/1/1819, Jasper, OM
DEAN, Nathaniel, decd, Unice Dean, wid, qualified as extrx of LWT 7/3/1820, Jasper, OM
DEAN, Shadrack, decd, LWT pvd by Owen J. Bowen and Wm Mackee 3/1813, Jackson, OM
DEAN, W. H., decd, Anna Dean, admx w/LWT annexed, C. H. Kytle, sec, 8/2/1870, White, AB
DEAN, Winnifred, decd, Williamson Dean issued L/A 1/4/1819, Laurens, AB
DEANE, Burkett, decd, Thomas C. Deane issued temp L/A 12/12/1825 and perm L/A 3/15/1826, Morgan, AB
DEANE, John A., decd., John L. Stephens, admr., 11/6/1843, Baldwin, AB

DEARING, Albin P., decd, Eugenia E. Dearing, wid, 6/30/1885, Clarke, LP
DEARING, Emma F. Dearing requests gdn be apptd for her dau, Margaret Thomas Dearing, only surviving child of late John T. Dearing of Madison Co., 4/3/1841; Wm Dearing apptd, Clarke, LP
DEARING, Marcella A., wife of Alfred L., Albin p. Dearing apptd trustee 9/10/1867, Clarke, LP
DEARING, Thomas H., decd, he d. 10/8/1890, widow, Edith St. John Dearing; ch: AlbinE ., age 22, M. G., age 20, Frank T. H., age 18, Harry T., age 16, Katherine Graham, age 3 (Albin E. lived Savannah), Clarke, LP
DEARING, Eugenia E. (Mrs), 2/19/1887 Albin P. Dearing, tr of mother per LWT of Sarah Hamilton; ch-T. H., John A., A. P. & W. D. Dearing, Marion D. Laurence (New Orleans, La), Eugenia D., Annie M., Marion S., Julie & Lulia Speer Clarke, LP
DEARING, William, decd, of Chatham Co., Albin P. Dearing issued L/A, sd decd d. 6/3/1853, his admr was Albin Dearing Sr., all prop has been administered except in Ga. and Miss, 1/26/1887, Clarke, LP
DEARMOND, William, (Capt.) decd, carpenter, Mary Dearmond, James Pearre, Wilson Woodroof issued L/A 7/30/1799, Walter Leigh, John O. Pearre, Hugh Magee, secs; Nathl Pearre, gdn of William, inf minor orph, Nelson Crawford, sec, Richmond, AB
DEAS, Jon, decd, Mr. Jenkins apptd gdn of orphs: Ella, Jades, Willie and Jon, 12/3/1894, Clarke, LP
DEASON, Benjamin, decd, Zachariah Deason apptd temp admr, 3/9/1805, Warren, MIC
DEATON, Elijah, decd, Charity Deaton, Elijah Perkle, admrs, William Vermillion, Jacob Perkle, secs, 11/1/1830, Hall, AB
DEAVERS, George, decd, LWT dtd 2/18/1829 pvd 1/1830 names wife, Rachel and ch: Abraham, John, Isaac, Christopher, Elizabeth Nole and Sarah McCracking, Habersham, MIC
DEBEAUREGARD, Lambert (Dr.), decd, Jane Mary Odette Kirblay issued L/A 4/5/1882, Frederick E. Gugas, John B. Guien, secs, Richmond, AB
DEDMAN, Ebolina, John R. Brown apptd gdn 3/1/1813, Franklin, OM
DEDMAN, John R. Brown apptd gdn 3/1/1813, Franklin, OM
DEDMAN, Sennica, John R. Brown apptd gdn 3/1/1813, Franklin, OM
DEEL, Shadrach, decd, of Montgomery Co., James Wales, admr, appr 4/17/1812, Emanuel, A
DEEL, Simon, decd, Edward Lane, admr, appr 11/29/1836, Emanuel, A
DEEN, Benjamin F., orph of Joel, decd, L/G issued Elizabeth Deen 5/6/1839, Washington
DEEN, Charity, orph of Richard, decd, Richard Deen, gdn, 9/4/1823, Laurens, GB
DEEN, Jesse E., orph of Joel, decd, L/G issued Elizabeth Deen 5/6/1839, Washington
DEEN, Joel, decd, Elizabeth Deen issued L/A 11/9/1836, Washington
DEEN, Joseph C., orph of Joel, decd, L/G issued Elizabeth Deen 5/6/1839, Washington
DEEN, Mickey Lailey, orph of Richard, decd, William Deen, gdn, 3/1/1819, Laurens, GB
DEEN, Moses H., orph of Joel, decd, L/G issued Elizabeth Deen 5/6/1839, Washington
DEEN, Nimrod, decd, Shadrach Deen issued L/A, James D. Gilmer, sec, Hall, AB
DEEN, Richard, decd, Robert W. W. Wynne issued L/A 9/6/1813, Laurens, AB
DEEN, Tarley, orph of Richard, decd, Winny Deen, gdn, 1/6/1816, Laurens, GB
DEEN, William E., decd, William and John Deen issued L/A 3/2/1818, Laurens, AB

82

DEES, James, decd, Henry W. McDaniel issued L/A 1/10/1859, Fulton
DEFOOR, James, decd, Martin Defoor, admr, 9/1/1856, Fulton
DEKLE, John L., decd, George Dekle, admr, appraisement 6/28/1828, Emanuel, A
DELACY, Henry M., decd, est 2/8/1870, Clarke, LP
DELANY, Daniel Sharp, decd, LWT probated, Samuel Clark, exr, 6/17/1816, Camden, MIC
DELAY, Hiram R., decd, Lucy H. Grifith, admx, 8/4/1856, Fulton
DELL, John, decd, Philip Dell apptd admr 1/4/1841, Bulloch, MIC
DELL, John, decd, inv and appr 2/27/1841 by John A. Fletcher, Luke P. Lanier, Wm P. Murdock, Robert M. Williams, Samuel Williams, Bulloch, Misc
DELLAH, Samuel, decd, Richard Knight, gdn, 1/8/1830, Butts, GB
DELONEY, Maria apptd gdn of her children: Martha, William and Robert 1/2/1837, Camden, MIC, GB
DELONEY, Martha (Mrs.), LWT pvd by witnesses taken in Savannah. Her son, Robert J. Deloney, qualified exr 1/1/1821, Camden, MIC
DELONEY, Martha (Mrs.), decd, Robert James Deloney offered her LWT for probate, 12/20/1820, Camden, MIC
DELONEY, R. J., decd, Maria Deloney gtd leave to sell ot 37, 10th dist Houston Co., lot 1194, 12th dist, 1st section, 6/4/1838, Camden, MIC
DELONEY, Robert J., decd, Robert Stafford, apptd admr, late mbr of ct, 6/3/1833, Camden, MIC
DELONEY, Rosa E., decd,d. 9/2/1897, Clarke, LP
DELONEY, William, decd, Martha Deloney apptd admx 1/8/1805, filed Retn, 2/5/1811, Camden, MIC
DELONEY, William G., decd, est 1/28/1864, Clarke, LP
DELPH, Natalie, minor wife of W. Delph who is apptd gdn 1898, Clarke, LP
DEMARY, Henry, decd, John G. Schenck issued L/A 1/9/1860, dismissed 7/1/1861, Fulton
DEMASS, Abraham, decd, Turner Thomasson issued L/A 4/6/1786, Benjamin Porter, sec, Richmond, AB
DEMERE, Raymond, decd, late of Chatham Co., Joseph Habersham, exr LWT,, gtd leave to sell 2000 acres on Midway Swamp, late the prop of Lyman Hall owned by decd at his death, 9/26/1814, Liberty, MIC
DEMORE, Nancy (Mrs.), decd, est 7/6/1885, Clarke, LP
DEMOT, John R., decd, commissioners apptd to set apart share of Margaret Proctor, admx 1/7/1834, Camden, MIC
DEMOTT, John, decd, Mrs. Margaret Demott, wid, apptd admr, 1/4/1820, Camden, MIC
DENHAM, Clement, decd, Margaret Denham, gdn to Samuel and Mary Ann, orphs, 1/6/1842, Mary Clements, sec, Richmond, GB
DENMARK, Allen, decd, inv and appr by Peter Cone, James Rawls, William Lee, Thomas Mills 3/2/1824, Bulloch, Misc
DENMARK, Allen, decd, inv of pers est 1/12/1824, Bulloch, Misc
DENMARK, Clarissa, minor of Redding, decd, Malachi Denmark apptd gdn 3/5/1821, Bulloch, MIC
DENMARK, James, decd, LWT pvd 9/7/1829, Malachi Denmark, Thomas Jones, exrs, wife, Nancy; est div by James Wilkinson, William Groover, Elander Nessmith, Allen Jones, 7 children not named, 9/8/1831, Bulloch, Misc
DENMARK, John, minor of Redding, decd, Malachi Denmark apptd gdn 3/5/1821, Bulloch, MIC
DENMARK, Redding, decd, acct of sale of stock of cattle by Malachi Denmark, gdn, 5/12/1821, Bulloch, Misc
DENMARK, Sarah, minor of Redding, decd, Malachi Denmark apptd gdn 3/5/1821, Bulloch, MIC
DENMARK, Stephen, decd, Allen Denmark and Robert Burton issued L/A 5/3/1819; acct of Seaborn Denmark mentioned 1/1/1821, Bulloch, MIC

DENMARK, Stephen, decd, appr of est by John Rawls, Aaron Cone, Charley Louder, Allen Denmark, Robert Burton, admrs, 6/11/1819, sale or property 1/4/1820, Bulloch, Misc
DENMARK, Stephen, decd, recd of Robert Burton, admr, $616, being bal of Jane Eliza Frances Rawls part of est, recd by Allen Rwls, admr of est of Thomas Rawls, decd; also gdn of child, Jane E. F. Rawls, 1/5/1824, Bulloch, Misc
DENMARK, Thomas, decd, Jacob Denmark L/A 3/1865, Webster, OD
DENMARK, Thomas, minor of Redding, decd, Malachi Denmark apptd gdn 3/5/1821, Bulloch, MIC
DENNARD, Kennedy, decd, R. R. Roby, admr, 7/1840; apprs: A. J. Snelling, John Thornton, Tomlinson Fort; purchasers at sale: Ivey, Green & C. C. Allen, Ichabod & Wm Cox, Sarah Dennard (wid), David, Jasper & Thomas Dennard, Stewart, Adms
DENNIS, Jesse, decd, Wm Fairchild, Sr. gtd L/A 7/1818, Jasper, OM
DENNIS, Jesse, decd, Samuel P. Dennis issued L/A 7/3/1820, John Barnes, sec, Morgan, AB
DENNIS, John, decd, Elizabeth C. Dennis, admx w/LWT annexed, David Berry, Stephen W. Price, James M. Bedsole, surs 1/3/1834; pd: H. F. Williams, Daniel Tye, Wm Dennis, Danl McCloud, Saml Griswold, A. G. & W. H. Atwood, Elizabeth C. Dennis, Gideon Pope, 5/25/1835; 1835 pd Peter Dennis his pt, 7/8/1835 Butts, ER
DENNIS, Joseph, decd, Charles A. Dennis issued L/A 5/2/1814, Putnam, AB
DENNY, John, decd, Thomas Elkins applies for adm 3/2/1829, Effingham, MIC
DENSMORE, David, decd, William Burt, admr, James L. Burt, sur on bond 8/21/1862, Dawson, WB
DENSON, Benjamin, decd, John B. Boyd, admr, 1/3/1801, Starling J. Pate, sur, Warren, AB
DENT, William C., orph of William, decd, Catherine Dent, gdn, 7/2/1821, Thomas C. Russell, sec; George Mahoney, gdn 1/12/1824, Lincoln, GB
DEPP, Samuel, decd, John Kogler, principal creditor, apptd admr, 9/1/1798, Effingham, Misc
DESAUXBLEAUX, L. P. B., decd, Lott Warren and William L. McKee issued L/A 7/2/1821, Laurens, GB
DESCLAUX, Joseph, decd, Margaret Desclaux qualified as exr 9/4/1826, Camden, MIC
DESCLAUX, Louisa Jane, decd, Mary M. Dufour apptd admx 6/3/1850, dismissed 6/2/1851, Camden, MIC
DESCLAUX, Louis Dufour, Mrs. Mary M. gdn´s bond 3/4/1850, Camden, MIC
DESHAROON, William H., orph of William, decd, Peyton Reynolds, gdn, 1/1835, Hollis Boynton, George R. McElvey, sur, Stewart, GB
DEVAUGHN, William, orph of Patrick, decd, George H. Page, gdn, Wm R. Head, sur, 6/1842, Fayette, GB
DEVILLERS, Lewis, decd, of Charleston, South Carolina, Nicholas Delaigle issued L/A 3/16/1831, Joseph Bignon, sec, Richmond, AB
DEWITT, Charles, Sr., decd, James May, Charles DeWitt, Jr., Joseph Burnett, in rt of wife, Ellen, John L. and Teresa DeWitt, heirs, appl for pers prop to be div amongst heirs, 1/5/1824; Charles DeWitt gtd leave to sell property 1/3/1835, Glynn, MIC
DICK, Robert, decd, list of debts due Robert Dick & Co. 1/1/1792 given by Will Kennedy, surviving co-partner and admr 2/3/1794, William Kennedy, admr, Richmond
DICKEN, Benjamin, decd, Presley Spinks, admr w/LWT annexed; caveat filed by Richard Snipes in behalf of himself and Lewis Dicken, 3/9/1802, Warren, MIC

DICKEN, Catharine, orph of Joseph, decd, 1810 retns of John Dicken, gdn, recd of Richard Dicken for use of Catharine, $60, Wilkins, Retns
DICKEN, Richard B., decd, est 9/1/1856, Milly Klutts apptd gdn of orphs: George H. and Milly M. M. P. 4/27/1865, Clarke, LP
DICKERSON, Ann M., minor of Griffith, decd, Thomas Hutchison, gdn, Robert Pritchett, sur, 12/7/1857, Cherokee, GB
DICKERSON, Griffith, late of Pittsylvania Co., Va., Thomas Hutcherson, admr, Robert Hutcherson, sur, 7/13/1857, Cherokee, AB
DICKERSON, Isaac, decd, William McTyeire issued L/A 5/2/1795, John Fox, sec, Richmond, AB
DICKERSON, John N., orph of Wilborn, decd, Middleton Thompson, gdn, 11/9/1847, Clarke, LP
DICKERSON, Sallie F., minor of Griffith, decd, Thomas Hutchison, gdn, Robert Pritchett, sur, 12/7/1857, Cherokee, GB
DICKERSON, Thomas, minor of Thomas, decd, James E. Rusk, gdn, Daniel C. Boger, sur, 2/18/1860, Cherokee, GB
DICKERSON, William, minor of Thomas, decd, James E. Rusk, gdn, Daniel C. Boger, sur, 2/18/1860, Cherokee, GB
DICKEY, George, decd, John B. Dickey, admr, makes retn 1/1843, Gilmer, Misc
DICKINSON, Stephen, decd, Jane Mahan, qualified admx 4/20/1783, Liberty, Ests
DICKS, David, Mrs. Susannah Dicks, Andrew Dicks, Thomas Sheppard, admrs, qualified 5/13/1785, Liberty, Ests
DICKSON, Conor, Michael Dickson, gdn, p. 98, Screven, OM
DICKSON, David, decd, LWT pvd by Alexander and Sarah Gillespie 11/7/1808, Jackson, OM
DICKSON, E. A., minor of D. W., petitions to have a gdn appointed for her; J. A. L. Born, gdn, 9/28/1869, Cobb, MIC
DICKSON, John, decd, Thomas Dickson and John G. Underwood issued L/A 5/6/1811, Laurens, AB
DICKSON, John, decd, Thomas Dickson and John G. Underwood issued L/A 5/6/1811, Laurens, AB
DICKSON, Windsor, decd, James Dickson, admr, p. 108, p. 147, p. 189, Screven, OM
DIGBY, John, decd, L/A gtd Bellinder Digby and William Penn 11/2/1818; Bellinder Digby, wid, claimed child's pt 5/3/1819, Jasper, OM
DIKES, Levi, decd, Jesse Dikes, apptd admr 8/24/1793, Effingham, Misc
DILDY, Isaac, orph of Eli, decd, Claiborn Vaughn Sr. & Jr., gdns, 6/12/1854, Cherokee, GB
DILDY, Levi, orph of Eli, decd, Claiborn Vaughn Sr. & Jr., gdns, 6/12/1854, Cherokee, GB
DILL, Andrew J., decd, Robert S. Dill issued L/A 9/1/1834, Jacob Dill, sec, 1839 retn pd H. Bowdre, gdn, pd B. F. Dill, D. W. Dill, R. S. Dill, Richmond, AB
DILL, Daniel, decd, Andrew J. Dill issued L/A 9/24/1816, Gabriel Clark, Henry Mealing, secs, Richmond, AB
DILLARD, Elizabeth, John J. Collier, gdn, 11/5/1840, Dooly, OD
DILLON, Sarah, decd, Robert Dillion issued L/A 3/3/1819, Isham Thompson, James A. Black, Adam Hutcheson, John McMillen, secs, Richmond, AB
DILWORTH, Araminta, minor, William Berrie apptd gdn, 6/3/1823, Camden, MIC
DILWORTH, Araminta, decd, John Hardee rendered his acctg of est 6/4/1805, retn 1/6/1808; John Hardee, exr, cited to make fair and full acctg of condition of est, 4/1/1805, Camden, MIC Camden
DILWORTH, Araminta (Mrs.), decd, Col. William Scott, Ephraim Cook, Nathan Atkinson apptd to div est, 1/8/1811, Camden, MIC

DILWORTH, George, decd, late of Camden Co., Catharine Dilworth issued L/A 11/16/1820, Elijah E. Jones, sec, Morgan, AB
DILWORTH, George, decd, Mrs. Catherine Ann Berrie, wife of William Berrie, wid of decd, allowed extn to file Retn, 6/3/1823, Camden, MIC
DILWORTH, George A., decd, William Berrie, gdn of heirs, dismissed 6/2/1834, Camden, MIC
DILWORTH, George A., decd, John Hardee, Mrs. Catherine Dilworth apptd admrs, 6/2/1817, Camden, MIC
DILWORTH, George J., decd, Major John Hardee produced copy of bond given in Morgan Co. by Catherine A. Dilworth, admx 11/16/1821, 1/6/1823, Camden, MIC
DILWORTH, George J., decd, Catherine Dilworth, gdn of Armenta M. and John H., 11/16/1820, Elizabeth Jones, Lucy Clark, secs, Morgan, GB
DILWORTH, James C., decd, LWT probated, John Hardee, Sr. exr 1/6/1823, Camden, MIC
DILWORTH, J. C., decd, Retn of Commrs to set aside dowry to Elizabeth M., wid, 8/4/1827, Camden, MIC
DILWORTH, John, minor, William Berrie apptd gdn, 6/3/1823, Camden, MIC
DIMON, Jesse, decd, Cabinet Maker, Robert Dimon issued temp LA 11/5/1822; 1/7/1823 Robert Dimon and Carlos Tracy issued perm L/A, Richmond, AB
DIMON, Robert, decd, Benjamin Picquet issued temp L/A 1825-1826, Antoine Picquet, Frederick Dugas, secs, Richmond, AB
DINBOCH?, Andrew B., Christian Biddenbach, admr, 9/17/1791, Effingham, Misc
DINEANS, William, decd, LWT pvd, Peter D. Dineans, admr 1/18/1791, Chatham, Adms
DINGLER, John, decd, Nancy and William Dingler issued L/A 3/18/1816, William Gill, sec; Nancy Dingler, gdn of orphs: Caty Kimble and Jonathan B. Dingler 9/1/1817, James Clark, sec, Morgan, AB, GB
DINKINS, Isham, decd, Roscoe Lipsey, gdn of orphs: John M., Leander J., Dusta M., James W. and Charles M., 11/7/1853, Houston, GB
DISMUKES, Betheny, decd, LWT pvd 11/5/1844, bro. Cary Cox of Putnam Co., and Joseph Day, exrs, Harris
DIX, Tandy, decd, Gabriel Dix, admr, 6/7/1831, Camden, MIC
DIXIE, James, decd, Thomas Mills, William Stephens, admrs, state that Nicholas Miller unfortunately keeps possession of effects of decd, 4/26/1787, Chatham, Adms
DIXON, Catharine, orph of Robert, decd, L/G issued Shadrack Dixon 5/2/1831, Washington
DIXON, Eliza C., decd, LWT proven, John J. Dixon qualified exr, Webster, OD
DIXON, Mary, petitions for child's part, p. 178, Screven, OM
DIXON, Mary M., orph of Robert, decd, L/G issued Shadrack Dixon 5/2/1831, Washington
DIXON, R. M., decd, Mrs. E. C. Dixon enters LWT 12/1862; John J. Dixon issued L/A 4/1869, Webster, OD
DIXON, Robert, orph of Robert, decd, L/G issued Shadrack Dixon 5/2/1831, Washington
DIXON, Thomas, decd, Thomas Mitchell, admr, 10/4/1819, Clarke, LP
DIXON, William, decd, LWT pvd, Moses Sheftall, exr, 4/21/1790, Chatham, Adms
DIXON, William, decd, Mary Dixon applied for L/A 4/19/1796, Elbert, AB
DIXON, William, decd, Elizabeth Dixon and William Dixon, admrs, 3/26/1796, Columbia, AB

DOBBINS, Jesse, orph of Joseph, decd, late of Franklin Co., Paul
Furr issued L/G, F. M. Gowden, sec, 11/4/1850, Hall, GB
DOBBINS, John, decd, John Miller was apptd admr 1/30/1790,
Chatham, Adms
DOBBINS, William, decd, Dr. James Nisbet and John Waddell applied
for L/A 2/3/1796, Greene, Misc
DOBBS, David, decd, cav LWT-Ella Fambro vs. David J. Dobbs; Furman
& Mary Robts, Ella Fambro, wit; Caroline Lyman, A. Q. York, Mrs.
E. F. Anderson, Mary Mason, Wm, Jas P., Jerry, Mrs. Jane, & W.
M. Dobbs, J. T. Haley, 8/16/1871, Cobb, MIC
DOBBS, Josiah, decd, Luzany and John Dobbs, admrs bond, Moses
Haynes, Sr., John Cunningham, sec, 7/2/1810, 400 acres Little
Cedar Cr., Elbert Co., 202-1/2 acres, Wilkinson Co., Elbert, AR
DODD, Catherine, decd, Benjamin Cleveland, admr, dismissed
1/1836, Habersham, MIC
DODD, William, decd, Elijah Dodd and Judah Dodd issued L/A, Henry
Morris, A. W. Bell, secs, Hall, AB
DODD, William, decd, Judah Dodd issued L/A of orphs: Cynthia,
Permelia, Susannah and Benson W., Wiley Dodd, sec, 3/1/1841,
Hall, GB
DODSON, Daniel, decd, est 9/20/1841, Clarke, LP
DODYRUS, Epa, decd, David Garvin, admr, 1/4/1803, Camden, MIC
DOGGETT, Chattin, decd, est 5/5/1817, Clarke, LP
DOGGETT, Chattin, Jr., decd, est 5/1/1820, Clarke, LP
DOGGETT, George, decd, 3/1844 est fr Oglethorpe Co, Royal
Flemming, admr per Wm & Thos Doggett, Jesse Kinnie (Fanny´s
husb), Oliver Higginbothom (Nancy´s husb), Elizabeth Daniel, wid,
Betsey Morton, wid, 1st cousins, only kin, Clarke, LP
DOGGETT, John, LWT pvd 3/10/1813, Rebecca Dickson´s ch (heirs of
John Dickson, decd), Jeremiah Smith (son of Griffin), heirs of
Asa Doggett; Bolin Smith, Asa Doggett, Richard Hughbanks, exrs,
Jasper, OM
DOGGETT, John, decd, Asa Doggett qualified as exr, LWT, caveat
entered 3/1/1813, on grounds of exclusion of some of lineal
descendants, LWT pvd by Wm Harvey, Bolin Smith, Anderson Worthy,
Obadiah West 3/8/1813, Jasper, OM
DOGGETT, Richard, decd, est from Arkansas 5/23/1848, Clarke, LP
DOLLY, Benjamin, decd, Gideon Dolly, admr, p. 38, Gideon and
Susannah gtd leave to sell property, p. 42, Screven, OM
DONAHOO, William W., decd, Elijah M. issued L/A 5/26/1866, Fulton
DONALDSON, H. W., decd, John W. Henry, temp admr, P. W.
McConnell, Telford McConnell, sur, 11/27/1874, Gwinnett, AB
DONALDSON, James, decd, Mrs. Dicey Donaldson apptd admx 1/4/1841,
filed retn 1841, Bulloch, MIC
DONALDSON, James W., Alexander Douglass, gdn, p. 147, Screven, OM
DONALDSON, Susan E. M. signed as having recd from W. M. McLane,
admr of est of R. G. F. Donaldson, sundry articles sold
10/26/1844, Bulloch, Misc
DONALDSON, William, Sr., decd, William G. Donaldson, etc., admr,
p. 121, p. 132, Screven, OM
DONOHOO, B. W., unsound mind, C. Donehoo, gdn, 1855, Cobb, BB
DONWORTH, Mary, decd, Richard and Mary Cooper, admrs qualified
12/20/1790, Liberty, Ests
DONWORTH, Patrick, decd, E. Henry Schmidt, admr qualified
1/13/1790, Liberty, Ests
DONWORTH, Peter, decd, E. Henry Schmidt, admr qualified
1/13/1790, Liberty, Ests
DOOLY, John, decd, Dianah Dooly, wid, apptd admx 4/16/1782; John
Dooly vs. Thomas Lee, caveat, Lee swears in Council that Dooly
still keeps possession of land 11/3/1778, Wilkes, MxR
DOOLY, Mary M., decd, James Netherland, William Anderson, A. M.
Barrett, admrs, 4/7/1862, Dawson, WB

DOPSON, Elvira Ann, decd, William B. Dopson applies for L/A 12/23/1831, Effingham, MIC
DORAN, John, decd, Martha Doran, widow, apptd admx, 4/28/1785, Chatham, Adms
DORMAN, John, decd, Alfred Dorman, admr, T. D. King, sur, 7/1850, 1851-1854 retns, Fayette, AB
DORMER, Charles, decd, James W. Bowie, etc., apprs, p. 139, Screven, OM
DOROTHY, Benjamin, decd, Silas Palmore, gdn of orphs: Francis, Susan and Nancy 11/3/1851, Lumpkin, GB
DOROUGH, James, decd, L/A to John Dorough 11/1/1813, Putnam, AB
DORSETT, John, decd, LWT 5/2/1796, Eleanor Dorsett and Theodore Dorsett, exrs, Columbia, L/A
DORSEY, Andrew, John Dorsey apptd gdn 8/7/1809, Franklin, OM
DORSEY, Andrew, decd, LWT filed 10/20/1865, wife, Nancy, admx, White, AB
DORSEY, Bazzel, decd, LWT names son, Andrew and children "when they arrive at inheritable age or marry"; Friends, John Dorsey and Elias Baker, exrs, dtd 6/16/1806, Franklin, IMW
DORSEY, Catherine, decd, late of Jefferson Co., George W. Collins issued L/A 7/1/1824, Benjamin Rowland, Jesse Kent, secs, Richmond, AB
DORSEY, Isaac, decd, James M. Dorsey issued L/A, Jones W. Roark, sec, 12/6/1852, Hall, AB
DORSEY, Isaac, decd, John R. Dorsey issued temp L/A 11/6/1848, H. J. Dorsey, sec, Hall, AB
DORSEY, Joel, decd, 1/26/1843; apprs: Benjamin Culpepper, Edmond Outlaw, Moses Pipkin; Daniel J. Bothwell, admr, Dooly, I&A
DOSS, Edward, decd, W. G. Woodward, S. Doss, admrs, B. E. Strickland, James W. Wilson, sur, 6/2/1873, Gwinnett, AB
DOSS, John, decd, LWT pvd 5/2/1842, wife, Sarah, extrx, Harris
DOSSEY, Daniel, minor of Elias, decd, John Milner, Jr. apptd gdn, Matthew Rainey, sur, 6/1802, Oglethorpe, MIC
DOSSEY, John, minor orph of Elias, decd, Jeremiah Boggas and Susannah Boggas apptd gdns, John Collier, John Gresham, surs, 6/1802, Oglethorpe, MIC
DOSSEY, Rebeccah, minor orph of Elias, decd, Jeremiah Boggas and Susannah Boggas apptd gdns, John Collier, John Gresham, surs, 6/1802, Oglethorpe, MIC
DOSTER, William, decd, Micajah Williamson apptd admr 10/25/1783, Wilkes, MxR
DOTHARD, Mary C., decd, of Anderson Dist, South Carolina, Samuel G. Pegg issued L/A 8/3/1857, Fulton
DOTY, Hull, decd, John Hardy qualified as admr 4/26/1783, Liberty, Ests
DOUBLEHEAD, Bird, orph, Zachariah Sims, gdn, 3/3/1817, Joseph Brown, Richard Shackleford, Richard Cox, L. A. Erwin, surs, Clarke, GB
DOUGHERTY, Charles, decd, Rebecca Dougherty, gdn of Jane R., Charles, William and Robert, orphs, 7/3/1815, Richard Cox, Thomas Moore, Surs, Clarke, GB
DOUGHTRY, Bryan, decd, Joseph Oswald, admr qualified 2/3/1785, Liberty, Ests
DOUGLAS, Daniel B., Alexander Douglas, gdn, p. 90, Screven, OM
DOUGLAS, Elizabeth, Alexander Douglas, gdn, p. 90, Screven, OM
DOUGLAS, Hannah W., Henry Bryan, gdn, p. 8, Screven, OM
DOUGLAS, John, decd, Eldred Swain, admr, appraisal 10/20/1832, Emanuel, A
DOUGLAS, John, decd, Alex Douglas, admr, p. 86, Screven, OM
DOUGLAS, John, decd, James Blackmon, etc., divides est, p. 86, Screven, OM

DOUGLAS, Thomas, decd, Edward Bond, admr, bond 12/22/1807, Peter
Randolph, Sur, Clarke, AB
DOUGLAS, William, decd, Samuel and Martin Douglas, admrs, 1810
retns, recd real estate for Thomas, Francis, William and Samuel
Douglas and Sterling and Francis Jenkins and John Sherman, signed
S. Douglas, Wilkes, Retns
DOUGLASS, Alexander, relieved from bond, p. 136, Screven, OM
DOUGLASS, Eugenious L., minor of William S., decd, Thomas
Douglass, exr, bd pd for 1839, Butts, ER
DOUGLASS, Francis, decd, Robert G. Dukes issued temp L/A, James
H. Stark, John Andrews, sur, 8/10/1847, permanent L/A issued
9/16/1847, Charles Bailey and Robert Douglass, surs, 9/16/1847,
Butts, AB
DOUGLASS, James, decd, inventory 9/9/1791, Effingham, Misc
DOUGLASS, Marcellus, minor of William S., decd, Thomas Douglass,
exr, 4/6/1840, Butts, ER
DOUGLASS, Martha R., orph of Robert F., decd, Robert G. Duke,
gdn, Richard G. Byars, James R. McCord, sur, 1/13/1851, Butts, GB
DOUGLASS, Narcissa, minor of William S., decd, Thomas Douglass,
exr, 4/6/1840, Butts, ER
DOUGLASS, Robert, decd, Edward Douglass issued L/A 6/6/1808, Mark
Mayo, sec, Laurens, AB
DOUGLASS, Robert F., decd, Sarah Jane Douglass, admx, Charles
Bailey, Robert Douglass, sur, 9/16/1847, Butts, AB
DOUGLASS, Samuel, decd, William L. & Robt Douglass L/A 7/4/1825;
Jos P. Pinick, gdn of legatee, Charles Coleman 11/7/1825; Wm
Douglass, gdn of Francis, Eliza, Martha, Elizabeth & Jane
11/7/1825, Morgan, AB, GB
DOUGLASS, Sarah Jane, orph of Samuel, decd, Francis Douglass,
gdn, Thomas Douglass, Robert G. Duke, sur, 7/3/1837, Butts, GB
DOUGLASS, Walter T., orph of Robert F., decd, Robert G. Duke,
gdn, Richard G. Byars and James R. McCord, surs, 1/13/18151,
Butts, GB
DOUGLASS, William F., orph of Robert F., decd, Robert G. Duke,
gdn, Richard G. Byars, James R. McCord, sur, 1/13/1851, Butts, GB
DOUGLASS, William S., decd, Thomas Douglass, exr pd from est of
William M. Williams, 2/6/1840; 1839 retn pd D. L. Bailey, John
McCord, J. Anderson, D. L. Bailey, Henry Duke, Butts, ER
DOUGLISS, Amaris, decd., Rhoda Dougliss, admx., A. C. Lanier,
Eldred Swain, sur., 9/3/1832, Emanuel, AB
DOUGLISS, David, orph. of John, decd., Prudence Dougliss, A.
Sumner, E. Swain, gdns., 9/3/1832 Emanuel, GB
DOUGLISS, James, orph. of John, decd., Prudence Dougliss, A.
Sumner, E. Swain, gdns., 9/3/1832, Emanuel, GB
DOUGLISS, John, decd., Prudence Dougliss, Wm. Dougliss, A. C.
Sumner, admrs., 9/3/1832, Emanuel, AB
DOUGLISS, Laura, orph. of John, decd., Prudence Dougliss, A.
Sumner, E. Swain, gdns., 9/3/1832, Emanuel, GB
DOUGLISS, Nancy, orph. of John, decd., Prudence Dougliss, A.
Sumner, E. Swain, gdns., 9/3/1832, Emanuel, GB
DOUGLISS, Rebecca, orph. of John, decd., Prudence Dougliss, A.
Sumner, E. Swain, gdns. 9/3/1832, Emanuel, GB
DOUGLISS, Susanna, orph. of John, decd., Prudence Dougliss, A.
Sumner, E. Swain, gdns., 9/3/1832, Emanuel, GB
DOURY, William, decd, LWT was admitted to record 3/4/1834,
Effingham, MIC
DOVE, Thomas, decd, LWT pvd by David Dove and Thomas Dove
1/10/1801, Warren, MIC
DOWNIE, Charles, decd, Samuel Goff and Daniel McMurphey issued
L/A 11/6/1817, George Adams, Wm Micou, secs, Richmond, AB
DOWNIE, David, decd, Samuel Goff and Charles Downie issued L/A
5/9/1817, George Adams, Henry Shultz, secs, Richmond, AB

DOWNING, Charlotte, late Whitman, decd, Isaac Whorton, Eli McConnell and Robert Dowdy, temp admrs, Benjamin Whorton, James and John McConnell, 1/2/1832, Hall, AB

DOWNING, George, decd, Richard Winn, admr w/LWT annexed, John Cain, James Law, secs, 5/7/1832, Hall, AB

DOWNS, James, decd, LWT pvd, L/T issued Nancy and Shelley Downs 9/1/1817, Jasper, OM

DOWNS, William, decd, LWT pvd by Thomas P. Bunkley; Winnifred Downs, Robert Stafford qualified exrs, 1/5/1830, Camden, MIC

DOWNS, William, decd, Robert Stafford, one of exrs, was dismissed, 6/3/1833, Camden, MIC

DOWSE, Gideon, decd, G. Dowse, admr, John Elliott, Thomas Bradwell, exrs qualified 3/17/1790, Liberty, Ests

DOYLE, John, decd, John Pond issued L/A 6/17/1820, Thomas Watkins, sec, Richmond, AB

DOZIER, Allen T., decd, R. M. Brown, admr, 11/7/1853, DeKalb, AB

DOZIER, Elias, decd, John Bailey, admr, and heirs being absent from State, Jacob T. Goodbread apptd to wind up est 1/7/1840, Camden, MIC

DOZIER, Elias, decd, LWT pvd by G. Pervical Cohen 3/7/1836, John Bailey qualified admr 1/3/1837, Camden, MIC

DOZIER, Elias, decd, Samuel Mew of Beaufort District, South Carolina pvd the marriage to Eliza M. Dozier 2/27/1840, decd´s daghter having right to negroes in hands of J. T. Goodbread; Eliza had interest in the slaves left to his son, Leonard Dozier, 1/7/1841, Camden, MIC

DOZIER, James, decd, James Dozier and John Dozier, L/T on LWT, pvd by William and Thomas Berry, 1/4/1808, Warren, MIC

DOZIER, L. W., Jr., decd, J. H. Carter, exr, 6/1862, Webster, OD

DRAKE, Sherrod, decd, Jesse White, admr, 5/5/1806, Samuel Alexander, sur, Warren, AB

DRAKE, John, LWT probated, 11/1/1813, Warren, MIC

DRAKE, John, decd, William Drake of North Carolina qualified as exr of LWT 1/7/1814, Warren, MIC

DRAKE, Matthew, decd, John Drake apptd admr 9/4/1809, Warren, MIC

DRAKE, Shimei, decd, Jesse White apptd temp admr, Samuel Alexander, sur 3/24/1806, Warren, MIC

DRAKE, Thomas, decd, LWT pvd by James Robinson, 9/20/1794, Warren, MIC

DRANE, James, decd, of Burn Pot, Nicholas Miller apptd admr 8/31/1789, Chatham, Adms

DREW, Alexander, decd, John Balfour issued L/A 11/9/1840, William Glendenning, sec, Richmond, AB

DREW, Jane Catherine, illeg, Thomas Drew, gdn, A. L. Kirkland, Levy Drew, sur, 9/6/1830, Emanuel, GB

DREW, Willis, decd, Thomas Moore and Margaret Drew issued L/A 7/6/1818, Laurens, AB

DRIGGORS, James, son of Jordan, to be bound unto Michael Young for 9 yrs 5/6/1822, Bulloch, MIC

DRIGGORS, Jonas, decd, Elenor Driggors issued L/A 11/3/1821, inventory and appraisement of estate, one tract in Walton Co. 3/4/1822, Bulloch, MIC, Misc

DRIGHAM, John, decd, Elizabeth Drigham issued L/A, Adam Johnston, sec, 7/6/1840, 1841 retn "support for myself and child during year", Richmond, AB

DRISCOLL, Dennis, decd, George Adams issued L/A, Peter Donaldson, Lewis Calfrey, secs, Richmond, AB

DRIVER, James, decd, James Blair 7/1833, Habersham, MIC

DRUMMOND, Francis E., minor of Matthew, decd, Micajah Fincher, gdn, C. Cox, N. H. Neely, sur, 1/10/1853, Cherokee, GB

DRUMMOND, Matthew, decd, Micajah Fincher, admr, Carr Cox, N.
Hutson Wiley, sur, 1/10/1853; James M. Fielder, admr, Henry G.
Ellison, sur, 11/7/1853, Cherokee, AB
DRUMMOND, Richard, orph of John, decd, James Drummond, gdn,
10/18/1826, Robert S. Hardaway, William F. Drummond, secs,
10/18/1826, Morgan, GB
DRUMMOND, William, James M. Fielder, gdn, James Haggert, sur,
4/10/1854, Cherokee, GB
DRUMMOND, William, minor of Matthew, decd, Micajah Fincher, gdn,
C. Cox, N. H. Neely, sur, 1/10/1853, Cherokee, GB
DRUSHER, George, decd, of Savannah, LWT pvd, L/T issued to Jacob
Casper, 11/11/1787, Chatham, Adms
DRYER, Edmund, orph, over 14 yrs old, William Ward apptd gdn,
1/4/1819, Liberty, MIC
DRYSDALE, Alexander, decd, John Jackson, admr qualified 3/1790,
Liberty, Ests
DRYSDALE, Sarah, decd, LWT pvd by H. A. Elbert, H. S. Pratt, Mary
and Charlotte Drysdale qualified exrs, 1/2/1838, Camden, MIC
DUBERRY, Jesse, decd, Mary and Henry Duberry, admrs, 12/10/1804,
Jacob Darden, sur, Warren, AB
DUBERRY, Jesse, decd, Henry Duberry, Harris McFarling, 10/1/1804,
temp admrs; 12/11/1804, Polly and Henry Duberry apply for perm
ltrs adm, Warren, MIC
DUBOSE, Ezekiel, decd, Lawrence Toombs, gdn for orphs: James R.,
William E., Martha Julian and Kaleb Sidney, 3/3/1823, Micajah T.
Anthony, sec, Lincoln, GB
DUBOSE, James, and wife gtd leave to sell prop, p. 7, p. 76,
Screven, OM
DUCKETT, Alfred H., decd, Malinda Duckett issued temporary L/A
6/25/1860, William and Champion Ferguson, secs; John and Malinda
Duckett issued L/A 8/6/1860, Wm Ferguson, Thomas Brock, Cary Cox,
secs, White, AB
DUCKWORTH, Gazaway, minor of William, decd, Joseph Duckworth,
gdn; Jeremiah Duckworth, his grandfather's est mentioned
3/1/1813, Warren, MIC
DUCKWORTH, Jeremiah, decd, Joseph Duckworth and Ranella?
Duckworth apptd admrs, 11/6/1809, Warren, MIC
DUCKWORTH, Joseph, minor of William, decd, Joseph Duckworth, gdn;
Jeremiah Duckworth, his grandfather's est mentioned 3/1/1813,
Warren, MIC
DUCKWORTH, Nelly, minor of William, decd, Joseph Duckworth, gdn;
Jeremiath Duckworth, her grandfather's est mentioned 3/1/1813,
Warren, MIC
DUCKWORTH, Polly, minor child of William, decd, being over 14,
chooses Joseph Duckworth as gdn; Jeremiah Duckworth, decd, her
grandfather's est mentioned 3/1/1813, Warren, MIC
DUCKWORTH, Rebecca, minor child of William, decd, being over 14,
chooses Joseph Duckworth as gdn; Jeremiah Duckworth, decd, her
grandfather's est mentioned 3/1/1813, Warren, MIC
DUCKWORTH, Samuel, decd, Joseph Culpepper, admr, 2/4/1822, Edward
Kinsey, William Terry, surs, Warren, AB
DUCKWORTH, Samuel, minor child of William, decd, being over 14,
chooses Joseph Duckworth as gdn; Jeremiah Duckworth, decd, her
grandfather's est mentioned 3/1/1813, Warren, MIC
DUCKWORTH, William, decd, Joseph Leonard, admr, 1/2/1827, David
Cody, Samuel Story, surs, Warren, AB
DUCKWORTH, William, decd, Rebecca Duckworth and Joseph Duckworth
apptd admrs 3/6/1809; Mrs. Rebecca Duckworth, relict, chooses her
1/3rd of estate 7/3/1810, Warren, MIC
DUDLEY, Benjamin, decd, estate 5/4/1840, Clarke, LP
DUDLEY, C., decd, James Dudley, minor, James Nunn, gdn, David Ees
Hutchen, surs, 5/7/1838, Emanuel, GB

DUDLEY, Guilford, decd, Bradford Jones applies for L/A 1/13/1846, ct decided he was not entitled to admn for reasons stated in caveat, 1/13/1846, Effingham, MIC
DUDLEY, James, minor, James Nunn, gdn., Wm. Phillips, Dempsey Phillips, sur., 1/12/1840, Emanuel, GB
DUDLEY, John, decd, James Dudley apptd admr 12/26/1792, apprs: Thomas Haney, Saml Spears, Manuel McConnell, Elbert, AB
DUDLEY, William H. chooses his mother for his gdn 9/6/1841, Effingham, MIC
DUFOUR, Lewis, decd, LWT pvd, Mrs. Mary Dufour qualified as extrx 1/3/1848; John J. and Alonzo B. Dufour, admrs 3/1/1852, Camden, MIC
DUFOUR, Mary M., decd, Jane Guebert apptd admx w/LWT annexed 1/5/1852, Camden, MIC
DUGGER, Emanuel D., decd, John Dugger gtd L/A 1/3/1831, Effingham, MIC
DUGGER, Hugh, decd, Harry Dugger applies for L/A 9/27/1841, Effingham, MIC
Dugger, John, decd, Paul Marlow and B. Edwards qualified exrs of LWT 3/6/1837; LWT declared null and void 3/6/1837; LWT admitted to record 7/5/1841, Effingham, MIC
DUKE, Ann, minor orph of Aristotle G., decd, Eli Conger, gdn, Thomas B. Burford, sur, 11/14/1840, Butts, GB
DUKE, Aristotle, minor orph of Aristotle G., decd, Eli Conger, gdn, Thomas B. Burford, sur, 11/14/1840, Butts, GB
DUKE, Aristotle G., decd, Charles A. Killgore, admr, appraisers: Robert Grimmett, John Jinks, Dory Taylor, Samuel P. Burford, Washington G. Atkinson, 9/9/1836; distributive shares pd to minors--- Ann, Polly, Coatsworth, William Elizabeth and Aristotle Duke; also to John Duke, Sarah Duke, William E. Jones, 12/2/1840, Butts, ER
DUKE, Aristotle S., Charles Killgore, admr, William Killgore, Henry Duke, sur, 9/5/1836, Butts, AB
DUKE, Charles, decd, retns of Dorothy Williams, formerly Duke, admx; 1814 pd William Killgore, Christobel, Rebecca and Lavinia Duke, Wilkes, Retns
DUKE, Elizabeth, minor orph of Aristotle G., decd, Eli Conger, gdn, Thomas B. Burford, sur, 11/14/1840, Butts, GB
DUKE, Henry, decd, LT pvd 11/14/1782, ch: Charles (under age), Mary, Thomas; bros: Thomas and James and Stephen Heard, exrs; "father and mother to live with my children", Wilkes, MxR
DUKE, Isom, decd, Epps Duke, present admr, revoked, he having failed to comply with the laws, 5/1/1815, Jasper, OM
DUKE, John, Archibald Hodges, gdn, 1/7/1839, Tattnall, GB
DUKE, John, decd, LWT pvd 3/6/1848, May Duke, James M. Walker, William B. Marshall, exrs, Harris
DUKE, Mary Ann, Archibald Hodges, makes retn as gdn 12/22/1836, Tattnall, I&A
DUKE, Polly Cotesworth, minor orph of Aristotle G., decd, Eli Conger, gdn, Thomas B. Burford, sur, 11/14/1840, Butts, GB
DUKE, Taylor, decd, henry Duke issued L/A 9/13/1823, E. Butler, sec, Morgan, AB
DUKE, William, minor orph of Aristotle G., decd, Eli Conger, gdn, Thomas B. Burford, sur, 11/14/1840, Butts, GB
DUKES, John, decd, Nancy Dukes produced the LWT 1/5/1824, Bulloch, MIC
DUKES, John, LWT refers to wife and children (not named), exrs: Edward Sikes, Nancy Dukes, 6/23/1820, Bulloch, Misc
DUKES, John, decd, inventory and appraisement of est by William Duggar, John Shuffield, John Rogers, 3/30/1824, Bulloch, Misc
DUKES, Robert, decd, Sarah Dukes and John Sessions issued L/A 5/2/1814, Laurens, AB

DULLANAY, William, decd, Ralph Kilgore, creditor apptd admr 10/15/1782, Wilkes, MxR
DUNAGAN, Ezekiel, decd, Benjamin Dunagan issued L/A 10/3/1837, Isaiah Dunagan, Jas M. McCleskey, David G. Eberhart, secs; Jas J. McCleskey, gdn of: Stephen R., Geo. W., Levi J., Daniel C. and Mary J., orphs, Dunagan, secs, Hall, AB, GB
DUNCAN, David, decd, Leonard Cecil, admr, qualified 2/20/1790, Liberty, Ests
DUNCAN, James E., decd, Catharine C. Duncan, gdn of orphs: James R., Clinton C. and Elliot E., 12/3/1855, Houston, GB
DUNCAN, James, Sr., decd., James Duncan, Jr., admr., 5/14/1834, Baldwin, AB
DUNCAN, William, decd, Edmund Duncan, Richard Pounds, admrs, 9/2/1839, Harris, AB
DUNHAM, Rebecca, decd, 11/2/1840 apprs apptd, Andrew McLean, admr, Richmond
DUNHAM, William, decd, Martin Willcox issued L/A 5/4/1838, James T. Barton, sec, Richmond, AB
DUNHAM, William, decd, Samuel Dunham gdn of minor orphs: Thomas and Mary Ann; Andrew McLean apptd gdn 9/2/1840, Richmond, GB
DUNHAM, William, decd, Joseph Law, John Dunham, admrs qualified 5/2/1783, Liberty, Ests
DUNKIN, Joseph (Capt.), decd, late of Wilkes Co., Matthew Dunkin issued L/A 12/2/1782; appraisers: Martain Malone, Wm Standford, Wm Wright, Richmond, AB
DUNKLEY, Carleton, decd, William J. Hobby issued L/A 8/1/1810, William Longstreet, sec, Richmond, AB
DUNN, Ann, free girl of color, dau of Sally, age 7, is bound to Turman Walthall for 14 yrs, William F. Stodgehill, sur, 7/7/1851, Butts, GB
DUNN, Benjamin, decd, Nehemiah Dunn issued L/A 1/8/1785, Isaac Prison, Samuel Johnston, secs, Richmond, AB
DUNN, Beverly, decd, James Law issued L/A 9/7/1846, M. W. Brown, sec, Hall, AB
DUNN, Henry, decd, appr 1/30/1800; John Hicks, admr; pd Nancy Dunn, Jeremiah, Hinchier & Danby Lary; 8/16/1806 recpts: Wm Rabun for wife's 1/3rd pt; Willie Hillard, gdn for orphs--Wm, Henry and Susannah; Wm Evans for his wife, Hancock, AA
DUNN, John, decd, Nancy Dunn, Joseph Jackson, Davis Harrison applied for L/A 1/23/1799, Greene, Misc
DUNN, Josiah, decd, Barnard Heard, R. P. gtd L/A to Nehemiah Dunn of Richmond Co. 7/1/1783, Wilkes, MxR
DUNNISEN, Daniel, decd, Darby Dunnisen apptd admr 5/17/1778, Wilkes, MxR
DUNNISEN, Darby, decd, Elizabeth Dunnisen, wid, apptd admx 10/15/1782, Wilkes, MxR
DUNY, John, decd, Thomas Elkins applies for adm 1/28/1829, Effingham, MIC
DUPREE, James, decd, LWT pvd 5/2/1836, Jacob Dupree, exr, Washington
DUPREE, Timothy R., decd, LWT pvd 9/6/1841, Permelia O. O. Dupree and James A. R. Kennedy, exrs, Washington
DURBIN, Luke, decd, L/A to Sarah Durbin 10/29/1803; petition of Agrippa Atkinson that Sarah Durbin, admx, make clear titles to land on Beech Creek 9/5/1808, Jackson, OM
DURHAM, General W., decd, William Sitton issued L/A 12/5/1853, E. M. Johnson, sec, Hall, AB
DURHAM, John C., decd, L/A issued Mrs. Casdra Durham 1/1870; non-cupative Will offered for probate, 2/1870, Webster, OD
DURHAM, Laura A. R., minor orph of William, decd, William McD. Durham, gdn, 11/5/1860, Fulton, GB

DURHAM, Mary, decd, J. L. C. Durham, admr, admits LWT to record 11/1868, Webster, OD
DURHAM, Mary Ann E., minor orph of William, decd, William McD. Durham, gdn, 11/5/1860, Fulton, GB
DURHAM, Thomas, decd, William A. Durham issued L/A 12/1865, Webster, OD
DURLEY, Thomas, Minnie Bell, Alvin, Katie and Vester, all minor children sent to Orphan's House in Decatur, Ga., sd minors being deserted by their father, and their mother dead, 12/21/1908, Clarke, LP
DUSKY, John, decd, caveat on LWT, land given to four sons equally, widow, sole extrx, by Nancy Dusky, 9/6/1819, Jasper, OM
DUVAL, Suzette, an insane person, investigation made by the ct into her affairs; Samuel Clarke, gdn, to make report, 6/6/1820; caveat filed by Samuel Clark, gdn, 9/18/1815, John Boog apptd gdn (Samuel Clark having been removed) 1/1/1821, Camden, MIC
DUVAL, Suzette, Lemuel Church, gdn of "free woman of color", reported, 1/7/1834, Camden, MIC
DUVAL, Suzette, R. Brunette petitions ct on behalf of his sister, Suzette, for Dr. Lemuel Church to be her gdn in lieu of John Boog, decd, 11/17/1825, Camden, MIC
DWELLE, Lemuel, apptd gdn of his ch: Charlotte F., Lemuel and Lucy A., minors, 5/16/1836, Richmond, GB
DYASS, Jeremiah, decd, Willoughby Barton issued temp L/A 12/4/1797, George and Littleton Wyche, secs; John Dyass apptd permt admr 6/16/1798, having filed caveat, Richmond, AB
DYE, Martin, decd, LWT pvd 1/4/1808 names sons---Stephen Mayfield Dye, Beckham Dye, George Dye, Benjamin Dye, John Dye, Prettyman Dye, Randolph Dye and Martin Dye; daus-Catharine Mayfield, wife of Edmund, Mary Jackson, wife of Micajah, Rebeccah Smith, wife of Joel; wf, Catharine, Franklin, OM
DYESS, Elizabeth, decd, Josiah H. Carter gtd L/A on 3/1856, Webster, OD
DYESS, George, decd, Elizabeth and William C. Dyess, admrs 1/1842; appraisers: Jonas Griffin, John Winzer, A. C. and Henry Spears, John O. Stapleton; purchasers at sale: George W., Thomas D. and Wingfield S. Dyess, etc., Stewart, Adms
DYESS, George, decd, Josiah H. Carter gtd L/A 3/1856, Webster, OD
DYESS, George H., decd, J. C. Carter gtd L/A 1/1862, Webster, OD
DYESS, George H., minor of G. H., decd, Mrs. M. A. Dyess apptd gdn 3/1864; Robert Parker gtd L/G 7/1864, Webster, OD
DYESS, John, decd, Robert Hendry, admr, makes retn 3/4/1836, Tattnall, I&A
DYKES, Angelina, William Dykes, gdn, Dooly, OD
DYKES, Daniel M., Norvell R. Truluck, gdn, Dooly, OD
DYKES, Hubbard, decd, appr 11/7/1798, John C. Peek, admr, Hancock, AA
DYKES, James R., William Dykes, gdn, Dooly, OD
DYKES, Jesse, decd, LWT admitted to record 11/2/1835, Effingham, MIC
DYKES, John E., decd, William N. Dykes, admr, Dooly, OD
DYSART, Cornelius (Dr.), decd, L/A issued to Charity Dysart and Samuel Jack 6/25/1800, William Longstreet, Samuel Barnett, secs, Richmond, AB
EADES, Thomas, minor heir of Thomas and Martha, decd, John B. Nichols, gdn, 12/14/1838, Hall, GB
EADY, Permelia, orph of James, decd, James Roberts, gdn, E. M. Johnson, sec, 10/4/1853, Hall, GB
EAMS, Zedekiah, decd, John Everitt allowed his account against est, 4/1/1816, Bulloch, MIC
EARLY, Gad, decd, Burkett Dean, admr, Clarke, AB

EASON, Elisha H., minor orph of Abraham, decd, chose Archelus
Pope, gdn, George Phillips, sec, 7/1807. Oglethorpe, GB, OM
EASON, Emily, minor of Rasberry, decd, J. R. Harbin for release
as security to be heard Dec term, the death of Emily suggested,
J. L. Eason apptd admr, 11/1/1869; pet of J. S. Eason for leave
to sell real est, 1/4/1869, Cobb, MIC
EASON, R., decd, O. R. Eason, admr, J. R. Harbin mismanagement to
be heard Dec term, 11/1/1869, Cobb, MIC
EASON, William, decd, Daniel Sikes, Michael M. Eason, exrs, file
retn 9/5/1836, Tattnall, I&A
EAST, Isaac, decd, John East issued temp L/A, Jeffrey A. Horton,
sec, 3/19/1849, Hall, AB
EASTEN, Phillip, decd, Daniel D. Denham, gdn of orphs, E. P.
Nickson, J. H. Elder, surs, 1/1841, 1841 retn, Fayette, GB
EASTEN, Silas G., decd, Elijah Cleckler, exr of LWT, 1851-1853
retns, Fayette
EASTER, Catherine, Polley Easter apptd gdn 9/7/1818, Jasper, OM
EASTER, Champion, William Easter, gdn, 1803 retn, Elbert, GR
EASTER, James, decd, Wm Thompson applied for L/A 4/19/1796,
Elbert, AB
EASTER, James Tucker, decd, Woodford Mabry apptd admr 1/8/1805,
Camden, MIC
EASTERS, John, decd, John L. Easters, admr, 1832, debts pd to:
Solomon Harrell, Andrew Orr, Henry Audulf, Dr. A. P. Pope, Joseph
Tooke, Thomas E. Rodgers, Stewart, Adms
EASTON, Charles, decd, Wm Davis applied for L/A 12/11/1792, inv
includes 200 acres in Va.; apprs: Richard Coulter, Hezekiah Gray,
Absolom Baker, Elbert, AR
EASTON, Eliza, minor orph of Abraham, decd, chose Archelus Pope,
gdn, George Phillips, sec, 7/1807. Oglethorpe, GB, OM
EASTON, John, decd, Sally and Reuben Easton apply for L/A
12/11/1792; apprs: Richard Coulter, Hezekiah Gay, Absolom Baker,
Elbert, AR
EASTON, Phillip, orph of John, decd, Stephen Grenade apptd gdn,
William Lay, sur, 7/1806, Oglethorpe, MIC
EATON, James, son of Sally, bound to Patrick Cash for 18 years,
7/9/1806, Jackson, OM
EATON, John, decd, LWT probated, Abraham Bessant, exr, 4/14/1807,
Camden, MIC
EATON, Joseph, John Brown, gdn, ordered that he receive sd
minor's share of John Eaton's est, 6/17/1816, Camden, MIC
EATON, Joseph, minor heir of John, decd, William Bailey apptd
gdn, 6/8/1819, Camden, MIC
EBERHART, James W., orph of John, decd, Jacob Eberhart, gdn,
James Saye, H. Jarratt, secs, 1/2/1838, Hall, GB
ECHOLS, Elijah, minor orph of Obediah, decd, James Echols apptd
gdn, James Rutledge, Thomas Dunn, surs, 6/18/1800; Joseph
Echols, gdn, 9/1806, Oglethorpe, OM, MIC
ECHOLS, Nancy (now Nancy Rutledge), dau of Obediah Echols,
releases her gdn, Joseph Echols, 6/17/1800, Oglethorpe, MIC
ECHOLS, Obediah, minor of Obediah, decd, Joseph Echols apptd gdn,
6/18/1800, John Hardman, James Rutledge, surs, Oglethorpe, MIC
ECHOLS, Philip H., decd, William Hartsfield, W. C. Osborn, J. C.
Gray, admrs, 3/7/1836, Harris
ECHOLS, Richard, decd, Jacob Loughridge, admr, prays to be
dismissed 1/7/1822, Jasper, OM
ECHOLS, Richard, decd, L/A gtd Jacob Lanthridge 3/4/1816, Isaac
R. Dyke, Benjamin Echols, surs, Jasper, OM
ECTOR, John, decd, LWT pvd, L/T gtd Asa Rogers (or Ragan), Robert
Freeman and Hugh W. Ector, 3/1/1819, Jasper, OM

EDDINGTON, James, decd, LWT dtd 10/2/1856, pvd 2/14/1860, names wife, Mary and ch: Hanibal A., Martha B. Stephens, wife of Thomas T., Leah Bennett, wife of Hiram, Annett A. Bennett, wife of Freeman, Cherokee

EDDY, Henry, Sarah Eddy, John K. Eddy, Jonathan Eddy, gdns, 12/19/1838, Harris

EDENFIELD, John, illegitimate son of Medcy Edenfield, James M. Tapley, gdn, A. E. Wiggins, sur, 9/6/1841, Emanuel

EDENFIELD, William, decd, Cooper, LWT dtd 8/18/1781, James Harnott and Alexander Cunningham, late of sd co., exrs, both are absent from State; Mary Edenfield apptd 12/12/1788, Chatham, Adms

EDMONDSON, Ambrose, decd, William G. Edmondson, admr, 9/6/1824, Hackakiah McMath, Henry Hinton, surs, Warren, AB

EDMONDSON, Benjamin C., decd, William Cook and John Wilson issued L/A 9/7/1818, Jasper, OM

EDMONDSON, Hilmary, decd, Thomas Edmondson, one of exrs, produced LWT 5/7/1821, Jasper, OM

EDMONDSON, Mary, decd, John Neal qualified as exr of LWT 1/7/1822, Jasper, OM

EDMONDSON, William, decd, Nathaniel W. Cocke issued L/A 1/5/1835, Western B. Thomas, sec, Richmond, AB

EDMONDSON, William, decd, William Hurt, admr, 2/14/1831, Henry Harris, Nathan Turner, surs, Warren, AB

EDMONSON, William, decd, Abner Zachery issued L/A 9/8/1823, George S. Bird, sec, Morgan, AB

EDWARDS, Anthony P., decd, James Edwards, gdn 1/20/1845, Effingham, MIC

EDWARDS, Edward M., decd, Robert J. Massey issued L/A 12/7/1865, Fulton

EDWARDS, Enoch, decd, LWT pvd 1/11/1831 names wife, Easter and ch: Enoch, Easter, William, Martha, Deborah, Elizabeth Wills, Thomas, James, Barbary Allen, Priscilla Flack; sons-in-law, John Whitaker and Newman Wills, Habersham, MIC

EDWARDS, Isaac, decd, LWT names son, William, "all my children", $500 note to Hannah Haiti to be raised from est, exrs: son, William Edwards, Joseph Edwards, dtd 7/2/1809, pvd 8/7/1809, Franklin, OM

EDWARDS, James, decd, Daniel A. McCollum issued temp L/A, W. T. Sears, sec, 10/2/1865, White, AB

EDWARDS, James, decd, John Hill, admr, 1811-1813 retns, expenses to Abbeville and Elbert Co., Wilkes, Retns

EDWARDS, James M., decd, Edward Edwards, admr, William F. Mullins, James M. Daniel, sur, 12/12/1855, Cherokee, AB

EDWARDS, John, orph of Charles, decd, bound to Richard Heath, no date, Jackson, OM

EDWARDS, Peter, decd, David Martin, admr, A. Chastain, sec, 11/4/1839, Hall, AB

EDWARDS, Robert, decd, William Edwards, Thomas Avera, admrs, 11/6/1820, Henry Hight, Richard Bray, surs, Warren, AB

EDWARDS, Susan A., minor, John Rivers, Jarrel Beasley, Francis Montune, Turner Hunt and John Jackson apptd to appraise property 1/7/1822, Jasper, OM

EDWARDS, Susan A., orph of Herbert of Brunswick Co., Virginia, chose John Moreland her gdn, having considerable property in Virginia, 9/29/1821, Jasper, OM

EDWARDS, William, decd, Catherine Edwards issued L/A 1/6/1787, Savage Littleton, James Wilkinson, secs; apprs Wm Stanford, Samuel Langston, Matthew Duncan, 10/18/1787, Richmond, AB

EDWARDS, William, decd, LWT pvd 11/4/1833, Effingham, MIC

EDWARDS, William, decd, Zachariah Brantley, admr, 11/4/1833, Washington

EDY, Elizabeth, decd, why W. Gunnells or other person should not be admr of est 11/1857, Webster, OD
EDY, James, decd, John Edy, gdn for orphs: William and Permelia 2/5/1838, Lincoln, GB
ELAM, A. G., decd, est set apart to widow and children 1/1863, Webster, OD
ELBERT, Samuel, decd, Elizabeth Elbert, extrx, 12/15/1789, Chatham, Adms
ELDER, John, decd, Richard Cox, gdn of Jack, Jerry, Joseph, David and Doctor Washington Patrick Henry Elder, orphs, 9/7/1812, David Holmes, Sterling Elder, surs, Clarke, GB
ELDER, John, decd, Sterling Elder, admr, 3/3/1812 bond, James Langford, Joseph Brown, Peter Randolph, surs, Clarke, AB
ELDER, Sterling, decd, Charles Clements, gdn for orphs: Howell, Sterling, Mary E. and Martha A., 5/1835, Fayette, GB
ELDER, William, decd, of Greene Co., John McAlister and Lydia Elder applied for L/A 1/28/1797, Greene, Misc
ELEBEE, Allen, statement of the amt of property recd by Jesse Elebee, gdn, from David Lastinger, his former gdn dtd 7/20/1824, Bulloch, Misc
ELEBEE, Isham, decd, recd of William Brown $111.00, etc. for Allen Elebee of sd estate, David Lastinger, gdn, 2/10/1822; retn of one of heirs, recd of William Brown for Allen Elebee of sd est, signed David Lastinger, gdn, 3/16/1822, Bulloch, Misc
ELEBEE, Isham, decd, recd of Mary Brown $457.91 being full amt of est by Allen Brown, decd, against heirs of Allen Brown, by R. T. Stanaland, gdn, Abraham Geiger, gdn, William Brown, gdn, Edward Elebee, Isham Elebee, 3/3/1821, Bulloch, Misc
ELERBEE, Allen, recd of Jesse Elerbee, my gdn, my pt of the share in full of est of my father, Isom Elerbee, decd, 4/8/1828, Bulloch, Misc
ELERBY, Allen, orph of Isham, decd, David Lastiner made retn 3/4/1822, Bulloch, MIC
ELERBY, Elizabeth, orph of Isham, decd, Abraham Geiger apptd gdn 1/1/1821, Bulloch, MIC
ELERBY, Jesse, orph of Isham, decd, Richard S. Stanaland apptd gdn 1/1/1821, Bulloch, MIC
ELERBY, William, orph of Isham, decd, Richard S. Stanaland apptd gdn 1/1/1821, Bulloch, MIC
ELKINS, Georgianna, Thomas Elkins apptd gdn 10/10/1836, Effingham, MIC
ELKINS, Herman, decd, Archibald Guyton applies for L/A 2/3/1836; 11/7/1836 div of est, Effingham, MIC
ELKINS, Lawrence T., Thomas Elkins apptd gdn 10/10/1836, Effingham, MIC
ELKINS, P. N., decd, Thomas Elkins applies for L/A 10/1846, Effingham, MIC
ELKINS, Solomon, decd, Selina Elkins applies for L/A 5/6/1830, Effingham, MIC
ELLINGTON, Celina H., orph of William, decd, Bethel B. Quillian, gdn, made retn 7/1837, Gilmer, Misc
ELLINGTON, Jervin F., orph of William, Coke A. Ellington, gdn, retn 7/1837, Gilmer, Misc
ELLINGTON, Priscilla, decd, Lewis D. Ellington, admr, 7/1837, Gilmer, Misc
ELLINGTON, Stephen, decd, Sr., expense, clothes for Stephen and Garland 1800; 1802 items-Jane & Robert, cloth, mother's coffin, etc.; 1798 items for Rice; heirs--Jno Langdon, Jr., Garland Ellington, Stephen, Ellington, Jr. and Rice Ellington; Wiley Thompson, admr, Elbert, AR

ELLINGTON, William, decd, inventory 4/28/1836; Priscilla, L. D. &
C. A. Ellington, gdns of orphs-William B. and Selina Ellington;
Lewis D. Ellington, admr; heirs recpts 11/1/1836--B. B. Quillian,
William P. King, C. A. Ellington and Priscilla Ellington, B. M.
Watkins, Gilmer, Misc
ELLIOT, Susan, Zack Elliot issued L/A 4/1871, Webster, OD
ELLIOTT, Abraham Bennet, minor, Elizabeth Elliott apptd gdn
11/2/1818, Jasper, OM
ELLIOTT, Alexander, decd, Rachel Elliott, John Elliott qualified
exrs of LWT, 1/5/1804, Camden, MIC
ELLIOTT, Alexander, minor, Richard Elliott apptd gdn 1/5/1804,
Camden, MIC
ELLIOTT, Alexander, pauper, ct directed Hezekiah Ponder be pd $24
from Poor Funds for maintaining; Ann Mizell allowed $15 for
supporting sd pauper, 1/6/1823, Camden, MIC
ELLIOTT, Cornelis C., Archibald Hodges retn as gdn 5/1/1837,
Tattnall, I&A
ELLIOTT, Irvine J., decd, Michael D. Garr, admr, William Thurman,
Sr., sec, 4/7/1862, Fulton, AB
ELLIOTT, James, decd, Mrs. Mary Elliott, wid, produced his LWT
for probate, 11/4/1816, Mary Elliott and Thomas Clark apptd admrs
w/LWT annexed 1/6/1817, Camden, MIC
ELLIOTT, James, decd, William Craig, in rt of wife, Mary, extrx,
gtd extn time to file Retn, 1/6/1823, Camden, MIC
ELLIOTT, James P., minor, Elizabeth Elliott apptd gdn 11/2/1818,
Jasper, OM
ELLIOTT, John, Rinchie Elliott, John Elliott, John Whitehead,
admrs, not dtd, Liberty, ests
ELLIOTT, John, decd, George Gales, admr, 5/6/1811, Camden, MIC
ELLIOTT, Martha, minor, Elizabeth Elliott apptd gdn 11/2/1818,
Jasper, OM
ELLIOTT, Martin V., decd, John C. Elliott, admr, 8/3/1857, James
S. Elliott, sur, DeKalb, AB
ELLIOTT, Mary E., minor, Elizabeth Elliott apptd gdn 11/2/1818,
Jasper, OM
ELLIOTT, Rachel, dau of Mary, decd, William Gibson, admr of James
Vincent est, gave his acct showing $3000 funds for Rachel; also
$3014.16 for ch of Ann Lane, decd, another heir, 1/5/1831,
Camden, MIC
ELLIOTT, Samuel, minor, Elizabeth Elliott apptd gdn 11/2/1818,
Jasper, OM
ELLIOTT, Summerville Haney, minor orph of Irvine J., decd,
William J. Hudson, gdn, Wesley Hudson, Benjamin Thurman, secs,
6/2/1862, Fulton, GB
ELLIOTT, Thomas, decd, Benjamin Elliott, sole exr 6/23/1789,
Chatham, Adms
ELLIOTT, Thomas, decd, Gideon Dowse, William Quarterman, Thomas
Sumner, exrs, LWT pvd 10/7/1783, Liberty, Ests
ELLIOTT, William, decd, James S. Elliott, admr, Martha Armstrong,
Thomas Fendrix, secs, Hall, AB
ELLIOTT, William, minor, Elizabeth Elliott apptd gdn 11/2/1818,
Jasper, OM
ELLIS, Elisha, decd, appr 5/14/1801, Hancock, AAAA
ELLIS, Mary, decd, Peter T. Bugg issued L/.A 5/2/1826, William A.
Bugg, sec, Richmond, AB
ELLIS, Radford, decd, LWT pvd by Daniel Smith, Richard Echols
and Luis McClain; L/T issued to Elizabeth, James and William
Ellis, 11/1812; legacies to wife, Elizabeth, ch: Wm, Amy (m. Jas
Stanley), Lucy McKessick, Jas, Elizabeth, Jno; grch: Radford
Berry, Presley Allen Berry, Jasper, OM
ELLIS, Shadrick, decd, A. N. Clardy, admr, 3/1/1852, Joseph
Caldwell, sur, DeKalb, AB

98

ELLIS, Thomas, decd, LWT pvd by Levi S. d´Lyon and E. Raiford, George W. Hardee qualified as exr 10/15/1851, Camden, MIC
ELLISON, Cunningham, decd, Benjamin Cleveland issued L/A 7/1832, Habersham, MIC
ELLISON, Ralph, decd, Dawson A. Walker issued L/A 11/5/1860, Fulton
ELMORE, James, decd, verbal LWT pvd, Simeon White, admr, 2/6/1815, Jackson, OM
ELROD, Abraham, decd, John Chastain, admr, Eaton Harris, John and Jacob Elrod, William Keith, secs, 11/20/1851, Hall, AB
ELROD, Adam, decd, of Carroll Co., Christopher Elrod, gdn, John Chastian, sec, of orphs: Isaac, Elizabeth, Westley and John, 5/3/1830, Hall, GB
ELSBERRY, Benjamin, decd, Benjamin Elsberry, exr, final retn 1/4/1808 pd Needham Norris and Absolom Sparks their pt, Nathan Sparks his pt, John Goodwin and Jeremiah Nisbet, their pt, Wilkes, Retns
ELTOFT, William, decd, George Pierson and George Morse issued L/A 5/5/1806, Daniel Bulger, Zachariah Bell, secs, Richmond, AB
ELTON, Charles, decd, LWT pvd 3/6/1837, Letha Elton, admx, Washington
ELY, Thomas L., decd, John Ely issued L/A 1/7/1820, Augustus Moore, Hosea Webster, George Webster, secs, 1822 retn pd 5 heirs: Seth, Abner L., Mary Ann Ely and Rev. John Ely as gdn, Horace Ely, Richmond, AB
ELZEY, Aaron, decd, Elizabeth Elzey apptd admr, 1805, Camden, MIC
ELZEY, Brittain, decd, Elizabeth Carney appl for dismission as admx, 1/3/1809, Camden, MIC
EMANUEL, Amos, decd, David, admr, p. 85, 103, Screven, OM
EMANUEL, Asa, decd, David, etc., admr, p. 112, 136, 155, 176, 183-187, Screven, OM
EMANUEL, Levi Jr., to pay $21.12 to Robert D. McKinnin, p. 71, Screven, OM
EMANUEL, Theophilus T., David Emanuel, gdn, p. 115 and 177, Screven, OM
EMBERSON, John, decd, John Stevenson and Galent Maxy, admrs, vs. Pascal Harrison and Thomas Watts, 2/1810, Morgan, SCW
EMEN, John, decd, Thomas C. Russell issued temp L/A 6/19/1811, Daniel Starnes, Zachariah Bell, secs; 6/14/1815 Dr. Alex Cunningham issued L/A, Richard H. Wilde, Thomas Glascock, secs, Richmond, AB
EMERSON, John, minor over 14 yrs, Reubin Rogers apptd gdn, 7/5/1813, Warren, MIC
ENGLAND, Joseph, decd, Matilda England issued temp L/A 5/2/1831; LWT dtd 4/9/1831, presented 7/3/1831 names ch: Powell, Harrison, Martin, Charley, Joseph, Arminda and Argin; sons-in-law, James McClain and J. H. Knox. Habersham, MIC
ENGLAND, Richard, decd, LWT dtd 6/5/1835, pvd 2/5/1836, names wife, Patsey, and "children", Habersham, MIC
ENGLISH, Jane, orph, Daniel Brinson, gdn, 8/2/1813, Tattnall, MIC
ENGLISH, Joseph, decd, Daniel Brinson, gdn of orphs: Nancy and Thomas 8/2/1813, Tattnall, MIC
ENGLISH, Thomas, orph, bound to James Corey for 8 yrs, 2/7/1814, Tattnall, MIC
EPERSON, Samuel, decd, inv 3/26/1796, Franklin, OM
EPERSON, Samuel, decd, Margaret Eperson, admx, 8/1838; apprs: Lewis Lee, L. Williams, John Whitaker; purchasers at sale: Mathew Brooks, A. Heath, Joseph Lawrence, H. H. Ramey, R. W. Simmons, Jordan Tucker, Thomas Walker, Stewart, Adms
EPSIE, William, decd, Henry Candler (Major) issued L/A, James Espie, Ignatius Few, secs, 1/6/1789, Richmond, AB

ERICK, Adam, Jr., decd, Darcus Erick, admr 10/8/1784; Catherine Erich, wid, 4/8/1788, Chatham, Adms

ERNST, Catharine, decd, James Ernst applies for L/A 12/15/1836, Effingham, MIC

ERNST, Gottlieb, decd, Ephraim Keiffer applies for adm 7/6/1829, Effingham, MIC

ERVIN, Elizabeth, decd, Thomas Hutchins, admr 5/4/1812, recpt of Matilda Hutchens for slave, etc., of William Jones for slave, etc. in rt of his wife, Phalba Hutchens, but now Phalba Jones, Wilkes, Retns

ERWIN, John, decd, Elijah Starr, E. Dorsey, Thomas Brock, Ely Qallet, James Dorsey, apprs, 3/1825; Catherine Erwin, gdn of heirs: William and Catherine C., 5/1825, Habersham, MIC

ESKEW, Richard H., decd, Joseph Walker w/LWT annexed, 7/7/1862, Francis Shumate, sur, DeKalb, AB

ESKEW, Thomas J., decd, Joseph Walker, admr, 7/7/1862, Francis Shumate, sur, DeKalb, AB

ESPEY, Thomas, decd, James Espey issued L/A 6/5/1783, Benjamin Few, John Pittman, planters, secs; apprs-Capt. Thomas Burke, Capt. Ignatius Few, Col. G. B. Lee, Capt. Rhesa Howard, B. Few 4/22/1784, Richmond, AB

ESTES, Robert, Sr., decd, L/A with LWT annexed gtd Baxter Estes 9/2/1816, Alsea Holefield, Zachary Estes, surs, Jasper, OM

EUBANKS, James, decd, 6/3/1839, apprs: Homer M. Powell, M. E. Moon, Daniel B. Sheffield, papers say "Baker Co"; purchasers at sale: E. O. Sheffield, John Andrews, Charles Nicholas, Daniel B. Sheffield, James L. Rowland, etc, Dooly, I&A

EUBANKS, James L., orph of William, decd, Isaac Willingham, gdn, 5/2/1836, Jefferson Winn, Wiley Jeter, secs, Lincoln, GB

EUBANKS, Orman, decd, Morgan Outlaw, admr, 7/1/1840, apprs: Benjamin Culpepper, Moses Pipkin, John C. Royal; purchasers at sale: Wm & John Eubanks, Morgan Outlaw, Montrevilla Ray, Irwin Brown, Emely Oliver, Thos. W. Pettee, etc, Dooly, I&A

EUBANKS, William, decd, 8/25/1843, Young P. Outlaw, Jane Eubanks, admrs; apprs: Benja. Culpepper, Edmond Outlaw, David Graham; 2/5/1847 Pleasant H. Key, admr, 10 acres to Jane Eubanks, bal to Pleasant H. Key, tr of Tempy Higdon, Dooly, I&A

EUBANKS, William, decd, James G. Hutchinson, gdn for orphs: James L. and Mary N., 11/2/1835, Jefferson Winn and Isaac Willingham, secs, Lincoln, GB

EUBANKS, William J., orph of William, decd, Thomas Curry, gdn, 11/3/1834, Allen Curry, sec, Lincoln, GB

EVANS, Andrew J., decd, John Evans, admr, Pleasant G. Light, sur, 7/27/1858, Cherokee, AB

EVANS, Arden (or Archie), Nathan Hackney issued L/A 9/11/1826, Henry Brown, Benjamin M. Peeples, Morgan, AB

EVANS, Arden, gdn of Rhody and Susannah, orphs of David, decd, 1813 and 1815 retns pd boarding, etc.; 1810 retn pd for land recd of Stephen and William Evans; William Evans, gdn, 1813-1815, Wilkes, Retns

EVANS, Columbus, orph of William and Mary of Greene Co., 11/1827 Retn filed 9/12/1834, William Duncan, gdn in 1827, James Webb, gdn in 1835, Stewart, L/G

EVANS, Daniel, decd, LWT pvd by John and Jacob Gerrard, 5/4/1807, Jackson, OM

EVANS, David, decd, Mary & Arden Evans, admrs, 1809-10 retns pd Jas Bates, heir; retn of Wm Evans, gdn of Rhoda; pd Mary Evans bd 1808-1810; retns of Wm Evans, gdn of Hannah; retns of Mary Evans, gdn of Sophia & Susannah, Wilkes, Retns

EVANS, Elizabeth, decd, George W. Evans issued L/.A 2/11/1822, Job S. Barney, Gabriel Clarke, secs, Richmond, AB

EVANS, George, decd, L/A to Sarah and Wilson Evans 1/7/1834, Hall

EVANS, George W., decd, Job S. Barney issued L/A 5/7/1824, Wm T. Hobby, Lyman Barney, secs, 1824 retn-shoes for Jane & Rebecca Evans, Wm & G. W. Evans, 1831 recpts from George W. & Wm E. Evans, George, tr for J. McNeil, Richmond, AB
EVANS, Henry, decd, Dorcas Evans issued L/A 1/5/1818, Jesse Everitt, Absolom Rhodes, Jr., secs, Richmond, AB
EVANS, Henry W., decd, Robert Cole and Mordecai Shackleford to sell pt of 25 acres in 18th dist, 1/1816, Jasper, OM
EVANS, Henry W., minor orph of Henry W., decd, John H. Trumble apptd gdn 7/1818, Jasper, OM
EVANS, Hiram, decd, David H. Bird, admr, 4/9/1855, Cherokee, AB
EVANS, James, orph of James, decd, Micajah Bennett, gdn, 1812 retns recept of Stephen and William Evans, admrs of James, decd, Wilkes, Retns
EVANS, Jesse, decd, John Evans, gdn of orphs: Betsy, Dorcas, William and George, 1/13/1820, James Woods, Thomas McCoy, secs, Morgan, GB
EVANS, John, decd, John Evans issued L/A 2/3/1820, Matthew Phillips, sec, Morgan, GB
EVANS, John, decd, LWT dtd 3/2/1826 names sole legatee Samuel Williams, Pike, MIC
EVANS, John G., decd, Joseph M. Evans issued L/A 9/15/1825, James Evans, William Stuckey, secs; Joseph M. Evans, gdns of orphs: Joseph C., John P., William T., Joel, Sarah Ann and Clara Ann, 1/7/1827, Morgan, AB
EVANS, John M., decd, Jane E. Evans, admx 9/11/1854; Jeremiah Warren, admr, Shem Carney, sur, 12/14/1857, Cherokee, AB
EVANS, Sarah, decd, David H. Bird, admr, 4/9/1855, Cherokee, AB
EVANS, Simeon, Thomas Hays, Thomas Simmons, gdns, 3/7/1836, Harris, GB
EVANS, Stephen, decd, Matthew J. Williams, admr, sale 5/3/1808, Elbert, AR
EVANS, William, decd, Lemuel Young issued L/A, Roger Triplett, sec, 5/27/1795, Richmond, AB
EVANS, William, decd, Nancy Evans, gdn of minor orphs: Andrew, William, Sarah, Columbus, Emily and Susan 4/5/1824; Thomas Murrah has intermarried w/Mary Evans, Morgan, GB
EVANS, William, decd, Royal Jenkins issued L/A 1/6/1823, Samuel Harris, sec, Morgan, AB
EVANS, William, decd, Wilmoth Evans and Edward Woodham issued L/A 10/4/1808, Putnam, AB
EVANS, William H., decd, Thomas D. Evans, admr, John M. Chambers, sur, 3/15/1858, Cherokee, AB
EVANS, W. T., decd, Alexander W. Norman issued L/A 11/1868, Webster, OD
EVERET, Alexander, decd, Molly Everet issued L/A 7/30/1799, Nathaniel Perin, Wm Duren, secs, Richmond, AB
EVERETT, Thomas, decd, John Everett qualified as exr of LWT 3/1864, Webster, OD
EVERINGHAM, John, decd, Hannah Everingham issued L/A 1/2/1790, John Baker Bennett, David Longstreet, secs; 1790 Britton Dawson, John Twiggs, George Wyche, Hugh Magee, Nathan Bostick, Hezekiah Beal, John Britt, admrs, Richmond, AB
EVERITT, Benjamin, decd, Benjamin Faircloth issued L/A 7/3/1820, John Barlow, sec, Laurens, AB
EVERITT, John, decd, LWT pvd 7/12/1828, names wife, Sarah; after her death est to be divided betwn: Joshua, Josiah, Enoch, Jehu, Aaron and John Everitt and day, Hann's two children, John and Sarah to have one of sd shares, Bulloch, Misc
EVERITT, John, decd, LWT pvd by Joan Deloatch and William Deloatch 1/4/1841; son-in-law, John Baxter, ch: Thomas, Asha Rodgers, Ervin G. Rodgers; grson, Ervin G. Rodgers, heirs of

Sarah Baxter, decd, Bulloch, MIC, Misc
EVERITT, William, decd, Maria Everitt apptd admx, 7/7/1832,
William R. Jackson, admr, 7/15/1833, Baldwin, AB
EVINS, John L., decd, James R. Evins issued L/A 9/4/1865, Fulton
EVINS, Naomi Z., minor orph of William H. C., Sr.., R. B. Jett
apptd gdn 4/25/1866, Fulton, GB
EVINS, R. W., minor orph of William H. C., Sr., R. B. Jett apptd
gdn 6/4/1866, Fulton, GB
EVINS, William H. C., Jr., minor orph of William H. C., Sr., R.
B. Jett apptd gdn 4/25/1866, Fulton, GB
EWIN, Thomas, decd, John Ashurst issued L/A 11/2/1812, Putnam, AB
EWING, Charles, a school boy, retn of Wm. A. D. Ewing, gdn, and
James Ewing's pt in full of sd est 2/22/1804, Elbert, GR
EWING, Jones H., decd, Miles E. Ewing, admr, John A. Moon, sur,
11/6/1876, Gwinnett, AB
EWING, Thomas, decd, Joseph Hudleston and James Hudleston issued
L/A 3/1/1813, Putnam, AB
EXLEY, John, decd, LWT pvd 11/7/1836, Effingham, MIC
EXLEY, Luke, decd, Solomon Exley applies for L/A 9/22/1841,
Effingham, MIC
EXPERIENCE, John, decd, John Holman, admr, William O. Hart,
Harriett E. Experience, sur, 3/16/1850, Bibb, AB
FAGAN, Andrew and Catherine, decd, Robert Leckie issued L/A
8/24/1820, John Cashin, Lindsey Coleman, secs, Richmond, AB
FAIL, Thomas, decd, purchasers at sale: James, Francis and Thomas
Fail, Hancock, AAAA
FAIN, Elizabeth, decd, LWT exhibited 3/3/1863, J. A. Fain, exr,
Fulton
FAIN, Eppy, decd, James Fain, admr, 12/31/1855, Cobb, BB
FAIN, John, decd, John J. Fain issued L/A 6/4/1867, Fulton
FAIRCHILD, Alexander, decd, William Parker, admr, John R.
Daniels, Benjamin Faircloth, sur, 1/3/1825; est appraised
6/28/1826, Emanuel, AB
FAMBROUGH, Anderson, decd, John A. Fambrough, gdn of Jesse, James
and Lucy, 6/2/1823, Wm Fambrough, sur, Clarke, GB
FANNIN, Elizer, orph of Isham, decd, Adam G. Saffold, gdn,
1/3/1825, O. Parker, sec, Morgan, GB
FANNIN, James H., orph of James W., decd, Augustus B. Fannin,
gdn, William F. Fannin, Benjamin B. Amoss, Henry Long, Jarrel
Pearley, sec, 11/6/1848, Troup, GB
FANNIN, Joseph, decd, John W. Porter, gdn of orphs: Marara and
Sarah, 10/18/1826, Reuben Mann, Morgan, GB
FANNING, John, decd, Bird Parks, admr, 1809-10 retns pd Matthew
Fabor boarding for four children, calico for Nancy, 1813 saddle
for Bryan Fanning, pd Matthew Favor for boarding of Patsy
Fanning, Wilkes, Retns
FARLEY, Benjamin, decd, Ann Farley, David Francis Bourquin, exrs
of LWT 6/21/1786, Chatham, Adms
FARMER, Eleanor, decd, Shadrick Farmer, admr, 4/4/1853, William
Jackson, Seth Morgan, surs, DeKalb, AB
FARMER, Jeremiah, relieved from bond, p. 67, Screven, OM
FARMER, Solomon, decd, William Garner, Frances E. Farmer, admrs,
Thomas G. Waldroup, sur, 4/4/1859, Paulding, AB
FARR, Milton, decd, James B. Jett, gdn of minor ch---Mary E.,
James B., Amanda C., Lucy C., Thomas J. and Charles M. 7/30/1866,
Fulton
FARRAR, Fields, decd, Thomas Townsend issued L/A 9/7/1790, James
Barnes, John E. Smith, secs, Richmond, AB
FARRAR, James H., decd, Stephen Stovall, gdn of orphs--Henry H.
and Nancy 7/5/1825, Peter Lamar, James Jennings, gdn, Lincoln, GB

FARRAR, William P., decd, Thomas P. Fleming, admr, J. J.
Thrasher, William McMillan, M. D. Garr, C. H. Elyea, secs,
12/2/1861, Fulton, AB
FARROR, Fields, decd, Thomas Townsend gtd L/A 9/7/1790 in
Richmond Co., Columbia, Ests
FARROW, Adam, decd, Josiah Smith, admr, 9/8/1812, Camden, MIC
FARROW, Perrin, decd, L/A to Penny Farrow 5/1/1809; admx to
give title to Adair Pool in Wilkinson Co 1/20/1808, Jackson, OM
FAULKNER, H. M., decd, Angus Johnson, temp admr, Emanuel Jackson,
sur, 1/26/1858; James H. Weaver admr de bonis non, S. L.
Strickland, 12/5/1859, Paulding, AB
FAY, Michael, decd, Louis Valentine issued L/A 7/5/1858, Fulton
FEARS, Absolom, decd, Ann Fears, wid, issued L/A 9/12/1791,
Philip Clayton, John Fury, secs, Richmond, AB
FEE, Michael, decd, Elizabeth and George Fee issued L/A
7/30/1799, William and John Fee, secs, Richmond, AB
FEEMAN, Timothy, decd, inv of est 3/20/1813 by Edwin Lambert,
John Morris, Thomas Ramsey; 1813 retn by Solomon Strickland,
Oglethorpe, MIC
FELDER, Aquilla S., decd, permanent L/A issued James M. Kennedy
11/1857; Abraham Loper, admr de bonis non 12/1862, Webster, OD
FELDER, G. D., decd, Sarah Felder issued L/A 1/1867, Webster, OD
FELDER, William, G. D. Felder, gdn, makes retn for ward 7/1862,
Webster, OD
FELPS, William, planter, decd, Elizabeth Felps issued L/A
5/19/1783, Wm Candler, Moses Marshall, secs, Richmond, AB
FELTON, John G., decd, Richard Felton, admr, Cobb, BB
FENDELL, Thomas H. (Dr.), decd, Sarah M. Fendall issued L/A
8/7/1823, William McGar, Daniel Savage, secs, Richmond, AB
FENLEY, Lucretia, decd, John Fenley, father apptd gdn of: Mary
Eliza, John R., William W., Nancy E., Nathan L. and Frances H.
Fenley, minor children of Lucretia. Rowland W. Hudson, Stephen G.
Lane, surs, 11/27/1848, Troup, GB
FENN, Eli, decd, LWT pvd 5/2/1842 by David Curry and Richard
Warthen, Washington
FENN, Elizabeth, minor orph of Travis, decd, Ashly Wood, gdn,
7/3/1815, Laurens, GB
FENN, George W., decd, Thomas A. Fenn issued L/A 10/2/1849, James
Roberts, Samuel Martin, secs, Hall, AB
FENN, Henry W., decd, Elizabeth Fenn, admx 10/16/1845; appraisers
of est: D. J. Bothwell, John Green, Willis Leonard, Dooly, I&A
FENN, Travis, decd, Mary Fenn and William Hawthorn issued L/A
5/7/1810; Lemuel Lassiter, gdn of Elizabeth Fenn, minor under 14,
9/7/1813, Laurens, AB
FENNEL, Clement, decd, Alexander Turner issued L/A 11/6/1821,
John Cacy and Ruth Fennell issued L/A 2/7/1820, Laurens, AB
FERENTON, Jacob, decd, Rebecca Ferenton, wid, apptd admx
2/25/1782, Wilkes, MxR
FERGUSAN, Jacob E., decd, temp L/A issued 12/30/1863 Milton
Moore, Michael T. Kenamore, sec; Milton Moore and Sarah Ferguson
issued L/A 6/6/1864, W. F. Sears, sec, White, AB
FERGUSON, John, decd, Rachael Ferguson issued temp L/A 4/18/1814,
W. Barton, sec, AB
FERGUSON, Joseph, decd, Dreadzil Pace and John Foster, exrs,
1/26/1799, Columbia, Ests
FERGUSON, Martha S., minor orph of William H., Sr., decd, William
C. Parker gdn 6/9/1866, Fulton, GB
FERGUSON, Neil, decd, Alfred W. Ferguson, admr, Francis Douglass,
John M. Pearson, sur, 3/2/1835, Butts, AB
FERGUSON, Neil, decd, inv and appr 6/9/1835; apprs: John M.
Pearson, Jason Greer, F. Douglass; Alfred W. Ferguson, admr;
purchasers at sale: Alfred W. Ferguson, Tarpley Price, Henry M.

Duke, Robert McGrady, E. S. Kirksey, etc., Butts, ER
FERGUSON, William and Joseph Sykes, late of Savannah, decd, Charles Jackson issued L/A 1790 or 1795, Richmond, AB
FERGUSON, William H., Jr., minor orph of William H., Sr., decd, William C. Parker, gdn, 6/9/1866, Fulton, GB
FERNANDEZ, Moses, being over age 14 applied to ct to apptd Archibald Clarke, atty, his gdn, 4/14/1807, Camden, MIC
FERRELL, John, decd, Martin Ferrell apptd admr 6/17/1793, Cuthberd Hudson, John Pollard, Wm Davis, appraisers, Elbert, AR
FERRELL, Micajah, decd, James A. McCune, admr, Samuel P. Burford, John Hendrick, sur, 11/7/1842, Butts, AB
FERRINGTON, Aaron, decd, Enoch James, admr, 5/4/1812 retn, pd James Platt bd for two orphs 1806-1811; pd bd for Nancy and Mandy to James Pratt, pd Henry Turner in rt of wife, Lucinda in 1812, Wilkes, Retns
FEW, Joseph, decd, Obediah M. B. Fielder and Mary Few issued L/A 5/7/1827, Terrell Fielder, Wm Lamberth, secs, Morgan, AB
FEW, William, Sr., decd, LWT dtd 7/21/1794, Benjamin and Ignatius Few and Rhesa Howard, exrs, Columbia, Ests
FIDLER, William, decd, Benjamin Allen, admr 1783, Wilkes, MxR
FIELD, Jeremiah, decd, Elijah M. Field and Elias Field, admrs, Joseph Donaldson, John D. Field, sur, 2/12/1855, Cherokee, AB
FIELDER, Mary C., minor orph of Thomas B., decd, Matthew Osborn issued L/G 4/7/1857, Fulton
FIELDER, Thomas B., decd, Mathew Osburn, admr, 9/5/1853, H. G. Dean, sur, DeKalb, AB
FIELDS, James, decd, merchant, Mrs. Ann Fields, admx, 12/16/1789, Chatham, Adms
FIELDS, Jeremiah, decd, LWT dtd 4/19/1854, pvd 2/1855, names wife, Anna and ch: James H. and William G. Field; grdau-Obedience Sutherland; dau-in-law, Obedience, wife of William G. Fields, Cherokee
FIELDS, William M., decd, L/A issued to Isaac Brown 8/1/1859, E. F. Starr, Wm A. Reaves, secs; William L. Sumter, gdn to John H., orph, 8/1/1859, E. J. Horton, Isaac Black, secs, White, AB, GB
FIELDER, William, decd, inv 1/15/1784, John ug, John and James Nall, apprs, "To Mary McDaniel, widow", Wilkes, MxR
FILPSE, David, decd, Alex Autrey, admr 2/25/1782, Wilkes, MxR
FINCH, Allen, decd, inv and appr 9/27/1831 by Frederick Lanier, Jesse Moore, James Hendrix, Charnick Selph, Charles Finch, Benjamin Lanier; Susannah Finch, admx, files retn 1837, 1/1/1838, Bulloch, Misc
FINCH, Ichabod, decd, Levi May, admr, 9/1/1820, James Rowland, Thomas Rowland, surs, Warren, AB
FINCH, Jeter, decd, James Hudgins issued perm L/A 1/1825, Habersham, MIC
FINCHER, Moses, inventory 7/28/1800, includes tomahawk, pair of compasses, Wm Arnold, Jeremiah Walker, J. M. Johnston, apprs, 8/30/1800 sale, Mary Fincher purchased horse, cotton wheel, etc., Elbert, AR
FINDLEY, Aaron, decd, LWT dtd 11/11/1858, pvd 12/1858, names wife, Matilda, of 25 yrs, "my five children", son-in-law, William E. Freeman, Cherokee
FINDLEY, John, decd, Stephen Findley, Asa Findley, Joseph Findley, admrs, 5/1/1822, Baldwin, AB
FINDLEY, John, decd, Stephen Findley, admr, appr 7/28/1826, Emanuel, A
FINDLEY, Richard, decd, Nancy Heckles issued L/A, Henry Heckles, sec, Richmond, AB
FINN, Richard, decd, John S. Holt issued L/A 3/10/1818, Welcome Allen, Daniel Savage, secs, Richmond, AB

FISH, William, decd, LWT pvd 1/6/1843, George W. Fish and Sarah Fish, exrs, Washington
FISHBOURNE, Benjamin, decd, Michael and Ann Burke issued L/A 8/16/1792, James Armstrong, Edward McFarland, secs, Richmond, AB
FISHER, Elizabeth, decd, Vincent Johnston, admr, James P. Elliott, sec, 1/4/1830, Hall, AB
FITTS, Walker, decd, Newton M. Fitts, admr files 1854 retn, Fayette, AB
FITZ, Edward, decd, Isaac Taylor issued L/A 1/1828, Richmond, AB
FITZGERALD, James, decd, David Fitzgerald, admr, Gideon Hayes, Josiah Drew, sec, William Rawls, Baldwin, AB
FITZGERALD, James, decd, Phillip Fitzgerald, gdn of orphs, 3/1849, 1852-1853 retns, Fayette, GB
FITZGERALD, James, decd, David Fitzgerald, admr, appraisal 5/28/1819, Emanuel, A
FITZGERALD, Mary, orph, Florence Area, gdn, 1834, Buford Spence, sur, Stewart, GB
FITZGERALD, William, decd, James Violean issued L/A 1/10/1809, James Hamilton, James Scott, secs, Richmond, AB
FITZPATRICK, Elizabeth Jane, Joseph Fitzpatrick, William Hays, gdns, 1/7/1839, Harris
FITZPATRICK, Polly, orph of Benjamin, decd, Bennett Fitzpatrick, gdn, 1/7/1822, Morgan, GB
FITZPATRICK, Susan (Mrs.), decd, LWT pvd, Mrs. Dorcas Sanchez apptd admx, 6/1/1811, Camden, MIC
FITZPATRICK, William, decd, apprs: Z. Phillips, Jas Simmens, P. Wier; Joseph Fitzpatrick, admr, retn 12/31/1808; purchasers at sale: Celia, Joseph, Elizabeth & Phillip; 1809 Retn exp boarding 6 ch (4 boys, 2 girls), Jasper, WAR
FITZSIMMONDS, E. L. W., decd, Mrs. Sally Fitzsimmonds and James Cooper applied for L/A 5/6/1799, Greene, Misc
FITZSIMMONS, Almyra, orph of Henry, decd, Almyra Munday, gdn, John McCarter, sur, 9/4/1848, Cherokee, GB
FITZSIMMONS, Mary Catherine, orph of Henry, decd, Almyra Munday, gdn, John McCarter, sur, 9/4/1848, Cherokee, GB
FITZSIMMONS, Patrick Washington, orph of Henry, decd, Almyra Munday, gdn, John McCarter, sur, 9/4/1848, Cherokee, GB
FITZSIMMONS, Patrick W., orph of Henry, decd, William M. Bearden apptd gdn, 12/3/1860, Dawson, WB
FITZSIMMONS, Rexany A., orph of Henry, decd, Almyra Munday, gdn, John McCarter, sur, 9/4/1848, Cherokee, GB
FITZSIMMONS, Torrence Emmet, orph of Henry, decd, Almyra Munday, gdn, John McCarter, sur, 9/4/1848, Cherokee, GB
FLANAGAN, Maria, Silas Payne, gdn, William H. Gregory, William Hill, sur, 8/1/1853, Cherokee, GB
FLANIGAN, Edward, decd, Henry Tate issued L/A 2/3/1806, Peter Jaillet, Thomas Lowry, secs, Richmond, AB
FLEMING, David, decd, Joshua Saunders issued L/A 10/22/1785; bill of John McMunn for keeping young child 18 mos. and keeping 2 young children, 6 mos, Richmond, AB
FLEMING, Duncan L., decd, Ferdinand Fleming, admr, Dooly, OD
FLEMING, Ellen, minor orph of James, decd, Jane A. Welch, gdn, 11/4/1867, Fulton, GB
FLEMING, E. M., decd, John C. Fleming, admr, Nancy J. Fleming, Daniel H. Fleming, sur, 8/3/1874, Gwinnett, AB
FLEMING, Jerry, a colored man, Henry Summerlin, gdn, John M. D. Bond, sur, 10/9/1834, Butts, GB
FLEMING, Martha, orph of William, decd, Benjamin Tutt, gdn, 1/22/1834, Francis F. Fleming, sec, Lincoln, GB
FLEMING, Robert, orph, R. A. Fleming, William Barden, gdns of orph 1/4/1836, Harris, GB

FLEMING, Samuel, decd, LWT pvd 12/8/1834, James Fleming, John F. Fleming, John F. Royal, exrs, Harris
FLEMING, Thomas, minor orph of James, decd, Jane A. Welch, gdn, 11/4/1867, Fulton, GB
FLEMING, William, decd, Susan Fleming, gdn of orphs: Emily, William, Newton and Martha 3/1/1830, Wm Curry, Hardy Leverett, secs; Benjamin Remson, gdn of Emily E. 1/7/1833, Lincoln, GB
FLENNIKEN, James, decd, LWT pvd 11/7/1789 names bro., John, 120 acres in Mecklenburg Co., N. C.; bro., Samuel, bro., David, bro., William, Greene, Misc
FLERL, Israel, decd, Lewis and Sarah Weitman, exrs produced accts 3/3/1828, Effingham, MIC
FLERL, Mary C., orph, Lewis Weitman, gdn, produced accts 3/3/1828, Effingham, MIC
FLERL, Sarah Ann Graline, orph, Lewis Weitman, gdn, produced accts 3/3/1828, Effingham, MIC
FLETCHER, Eliza, illegitimate, 5/5/1834, retn of Muscogee Co. land, signel '. Fletcher, gdn, Bulloch, Misc
FLEWELLEN, James, decd, Elizabeth Flewellen, admx, Nicholas W., Amos J., John Flewellen, sur, 1830, Bibb, AB
FLEWELLEN, Louisa C., orph, James C. Dunselsieth, gdn, 5/15/1829, Butts, GB
FLEWELLIN, Archelaus, decd, Thomas Flewellin, temp admr 1/5/1824, Wm H. Blount, James Shivers, Thomas Berry, surs, Warren, AB
FLEWELLIN, Nancy, decd, James Flewellin, admr, 3/5/1827, James Shivers, Henry Hight, Wm Hurt, surs, Warren, AB
FLINN, James, decd, LWT, John I. Flinn, Martha Tridwell, exrs, Harris
FLINN, Richard, decd, James Williams apptd admr, 1/4/1814, Camden, MIC
FLIRSHELL, David, decd, Joseph Flirshel issued L/A 6/3/1868, Fulton
FLOOD, Lewis M., illegitimate child, Joshua Sutton, gdn, 3/1/1830, Habersham, MIC
FLORENCE, Levi, decd, John S. Cohen issued L/A 11/14/1831, Jacob Moise, sec, retns list board for Mrs. Florence and four children, Richmond, AB
FLORENCE, Obediah, decd, B. P. Florence, admr, A. J. Florence, J. H. Turner, sur, 2/5/1856, Paulding, AB
FLORENCE, Thomas, decd, Wiley G. Tatom, gdn of orphs: Sophronia, Lavina and Angeline, 3/2/1835, Wm H. Norman, Hardy Leverett, secs, Lincoln, GB
FLORET, Joseph, mariner, decd, Francis Durant apptd admr, nearest of kin, 9/6/1813, Camden, MIC
FLOURNOY, Betsey, orph of Gibson, decd, William H. Miles, gdn, asked to remove proceedings from Greene to Jasper Co., 9/1811, Jasper, OM
FLOURNOY, Jacob, decd, William Flournoy, gtd L/A 9/19/1802, Robert Abercrombie, John B. Flournoy, surs, 6/23/1802, Warren, AB, MIC
FLOURNOY, Nancy, orph of Gibson, decd, William H. Miles, gdn, asked to remove proceedings from Greene to Jasper Co., 9/1811, Jasper, OM
FLOURY, Henry, decd, LWT pvd 9/4/1837, Harris
FLOWER, John, decd, Rudolph Strawhager, admr, 4/18/1786, Chatham, Adms
FLOWERS, Edward, LWT dtd 12/26/1820 pvd 2/1821, wife, Elizabeth; ch: William, James M., Theophilus, Catherine, Eliza; grch: Adaline, dau of Catherine; exr, friend, John Heard, bro., Sanders Vann, and son, James Flowers, Jasper, Retns
FLOWERS, Edward, decd, LWT pvd, John Heard, Sanders Vanner, James Flowers, exrs, 3/5/1821, Jasper, OM

FLOYD, Catherine, inf, Charles R. Floyd apptd natural gdn 6/7/1831, Camden, MIC
FLOYD, Charles S., orph of Stephen, decd, Samuel B. Hoyt, gdn, 6/7/1858; James Craig, gdn, 5/4/1863, Fulton, GB
FLOYD, Grandbury signed as having recd of Simon Smith and Nicey Smith, admrs of est of Middleton Smith, decd his share 10/26/1836, Bulloch, Misc
FLOYD, Letty C., orph of Stephen, decd, Samuel B. Hoyt, gdn, 6/7/1858; James Craig, gdn, 5/4/1863, Fulton, GB
FLOYD, Lewis, decd, John Trussell, admr, p. 46, Screven, OM
FLOYD, Stephen, decd, late of Cass Co., Robert M. Clarke qualified as admr 3/4/1857, Fulton
FLUWELLIN, Betty, decd, Alexander Fluwellin, admr, 8/11/1800, applies for ltrs dismission, 8/11/1800, Warren, MIC
FLUWELLIN, Stephen, decd, John Matthews gtd L/A 6/10/1802, Henry Kendall, Jesse Matthews, sur, 6/10/1802, Warren, AB, MIC
FLYNT, John, minor orph of Tapley, decd, Charles Stewart apptd gdn, Alexander Gordon, sur, 6/21/1803, Oglethorpe, MIC
FLYNT, Rachel, minor orph of Tapley, decd, Charles Stewart apptd gdn, Alexander Gordon, sur, 6/21/1803, Oglethorpe, MIC
FLYNT, Sarah, minor orph of Tapley, decd, Charles Stewart apptd gdn, Alexander Gordon, sur, 6/21/1803, Oglethorpe, MIC
FLYNT, Tapley, decd, ordered that Charles Stewart, gdn of orphs, be released from guardianship, 1/1804, Oglethorpe, MIC
FLYNT, William, minor orph of Tapley, decd, Charles Stewart apptd gdn, Alexander Gordon, sur, 6/21/1803, Oglethorpe, MIC
FOARD, Wyatt, decd, Mary Foard, admx, 2/21/1831; Richard B. Green, admr 1/17/1833, Baldwin, AB
FOLL, George, decd, Lucy Moore Foll and George Pearson issued L/A 7/16/1803, Martin Wiseman, Robert Reid, secs, Richmond, AB
FOLLY, Asa, minor orph of Thomas, bound to James Folly, 7/7/1817, Jasper, OM
FOLLY, James, orph of Thomas, decd, Zachariah Estes apptd gdn 1/7/1822, Jasper, OM
FOLLY, James, orph, bound to John L. Ponder, Zacheus Estes, sur on bond, 11/1814, Jasper, OM
FOLLY, Matilda, orph of Thomas, decd, Zachariah Estes apptd gdn 1/7/1822, Jasper, OM
FOLLY, Thomas, decd, L/A issued Zachary Estes 5/2/1814, Alfred Holefield, Jordan Compton, surs, Jasper, OM
FONTAIN, Peter, decd, Mary Fontain issued L/A 9/1/1789, John E. Smith, James Barnes, secs, Richmond, AB
FONTAINE, Thomas, decd, John Fontaine qualified as jt exr with James Allen on LWT, 3/6/1809, Warren, MIC
FONTAINE, Thomas, decd, LWT pvd by Cader Wesley & Sally Fontaine; James Allen, exr. Elisha Hart, John Fontaine named exrs in LWT relinquish rts to serve. Sally Fontaine relinquished rt as legatee, 11/7/1807, Warren, MIC
FORBES, William, decd, John O. Boon, gdn of orphs: George J. and Tabitha, 1/15/1833, Habersham, MIC
FORBS, Benjamin, decd, Joseph Forbs, Isaac Tull issued L/A 3/13/1843, Washington
FORBS, Benjamin, orph of Benjamin, decd, Joseph Forbs issued L/G 3/13/1843, Washington
FORBS, Enoch, decd, Charles and C. Forbs issued L/A 3/7/1814, Putnam, AB
FORBS, Robert, orph of Benjamin, decd, Joseph Forbs issued L/G 3/13/1843, Washington
FORCE, Henry O., decd, John P. Force issued temp L/A 10/3/1826, Richmond, AB
FORD, John, decd, William Ford was gtd L/A 10/2/1793, Columbia Co., Ests

FORD, Joseph, decd, William W. Ford, admr, 7/5/1819, Jeremiah Butt,Kendall McTyeire, James Neal, Sr., surs, Warren, AB
FORD, Norman M., decd, Nancy Ford, admx, 4/6/1863, Elizabeth Ford, W. A. Wilson, surs, DeKalb, AB
FORD, William, decd, James A. Fowler, admr, F. W. King, sur, 1/11/1857, Cherokee, AB
FORD, William, decd, Joseph Habersham apptd admr, 4/9/1791, Chatham, Adms
FOREHAND, Francis, decd, 3/31/1842, apprs: Adam Butler, Thomas Swearingen, Charles B. Johnson; purchasers at sale: John A. Forehand, Matthew Butler, John Swearingen, Jordan F. Harvard, Moses Johnson, David Butler, etc. Dooly, I&A
FOREMAN, David, decd, L/A to John Hamilton 9/2/1822, Laurens, AB
FOREMAN, Ira, son of Sally, an illegitimate child, John Greer apptd gdn, Thomas Mangram, sur on bond, 7/4/1814, Jasper, OM
FORMWALT, Moses W., decd, Joseph Thompson, admr, 7/6/1852, William Ezzard, sur, DeKalb, AB
FORRISTER, Owen, decd, Christopher Baker and Eleanor Forrister issued L/A 2/16/1803, inv 8/3/1804, Franklin, OM, IMW
FORSYTH, James, decd, William Pugh, gdn of orphs, Harris, GB
FORSYTH, Mary, decd, Davis Austin, qualified admx, 4/3/1784, Liberty, Ests
FORSYTH, Robert, decd, Benjamin Forsyth issued L/A 3/12/1794, Nathl Pendleton, Joshua Meals, secs, pt of property appraised Galphinton, Washington Co.; 3/20/1796 Mrs. Fanny Forsyth, admx, Wm Poe, sec, Richmond, AB
FORT, Dolly, minor, having no gdn, and being disagreeably retained by Daniel Greene, Mrs. Elizabeth Williams was named as her gdn 4/3/1809, Camden, MIC
FORT, Mary Ann, orph of Arthur P., decd, Samuel Smith issued L/G 11/9/1855, Washington
FORT, Moses, decd, Endocia W. Fort, admx, 3/2/1846, Baldwin, AB
FORT, Richard, orph of Arthur, decd, of Twiggs Co., Tomlinson Fort, gdn, 12/23/1834, Stewart, Adms
FORT, Winneford, Sr., of 96th Dist, S. C. to Arthur Fort of same place, a slave, 10/1/1779, Wilkes, MxR
FORTH, Thomas, decd, L/A Andrew E. Wells 3/2/1829, Washington
FORTNER, J. Y., illegitimate orph of Sarah Fortner, Mitchel G. Fortner, gdn, Emanuel, GB
FORTSON, Richard, decd, Samuel Thurman, Tavner W. Fortson, admrs, 12/12/1836, Harris
FORTSON, Richardson, decd, LWT pvd 11/16/1836, Harris
FOSTER, Alfred, decd, A. H. Vandiner issued L/A 10/6/1862, David M. Hortman, sec, White, AB
FOSTER, Arthur, decd, L/A to Harmon Holt 7/3/1809, Jackson, OM
FOSTER, Bazzel, decd, inv 2/14/1801; purchasers: John Foster, Thos Smith, Wm Rimes, Nicholas Booty, Asa Sutton, Salley Foster; heirs: John Garrett, gdn for Judah, Polley and Frederick, Martha Foster; Robt Clark, admr, Hancock, AAAA

FOSTER, Daniel J., son of Philemon, decd, William J. Ellison, gdn, Larkin Nix, James M. Fields, sur, 4/10/1854, Cherokee, GB
FOSTER, Eliza, orph of Philemon, decd, William J. Ellison, gdn, Elijah L. Ellison, sur, 3/10/1855, Cherokee, GB
FOSTER, Frances Jane, orph of Francis, decd, Amy Foster, gdn, James Andrew J. Alford, John Edwards, James E. Ridgeway, sec, 7/2/1849, Troup, GB
FOSTER, George, decd, Samuel Lewis, admr, 1811, partner with Josiah Stewart, merchant of Liberty Co., Bryan, MSC
FOSTER, Ira M., orph of Francis, decd, Amy Foster, gdn, James Andrew J. Alford, John Edwards, James E. Ridgeway, sec, 7/2/1849, Troup, GB

FOSTER, John, decd, John Way, Samuel Jones, qualified exrs
10/26/1790, Liberty, Ests
FOSTER, John E., orph of Francis, decd, Amy Foster, gdn, James
Andrew J. Alford, John Edwards, James E. Ridgeway, sec, 7/2/1849,
Troup, GB
FOSTER, Jones, William J. Ellison, gdn, Larkin Nix, sur,
1/8/1855, Cherokee, GB
FOSTER, Martha Ann, orph of Philemon, decd, Larkin Ellison, gdn,
4/1/1854, Cherokee, GB
FOSTER, Philemon, decd, Larkin Nix issued L/A 7/27/1853; Nancy
Foster, Thomas N. White, admrs 9/5/1853, Burton Buice, Phillip
Wells, sur, Cherokee, AB
FOSTER, Ransom, decd, LWT "of Forsyth Co.", bond blank, dtd abt
1855, Cherokee, AB
FOSTER, Sarah E., minor orph of William T., decd, Benjamin F.
Boman, gdn, 8/6/1860, Fulton, GB
FOSTER, Susan A., orph of Francis, decd, Amy Foster, gdn, James
Andrew J. Alford, John Edwards, James E. Ridgeway, sec, 7/2/1849,
Troup, GB
FOWLER, Andrew H., orph of John, decd, Jesse Burtz, gdn, Isaac L.
Mothershed, sur, 4/9/1855, Cherokee, GB
FOWLER, Easter, orph of John, decd, Jesse Burtz, gdn, Isaac L.
Mothershed, sur, 4/9/1855, Cherokee, GB
FOWLER, Hays B., decd, Francis S. Bell issued temporary L/A
10/1864, perment ltrs 11/1864, Webster, OD
FOWLER, James, decd, Irving J. Fowler, admr, John A. McWhorter,
sur, 7/1858, Cherokee, AB
FOWLER, John, decd, James T. Hendrix, gdn of orphs: William A.
and Joel H., 3/1/1852, J. N. Alexander, sec, Hall, GB
FOWLER, Lemuel J., decd, James W. Johnson, admr, William J.
Johnson, sur, 11/22/1859, Cherokee, AB
FOWLER, Margaret E., orph of John, decd, Jesse Burtz, gdn, Isaac
L. Mothershed, sur, 4/9/1855, Cherokee, GB
FOWLER, Mariah Ann, orph of John, decd, Jesse Burtz, gdn, Isaac
L. Mothershed, sur, 4/9/1855, Cherokee, GB
FOWLER, Nathan, decd, formerly of Wilkes, now Warren Co.,
6/30/1823, Zephaniah Fowler, temp admr de bonis non of certain pt
of undivided pt of est, Elijah Jones, surs, Warren, AB
FOWLER, Thomas, decd, James S. and William J. Fowler issued L/A
3/7/1859, Fulton
FOWLER, William J., orph of John, decd, Jesse Burtz, gdn, Isaac
L. Mothershed, sur, 4/9/1855, Cherokee, GB
FOX, Benjamin, decd, planter, David Francis Bourquin, planter,
admr, 4/21/1785, Chatham, Adms
FOX, David, decd, Joseph Fox apptd admr 8/22/1783, Chatham, Adms
FOX, Elijah, decd, late of Morgan Co., Alex Bryan issued L/A
2/1/1825, Wm J. Hobby, George P. Turpin, secs, Richmond, AB
FOX, James, decd, Sarah Fox gtd L/A 9/7/1790 in Richmond Co.,
Columbia Co., Ests
FOX, James, decd, Sarah Fox issued L/A 9/11/1790, Michael Burke,
Abraham Jones, secs, Richmond, AB
FOX, Joseph, decd, T. A. Browning, admr, 8/6/1855, W. C. Russian,
James Millican, surs, DeKalb, AB
FOX, Matthew, decd, Anna Fox, gdn of minor orphs 7/7/1817: James,
Wm, George, Sarah and Nicholas, Richmond, GB
FOX, Richard, decd, planter, Francis Courvoisie of Savannah gtd
L/A, LWT dtd 4/15/1771, pvd by exrs who are since dead 2/4/1785,
Chatham, Adms
FOX, Robert, decd, John Sandifer, gdn of orphs: Sebastian C.,
Theresa and Mary Anna 5/6/1822, Morgan GB
FOX, William B., decd, Ann Fox issued L/A 11/15/1827, Wm Jackson,
A. R. Ralston, secs, Richmond, AB

FOYE, George, decd, LWT pvd 5/20/1805, John Swilley, Sr. L/A;
6/2/1806 George Browning qualified as exr of LWT to acct w/wife,
Frances Browning, formerly Foye; apprs: Asa Travi, Littleton
Wyche and Clement Dozar, 3/3/1807, Tattnall, MIC
FOYE, James, Joseph Rickerson, gdn, 4/23/1807, Tattnall, MIC
FRANCIS, Cordall, decd, LWT pvd 9/7/1840, William Smith, exr,
Washington
FRANCIS, James C., decd, William Smith, Mary Francis issued L/A
5/1/1843, Washington
FRANKLIN, James M., decd, Samuel O. Franklin issued L/A 1/8/1838,
Washington
FRANKLIN, John, decd, David and Fanny Franklin issued L/A
9/1/1817, Burnel Russell, Wm Williams, secs, Morgan, AB
FRANKLIN, Mary, decd, Davis Smith issued L/A 11/5/1821, Simeon
Ellington, sec, Laurens, AB
FRANKLIN, Mary G., decd, LWT pvd 8/1858-decd dau, Ann's ch-Mary
Ann Atkinson, Ella D. McDonald and Charles M. McDonald, Jr.
(father, Charles McDonald); sons-Benjamin C. of Texas, Leonidas
of Clarke Co. & Marcus A. of Bibb Co.; Cherokee
FRANKLIN, Nancy, orph child 3 mos old the 25th inst, bound to
Edward Harris until 21 yrs old, 12/1827, Habersham, MIC
FRASER, John, decd, ordered that Clk pay John C. Rahn for making
coffin of decd who died in Ebenezer 11/1/1830, Effingham, MIC
FRASER, William, decd, Simon Fraser, admr, 5/28/1857, Cobb, BB
FRAZE, Barrer, decd, inv. dtd 4/1792, Effingham, Misc
FRAZER, Arthur, decd, Wm Addison Frazer, gdn for orphs: Lucinda
Alvisa and Amelia 1/3/1833, Lincoln, GB
FRAZER, John, decd, Alexander Frazer, gdn of orphs: Nancy and
Mary 11/2/1835, Wm M. Larkin, sec, Lincoln, GB
FRAZER, Samuel, decd, Shepherd Guice, gdn for orphs: Martha,
Jeremiah and Thomas A. 1/7/1833, John Guice, James Moncrief,
secs, Lincoln, GB
FRAZIER, Arthur, decd, Addison Frazier, John H. Frazier, gdn of
orphs 9/4/1837, Harris
FRAZIER, Dyer, decd, Mrs. Elizabeth, relict, applies for adm
11/29/1791, apptd 1/5/1792, Effingham, Misc
FRAZIER, Elijah, decd, Joshua D. and Mary Ann Frazier issued L/A
11/1814, Putnam, AB
FRAZIER, Samuel, decd, David Frazier, gdn of orphs: Martha,
Jeremiah and Thomas 1/12/1824, Thomas Florence, sec, Lincoln, GB
FRAZIER, Stephen, decd, L/A issued John Curry 11/4/1833,
Washington
FREDERICK, Joseph, decd, John Richmond issued L/A 2/2/1837,
Joseph Gauter, sec, Richmond, AB
FREEMAN, Abigail and John, gtd leave to sell perishable property,
p. 37, 40, Screven, OM
FREEMAN, Abigail, John Freeman, Jr., gdn, p. 60, Screven, OM
FREEMAN, Alexander, decd, A. F. Underwood issued temp L/A
5/3/1868, White, AB
FREEMAN, Benjamin, accout of $450 ordered pd, p. 25, 29, Ferribee
Freeman, admx, p. 175, Screven, OM
FREEMAN, Benjamin bound to Joseph McGowin, p. 157, Screven, OM
FREEMAN, Holman, Sr., decd, died intestate, to Holman Freeman,
Jr., Merchant, Wilkes, MxR
FREEMAN, Irby, decd, M. T. Kenamore and Rebecca E. Freeman issued
L/A 1/11/1864, W. B. West, sec, White, AB
FREEMAN, Jacob, decd, of Troup Co., Hilliard M. Harris of Morgan
Co. issued L/G of orphs--Martha Jane Freeman, Dorothy Owen
Freeman and Emanuel Francis Freeman 5/5/1856, Fulton

FREEMAN, Jacob, decd, Roger McKinney and Jordan Floyd, exrs, p. 56, Screven, OM
FREEMAN, James, John Freeman, gdn, p. 78, Screven, OM
FREEMAN, Job, bound to Job Herrington, p. 46, Screven, OM
FREEMAN, John, decd, L/A gtd Zephaniah Hardy, John Greer, sur, 7/3/1815, Jasper, OM
FREEMAN, John, decd, Thomas Colding, et al, apprs, p. 59, Screven, OM
FREEMAN, John (Capt), decd, Shaler Hillyer, admr, 1807 retn includes expenses of trip to Oglethorpe Co., Milledgeville and Savannah to Federal Court; also to Athens and Greensboro, 7/1/1816, Wilkes, Retns
FREEMAN, John L., embecile, Jesse Hunt, gdn, 9/8/1863, White, GB
FREEMAN, Josiah, decd, Azel R. Freeman, admr, John B. Wick, Edward W. Wright, sur, Bibb, AB
FREEMAN, Josiah, decd, Azel R. Freeman, admr, John B. Wick, sur, Newton, AB
FREEMAN, Mahala, Jacob Freeman, gdn, p. 101, 132 and 137, Screven, OM
FREEMAN, Mary, formerly Mary Taylor, acct with Charles Bailey, her late gdn to 12/31/1830, Butts, ER
FREEMAN, Nancy, Jacob Wolf, gdn, p. 37, Screven, OM
FREEMAN, Rachel, John Freeman, Jr., gdn, p. 57, Screven, OM
FREEMAN, Sarah, John Freeman, Jr., admr, p. 55, 74, John L. Emanuel, etc. divide estate p. 52, Screven, OM
FREEMAN, Shadrack, son of Polly, age 3, bound 6/24th to Andrew Miller until age 21, 6/4/1794, Oglethorpe, MIC
FREEMAN, Toby and William, bound to Richard Herrington, p. 57, Screven, OM
FREEMAN, Wiley, decd, James Freeman issued L/A 6/28/1870, Henry L. Meeks, sec, White, AB
FREENY, L. J. A., decd, Joel Renfroe, admr, 9/13/1855, Cobb, BB
FRENCH, Ella, decd, David Mayer qualified as admr 1/14/1866, Fulton
FRETWELL, Micajah H., decd, L/A gtd Wm Cook 7/7/1814, Jasper, OM
FREYERMUTH, Ebeline, Gottlieb Seckinger chosen gdn 1/2/1832, Effingham, MIC
FREYERMUTH, John, decd, Peter Freyermuth applies fod L/D 1/3/1831, Effingham, MIC
FRIARWOOD, Sarah, deed of gift dtd 10/10/1792 to daughter, Mary Thornton; also to daughter, Elizabeth Crosby, wife of Aaron Crosby; also Henry Crosby, son of sd Aaron and Elizabeth, Effingham, Misc
FRILSOME, Stephen, decd, George Granberry, John Murphy, admr, 9/18/1837, Harris, AB
FULCHER, Armsted, decd, Nancy, Jas & Jno Fulcher L/A 1823; Ann Fulcher, minors' gdn (1831 Nancy Salisbury, gdn)-Jas, Henry, Martha, Mary, Jinnett, Jefferson, Jos, Armsted; Henry Smith, Jno C. Walton, David Salisbury for wives, Richmond, AB
FULGHAM, Matthew, decd, Stephe Fulgham applied for L/A 7/27/1791, John Smith, Peter Sheppard, apprs, Elbert, AR
FULLILOVE, Temperance, recd of Benjamin Taylor, gdn, in full of her pt of est of John Tatom, decd and all claims she might have against sd Taylor as gdn, 1/1/1803, Oglethorpe, MIC
FULLILOVE, Templey, minor dau of John, Benjamin Taylor apptd gdn, William and Josiah Freeman, surs, 6/17/1800, Oglethorpe, MIC
FULTON, James, decd, Thomas H. Fulton apptd gdn for minors, Dooly, OD
FULWOOD, Andrew, gdn, to show cause, p. 64, 72, Screven, OM
FURCRON, Oscar D., minor orph of William C., decd, J. W. Kennedy, gdn, 1/8/1866, Fulton, GB

111

FURCRON, William C., decd, James F. Alexander issued L/A 1/11/1858, Fulton
FURCRON, William C., decd, James W. Kennedy, admr de bonis non 9/6/1866, Fulton, AB
FURCRON, William H., minor orph of William C., decd, J. W. Kennedy, gdn, 1/8/1866, Fulton, GB
FURGASON, William, decd, Charles Jackson gtd L/A 9/13/1790 in Richmond Co., Columbia Co., Ests
FURGERSON, Howell, son of Bettey, a boy of color, bound to William Brown, to learn trade, 3/2/1807, Oglethorpe, OM
FUTCH, Jacob, decd, acct of sale of personal property 1/10/1825; inventory and appraisement by Garrett Williams, Michael Young, John Anderson 8/16/1824, Bulloch, Misc
FUTCH, Solomon, Sr., decd, LWT pvd 7/1836, names wife, Sally and ch: Isaac, Betsey, Zachariah, John, Thomas, Jacob, Rowan, and Solomon Futch, Mary Ann Duggar, Sarah Baxter, Delila Strickland, Betsey Swea; 5/1837 heirs agreement, Bulloch, Misc
FYFEE, Isaac W., decd, Archibald Ramsay issued L/A 5/3/1830, Henry H. Cook, sec, Richmond, AB
GAAR, Joel, decd, Alexander McAlpin apptd gdn of orphs: Michael A., Margaret and Russell W. Gaar, 3/15/1826, John Barton, sec, Morgan, GB
GAAR, Joel, decd, Alexander McAlpin, gdn of orphs: Permelia, Benajah L., Elizabeth W., 11/1/1824, Morgan, GB
GAAR, Michael, decd, pd Jas Brown, Abraham Gaar, Nicodemus Colbert 1795; Virginia travel expense; settlement by Joseph Rucker and Lewis Gaar; Benjamin Gaar, exr of Adam Gaar, Sr.; Adam Gaar, gdn of minors--Sally, Joel, Wm, Nancy, Frances and George Gaar, Elbert, AR
GABLE, Oham, decd, Mrs. Elizabeth Susannah Gable, extrx and John Nicholas, exr, 3/7/1790, Chatham, Adms
GACHET, Charles, decd, Henry W. Jernigan, James E. Gachet, exrs, 1832, Stewart, Adms
GAITHER, Elizabeth, decd, Daniel Newnan issued L/A 1/11/1813, Putnam, AB
GALACHE, James, decd, planter, Mrs. Elizabeth Ann Galache and John Parlen, exrs of LWT 12/28/1790, Chatham, Adms
GALE, William, decd, Andrew Rhodes, admr, gtd leave to sell 1/6/1812, Liberty, MIC
GALPHIN, George, minor orph of Thomas, decd, Joseph Grant, gdn, 5/1/1820, John and Barna McKinne, secs, Richmond, GB
GALT, Francis W., decd, Sarah W. Galt issued L/A 1/10/1859, Fulton
GAMAGE, Thomas M., orph of William, decd, Floyd Gamage, gdn, F. M. Nix, 3/1851, Fayette, GB
GAMBLE, Cochran, decd, James Love of Savannah, silversmith, admr, 1/7/1786, Chatham, Adms
GAMBLE, James, etc., order for execution, p. 123, Screven, OM
GAMBLE, John N., decd, John N. Harris, admr, William Gamble, sur, 5/24/1849, Bibb, AB
GAMBLIN, Sion, decd, William Gamblin issued L/A 12/5/1853, Ambrose Little, Isaac M. Jay, secs, Hall, AB
GAMEY, James, decd, John Linch issued L/A 11/3/1862, Fulton
GAMMAGE, N., recpts for himself and as gdn of William, Samuel and Lydia Gammage for "my share of my father, William Gammage's estate" dtd 12/29/1808; recpt of Charity Gammage, gdn of Sarah, Mary, William, Davis and Fanny Gammage, orphs of William, decd, Wilkes, Retns
GANCY, Charles, decd, Ezekiel Gancy, admr, 1/6/1817, Jackson, OM
GANGARELL, James Alfred, free person of color, Lemuel Church apptd gdn 1/6/1823, Camden, MIC

GANGARELL, James Alfred, free person of color, Lemuel Church apptd gdn, 1/6/1823, Camden, MIC
GANN, Ann, illegitimate child of Elizabeth, William P. Jackson, gdn, 3/2/1818, John Nutt, sur, Clarke, GB
GARDNER, Etheldred, decd, Lydia Gardner, admx 2/28/1821, orphans: John E. and Hillary A., Jasper, Retns
GARDNER, Etheldred, decd, Patrick Henry Gardner and Lydia Gardner gtd L/A 12/23/1820, Jasper, OM
GARDNER, H. B., decd, C. R. Gardner apptd gdn of orphs: Charles C. and Eddie P., 5/4/1863, Fulton, GB
GARDNER, Hezekiah, decd, of Capt. Gouche's Troop, Col. Andrew Burns applied for L/A 5/7/1796, Greene, Misc
GARDNER, Jane, decd, LWT pvd 9/6/1847, John McKee, exr, Harris
GARDNER, John, decd, Benjamin Webley, apptd admr, 10/6/1787, Chatham, Adms
GARDNER, John, decd, Sterling Gardner of N. C., at present Savannah, planter, admr, 9/17/1787, Chatham, Adms
GARDNER, Mary, orph of Timothy, decd, Patrick Gardner, gdn, 2/6/1860, Fulton, GB
GARDNER, Nancy G., decd, John S. Moreman applies for L/A 2/20/1860, John B. Gilbert, G. J. Wright, sur, Lee
GARDNER, Patrick, decd, Michael Gardner issued L/A 9/9/1867, Fulton
GARDNER, Samuel, decd, William Johnston issued L/A 1/11/1819, Lancelot Johnston, sec, Morgan, AB
GARDMER, Thomas, decd, of Chatham Co, Mrs. Ann Gardner L/A 11/6/1822; Chatham, Richmond Co. land; ch: Ann & Henry K.; heirs: Jas T., W. N. & M. W. Gardner, J. P., for wf, Mary, T. F. Foster, for wf, E. G. Foster, J. M. Gardner, Richmond, AB
GARDNER, Timothy, decd, Michael Gardner issued L/A 9/9/1867, Fulton
GARNER, James, decd, Emard Cronin issued L/A 11/11/1835, Baldwin
GARNER, John, decd, John A. Jordan, Henry Y. Garner, temp admrs, William A. Jordan, sur, 10/2/1874; John A. Jordan, Henry Y. Garner, admrs, file inv 11/2/1874, Gwinnett, AB
GARNER, Richard, decd, John and William Vaughn issued L/A 5/7/1827, Thomas and Benjamin Brown, secs, Morgan, AB
GARNER, Samuel, decd, Cyrus M. Lee issued L/A de bonis non 3/1857, Webster, OD
GARNER, Stephen, decd, 1799 retn by Daniel Orr, Wm Hendon, Mary Garner; 1800 retn, Daniel Orr, admr, pd schooling of orphs; inv, Anthony Oliver, Wm Easton, Capt. Robert Cowden, apprs, Elbert, AR
GARNER, William S., decd, Thomas Watts, gdn of orphs: Mary Ann and John 5/7/1827, Benjamin S. Ogletree, Morten Sparks, secs, Morgan, GB
GARNETT, Anthony, decd, Joseph Garnett and John Shackleford of Columbia Co. issued L/A 10/18/1794, David Miller, secG; purchasers at sale-Zachariah Lamar, Joseph Garnett, Benjamin Daly, John Shackleford, Rachel Garnett, wid, Richmond, AB
GARNETT, John, decd, Zachariah Lamar apptd admr 2/26/1782, Wilkes, MxR
GARNETT, Thomas, decd, Jacob Kittles gives receipt at Savannah 1/28/1797 to Wm Porter for his pt of est, wit: James Porter, David Porter, Charles Cope, Effingham, Misc
GARRETT, Asa, decd, Charity Garrett and Robert McCoombs issued L/A 5/16/1809, George Pearson, Wiley Brazel, secs, Richmond, AB
GARRETT, James, decd, LWT pvd 4/13/1795, wife, Mourning, ch: Ann Ford, Elizabeth Barksdale, Susannah Butler, Mary, William, Charity, James Kelly Garrett, wife, Edmund Butler, Sr., Jonadab Reid and Joseph Barksdale, exrs, Greene, Misc

GARRETT, Riley, a poor child abt 11 yrs old, bound to Lewis Peacock 9/1821, Jasper, OM
GARRETT, Samuel, decd, Thomas B. Applewhite issued L/A 3/1856, Webster, OD
GARRISON, Mary Ann Letha, minor orph of James Douglas, decd, Benjamin Little, gdn, 3/4/1867, Fulton, GB
GARRISON, Mary B. (Mrs.), decd, John C. Garrison, admr, Nehemiah Garrison, sur, 10/9/1854, Cherokee, AB
GARRISON, William Jasper, minor orph of James Douglas, decd, Phebe Garrison, gdn, 3/4/1867, Fulton, GB
GARTRELL, Joseph, decd, Rebecca Gartrell, extrx, 5/6/1817 retn, Wilkes, Retns
GARTRELL, Mary Ann, orph of Jeremiah, decd, Wm Jeter, gdn, 1/16/1826, Charles Jennings, Micajah Henley, secs; Harvey What, gdn, 2/6/1829, Lincoln, GB
GARVER, William P., decd, Nancy M. Garver, admx, Jeremiah Warren, Jasper L. Keith, sur, 12/14/1857, Cherokee, AB
GARVIN, Daniel, decd, Wm Dunlap gtd L/A 7/1/1811 & apptd gdn of: Robt M., Jno E. & Wm D., orphs; exp of Jas Hannah from Abbeville, Jackson & Lincoln Co.'s, Jane Garvin, admx, 1807 retns pd school for Nancy & Robt, Elbert, AR
GARVIN, David, decd, Lucinda B. Garvin issued L/A 7/4/1853, W. P. Reid, John Clark, secs, Hall, AB
GARY, Amlinda, orph of David, decd, Wm Gary apptd gdn 11/1/1819, Jasper, OM
GARY, William Bluford, orph of David, decd, Wm Gary apptd gdn 11/1/1819, Jasper, OM
GARY, William L., orph of William L., Elizabeth N. Wood issued L/A 9/8/1842, Washington
GASCOIGNE, Richard, decd, William Gibson qualified as exr, 6/9/1802, 1804 retn, admr applied for leave to sell property of estate 8/5/1806, Camden, MIC
GASKINS, Rusannah, decd, LWT dtd 11/14/1799, pvd 10/31/1800 of St. Peters Parish, Beaufort, South Carolina, to ch: Amos, Rosannah & Wm Gaskins, Elizabeth Williams; grsons, John Harril Gaskins and Wright Harril Gaskins, Effingham, Misc
GATEWOOD, Richard, decd, 1794-1808 retns includes trip to Va; heirs: Sally Gatewood, Flemming Greenwood, Robert Laurimore, James Floyd, John Gatewood, admr, Elbert, AR
GATEWOOD, Z. B., decd, John F. Ezzard, admr, William Ezzard, sec, 4/7/1862, Fulton, AB
GATT, Jabez, decd, Joel Gatt, admr, Thomas Gatt, John R. Gatt, John G. Vernon, sur, 1/13/1851, Cherokee, AB
GAWLEY, Robert, decd, of Lumpkin, Artimesa Lewis 2/1840; apprs: Elijah Pearce, W. A. May, E. T. Beall, Stewart, Adms
GAY, Abraham, decd, Sarah Gay, wid, and John Beatty, practitioner of physick, admrs, 4/11/1785, Chatham, Adms
GAY, Boran Fay, minor of Mathew, decd, Mitchell Gay, gdn, William Thigpen, sur, 3/4/1844, Emanuel, GB
GAY, Gilbert, decd, Thomas B. and Isaac T. Gay, exrs, 1853-1854 retns, Fayette
GAY, Joel bound to John Reid 9/5/1814, Archibald Quimmilly, sec; bound to Sherod H. Gay 1/7/1817, Jasper, OM
GAY, Martha, decd, LWT pvd 5/7/1821, Jasper, OM
GAY, Mathew, decd, Lewis Gay, admr w/LWT annexed, John Oglesby, sur, 1/2/1844, Emanuel, AB
GAY, Mathew, decd, Mitchel Gay, admr w/LWT annexed, Henry Parrish, sur, 1/4/1844, Emanuel, AB
GAY, Polly Ann, minor of Mathew, decd, Mitchell Gay, gdn, William Thigpen, sur, 3/4/1844, Emanuel, GB
GAY, Sarah (Mrs.), wid, decd, of Savannah, John Beatty, admr, 2/12/1791, Chatham, Adms

GEDDY, Francis, decd, William S. Morgan issued temporary L/A 3/2/1814, Putnam, AB
GEESLAND, William, decd, Sally and Benjamin Geesland, admrs, 8/15/1804, John Jones, John Moses, surs, Warren, AB
GEIGER, John, LWT pvd 3/6/1826, names wife, Sarah, dau, Mary Denmark, bro, Abraham Geiger, pvd 3/6/1826; inventory and division of est betwn Mrs. Sary Geiger and Mrs. Mary Denmark, divided by A. Rawls, Alexander Knight, A. Richardson, 4/13/1826, Bulloch, Misc
GEIGER, John, decd, recd of Mrs. Sarah Geiger, extrx of LWT cattle & furniture, 4/13/1826, Bulloch, Misc
GEORGE, Bailey, decd, William and Delilah McNess, gdns of Mary, James, William and George, orphs, 1/4/1819, Clarke, GB
GEORGE, Bailey, decd, Robert Stewart gdn of orphs: Mary, James and William, 9/2/1822, Parmenus Haynes, Richard Cox, James Langford, Edward Conner, surs, Clarke, GB
GEORGE, Ella, minor of Henry, decd, William Adams issued L/G 5/1855, Webster, OD
GEORGE, James, decd, L/A gtd James Griggs 1/1820, Jasper, OM
GEORGE, James G., orph of Bailey, decd, John H. Lowe, gdn, 4/5/1824, Milner Echols, sur, Clarke, GB
GEORGE, William, decd, Capt. John McAllister applied for L/A 1/31/1796, Greene, Misc
GEORGE, William H., decd, LWT pvd 3/6/1848, W. T. James, James T. George, William Glass, exrs, Harris
GERDAN, Joseph, decd, Thomas Gerdan issued L/A 2/11/1806, Franklin, IMW
GERMANY, James, decd, Joseph Slaton and Bridget, his wife, issued L/A 6/5/1786, Richmond, AB
GERMANY, William, decd, L/A to Sarah Germany 1786, Richmond, AB
GHOLSON, Anthony, decd, Archibald Standifer, admr applies for L/D 11/5/1821, Jasper, OM
Gholston, G. C., decd, G. C. Gholston, admr, John C. Austin, A. Vaughn, surs, DeKalb, AB
GHOLSTON, William D., decd, Sarah E. Gholston, admx, 9/1/1862, William Sheppard, sur, DeKalb, AB
GHOLSTON, Zachariah, decd, R. McAlister, admr, 3/1/1852, Joseph Walker, John M. Fowler, Joseph A. Reeve, J. L. Williams, J. S.
GIBBON, George, decd, LWT exhibited 7/6/1868, George E. Gibbon, exr, Fulton
GIBSON, Alexander, decd, Winneford Gibson issued L/A 12/24/1799, Richard Bullock, sec, Richmond, AB
GIBSON, Clarisa, decd, David G. Jones, apptd admr, 1/5/1824; Rebecca Jones apptd admx 6/7/1824, Camden, MIC
GIBSON, John, decd, Persons Bass, admr, 9/16/1822, Samuel Fuller, Thomas Gibson, surs, Warren, AB
GIBSON, Robert, decd, Daniel Gibson, exr of LWT, 3/8/1790, Chatham, Adms
GIBSON, S. B., James Barr, gdn 12/1869, Webster, OD
GIBSON, S. B., decd, James Barr issued L/A 1/4/1869, Webster, OD
GIBSON, William, decd, Henry R. Fort apptd admr de bonis non, 9/1849, Camden, MIC
GIDDINS, William, decd, Francis Giddins, admr, 1796 retn pd Wm Bostwick for coffin, 1806 bt of Wm and F. Gilbert for Rachel, 1809 cash pd Roger Giddins; Francis Giddins, Jr., debtor to one horse, etc., Wilkes, Retns
GIDEON, Berry, orph of James, decd, Hosea Camp apptd gdn 5/6/1816, Jackson, OM
GIDEON, Francis, decd, Lucius J. Gartrell qualified as admr w/LWT annexed 9/30/1853, Fulton
GIDEON, Hosea, orph of James, decd, chooses Hosea Camp as gdn, 5/6/1816, Jackson, OM

GIDEON, James, decd, Nathan Camp and Elizabeth Gideon issued L/A, 1802; admrs to render acctg of est, 3/4/1816, Jackson, OM
GIGNILLIAT, Gilbert, decd, div ordered betwn heirs, 6/4/1826, Glynn, MIC
GIGNILLIAT, James, decd, John and Henry Gignilliat, the natural gdns of their respective children, petition to divide est betwn heirs 6/4/1826, Glynn, MIC
GIGNILLIAT, John M., decd, division betwn heirs--M. C. Gignilliat and child, J. W. Frost, S. C. Gignilliat, John H. and Robert D. Hall, H. G. and John Gignilliat, and T. S. Hopkins, not dtd, abt 1850, Glynn, MIC
GIGNILLIAT, Norman P., minor, chose Henry T. Hall, gdn, 6/4/1826, Glynn, MIC
GILBERT, Eli, decd, Israel Gilbert issued L/A 9/9/1828, James M. Prescott, sec, Richmond, AB
GILBERT, Elizabeth H., minor orph of William, decd, Jeremiah S. Gilbert, gdn, 1/8/1866, Fulton, GB
GILBERT, Felix H., decd, William G. Gilbert, exr, 1815 retns pd David P. Hillhouse, John Taylor's legacy, Nancy Hay, Betsy Shepherd, Caroline Gibson, Maria Hay, $2000 each, Wilkes, Retns
GILBERT, Isaac, William Gilbert apptd gdn of his own son, Isaac, to take possession of legacy left the boy by Jacob Strickland, Sr., decd, George Hampton and Josiah Lester, secs, 7/1807, Oglethorpe, OM, GB
GILBERT, John, LWT pvd 8/3/1804, names wife, Mary and ch--William, James, Nancy, Elizabeth; inventory by Dudley Jones, Russell Jones, James Hargrove, apprs, Franklin, IMW
GILBERT, John, decd, LWT pvd 10/1/1804, names wife, Mary and ch--William, James, John, Elizabeth, and Nancy, dtd 4/4/1803, Franklin, OM
GILBERT, L., decd, A. J. Walraven, admr, 10/5/1852, William Gilbert, sur, DeKalb, AB
GILBERT, Marnes, William Parker and James Scarborough, gdns 1/4/1819, Emanuel, GB
GILBERT, Mary, decd, LWT dtd 4/6/1804 names ch--Jane, Elizabeth, William; grch--William, son of John Gilbert, Edward Komings, Mary Komings (ch of Elizabeth Komings), Edward Gilbert, Mary Gilbert, Franklin, IMW, OM
GILBERT, Nancy, decd, Robin K. Gilbert, admr, James B. Green, sur, 1/20/1852, Bibb, AB
GILBERT, Nancy, William Parker and James Scarborough, gdns, 1/4/1819, Emanuel, GB
GILBERT, Richard M., decd, Alexander Fitzpatrick issued L/A 7/15/1824, P. Fitzpatrick, sec, Morgan, AB
GILBERT, Robert of Houston Co., Ga., decd, Edward Gilbert, admr, Julius J. Gilbert and L. Mimms, surs, 7/10/1848, Bibb, AB
GILBERT, Thomas, decd, Eady Gilbert and John Ray issued L/A 2/2/1810, Laurens, AB
GILBERT, William, decd, L/A to J. T. Gilbert 12/4/1865, Fulton
GILBERT, Winnie, William Parker and James Scarborough, gdn, 1/4/1819, Emanuel, GB
GILES, Barnabas M., made gdn of his ch--Isaac C. and William S. 4/28/1852, Houston, GB
GILES, John, decd, William J. Hobby applied for L/A 11/23/1795; 1800-1801 retns, John Russell, admr, Elbert, AB
GILL, Days, decd, Bailes Gill issued L/A 9/3/1834, Baldwin
GILL, Jacob bound to Thomas Brown, p. 144, Screven, OM
GILL, Jane, decd, LWT exhibited 2/8/1867, William R. Venable, exr, Fulton
GILL, John, decd, late of Charleston, South Carolina, Peter Murphy and Francis Grace issued L/A 12/9/1824, Richmond, AB
GILL, Maria bound to Thomas Brown, p. 144, Screven, OM

GILLELAND, Rhoda, decd, John Gindrat issued L/A 12/7/1818, Thomas
Quisenberry, John H. Manns, secs, Richmond, AB
GILLESPIE, Samuel, decd, Alexander D. Brown, admr, A. Dwight,
Roland Cook, Lewis H. Gregory, secs, 1831, Bibb, AB
GILLETT, William, decd, Hannah Gillett, admx, William H. Kean,
admr, 9/7/1812, Camden, MIC
GILLEY, Margaret M., minor orph of George N., decd, James L.
Adair, gdn, Thomas Moodh, sur, 12/12/1859, Paulding, GB
GILLILAND, Hugh, decd, Thomas Gilliland, father, apptd admr,
1781, Wilkes, MxR
GILLILAND, Thomas, Sr., deed of gift 6/26/1778 to grson, Thomas
Winters, son of John and Mary Winters, on the line of his
grfather Gilliland, froever, one slave, Wilkes, MxR
GILLIS, Christian, orph of Murdock, decd, Angus Gillis, John
Gillis, gdns, 9/1/1834, Emanuel, GB
GILLIS, Mary, orph of Murdock, decd, Angus Gillis, John Gillis,
gdns, 9/1/1834, Emanuel, GB
GILLIS, Nancy, orph of Murdock, decd, Angus Gillis, John Gillis,
gdns, 9/1/1834, Emanuel, GB
GILMER, Robert, decd, John Guice, gdn for orphs--Ruth and Ebby,
7/1/1822, Stephen Stovall, sec, Lincoln, GB
GILMORE, Almarine, orph of Thomas, decd, Hugh Gilmore, gdn, 1830,
Washington, GB
GILMORE, Aquilla, decd, Josiah Hardy, admr, 1838-1839 retns,
Butts, ER
GILMORE, Francis, decd, Agnes C. and Obed B. Gilmore issued L/A
12/5/1853, N. K. Wright, C. R. Simmons, secs; Nancy A. Gilmore,
gdn of minor ch--Ezekiel, Solomon, Alfred C., Levinna A.,
1/8/1855, Hall, AB, GB
GILMORE, Hugh, orph of Thomas, decd, Hugh Gilmore, gdn, 1830,
Washington
GILMORE, James, orph of Thomas, decd, Hugh Gilmore, gdn, 1830,
Washington
GILMORE, Narcissa, orph of Thomas, decd, Hugh Gilmore, gdn, 1830,
Washington
GILMORE, Thomas W., decd, Lorenzo D. Newson issued L/A 1/7/1839,
David Solomon Issued L/A 3/9/1840, Washington
GILMORE, William, decd, Benjamin riant issued L/A 8/7/1815,
Jackson, AB
GILMORE, W. W., decd, John H. Gilmore applies for L/A 3/16/1857,
John H. Kitchens, Samuel Sullivan, surs, Lee
GILPHIN, William, decd, Ephraim Sanders issued L/A 12/6/1790,
Randolph Ramsey, John Ramsey, secs, Richmond, AB
GILSTRAP, John M., decd, H. H. Bowen issued temporary L/A
10/27/1865, permanent L/A issued 5/7/1866, William H. Brown, sec,
White, AB
GILSTRAP, Milton H., H. H. Bowen, gdn, 1/7/1867, White, GB
GINDRACH, Joseph H., decd, George Wood, gdn of Henry, David and
Elizabeth 1/1/1838, Randolph, GB
GINDRAT, Dorcas, decd, LWT dtd 9/9/1797 pvd 9/1797 with assent by
husband, Henry; names daughters, Mary Stafford, Dorcas Gindrat,
Henrietta Gindrat, Elizabeth Tison; sons, William Stafford
Gindrat and Seth Stafford Gindrat, Effingham, Misc
GINDRAT, Henry, planter, decd, LWT pvd 2/23/1801 names wife,
Dorcas, ch--Henrietta Gindrat, Rhoda Gilleland, Mary H. Mark,
Abraham Gindrat, Susannah Morrell, John Gindrat, Effingham, Misc
GINDRAT, William Stafford, decd, Mrs. Dorcas Gindrat and her
husband, Henry, apply for L/A 5/3/1799, Effingham, Misc
GIPSON, Elbert A., orph of Samuel, decd, William Worley, gdn,
9/1829, Habersham, MIC

117

GIPSON, Mary A. F., orph of John T. A., decd, Joseph Ragsdale, gdn, Sarah Ragsdale and Daniel H. Bond, surs, 11/5/1849, Cherokee, GB

GIPSON, Zimolia D., orph of John T. A., decd, Joseph Ragsdale, gdn, Sarah Ragsdale and Daniel H. Bond, surs, 11/5/1849, Cherokee, GB

GIRARDEAU, Isaac, decd, William Girardeau qualified as admr 5/26/1783, Liberty, Ests

GIRARDEAU, John B., decd, Mrs. Ann Girardeau, relict, applied for leave to sell three tracts of land, viz: Cedar Grove (decd´s homeplace) and two 1000-acre tracts on Turtle River in Glynn Co., 1/31/1806, Liberty, MIC

GLASCOCK, Thomas (General), decd, John Willson, Jr. and William Bacon issued L/A 10/21/1810, John Willson, gdn of Edmund B., minor over age of 14, Richmond, AB, GB

GLASS, Richard, decd, Nancy and James D. Glass, exrs, L/T issued 1/1841; 1842 retn, Fayette, AB

GLASSON, Henry, orph of Hugh, decd, Sylvanus C. Doolittle, gdn, 9/6/1813, William Dyson, sur, Clarke, GB

GLASTER, Robert, decd, Abraham Jones issued L/A 7/2/1804, Thomas Moore, sec, Richmond, AB

GLEATON, Joseph, decd, Mary Gleaton and James C. Gleaton, admrs, Dooly, OD

GLENN, Clement, decd, William Glenn, admr, Groves Howard, James Olive, secs, 1/1809, Oglethorpe, MIC

GLENN, Duke, decd, LWT pvd 12/9/1788, lands in North Carolina on Pee Dee River, ch--David, Ann, Lucy; wife, Ann, Greene, Misc

GLENN, Jefferson, late of Baltimore, Maryland, decd, John Bessant dismissed as admr 6/2/1835, Camden, MIC

GLENN, Joseph, Sr., decd, LWT pvd 5/7/1810 names wife, Nancy and ch--John, William, Thornton, Jopson, Matthew H. and Simeon Gollandon Glenn, Lucy Brown, Sally Barnett, Polly Emory; caveat of Joseph Ewing vs. Isaac Barrett and wife and exrs 3/1/1813, Franklin, OM

GLENN, William, decd, L/A to Patience Glenn 7/22/1839, dismissed 11/1843, notice given iN Sandersville Telescope, Washington

GLOVER, Absolom, decd, L/A to Mary Glover 1/14/1839, Washington

GLOVER, James F., decd, L/A to Talitha Glover 1*7/1867, White, AB

GLOVER, Jefferson, decd, John Bessant qualified as admr, 9/2/1833, Camden, MIC

GLOVER, John, decd, late of Edgefield District, South Carolina, William Moody issued L/A 7/5/1835, John Marshall, William Jackson, secs, Richmond, AB

GNANN, Andrew, decd, LWT pvd 8/17/1801 names ch--Christopher, Benjamin, Timothy, Andrew, Hannah, Salome, Catherine, exrs, brother, Solomon Gnann & Christopher Gnann, exrs, Effingham, Misc

GNANN, Emanuel, decd, ordered that Jacob Gann, Jr. have leave to sell negroes to make division to heirs 9/1/1838, Effingham, MIC

GNANN, Sarah, decd, widow of Solomon, Andrew Griner applied for admn 11/3/1828, qualified 1/5/1829, Bulloch, MIC

GNANN, Solomon, Jr., decd, Joshua Gnann, admr, 7/7/1828 accts, Effingham, MIC

GNANN, Solomon, Sr., decd, Joshua Gnann applies for adm 9/27/1827, Bulloch, MIC

GOBER, Sarah F., orph of Robert H., decd, Samuel Cobbs, gdn, Phillip Graham, George R. McCurdy, sur, 7/14/1856, Cherokee, GB

GODDARD, Bailey, decd, James Goddard, admr, Jerry Cowls, William Cook, sur, 1/9/1832, Bibb, AB

GODSON, Anthony, decd, L/A issued Archibald Stand and Robert Owen 1/1819, Jasper, OM

GOFFE, Jane (Mrs) decd, of Savannah, Owen Owens, exr of LWT, 2/1/1791, Chatham, Adms

GOIN, Jane, decd, David Smith, admr, Hubbard Williams, Joseph Summerlin, sur, 12/12/1837, Butts, AB
GOLDEN, Arminda, decd, Robert R. Golden, admr, Dooly, OD
GOLDEN, David, decd, Phillip Brantley apptd admr, 9/4/1809, Warren, MIC
GOLDEN, Henry, decd, Sarah Golden and Solomon Nusom, admrs 1/15/1784, Wilkes, MxR
GOLDING, John R., orph of John R., decd, John Brown, gdn, 1/3/1825, Josiah Newton, Ebenezer Newton, surs, Clarke, GB
GOLDSBY, William, decd, Letty Goldsy, wid, to keep in her possession the plantation for maintenance of herself and children, 11/1/1819, Jasper, OM
GOLDSMITH, William, decd, B. F. Veal, Andrew J. Goldsmith, admrs, 12/6/1852, John L. Hamilton, Thomas Johnson, William Johnson, S. Howard, surs, DeKalb, AB
GOLDWIRE, Benjamin, decd, Charles White, Benjamin Roul, admrs, 4/22/1788, Chatham, Adms
GOLDWIRE, Frances, decd, James O. Goldwire applies for L/A, Effingham, MIC
GOLDWIRE, Francis, minor orph of John, decd, James O. Goldwire apptd gdn 5/5/1834, Effingham, MIC
GOLDWIRE, John, decd, Francis and James O. Goldwire applied for L/A 7/12/1832, Effingham, MIC
GOLDWIRE, John, Sr., decd, John Goldwire, admr, applies for dismission, 9/22/1792, Effingham, Misc
GOLDWIRE, Mary Ann, minor orph of John, decd, James O. Goldwire apptd gdn 5/5/1834, Effingham, MIC
GOLDWIRE, Obedience A., minor orph of John, decd, James O. Goldwire apptd gdn 5/5/1834, Effingham, MIC
GOLDWIRE, Rebecca, minor orph of John, decd, James O. Goldwire apptd gdn 5/5/1834, Effingham, MIC
GOLDWIRE, Sarah Jane, minor orph of John, decd, James O. Goldwire apptd gdn 5/5/1834, Effingham, MIC
GOLDWIRE, William Joseph J., minor orph of John, decd, James O. Goldwire apptd gdn 5/5/1834, Effingham, MIC
GOLEY, Robert, decd, William Cameron and John Williams issued L/A 1/6/1817, John L. Pearcy, Thomas Lewis, secs, Morgan, AB
GOLIGHTLY, James, decd, Nancy Brown, admx w/LWT annexed 1/8/1838, Morgan Brown issued L/A 5/7/1838, Washington, AB
GOLIGHTLY, Thomas, decd, Morgan Brown issued L/A 5/7/1838, Washington
GOOD, Isham, orph of Theophilus, Obadiah Edge apptd gdn 1/7/1822, Jasper, OM
GOOD, Martha, orph of Theophilus, Obadiah Edge apptd gdn 1/7/1822, Jasper, Om
GOOD, Nancy, orph of Theophilus, Obadiah Edge apptd gdn 1/7/1822, Jasper, OM
GOOD, Polly, orph of Theophilus, Obadiah Edge apptd gdn 1/7/1822, Jasper, OM
GOOD, Starling, decd, L/A issued William Peddy and Elizabeth Good 5/7/1821, leave gtd to sell 250 acres in Early Co., Jasper, OM
GOODBREAD, Samuel, decd, Thomas Goodbread apptd admr, 1/7/1840, Camden, MIC
GOODE, Agnes, Nicholas Hobson petitions to be apptd gdn, William Bailey, John Stiles, Wm Clift, surs, 12/1/1796, Oglethorpe, MIC
GOODE, Mackimus, decd, 11/1842, apprs: James Pace, William* Lowe, Michael Duskin, James Lowe, Stewart, Adms
GOODE, Phillip, decd, Adam Alexander qualified as admr 11/15/1786, Liberty, Ests
GOODGAME, Alexander, orph of Alexander, decd, William Bates, gdn, 9/2/1833, Washington, GB

GOODGAME, Elizabeth, orph of Alexander, decd, William Bates, gdn, 9/2/1833, Washington, GB

GOODGAME, George H., orph of Alexander, decd, William B. M. Goodgame, gdn, 9/7/1835, Washington, GB

GOODHUE, Nathaniel, decd, Michael Fitzgerald issued L/A 12/13/1867, Fulton

GOODIN, Bethena, Authora A. Couch, gdn, Mitchell Beasley, Alexander Timons, sur, 9/8/1856, Cherokee, GB

GOODIN, Milly Jane, Authora A. Couch, gdn, Mitchell Beasley, Alexander Timons, sur, 9/8/1856, Cherokee, GB

GOODIN, Sally, Authora A. Couch, gdn, Mitchell Beasley, Alexander Timons, sur, 9/8/1856, Cherokee, GB

GOODIN, William J., Authora A. Couch, gdn, Mitchell Beasley, Alexander Timons, sur, 9/8/1856, Cherokee, GB

GOODMAN, Aden T., James Brown, gdn, Dooly, OD

GOODMAN, David, decd, LWT pvd 9/30/1817, Sarah Goodman, admx, apprs: Sharrod McCall, William Wright, Bulloch, Misc

GOODMAN, David, LWT pvd 1/1/1821, Jane: ch: Jesse, Henry, Wm, Elizabeth, Frances, Margaret; dau-in-law, Sary, wid of David Jr., gdns of grson John Goodman, son of David, decd. grfather, Aaron Cone; uncles Peter & Wm Cone, Bulloch, Misc

GOODMAN, David, Jr., Sarah Goodman to receive $19 from est, 5/3/1819, Bulloch, MIC

GOODMAN, David Sr., decd, inv 10/31/1823, apprs: Jehu Everitt, John Wise, Aaron Everitt, Bulloch, Misc

GOODMAN, Elizabeth, James Brown, gdn, Dooly, OD

GOODMAN, Henry, decd, Charles Higdon, admr, Dooly, OD

GOODMAN, Henry, decd, Timothy Goodman, admr 11/30/1846; appraisers of est: Jacob Slappy, William Posey, Simeon Royal, William W. Brown w/ Mary Goodman, John Goodman, buyers at sale, Dooly, I&A

GOODMAN, James, James Brown, gdn, Dooly, OD

GOODMAN, John, orph of David, Jr., decd, William, Aaron and Peter Cone apptd gdns 1/1/1821, Bulloch, MIC

GOODMAN, Mary, James Brown, gdn, Dooly, OD

GOODWIN, Charles G., decd, Solomon Kemp, admr, retns for 1851-1853, 1/29/1859, Cobb, BB

GOODWIN, Gustin, decd, James M. Reeve, admr, 12/1/1862, William Wright, G. L. Humphries, surs, DeKalb, AB

GOODWIN, Hey, minor, Solomon Kemp, gdn, 1852-53 retns, 5/12/1859, Cobb, BB

GOODWIN, Ivey, minor, Solomon Kemp, gdn, 1852-53 retns, 5/12/1859, Cobb, BB

GOODWIN, John, minor, Solomon Kemp, gdn, 1852-53 retns, 5/12/1859, Cobb, BB

GOODWIN, Jones F., decd, John A. White, admr de bonis non w/LWT annexed, William Collins, sur, 2/9/1849, Bibb, AB

GOODWIN, Narcissa, minor, Solomon Kemp, gdn, 1852-53 retns, 5/12/1859, Cobb, BB

GOODWIN, Peter, decd, Elizabeth Goodwin, applies for L/A, 4/26/1798, Harmon Wilkinson and Peter Castleberry, sur, Warren, AB, MIC

GOODWIN, Vester, minor, Solomon Kemp, gdn, 1852-53 retns, 5/12/1859, Cobb, BB

GOODWIN, Wyche, decd, Jacob Danford issued temp L/A 9/12/1803, George Pearson, Angus Martin, secs, Richmond, AB

GOOLEY, John, decd, Isaac M. Connell, admr, James S. Olive, sur, 10/30/1855, Cherokee, AB

GOOLRICH, Doyle S., decd, John Edgar issued L/A 9/25/1827, H. Cook, Fields, Kennedy, sec, Richmond, AB

GRAY, Jacob, decd, David Rogers, admr de bonis non 7/1/1816, Jackson, OM
GRAY, James, decd, Lewis H. Fargason, admr, pd: Elizabeth Gray, gdn for Rachel, William, James, Allen, and Johnson Auster Gray, Hardy Pace, 11/10/1835, Butts, ER
GRAY, James, decd, Lewis H. Ferguson, admr, Johnson Ferguson, William H. Wyatt, sur, 9/5/1831, AB
GRAY, James, decd, Mary Gray issued L/A 4/26/1794, Philip Clayton, sec; Mary, wid and relict now Mary Briscoe, chooses child's pt 9/16/1801, Richmond, AB
GRAY, James, late of Henry Co., Mrs. Harriet N. Gray issued L/A 3/3/1845, Baldwin
GRAY, James, orph of James, decd, Elizabeth Gray, gdn, Thomas Pair, sur, 5/5/1834, Butts, GB
GRAY, James, decd, Lewis H. Ferguson, admr, Johnson Ferguson, William H. Wyatt, sur, 9/5/1831, AB
GRAY, James, Sr., decd, James Gray, admr, 5/6/1822, Thomas Lockett, Micajah Rogers, David Sallis, surs, Warren, AB
GRAY, Jane (Mrs.), decd, Mrs. Elizabeth Green and William Maxwell, admrs, 4/23/1790, Chatham, Adms
GRAY, John C., orph of John M., decd, 3/7/1837, Harris
GRAY, John M., decd, John C. Gray, William L. Hartsfield, gdn of orphs 3/7/1836, Harris
GRAY, John W., LWT pvd by James McDonald; exrs named therein declined to qualify; ct apptd A. J. Bessant as admr, directed to keep plantation of decd on Cumberland Isl and cultivate it, 1/7/1851, Camden, MIC
GRAY, Johnson, orph of James, decd, Elizabeth Gray, gdn, Thomas Pair, sur, 5/5/1834, Butts, GB
GRAY, Levisa, orph of William, decd, Rachel Gray, gdn, 12/2/1822, S. Brown, sur, Clarke, GB
GRAY, Lucinda, orph of William, decd, Rachel Gray, gdn, 12/2/1822, S. Brown, sur, Clarke, GB
GRAY, Nancy, decd, LWT pvd 9/4/1843, George Granberry, exr, Harris
GRAY, Nancy, orph of John, decd, 10/7/1834, Harris
GRAY, Pleasant bound to Shelton White to learn farming 5/4/1812, Elbert, GB
GRAY, Rachel, orph of James, decd, Elizabeth Gray, gdn, Thomas Pair, sur, 5/5/1834, Butts, GB
GRAY, William, orph of James, decd, Elizabeth Gray, gdn, Thomas Pair, sur, 5/5/1834, Butts, GB
GRAY, William, decd, William Watkins issued L/A 4/20/1852, Rufus M. Love, sec, Lumpkin, AB
GREEN, Abner, rule to show cause, p. 81, Screven, OM
GREEN, Alexander, decd, Hugh Knox, admr de bonis non, 7/8/1844, Baldwin
GREEN, Amos, decd, Andrew J. Green, admr, Edmond Sebastian, John Gilmore, sur, 1/15/1857, Cherokee, AB
GREEN, Ann, decd, David Delegal qualified as admr 2/1/1791, Liberty, Ests
GREEN, Christopher C., minor of Rebecca, decd, Thomas Moore, gdn, Mary Moore, sur, 9/1/1844, Emanuel, GB
GREEN, Elizabeth, Thomas Green, gdn, p. 8, 16, Screven, OM
GREEN, Elizabbh, decd, James Stubbs, admr, 3/5/1838; heirs: Samuel A. Green, John B. Ogletree, Leroy Jenkins, Zachariah Bailey, Moses, Elizabeth and Felix Green, Randolph
GREEN, George, decd, L/A to Mrs. Catharine Green 2/6/1866, Fulton
GREEN, Isaac, decd, John Wilson issued L/A 7/11/1789, David Robeson, Sr. and Jr., secs, Richmond, AB
GREEN, Isaac, decd of Richmond Co., 7/7/1789 John Wilson gtd L/A, Columbia, Ests

GOULDING, William, decd, Sarah and Peter Goulding, Thomas Graves, qualified admrs 6/6/1787, Liberty, Ests

GOULDSMITH, Richard, decd, Sarah G. Gouldsmith issued L/A 4/1/1867, Fulton

GOUNDERS, Mary, decd, LWT pvd 7/7/1845, Effingham, MIC

GOWDER, Frederick, decd, Frederick M. Gowder and Stephen G. Furr issued L/A 7/2/1850, S. G. and Paul Furr, secs, Hall, AB

GOWER, Robert M., decd, D. S. Gower, David Hamilton, admrs w/LWT annexed, Mildred T. Gower, P. H. B. Gower, sur, 5/5/1874; inv 6/1/1874, Gwinnett, AB

GOZA, Robert J., decd, W. F. Gholsten, admr w/LWT annexed, Thomas H. Liddele, sur, 6/7/1875, Gwinnett, AB

GRACE, John, decd, LWT dtd 9/29/1839, pvd 1/1840, wife, Nancy, ch: Mary Carmichael, son-in-law, John Carmichael, Tattnall, I&A

GRACE, Samuel, decd, John Laidler, Jr., gdn of orphs: Andrew H., Samuel, Nancy S., 9/4/1854, Houston, GB

GRACIE, Daniel, decd, Archibald Clarke, temp admr, gtd leave to sell perishable prop of est, 9/2/1822, Camden, MIC

GRADY, Jackson, orph of Grigsby, decd, William Prady, gdn, James Gorman, sec, 7/6/1829, Hall, GB

GRADY, William, decd, Andrew Hampton issued L/A 7/1/1816, Laurens, AB

GRADY, William, decd, James M. Thompson issued L/A 9/27/1822, Milton Antony, sec, Richmond, AB

GRAHAM, Alexander, decd, Mrs. Graham and Joseph Jackson apptd admrs w/LWT annexed, 1/5/1804, Camden, MIC

GRAHAM, Ann (Mrs.), LWt pvd 6/7/1808, Camden, MIC

GRAHAM, Archibald, decd, Archibald Graham issued L/A 1/1825; Archibald and Jane Graham, temp L/A 1/23/1826, Habersham, MIC

GRAHAM (or Tutte), Carolina Amanda, Margaret Ann Graham objects to James Tutt becoming gdn because she is the mother of sd Caroline 6/1/1836, Effingham, MIC

GRAHAM, James, decd, Rufus Knight, admr, Henry Durden, sur, 5/6/1837, Emanuel, AB

GRAHAM, James, decd, L/A to Williamson Wynne 5/1/1815, Jasper, OM

GRAHAM, John, decd, Jesse Graham applies for L/A, with LWT annexed 8/30/1839, Effingham, MIC

GRAHAM, John, decd, LWT pvd 1/4/1836, Effingham, MIC

GRAHAM, John, decd, Thomas H. Brewer gtd L/A 10/10/1836; Seleta Graham made choice of child's pt of husband's est 11/7/1836; Letitia Graham, extrx, gtd leave to sell real est 7/2/1837. Effingham, MIC

GRAHAM, Richard, decd, Roger Quarles issued L/A 11/15/1788, Thomas Jones, John Kindrick, secs, Richmond, AB

GRAHAM, Sebler, decd, LWT pvd by Samuel Hodges 9/2/1839, Effingham, MIC

GRAHAM, Selita Duncan, Jesse and Alexander chose their mother gdn, Selita Graham 9/3/1838, Effingham, MIC

GRAHAM, William H., decd, L/A to J. J. Deamond 8/1/1853, Y. J. Marbut, Henry Holmes, B. Smith, D. G. Waldrup, surs, DeKalb, AB

GRANBERRY, Silas, decd, LWT dtd Monroe Co., pvd 1/11/1847, wife, Emaline, extrx, Geo. Granberry, Early Cleveland, exrs, Harris

GRANBURY, Moses, decd, Nowell Robertson and George Granberry presented LWT, they were apptd exrs 3/7/1808, Warren, MIC

GRANNIS, John, decd, George Langford issued L/A 3/6/1826, John W. Langford, P. Fitzpatrick, secs, Morgan, AB

GRANT, Andrew, decd, Mark Mayo and Benjamin Daniel issued L/A 3/2/1812, Laurens, AB

GRANT, Daniel, decd, Archibald Clark, temp admr, produced inv, 1/4/1832, dismissed 6/3/1834, Camden, MIC

GRANT, John, decd, James Grant issued L/A 11/1/1842, W. B. Grant, sec, Hall, AB

GRANT, Nancy, orph of Andrew, decd, minor above age 14, John Parramore, gdn, 9/7/1812, Laurens, GB
GRANT, Peter, orph of Andrew, decd, Peter Sanderson, gdn, 1/5/1819; John McDaniel, gdn, 5/3/1819, Laurens, GB
GRANT, Polly, orph of Andrew, decd, minor under age 14, Mark Mayo, gdn, 9/7/1812, Laurens, GB
GRATEHOUSE, Purnine, bastard child of Sarah Gratehouse, Isaac Funderburk, gdn, 9/6/1813, John Cohoon, Moses H. Cogburn, surs, Clarke, GB
GRAVES, Charles, decd, Elizabeth Graves, extrx of LWT, 8/1853, 1854 retn, Fayette, AB
GRAVES, David, decd, Malinda Graves, admx, Minten and John Graves, Hilby Cleckler, Jesse Ward, surs, 1/1853, 1853-1854 retns, Fayette, AB
GRAVES, George, decd, Mary Graves, gdn of minor orphs 4/5/1826: George, Caroline, Thomas and John, Augustine Slaughter, sec, Richmond, GB
GRAVES, Robert, decd, LWT pvd 8/9/1796, Marah Graves, extrx, Columbia, Ests
GRAVES, Thomas, decd, John and Rebecca Graves, admrs, 2/2/1790, Liberty, Ests
GRAVES, Thomas, decd, LWT pvd 3/5/1791, Perry Graves, exr, Columbia, Ests
GRAVES, William, decd, Rebecca Graves, William Graves, Thomas Graves, exrs qualified 5/5/1783, Liberty, Ests
GRAVES, William, Jr., decd, Col. John Baker, Thomas Graves, admrs 2/14/1785, Liberty, Ests
GRAY, Adeline T., decd, James L. Rogers qualified as admr 11/3/1862, dismissed 7/5/1866, Fulton
GRAY, Amy, decd, 10/7/1826 James Gray, admr, John Davidson, sur, Warren, AB
GRAY, Andrew, late of Ala, decd, Allen Gray, admr, Edward W. O'Nail, sur, 3/6/1837, Butts, AB
GRAY, Ann Eliza and Annis, illegitimate children of Harriett Gray, George T. Gray, gdn, 1/4/1841, Tattnall, GB
GRAY, Daniel W., decd, James Baird gtd leave to sell wearing apparel, 1/2/1815, Glynn, MIC
GRAY, George, decd, est 10/4/1852, Clarke, LP
GRAY, Jacob, decd, David Rogers, admr de bonis non 7/1/1816, Jackson, OM
GRAY, James, decd, Lewis H. Fargason, admr, pd: Elizabeth Gray, gdn for Rachel, William, James, Allen, and Johnson Auster Gray, Hardy Pace, 11/10/1835, Butts, ER
GRAY, James, decd, Lewis H. Ferguson, admr, Johnson Ferguson, William H. Wyatt, sur, 9/5/1831, AB
GRAY, James, decd, Mary Gray issued L/A 4/26/1794, Philip Clayton, sec; Mary, wid and relict now Mary Briscoe, chooses child's pt 9/16/1801, Richmond, AB
GRAY, James, late of Henry Co., Mrs. Harriet N. Gray issued L/A 3/3/1845, Baldwin
GRAY, James, orph of James, decd, Elizabeth Gray, gdn, Thomas Pair, sur, 5/5/1834, Butts, GB
GRAY, James, decd, Lewis H. Ferguson, admr, Johnson Ferguson, William H. Wyatt, sur, 9/5/1831, AB
GRAY, James, Sr., decd, James Gray, admr, 5/6/1822, Thomas Lockett, Micajah Rogers, David Sallis, surs, Warren, AB
GRAY, Jane (Mrs.), decd, Mrs. Elizabeth Green and William Maxwell, admrs, 4/23/1790, Chatham, Adms
GRAY, John C., orph of John M., decd, 3/7/1837, Harris
GRAY, John M., decd, John C. Gray, William L. Hartsfield, gdn of orphs 3/7/1836, Harris

GRAY, John W., LWT pvd by James McDonald; exrs named therein declined to qualify; ct apptd A. J. Bessant as admr, directed to keep plantation of decd on Cumberland Isl and cultivate it, 1/7/1851, Camden, MIC

GRAY, Johnson, orph of James, decd, Elizabeth Gray, gdn, Thomas Pair, sur, 5/5/1834, Butts, GB

GRAY, Levisa, orph of William, decd, Rachel Gray, gdn, 12/2/1822, S. Brown, sur, Clarke, GB

GRAY, Lucinda, orph of William, decd, Rachel Gray, gdn, 12/2/1822, S. Brown, sur, Clarke, GB

GRAY, Nancy, decd, LWT pvd 9/4/1843, George Granberry, exr, Harris

GRAY, Nancy, orph of John, decd, 10/7/1834, Harris

GRAY, Pleasant bound to Shelton White to learn farming 5/4/1812, Elbert, GB

GRAY, Rachel, orph of James, decd, Elizabeth Gray, gdn, Thomas Pair, sur, 5/5/1834, Butts, GB

GRAY, William, orph of James, decd, Elizabeth Gray, gdn, Thomas Pair, sur, 5/5/1834, Butts, GB

GRAY, William, decd, William Watkins issued L/A 4/20/1852, Rufus M. Love, sec, Lumpkin, AB

GREEN, Abner, rule to show cause, p. 81, Screven, OM

GREEN, Alexander, decd, Hugh Knox, admr de bonis non, 7/8/1844, Baldwin

GREEN, Amos, decd, Andrew J. Green, admr, Edmond Sebastian, John Gilmore, sur, 1/15/1857, Cherokee, AB

GREEN, Ann, decd, David Delegal qualified as admr 2/1/1791, Liberty, Ests

GREEN, Christopher C., minor of Rebecca, decd, Thomas Moore, gdn, Mary Moore, sur, 9/1/1844, Emanuel, GB

GREEN, Elizabeth, Thomas Green, gdn, p. 8, 16, Screven, OM

GREEN, Elizabeth, decd, James Stubbs, admr, 3/5/1838; heirs: Samuel A. Green, John B. Ogletree, Leroy Jenkins, Zachariah Bailey, Moses, Elizabeth and Felix Green, Randolph

GREEN, George, decd, L/A to Mrs. Catharine Green 2/6/1866, Fulton

GREEN, Isaac, decd, John Wilson issued L/A 7/11/1789, David Robeson, Sr. and Jr., secs, Richmond, AB

GREEN, Isaac, decd of Richmond Co., 7/7/1789 John Wilson gtd L/A, Columbia, Ests

GREEN, James, decd, Isaac Green apptd admr, 8/3/1835, Camden, MIC

GREEN, John, decd, James Habersham qualified as admr, 8/12/1784, Chatham, Adms

GREEN, John, decd, Jane Green, extrx, made retns in 1809, Jackson, OM

GREEN, John, decd, Joseph Chairs and Mourning Green issued L/A 7/3/1809, Laurens, AB

GREEN, John (Colonel), decd, Benjamin Harris issued L/A 11/1/1802, Lewis Harris, sec, Richmond, AB

GREEN, John R., decd, Sally Green, gdn of Lucy, Rebecca, Dorothy, Wm and John, orphs, 9/1/1817, James Meriwether, sur, Clarke, GB

GREEN, Mary, decd, LWT pvd 8/24/1866, Jane Kelly, extrx, Fulton

GREEN, Nancy, minor, Joab Horn, gdn, to furnish with sufficient board, clothing, etc., 1/7/1812, Laurens, GB

GREEN, Oliver P., idiot, Andrew J. Green, gdn, John Gilmer, Jonathan Williams, sur, 5/1858, Cherokee, GB

GREEN, Thomas A., decd, Mary G. Green, etc., admx, p. 69, Screven, OM

GREEN, Uriah, decd, Mrs. Mary Green qualified admx 10/26/1790, Liberty, Ests

GREEN, W. C., decd, H. M. Mayes, exr, applies for L/D 8/2/1869; Davis Irwin, atty for John Anderson, gdn of minor heirs of decd & P. M. Green, wid, A. N. Simpson, and M. P. Gartrell and Winn

appear regarding est comm, 12/22/1869, Cobb, MIC
GREEN, William E., decd, L/A to Robt C. Green 10/15/1867, Fulton
GREENE, Nathaniel (General), decd, Nathaniel R. Greene applied
for Rule Nisi to issue against admr and exr of his late father,
and his mother, Mrs. Catherine Miller, requiring them to make
settlement for the ests, 1/5/1819, Camden, MIC
GREENE, Nathaniel (General), decd, Russell Goodrich qualifies as
exr; Mrs. Louisa Shaw also offers to qualify as extrx,
4/10/1815; exr reports bal due est, James and Louisa C. Shaw as
exrs report bal 3/1/1819, Camden, MIC
GREENE, William A., decd, C. C. Greene and W. A. Wilson issued
L/A 3/5/1860, Fulton
GREENLEA, Eliza, decd, L/A issued to Jane Howard 3/2/1829, Baldwin
GREER, Aaron, decd, Robert Greer, Jr. issued L/A 1/1816, sells
land in Wilkinson Co., 26th dist, 11/4/1816, Jasper, OM
GREER, Aquilla, decd, LWT pvd 10/3/1790, wife, Elizabeth, ch:
Sary Haynes, James, William, Elizabeth Starkey, Vinson, Delia
Haynes, and Yel, Greene, Misc
GREER, Benjamin, decd, Durham Kelly, gdn of Elizabeth, William
and Cetilla, orphs, 7/1/1811, Joseph Cowlin, sur, Clarke, GB
GREER, Robert D., decd, Augustus L. Pitts, Mary Ann Greer, admrs,
9/3/1860, Joseph Pitts, James Paden, surs, DeKalb, AB
GREER, Thomas, decd, Amesa R. Moore, Hiram Reid, admr for orphs
1/5/1835, Harris, GB
GREER, Thomas, decd, L/A to Thos Greer 12/11/1792, Columbia, Ests
GREER, William, decd, Josiah Greer, admr, 1855, Cobb, BB
GREESON, George W., decd, Benjamin Thomas, admr, G. W. Thomas, A.
N. Thomas, James Farr, W. P. Bell, sur, 2/5/1872, Gwinnett, AB
GREGG, John, orph of George, decd, bound to Payton Chapman, 1809,
Jackson, OM
GREGG, John, decd, Wm Wood issued L/A 9/5/1808, Jackson, OM
GREGG, Thomas, decd, Howard Cash and Johannah Gregg, admrs,
2/29/1808, Elbert, AR
GREGGS, Lee, orph of Lee and Hannah, decd, Cullin Pope, Jesse
McKinsey Pope, William Horton, gdns, 5/4/1812, Jones, GB
GREGORY, Algarim, illegitimate, William C. Phillips, gdn,
2/3/1838, Anthony Phillips, Neill McLeod, Montgomery, GB
GREGORY, Emanuel, decd, Lewis H. Gregory issued L/A 5/11/1821,
Simeon Russell, Thomas Quisenberry, secs, Richmond, AB
GREGORY, Howell, decd, Francis Beall, admr, 3/2/1812, Samuel
Beall, sur, Warren, AB
GREGORY, Ossian?, decd, of Butler Co., Amherst W. Stone issued
L/A 9/1/1862, Fulton
GRENADE, Adam, decd, Joseph Ansley, admr, 11/5/1832, George W.
Ray, Aaron Adkins, surs, Warren, AB
GRENADE, Benjamin, decd, James Grenade, admr, 9/6/1813, Jeremiah
Burkhalter, sur, Warren, AB
GRESHAM, Betty, decd, LWT pvd 7/1807, Oglethorpe, OM
GRESHAM, Davis, decd, Archibald, Littleberry and Young Gresham,
admrs, 3/16/1819 bond, D. Meriwether, Hundley Brewer, surs,
Clarke, AB
GRESHAM, Mary, decd, LWT pvd, Harris Gresham, exr, 9/1806,
Oglethorpe, OM
GRESHAM, Thomas, orph of Thomas, decd, James D. Gresham, gdn,
1812-1815 pd bd and tuition to Moriah Mercer and William Booker,
Wilkes, Retns
GREY, Jane, decd, 1799 est, Bryan, CR
GRIER, Josiah, decd, Catherine Grier applies for L/A 10/19/1869,
Cobb, MIC
GRIERSON, Abram, decd, Susannah Grierson, admx, 4/25/1829, Howell
Hight, Ambrose, Hight, surs, Warren, AB

GRIFFIN, Abel, decd, Hiram Mott issued L/A 9/3/1838, Washington
GRIFFIN, Abel, idiot and orph of Asa, decd, Hiram Mott, gdn, 1/22/1838, Washington, GB
GRIFFIN, Adeline, orph of Robert T., decd, Green Griffin, gdn, James S. Dial, sec, 1/8/1849, Cherokee, GB
GRIFFIN, Andrew, decd, LWT pvd 11/8/1794, wife, Nancy, ch: Jinney, Peggy, Nancy, Polly, Thomas, Greene, Misc
GRIFFIN, Andrew J., decd, John J. A. Griffin issued L/A 1/8/1849, Asa Griffin, Joseph Dunagan, secs, Hall, AB
GRIFFIN, Charles, orph of James, decd, of Wilkes Co, bound until age 21 to George W. Pace as apprentice to learn art of farming, 1/9/1832, Butts, GB
GRIFFIN, Edward, decd, Henry G. Ross, admr, Luke Ross, Irwin Bullock, sec, 11/5/1832, Bibb, AB
GRIFFIN, Eliza, decd, John C. Blance gtd leave to sell negro 9/1/1828, Effingham, MIC
GRIFFIN, Ezekiel, Jr., orph of John, decd, Sarah J. Griffin, gdn, Ezekiel Griffin, sur, 8/11/1859, Paulding, GB
GRIFFIN, George, orph of Robert T., decd, Green Griffin, gdn, James S. Dial, sec, 1/8/1849, Cherokee, GB
GRIFFIN, Henry, decd, James and John Griffin applies for L/A 3/10/1835, Effingham, MIC
GRIFFIN, James, decd, David Griffin apptd admr 9/5/1842, Effingham, MIC
GRIFFIN, John, decd, Ezekiel Griffin, admr, G. W. Foote, sur, 6/11/1859, Paulding, AB
GRIFFIN, John, decd, Elizabeth Griffin, wid, apptd admx, inv 2/7/1784, Edward Nugent, Nathl Cots, Wm West, apprs, Wilkes, MxR
GRIFFIN, John T., orph of John, decd, Sarah J. Griffin, gdn, Ezekiel Griffin, sur, 8/11/1859, Paulding, GB
GRIFFIN, Joseph, orph of James, decd, of Wilkes Co, bound until age 21 to George W. Pace as apprentice to learn art of farming, 1/9/1832, Butts, GB
GRIFFIN, Martha, decd, LWT pvd 6/11/1787, James Jackson, Thomas Mills, admrs, Chatham, Adms
GRIFFIN, Mary, orph of Robert T., decd, Green Griffin, gdn, James S. Dial, sec, 1/8/1849; Thomas Boring, gdn, 3/14/1849, Isaac Boring, sec, Cherokee, GB
GRIFFIN, Mary F., orph of John, decd, Sarah J. Griffin, gdn, Ezekiel Griffin, sur, 8/11/1859, Paulding, GB
GRIFFIN, Rial B., decd, Lewellen Phillips, admr, 1/1844; apprs: William T. Park, James Lunsford, Thomas R. Woodall, Abel Champion; purchasers at sale: Langston & Lyddal Bacon, R. A. Bell, John W., Marty & William Griffin, Stewart, Adms
GRIFFIN, Sarah, orph of Robert T., decd, Green Griffin, gdn, James S. Dial, sec, 1/8/1849, Cherokee, GB
GRIFFIN, Thomas, decd, L/A Lucy Griffin 8/3/1812, Tattnall, MIC
GRIFFIN, Waldon apptd gdn of minor children of James, decd, 1/13/1845, viz: Martha, Maria, James and Margaret, Effingham, MIC
GRIFFIS, Casandra, minor orph of John, decd, Sarah Griffis, gdn, 2/6/1826; Robt Higdon, gdn, Jno Higdon, Henry Durden, Danl Kenady, surs, 5/1/1837, Emanuel, GB
GRIFFIS, John, decd, John R. Daniell, admr, William D. Nabb, Owen Fountain, Wm Parker, F. T. Hotton, Wm Lasenby, Nathaniel Hotton, Hambleton G. Daniell, John Chasen, sur, 9/5/1825, AB
GRIFFIS, John, decd, Sary Griffis, admx, John C. Neel, David Anderson, sur, 9/5/1825, Emanuel, AB
GRIFFIS, John, decd, Sarah Griffis, admx, est appraised 9/21/1824, Emanuel, A
GRIFFIS, Mary, orph and minor of John, decd, Robert Higdon, gdn, John Higdon, Henry Durden, Daniel Kenady, surs, 5/1/1837, Emanuel, GB

GRIFFIS, Mary and Milly, minors of John, decd, Sarah Griffis, gdn, 2/6/1826, Emanuel, GB
GRIFFIS, Reuben, minor orph of John, decd, Robert Higdon, gdn, John Higdon, Henry Durden, Daniel Kenady, surs, 5/1/1837, Emanuel, GB
GRIFFIS, Reuben N., minor of John, decd, Sarah Griffis, gdn, 2/6/1826, Emanuel, GB
GRIFFITH, John, decd, LWT pvd by William Harvie and Thomas Meriwether, Ann Griffith, extrx, 7/1809, Oglethorpe, MIC
GRIFFITH, John, decd, Robert and Martha Griffith, admrs, 4/17/1799 inventory, 200 acres north fork of Oconee River; Saml Nelson, John McEny, Robt Cowden, apprs, Elbert, AR
GRIGGS, Bryant, decd, B. O. Jones, gdn of orphs, T. M. Jones, sur, 5/1849, 1/1851-1852 retns, Fayette, GB
GRIGGS, Bryant, decd, James F. Johnson, admr de bonis non, T. D. King, Patrick Allen, 7/1849, 1851-1853 retns, Fayette, AB
GRIGGS, John J., decd, L/A issued Wesley and Harriett H. Griggs 8/22/1854, Webster, OD
GRIGGS, Powell, decd, carpenter, Jane Griggs, admx, 12/12/1785, Chatham, Adms
GRIGSBY, James, decd, John Moody, gdn of orphs: Betholm R. and Thomas K. 3/8/1824, John H. Porter, sec, Morgan, GB
GRIMES, Lewis, decd, Clk or L. R. Redding to show cause why they should not administer est 11/1857, Webster, OD
GRIMES, Patsy, retn of gdn, John Wilhite, 1802, Elbert, GR
GRIMES, Thomas, gdn of his children: Marshall, Elizabeth Ann, Caroline, George K., 1834, Stewart, Adms
GRIMES, William, decd, Samuel Brooks, admr, 7/1837; apprs: Charles Sapp, Donald McLeod, Tomlinson Fort, and wid, Mary Grimes, Stewart, Adms
GRIMES, William, decd, heirs of father's est-Jno Wilhite, gdn, Wm Grimes/gdn of Thos Grimes, Wm & Elizabeth Carter, Robt Moon; 1795 pd Abraham Hill, boarding Wm Grimes, Jr., Jno Wilhight, exr; 1808 retn of Wm Grimes, gdn ofThos M. Grimes, Elbert, AR
GRIMMER, Eleanor, decd, Williard Boynton, admr, 1834; purchaser at sale: F. H. Boynton, Stewart, Adms
GRIMMET, Robert, decd, Aaron Levingson and William Grimmet applied for L/A 9/1/179; inv shows notes of Robert Greer, Dozier, Grimmet, Wm Grimmet, Robt. Grimmet, Jr. 10/31/1791, Greene, Misc
GRIMMET, Robert, decd, James N. Grimmet, admr, Alfred L. Grimmet, Thomas L. Grimmet, Thomas B. Burford, sur, 6/1/1839, Butts, AB
GRIMMETT, Robert, decd, 2/1840 DeKalb Co land, A. J. Grimmet, admr (gdn of Robt); ch-Jas H., Wm M., Thos L. Grimmet, Mary May, Geo. E. Hodge; heirs-Geo. Hodge, Mary, A. J., Thos L., Hiram, Robert Grimmet, Jas Stewart, Butts, ER
GRIMMET, Robert M., minor of Robert, decd, Alfred J. Grimmet, gdn, Mary Grimmet, Ezekiel Watkins, sur, 1/14/1840, Butts, GB
GRINAGE, Alexander, decd, LWT pvd 7/1/1839, Toliver Jones, exr, Harris
GRINAGE, Joshua, decd, Wm H. Harper, gdn for orphs: Josephine and Laurence, 9/1/1823, Wm Harper, Peter Lamar, Stephen Stovall, secs, Lincoln, MIC
GRINDER, Timothy, to produce orphan child, p. 39, Screven, OM
GRINER, Andrew, decd, L/A to Caleb Griner /2/1837, Effingham, MIC
GRINER, Benjamin, Philip Griner apptd gdn 11/6/1815, Bulloch, MIC
GRINER, Caroline, James Griner apptd gdn 11/6/1815, Bulloch, MIC
GRINER, James A. signed as receiving from est, Wm Grimmet, Robt. Grimmet, Jr. 10/31/1791, Greene, Misc
GRINER, Martin signed as having recd his share of est of John Wise from Rachel Wise, admx 9/5/1836, Bulloch, Misc

GRINER, Philip, decd, James Griner issued L/A 5/3/1819, David Goodman, Sr., Robert Donaldson, Joshua Hodges, Aaron Everitt, Samuel Wilson to divide property, 11/6/1815, Bulloch, MIC

GRINER, Samuel, decd, Isaac Waters, admr, p. 100, Screven, OM

GRINER, W. B. recd from Sarah Griner, admx of est of James Griner, decd, his full share of the est 3/30/1844, Bulloch, Misc

GRINSLATE, John, decd, Andrew J. Miller issued L/A 10/19/1829, Peter F. Boisclair, sec, Richmond, AB

GRISHAM, Joseph, decd, LWT pvd 6/1857-ch:-Jno Overton Grisham, Susan Brewster, wf of Patrick, Elizabeth Brown; sis-Malinda Watson; grsons-Jos. & Jno O. Grisham; nephew-Jos. Watson; niece-N. E. Watson; Jno Brewster & Birdwell Hill est, Cherokee

GRIZZLE, Thomas W., decd, Lettice Grizzle, admx, 1/2/1825, William H. Blount, Lewis Jackson, surs, Warren, AB

GRIZZLE, Wilie, decd, 5/5/1823, Thomas Gibson, admr, Arthur Moncrief, Gerrard Camp, surs, Warren, AB

GROCE, James E., orph of Shepherd, decd, James N. Harper, gdn, 3/2/1829, Wm Jones, sec, Lincoln, GB

GROCE, John B., decd, C. Carloss, admr, George F. Cowart, Richard A. Cane, sur, 5/10/1854, Bibb, AB

GROCE, Sarah, orph, John J. Hendricks has been damaged by Moses Fagan, gdn; ordered that sd Fagan bond be delivered to Thomas J. Rusk, 7/1832, Habersham, MIC

GROCE, Shepherd, decd, Peter Lamar, gdn for orphs: Jared E., Benton, George L., 3/2/1829, Thomas Simmons, James N. Harper, secs; Jared E. Groce, gdn for Benton, George L., 9/6/1831, Lincoln, GB

GROCE, Solomon J., decd, Richard B. Roddenbury, admr, Thomas P. Stubbs, Mary Ann Groce, sur, 3/3/1851, Bibb, AB

GROFF, John, decd, L/A to John A. Cuthbert 11/11/1835, Baldwin

GROGAN, David, decd, late of formerly DeKalb, now Fulton Co., Bartholomew Grogan, admr de bonis non 1/11/1858, Fulton

GROOVER, E. recd her legacy from est of Charles Groover, decd from Sarah R. Jones, gdn for minor heirs 4/5/1845, Bulloch, Misc

GROOVER, John David, Sarah Metzger, gdn, 5/4/1841, Effingham, MIC

GROOVER, Joshua, decd, Elishu Wilson, apptd admr 9/28/1830, Effingham, MIC

GROSS, James, decd, Alexander Wilde, James C. Johnson, Griffin Campbell, gdn of orphs 5/1/1837, Harris, GB

GROVENSTEIN, Henry L., decd, Hannah Grovenstein applies for L/A 1/12/1833, Effingham, MIC

GROVENSTEIN, Shadrack chose Benjamin Grovenstein as gdn 11/1/1841, Effingham, MIC

GRUBBS, Mary, decd, James Francis issued L/A 11/6/1820, Robert Cone, W. Lamkin, secs, Richmond, AB

GRUBBS, S. M., decd, L/A Martha S. Grubbs 2/1864, Webster, OD

GRUBBS, Thomas, decd, L/A to Ann Grubbs 9/26/1783, David Harris, Wm Bryant, secs; Thomas Grubbs apptd gdn of Sarah, minor orph, Richmond, AB

GUEST, Thomas, decd, Wm Anderson, exr, 1809 retn pd Elizabeth and Thomas Guest, 1811 pd Sarah Perkins, trustee for Elizabeth Guest, Wilkes, Retns

GUGEL, David, decd, John Charlton caveats application of J. R. Saussy for admn 4/22/1844, Effingham, MIC

GUGEL, David, decd, L/D to John Charlton, exr, 7/4/1846, Effingham, MIC

GUGOLE, John, decd, LWT pvd 5/27/1788, L/T issued Christopher and Samuel Gugole, Chatham, Adms

GUICE, Jonas, decd, Francis F. Fleming, gdn for Seymore C., orph, 5/4/1829, Peter Lamar, sec, Lincoln, GB

GUIEN, Belfort, inf of 6 yrs, orph of John B., decd, late of City of Marseilles, France, decd, Joseph Arnold Guien apptd gdn 1/4/1813, Nicholas Delaigle, Francis Bonyer, secs, Richmond, GB

GUILFORD, John, decd, Houston Co., LWT pvd 7/1839, ch: Matty Conyns, Polly Mitchell, Susannah Garrison, Colson and John Guilford, Jr., Randolph

GUIN, Richard, decd, Mrs. Elizabeth Guin, relict, applies for L/A, 7/27/1793, dismissed 6/29/1794, Effingham, MIC

GULLETT, William, decd, David Mizell and Jehu Mizell, sur on bond of Mrs. Hannah Gullett, admr, asked to be released because she is abt to remove from the co., 1/4/1816, Camden, MIC

GUN, Gabriel, decd, LWT pvd by E. A. Stroud, Richard Daniel, L/T gtd Gabriel Gun and Wm Cameron, 5/2/1814, Jasper, OM

GUNBY, John H., minor son of Levin, decd, Elizabeth Bowen, gdn, 6/2/1835, Camden, MIC

GUNBY, Levin, decd, Elizabeth Bowen, admx w/LWT annexed 6/3/1834, gtd leave to sell prop, 1/6/1835; Dr. Henry Bacon admr /LWT annexed 3/7/1836, dismissed 1/3/1837, Camden, MIC

GUNBY, Levin, decd, LWT pvd 8/7/1826, Camden, MIC

GUNBY, Mary, decd, Elizabeth Bowen, admx, 6/3/1834; Dr. Henry Bacon dismissed as admr 1/3/1837; Wm T. Hopkins, John Bachlott, John Pottle to divide est betwn heirs, 6/3/1836, Camden, MIC

GUNN, Archelaus, orph of Daniel, decd, Green G. Gunn, gdn, 3/1/1852, Houston, GB

GUNN, Daniel, decd, Daniel F. Gunn, gdn of orphs: Julia, Brooks, Mlynn and Valeria, 4/5/1852, Houston, GB

GUNN, Gabriel, orph, Johnson Wellborn, trustee, 1810-1811 retn, Wilkes, Retns

GUNNELLS, M. L., decd, Wm Gunnells pvd LWT 12/1871, Webster, OD

GUNNOLDS, Daniel, decd, Merril Bridges, admr, 9/1806; Merrel Bridges apptd gdn of minor orphs--Joseph and Mary 3/2/1807, Jonathan Bridges, Abner Ponder, secs, Oglethorpe, AB, MIC

GUNNOLDS, Joseph, minor orph of Daniel, decd, Merrel Bridges, gdn, Jonathan F. Bridges, Abner Ponder, secs, 3/2/1807, Oglethorpe, GB, MIC

GUNNOLDS, Mary, minor orph of Daniel, decd, chose Merrel Bridges for her gdn 3/2/1807, Oglethorpe, GB, MIC

GUTHREY, Beverley, decd, L/A gtd Sarah Guthrey; James Colquitt, George Cross and William Guthrey, secs, 7/1809, Oglethorpe, OM

GUTHREY, Leroy, decd, Martin Chamlee and John Liles issued L/A 1/10/1848, John Tumblin, Burwell Miller and Richard Miller, secs, Hall, AB

GUTHREY, Reuben, idiot son of Leroy, decd, Charlotte Guthrey, gdn, Charles Hulsey, sec, 9/6/1847, Hall, GB

GUY, John, decd, late of U. S. Service, Robert Ripley, admr, 12/14/1813, Camden, MIC

GUYER, Ernst M., decd, Jacob Hinely applies for L/A 9/6/1839, Effingham, MIC

HAAS, Jacob, decd, of Philadelphia, pennsylvania, A. J. Brady qualified as admr 2/2/1857; David Mayer, admr, 2/6/1860, Fulton

HACKET, Patrick, decd, Thomas King of St. Mayrs apptd admr 1/3/1809, Camden, MIC

HADDOCK, Charles, decd, appraisers of estate 6/24/1842, Adam Butler, Henry Wright, Jordan P. Harvard; purchasers from sale: Frances Haddock, LeGrand Guerry, Robert Golden, Lewis Clewis, Josiah Wheeler, John Hustice, Jacob Butler, Dooly, I&A

HADDOCK, Lewis F., orph of William L., decd, William H. Stanley, gdn, 2/5/1855, Houston, GB

HADDOCK, William, Thomas C. Coleman, gdn, Dooly, OD

HADDOCK, William L., decd, James G. Gaskin, gdn of orphs--James William and Lewis Franklin Haddock 2/28/1852, Houston, GB

HADLEY, Simon Peter, orph of Thomas, decd, of lawful chose, chose
John W. Compton as his gdn, with Jordan Compton, sur, 5/1818,
Jasper, OM
HADLEY, Thomas, decd, John W. Compton, admr in rt of wife, apptd
gdn of: Simon Thomas, Reeves and Henry Hadley, children of decd,
3/3/1817, Jasper, OM
HADLEY, Thomas, decd, Joseph Beavers, Joel Crawford, William
Brown, apprs, 4/2/1818 div of negroes among legatees: John M.
Compton, in rt of wife; Simon P. Hadley; Thomas T. Hadley; Henry
D. Hadley; Lewis L. Hadley; John H. Compton, admr, 1/1819 retn;
1823 retn, tuition pd John Brown, Hiram Glazier, William W.
Oslin, Jasper, Ests
HAGAN, James, decd, Ann and Edward Hagan applied for L/A
7/12/1790; apprs: Joseph Phillips, Saml Hemphill, Ez. Park, Zach.
Phillips, George Clough; inv $544.17 10/5/1798, Greene, Misc
HAGGARD, Samuel, decd, LWT pvd by Solomon Stephens 7/1/1811,
Margaret McMullen, admx, 11/4/1811, makes retn, Jackson, OM
HAGGINS, Conmack, decd, Moses Trimble given final L/A on est
7/8/1801; inv appraised 8/25/1801 by Stephen Westbrook, William
Gober, Obadiah Hooper, Franklin, OM
HAGGOOD, Greene B., decd, LWT pvd 1/1863, Martha A. Haggood,
extrx, Fulton
HAGIN, Absalom, decd, LWT pvd 9/29/1838-ch-Mary Wilson, Johnson
Colson Hagin, Absalom, Sarah, Eliza Ann, Solomon, Etheldred
James & Martha Hagin; grch-Milton, John & Georgia Ann Sheppard;
Henry Dutton, admr, 1840-1 retns, Bulloch, Misc
HAGIN, Etheldred, decd, Appraisal by Andrew Wilson, William Lee,
Joseph Hagin 5/12/1832; heirs receipts: George Grooms, James
Corner, Jeptha Hagin, Rebecca Hagin, Isom Hagin, Happy Hagin from
Margaret Hagin, gdn 7/20/1833, Bulloch, Misc
HAGIN, John, decd, LWT pvd, Malachi Hagin, William A. Knight
qualified as exrs, 11/4/1822, Camden, MIC
HAGIN, Solomon, decd, LWT pvd 10/7/1835 names ch: Tabitha Mikell,
James Hagen, Mourning Denmark, wife of John, Allen, Sheppard,
Mary, Martha, Margaret and Malachi Hagin; wife, Margaret, extrx,
filed retn 1839, 3/2/1840, Bulloch, Misc
HAIL, Nancy H., decd, James L. Hail, admr, 1856, Twiggs, Misc
HAILES, John, decd, Elizabeth Hailes, gdn of Biddy, Matilda,
Allen I., William T., orphs, 3/7/1825, Abner R. Wright, John
Hailes, surs, Clarke, GB
HAINES, Stephen, Sr., decd, Moses Haines applies for L/A
11/23/1795, Elbert, AB
HALE, James, orph of Andrew, decd, Thomas Jennings, gdn, John
Shank, sec, 3/5/1849, Troup, GB
HALE, James R., decd, Elizabeth E. Hale, admx, David P. Phillips,
Ezekiel Mathews, sur, 10/4/1875, Gwinnett, AB
HALE, Jerry, decd, L/A to James Westmoreland, 1/1820, Jasper, OM
HALE, J. J., decd, William F. Roberson issued L/A 9/1861,
Webster, OD
HALE, Joel, decd, John Selman, gdn of Jonas, Silas, Brantley,
Sally, Polly, Lucinda and Nancy, orphs, 1/4/1819, James Langford,
sur, Clarke, GB
HALE, Joshua, decd, Gershom Selleckmapp issued L/A 1/21/1818,
Gilbert Longstreet, Thomas H. Penn, secs, Richmond, AB
HALE, Pamelia Ann, minor of Jose, late of Jones Co., decd, Reuben
Westmoreland, gdn, 11/7/1826, John and Mark Westmoreland, secs,
Pike, MIC
HALE, Thomas, orph of Andrew, decd, Robert H. Jennings, gdn, John
Shank, Robert W. Brown, sec, 9/4/1848, Troup, GB
HALEY, Addison, orph of Holliday, decd, Harris
HALEY, Holliday, decd, George C. Hodge, John I. Harper, admrs,
11/7/1836, Harris

HALEY, James M., decd, Jasper L. Keith, apptd admr, 9/8/1856, Cherokee, AB
HALL, Albert, minor son of Nathaniel D. and Martha E., Jackson Co., Ala., David L. Hall applied for L/G 11/11/1858, Dawson, WB
HALL, Albert H. W., Daniel P. Monroe and James L. Baird, gdn, 12/14/1858, Dawson, WB
HALL, America, Jesse Watson, gdn, Dooly, OD
HALL, Blake, decd, L/A to John Spears 9/19/1836, Habersham, MIC
HALL, David L., of Jackson Co, Ala, gdn minor ch of M. E. B. Hall, decd of Forsyth Co, Ga appts Nathaniel P. Hall of Jackson Co, Ala, atty to sue Reuben Hill est left dau, Belariah Wilkins, decd, now due sd minors, 11/13/1858, Dawson, WB
HALL, D. Hall, Daniel P. Monroe and James L. Baird, gdn, 12/14/1858, Dawson, WB
HALL, Harriet E. (Mrs.), decd, Joseph S. Morrell and William Hansell Hall, admrs, 1/19/1852, Baldwin, AB
HALL, Hugh, decd, Frances Lewis and Dixon Hill issued L/A 3/4/1811, Putnam, AB
HALL, James, decd, Mary Hall applied for L/A 3/16/1799, Greene, Misc
HALL, James, orph of James, decd, Mitchel Neel, gdn, Noah Dison, sur, 9/7/1835, Emanuel, GB
HALL, James J., Henry Collier, gdn, Dooly, OD
HALL, J. J., orph of James, decd, Mitchel Neel, gdn, Noah Dison, sur, 9/7/1835, Emanuel, GB
HALL, John, orph of James, decd, Mitchel Neel, gdn, Noah Dison, sur, 9/7/1835, Emanuel, GB
HALL, Joseph, orph of Susannah, decd, Stanley Hall, gdn, 7/1/1822, Francis Rountree, sec, Morgan, GB
HALL, Malinda S. J., minor child of Nathaniel D. and Martha E., Jackson Co., Ala., David L. Hall applies for L/G 11/11/1858; Daniel P. Monroe and James L. Baird, gdns, 12/14/1858, Dawson, WB
HALL, Martha Ann, dau of James B., Wm Kennedy apptd gdn 7/12/1820, John H. Mann, Gabriel Clarke, secs, Richmond, GB
HALL, Mary, Jesse Watson, gdn, Dooly, OD
HALL, Matthew, decd, inventory of est 7/25/1807 by Moses Sanders, Michael Box, Thomas Lenoir, appraisers, Franklin, OM
HALL, Nathaniel, decd, LWT pvd 1/6/1817, Emanuel Co., names wife, Sarah, ch: Mary Maclean, Ann Elizabeth Hall, Nathaniel G. Hall; property appraisement, property divided betwn: Robert Williams, Nathaniel G. Hall by Arthur Kerby, Moses Wilson, Ely Kennedy 1/9/1826; 1825 lots drawn by: Mrs. Sarah Hall, Robert Williams, N. Hall, Bulloch, Misc
HALL, Nathaniel G., decd, inventory and appraisement by Wm H. McLane, Moses Wilson, Wm Lester 12/15/1844, Bulloch, Misc
Hall, Nathaniel, decd, 6/21/1828 div of negroes to: Nathaniel Lang, gdn of Nathaniel G. Hall; land div betwn Robert Williams, an heir and Nathaniel Green Hall, heir 3/10/1830, Bulloch, Misc
HALL, Patrick, orph of Geneper, Sr., Isaac M. Norman, gdn, 5/5/1828, Emanuel, GB
HALL, Richard, decd, J. A. Juhan and N. S. Juhan, admrs, 8/27/1862, James M. Hart, J. A. J. Duncan, John R. Mehaffey, surs, DeKalb, AB
HALL, Robert, decd, John A. Dalton, admr, B. A. Blakey, V. Dalton, sur, 9/8/1873, Gwinnett, AB
HALL, Sarah, orph of James, decd, William Hall, gdn, Thomas Hutcheson, sur, 3/1/1841, Emanuel, GB
HALL, Sarah Ann E., minor child of Nathaniel D. and Martha E., Jackson Co., Ala., David L. Hall applies for L/G 11/11/1858; Daniel P. Monroe and James L. Baird, gdn, 12/14/1858 Dawson, WB
HALL, Sarah Hall, orph of James, decd, Mitchel Neel, gdn, Noah Dison, sur, 9/7/1835, Emanuel, GB

HALL, Susan, Henry Collier, gdn, Dooly, OD
HALL, Thomas, decd, LWT dtd 3/12/1840 pvd 7/6/1840 names ch:
Martin (his dau, Nanc), Zachariah and Betsy Morgan, L/A issued
Lewis and Enoch Hall, 8/5/1811, Tattnall, MIC
HALL, Thomas (Lieut), Lydia Hall and Richard B. Fletcher apply
for L/T on LWT, pvd by Daniel Saunders and Mary Ann Wilkins,
11/29/1799, Warren, MIC
HALL, Thomas H., decd, Harriet E. Hall issued L/A 3/19/1849;
Joseph S. Morrell and William Hansell Hall, admrs de bonis non
1/19/1852, Baldwin, AB
HALL, Thomas Lent, decd, Richard Fletcher applies for admn,
1/23/1804, Warren, MIC
HALL, William, decd, William Head makes oath that decd died
w/LWT, asks for L/A 9/7/1812, Tavneah Head, John Daniel, sec;
Thomas S. Carter apptd gdn of: Blake, Alcy, John and Thomas,
orphs, 5/4/1812, Elbert, AB
HALL, William, decd, inventory and appraisement 8/28/1838,
appraisers: J. J. Collier, Isaiah Powell, Pearson Brown.
Purchasers at sale: Macon, Nathan, Joseph, Sarah, Harmon,
Caroline, Hiram Hall, Dooly, I&A
HALL, William W., Henry Collier, gdn, Dooly, OD
HALL, Wingate, decd, Samuel Hall issued L/A 1/8/1836, Baldwin
HALLMAN, Adam, son of Sally, John Groover, Jr. to indenture
7/5/1819, Bulloch, MIC
HALLMAN, Andrew, son of Sally, John Groover, Jr. to indenture
7/5/1819, Bulloch, MIC
HALLONS, William, decd, Edward Rich, admr, William R. Wilson,
Hardy Parker, sur, 3/1/1844, Emanuel, AB
HALY, Isaiah, decd, inv of est 7/5/1800, Franklin, OM
HAM, Bartlett, decd, Robert G. Turman, debtor, schooling and
board for 1810, A. Jarrett protesting because orph was bound to
sd Ham, Elbert, GR
HAMBLETON, Francis, decd, James Cosby applied for L/A 4/26/1792,
Elbert, AB
HAMBRICK, Burwell, minor son of Thomas, decd, , has prop in hands
of admrs of decd father as stated by his bro, Joseph Hambrick;
Joseph apptd gdn of sd Burwell, 7/22/1805, Jackson, OM
HAMBRICK, Joseph, decd, LWT pvd 8/7/1792, wife, Margaret, ch:
Ann, Margaret, Elizabeth, Sarah, Mary, Susannah; wife, Margaret,
Greene, Misc
HAMBRICK, Thomas, decd, Jacob Parker applied for L/A 11/14/1791,
Greene, Misc
HAMBRICK, William, Arthur Foster apptd gdn, 1802, Jackson, OM
HAMBY, Emanuel L., decd, M. Rapier, admr, William Dell, sur,
7/4/1847, Bibb, AB
HAMBY, Leonard, decd, N. K. Butler issued L/A 10/15/1827, William
P. Dearmond, sec; 1829-37 retns pd Saml Smith board for child,
Susan, recpts from Perry Dillard, heir by marriage to Susan, land
in Lee and Muscogee Co.'s, Richmond, AB
HAMILL, John, decd, Susannah Hamill apptd gdn 3/31/1815 of minor
orphs: Catherine and William Stith Hammill, Richmond, GB
HAMILTON, Duncan, decd, Sherrod Hamilton issued L/A 11/6/1837,
Washington
HAMILTON, Evan, orph of Calvin, decd, John B. Massey issued L/G
1/8/1838, Washington
HAMILTON, Irwin, orph of Calvin, decd, John B. Massey issued L/G
1/8/1838, Washington
HAMILTON, Joseph, orph of Calvin, decd, John B. Massey issued L/G
1/8/1838, Washington
HAMILTON, Robert, decd, Amy Hamilton, gdn of orphs: Mary and Anna
9/1/1817, William Lewis, sec, Morgan, GB

HAMILTON, Sarah Ann, orph of Calvin, decd, John B. Massey issued L/G 1/8/1838, Washington
HAMILTON, Steward, decd, Clary Hamilton issued L/A w/LWT annexed 11/7/1831, Malcolm Currie, sec, Montgomery, AB
HAMILTON, Thomas, decd, Concord Hamilton, Isaiah Wright and Henry Dindale make inv, 5/3/1798, Columbia, Ests
HAMILTON, Waddy T., decd, William Hamilton, admr, intends to sell real est 1/1827; pet of Richard L. Powell that Waddy T. Hamilton, decd, executed bond to Wm Edwards for land in Clarksville-admr to make title 9/8/1828, Habersham, MIC
HAMILTON, William, decd, Sherrod Hamilton issued L/A 11/6/1837, Washington
HAMILTON, Winney, decd, LWT pvd by Smith Garrison, L/T issued William Traylor, 1/3/1814; dismissed 7/7/1817, Jasper, OM
HAMMET, Carter bound to Mason Ezzard for 15 yrs, 7/9/1806, Jackson, OM
HAMMOCK, Hugh, decd, died intestate, inv 10/15/1783, Robert and Nancy Hammock, purchasers, Wilkes, MxR
HAMMOCK, Jeremiah, decd, Payton H. White, admr, D. T. Deupree, sur, 4/5/1832, Butts, AB
HAMMOCK, John, decd, L/A to Lemuel Hammock 1/5/1821, Laurens, AB
HAMMOCK, Thomas, decd, Joseph Henderson, admr 9/2/1816, Wilkes, Retns
HAMMOCK, Thomas B. gdn for Eliza, Susannah, Jeremiah, John, Mariah, Thomas J. and Mary Ann, 9/7/1835, John B. Hammock, Robert Mumford, secs, Lincoln, GB
HAMMOND, Henrietta, orph of Leroy, decd, Hardy Strickland, gdn, Henry B. McConnell, J. A. Maddox, R. F. Daniel, surs, 1/5/1855, Cherokee, GB
HAMMOND, Jefferson C., orph of William, decd, William W. McCutchen, gdn, William McCutchen, Herndon Haralson, sec, 1/10/1848, Troup, GB
HAMMOND, Leroy, decd, Eli McConnell, Hardy Strickland, admrs, R. F. Daniel, John R. Galt, N. J. Harrison, William P. Hammond, sur, 8/14/1854, Cherokee, AB
HAMMOND, Lewis, orph of Leroy, decd, Hardy Strickland, gdn, Henry B. McConnell, J. A. Maddox, R. F. Daniel, sur, 1/5/1855, Cherokee, GB
HAMMOND, Martin, decd, acct of sale 3/31/1798; purchasers: James Turner, Susannah Hammond, Isaac Ellis; Susannah Hammond, James Turner, admrs, Hancock, AA
HAMMOND, Mary Ann (Miss), (now Mrs. Barnes) Retns of John Course, gdn 2/5/1807, Richmond, GR
HAMMOND, Susannah, decd, Ira Burton issued L/A 2/24/1829, Philip H. Mantz, sec, Richmond, AB
HAMMOND, William J., minor of Charles, decd, Charles Hammond, gdn, Thomas Foster, William McElhaney, sur, 1/5/1838; Charles Hammond, gdn, retn 1/17/1842, Butts, GB, ER
HAMON, Charles Monroe, orph of James, decd, age 5 yrs, bound to John King, gdn, for 15 yrs, Lazarus Hood, J. B. Lively, sur, 3/12/1855, Cherokee, GB
HAMON, David Walker, orph of James, decd, age 8, bound for 13 yrs to Lazarus Hood, gdn, John King, J. B. Lively, sur, 12/3/1855, Cherokee, GB
HAMON, Elizabeth Ann, orph of James, decd, J. B. Lively, gdn, Lazarus Hood, John King, sur, 3/12/1855, Cherokee, GB
HAMPTON, William S., decd, Martha W. Hampton, admx, 2/4/1861, Andrew J. Minor, sur, DeKalb, AB
HANBERRY, Israel, decd, Thomas Drew, admr, appr 7/13/1833, Emanuel, A
HANCOCK, Albert G., decd, Alexander L. Huie, admr, 3/1847, 1850-1851 retns, Fayette, AB

HANCOCK, John, decd, Wm Hancock issued L/A, 5/2/1814, Jackson, OM
HANCOCK, Marian, William Hartsfield, Willis Jones, gdn, 1/10/1839, Harris
HANCOCK, William, decd, Martha Hancock, gdn of orphs: Robert E. and Elizabeth A., 9/6/1852, Houston, GB
HANDLEY, George (Colonel), decd, Sarah Handley issued L/A 12/31/1793, John Cobbison, P. Clayton, secs, Richmond, AB
HANDLEY, William, decd, John McIntosh apptd admr, 2/4/1784, Chatham, Adms
HANDLEY, William, decd, Merchant, George Handley, admr, 4/15/1791, Chatham, Adms
HANEY, Caroline, orph of Timothy, decd, Joshua S. Haney, gdn, Frederick Freeman and William W. Hawkins, surs, 10/12/1857, Cherokee, GB
HANEY, Timothy, decd, Joshua S. Haney, admr, Jacob Haney, James H. Bell, sur, 3/10/1856, Cherokee, AB
HANGAL, Sarah, decd, Charles Blount, admr, makes retn 2/13/1837, Tattnall, I&A
HANGLEITER, John, decd, John Grabenstine and Mrs. Catherine Hangleiter apply for admn, 9/3/1796, apptd 10/1/1796, Camden, MIC
HANSBY, George, decd, L/A issued Martha Hansby with John and Wiley Phillips, surs, 7/1818, Jasper, OM
HANSELL, A. J. (General), T. R. Huson, admr, 12/9/1854; C. C. Bostick, admr, 1855; Robert B. Bostick, admr, 1855, Cobb, BB
HANSFORD, Charles, made gdn of his ch, Charles and Eliza 4/4/1814, Wilkes, Retns
HANSON, George W., orph of Samuel, decd, Nathan Aldridge, gdn, 11/3/1823, Morgan, GB
HANSON, John, decd, Mary Hanson, extrx, 1813 retns, Wilkes, Retns
HANSON, John, decd, Walton Harris, acting admr w/Hugh Montgomery claims they cannot make retns because of demand vs. est by Edward Paine, 9/5/1814; Hugh Montgomery and Walton Harris, admrs, ask to be dismissed 8/7/1815, Jackson, OM
HANSON, Thomas, decd, LWT pvd by Walton Harris and David Rogers 3/2/1812; Mrs. Maria Hanson, wid, apptd gdn of orphs: Virginia & John Augustus, Jackson, OM
HANSON, Thomas, Jr., L/A Thos Hanson, Sr. 3/2/1812, Jackson, OM
Hanson, Thomas N., decd, John N. Hanson, gdn of orphs: Ludza Tally, Thomas and John A., 7/6/1821, Morgan, GB
HARALSON, Paul A., decd, James F. Leonard, Camillus A. Haralson issued temporary L/A 2/2/1852, M. B. Haralson, James J. Dean, Henry Holmes, Elijah Stewart, surs, DeKalb, AB
HARBIRT, Thomas, decd, LWT dtd 4/2/1799 names ch: John, George, Thomas; grdau: Alice Wright Harbirt; grson: Hardy, son of John Harbirt; son-in-law, Burrell Cook; exrs, John, George and Thomas Harbirt, pvd 5/27/1799, Hancock, AA
HARBUCK, John, decd, William Harbuck qualified as admr 11/7/1814, James Neal, sur, Warren, MIC
HARBUCK, William, decd, William Harbuck, admr, 11/13/1830, Michael Harbuck, James Harbuck, surs, Warren, AB
HARDAGE, Jesse D., decd, Jonathan Martin and Neverson Cook issued L/A 11/6/1843, Jacob Cagle, Wm Cagle, Lewis Jones, secs, Hall, AB
HARDAMAN, John N., orph of William, decd, Mariah Wood, gdn, John Ford, sur, 1/11/1858, Cherokee, GB
HARDAMAN, Sarah F., orph of William, decd, William Dinsmore, gdn, Lawson Fields, John P. Reavis, sur, 4/13/1857, Cherokee, GB
HARDAMAN, Thomas, decd, inv. of est. 8/27/1791, Effingham, Misc
HARDAMAN, William, decd, John J. Ford, admr, Lawson Fields, sur, 7/10/1854, Cherokee, AB
HARDAWAY, John, decd, Washington Hardaway, admr, 7/4/1814, John Burkhalter, sur; Mrs. Martha Hardaway, wid, chose child's pt 11/7/1814, Warren, AB

HARDAWAY, Stith, orph of John, decd, Thomas Maddux apptd gdn
11/7/1814, Warren, MIC
HARDAWAY, Thomas, orph of John, decd, Thomas Maddux apptd gdn
11/7/1814, Warren, MIC
HARDEE, John, decd, LWT pvd by John Bailey and Joseph Hull, and
the codicil by Joseph Hill, Lewis Demere and Andrew M. Ross,
1/8/1839, Camden, MIC
HARDEE, Sarah (Mrs), LWT pvd, George W. Hardee qualified as extr
3/5/1849; George W. Hardee, exr, dismissed 6/2/1851, Camden, MIC
HARDEE, Thomas E., decd, Mrs. M. A. admx, 1/4/1841, Camden, MIC
HARDEN, Alberta, orph of Martin, decd, Moses Hutcherson, Noah
Sison, gdns, 9/7/1835, Emanuel, GB
HARDEN, Henry, planter, decd, John G. Maxwell apptd admr, 1825,
Bryan, CR
HARDEN, Janus Harden, decd, Ann Harden, admx, John Higgs, sec,
5/3/1830, Bibb, AB
HARDEN, William, (Colonel) decd, LWT names ch: Martin, Richard,
Cynthia, Sarah and Sucka dtd 10/17/1803 pvd 9/3/1810 inv
9/19/1810, Franklin, OM
HARDEN, William, decd, Edward Harden, admr, 5/13/1799, Bryan, CR
HARDEN, William, decd, LWT, William Harden, exr, 4/6/1789,
Chatham, Adms
HARDIN, Arthur F., orph of Reuben N., decd, Samuel Robison, gdn,
11/1/1841, Washington, GB
HARDIN, Hiram, orph, James Hardin, gdn, Henry Knight, sur,
3/3/1834, Butts, GB
HARDIN, Nancy, minor, John Hardin, gdn, 11/4/1833, Washington, GB
HARDIN, Nancy R., orph of Reuben N., decd, Samuel Robison, gdn,
11/1/1841, Washington, GB
HARDIN, Thomas, minor, John Hardin apptd gdn, 11/4/1833,
Washington, GB
HARDIN, Thomas R., decd, Allen Smith issued L/A 11/4/1839; John
Hardin issued L/A 11/6/1840, Washington
HARDING, Stirling R., decd, George W. Marks, Penell Truett, admr,
11/6/1837, Harris, AB
HARDISON, Francis E., orph of Thomas, decd, James W. Hardison,
gdn, 6/5/1854, Houston, GB
HARDMAN, Allen, decd, R. J. Hardman, admr, 2/6/1854, Jonathan
Pennell, sur, DeKalb, AB
HARDMAN, John, decd, Charles Hardman, exr dismissed from making
retns on sd est, 3/2/1807, Oglethorpe, OM
HARDSHIP, John W., Carpenter, decd, Francis Septimus, admr,
11/7/1786, Chatham, Adms
HARDWICK, Hazlewood, decd, John Tidwell, gdn of orphs: David and
William 1/6/1818, Morgan, GB
HARDWICK, William, decd, Robert Mitchell, exr of LWT and having
declined to perform duties, L/T gtd are repealed, 9/7/1818,
Jasper, OM
HARDY, Gardner, orph of Robert, decd, Robert Kelly apptd gdn
3/5/1821, Bulloch, MIC
HARDY, George, orph of Robert, decd, Robert Kelly apptd gdn
3/5/1821, Bulloch, MIC
HARDY, Jesse, decd, Buck Jeter, gdn for orphs: Whitmel H. and
Dicey L., 1/5/1829, John H. Little, sec;
Shadrach Gather, gdn, 1/14/1833, Lincoln, GB
HARDY, John, decd, Mary Hardy, Joseph T. Hardy, John Graves
qualified as admrs 5/26/1790, Liberty, Ests
HARDY, Theophilus, decd, of Lumpkin, James Griffin, admr 1/1836,
John Talbot, Thomas Justice, sur; apprs: John Talbot, Wade Ball,
John G. Perry; purchasers at sale: James & Henry Hall, Henry
Jones, James Leary, Isaac Redmond, Stewart, Adms

HARGRAVES, John S., decd, George W. Walker issued L/A 1/14/1828, Holland McTyeire, sec, Richmond, AB
HARGROVE, Clayton S., decd, Robert W. Baskin, gdn of orphs: Mary Francis and Temperance Maria, 3/6/1854, Houston, GB
HARGROVE, Edmund, decd, Howel Hargrove issued L/A 3/6/1815, Laurens, AB
HARGROVE, Hanse, minor orph of J. B., decd, Edmund W. Holland, gdn, 2/3/1862, Fulton, GB
HARGROVE, Mary Ann E., decd, LWT pvd 5/5/1862, E. W. Holland, exr, Fulton
HARGROVE, Rameth R., minor orph of J. B., decd, Edmund W. Holland, gdn, 2/3/1862, Fulton, GB
HARGROVES, William, decd, Patience and Dudley Hargroves and Myles Green issued L/A 9/5/1808, Putnam, AB
HARINGTON, Richard S., orph of Richard, decd, William Malone apptd gdn 7/9/1805, Franklin, IMW
HARKNESS, William, decd, Oswell Eve issued L/A 12/3/1804, Anderson Watkins, sec, Richmond, AB
HARLEY, Charles S., decd, Charles G. Campbell issued L/A 4/5/1852, Baldwin
HARP, Henry, decd, LWT pvd by Jesse Ward and Charles Beddingfield; Solomon Beddingfield qualfied as exr, 10/15/1805, Warren, MIC
HARPE, James, decd, Oliff Harpe, admr, 1/23/1844, apprs: D. J. Bothwell, James McLain, Edmond Outlaw. Purchasers at sale: Olive Harpe, Aaron Harpe, Henry Harpe, William Harpe, Allen Waters, Thomas B. Donally, Thomas Mobley, Dooly, I&A
HARPER, ALexander, decd, LWT pvd, Tabitha Harper, extrx, 3/6/1815, Jackson, OM
HARPER, Amon L., decd, L. Solomon Harper, Thomas H. Moore, admrs, Harris, AB
HARPER, G. A., decd, J. M. Summers? makes final retn 5/1862, Webster, OD
HARPER, John, decd, John Clarke issued L/A 2/15/1817, John Campbell, John Moore, secs, Richmond, AB
HARPER, Robert, decd, John Clark issued L/A 1/26/1813, John John Campbell, Wm Ross, secs; also, Alex Matheson apptd admr on credits of Robt Harper and Duncan Matheson, lately trading as Harper & Matheson, Richmond, AB
HARRELL, James, decd, LWT pvd by James Byrum, Lundy Huff and Wm Willingham, L/T gtd John Cargile 1/6/1823, Jasper, OM
HARREL, J. P., Clk of Superior Court to issue citation for L/a de bonis non be issued 12/1864, Webster, OD
HARREL, T. P. (Mrs.), decd, John S. Harrell issued L/A 10/1865, Webster, OD
HARRELL, Abner, Sr., decd, Abner Harrell apptd admr, 1/5/1836, Camden, MIC
HARRELL, Jesse P., decd, James Nicholson issued L/A 3/1856, Webster, OD
HARRIGAL, Sarah, decd, inv dtd 11/14/1835, apprs: Seth Knight, James Anderson, Joseph Dubanly, Tattnall, I&A
HARRINGTON, Jeptha B., decd, Wm S. Barton issued L/A 4/5/1852, Wiley A. Harrington, Thomas Suddeth, secs; Elizabeth Harrington, gdn of orphs 11/1/1852: Frances L., Margaret C. and Jeptha B., Jonathan Martin, John Crow, secs, Hall, AB, GB
HARRINGTON, Richard S., orph of Richard, decd, William Malone apptd gdn 2/11/1806, Franklin, OM
HARRIS, Alexander Evin, orph of Alexander E., decd, John J. Harris, gdn, 9/4/1854, Houston, GB
HARRIS, Ann S., orph of Stephen, decd, John West, gdn, 3/1836, Dr. Seymour Catchings, sur, Stewart, GB, Adms

HARRIS, Augustine, decd, Iverson L. Harris issued L/A 9/5/1836, Baldwin

HARRIS, Augustine H., orph of Walton, decd, Robert R. Billups, gdn, 1/13/1824, George W. Moore, sur, Clarke, GB

HARRIS, Baker, orph of Baker, decd, Thomas Wheeler, gdn, 12/6/1819, Sterling Elder, John H. Lowe, surs, Clarke, GB

HARRIS, Benjamin, decd, Mary Sophia Harris issued L/A 9/6/1822, William A. Bugg, R. R. Reid, secs, signed Polly S. Harris, Richmond, AB

HARRIS, Benjamin, decd, Sophia Harris issued L/A 1/8/1817, Robert R. Reid, Benjamin Picquet, secs, Richmond, AB

HARRIS, Brittain, decd, L/A issued Celia Harris with William Ragland and Woody Dozier, surs, 11/4/1822, Jasper, OM

HARRIS, Caroline Augusta, decd, John L. Harris, admr, 1/12/1852, Benjamin F. Harris, sur, DeKalb, AB

HARRIS, Charles P., orph of Stephen, decd, John West, gdn, 3/1836, Dr. Seymour Catchings, sur, Stewart, GB, Adms

HARRIS, Edward Charles, decd, Laird M. Harris issued L/A 2/14/1796, Thomas M. C. Harris, sec; apprs apptd in Greene Co.- John Harrison, John Armour, Ezekiel Park, Payton Smith, Thomas Baldwin, Richmond, AB

HARRIS, Elbert, decd, John J. Whitaker, admr, S. T. Whitaker, sur, 9/1854, Fayette, AB

HARRIS, Ezekiel, decd, John B. Pounds issued L/A 9/5/1843, Baldwin

HARRIS, Francis Epps, orph of Alexander E., decd, John J. Harris, gdn, 4/2/1855, Houston, GB

HARRIS, Henry, decd, P. W. Gunnels issued L/A 2/1864, Webster, OD

HARRIS, James, decd, Dorcas Evans issued L/A 11/3/1819, Josiah Brunson, William B. Burton, secs, Richmond, AB

HARRIS, James, decd, William Parkes, gdn for orphs: Robert T., Albert B. and Andrew J., 11/7/1825, Lewis Parker and Jeremiah Tomson, secs, Lincoln, GB

HARRIS, Jeremiah, decd, Eleanor Harris, admx 9/5/1825 bond, James A. Groves, Nathan and Zephaniah Beal, surs, Clark, AB

HARRIS, Jeremiah, decd, L/A gtd to Thomas Harris 4/13/1791, Greene, Misc

HARRIS, John, age 7, minor orph of Richard, decd, to be bound to George Brittain, Jr., farmer, until 21. Alexander McEwen, sec, 1/1807, Oglethorpe, GB

HARRIS, John, decd, Mrs. Mary Harris, admx 6/4/1827, Glynn, MIC

HARRIS, John W., orph of Stephen, decd, John West, gdn, 3/1836, Dr. Seymour Catchings, sur, Stewart, GB, Adms

HARRIS, Joseph F., decd, Nathan M. Harris issued L/A 4/1/1867, Fulton

HARRIS, Joseph T., orph of James, decd, Albert B. Harris, gdn, 11/21/1831, Wm C. Stokes, Wm Dallas, secs, Lincoln, GB

HARRIS, Joshua, decd, Mrs. Jane Harris and John Kerr applied for L/A 10/26/1795, Greene, Misc

HARRIS, Morris, decd, Abner Camp, exr of LWT, 1852-1854 retns, Fayette

HARRIS, Olive (Miss) decd, John Baker, admr, 9/12/1812, Nicholas Williams, Thomas Battle, surs, Warren, AB

HARRIS, Robert S., orph of Walton, decd, Milner Echols, gdn, 1/12/1824, Edward Paine, sur, Clarke, GB

HARRIS, Sampson, decd, John Cook vs. Stephen W. and Susannah Harris, admrs, 2/1809, Morgan, SCW

HARRIS, Samuel, decd, LWT pvd 11/7/1789, ch: Robert, Thomas, Samuel, John, William, Laird, Matthew; wife, Martha; son-in-law William Wylie; grandson, Moses Wylie; names Thomas McCaul, Greene, Misc

HARRIS, S. J., decd, Mary C. A. Harris applies for L/A 11/1/1869, Cobb, MIC
HARRIS, Thomas (Major), decd, L/A gtd Mrs. Mary Harris, S. B. Harris and Andrew Baxter 8/11/1798, Greene, Misc
HARRIS, Thomas, age 11, minor orph of Richard, decd, to be bound to George Brittain, Jr., farmer, until 21. Alexander McEwen, sec, 1/1807, Oglethorpe, GB
HARRIS, Thomas, orph of Jeremiah, decd, Eleanor Harris, gdn, 9/5/1825, James A. Groves, N. H. Beal, Zephaniah Beal, surs, Clarke, GB
HARRIS, Walton, decd, Virginia B. Harris, gdn of Walton, Mary Ann, Young L., Jeptha and Willis, orphs, 1/13/1824, West Harris, John Jackson, surs, Clarke, GB
HARRIS, William, decd, John Harris, admr, 11/19/1814, Glynn, MIC
HARRIS, William, decd, of Wilkes Co., Patrick Cunningham Harris and Major Andrew Baxter applied for L/A 7/4/1795, Greene, Misc
HARRIS, William Thomas, decd, William Thomas Harris qualified exr, 1786, Liberty, Ests
HARRISON, Benjamin, decd, Charity and James Harrison and Daniel O'Neal issued L/A 3/2/1812, Noah Stringer, Daniel Odom, secs; Charity Harrison apptd gdn of orphs, Charlotte and Dorcas 1/2/1815, Laurens, AB, GB
HARRISON, Benjamin, decd, Mary Harrison and Samuel Payne issued L/A 11/20/1790, Richmond, AB
HARRISON, Benjamin, decd, of Richmond Co., Mary Harrison and Samuel Payne, Jr., exrs, 11/20/1790, Columbia, Ests
HARRISON, Berryman H., decd, Zephaniah Franklin, admr, 4/17/1830, Henry Hight, sur, Warren, AB
HARRISON, Bieon, decd, Mary and David Harrison applied for L/A 3/15/1797, Greene, AB
HARRISON, Dinwiddie R., decd, Adam Jones, admr, 1/29/1821, Daniel Owens, John Moore, Asa Chapman, surs, Warren, AB
HARRISON, Edward, decd, Ambrose Kennedy issued L/A 9/2/1839, Elias Miller, sec; Ambrose Kennedy apptd gdn of orphs 4/7/1846: Edward, Elizabeth, James and Gideon, Hall, AB
HARRISON, Edward, decd, Roger Gideon and Susan Harrison issued L/A 1/6/1834; Ambrose Kennedy, admr 9/7/1835 and 5/12/1835 made gdn of orphs: Edward, Elizabeth, James and Gideon, Hall
HARRISON, Edward L., decd, Mary C. Harrison applies for L/A 6/22/1838, Effingham, MIC
HARRISON, Elizabeth, minor of James, decd, William Harrison, gdn, 1838 retn, Butts, ER
HARRISON, Elizabeth, orph of James, decd, Rufus McCune, gdn, James A. McCune, Thomas B. Burford, sur, 1/10/1848, Butts, GB
HARRISON, Elizabeth, orph of James, decd, William Harrison, gdn, Wesley C. Welch, sur, 5/4/1835, Butts, GB
HARRISON, James, decd, Robert Hazlehurst applied to be dismissed 9/4/1820, Glynn, MIC
HARRISON, James, decd, William Harrison, admr, Wesley C. Welsh, sur, 7/23/1834; 1838 retn, Butts, AB
HARRISON, John, decd, Robert Hazlehurst applied to be dismissed 9/4/1820, Glynn, MIC
HARRISON, Joseph, orph of Edward, decd, Isaac B. Payne, gdn 9/7/1835, Hall, GB
HARRISON, Martha, decd, Robert Hazlehurst applied to be dismissed 9/4/1820, Glynn, MIC
HARRISON, Robert, decd, LWT pvd 12/10/1844, Harris
HARRISON, Thomas, minor orph of James, decd, William Harrison, gdn, Wesley C. Welch, sur, 5/4/1835; 1838 retn, Butts, GB, ER
HARRISON, Thomas, orph of James, decd, Rufus McCune, gdn, James A. McCune, Thomas B. Burford, sur, 1/10/1848, Butts, GB

HARRISS, Charity apptd gdn of persons and estates of James Nap, Charity Nap, Patsey Nap, and William Harriss, her children, Lemuel Crawford, Thomas Jones, sec, 5/1808, Oglethorpe, OM, GB

HARROLL, Catharine, decd, James O'Brien issued L/A 1/12/1845, Baldwin

HARSHAM, A. L., decd, E. P. Williams issued L/A 10/6/1862, E. J. Houston, sec, White, AB

HART, Edward, decd, James Walker issued L/A 12/1793; decd partner of James Walker (merchants), Richmond, AB

HART, Fanny and Ginsey to be furnished board, clothing support, etc. by George G. Gaines, gdn, 11/5/1811, John G. Underwood apptd gdn 9/6/1813, Laurens, GB

HART, Jesse, minor son of Mary Fenn, Thomas G. Underwood apptd gdn 11/5/1811, Laurens, GB

HART, Murray, decd, James Pearre issued L/A 1/15/1813, Anthony Labuzan, Angus Martin, secs, Richmond, AB

HART, Robert, decd, Wm O'Neal and Mary Hart issued L/A 6/6/1808, James Thompson, sec, Laurens, AB

HART, Samuel, decd, Esther Hart and Joel Cloud issued L/A 10/23/1787, Noble Butler, Duncan McCowen, secs, Richmond, AB

HART, Warren, son of Robert, decd, being a minor, ct appts John G. Underwood, gdn, 11/5/1812, Laurens, GB

HART, Wiley, decd, A. J. Tison and J. W. Sessions, exrs, est to be sold in Coffee Co. 1st Tues in Sept, 7/5/1855, Lee, MSC

HART, William, decd, Elizabeth Hart issued L/A 2/2/1819, Isaac Low, George Twiggs, secs; 12/28/1825 div to: Mrs. Elizabeth Hart, Elbert A. Holt in rt of wife, Rebecca, Elbert Hold, gdn for Grace Hart, Richmond, AB

HART, William, orph of Charles, decd, Robert Reynolds, gdn, 9/17/1821, Peter Lamar, sec, Lincoln, GB

HARTFIELD, George, decd, John Hartfield and Anna Powers issued L/A 3/21/1789, David Evans, John Furey, secs, Richmond, AB

HARTFIELD, George, decd, Lydia Hartfield, admx, gtd ltrs dismission, 2/11/1801, Warren, MIC

HARTHORN, Stephen, decd, John Campbell qualified as admr 10/21/1791, Liberty, Ests

HARTLEY, Polley, orph and minor of Thomas, decd, to receive legacy left her by her grandmother, Mary Bell, decd, John Beasley, sec, 7/1809, Oglethorpe, OM, GB

HARTLEY, Thomas, decd, John Bell gtd L/A, 1/1807, Oglethorpe, OM

HARTSFIELD, Andrew N., decd, Josiah B. Holmes, admr 5/4/1814, Wilkes, Retns

HARTSFIELD, George, decd, Lydia Hartsfield, admx, 8/11/1800, Benjamin Howard, sur, Warren, AB

HARTSFIELD, Godfrey, decd, Josiah B. Holmes & Alsey Hartsfield, exrs, 5/5/1812 pd Andrew N. Hartsfield; recd of Alsey Hartsfield which was pd to Warren Hartsfield, legatee, pd Anderson Hartsfield, pd Luke Williams, heir, Wilkes, Retns

HARTSFIELD, Sarah, decd, LWT pvd by Evan Evans and Davenport Graves, L/T issued Luke Williams, 5/1817, Jasper, OM

HARVAL, Mason, decd, LWT dtd 12/9/1820, pvd 3/1821, names wife, Nancy; wit: P. C. Haggason, James Stewart, John P. Stewart, Jasper, Retns

HARVELL, Wilson, decd, Riley Harvell, admr, 1855, Cobb, BB

HARVEY, Caleb W., decd, John P. Harvey, admr, Dooly, OD

HARVEY, Mary S., orph of William, decd, Vandevas Leonard, gdn, 10/14/1822, Asbury Hull, Patrick Leonard, surs, Clarke, GB

HARVEY, Thomas, decd, John Harvey of Washington Co., Michael Harvey, Evan Harvey and James Harvey of Greene Co. applied for L/A 4/3/1792, Greene, Misc

HARWELL, H. I., decd, LWT pvd 3/2/1840, Harris

HASKINS, Thomas, decd, Sarah and Thomas Haskins, Archibald Gresham applied for L/A 2/19/1799, Greene, Misc

HASLIP, Randal G., minor of Randal G., decd, W. B. Daniels, gdn, James M. Daniels, Nathaniel Holton, Frances F. Holton, surs, 9/2/1833, GB

HASTINGS, Archibald, decd, Elizabeth and Catherine Hastings qualified as exrs 2/1/1790, Liberty, Ests

HATCHER, Archibald, decd, Mary Hatcher and James Meriwether issued L/A 3/30/1808, Littleberry Bostwick, Chesley Bostwick, Hezekiah Beal, secs, Richmond, AB

HATCHER, Edward, decd, Benjamin F. Harris and Henry Hatcher issued L/A 3/25/1808, Bird Booker Tindall, Holland McTyeire, Owen McGar, Matthias Liverman, Basil Lamar, apprs, Richmond, AB

HATCHER, Isaac, decd, LWT pvd by Isaac Tucker, offered for probate by Joseph Crews, 6/4/1832, Camden, MIC

HATCHER, Isham, decd, John Hatcher, admr, 1/5/1830, Camden, MIC

HATCHER, James, decd, Mrs. Maria Hatcher apptd admx w/LWT annexed 8/8/1833, Camden, MIC

HATCHER, Jonathan J., decd, L/A to Mary C. Hatcher 9/3/1866, Fulton

HATCHETT, John, decd, Sally Hatchett, admx, asked to be dismissed, 7/1807, Oglethorpe, OM

HATCHETT, John B., decd, LWT pvd 8/17/1847, William, Patrick and James Hatchett (sons), exrs, and brother,? Hatchett; wife, Eliza Hatchett, Harris

HATFIELD, James C., minor orph of James, decd, Thomas Whitsett apptd gdn 1/17/1859, Lee

HATFIELD, Joseph W., minor orph of James, decd, Thomas Whitsett apptd gdn 1/17/1859, Thomas Green, sur, Lee

HATHCOCK, Mary C., minor of William, Arminda Hathcock, gdn, 9/1/1856, Fulton

HATHCOCK, Tempy Ann Margaret, minor of William, decd, William M. Hathcock, gdn, 11/3/1856, Fulton

HATHCOCK, William, decd, Azariah Mimis qualified as admr 8/6/1855, Fulton

HATHCOX, Mary Ann, orph of Isaac, decd, late of Russell Co., Ala, James Oliver, gdn, Thomas Hardy, Walter Dunson, sec, 3/5/1849, Troup, GB

HATHCOX, Sarah, orph of Isaac, decd, late of Russell Co., Ala., James Oliver, gdn, Thomas Hardy, Walker Dunson, sec, 3/5/1849, Troup, GB

HATHORN, Benjamin, decd, Henry Sharp and Elizabeth Hawthorn issued L/A 1/6/1820, Morgan, AB

HAVER, Timothy, decd, Robert White, admr w/LWT annexed 9/5/1808, Putnam, AB

HAWES, Edmund, decd, Samuel Hawes issued L/A 3/5/1822, Thomas Crayton, John W. Reid, secs, Richmond, AB

HAWES, Elizabeth, orph of Spencer, decd, James B. Turner, gdn, 3/5/1832, James Jennings, Robert Walton, secs, Lincoln, GB

HAWES, Peyton, decd, Mosley Hawes, gdn for orphs: Ellington C. and Samuel G. 5/6/1839, TG. W. Norman, Isaac Willngham, secs, Lincoln, GB

HAWKINS, Abimeleck, decd, Sarah Hawkins issued L/A 7/30/1799, Ezekiel Harris, Collin Red, secs, Richmond, AB

HAWKINS, Alexander, Sr., LWT pvd, Nicholas Hawkins, exr, 1/1807, Oglethorpe, OM

HAWKINS, James, decd, Jeremiah Hawkins issued L/A 2/5/1855, Jonathan Martin, sec, Hall, AB

HAWKINS, James, decd, Nicholas Hawkins apptd admr 9/9/1783, Wilkes, MxR

HAWS, Claiborn, decd, LWT pvd 6/1/1863, Emma R. Haws and N. A. Wilson, exrs, Fulton

HAWS, Moseley, orph of Peyton, decd, Eliel Lockhart, gdn, 1/13/1834, Peter Lamar, sec, Lincoln, GB
HAWS, Spencer, decd, Fincher Thomas, gdn of orphs: Thomas, Elizabeth, Claiborn, 3/1/1824, Charles Jennings, Wm Curry, secs, Lincoln, GB
HAWS, William L., orph of Peyton, decd, Mosley Haws, gdn, 2/4/1839, Lincoln, GB
HAWTHORN, Benjamin, William Hawthorn, gdn, 11/1856, Webster, OD
HAY, Betey J., orph and minor of James, decd, Thomas Stone apptd gdn, Matthew Gage, John Walton, sec, 1/1807, Oglethorpe, OM
HAY, John, decd, L/A issued Benjamin Foy, Alfred Holefield, Jesse Crede, surs, 5/2/1814, Jasper, OM
HAY, John, decd, Elihu Atwater and Isaac Crews, atty for William Hay, admr, files retn, 4/1/1805, Camden, MIC
HAY, Melissa, orph and minor of James, decd, Thomas Stone apptd gdn, Matthew Gage, John Walton, sec, 1/1807, Oglethorpe, OM
HAY, Reubin, decd, George M. Hay, temporary admr, 3/1854, Webster, OD
HAY, Sarah E., minor of Reuben, decd, over age 14, L/G gtd George M. Hay, 4/1855, Webster, OD
HAY, William, decd, on motion of council, Gilbert Hay, surviving exr, published his notice to sell real estate for benefit of heirs--150 acres in Franklin Co., 107 acres on Broad River, 50 acres, 292 acres on Tugalo River, 11/2/1813, Franklin, OM
HAY, William T., decd, L/A issued Thomas Stone, Paschal Murphy, sur, 1/6/1817, Jasper, OM
HAY, William T., orph and minor of James, decd, Thomas Stone apptd gdn, Matthew Gage, John Walton, sec, 1/1807, Oglethorpe, OM
HAYES, A. J., orph of Lewis, decd, P. H. Allen, gdn, 1851-1854 retns, Fayette, GB
HAYES, Martha A. E., orph of John A., decd, Lemuel M. Murphy, gdn, David Haines, sur, 3/1849, 1851-1854 retns, Fayette, GB
HAYES, James, decd, inv of est by appraisers Jacob Hollingsworth, Elijah Martin, Samuel Hollingsworth 9/8/1796, Franklin, OM
HAYES, Patrick, Merchant, decd, John Wilson issued L/A 2/15/1797, John Fox, Henry Smerdon, secs, Richmond, AB
HAYLES, Emma, John Hayles apptd gdn of his minor dau 3/26/1823, Burwell W. Bracewell, Richard H. Wilde, secs, Richmond, GB
HAYLES, John, decd, L/A to Western B. Thomas 1818, Richmond, AB
HAYMAN, Famariah, decd, Jacob and Solomon Futch, James and Daniel Newman, Samuel Futch appr est 9/4/1837, Bulloch, MIC
HAYNES, Anthony, decd, David Maxwell and Thomas Haynes, exrs, 6/20/1795, Columbia, Ests
HAYNES, Elizabeth, decd, LWT pvd 1/1808, Oglethorpe, OM
HAYNES, Reuben, decd, W. A. Haynes, admr, 2/2/1857, Fulton
HAYNES, Stephen, decd, 1/11/1796 sale, Moses Haynes, admr; purchasers: Moses Haynes Sr. and Jr. and Stephen Haynes; Moses Haynes, admr and gdn for heirs: James, Sarah, William, Robert, Mary and Walter, Elbert, AR
HAYNES, Thomas, decd, Carey Cox issued L/A 1/12/1845, Baldwin
HAYNES, Thomas, decd, Reuben Haynes, admr, 9/5/1853, W. E. Oglby, sur, DeKalb, AB
HAYNIE, Bridger, decd, 1807 retns pd Thomas Going, Wm Haynie, Richard Saunders, Jonas Broach, recd of Charles Haynie on note, Bridger Haynie, admr, Elbert, AR
HAYNIE, Margaret, decd, George Haynie applied for L/A 7/7/1812 for his wife, formerly Margaret Holliday, refused because he relinquished all rt to same, Jackson, OM
HAYNIE, Richard, decd, 5/10/1807 inv, Elbert, AR
HAYS, Epsey, minor orph of Gideon, decd, Joseph Anderson, gdn, John R. Daniell, Owen Fountain, sur, 5/7/1827, Emanuel, GB

HAYS, Garsey, minor of Gideon, James Marsh, gdn, Henry Durden, Samuel Ramsay, sur, 3/1/1824, Emanuel, GB
HAYS, Gideon, decd, "received of Samuel Kenedy $1282 in full of all moneys due est of Gideon Hays." signed Gideon M. Keneday, 2/23/1839, Emanuel, AB
HAYS, Gideon, decd, Jesse Brown, James Marsh, admrs, 5/26/1820, appr, Emanuel, A
HAYS, Green, orph of Gideon, decd, Susannah Hays, Uriah Anderson, Stephen Beck, gdns, 7/1/1822, Emanuel, GB
HAYS, Halsey, minor of Gideon, Susannah Hays, Uriah Anderson, Stephen Beck, gdns, 7/1/1822; Susannah Hays, gdn, William Daniell, Bluford Spencer, sur, 3/1/1824, Emanuel, GB
HAYS, Hezekiah, minor of Gideon, decd, Susannah Hays, gdn, Joseph Anderson, sur, undtd, Emanuel, GB
HAYS, John, decd, William Hay apptd admr, 6/9/1802, Camden, MIC
HAYS, Owen S. E., Decd, A. Nicholson issued L/A 7/1863; J. H. Carter issued L/A de bonis non 12/1864, Webster, OD
HAYS, Thomas, who is blind and infirm with age has a lifetime support in Est of H. B. Fowler; ordered that Mrs. F. S. Bell, admx, make arrangements to support him, 12/1868, Webster, OD
HAYSLIP, James, decd, William H. Green, exr, 5/11/1854, Lee, MSC
HEAD, Harrison, decd, Jane A. Head, admx, A. T. Baugh, Scott L. Baugh, sur, 4/7/1873, Gwinnett, AB
HEAD, William, decd, William Head issued L/A 7/5/1808, Putnam, AB
HEAD, William R., decd, O. J. Head, David P. Elder, admrs, Joshua Elder, S. T. Whitaker, surs, 7/1850, 1851-1854 retns, Fayette, AB
HEADEN, William, decd, LWT pvd 1/4/1808, Jackson, OM
HEADS, Sarah H., Sharp S. Reynolds, gdn, 3/5/1855, Hiram Kelton, sec, Hall, GB
HEARD, George, John Ramey, gdn, vs. Gates F. Fawley, 2/1807, Morgan, SCW
HEARD, George, orph of George W., decd, 11/4/1839, Harris
HEARD, Martha, decd, John Heard issued L/A 11/14/1808, John Cashin, Holland McTyeire, secs, Richmond, AB
HEARD, Samuel C., decd, Charles M. Heard issued L/A 7/5/1852, Mary Stewart, sec, Lumpkin, AB
HEARD, Stephen, decd, John Heard, admr, pd Allin Martin, George Crain, Henry C. Dawson, Stephen G. Heard, William Dawson, Elizabeth Heard, heirs, 3/2/1812, Wilkes, Retns
HEARD, Thomas, decd, Joseph Heard, Wilson Whatley and Henry Ware make retn on est through 1819, slaves already divided among ch-- W. T., Hubbard P., George, Amelia, Thomas W. and Mary F. Heard, 1/25/1821, Jasper, Ests
HEARD, Thomas of Randolph Co., Ga., decd, names ch--Mary F., Wyatt, Hubbard, George, Thomas, Amelia, Polley F.; wife, Polley, LWT dtd 11/22/1810, Jasper, Ests
HEARD, Thomas, decd, exrs of LWT order division f estate 9/2/1816, Jasper, OM
HEARDON, Joseph, decd, Samuel Robison issued L/A 9/2/1833, Washington
HEART, Samuel, decd, LWT pvd by Septimus Weatherby and John Myrick; Isaac Heart qualified as exr; LWT and proceedings retd to Washington Co., Ga., 3/3/1806, Warren, MIC
HEARTFIELD, George, decd, Lydia Heartfield applies for admn, Benjamin Howard, sur, 3/18/1800, Warren, MIC, AB
HEATH, Adam, decd, Richard Heath, Peter Clower, admrs, 5/6/1816, Hardy Pitts, Benjamin Sandiford, surs, Warren, AB
HEATH, Edmond P., decd, Peterson Heath, admr, 11/7/1831, Curtis Lowe, D. Dennis, Nicholas H. Jones, surs, Warren, AB
HEATH, Henry, decd, Winneford Heath, admx, David Anderson, sur, 3/5/1827, appraisal 7/14/1827, Emanuel, AB, A

HEATH, Joel, decd, LWT pvd, Hartwell Heath and Robert Bonner qualified exrs, 5/7/1810, Warren, MIC
HEATH, Lewis, decd, Winniford Heath, admx, James Waters, Jean Kirkland, Nathan Vickers, sur, 5/14/1819, Emanuel, AB
HEATH, Lewis, decd, Winniford Heath, admx. appr 7/9/1819, Emanuel, A
HEATH, Mark, decd, Henry Heath, admr, 8/7/1820, Joseph Hill, Chappell Heath, surs, Warren, AB
HEATH, Millie (Mrs.), decd, John Hobson, admr, to sell negroes; she was sole heir of Wm Stith, decd, 2/4/1811, Warren, MIC
HEATH, Richard, decd, Chapple Heth and Joseph Hill applied for adm w/LWT annexed, pvd by John Baker, William Baker, 1/4/1808, Warren, MIC
HEATH, Richard, decd, George W. C. Shivers, admr, 5/21/1832, Sterling J. Pate, John L. Burkhalter, surs, Warren, AB
HEATH, Sterling, decd, Henry Butts issued temporary L/A 3/25/1814, Putnam, AB
HEATH, Stokes, decd, Wiley Heath issued L/A 9/22/1815, Gabriel Clarke, Jacob Dill, secs, Richmond, AB
HEATH, William, LWt pvd, 7/4/1814, Warren, MIC
HEBBARD, John, decd, Mrs. Elizabeth A. Hebbard apptd admx, 9/2/1850, Camden, MIC
HEBBARD, Winnifred (Mrs.), decd, LWT pvd, M. H. Hebbard qualified exr 7/10/1839, Camden, MIC
HECKLE, Christopher, decd, Nancy Heckle issued L/A 4/6/1829, John Heckle, James Murphy, secs, Richmond, AB
HECKLIN, Reuben N., decd, Elizabeth Hecklin, admx, 1/3/1832; Samuel Tompkins issued L/A 3/6/1837; William P. Hecklin, admr de bonis non 11/13/1843, Washington, AB
HECKLIN, Sarah, decd, LWT pvd 3/7/1842, William Hall, Sr., exr, Washington
HECKLIN, William P., orph of Reuben N., decd, Samuel Robison, gdn, 11/1/1841, Washington, AB
HEDGEPATH, Riley, age abt 10 yrs, Wilson Byers apptd gdn for 11 yrs, William Presley, sur, 3/8/1833, Butts, GB
HEETH, William W., illeg child of Sarah Heeth, Hardy V. Heeth, gdn, Henry Durden, David Connady, sur, 11/2/1835, Emanuel, GB
HEFFLIN, James, decd, Samuel Alexander, admr, 3/2/1807, John Simmons, sur, Warren, AB
HEFLIN, James, decd, Samuel Alexander as the greatest creditor applies for L/A; Will of decd not proven, 2/2/1807, Warren, MIC
HEIDT, Abigail, decd, of Chatham Co., Matthew Heidt applies L/A 11/28/1838, Effingham, MIC
HEIDT, Solomon, decd, L/A to Lewis Hinely 3/25/1847; Caroline M. Heidt, wid, applied for L/A 11/9/1842, Effingham, MIC
HELMLY, David, decd, Frederick Hinely applies for L/A 3/25/1847, Effingham, MIC
HELTON, Samuel, decd, Henry Graybill, admr, 11/19/1794, Aaron Benton, sur, Warren, AB
HELVENSTEIN, John and Jacob, decd, Mrs. Blandina Magdalena Helvenstein admx w/LWT annexed 10/10/1801, Camden, MIC
HELVENSTINE, John, decd, LWT dtd 12/4/1774, pvd 10/16/1801, bequeaths to father 100 acres he bt from George Burkholder, etc, pair of breeches to bro, Jacob; sister, Hannah; bro., Daniel, Effingham, Misc
HELVENSTINE, John, decd, LWT dtd 12/4/1774, pvd 10/16/1801, leaves father 100 acres, a hat to bro, Jacob, sister, Hannah, bro, Daniel, Camden, MIC
HELVENSTINE, John Frederick, decd, planter, LWT pvd 4/5/1793--to wife, Blandina Magdelina, ch: Jacob, Daniel, Joshua, Mary Magdalena, Mary Christina. Recpts of Joseph & Maria Christina Helvenstine & Maria Magdalena Gromet, Effingham, Misc

HELVENSTON, Joseph, decd, LWT pvd 7/5/1830, Effingham, MIC
Helveston, Jeremiah, decd, R. McGillis apptd admr, 4/12/1808,
Camden, MIC
HEMBREE, A., decd, J. L. and E. M. Hembree, exrs, 1855, Cobb, BB
HEMPHILL, Tilmon, decd, Wade Hemphill and George Langford issued
L/A 2/14/1825, A. Fitzpatrick, sec, Morgan, AB
HENAMAN, William, decd, George Hill issued L/A 7/31/1824, Daniel
Meigs, A. G. Raiford, secs, Richmond, AB
HENDERSON, Alary A., orph of John, decd, Beverly Adams apptd gdn
1/7/1822, Jasper, OM
HENDERSON, Andrew M., orph of Mitchel, decd, Robert C. Porter,
gdn, Hugh Porter, sur, 5/1850, 1851-1853 retns, Fayette, GB
HENDERSON, Beverly A., orph of John, decd, Beverly Adams apptd
gdn 1/7/1822, Jasper, OM
HENDERSON, Caty, late Caty Thornton, Elisha Reid, gdn, pd her pt
of est two slaves, 1/7/1817, Wilkes, Retns
HENDERSON, Daniel, decd, John Hodges applies for L/A 9/6/1832,
Effingham, MIC
HENDERSON, Hannah, gdn of Dolly, Hannah & John, minors, bd for
1813; pd John & Hannah Henderson, John Heard, gdn of Josiah,
Elisha, William & Thomas Henderson, James Henderson, Hannah
Henderson, gdn of Hannah & John, Dolly; pd William B. Simmons,
James, Henry, William and Elisha Henderson, heirs,
12/29/1815, Wilkes, Retns
HENDERSON, James, decd, Hannah Henderson and Phenail Wilson
issued L/A 3/7/1814, Jackson, OM
HENDERSON, James, decd, late of North Carolina, Alexander
Johnston gtd L/A, 6/22/1795, Columbia, Ests
HENDERSON, James B., orph of John, decd, Beverly Adams apptd gdn
1/7/1822, Jasper, OM
HENDERSON, John, decd, L/A issued Matilda J. Henderson and
Beverly Allen 3/5/1821, Jasper, OM
HENDERSON, John, minor of William, James Henderson apptd gdn
1/1820, Jasper, OM
HENDERSON, John A., orph of John, decd, Beverly Adams apptd gdn
1/7/1822, Jasper, OM
HENDERSON, Joseph, decd, Catherine Henderson, gdn of orphs: Hugh,
Eliza, James, Robt, Joseph, Lee, Mariah and Green, 5/2/1825; Hugh
Henderson, gdn, 10/8/1833, Lincoln, GB
HENDERSON, Joseph W., orph of John, decd, Beverly Adams apptd gdn
1/7/1822, Jasper, OM
HENDERSON, Josiah T., decd, Benjamin F. Cock, admr, Lee, MSC
HENDERSON, Mary (Mrs.), decd, of Augusta, Robert Henderson issued
temp L/A 6/15/1802, perm admx 8/2/1802, John Turman, Wm Foster,
secs, Richmond, AB
HENDERSON, Mitchel, decd, Robert C. Porter, exr of LWT, 1851-1854
retns, Fayette, AB
HENDERSON, William, decd, Benjamin Stovall and Hannah Henderson,
admrs, 7/1/1811 retn, Wilkes, Retns
HENDLEY, Abetha, orph of William, decd, Ely Roberts, gdn, Josiah
Drew, David E. Rich, sur, 11/7/1836, Emanuel, GB
HENDLEY, Elizabeth, minor of William, decd, John Rountree, gdn,
Zaccheus Evans, sur, 11/4/1839, Emanuel, GB
HENDLEY, Elizabeth, orph of William, decd, Ely Robarts, gdn,
Josiah Drew, David E. Rich, sur, 11/7/1836, Emanuel, GB
HENDLEY, Gary, orph of William, decd, Zaccheus Evans, gdn, John
Rountree, sur, 1/1840, Emanuel, GB
HENDLEY, James, decd, ordered that James Nessmith have leave to
sell Cass Co. land, 80 acres; made his retn as gdn of heirs for
1839, Bulloch, MIC
HENDLEY, John F., orph of James, decd, James Nessmith, gdn, made
1840 retn, 5/8/1841, Bulloch, MIC

HENDLEY, Sarah, orph of William, decd, Ely Roberts, gdn, Josiah Drew, David E. Rich, sur, 11/7/1836, Emanuel, GB`

HENDLEY, Tabitha, orph of William, decd, Zaccheus Evans, gdn, John Rountree, sur, 1/1840, Emanuel, GB

HENDLEY, William, decd, James Scarborough, admr, Silas Scarborough, John Hart, sur, 9/5/1836, Emanuel, AB

HENDLEY, William, decd, Lewis Collins, admr, 10/17/1836, appr, Emanuel, A

HENDLEY, William ordered to support his wife, Jane Hendley, Thomas Camp, apptd her gdn, 3/7/1808, Jackson, OM

HENDON, Elijah, orph of Isham, decd, James Thomason, gdn, 5/7/1812, Daniel Conner, Parmenus Haynes, surs, Clarke, GB

HENDON, Isham, decd, Patience and Elijah Hendon, exrs, made retn 10/25/1802, Jackson, OM

HENDRICK, Martin, decd, Alford Clopton and Jane Hendrick issued L/A 3/1/1813, Putnam, AB

HENDRICKS, Abijah, decd, 6/1/1809 est appraised by Barnabas Pace, John Certain, John Turner, John Bray; purchasers at sale: Elias, William, Camnel and Anna hendricks, John Bray; Elias and Anna Hendricks, admrs, Elbert, AR

HENDRICKS, David & Sarah, decd: Heirs agrmt betwn William Hendricks, Allen Finch, James Hendricks (for himself & gdn of Griffin Hendricks, his bro), 9/10/1822; div. betwn: James, William, Griffin and Allen Hendricks, Bulloch, Misc

HENDRICKS, Isaac, decd, LWT dtd 5/25/1803 pvd 7/9/1805; Will names ch: Nancy, Isaac, Japeth, Anniss, Moses, Joseph, James and Andrew, Franklin, OM

HENDRICKS, Isaac, Sr., LWT pvd 7/9/1805, ch: Isaac, Nancy, Jepthah, Anness, Moses, James; Andrew and Fennett Wilson, exrs, Franklin, IMW

HENDRICKS, John, decd, appr 2/24/1838, by Emanuel Brewton, Cullin Barrow, Uriah A. Rogers, lots in Screven, Cherokee, Ware Co.´s, Bulloch, Misc

HENDRICKS, William, decd, Ethelred Tarvin, Isabel Hendricks, Ezekiel Smith, admrs, 10/8/1811, Jones, AB

HENDRICKS, William E., decd, Benjamin Palmer issued L/A 1/2/1821, Etheldred Tarver, sec, Richmond, AB

HENDRICKS, William E., minor orph of William, decd, Etheldred Tarver, gdn 1/6/1817, Moses Collins, Jeptha Daniel, secs, Richmond, GB

HENDRICKS, William E., orph of William, Isabel Hendricks, Ethelred, gdns, Peter Wynch, William Cabiniss, sur, 1/7/1812, Jones, LG

HENDRIX, (or HENDRICKS) Daniel, decd, inv and appr by Wm Brack, Wm Busby, James Young, James Hendrix; heirs: Wyley, Laborn, John and McGinty Hendrix, 2/5/1833, Bulloch, Misc

HENDRIX, David, lunatic, petition of Mrs. Chira Hendrix that he be committed to asylum, 2/23/1866, Cobb, MIC

HENDRIX, Griffin, orph of David, decd, Luke Mizell apptd gdn 3/3/1817; James Hendrix apptd gdn 9/2/1822, Bulloch, MIC

HENDRIX, Jack, decd, pet of Reuben Thornton states that decd gave J. Hoxey bond on 1/5/1805 that he would make title to land whereon Thomas Thornton now lives, 11/1/1811; admrs ordered to make title 11/1811, Franklin, OM

HENDRIX, Jackson, orph, Thomas T. Tate, gdn, Thomas Holland, Barrett Jackson, secs, 1/8/1833, Hall, GB

HENDRIX, James, decd, Hannah Hendrix and Fannie Wilson, admrs, file retns 2/6/1816, Jackson, OM

HENDRIX, James, decd, widow allowed to have land for ensuing yr for yer support, 1814, Jackson, OM

HENDRIX, John, decd, Mrs. Jemima Hendrix made 1838 retn as admx 11/4/1839; leave to sell Lee, Randolph and Screven Co. lands of decd 3/2/1840, Bulloch, MIC
HENDRIX, Mary, orph of David, decd, Luke Mizell apptd gdn 3/3/1817, Bulloch, MIC
HENDRIX, Susannah, orph of David, decd, Luke Mizell apptd gdn 3/3/1817, Bulloch, MIC
HENDRY, Barbara and Sarah, Alex Hendry, Jr, gdn, p. 179, 195, Screven, OM
HENLEY, Lott, John W. Henley, gdn, 1855, Cobb, BB
HENNING, George, decd, Margaret Henning, gdn of Harriet C., Caroline W., Elizabeth I., Louisa P., Polly N., George T., orphs, 5/5/1816, Augustine S. Clayton, sur, Clarke, GB
HENNON, Martha Avarella, dau of Fanny, aged abt 6 yrs, bound to Wiley Potty until age 21, 5/10/1858, Cherokee, GB
HENDRY, Celia, decd, Wiley Massey, admr, 12/1838; apprs: John Upton, Patrick Monroe, Sheldon Swift, James M. Dunaway; purchasers at sale: T. F. Henry, Aaron P. Moon, T. H. Traywick, Wiley and Simeon Massey, Isaiah Smith, Stewart, Adms
HENRY, Stephen, decd, appr 7/9/1803, David Henry, admr; purchasers at sale: David Henry, James Reid, Joseph Johnson, Abner and Fanny Reid, Elizabeth and Levy Foster, Hancock, AAAA
HENRYMAN, Pleasant, decd, Jacob Miller reports that he d. at his home in Sept. and left a trunk of clothing; sheriff directed to sell same, 6/2/1818, Camden, MIC
HENSON, David, decd, Judy Henson extrx of LWT, ordered to show cause why she should not be removed 5/7/1821, Jasper, OM
HERB, Frederick, decd, William N. Hubard, John Frederick Herb, exrs of LWT, 11/2/1790, Chatham, Adms
HERRIN, C. L., decd, John Herrin, Aaron Herrin, admrs 3/2/1840, Harris, AB
HERRING, Abraham, decd, Richard Ricks and Harman Neill issued L/A 2/3/1812, Laurens, AB
HERRING, Francis, orph of Thomas, decd, Wm J. Russell, gdn, 1851-1854 retns, Fayette, GB
HERRING, John, decd, Hollen Herring and James Phillips issued L/A 7/7/1823; James Phillips, gdn of orphs: Jesse and Patsy, 7/12/1823, Samuel Patton, Morgan, AB, GB
HERRING, Jonathan, orph of Thomas, decd, Wm J. Russell, gdn, 1851-1854 retns, Fayette, GB
HERRING, Marcus, orph of Thomas, decd, Wm J. Russell, gdn, 1851-1854 retns, Fayette, GB
HERRING, Thomas, decd, William J. Russell, admr de bonis non, Charles Clements, sur, 1/1850, 1851-1852 retn, Fayette, GB
HERRING, William, decd, John Johnson Cox, gdn of Jane F., Elvira and John, orphs, 1/25/1819, Thomas Moore, George W. Moore, surs, Clarke, GB
HERRSON, Johannah Christiana, decd, of near Ebenezer, wid, LWT dtd 2/12/1802 pvd 4/15/1802, to: son, Gottlief Ernst, Camden, MIC
HERSON, Hergan, decd, Mrs. Hannah Herson applies for adm 2/27/1797, apptd 6/5/1797, Camden, MIC
HERY, Patrick I., decd, Neill Munroe issued L/A 1/8/1822, Laurens, AB
HESTER, Joseph, decd, LWT recd 1/13/1845; William Hester applies for L/A 12/3/1844, Effingham, MIC
HESTER, Joseph, orph of Stephen, decd, Wyatt Hester, gdn, 7/4/1825, Elizabeth Hester, sur, Clarke, GB
HESTER, Stephen, decd, Elizabeth Hester, gdn of Elizabeth, Sherwood, Sarah and Martha, orphs, 7/4/1825, Stephen C. Hester, sur, Clarke, GB
HEUTEN, D., decd, LWT pvd 3/1875, Webster, OD

HEWET, John, decd, L/A to Gilbert M. Stokes 10/18/1858, Lee
HIBBARD, Elihu, decd, William King exr of LWT, says estate is not
sufficient to support orphs of decd. Malatiah Haley Hibbard, one
of minors, ordered bound out to a machanical trade for 4 yrs,
7/16/1812; William King abt to remove from the State, resigned as
exr of est 6/18/1816; M. H. Hibbard qualified as admr w/LWT
annexed 1/4/1820, Camden, MIC
HIBBARD, John, James Vincent apptd gdn, 2/5/1816 and 1/6/1823,
Camden, MIC
HICKMAN, William, decd, LWT pvd 9/2/1816, Jasper, OM
HICKS, George, decd, John Collier was gtd L/A 3/2/1807,
Oglethorpe, OM
HICKS, James, a minor, decd, William Beck issued L/A 9/6/1819,
Laurens, AB
HICKS, Jefferson, a poor child, to be bound out to John Jones
McKleroy until age 21, 5/1817, Jasper, OM
HICKS, Joseph, decd, L/A gtd to William Philips 9/29/1821,
Jasper, OM
HICKS, Lewis, decd, Daniel Hicks, admr and gdn of orphs--Bunetta
and Esther 1/6/1815; John Fullwood, gdn of Narcissa and James
1/6/1815; William O'Neal, gdn of Benjamin H. 1/6/1815; Jethro B.
Spivey, gdn of John 3/6/1815, Laurens, GB
HICKS, Mary, orph of Daniel, decd, John McCoy, gdn, 2/4/1822,
Amos Hicks, sur, Clarke, GB
HICKS, Nathaniel, decd, Edmund B. Hicks issued L/A 12/20/1794,
Leonard Nobles of Burke Co. and James McCoy of Winton Co., South
Carolina, secs; Edmund B. Hicks mother, Ruth Hicks, alias Ruth
Townsend, Richmond, AB
HICKS, Timothy, decd, Agnes Perritt issued L/A 7/15/1783, John
Stewart, Sarah Baldwin, secs, Richmond, AB
HIGDON, Bud, decd, Jeremiah Covey and Robert Higdon issued L/A
9/8/1820, Laurens, AB
HIGDON, Charles H., decd, Amos D. and Winfrey Higdon, admrs (not
dtd), Dooly, OD
HIGDON, Robert had illegitimate daughter, Amanda E. Smith; Robert
Higdon apptd gdn, Daniel E. Rich, sur, 9/4/1837, Emanuel, GB
HIGDON, Robert, decd, Robert Higdon, admr, William Phillips,
Rufus Knight, sur, 7/6/1835; decd Emanuel, AB
HIGGINBOTHAM, Larkin, orph of Benjamin, decd, John S.
Higginbotham apptd gdn 1/7/1811, John Ham, Francis Higginbotham,
sec, Elbert, GB
HIGGINBOTHAM, Mary, orph of Benjamin, decd, Francis Higginbotham
apptd gdn 1/7/1811, Charles Carter, John Ham, sec, Elbert, GB
HIGGINBOTHAM, Peter, orph of Benjamin, decd, John S. Higginbotham
was apptd gdn 1/7/1811, John Ham, Francis Higginbotham, sec,
Elbert, GB
HIGGINBOTHAM, Samuel (Colonel), decd, 8/10/1803 inv, John S.
Higginbotham, adm, Elbert, AR
HIGGINS, Nancy, decd, David Higgins, admr, Sterling T. Higgins,
sur, 7/13/1844, Butts, AB
HIGGS, Elizabeth, illegitimate, Patience Higgs, gdn of her dau,
1/2/1832, John Higgs, sec, Montgomery, GB
HIGHNOTE, Eda gtd L/G for: William, John W., James and Mary E.
Highnote, orphs & minors under age of 14 yrs, 4/1856, Webster, OD
HIGHNOTE, Henry, decd, Cader A. Parker, admr, 7/1835; apprs:
Henry Audulf, James & Stephen Jackson; purchasers at sale: Abner
& George Banks, Isaac Brooks, William Burgamy, Philip & Sara
Highnote, Malachi & Wilson Josey, Stewart, Adms
HIGHNOTE, Philip, decd, Eda Highnote gtd L/A w/LWT annexed
9/1856, Webster, OD
HIGHSMITH, James, decd, Beady Highsmith issued L/A 1/5/1815,
Tattnall, AB

147

HIGHTOWER, Andrew M., Joel Hightower, gdn, Dooly, OD
HIGHTOWER, Echols, decd, Joel Hightower and Thomas B. Fuqua, admrs, Dooly, OD
HIGHTOWER, Henry A., Joel Hightower, gdn, Dooly, OD
HIGHTOWER, Mary, Joel Hightower, gdn, Dooly, OD
HIGHTOWER, Nancy, decd, Joel W. Hightower, admr, Dooly, OD
HIGHTOWER, William, decd, D. P. Hightower, admr, M. L. Thompson, sur, 7/7/1847, Bibb, AB
HILBURN, Nathaniel G., decd, Martha H. A. Hilburn, admx, 1/12/1852, John Bird, William H. Harville, H. P. Ivey, surs, DeKalb, AB
HILL, Adam, decd, L/A with LWT annexed gtd Habukkuk Wright, 10/3/1794, Warren, MIC
HILL, Arabella E., orph of Asaph, decd, Andrew H. Hill, gdn, 6/4/1860, Dawson, WB
HILL, Asaph, decd, Andrew H. Hill and John W. Hill, admrs, James L. Harris, James Hill, Samuel C. Taylor, A. J. Taylor, D. H. Logan, surs on bond 10/3/1859, Dawson, WB
HILL, Augusta M. (Miss), orph, Joseph Winship, gdn, 4/1863, dismissed 8/26/1867, Fulton
HILL, Barbary L., minor orph of Asaph, decd, Andrew Hill, gdn, 6/4/1860, Dawson, WB
HILL, Benjamin, decd, L/A issued Leonadas W. Hill 5/1854, Webster, OD
HILL, Birdwell, decd, Francis Hill, admr, David H. Bird, sur, 8/13/1855, Cherokee, AB
HILL, Christian, decd, Henry Hill, admr, Archilous Hill, Miles Hill, sec, 9/1809, Oglethorpe, OM, AB
HILL, Clementa D., minor orph of Asaph, decd, Andrew Hill, gdn, 6/4/1860, Dawson, WB
HILL, David B., decd, Eli G. Hill, Theodore A. Goodwin and Matilda Hill issued L/A 3/4/1844, Baldwin
HILL, E., decd, Elisha Hill, gdn of orphs and minors, Wm L. Chambers, sur, 1847 retn, Fayette, GB
HILL, Edward, decd, David Castleberry and Joshua Hill apptd admrs 1/6/1817, Jackson, OM
HILL, Eliza, orph and minor of William, decd, L/G gtd Isaac Hill 3/4/1816, Jasper, OM
HILL, George, decd, Mary Hill issued L/A 12/12/1814, Putnam, AB
HILL, Greenberry, minor orph of Theophilus, decd, Amey Castello apptd gdn 9/7/1818, Jasper, OM
HILL, Henry, decd, Frances Hill, extrx, gtd dismission, 8/10/1801, Warren, MIC
HILL, Hill, Isaac, Jr., retn 1813, signed Henry Peddy, Jr. in rt of his wife, 1/5/1814, Jasper, OM
HILL, Isaac, decd, Penny Hill, admx, Richard Head, Wright Hill, surs, ask to be discharged from securityship, Penny Hill now Penny Peddy, 9/1812; Henry Peddy gave sec for Eli Clark for adm of Penny Hill on est 3/1813, Jasper, OM
HILL, Isaac, orph of Isaac, decd, Henry Peddy apptd gdn 1/7/1817, Jasper, OM
HILL, John, decd, merchant, Mrs. Mary Hill and John Carmichael issued L/A 9/15/1815, John Cumming, Angus Martin, secs; div to Mary Louise Hill, slaves, etc., to wid, land in Wilkinson Co., Richmond, AB
HILL, John E., caveat filed by James May to apptmt of Dr. William Dicks as admr (overruled), 7/5/1813, Glynn, MIC
HILL, Joseph, decd, Zephaniah Franklin, admr, 10/3/1832, Q. L. C. Franklin, David Mims, D. Dennis, surs, Warren, AB
HILL, Joshua, decd, John Hill and Isaac Edward, admrs, Nathaniel Boley, B. A. Boley, B. A. Blakey, James O. Jones, sur, 4/8/1875, Gwinnett, AB

HILL, Joshua, decd, Sarah Hill applies for L/A, Adam Jones, Wyatt
Bonner, sec, 2/16/1796, Warren, MIC, AB
HILL, Lawrence, decd, L/A gtd James Reid 1/6/1817, James Hines,
Richard Bird, surs; Elizabeth Hill, wid, elected to take child's
pt 5/1817, Jasper, OM
HILL, Lovery D., decd, Leonadas W. Hill apptd admr 1/1855,
Webster, OD
HILL, Lovice, orph and minor of William, decd, L/G gtd Isaac Hill
3/4/1816, Jasper, OM
HILL, Luaunda Patsey, orph of Isaac, decd, Henry Peddy apptd gdn
1/7/1817, Jasper, OM
HILL, Lucinda, orph of Isaac, decd, retn for 1817, Jasper, OM
HILL, Lucinda C., orph of Asaph, decd, Andrew H. Hill, gdn,
6/4/1860, Dawson, WB
HILL, Martha J., minor orph of Asaph, decd, Andrew Hill, gdn,
6/4/1860, Dawson, WB
HILL, Mountain, decd, Ambrose Heath, admr, 1/14/1827, Abner
Rogers, John Wright, surs, Warren, AB
HILL, Polley, minor orph of Theophilus, decd, Amey Castello apptd
gdn 9/7/1818, Jasper, OM
HILL, Polley, orph of Isaac, decd, Henry Peddy apptd gdn
1/7/1817, Jasper, OM
HILL, Reuben, decd, Alfred Webb, admr, David and Asaph Hill, surs
on bond, 9/6/1858, Dawson, WB
HILL, Reubin, orph of Asaph, decd, Andrew H. Hill, gdn, 6/4/1860,
Dawson, WB
HILL, Richard, decd, Frances Hill, admx asks to be dismissed,
4/7/1800, Warren, MIC
HILL, Richard A., decd, LWT pvd 8/3/1835, Mary F. Hill, widow,
qualified as extrx of LWT 9/16/1835, Camden, MIC
HILL, Samuel Berry, decd, 11/13/1795 appr of est, Robert Berry
Hill, admr, Richmond, AB
HILL, Sarah, decd, Abraham and John Hill, exrs, 1813 retn,
Wilkes, Retns
HILL, Sarah Parham, age over 14 yrs, James Bonner apptd gdn,
12/2/1811, Warren, MIC
HILL, Sophrona, decd, William N. Hill, admr, J. P. Allen, sur,
5/1855, Fayette, AB
HILL, Susanna, orph of Isaac, decd, Henry Peddy apptd gdn
1/7/1817, Jasper, OM
HILL, Theophilus, decd, Isaac McClendon and John Castellow, admr,
to sell 135 acres, 1/7/1817; adm on est presented on acct against
est $186.69 9/5/1814, Jasper, OM
HILL, Theophilus, decd, late of Randolph Co., Ga., inventory and
appraisement 9/14/1810, div 1816, heirs: Elizabeth, Martha,
Winney, Nancy; 1819 Retn, Anny Castello, gdn, Isaac McClendon,
admr of ch: Mary, Harriet, Kinney, Martha, Sary and Winney.
Jasper, Ests
HILL, Thomas, decd, Phoebe Hill, admx, 5/1/1794, Richard Hill,
sur, admx dismissed 5/10/1795, Warren, AB, MIC
HILL, Thomas C., decd, John A. Hill, admr, 3/1/1858, Thomas Kile,
sur, DeKalb, AB
HILL, William, decd, George Parham, admr, 7/3/1810, Warren, MIC
HILL, William, decd, LWT pvd 7/1846, Harris
HILL, William, decd, Lindsey Coleman issued L/A 11/28/1805,
William J. Hobby, Eli Pearre, secs, Richmond, AB
HILL, William, decd, pd Isaac Hill, in rt of wife, Lydia Hill,
admx, 1813; Eliza and Lovice Hill, orphs of William, Jasper, Ests
HILL, William, decd, Moses Speer, Lydia Hill, admrs, appl of
Moses Speer, one of admrs, to make title to John Shackleford for
land in Greene Co., 70 acres, which land decd sold sd
Shackleford, 3/8/1813, Jasper, OM

HILL, Joshua, decd, Sarah Hill applies for L/A, Adam Jones, Wyatt Bonner, sec, 2/16/1796, Warren, MIC, AB
HILL, Lawrence, decd, L/A gtd James Reid 1/6/1817, James Hines, Richard Bird, surs; Elizabeth Hill, wid, elected to take child's pt 5/1817, Jasper, OM
HILL, Lovery D., decd, Leonadas W. Hill apptd admr 1/1855, Webster, OD
HILL, Lovice, orph and minor of William, decd, L/G gtd Isaac Hill 3/4/1816, Jasper, OM
HILL, Luaunda Patsey, orph of Isaac, decd, Henry Peddy apptd gdn 1/7/1817, Jasper, OM
HILL, Lucinda, orph of Isaac, decd, retn for 1817, Jasper, OM
HILL, Lucinda C., orph of Asaph, decd, Andrew H. Hill, gdn, 6/4/1860, Dawson, WB
HILL, Martha J., minor orph of Asaph, decd, Andrew Hill, gdn, 6/4/1860, Dawson, WB
HILL, Mountain, decd, Ambrose Heath, admr, 1/14/1827, Abner Rogers, John Wright, surs, Warren, AB
HILL, Polley, minor orph of Theophilus, decd, Amey Castello apptd gdn 9/7/1818, Jasper, OM
HILL, Polley, orph of Isaac, decd, Henry Peddy apptd gdn 1/7/1817, Jasper, OM
HILL, Reuben, decd, Alfred Webb, admr, David and Asaph Hill, surs on bond, 9/6/1858, Dawson, WB
HILL, Reubin, orph of Asaph, decd, Andrew H. Hill, gdn, 6/4/1860, Dawson, WB
HILL, Richard, decd, Frances Hill, admx asks to be dismissed, 4/7/1800, Warren, MIC
HILL, Richard A., decd, LWT pvd 8/3/1835, Mary F. Hill, widow, qualified as extrx of LWT 9/16/1835, Camden, MIC
HILL, Samuel Berry, decd, 11/13/1795 appr of est, Robert Berry Hill, admr, Richmond, AB
HILL, Sarah, decd, Abraham and John Hill, exrs, 1813 retn, Wilkes, Retns
HILL, Sarah Parham, age over 14 yrs, James Bonner apptd gdn, 12/2/1811, Warren, MIC
HILL, Sophrona, decd, William N. Hill, admr, J. P. Allen, sur, 5/1855, Fayette, AB
HILL, Susanna, orph of Isaac, decd, Henry Peddy apptd gdn 1/7/1817, Jasper, OM
HILL, Theophilus, decd, Isaac McClendon and John Castellow, admr, to sell 135 acres, 1/7/1817; adm on est presented on acct against est $186.69 9/5/1814, Jasper, OM
HILL, Theophilus, decd, late of Randolph Co., Ga., inventory and appraisement 9/14/1810, div 1816, heirs: Elizabeth, Martha, Winney, Nancy; 1819 Retn, Anny Castello, gdn, Isaac McClendon, admr of ch: Mary, Harriet, Kinney, Martha, Sary and Winney. Jasper, Ests
HILL, Thomas, decd, Phoebe Hill, admx, 5/1/1794, Richard Hill, sur, admx dismissed 5/10/1795, Warren, AB, MIC
HILL, Thomas C., decd, John A. Hill, admr, 3/1/1858, Thomas Kile, sur, DeKalb, AB
HILL, William, decd, George Parham, admr, 7/3/1810, Warren, MIC
HILL, William, decd, LWT pvd 7/1846, Harris
HILL, William, decd, Lindsey Coleman issued L/A 11/28/1805, William J. Hobby, Eli Pearre, secs, Richmond, AB
HILL, William, decd, pd Isaac Hill, in rt of wife, Lydia Hill, admx, 1813; Eliza and Lovice Hill, orphs of William, Jasper, Ests
HILL, William, decd, Moses Speer, Lydia Hill, admrs, appl of Moses Speer, one of admrs, to make title to John Shackleford for land in Greene Co., 70 acres, which land decd sold sd Shackleford, 3/8/1813, Jasper, OM

HOBBS, Wiley, decd, William Fountain issued L/A 11/4/1839, Washington

HOBSON, Christopher, decd, L/A gtd Harriet H. Hobson and John Willson 11/4/1822, Jasper, OM

HOBSON, Nicholas, decd, LWT pvd, L/T gtd to John, Matthew and Baker Hobson, 5/1/1809, Jackson, OM

HODGE, Henry, decd, LWT pvd 9/12/1830 by Wiley T. Hodges, exr, Washington

HODGE, Joseph S., decd, Hezekiah Ponder, temp admr, offered non-cupative will of decd, 1/6/1823, Camden, MIC

HODGE, Joseph S., decd, leave gtd to Hezekiah Ponder, temp admr to sell perishable prop of est, cattle & clothing, 6/4/1822, Camden, MIC

HODGE, William B., minor orph of William, decd, Collin Shackleford was apptd gdn, James Shackleford, sur, 7/7/1817, Jasper, OM

HODGE, William, decd, Edmond Peters applied for L/A 3/18/1794, Greene, Misc

HODGE, William, decd, L/A gtd James Hodge, William H. Morrow, sur, 1/1816, Jasper, OM

HODGES, Elias, decd, of Granville Co., S. C., LWT dtd 8/19/1779, pvd 10/25/1800, leaves cousin Drury Hodges when 16 cattle, etc; to Mary, wife, exrs: wife, Mary, and bro, Robert Hodges, Effingham, Misc

HODGES, Henrietta, Elijah Butts, gdn, Dooly, OD

HODGES, James Montgomery, orph of Sarah, decd, (bond shows Samuel) -Willis A. Hodges, gdn, 3/3/1851, Camden, MIC

HODGES, John, decd, 6/25/1841, apprs: Samuel P. Bond, Allen Waters, J. Sutton; purchasers at sale: William H. C. and James H. Hodges, Silas Powell, Wm Humphrey, Nathan Futrell, Green Bryan, D. McLeod, Dooly, I&A

HODGES, Joshua, decd, LWT pvd 11/1/1841 by John J. B. Hughs, Nathl G. Hall, Nathl Hodges; wife, Rebecca, ch-James D., Benjamin, Moses L., George Wm Asbury Washington, Frances C., Rhoda, Joshua F. Hodges and Nancy Brannen, Bulloch, Misc

HODGES, Julia, Elijah Butts, gdn, Dooly, OD

HODGES, Margaret Jane, orph of Sarah, decd, (bond shows Samuel) - Willis A. Hodges, gdn, 3/3/1851, Camden, MIC

HODGES, Robert, Elijah Butts, gdn, Dooly, OD

HODGES, Sarah Clarky, orph of Sarah, decd, (bond shows Samuel) - Willis A. Hodges, gdn, 3/3/1851, Camden, MIC

HODGES, Seabourn M. recd of Miss Jemima Hendricks, admx of John Hendricks, decd, his sh of prop of est 5/1/1843, Bulloch, Misc

HODGES, Solomon, decd, George W. Duncan, admr, 10/4/1858, John N. Pate, N. H. Austin, surs, DeKalb, AB

HODGES, Susan C., Elijah Butts, gdn, Dooly, OD

HODGES, Wiley F., decd, Redding Hodges issued L/A 7/7/1843, Washington

HODGINS, William, abt 8 yrs old, bound out to Richard Bray until 21 to learn carpenter's trade, 5/4/1812, Warren, MIC

HODNETT, Lovet, orph of Benjamin, decd, Elizabeth Hodnett apptd gdn 9/1821, Jasper, OM

HOFFMAN, Jacob, decd, Simeon Travis allowed his acct against est for 1815, 1/1/1815; sd Hoffman to pay Mary Hoffman money collected by heirs, 1/6/1817, Bulloch, MIC

HOGAN, James, decd, J. W. Cato, Jemimah Hollman, gdns of orphs, 1/3/1837, Harris

HOGAN, M. T., decd, G. A. Owens, temp admr, James Hogan, B. H. Adams, sur, 2/20/1866, Paulding, AB

HOGG, William, decd, LWT pvd 10/5/1795, wife, Martha, ch: John, Samuel, Mary, Martha, Greene, Misc

HOGGINS, Harris, decd, Elijah Puckett issued L/A 3/5/1855, James Roberts, sec, Hall, AB
HOGINS, Robert, decd, Zilphia Hogins and James Hogins apply for adm 1/1/1802, Warren, MIC
HOLBROOK, John B., decd, LWT exhibited 4/6/1863, John B. Holbrook qualified as exr 4/1863, dismissed 6/6/1866, Fulton
HOLBROOKS, John, LWT names son, Caleb (ch of Caleb-John & Jince); grch: John Baker (son of Wm), John Baker (son of Benjamin), John Baker (son of Elias), John (son of Wm), John (son of Vachel), ch: Jacob & Nelly, dtd 8/15/1804, Franklin, IMW
HOLCOMB, Benjamin C., decd, LWT dtd 2/13/1863, pvd 1/20/1866 names wife, Malinda, and "my children", White, AB
HOLCOMB, Jasper W., decd, William C. Ally issued L/A 12/29/1862, Edward P. Williams, sec, White, AB
HOLCOMB, Jesse, decd, Green B. Holcomb issued L/A 11/3/1862, James Edwards, sec, White, AB
HOLDER, Daniel, inf son and orph of Evan, decd, Celia Holder apptd gdn 2/5/1828, "Whereas on 5th Feb last, an order was granted directing an infant.....be taken from his mother, Jane Holder, and delivered to his grandmother, Celia Holder...", 6/3/1838, Camden, MIC
HOLDER, Daniel, minor, Daniel Holder, gdn 1/6/1829, Camden, MIC
HOLDER, Daniel, decd, N. J. Patterson, Jr., Robt Tompkins, C. M. Pratt divs to heirs: Mrs. Charlotte Holder, wid; Jos. H. Findley, rt of wf, Eliza; Ann W. Ratcliff, admx of decd husb & Robert Moody who m. Elizabeth, 1/6/1851, Camden, MIC
HOLDER, Samuel, minor, chose Gabriel Skipper his gdn 2/7/1826, Camden, MIC
HOLDER, William, decd, Lydia Holder, admx, 9/3/1827, John Mays, Joshua Lazenby, surs, Warren, AB
HOLEBROOK, John, decd, LWT pvd 7/9/1805-ch: Caleb, Nelly, Jacob, Wm; Jincy, dau of Caleb; grsons-Jno Baker, son of Wm, Jno Baker, son of Benja., Jno Baker, son of Elias, Jno Holbrook, son of Wm, John Holbrook, son of Rachel, Franklin, OM
HOLEBROOK, John, decd, LWT pvd 7/9/1805-ch: Caleb, Nelly, Jacob, Wm; Jincy, dau of Caleb; grsons-Jno Baker, son of Wm, Jno Baker, son of Benja., Jno Baker, son of Elias, Jno Holbrook, son of Wm, John Holbrook, son of Rachel, Franklin, OM
HOLIDAY, Tabitha, (Mrs.), decd, 1807 retn pd John Gatewood and John Rowsey their legacies; John Ham, Absolom Stinchcomb, exrs, Elbert, AR
HOLIFIELD, Christopher, orph of Wiley, decd, Willis Holifield, gdn, Simon H. Saunders, sur, 3/6/1843, Butts, GB
HOLISTER, J. G., decd, D. H. Whitfield, admr, 1855, Cobb, BB
HOLLAND, Archibald, decd, LWT names wife, Sarah, children: William, Frankey, Cassey, John, Harris, Isaiah, Elijah, Jacob & Nancy, 8/24/1848, Cherokee, WB
HOLLAND, Henry, decd, Wm Harris applied for L/A 1/14/1794, inv includes notes of Henry Stewart, Wm Harris, Dawson Grimes, James Houghton, James McDowell, Greene, Misc
HOLLAND, Jacob, decd, Merchant, Henry W. Jernigan, admr, 1837; apprs: Thomas Gardner, Joseph Reese, William Stafford, A. P. Rood, Stewart, Adms
HOLLAND, James, decd, John Hendricks apptd admr, 7/1/1816; James C. Mangham, admr, gtd leave to sell, 9/5/1824; James C. Mangham, admr, asks that est be divided betwn heirs 3/6/1826, Glynn, MIC
HOLLAND, Talton and Susan, Talton Holland, gdn of heirs, L. C. Smith, sur, 11/1850, 1852 retn, Fayette, GB
HOLLAND, Thomas, decd, late of Mobile, Ala., Ralph S. Law issued L/A 7/2/1850, Martin Graham, sec, Hall, AB
HOLLAND, William, decd, Martha Holland issued L/A 7/1/1839, John Holland, Jr., sec, Tattnall, I&A

HOLLEMAN, Ezekial, decd, David Holleman issued L/A 5/2/1814, Putnam, AB
HOLLEY, James R., decd, L/A issued John B. Holley 2/23/1869, Webster, OD
HOLLIDAY, Ambrose, decd, Elijah Worthen, Margaret Holliday, admrs, 5/4/1802, William Worthen, sur, Warren, AB
HOLLIDAY, Jane, decd, Bennett S. Johnson, apptd admr, 1/1/1855, Cobb, BB
HOLLIDAY, Jeremiah, decd, L/A gtd Margaret Holliday 2/10/1803, Hugh Montgomery and Edward Adams apptd gdns for orphs: Fanny, Nancy and Martin, 2/5/1810; George Haynie, admr in rt of wife, makes retns 1/6/1807; division of est for Martin Holliday, one of heirs, 1814; 3/6/1815 Hugh Montgomery and Edward Adams, gdns of orphs, to sell 202-1/2 acres in Twiggs Co., Jackson, OM
HOLLIDAY, John, orph of Jeremiah, decd, Capt. Robert Martin, gdn, 1/1/1810, Jackson, OM
HOLLIDAY, Robert, decd, 1/11/1803 inv of slaves, negro man ran away to Virginia, acct of John Holliday, #260 Va. money, acct of Jeremiah Holliday #175 Va. money, Elbert, AR
HOLLIDAY, Simeon L., decd, Sarah E. Holliday, admx, Dooly, OD
HOLLIDAY, William, decd, Elizabeth Holliday applied for L/A 6/9/1791 on her decd husband's est, Greene, Misc
HOLLIMAN, David, decd, LWT pvd 7/9/1783, Absalom and Charity Holliman, exrs, ch: David, Samuel, Alcy, Mark, Wilkes, MxR
HOLLINGER, William, decd, Eleazer Brack and John Allen issued L/A 12/4/1815, Laurens, AB
HOLLINGER, William, decd, John Allen, gdn of orphs: Brack and Littleton, 12/4/1819, Laurens, GB
HOLLINGSWORTH, Henry came into ct and chose Benjamin Hollingsworth his gdn 9/7/1812, Franklin, OM
HOLLINGSWORTH, Henry, decd, of S. C., LWT dtd 2/26/1865, pvd 10/1/1865, Charles L. Williams, exr (dim), White, AB
HOLLINGSWORTH, Jacob, ordered that citation be issued Thomas Lenoir, gdn, to show cause at next ct why his gdnship should not be revoked 8/7/1809, Franklin, OM
HOLLINGSWORTH, Jeremiah, decd, Richard Lang apptd admr, 1/4/1815, Camden, MIC
HOLLINGSWORTH, John, minor of Samuel, decd, Thomas Hollingsworth apptd gdn 3/7/1808, Franklin, OM
HOLLINGSWORTH, Polly, illegitimate child, Ephraim McClain apptd gdn 11/1830, Habersham, MIC
HOLLINGSWORTH, Samuel, decd, Jacob and Mary Hollingsworth gtd L/A 8/6/1802; inv 9/27/1802, Franklin, OM
HOLLINGSWORTH, Samuel, decd, ct orders that gdn be apptd for five minor children of decd; Thomas Linore apptd gdn, 2/11/1806, Franklin, IMW
HOLLINGSWORTH, Timothy, decd, LWT produced by William Hollingsworth, qualifying as exr 11/6/1815, Camden, MIC
HOLLINGSWORTH, Valentine, decd, William Wates issued L/A 11/7/1808, Jackson, OM
HOLLINSHED, John, decd, Robert B. Lewis and Jacob Hollinshed issued L/A 1/12/1852, Lumpkin, AB
HOLLMAN, Andrew, orph of John, decd, Dempsey Stanaland apptd gdn 7/7/1823, Bulloch, MIC
HOLLOWAY, Ailsey, minor orph of Isaac, decd, James Brown apptd gdn 7/3/1815; Judith Holloway apptd gdn 1/5/1818, Jasper, OM
HOLLOWAY, Asa, decd, LWT pvd 1/23/1804, wife, Anne, ch: Ruth Holloway, Thomas Holloway, Nancy Gardner, Clarke, AB
HOLLOWAY, Elizabeth, minor orph of Isaac, decd, James Brown apptd gdn 7/3/1815; Judith Holloway apptd gdn 1/5/1818, Jasper, OM

HOLLOWAY, Isaac, decd, L/A gtd to Judith and Joseph Holloway 1/3/1814, John C. Willis, Isaac Newton, Martin Stanley, surs, Jasper, OM
HOLLOWAY, James, decd, LWT pvd 7/3/1844 names: Mrs. William Holloway, Timothy Kirkland, Malachi Messer, Lewis Lanier, Hilliard Janes, Alexander Waters; Mitchell, Redding and Stephen Holloway; wife, Catherine Holloway, Bulloch, Misc
HOLLOWAY, James, minor orph of Isaac, decd, Martin Stanley apptd gdn 7/3/1815, Jasper, OM
HOLLOWAY, Jesse, decd, LWT pvd by Martin Stanley, Elizabeth Mitchell, William Brown, L/T gtd William Holloway and Martin Stanley, 1/6/1823, Jasper, OM
HOLLOWAY, Joham, decd, Judith Holloway, admx, asks for leave to sell land in 15th dist., 1/5/1818, Jasper, OM
HOLLOWAY, Rebecca, minor orph of Isaac, decd, Martin Stanley apptd gdn 7/3/1815, Jasper, OM
HOLLOWAY, Samuel, Judith Holloway apptd gdn 1/5/1818, Jasper, OM
HOLLOWAY, Samuel, decd, LWT pvd, L/T issued William Holloway, John Hughes, exrs, 7/7/1817, Jasper, OM
HOLLOWAY, William, decd, Anthony Holloway issued L/A 6/6/1814, Putnam, AB
HOLLY, James R., decd, John Holly, admr, asks leave to sell property, 9/1871, Webster, OD
HOLMAN, David, decd, Drury Rogers, planter, admr, Wilkes, MxR
HOLMES, Benjamin, decd, George W. Fuller, gdn of orphs: Mary, Thomas and Jonathan, John Fuller, sec, Morgan, GB
HOLMES, Horatio N., decd, Margaret M. Holmes issued L/A 1/16/1828, James Primrose, James May, secs, Richmond, AB
HOLMES, Isaac, decd, Louisa Holmes, admx, Randolph L. Mote, atty in fact, 8/9/1847, Bibb, AB
HOLMES, James, decd, Ann Holmes apptd gdn of orphs: Mary and Sophronia 5/4/1807, Jackson, OM
HOLMES, John, decd, Harvey Wheat, gdn for Bustah, 9/3/1821, Lincoln, GB
HOLMES, John, decd, John Marable, gdn of orphs: Isaac and Lucy, 8/5/1811, A. S. Clayton, Thomas Moore, surs, Clarke, GB
HOLMES, Lewis, decd, L/A issued Drewry Jenkins 1829, Washington
HOLMES, Robert, decd, 1796 est, Bryan, CR
HOLMES, Robert, decd, David Holmes, son and heir, 11/2/1804, Bryan, CR
HOLMES, Sarah T., decd, LWT exhibited 1/1864, Solomon L. Beach, exr, Fulton
HOLMES, Thomas, decd, Margaret Holmes and Stephen Hester issued L/A 3/5/1821, Laurens, AB
HOLSWRITE, William, decd, William Niblack, admr, filed his retn, 4/3/1809, Camden, MIC
HOLT, Abner F., decd, G. W. Rains, admr, William S. Holt, sur, 1/16/1848, Bibb, AB
HOLT, Andrew J., decd, John C. Ragsdale, admr, 2/1/1858, E. A. Davis, sur, DeKalb, AB
HOLT, Paschal, decd, Julian A. Juhan, admr, 3/4/1861, James M. Hall, sur, DeKalb, AB
HOLT, Richard, decd, John W. Scruggs, Nathaniel S. Juhan, admrs, 10/1862, William N. Duncan, J. H. Kimbrell, H. R. Hannah, J. A. Juhan, surs, DeKalb, AB
HOLT, William B., gdn of his minor children: David M. and William B., 1/6/1823, James Meriwether, sur, Clarke, GB
HOLT, W. N., J. N. Holt issued L/G 2/26/1867, Webster, OD
HOLTON, William, decd, Mark Holton, admr, 6/15/1822, Emanuel, A
HOLTON, William, minor of William, decd, Stephen Swain, gdn, Reuben Thomson, sur, 3/7/1825, Emanuel, GB

HOLWECK, Reinhard L., decd, John Osborne, mercht, admr, 10/15/1787, Chatham, Adms
HONEA, William, decd, Sion Honea, John L. Honea, Eleazor Edwards, admrs, Wm M. Dell, Jacob Martin, surs, 2/6/1848, Cherokee, W&B
HONIKER, Benjamin, decd, late of St. Marys, Abraham Bessant applied for adm, 2/5/1811, Winnifred Hibbard apptd admx 11/6/1815, Camden, MIC
HONIKER, Jacob, decd, M. H Hibbard, admr 1/6/1835, Camden, MIC
HONIKER, Jacob, minor, Darius Couch, gdn, 6/2/1818, Camden, MIC
HOOD, Joseph, decd, Sherrod Hood issued L/A 9/5/1836, Washington
HOOD, Nathaniel, decd, LWT pvd by William Hardin and Sampson Ivy 2/1/1795, Warren, MIC
HOOD, Peter C., decd, Manerva A. Hood and Jesse Hunt issued L/A 1/17/1863, William A. Reaves, Robert Hood, secs, White, AB
HOOD, Wiley, decd, LWT pvd 11/4/1813 by Alexander Bohannon and George Fielder; decd, in his lifetime, gave obligation to sd Bohannon to title land in 18th dist, Jasper, OM
HOOKS, Bardon, decd, Sarah Hooks, William Hoos, exrs, 4/28/1845; apprs: Middleton Patrick, Jesse Walters, Solomon Fokes; LWT rec Superior Ct Mt Bk 1847-52, P. 187, Dooly, I&A
HOOKS, Jacob, decd, LWT dtd 3/3/1855, pvd 5/1855, names ch: Sarah H. and Elizabeth (latter begotten by former wife), Cherokee
HOOKS, John G., decd, John T. Howard applies for L/A 6/28/1855, Lee, MSC
HOOPER, John, decd, Bathaser Shaffer, tailor, admr, 1/14/1786, Chatham, Adms
HOOPER, Obadiah, decd, LWT pvd 8/3/1804 names ch: Mary White, James, Thomas, John, Obadiah, Matthew, Nancy Goodlet, Richard, Milla Munro, Susannah Perry, Franklin, OM
HOOPER, Toliver ordered to be bound to Isaac Brown during minority 5/3/1813, Franklin, OM
HOPKINS, Edward H. apptd gdn of Mary Eliza, Carolanus, Rebecca and George Hopkins, his children, 6/4/1849, Camden, MIC
HOPKINS, Emily, illegitimate child of Susannah, 9/3/1821 David Shay, gdn, James Hendon, Leonard Ward, surs, Clarke, GB
HOPKINS, Joshua, decd, Susannah Hopkins, admx, 7/3/1815, Chappel Heath, Joseph Roberts, surs, Warren, AB
HOPKINS, Lambeth, decd, William and Palasiah Stallings, gdn of orphs: Osborn and Lambeth 9/7/1819; Archibald Lee apptd gdn 1/11/1819, William Stallings, sec, Morgan, GB
HOPKINS, Martha, decd, LWT pvd 11/6/1843, John A. and William Hopkins, exrs, Harris
HOPKINS, Susan A., inf, Mrs. Elizabeth H. Hopkins apptd natural gdn, 3/5/1849, Camden, MIC
HOPKINS, Thomas S. apptd gdn of Louisa, Francisco and Cecilia Hopkins, his minor children, 6/4/1849, Camden, MIC
HOPKINS, Timothy, decd, LWT pvd, William T. Hopkins qualified as exr 6/3/1833, exr dismissed 6/7/1842, Camden, MIC
HOPKINS, William, minor child of Susan, William B. Parker, gdn, 12/3/1821, West Parker, sur, Clarke, GB
HOPKINS, William T., decd, LWT pvd, Mrs. Elizabeth H. Hopkins, George W. Thomas, John Bessant and George Lang qualified as exrs 6/15/1848, Camden, MIC
HOPKINS, William T., decd, the children of John Bessant and George Lang (legatees) under LWT directed to give bond as gdns for their children's shares of est, 6/15/1848; exers authorized to amend inv as filed by adding in certain property (slaves) devised by late Timothy Hopkins in his LWT to Mrs. Susan H. Hopkins and now in her possession, 1/4/1850, Camden, MIC
HORN, Edward, decd, James Butler issued L/A 11/6/1820, John Barton, sec, Morgan, AB
HORN, Elizabeth C., John H. Horn, gdn, 1/10/1853, Houston, GB

HORN, Henry, John H. Horn, gdn, 1/10/1853, Houston, GB
HORN, Jacob, decd, john, exr of LWT, dismissed, 7/10/1800, Warren, MIC
HORN, Jesse, decd, Robert Bowdry and Andrew Hais, exrs. LWT pvd 12/26/1794, Columbia, Ests
HORN, Samuel, decd, Henry Horn apptd sole exr of LWT, 3/1789, Chatham, Adms
HORN, T. J., decd, E. E. Little issued L/A 7/1863, Webster, OD
HORNBY, Thomas, decd, Eleanor Hornby issued L/A 3/6/1820, Absolom Rhodes, Sr., James B. Robinson, Robert Allen, Waddell Allen, Nicholas Murphy, appraisers, Richmond, AB
HORNSBY, Noah, decd, LWT exhibited 6/1/1863, Joseph Hornsby, exr, Fulton
HORSFELL, James W., decd, an alien, d. intestate without known heirs, 12/7/1814, Camden, MIC
HORTON, Amos, decd, John H. Powell, R. Horton, admrs, John Bailey, Bryant Bateman, Simon Park, sec, 11/5/1832, Bibb, AB
HORTON, Gilley Frances, orph of Walker, decd, Elisha Williams, gdn, Robert D. A. Tharp, Seaborn A. Johnson, sur, 11/5/1849, Troup, GB
HORTON, Hugh, decd, John H. Powell, Remchesant Horton, admrs, Bryant Bateman, John Bailey, sec, 11/5/1832, Bibb, AB
HORTON, Levicia, orph of George W., decd, David Cox issued L/G 5/6/1839, Washington
HORTON, Mary Jane, orph of Walker, decd, Elisha Williams, gdn, Robert D. A. Tharp, Seaborn A. Johnson, sec, 11/5/1849, Troup, GB
HORTON, Nancy F., orph of Walker, decd, Elisha Williams, gdn, Robert D. A. Tharp, Seaborn A. Johnson, sec, 11/5/1849, Troup, GB
HORTON, Roxanna, orph of George W., decd, David Cox issued L/G 5/6/1839, Washington
HORTON, Thomas, decd, Henry Mitchell, admr, 3/5/1795, Warren, AB
HORTON, Walker V., orph of Walker, decd, Elisha Williams, gdn, Robert D. A. Tharp, Seaborn A. Johnson, sur, 11/5/1849, Troup, GB
HOTTON, William, decd, Richard L. Tailor, Jesse Parker, Mark Hottan, admrs, 1/7/1822, Emanuel, AB
HOUGHTON, Ann Eliza, orph of Matthew, decd, William King, W. T. King, James Pollard, gdns, 5/4/1840, Harris
HOUGHTON, Edward, decd, A. G. Raiford issued L/A 1/7/1824, B. D. Thompson, John Dent, secs, Richmond, AB
HOUGHTON, Joshua, decd, LWT pvd 10/22/1790, ch: Thomas, Joshua, Deborah, William; wife, Sarah, Greene, Misc
HOUGHTON, Josiah, decd, LWT pvd 7/7/1817, L/T issued to Betsey Houghton, Banister Crawford, exrs, Jasper, OM
HOUSE, Brinkley, decd, John Millican, admr 7/1806, Elbert, AB
HOUSE, Zachariah, son of Winney, bound to John Watson, farmer, for 8 yrs, John Hambleton, sec, Oglethorpe, OM, GB
HOWARD, Abell, decd, LWT pvd by Isaac David and Nathan Johnson; Groves Howard and Clement Glenn, exrs, 5/1808, Oglethorpe, OM
HOWARD, A. M., orph of Solomon, decd, L/G issued to Sarah Howard 1/19/1835, Washington
HOWARD, Andrew J., orph of Solomon, decd, David Barrow issued L/G 1/19/1834, Washington
HOWARD, Anna, Elizabeth Howard, gdn, p. 192, 120 and 123, Screven, OM
HOWARD, Asa J., orph and minor of Abel, decd, William Glenn, gdn, Joseph Embry, William Glenn, Jr., sec, 1/1810, Oglethorpe, OM
HOWARD, Devine, orph and minor of Abel, decd, William Glenn, gdn, Joseph Embry, William Glenn, Jr., sec, 1/1810, Oglethorpe, OM
HOWARD, Elizabeth, Abram Hunter, gdn, p. 177, Screven, OM
HOWARD, Fannin A., decd, LWT exhibited 11/1863, Charles G. Moore, exr, Fulton

HOWARD, G. G., decd, LWT pvd 4/1/1863, Rufus A. Howard, exr, Fulton

HOWARD, Groves, orph and minor of Abel, decd, William Glenn, gdn, Joseph Embry, William Glenn, Jr., sec, 1/1810, Oglethorpe, OM

HOWARD, James, decd, John R. Howard issued L/A 1/3/1832, Washington

HOWARD, James, orph of James, decd, John Wicker issued L/G 5/4/1835, Washington

HOWARD, John, decd, Andrew Burns issued L/A 4/9/1785, Samuel Jack, Moody Burt, secs, Richmond, AB

HOWARD, John, decd, Nicholas Howard issued L/A 3/15/1823, C. Campbell, sec, Morgan, AB

HOWARD, John J., orph of Solomon, decd, L/G issued to Sarah Howard 1/19/1835, Washington

HOWARD, Joseph, decd, LWT dtd 1/30/1803, Jesse Sandford, exr, ch: Nancy, Luraine, Sarah, wife "now pregnant"; exrs, bro., Isaac Howard, Jesse Sandford, wife, Mary Howard, Hancock, AAAA

HOWARD, Joshua, minor, Gotlieb Zitterauer apptd gdn 2/18/1800, Effingham, Misc

HOWARD, Lemuel, decd, from Harford Co., MD., Martha Howard gtd L/A, 7/18/1795, Columbia, Ests

HOWARD, Levi and Mose, exrs, give acctg of appraisement & sales, p. 40, Screven, OM

HOWARD, Lucy H. chose William Glenn as her gdn, 1/1810, Oglethorpe, OM

HOWARD, Martha, orph of James, decd, John Wicker issued L/G 5/4/1835, Washington

HOWARD, Martha E., orph of Naugheflight, decd, James Boatright issued L/G 7/2/1839, Washington

HOWARD, Martha E., orph of Naugheflight, decd, John Wicker issued L/G 11/10/1834, Washington

HOWARD, Missouri, orph of James, decd, John Wicker issued L/G 5/4/1835, Washington

HOWARD, Morgan, orph of James, decd, John Wicker issued L/G 5/4/1835, Washington

HOWARD, Nancy J., orph of Naugheflight, decd, John Wicker issued L/G 11/10/1834, Washington

HOWARD, Rhesa, decd, William Few and John Howard gtd L/A 6/10/1799, Columbia, Ests

HOWARD, Samuel, decd, LWT pvd 5/4/1829 by John J. Long and William L. Hardwick, exrs, Washington

HOWARD, Samuel, orph of James, decd, John Wicker issued L/G 5/4/1835, Washington

HOWARD, Sidney, orph of Solomon, decd, L/G issued to Sarah Howard 1/19/1835, Washington

HOWARD, Thomas, decd, Henrietta Howard, gdn of orph: Hannah F., 3/6/1843; George W. Harrison, gdn of orph: Albert, 3/6/1843, Randolph

HOWARD, Thomas, decd, John Wicker issued L/A 3/3/1834, Washington

HOWARD, William H., decd, Samuel Strong, admr, 9/18/1806, Oglethorpe, OM, AB

HOWARD, Winneford H., orph of Naugheflight, decd, James Boatright issued L/G 7/2/1839; William Davis issued L/G 3/7/1842, Washington

HOWE, William, decd, apprs: John Patrick, Alex. Curry, Robt. Curry, 2/13/1796, Greene, Misc

HOWELL, Caleb, Mahala Howell, admr, p. 117, Screven, OM

HOWELL, Caleb, receipt for $20, p. 38, Screven, OM

HOWELL, Catherine (Mrs.), decd, LWT pvd by James Bentham, Archibald Clark, exr, 8/4/1826, Camden, MIC

HOWELL, Daniel, Mahala, gdn, p. 134, Screven, OM

HOWELL, Daniel, decd, LWT ordered recorded p. 3, 48, Cassandria Howell, admr, p. 116, Wm Barnes and Daniel Conyers, admrs, p. 117, James Boston, etc., apprs, p. 116, Screven, OM
HOWELL, E., decd, LWT pvd 3/1875, Webster, OD
HOWELL, Emiline, decd, LWT pvd 2/1875, Webster, OD
HOWELL, Henry, decd, Isaac Parker issued L/A 1/3/1809, Putnam, AB
HOWELL, John, decd, Catherine Howell apptd admx, 1/17/1814, Camden, MIC
HOWELL, John H., decd, Mary Howell apptd admx, 5/30/1788, Chatham, Adms
HOWELL, Matthew, decd, Sarah Howl and Lewis Williams request L/A 1/5/1807, gtd 9/7/1807, Franklin, OM
HOWELL, William, decd, of S. C., Elizabeth & Malachi Howell, Ethel Heath issued L/A 3/14/1796, Edward Rowell, Hugh McGee, secs; Malachi Howell, gdn of minor orphs: Gracy, Wm, Elizabeth, Lucy, 3/17/1800, Richmond, AB
HOWSER, Robert, decd, Henry Howser, admr, A. J. Logan, sur on bond, 4/7/1862, Dawson, WB
HOY, Amos E., decd, Bailey A. Abrey, admr, James S. Dukes, sur, 7/1/1850, Bibb, AB
HOYLE, George S., decd, N. F. Rhinehardt, admr, Lewis W. Rhinehardt, sur, 4/13/1857, Cherokee, AB
HUBBARD, Daniel, decd, Hannah Hubbard issued L/A 7/10/1817, Samuel Hale, Richard Allen, secs, Richmond, AB
HUBBARD, Henry, Sr., decd, Peterson Hubbard, Phillip Fitzgerald, admrs, 1/1840, 1843 retn, Fayette, AB
HUBBARD, Nancy, John B. Whatley apptd gdn 3/2/1818, Jasper, OM
HUBERSON, William, decd, James Blue, admr, 3/6/1826, Glynn, MIC
HUBERT, Benjamin, decd, Matthew Hubert and David Hubert and John Rutherford issued dismission as admrs, 3/2/1802, Warren, MIC
HUBERT, Gabriel, decd, 6/25/1811 bond, Elizabeth Hubert and James Meriwether apptd admrs, David Meriwether, Josiah Bonner, surs, Clarke, AB
HUBERT, James, orph of Gabriel, decd, Josiah Bonner, gdn, 10/5/1812, Jack F. Cook, George Y. Farra, surs, Clarke, GB
HUBERT, James, orph of Gabriel, decd, Josiah Bonner, gdn, 1832, Clarke, LP
HUCKEBEE, Isham, decd, LWT dtd 5/28/1801, names wife, Sarah and 8 ch: Mary Faner, John, Nancy, Kesiah, Jeremiah, James, Josiah and Betsey, Hancock, AAAA
HUCKLES, Martha, orph of John, decd, Edward Megar, gdn, Thomas Drew, Benjamin Sherrard, sur, 7/6/1835, Emanuel, GB
HUCKLES, Robert, orph of John, decd, Edward Megard, gdn, Thomas Drew and Benjamin Sherrard, surs, 7/6/1835, Emanuel, GB
HUCKY, Joseph S., decd, Robert M. Brown apptd admr 12/6/1853, DeKalb, AB
HUDSON, Christopher, decd, James M. Stewart, Isaac Hudson qualified as admrs 2/10/1790, Liberty, Ests
HUDSON, Christopher, Sr., decd, Nathaniel Lunday and Christopher Hudson apply for admn 8/6/1792; Christopher Hudson apptd admr of his decd father 12/5/1793 in place of himself and Nathaniel Lunday, Effingham, Misc
HUDSON, David, decd, Nathaniel and Nancy Hudson applied L/A 1/11/1797, inventory includes 300, 180, 250 acres, Franklin Co., Ga. 1798 pd expenses of Anne Hudson's tobacco, Nancy Hudson's dower; 1808 recpt of Edward Carrell for wife's share, Elbert, AR
HUDSON, David B., decd, William Newsom applied for L/A 6/12/1855, Lee, MSC
HUDSON, James, decd, Robert M. Hudson, admr, p. 111, James Hudson, admr, p. 126, Screven, OM
HUDSON, James, decd, James Love applies for admn 12/7/1845, Effingham, MIC

HUDSON, James W., minor of James J., decd, Charles T. King issued L/G 6/1856, Webster, OD

HUDSON, Joakim, decd, proven accts vs est, John Weems swore Hudson was indebted to him for $1 for smith work, 11/26/1808, Franklin, OM

HUDSON, Joseph, decd, Ann Hudson and Joshua Hudson issued L/A 9/5/1808, Franklin, OM

HUDSON, Lewis B., orph of Madison E., decd, Samuel M. Weil, gdn, Jasper L. Keith, sur, 7/13/1857, Cherokee, AB

HUDSON, Mary D., orph of David, decd, 1809 retns of est pd Asa Allen, gdn, Elbert, AR

HUDSON, Mary D., orph of David, decd, of Elbert Co., Asa Allen, gdn, makes retns 1/5/1813, Franklin, OM

HUDSON, Rhoda, relict of Robert, Jr., late of Effingham Co., decd, makes deed of gift to her children: Samuel, Robert, Mary, Maxwell, conveying thre slaves, etc, 7/1/1792, Effingham, Misc

HUDSON, Robert, planter, makes deed of gift 6/20/1789 to grson, Robert Hudson, minor son of his decd son, Robert Hudson, the younger, slave now in possession of Rhoda Hudson, relict of decd, Effingham, Misc

HUDSON, Samuel, decd, Robert Hudson recpt to Christopher Hudson, admr 9/27/1769 his sh of father's est; from Wm Thomson to Robert 3/27/1769, 1650# decd owed him; recpt of Samuel & Charles Hudson, John Brady to 2/29/1769, Effingham, Misc

HUDSON, Virginia, orph of David, decd, 1809 retns of est pd Asa Allen, gdn, Elbert, AR

HUDSON, Virginia, orph of David, decd, of Elbert Co., Asa Allen, gdn, makes retns 1/5/1813, Franklin, OM

HUDSON, Ward, minor orph of John, decd, Seth Ward apptd gdn, John Beasley, sur, 1/19/1802, Oglethorpe, MIC

HUEY, Jesse M., decd, Samuel C. Clay, admr, 1/12/1863, Robert H. Webb, Eli Clay, surs, DeKalb, AB

HUEY, Robert C., decd, A. L., Nelly, A. B. and Samuel Huey, admrs, 11/7/1836, Harris

HUEY, Robert D., decd, W. C. Osborne, William Johnson, J. Daniel, gdn of orphs of decd 9/4/1837, Harris

HUFF, Abner, decd, Jonathan Huff, admr, 12/4/1822, Middleton Huff, Wm Standford, surs, Warren, AB

HUFF, Edwin, decd, James Harrison, admr w/LWT annexed, Thomas W. Baxter, sec, 3/4/1833, Bibb, AB

HUFF, James, decd, W. W. Thornton, exr, LWT pvd 9/6/1839, Harris

HUFF, John, decd, Harriet E. Huff, admx, Andrew J. Shaffer, sur, 9/7/1874, Gwinnett, AB

HUFF, Jonathan, decd, William Huff was gtd L/A, 12/31/1796, Columbia, Ests

HUFF, Richard H., decd, LWT pvd 7/5/1847, James M. Huff, Marshall Stevens, exrs, Harris

HUFF, Thomas, decd, inventory and appraisement by Avington Williams, John Reid, James Stephens 2/15/1812; Tabitha Huff principal purchaser. 1812 Retn by Joshua Callahan & Tabitha Huff, admrs; orphs-- Ransom and Silvey Huff, under 7, Jasper, Ests

HUGHES, Eliza M. and Rosamond, William Young, etc., to divide est, p. 13, Screven, OM

HUGHES, Hubert, decd, Williamson Norwood, gdn of orphs: Evelina S., Caroline S., Andrew and Thomas, 3/17/1821, Silas Tatom, Wm C. Stokes, Shepherd Groce, secs, Lincoln, GB

HUGHES, Isaac, decd, John Huie, admr, T. M. Jones, G. C. King, Eli Edmondson, surs, 7/1842, Fayette, AB

HUGHES, Philip, decd, Paul Hamilton Wilkins, admr, 7/14/1790, Chatham, Adms

HUGHES, Robert, decd, Frederick Thompson, Wm Lewallen apptd admrs 3/1/1813, Jackson, OM

HUGHES, William, decd, LWT dtd 2/1/1829, pvd 9/1829, names bro.,
Alfred, Father, Samuel, and bro., Gabriel, Habersham, MIC
HUGHES, William, decd, Willis H. Hughes, admr, Sarah Hughes, Lucy
Ann Jewell, sur, 2/14/1848, Bibb, AB
HUGHES, Willis H., decd, Frances M. Hughes, admx, James D.
Strobecker, Henry G. Ross, sur, 3/17/1851, Bibb, AB
HUGHS, Duncan, decd, Hugh and Neill Hughs issued L/A 9/8/1838,
Montgomery, AB
HUGHS, John Thomas, orph of Littleton J., decd, Jane Hughs, gdn,
William Griffin, Nathaniel Griffin, sur, 1/13/1851, Cherokee, GB
HUGHS, Phillip L., orph of Littleton J., decd, Jane Hughs, gdn,
William Griffin, Nathaniel Griffin, sur, 1/13/1851, Cherokee, GB
HUGHS, Richard P., orph of Littleton J., decd, Jane Hughs, gdn,
William Griffin, Nathaniel Griffin, sur, 1/13/1851, Cherokee, GB
HUGHS, William H. H., orph of Littleton J., decd, Jane Hughs,
gdn, William Griffin, Nathaniel Griffin, sur, 1/13/1851,
Cherokee, GB
HUGULEY, Allcy, gdn of Amos, Sarah, Nancy, George, Allcy and
Betsey Huguley, orphs of Job, decd, 7/1/1816, Wilkes, Retns
HUGULEY, Job, decd, George and Allcy Huguley, admrs, recpts of
John Huguley for $50, etc.; retns of John W. Cooper, gdn of
Zachariah pd Allcy Huguley, tuition and bd, 3/6/1815, Retns,
HUGULEY, Zachariah, receipt to his gdn, John W. Cooper for his pt
of his decd father, Job Huguley's est 2/17/1817, Wilkes, Retns
HULL, George Irvin, decd, Sarah Hull issued L/A 4/5/1802,
Benjamin Harris, sec, Richmond, AB
HULSEY, Adley, Jr., decd, Charles Hulsey issued L/A 5/4/1840;
Charles, gdn of orphs: Rolan, William and Sarah, Charles H.
Harrington, sec, 1/10/1853, Hall, AB, GB
HULSEY, Anna, decd, Pleasant Hulsey, admr, Nelson Dickison,
Obadiah Light, secs, 9/5/1831, Hall, AB
HULSEY, Elijah, orph of Adler, Jr., decd, Charles Hulsey, gdn,
James J. Hulsey, sec, 9/7/1846, Hall, AB
HULSEY, Jennius J., minor orph of William M., decd, Marcus A.
Bell, gdn, 1/9/1860, Fulton, GB
HULSEY, Jesse, decd, Salathiel Hulsey issued L/A 9/4/1843, J. B.
Hulsey, Wilkerson Smallwood, secs, AB
HULSEY, Polly, orph of Adler, Jr., decd, William Cagle, gdn,
Jonathan Martin, sec, Hall, GB
HULSEY, William M., decd, Samuel B. Crawford, admr, 1/10/1852,
William W. Right, Thomas A. West, surs, DeKalb, AB
HUMBART, David, decd, Albert Porter applies for L/A 10/5/1838,
Effingham, MIC
HUMBART, Harriet, Albert G. Porter, gdn, 1/7/1839, Effingham, MIC
HUMBER, Charles, orph of Robert, decd, Hubbard Williams, gdn,
Benjamin F. Ward, sur, 7/12/1847, Butts, GB
HUMBER, Elendor, decd, John S. Anderson,admr, William J.
Anderson, sur, 3/5/1849, Butts, AB
HUMBER, Elizabeth, orph of Robert, decd, William J. Anderson,
gdn, William K. Anderson, William H. C. Mickelberry, sur,
7/6/1847, Butts, GB
HUMBER, John, orph of Robert, decd, William J. Anderson, gdn,
William K. Anderson, William H. C. Mickelberry, sur, 7/6/1847,
Butts, GB
HUMBER, Mary C., orph of Robert, decd, Hubbard Williams, gdn,
Benjamin F. Ward, sur, 7/12/1847, Butts, Gb
HUMBER, Robert, decd, William J. Anderson, gdn of orphs: John and
Ann E., 11/6/1854, Houston, GB
HUMBER, Robert C., orph of Robert, decd, Hubbard Williams, gdn,
Benjamin F. Ward, sur, 7/12/1847, Butts, GB
HUMBER, William C., orph of Robert, decd, Hubbard Williams, gdn,
Benjamin F. Ward, sur, 7/12/1847, Butts, GB

HUMBLE, John, decd, late of Edgefield Dist, S. C., Augustin
Slaughter and Charles Labuzan issued L/A 12/4/1823, Alexander
Cunningham, sec, Richmond, AB
HUMPHREY, Mitchell B., illegitimate child, James Jones, gdn,
1829, Washington, GB
HUMPHREYS, Spencer, decd, James Harvey qualified as admr
8/1/1790, Liberty, Ests
HUMPHRIES, Joseph, decd, George Humphries, admr, makes retns
1/6/1817, Jackson, OM
HUMPHRIES, Joseph, decd, exrs of LWT, George, Shadrack and Uriah
Humphries, ask for leave to sell land 9/3/1810, Jackson, OM
HUMPHRIES, Merrill, decd, P. F. Hoyle, admr, 6/4/1855, Thomas R.
Hoyle, sur, DeKalb, AB
HUMPHRIES, Thomas K., decd, James M. Reeve, admr, 9/1/1862, Moses
Robinson, Harris Goodwin, surs, DeKalb, AB
HUMPHRIES, Uriah, decd, Nancy Humphries, gdn of Joseph, Patsy,
Elijah, Presley Thornton, Madison Tigner, and Julian Humphries,
7/7/1817, George W. Moore, David Nowlin, surs, Clarke, GB
HUNCK, Mary, decd, Jesse Davis applies for L/A 8/15/1831,
Effingham, MIC
HUNDLEY, Jared, decd, L/A to Terrel Higdon 8/7/1809, Laurens, AB
HUNOLT, John, decd, Emanuel and David Zeigler apply for adm
8/1/1796, dismissed 1/6/1800, Effingham, Misc
HUNT, Jesse, decd, L/A gtd Spencer Crain, Jr., 1/1820, Jasper, OM
HUNT, John, decd, LWT dtd 1/13/1799, wife, Rebekah, ch: Henry,
Thomas, Daniel (land in Washington Co.), Letty, Michael C.,
Daniel, Thomas and Curtis, pvd by Richard Grimsley 3/1/1799,
Hancock, AA
HUNT, Richard S., decd, John Richardson, admr, Thomas Hutcherson,
sur, 12/15/1858, Cherokee, AB
HUNT, Ruth (Mrs.), decd, Wm J. Hobby issued temp L/A 7/8/1800 and
perm L/A 1/3/1801, Edmund B. Jenkins, sec, Richmond, AB
HUNT, Spencer, Jr., decd, Elizabeth Hunt, issued L/A 3/3/1851,
Baldwin
HUNT, Thomas, LWT names wife, Elizabeth; ch: Dennis A., Carson,
Calvin, dtd 5/12/1847, Cherokee W&B
HUNT, Timothy, decd, LWT names wife, Lettitia, children:
Greenbury Hunt, Elizabeth, wife of Ephraim B. Sergeant,
12/12/1848, Cherokee, WB
HUNT, Turner apptd gdn of Susannah D., Tabitha and Joseph, minors
of Turner Hunt, 9/1821, Jasper, OM
HUNT, William H., decd, D. M. & S. E. Young, admrs 1854, Cobb, BB
HUNTER, Henry, orph of Samuel S., decd, Alexander Hunter, gdn,
4/7/1817, John Selman, sur, Clarke, GB
HUNTER, James, decd, Andrew J. Sweat, admr, Ephraim Sweat, sur,
5/1850, Fayette, AB
HUNTER, James, decd, LWT dtd 6/15/1827, L/A issued James R. Wyly
3/1828; names bro., George V. and sisters, Delilah and Ann M.
Hunter, dtd 6/15/1827, Habersham, MIC
HUNTER, J. C., decd, John Gibbs, admr, Matthew M. Gibbs, sur,
11/9/1857, Cherokee, AB
HUNTER, Joseph R., decd, LWT pvd 7/7/1854, Mrs. Priscilla W.
Hunter, extrx, Fulton
HUNTER, Lydia Isabella, orph of Robert W., decd, Joel T. Crawford
appd gdn, Harris, 1/6/1841, Butts, ER
HUNTER, Lydia Isabellah, orph of Robert W., decd, Alexander
Hunter, gdn, Lewis Moore, sur, 1/25/1845, Butts, GB
HUNTER, Robert, decd, Joel T. Crawford, William Crawford, gdn of
orphs 12/14/1840, Harris
HUNTER, Robert W., decd, Alexander Hunter, admr, Lewis Moore,
Thomas B. Burford, sur, 11/4/1839, inv 11/4/1839, Alexander
Hunter, Sr., admx, Butts, AB, ER
HUNTER, Sarah Ann, orph of Samuel S., decd, James Worthington,
gdn, 3/4/1817, Betsey Hunter, sur, Clarke, GB

ISOM, James M., decd, L/A to William M. Isom 10/1/1866, Fulton
ISOM, William, decd, inv 4/13/1804, appraisers: John Baugh, Samuel Jackson, Jesse Blackwell, Franklin, OM
IVERSON, Robert, decd, Henry Branham, John Harvey and Margaret Iverson issued L/A 6/6/1814, Putnam, AB
IVEY, F. W., decd, William F. Ivey, admr, 7/6/1852, Thomas Kile, H. T. Ivey, surs, DeKalb, AB
IVEY, George, decd, Earnest C. Wittick, gdn of orphs: William and Elizabeth, 6/20/1822, Morgan,GB
IVEY, Jeremiah, decd, Jeremiah Ivey, gdn of orphs: Levy, Mahala and Anny, 7/7/1823, Morgan, GB
IVEY, Lott, decd, LWT pvd by William Leverett and Bacey Leverett 11/1812, Jasper, OM
IVIE, Lot, decd, LWT names wife, Winifred, and ch: Benjamin, John, Sally; grson: Russel Jones, dtd 8/11/1812, Jasper, WAR
IVY, Myrick, decd, Alexander Meriwether, admr, Dooly, OD
JACK, James W., decd, Jane H. Jack, and James W. Jack, exrs, 8/5/1844, James J. Jarrett, gdn, Harris
JACK, Samuel (Colonel), John Hodges, gdn of Evalina, John McCormick, William Dysert and Amanda Melvina Jack, orphs, 12/5/1814, Young Gresham, George W. Moore, surs, Clarke, GB
JACK, William, decd, Elizabeth Jack, admx 1/7/1817, Jackson, OM
JACKSON, Andrew, James G. Cotton, W. C. Osborne, gdns, 3/5/1838, Harris, GB
JACKSON, Catharine, decd, appraisal by Robert R. Williams, Mathew Donaldson, Moses Wilson 12/28/1842, Nathaniel Hodges, admr; 7/3/1844 heirs receipts: John D. Hodges, Nancy Brannen, C. J. Fletcher, Moses L., Asbury, Rhoda, Joseph G., James C., Judge M., Hardy, and Jane Hodges Bulloch, Misc
JACKSON, Coleby, decd, LWT pvd, L/T issued Charity Jackson and Benjamin Cook 7/1818, Jasper, OM
JACKSON, Daniel, decd, Mrs. Betsey Jackson, admx, Daniel M. Jackson, James B. Daniel, Jasper L. Keith, sur, 4/20/1854, Cherokee, AB
JACKSON, Drury, decd, Stephen Jackson, temp admr 10/9/1823 bond, Edmund Jackson, sur, Clarke, AB
JACKSON, Edward, decd, Mary and David Jackson and Nathaniel Ross applied for L/A 12/31/1796, Greene, Misc
JACKSON, Edward J., decd, of Laurens Co., John Martin, admr, applies for leave to sell real estate 8/7/1827, Habersham, MIC
JACKSON, Isaac, decd, L/A issued Robert H. Mann, Enoch and Henry Jackson, surs; Robert K. Mapp and Nancy Jackson, admrs, applied for leave to sell real est, 7/1820, Jasper, OM
JACKSON, James, decd, L/A issued John Martin 1/23/1826, Habersham, MIC
JACKSON, James, decd, late of Jasper Co., inv of est 3/13/1813-purchasers: James, Henry, and Littleton Jackson and Elijah Bankston, 1/1813, Jasper, Ests
JACKSON, James W., decd, LWT headed Muscogee Co., pvd 7/3/1848, Moses Jones, Daniel Huff, exrs, Harris
JACKSON, Jarvis, decd, Catharine, admx, 9/4/1815, Bulloch, MIC
JACKSON, J. C., decd, John Smith, M. M. Fleming, admrs 7/1837; apprs: B. D. Brown, John Upson, Stewart, Adms
JACKSON, John of Randolph Co., Ga., decd, LWT names ch: Nancy Cimbrul, Sam, Henry, Littleton, Betsey, John; bro., James Jackson and William Scott, exrs, 1/1813, Jasper, Ests
JACKSON, John, decd, LWT pvd by James Bankston and Littleton Jackson 1/1813, Jasper, OM
JACKSON, John, decd, apprs: John White, Julian Alford 1/19/1790, Greene, Misc
JACKSON, Lowe, LWT pvd 7/5/1813, Warren, MIC

JACKSON, Thomas, decd, LWT pvd, L/T gtd James Ballard, exr, 9/29/1821, Jasper, OM
JACKSON, William, decd, LWT pvd 2/19/1798, Elizabeth Jackson, extrx, Columbia, Ests
JACOBS, Andrew J., decd, Elizabeth C. Jacobs, admx, Thomas Hall, sur, 11/6/1871, Gwinnett, AB
JAMERSON, Elizabeth, orph of David, decd, of Twiggs Co., Alexander Nelson dischgd as gdn 5/1830, Stewart, Adms
JAMERSON, Seaborn, orph of David, decd, of Twiggs Co., Alexander Nelson dischgd as gdn 5/1830, Stewart, Adms
JAMES, Aaron, decd, Enoch James, admr, 1808 retns pd Dudley Meland for boarding two orphs--Nancy and Amanda Ferrington for 1807, Wilkes, Retns
JAMES, Elvira, decd, Ezekiel Andler issued L/A 1/7/1824, Zachariah Florence, sec, Richmond, AB
JAMES, John, decd bound until age 21 to Hugh B. Greenwood 9/2/1811, Franklin, OM
JAMES, John P., decd, John Hail, Nancy A. James, admrs, James Bledsoe, sur, 1/10/1848, Butts, AB
JAMES, Joseph, decd, Simon Banks, admr, 5/2/1822, Baldwin, AB
Jameson, John, decd, Mrs. Sarah Jameson apptd admx, 4/9/1811, Camden, MIC
JAMIESON, Thomas, decd, William Rhodes issued L/A 6/8/1808, George Fee, Peter Gaillet, secs, Richmond, AB
JARNETT, Alexander, decd, Hannah Jarnett, admx, 9/1/1806, James Edge, Nehemiah Edge, surs, Warren, AB
JARRATT, James D., decd, Asbury A. Adams, admr de bonis non, 11/4/1850, Baldwin, AB
JARRATT, James D., decd, Isaac Boring issued L/A 3/13/1843, Baldwin
JARRATT, William D., decd, Archibald and William Jarratt gtd L/A 3/1/1841, Baldwin
JARRELL, William, decd, Polly Jarrell, admx, Richard Stilwell, Jesse Henley, Robert P. Smith, sur, 1/26/1848, Butts, AB
JARRETT, Alexander, decd, Mary Jarrett apptd temp admr 6/14/1806, Warren, MIC
JARRETT, Deveraux, decd, L/T gtd Milley, extrx of LWT 1/10/1784, Wilkes, MxR
JARRETT, Howell, decd, Nathaniel Jarrett apptd admr 7/1/1811, Jackson, OM
JARRETT, Nicholas, decd, Patsy Jarrett apptd admx 7/1/1816,Jackson, OM
JEFFERS, Amanda H., minor of Henley S., decd, Mary Jeffers, gdn, George Allen, Sur, 6/7/1858, Paulding, GB
JEFFERS, Henley S., Jr., minor of Henley S., decd, Mary Jeffers, gdn, George Allen, sur, 6/7/1858, Paulding, GB
JEFFERS, John P., decd, Edward G. Jeffers, admr, Lewis H. Hughes, Henry Moore, sur, 9/4/1848, Bibb, AB
JEFFRIES, James, decd, Nancy jeffries, Colonel John Baker qualified as admrs 3/18/1789, Liberty, Ests
JEFFRIES, Thomas H., orph of Henry F., decd, Thomas Moore apptd gdn 12/1/1856, Fulton
JENKINS, Betty, orph and minor of William, decd, John Keen apptd gdn, William Brown, James Jones, surs, 1/1805, Oglethorpe, MIC
JENKINS, Catharine, minor heir of Charles C., decd, Thomas M. Jenkins, gdn, Enoch Johns, Hamilton G. Daniell, sur, 9/2/1833, Emanuel, GB
JENKINS, Clark, orph of John, decd, Elizabeth Jenkins, gdn, 5/1835, C. Parker, Henry Jenkins, Henry Riley, Thomas E. and David Rogers, James E. C. Beard, surs, Stewart, GB, Adms
JENKINS, Cyrus R., orph of William, decd, Hardy Crawford apptd gdn 11/1/1819, Jasper, OM

JENKINS, Elizabeth, orph of John, decd, Elizabeth Jenkins, gdn, 5/1835, C. Parker, Henry Jenkins, Henry Riley, Thomas E. and David Rogers, James E. C. Beard, surs, Stewart, GB, Adms
JENKINS, James, orph and minor of William, decd, John Keen apptd gdn, William Brown, James Jones, surs, 1/1805, Oglethorpe, MIC
JENKINS, Jane, decd, Francis Douglass, admr, appr of prop, two notes on William Barkley and William C. Jenkins; apprs: Jason Greer, Robert Bickerstaff, Thomas Douglass, 12/25/1835, Butts, ER
JENKINS, Jennett E., minor orph of David, decd, Jesse Jenkins apptd gdn 1/12/1857, Fulton
JENKINS, John, decd, of Jones Co., Elizabeth Jenkins, wid, admx, Henry M. Jenkins (son), E. C. Beard, Thomas E. Rogers, surs, 6/1828, Stewart, AB, Adms
JENKINS, John, orph of John, decd, Elizabeth Jenkins, gdn, 5/1835, C. Parker, Henry Jenkins, Henry Riley, Thomas E. and David Rogers, James E. C. Beard, surs, Stewart, GB, Adms
JENKINS, John, orph of Sampson, Jr., Elizabeth Jenkins, gdn, John Moore, Henry Durden, sur, 5/6/1839, Emanuel, GB
JENKINS, John, orph of Sampson, decd, Neill McLeod, gdn, Duncan McLeod, John Gillis, sur, 1/11/1840, Emanuel, GB
JENKINS, John A., decd, Arrington L. Goldsmith issued L/A 9/4/1866; Mrs. Elizabeth Jett, gdn of minor orphs: A. C. and Charity, 9/5/1859, Fulton, GB
JENKINS, John M., orph of Samuel, decd, Joseph Tipton, gdn, John J. Hart, sur, 11/2/1835, Emanuel, GB
JENKINS, Lewis, decd, L/A issued to Drury Jenkins 1/7/1834, Washington
JENKINS, Louisa, orph of Sampson, Jr., Elizabeth Jenkins, gdn, John Moore, Henry Durden, sur, 5/6/1839, Emanuel, GB
JENKINS, Margaret, minor heir of Charles C., decd, Thomas M. Jenkins, gdn, Enoch Johns, Hamilton G. Daniell, sur, 9/2/1833, Emanuel, GB
JENKINS, Mary, decd, James R. Nunn, admr, Jesse Edenfield, William Philips, sur, 3/2/1840, Emanuel, AB
JENKINS, Mary, decd, Wilson J. Kerce, admr, appraisal 11/16/1839, Emanuel, A
JENKINS, Mary Ann, orph of Samuel, decd, Joseph Tipton, gdn, John J. Hart, sur, 11/2/1835, Emanuel, GB
JENKINS, Mary E., minor orph of David, decd, Jesse Jenkins apptd gdn 1/12/1857, Fulton
JENKINS, Nancy, orph of John, decd, Elizabeth Jenkins, gdn, 5/1835, C. Parker, Henry Jenkins, Henry Riley, Thomas E. and David Rogers, James E. C. Beard, surs, Stewart, GB, Adms
JENKINS, Owen, decd, Solomon Kemp, etc., admr, p. 89, Screven, OM
JENKINS, Penelope, orph of Samuel, decd, Joseph Tipton, gdn, John J. Hart, sur, 11/2/1835, Emanuel, Gb
JENKINS, Robert, decd, Robert Jenkins and Anson Beall apptd admrs 7/3/1809, Warren, MIC
JENKINS, Rowan, orph of Samuel, decd, Joseph Tipton, gdn, John J. Hart, sur, 11/2/1835, Emanuel, GB
JENKINS, Sally, orph and minor of William, decd, John Keen apptd gdn, William Brown, James Jones, surs, 1/1805, Oglethorpe, MIC
JENKINS, Sampson D., decd, Seaborn A. H. Jones issued L/A 1/7/1837, Washington
JENKINS, Stephen, decd, d. intestate; heirs: widow, Mary, Lucretia (wife of Henry Spencer), Esther Towers and Mary, 3/9/1808, Bryan, CR
JENKINS, Sterling, Jr., decd, Thomas Douglas and Martha Jenkins, admrs, 1812 retns, Wilkes, Retns
JENKINS, William, bound to William Smith, p. 63, Screven, OM
JENKINS, William, orph of Sampson, Jr., Elizabeth Jenkins, gdn, John Moore, Henry Durden, sur, 5/6/1839; Neill McLeod, gdn

1/11/1840, Duncan McLeod, John Gillis, surs, Emanuel, GB
JENKINS, Willis C., decd, Sterling G. Jenkins, admr, Francis
Douglass, Thomas Douglass, sur, 3/1/1841, Butts, AB
JENNINGS, Charles, decd, James Jennings, gdn of orphs: Prudence,
Richard and Nancy 11/4/1839, Eliel Lockhart and Hardy Leverett,
secs, Lincoln, GB
JENNINGS, Charles, orph of Charles, decd, Wyatt L. Chamblin, gdn,
1/7/1839, Hardy Leverett, sec, Lincoln, GB
JENNINGS, John A., decd, Sarah F. Jennings, admx of LWT, no date,
Fayette, AB
JENNINGS, John M., orph of Charles, decd, Thomas J. Jennings,
gdn, 2/4/1839, John Eady, sec, Lincoln, GB
JENNINGS, Priscilla, decd, Miles Jennings issued L/A w/LWT
annexed 1/6/1816, Robert Jennings, Thomas Yarbrough, secs,
Morgan, AB
JERMAN, Robert, decd, Nancy Jerman and Leonard M. Peek issued L/A
1/7/1810, Putnam, AB
JERNIGAN, Henry, decd, John Grayhill, William and Elizabeth
Jernigan issued L/A 1/6/1812, Putnam, AB
JERNIGAN, Jesse, decd, Jane Gray issued L/A; apprs: David
Kennedy, Edmond Warren, Sheppard Williams, Ely Kennedy 3/5/1821,
Bulloch, MIC
JERNIGAN, Jesse, decd, inventory and appraisement by Sheppard
Williams, Ed Warren, Ely Kennedy 3/28/1821, Bulloch, Misc
JERNIGAN, Mary J., Jane Gray apptd gdn, 11/3/1821, Bulloch, MIC
JESTER, James, decd, Henry Jester, admr, Benjamin Jester, Abner
Jester, William F. Mapp, Calvery F. Knight, Henry Knight, sur,
5/1/1837; Henry Jester, admr w/LWT annexed, Benjamin Jester,
Abner Jester, Samuel Billak, Dolphin Lindsey, sur, 5/17/1838;
1839 retn of Henry Jester, admr; legatees receipts: Benjamin,
Abner, and Mary Jester, William Foster in rt of wife, Mary
Foster, 2/26/1840, Butts, AB, ER
JESTER, James, decd, John Lofton, admr, Gustavus Hendrick, John
H. McDaniel, sur, 9/2/1837, Butts, AB
JESTER, Levi, decd, LWT names wife, Rosanna and ch: Mary, Henry,
Benjamin, Abner, Sarah Lofton, wife of John, Nancy Hammond, wife
of Charles; grch: Jain Mason, wife of Lenerd, Butts, ER
JETER, Keziah, orph of Thomas, decd, Charles Jennings, gdn,
1/4/1833, Wm Curry, Stephen Stovall, secs, Lincoln, GB
JETER, William, orph of Thomas, decd, Wiley Jeter, gdn, 5/2/1836,
Isaac Willingham, sec, Lincoln, GB
JETT, Ferdinand, decd, Richard B. Jett issued L/A 4/5/1858,
dismissed 8/1/1859, Fulton
JEWELL, Joseph, decd, Jane and James Jewell apply for L/A 7/1809,
Oglethorpe, OM
JILES, John, minor over 14 yrs, Wylie Jiles Brady apptd gdn,
9/2/1811, Warren, MIC
JIMERSON, John, decd of Richmond Co., LWT 6/27/1787, pvd by
Daniel Cocke, one of exrs, 7/22/1789, Columbia, Ests
JINKINS, Betsey, orph and minor of William, decd, William Brown,
gdn, Samuel Whitehead, Richard Banks, sec, 5/1808, Oglethorpe, OM
JINKINS, James, decd, James Jinkins, admr, asked for dismission,
7/1807, Oglethorpe, OM
JINKINS, James M., orph and minor of William, decd, William
Brown, gdn, Samuel Whitehead, Richard Banks, secs, 5/1808,
Oglethorpe, OM
JINKINS, Jane, decd, Francis Douglass, admr, John M. Pearson,
sur, 7/6/1835, Butts, AB
JINKINS, Jane, orph of Francis, decd, Francis Douglass, gdn,
Jason Greer, sur, 11/7/1833, Butts, GB
JINKINS, Salley, orph and minor of William, decd, William Brown,
gdn, Samuel Whitehead, Richard Banks, sec, 5/1808, Oglethorpe, OM

JINKS, Burwell, decd, Gales Jinks, temp admr, Alfred King, Amos
A. Conger, sur, 9/17/1844; Gales Jinks, admr 11/5/1844, Samuel P.
Burford, sur, Butts, AB
JINKS, Matthew, decd, Isaac Jinks, exr, pd: Henry Barron, J. W.
Watkins, Wm Hamilton, James A. McCune, Matthew Gaston in 1835,
1/15/1836, Butts, ER
JINNINGS, Allen, decd, William Jinnings, admr w/LWT annexed, Wm
Whatley, Wm Jinnings, Sr., A. M. Parker, surs, 11/1849, 1851-1852
retns, Fayette, AB
JINNINGS, Elizabeth, orph of Allen, decd, Nathaniel Stinchcomb,
Burrell A. Ware, surs, 11/1850, 1851-1853 retns, Fayette, GB
JINNINGS, Keziah, orph of Miles, decd, under age 21, Jonathan and
Solomon Jinnings apptd gdns, 1/4/1799, Oglethorpe, MIC
JINNINGS, Leathe, orph of Miles, decd, under age 21, Jonathan and
Solomon Jinnings apptd gdns, 1/4/1799, Oglethorpe, MIC
JINNINGS, Levy, orph of Miles, decd, under age 21, Jonathan and
Solomon Jinnings apptd gdns 1/4/1799, Oglethorpe, MIC
JOHNS, Almy, infant of late Jacob, decd, Levi Johns, trustee,
seeks to remove orph´s cattle; he to leave State; orphs to remain
w/mother, Elizabeth Crews, who may take sd cattle if husband,
John Crews, files bond 1/4/1831, Camden, MIC
JOHNS, Archibald, minor under age 14, John Lee apptd gdn
6/7/1824, Camden, MIC, GB
JOHNS, Archibald, orph of Levi, decd, John Lee, gdn, gtd leave to
sell Monroe Co. land, drawn by minors, 6/16/1825, Camden, MIC
JOHNS, Charles, orph of Griffeth, Mary Johns, gdn, D. C. Rich,
sur, 7/2/1832, Emanuel, GB
JOHNS, Griffeth, decd, William Daniels, admr, Francis Hotton,
sur, 9/5/1825, Emanuel, AB
JOHNS, Jacob, minor over age 14, chose John Lee as gdn 6/7/1824,
Camden, MIC, GB
JOHNS, Jacob, orph of Levi, decd, John Lee, gdn, gtd leave to
sell Monroe Co. land, drawn by minors, 6/16/1825, Camden, MIC
JOHNS, James, decd, Keziah harrell and Andrew Harrell apptd
admrs; Jeremiah Johns, Stephen McCall, Isaac Hatcher, apprs of
est, 3/4/1850, Camden, MIC
JOHNS, Jeremiah, minor under age 14, John Lee apptd gdn
6/7/1824, Camden, MIC, GB
JOHNS, Jeremiah, orph of Levi, decd, John Lee, gdn, gtd leave to
sell Monroe Co. land, drawn by minors, 6/16/1825, Camden, MIC
JOHNS, Jonathan, decd, appr 6/12/1802, Anthony Butts, admr,
Hancock, AAAA
JOHNS, Levi, decd, John Lee, gdn of orphans, applied to div est,
consisting of stock and cattle, 6/3/1828, Camden, MIC
JOHNS, Levi, minor over age 14, chose John Lee as gdn 6/7/1824,
Camden, MIC, GB
JOHNS, Levi, orph of Levi, decd, John Lee, gdn, gtd leave to sell
Monroe Co. land, drawn by minors, 6/16/1825, Camden, MIC
JOHNS, Louisa, minor heir of Charles C., decd, Thomas M. Jenkins,
gdn, Enoch Johns, Hamilton G. Daniell, sur, 9/2/1833, Emanuel, GB
JOHNS, Malinda, infant of late Jacob, decd, Levi Johns, trustee,
seeks to remove orph´s cattle, he to leave State; orphs (Almy and
Malinda) to remain w/mother, Elizabeth Crews, who make take sd
cattle if husband, John Crews, files bond 1/4/1831, Camden, MIC
JOHNS, Nancy, decd, William Statings issued L/A 12/16/1815,
Morgan, AB
JOHNS, Nancy McRight, orph of Griffeth, Mary Johns, gdn, D. C.
Rich, sur, 7/2/1832, Emanuel, GB
JOHNS, Sarah Ann, minor child of Enoch, decd, Charlton P. Sutton,
gdn, 8/20/1855, Lee, MSC
JOHNSON, Aaron, decd, John Sterling issued L/A 9/12/1829,
Washington

JOHNSON, Abner, decd, David Chestnut issued temporary L/A 11/16/1855, Robert Baxter, Rufus Henderson, surs, DeKalb, AB
JOHNSON, Abraham, decd, William Rhodes issued L/A 6/8/1808, Absolom Rhodes, John Cashin, secs, Richmond, AB
JOHNSON, Allen, decd, Martha Johnson, extrx, makes retn for period 1825-1828; inv 1/29/1836, apprs: B. W. Gunn, J. B. Stripling, Thomas Grace, Tattnall, I&A
JOHNSON, Allen C., decd, L/A to Mrs. M. J. Johnson 11/9/1865, Fulton
JOHNSON, Allis L., orph of William, decd, Turman Watthall, gdn, William F. Stodgehill, sur, 9/1/1851, Butts, GB
JOHNSON, Andrew, decd, Thomas and William Johnson, John L. Hamilton, admrs, temporary L/A issued 4/19/1852, permanent L/A issued 6/7/1852, John L. Hamilton, George K. Hamilton, surs, DeKalb, AB
JOHNSON, Arnold, Yelventon Thaxton, gdn, retns 1838-41, Butts, ER
JOHNSON, Arnold, orph of Arnold, decd, Yelventon Thaxton, gdn, Green C. Thaxton, Samuel W. Thaxton, sur, 10/1/1837, Butts, GB
JOHNSON, Benjamin, decd, div completed by William Johnson, admr, 9/18/1806, Oglethorpe, OM
JOHNSON, Burwell, orph of Arnold, decd, Yelventon Thaxton, gdn, Green C. Thaxton, Samuel W. Thaxton, sur, 10/1/1837, Butts, GB
JOHNSON, Clary, a minor age 14, chose Henry Pope as her gdn, 6/28/1797, Oglethorpe, MIC
JOHNSON, Daniel C., minor orph of Allen E., decd, James E. Williams apptd gdn 12/7/1857, Fulton
JOHNSON, David, minor son of Benjamin, decd, bound to Wm Johnson until 19 yrs old, Patton Wise, sur, 1/1804, Oglethorpe, MIC
JOHNSON, Dennis, decd, Rowland Johnson issued temp L/A 1/21/1851, Edward Goode, sec, Hall, AB
JOHNSON, Dorcas, orph of John, decd, James Sanders apptd gdn 11/28/1797; Joseph Johnson apptd gdn 1/14/1799, Oglethorpe, MIC
JOHNSON, Drury, decd, bill of appr, drawn by widow Jones, Samuel Williams, Col. Sheppard Williams, gdn of Benjamin Jones, Capt. John Dell, William F. Bridger, 1/30/1818, Bulloch, Misc
JOHNSON, Frances Marion, orph of William, decd, Turman Watthall, gdn, William F. Stodgehill, sur, 9/1/1851, Butts, GB
JOHNSON, Frank M., decd, Mrs. Harriett Johnson issued L/A 3/25/1868, Fulton
JOHNSON, Henry, decd, LWT pvd 9/4/1843, Samuel Smith, exr, Washington
JOHNSON, Henry, decd, Vinson Johnson, admr, 4/5/1831, James T. Dicken, Wm Hurt, Warren, AB
JOHNSON, Henry, minor orph of Charles, decd, James Johnson, Jr., gdn, 7/8/1817, James Johnson, Sr., sec, Richmond, GB
JOHNSON, Hugh O., orph of Robert, decd, Seaborn A. Johnson apptd gdn, Alexander Mooty, Jr., Robert D. A. Tharp, sec, 1/8/1849, Troup, GB
JOHNSON, Isaac, decd, LWT pvd 11/1/1847, Josannah Embry, gdn for orphs, Harris
JOHNSON, Isaiah, decd, adm gtd to Patton Wise, 3/1808, Oglethorpe, OM
JOHNSON, Isaiah, orph of John, decd, James Sanders apptd gdn 11/28/1797; Joseph Johnson apptd gdn 1/14/1799, Oglethorpe, MIC
JOHNSON, Jackson L., decd, John L. Evins, admr, 10/6/1856, James S. Elliott, sur, DeKalb, AB
JOHNSON, Jacob, decd, Jacob Smith, admr, 2/14/1827, John Smith, James Grenade, surs, Warren, AB
JOHNSON, James, decd, David Gillies, Simon Fraser, qualified exrs, 4/13/1784, Liberty, Ests
JOHNSON, James H., minor orph of Allen E., decd, James E. Williams, gdn, 7/12/1857, Fulton

JOHNSON, James R., "received of my mother, Delila Rountree, exr
of my father's estate, William Johnson, decd," signed James R.
Johnson, 9/28/1819, Bulloch, Misc
JOHNSON, Jarvis, decd, statement of money pd by Catherine
Jackson, admx, 2/14/1819, Bulloch, Misc
JOHNSON, Jesse J., orph of William, decd, Turman Watthall, gdn,
William F. Stodgehill, sur, 9/1/1851, Butts, GB
JOHNSON, John, "received of my mother, Delila Rountree, exr of
est of William Johnson, decd one negro boy as part of my dowry,
2/6/1818, Bulloch, Misc
JOHNSON, John, orph of Richard, decd, Benjamin Baldwin apptd to
have bound out, 6/17/1800, Oglethorpe, MIC
JOHNSON, John, Jr., decd, Thomas Drew, admr, 3/25/1837 appraisal,
Emanuel, A
JOHNSON, John P., orph of Robert, decd, Seaborn A. Johnson, gdn,
Alexander Mooty, Jr. and Robert D. A. Tharp, secs, 1/8/1849,
Troup, GB
JOHNSON, John S., orph of Allen E., decd, James E. Williams apptd
gdn 12/7/1857, Fulton
JOHNSON, Joseph, decd, LWT names wife, Rebeccah, "my children"
mentioned, Benjamin Tucker, Rebeccah Johnson, wid, exrs, dtd
3/24/1808, pvd 1/2/1809, Franklin, OM
JOHNSON, Letitia, orph of James, decd, Richard Cox, gdn,
11/2/1818, David Holmes, sur, Clarke, GB
JOHNSON, Levi, decd, John Collins, admr, A. J. Shaffer, sur,
8/3/1874, Gwinnett, AB
JOHNSON, Louisenda, orph of John, decd, Benjamin Lane, gdn, A. L.
Strickland, Edward Lane, sur, 1/4/1844, Emanuel, AB
JOHNSON, Martha, decd, LWT pvd 1/1840 names grandson, Andrew H.
Thomas and Margaret Stripling, wife of James B., Tattnall, I&A
JOHNSON, Martin, orph of Richard, decd, Benjamin Baldwin apptd to
have bound, 6/17/1800, Oglethorpe, MIC
JOHNSON, Mary Ann, minor orph of Charles, decd, Asaph Waterman,
gdn, 7/8/1817, Richmond, GB
JOHNSON, Newton, orph of Abner, decd, Jasper, gdn, 1/4/1840,
Gilmer, GB
JOHNSON, Pickens, orph of Arnold, decd, Yelventon Thaxton, gdn,
Green C. Thaxton, Samuel W. Thaxton, sur, 10/1/1837, Butts, GB
JOHNSON, Pleasant, orph of Arnold, decd, Yelventon Thaxton, gdn,
Green C. Thaxton, Samuel W. Thaxton, sur, 10/1/1837, Butts, GB
JOHNSON, Polly, orph of Richard, decd, Benjamin Baldwin apptd to
have bound out, 6/17/1800, Oglethorpe, MIC
JOHNSON, Robert, decd, Littleton Johnson, admr, 9/10/1821, Edmond
Johnson, John P. Carr, surs, Warren, AB
JOHNSON, Robinson, decd, LWT names ch: Eudenia Bayls, wife of
William (land in Catawba Co., N. C.) and Hiram Johnson, dtd
9/2/1854, pvd 2/16/1860, Cherokee
JOHNSON, Samuel, decd, Burwell, Arnold, Pickins and Pleasant
Johnson, minors of decd, in acct with Yelventon Thaxton, gdn,
1837-1839, Cherokee Co. land, Butts, ER
JOHNSON, Samuel, orph of Arnold, decd, Yelventon Thaxton, gdn,
Green C. Thaxton, Samuel W. Thaxton, sur, 10/1/1837, Butts, GB
JOHNSON, Sarah, Patton Wise apptd gdn 1/1804; ordered that clk
cite Patton Wise, gdn, to answer complaint of Sarah Sanders,
dismissed by default, 6/18/1805, Oglethorpe, MIC
JOHNSON, Sarah, decd, L/A to James Fruman 3/1/1812, Putnam, AB
JOHNSON, Sarah, orph of William, decd, Turman Watthall, gdn,
William F. Stodgehill, sur, 9/1/1851, Butts, GB
JOHNSON, Seaborn, decd, Mary Ann Johnson, William Johnson, admrs,
3/4/1844, Emanuel, AB

JOHNSON, Sherod B., decd, Hope Ogletree, gdn of orphs, Absolom Ogletree, Jr., Thomas Ogletree, Solom Bearden, Elijah Glass, surs, 1/1842, 1842 retn, Payette, GB
JOHNSON, Smith, decd, est settled by exr, Minor Johnson, 9/18/1806, Oglethorpe, OM
JOHNSON, Thomas, decd, Mary J. and Nathan Z. Johnson, admrs, 4/6/1863, E. J. Bailey, E. A. Tanner, surs, DeKalb, AB
JOHNSON, Thomas, minor orph of Allen E., decd, Martha J. Johnson apptd gdn 12/7/1857, Fulton
JOHNSON, Walter, decd, LWT produced by Ruthy Johnson, wid, 3/3/1821, Jasper, OM
JOHNSON, Walter, decd, of Walton Co., LWT pvd 3/1821, names wife, Ruthy; Mrs. Ann Shepherd, Sarah Saunders, Riley Wise; sister, Dorcas Freeman's children; sister, Elizabeth Wyse's children, Jasper, Rtns
JOHNSON, Walter, decd, whereas decd by his LWT left a certain pt of est to children of Elizabeth and Riley Wise; one of children of sd Elizabeth, chose Parham Lindsey for her gdn 5/7/1821, Jasper, OM
JOHNSON, Walter, orph of John, decd, James Sanders apptd gdn 11/28/1797; Joseph Johnson apptd gdn 1/14/1799, Oglethorpe, MIC
Johnson, William, LWT pvd 5/7/1810 names ch: James, John, Nancy, William, Catherine, Nathan and Patty. extrx, wife, Delila Johnson, Bulloch, Misc
JOHNSON, William, decd, LWT pvd by William Mobley, Polly O. Johnson, Nicholas Johnson and William Johnson, exrs, 9/1821, Jasper, OM
JOHNSON, William, decd, LWT pvd by Wm Mobley; Polly O. Johnson, Nicholas Johnson and William Johnson, exrs, Jasper, OM
JOHNSON, William, decd, William Johnson, admr, 7/4/1831, James and Randolph Johnson, surs, Warren, AB
JOHNSON, William, decd, receipts from Delila Rountree, extrx, one signed by Nathan Brown, heir by marriage; one from Nathan Johnson; one from Nancy Johnson and William Johnson, 8/19/1826, Bulloch, Misc
JOHNSON, William, minor orph of Allen E., decd, Martha J. Johnson apptd gdn 12/7/1857, Fulton
JOHNSON, William, orph of Richard, Jr., decd, John Laidler, gdn, 11/2/1852, Houston, GB
JOHNSON, William R., decd, LWT pvd 2/6/1867, Willis A. Johnson issued L/A, Fulton
JOHNSTON, Abraham, decd, LWt pvd by Ezekiel Alexander, 7/1806, Warren, MIC
JOHNSTON, Charles, decd, Henry Zinn issued L/A 1/15/1813, Geo. Adam, Zachariah Bell, secs; 1815 retn pd for Henry & Mary Ann, pd Susannah johnston, James Johnston (son), pd for digging grave for Susan, relict of decd, Richmond, AB
JOHNSTON, Daniel, decd of Richmond Co., LWT, Verlinda Johnston, extrx to give inv, 5/6/1789, Columbia, Ests
JOHNSTON, James A., decd, Nathaniel Smith issued L/A 7/26/1836, Fulton
JOHNSTON, James Monroe, orph of William H., decd, Littleton Johnston, gdn, Robert W. Smith, Robert Lawson, John Greer, sur, 9/3/1838, Butts, GB
JOHNSTON, John, decd, Rowan Johnston and Seborn Johnston, admrs, 7/1/1839, Emanuel, AB
JOHNSTON, Malcolm, decd, Anna Terrell Johnston applies for L/A 8/12/1795, Warren, MIC
JOHNSTON, Malcolm, decd, Jacky Davenport gtd ltrs dismission 8/2/1801, Warren, MIC

JOHNSTON, Martha, orph of Hiram, decd, James Brown, gdn, James Tippens, sur, 9/2/1850; George W. Tippens, gdn, William Tippens, sur, 3/10/1856, Cherokee, GB
JOHNSTON, Mary Sophronia, orph of Hiram, decd, Robert W. Trout, gdn, James Tiffin, sur, 5/8/1854, Cherokee, GB
JOHNSTON, Mary, decd, George Stovall apptd gdn of orphs: William, Lindsay, Equincy, James and Marshall, orphs, George and William Oglesby, sec, 1/6/1812, Elbert, GB
JOHNSTON, Milly, orph of Hiram, decd, James Brown, gdn, James Tippens, sur, 9/2/1850; George W. Tippens, gdn, William Tippens, sur, 3/10/1856, Cherokee, GB
JOHNSTON, Robert, decd, John, Samuel and Posey Johnston issued L/A 7/3/1830, William R. Williams, sec, Morgan, GB
JOHNSTON, Robert, decd, Samuel Johnston, gdn of orphs: Richard and Chandler 1/8/1822, Martin P. Sparks, sec, Morgan, GB
JOHNSTON, Sarah Jane, dau of William, decd, chose William Sinclair as her gdn, 11/1/1819, Camden, MIC
JOHNSTON, Sarah Starret Cordelia, dau of William, decd, William Gibson apptd gdn, 11/1/1819, Camden, MIC
JOHNSTON, Sarah, William Gibson resigned as her gdn; she selected William Sinclair as her gdn 1/3/1825, Camden, MIC, GB
JOHNSTON, Thomas, decd, James H. Johnston apptd admr, 6/4/1827, Camden, MIC
JOHNSTON, William, decd, James Hughey issued L/A 11/6/1820, Martin P. Sparks, sec, Morgan, AB
JOHNSTON, William, decd, LWT pvd, William Gibson, exr, 11/1/1819, Camden, MIC
JOHNSTON, William, decd, appr 4/2/1803, Rebekah Johnston, admx, Hancock, AAAA
JOHNSTON, William H., decd, Thomas Hairston, admr, Robert Lawson, Pleasant M. Compton, sur, 9/5/1836; Moses B. Hairston, admr de bonis non, Robert Lawson, Benjamin F. Ward, sur, 10/13/1838, Butts, AB
JOHNSTON, William H., orph of William J., Joseph Stroup, gdn, Daniel H. Bird, sur, 11/5/1849, Cherokee, GB
JOHNSTON, William Jefferson, orph of William H., decd, Littleton Johnston, gdn, Robert W. Smith, Robert Lawson, John Greer, sur, 9/3/1838, Butts, GB
JOHNSTON, Young, decd, Harry P. Strickland, admr de bonis non, R. Bassett, Samuel Ray, sur, 3/6/1847, Bibb, AB
JOLLY, Jesse, decd, Bazaleel Langford, admr, 12/3/1860, Edward Wates, J. R. McAlister, surs, DeKalb, AB
JOLLY, John, decd, William Jolly issued L/A 7/6/1835, Baldwin
JONES, Abraham, decd of Richmond Co., Stephen Meers given ltrs dismission 11/22/1790, Columbia, Ests
JONES, Abraham, decd, William Coal, admr, John McBreyer, James Coal, sur, 1/11/1858, Paulding, AB
JONES, Absalom, decd, William Coal, admr, 12/5/1859, Paulding, AB
JONES, Allen, decd, LWT dtd 8/4/1799 pvd 1/16/1800, mentions wife and children (no names), wife, sole extrx, Hancock, AA
JONES, Alonzo W., decd, L. Stripling, admr, Jones T. Tinley, James Holmes, sur, 8/3/1851, Bibb, AB
JONES, Amelia, orph of Henry Jones, Jr., decd, Seaborn Jones, gdn, 1804 retn pd money as exr of Henry Jones, Jr. of Burke Co.; 1814 retn shows Mrs. Fanny Jones, gdn, Richmond, GR
JONES, Anderson G., decd, J. W. Mays, Toliver Jones, Moses Jones, Thomas Mahone, admrs, Harris
JONES, Ann and John, John Jones, gdn, p. 112, Screven, OM
JONES, Aquilla, decd, Hannah Jones, admx, 7/7/1806, Henry Williams, Isaac Davis, surs, Warren, AB
JONES, Archibald, decd, James Blair apptd admr, 11/8/1812, Camden, MIC

JONES, Arthur, decd, L/A issued to Tignal Jones 2/12/1803; admrs ordered to make title to James Sartain of land 8/3/1804, Franklin, OM
JONES, Arthur, ordered that title be made to James Sartain for land given decd in his lifetime to sd Sartain, 8/3/1804, Franklin, IMW
JONES, Barnabas, decd, LWT pvd by Joseph Bonner; Anthony and Henry Jones gtd ltrs of guardianship for orphans of decd, 9/7/1812, Warren, MIC
JONES, Barnabas, son under 14 yrs of Barnabas, decd, Anthony Jones apptd gdn, 3/2/1812, Warren, MIC
JONES, Basil, decd, Ann Jones, extrx, 1/23/1799, Columbia, Ests
JONES, Bazel, orph of Bridger, decd, Jehu Everitt apptd gdn 1/3/1820, Bulloch, MIC
JONES, Benjamin, decd, Levicy Jones, admx, ordered to appear next term of ct 11/3/1823, Bulloch, MIC
JONES, Benjamin, decd, Nathan Fowler issued L/A 5/4/1812, Jackson, OM
JONES, Benjamin, decd, list of appr by Samuel S. Lockhart, Ezekiel Self, Henry Clifton 1/18/1823, Bulloch, Misc
JONES, Berry, decd, James Wilkinson, admr, 11/29/1825 John Matthis, Garrott Williams, Seth Williams, apprs, Bulloch, Misc
JONES, Berry, decd, Rebecah Jones, issued L/A 3/2/1822; inv and appr by Seth Williams, Garrett Williams, Thomas Brannen, 3/16/1822, Bulloch, MIC, Misc
JONES, Betsey, orph of James, decd, Francis Jones apptd gdn 5/5/1823, Bulloch, MIC
JONES, Bridger, planter, decd, LWT, names wife, Rachel; ch: Berry, Briant, Josiah, Bassel, Buckner Jones; Mary Everitt, Rachel Wise, Nancy Jones, 5/1/1819, Bulloch, Misc
JONES, Buckner, orph of Bridger, decd, Jehu Everitt, gdn, 3/5/1821, Bulloch, MIC
JONES, Charles S., minor orph of H. P., decd, Charles A. Jones, gdn, 1/14/1861, Fulton, GB
JONES, Chauncy, decd, Mary H. Jones issued L/A 9/5/1823, Lucy M. Yarnold, sec; final div 4/24/1824-heirs: Hastings Warren, gdn of Lucy Matilda Jones, Hatton H. Pemberton, in rt of wife, Mary H., Richmond, AB
JONES, Council B., decd, L/A to Wm B. Hunt 5/5/1843, Washington
JONES, Daniel, decd, Nathaniel Jones, admr, authorized to make titles to John M. Geiger for land in Early Co. sold by decd to Geiger but never executed, 1/14/1828, Glynn, MIC
JONES, Daniel, decd, Nathaniel Jones, exr, gtd leave to sell, 1/9/1826, Glynn, MIC
JONES, David, decd, Daniel L. Harrison, apptd admr de bonis non, Dooly, OD
JONES, David, orph of Nathan, decd, Arthur Jones apptd gdn, Wm Dunlap, sec, 6/1/1811, Elbert, GB
JONES, David, decd, Eliab Jones, admr, 3/12/1845; apprs: Churchwell Patrick, Abel Hotton; purchasers at sale: L. R. Felton (family bible), L. G. Cotton, Benja. Oliff, Jonas Rackleyh, Roscoe Lipsey, A. A. Morgan, Jas G. Oliver, Dooly, I&A
JONES, David G., decd, John Hardee apptd admr after caveat to his apptmt by Archibald Clark was overruled, 6/7/1824; John Hardee gtd L/D 8/7/1826; John Hardee apptd admr 3/6/1835; admr gtd leave to sell lot 282, 19th dist, Jasper Co., 6/3/1836, Camden, MIC
JONES, Drury, Jr., decd, perishable property sold by Sheppard Williams, gdn for children of decd 2/1/1818; inventory and appraisal by: Allen Lanier, Hamilton Hudson, 2/14/1819; Sheppard Williams, John Dell issued L/A 12/7/1818, Francis Jones, James Young, Henry Parrish, Thomas Jones to appraise estate 1/5/1824; sale 2/26/1824, Bulloch, MIC, Misc
JONES, Elizabeth chose Bradford Jones for her gdn 11/6/1837, Effingham, MIC

171

JONES, Frances, John Jones, gdn, p. 17, 28, 86, 99, 165, 187, 192, 108, Screven, OM
JONES, Francis M., decd, Andrew J. Munday, admr, 12/1853 temp L/A issued, Fayette, AB
JONES, Hamilton, decd, LWT admitted to probate, 9/25/1809, Elihu Atwater applies for adm 1/8/1811, Camden, MIC
JONES, Harriett, orph of James, decd, Francis Jones apptd gdn 5/5/1823, Bulloch, MIC
JONES, Henry, Rule Nisi issued against Elizabeth Green (formerly Jones), Hardy Green her present husband, admrs of decd, requiring them to appear at next term to show cause why retns not filed, 9/6/1813, Warren, MIC
JONES, Henry, decd, Thomas Jones apptd temporary admr 3/5/1804; Elizabeth Jones, admx, 12/15/1804, John Nunn, William Jones, surs, Warren, AB
JONES, Henry, minor orph of Joseph, decd, William Jones apptd gdn, John M. Sims, Dudley Rutledge, surs, 1/1804, Oglethorpe, MIC
JONES, Henry, decd, Levan McGee asked for deed-that Henry Jones in lifetime agreed to title 270 acres, both sides of Georgetown-Augusta Rd 1/17/1803; Rule Nisi to Elizabeth Jones, admx, to show cause next term of ct, 3//1808, Warren, MIC
JONES, Henry W., minor orph of Seaborn, decd, Henry Strickland, gdn, 9/5/1859, Fulton, GB
JONES, Hugh, decd, 1808 retn payments for clothing for Betsey, Lydia and Polley Jones. Lydia Hill recd $35 for boarding Polley in 1810, Jasper, Ests
JONES, Hugh, decd, apprs: James Knoles, Elijah Cooper, William Hill, 6/2/1798, Greene, Misc
JONES, Hugh, decd, of Greene Co., LWT 7/8/1797, names wife, Lydia, Jasper, Ests
JONES, J. Merrill, decd, William R. Phillips issued L/A 12/7/1865, Fulton
JONES, Jacob, decd, Rachel Jones, relict applied for L/A 1/10/1791, Greene, Misc
JONES, James, decd, 1807 retn pd heirs: James Jones, Richard Hubbard, Shadrick Floyd, Nancy, Polly, John, Stanby and George Jones and Thomas and William Jones, minors, by admr, Elbert, AR
JONES, James, decd, Betsey Jones and Francis Jones issued L/A 3/3/1823, Bulloch, MIC
JONES, James, decd, Clara Jones apptd admx, Henry Eady, sur, Jasper, OM
JONES, James, decd, Elizabeth Jones, Allen Smith issued L/A 3/1/1841, Washington
JONES, James, decd, James Few issued L/A 2/8/1817, Joseph Fannin, James Few, Jr., secs, Morgan, AB
JONES, James, decd, LWT pvd by Stephen McCall; Harley and James Jones qualified as exrs 9/1849, Camden, MIC
JONES, James, decd, Martha Jones, William Copeland, Lewis Ethridge, admrs, 9/1/1833, Harris, AB
Jones, James, decd, Mary Jones, admx, pet of Agrippa Atkinson, one of secs on bond, to be relieved because sd Mary abt to move out of county, 1/2/1809, Jackson, OM
JONES, James, decd, Polly Jones issued L/A 3/22/1808, James Scott, Benjamin Darling, secs, Richmond, AB
JONES, James, decd, William Jones and James Jones apptd temp admrs, Michael Burkhalter, Thomas Dent, sur, 10/1804, Warren, MIC, AB
JONES, James, decd, William and James Jones, admrs, 12/10/1804, Michael Burkhalter, Thomas Dent, surs, Warren, AB
JONES, James, decd, inv and appraisal of stock of cattle in Appling Co. by John Jones, Berry Jones and James Young, 1/2/1824, Bulloch, Misc
JONES, James, orph of Samuel, decd, Robert Jones apptd gdn 6/4/1849, Camden, MIC, GB

JONES,, James, decd, retn of div of negroes to: Francis, Michael, William E., Thomas, Harriet, E., Matthew, and Berry Jones, and James Young, 1/24/1824, Bulloch, Misc
JONES, James, decd, inv. and appr by Moses Wilson, R. Whitaker, James Young, James Lanier, 11/1/1819, Bulloch, Misc
JONES, James, Sr., decd, Harley and James Jones dismissed as exrs, 6/3/1850, Camden, MIC
JONES, Jane, minor orph of Thomas, decd, late of Effingham Co., Benjamin Sims apptd gdn, Henry Sims, Benjamin G. Sims, secs, Richmond, GB
JONES, Jarvis, decd, 7/27/1816, 608 acres on road and river to Elijah Bragg, 40 acres of island to Joseph Sheppard, pine land to Samuel Lockhart, signed Catharine Jackson, admr, Bulloch, Ests
JONES, Jesse, decd, 11/6/1806 inv, John Allgood, James Butler, James Childers, apprs; Thomas Jones & Arthur Jones, admrs, Elbert, AR
JONES, Jesse, gdn for Robert and Harrison Jones, John McLean, Wm B. Jones, surs, 11/1847, Fayette, GB
JONES, John, decd, James Worth gtd L/A 3/18/1799, Columbia, Ests
JONES, John, orph over 14 of Barnabas, decd, chose Henry Jones as gdn, 5/4/1812, Warren, MIC
JONES, John H., decd, John N. Pate, admr, 4/1/1861, Robert Jones, sur, DeKalb, AB
JONES, Joshua, orph of Samuel, decd, Robert Jones apptd gdn 6/4/1849, Camden, MIC, GB
JONES, Josiah, orph ot Bridger, decd, Jehu Everitt apptd gdn 1/3/1820, Bulloch, MIC
JONES, Judge, orph of Drury, decd, Sheppard Williams apptd gdn 1/5/1818, Bulloch, MIC
JONES, Julius C., decd, John Jones, admr, 3/1/1824, Henry Gibson, sur, Warren, AB
JONES, Lucreasy, orph of Drury, decd, Sheppard Williams apptd gdn 1/5/1818, Bulloch, MIC
JONES, Lucy Matilda, minor orph of Chauncy, decd, Hastings Warren, gdn, 5/15/1823, Richmond, GB
JONES, M., gdn of J. E. and C. T. Jones, 12 and 13 yrs old, 6/1872, Webster, OD
JONES, Martha, orph of Thomas, decd, James Butts, gdn, 2/4/1816, Thomas Hogg, sec, Morgan, GB
JONES, Martha, orph over 14 of Barnabas, decd, chose Henry Jones as gdn, 5/4/1814, Warren, MIC
JONES, Mary T., orph of Thomas L., decd, Thomas Stock, gdn, 2/8/1820, Faulkner Heard, Woodson Heard, William Stocks, secs, Morgan, GB
JONES, Mathew, LWT presented by James Jones, p. 101, Screven, OM
JONES, Matilda, decd, Joseph L. Jones, admr, John W. Wilkie, sur, 5/2/1853, Cherokee, AB
JONES, Mitchell, orph of James, decd, Francis Jones apptd gdn 5/5/1823, Bulloch, MIC
JONES, Moses, orph of Moses, decd, Mason Jones, gdn, 3/1/1830, Tolliver Jones, sec, Lincoln, GB
JONES, Nancy, decd, William Stallings issued L/A 3/4/1816, Jesse Moseley, sec, Morgan, AB
JONES, Nathan, decd, LWT pvd 9/3/1844, wife, Sarah M. Jones, Bulloch, Misc
JONES, Nathan, decd, late of Greene Co., Ga., Betsey, relict, applied for L/A 3/2/1799, Greene, Misc
JONES, Nathan, decd, 1/28/1808 heirs receipts: Allen Jones, John Hatchcock and Denton Hatchcock, James Childers, Arthur Jones, Darvin Harris, Thomas & John Jones, exrs of Jesse Jones, decd, Elbert, AR
JONES, Philip, decd, Elizabeth Jones and Nathaniel Zettler apply for L/D 5/17/1837, Effingham, MIC

JONES, Phillip, son under 14 yrs of Barnabas, decd, Anthony Jones apptd gdn, 9/6/1813, Warren, MIC
JONES, Polley, orph and minor of Joseph, decd, William Jones apptd gdn, John M. Sims, Dudley Rutledge, surs, 1/1804, Oglethorpe, MIC
JONES, Polly, dau under 14 yrs of Barnabas, decd, Anthony Jones apptd gdn, 3/2/1812, Warren, MIC
JONES, Polly, minor orph of Hugh, Sr., decd, Archibald Standerford, gdn, John Knight, Benjamin Irvin, surs, Jasper, OM
JONES, Priscilla, orph of Samuel, decd, Robert Jones apptd gdn 6/4/1849, Camden, MIC, GB
JONES, Repp, orph of Benjamin, decd, Levicy Jones apptd gdn 9/1/1823, Bulloch, MIC
JONES, Robert, decd, Fanny and Henry Jones, Jr. issued L/A 3/22/1792, Daniel and John Evans, secs, land in Burke and Richmond Co.´s, Richmond, AB
JONES, Sam, decd, Robert Jones, admr, 1/3/1848, Camden, MIC
JONES, Samuel, decd, Hardin Pruitt, admr, 6/6/1814, Thomas Maddux, sur, Warren, AB
JONES, Samuel, decd, William J. Jones, James J. Jones, admrs, James McDaniel, sur, 9/7/1874, Gwinnett, AB
JONES, Sarah, minor orph of Seaborn, decd, Augustus S. Jones, apptd gdn, 5/28/1821, Reuben Wilkinson, Patrick Carnes, secs, Richmond, GB
JONES, Seaborn, decd, Ezekiel A. Davis, admr, 5/5/1856, R. M. Brown, sur, DeKalb, AB
JONES, Smith, decd, Robert Jones and Rhesa Bostick issued L/A 3/7/1820, Nathan L. Strugis, Wm P. Dearmond, secs, Richmond, AB
JONES, S. R., decd, E. E. Little issued L/A 3/1863, Webster, OD
JONES, Tamerlane, decd, Sally Jones, admx, 1/2/1808, Warren, MIC
JONES, Thomas, decd, John Lamar, admr, dismissed, 3/4/1811, Warren, MIC
JONES, Thomas, decd, LWT pvd 2/5/1778, ch: Mary, Samuel, Sarah, John, Thomas, Nancy, William; grson, James Welch; James Graves and Nancy Jones, exrs, Wilkes, MxR
JONES, Thomas, decd, Martha Jones apptd temp admr; perm adm gtd her and John Lamar 7/6/1807, Benjamin Sansford, Matthew Hubert, sur, Warren, MIC
JONES, Thomas, decd, Mary Jones issued L/A 4/26/1803, Jackson, OM
JONES, Thomas, decd, Mrs. Martha Jones, wid, elected to take child´s pt of est, 7/5/1841, Bulloch, MIC
JONES, Thomas H., decd, Joshua Jones issued L/A 11/12/1821, Joshua Sego, Armsted Fulcher, secs, Richmond, AB
JONES, Thomas L., decd, Richard and Mary D. Jones issued L/A 5/4/1818, Harris Jones, Samuel Harper, secs, Morgan, AB
JONES, Wiley, decd, Nancy Jones issued L/A 5/5/1856, Paulding
JONES, William, decd, David G. Jones, admr, gtd leave to sell, 4/12/1808, Camden, MIC
JONES, William, decd, James M. Jones, temporary admr 1/1857, Webster, OD
JONES, William, decd, Richard H. Jones, admr, 1/7/1828, Hartwell Heath, Lewis Parham, surs, Warren, AB
JONES, William, decd, Sarah Jones applied for L/A 10/1/1791, Greene, Misc
JONES, William, decd; Sinar Jones issued L/G for orphs: Elisha, Sarah A., Benjamin and Rebecca J., 3/1857, Webster, OD
JONES, William, orph of Mason, decd, Wm M. Lampkin, gdn, 11/4/1839, Wm E. DuBose and John McDowell, secs, Lincoln, GB
JONES, William H., minor orph of H. P., decd, Charles A. Jones, gdn, 1/14/1861, Fulton, GB
JONES, Willis, decd, Davis Gray, George H. Bryan, Felix Leslie, Anderson W. Redding, gdn of orphs 1/6/1840, Harris
JONES, Willis, decd, Felix Leslie, Medium Jones, John W. Cooper, W. Thornton, admrs, 11/7/1837, Harris

JONMEL?, Phillip J., decd, Peter Huge issued L/A 11/4/1861, Fulton

JORDAN, Albert W., orph of Britton, decd, Francis T. Tennille issued L/G 9/4/1837, Washington

JORDAN, Asa, decd, Josiah Amason issued L/A 9/2/1839, Washington

JORDAN, Elbert P., decd, John G. Glore, admr, applies for leave to sell, 9/6/1869; Francis Jordan, wid, applies for yr's support for herself and eight minor children, 11/1/1869, Cobb, MIC

JORDAN, Elizabeth, legatee of Martha Harvee, decd, Reuben Jordan apptd gdn 1/1804, Oglethorpe, MIC

JORDAN, Elizabeth, orph of Isham, decd, Abner Weathersby, gdn, Benjamin F. Gunn, George Weathersby, sur, 9/11/1854, Cherokee, GB

JORDAN, George W., orph of Britton, decd, Francis T. Tennille issued L/G 9/4/1837, Washington

JORDAN, Henry H., a lunatic, Reuben Whitfield issued L/G 3/3/1834; Arthur G. Ware issued L/A 11/4/1839, Washington

JORDAN, Jesse, decd, LWT dtd 9/5/1814 pvd 1/14/1833, Britton Jordan, exr, Washington

JORDAN, John A., orph of Britton, decd, Francis T. Tennille issued L/G 9/4/1837, Washington

JORDAN, John P., decd, of Richland, 1/1842, Loverd Bryan, Jacob G. Mathews, George W. Jordan, John Perry, John Talbot; purchasers at sale: James B. Boyer, Joseph Collier, Hewey & J. T. Davis, Isaac Dennard, etc., Stewart, Adms

JORDAN, Levi, decd, Jorden and Lizia Jordan issued L/A 11/6/1809, Putnam, AB

JORDAN, Margaret, legatee of Martha Harvee, decd, Reuben Jordan apptd gdn 1/1804, Oglethorpe, MIC

JORDAN, Mary A., orph of Britton, decd, Francis T. Tennille issued L/G 9/4/1837, Washington

JORDAN, Oliver W., orph of Britton, decd, Francis T. Tennille issued L/G 9/4/1837, Washington

JORDAN, Sterling, decd, appraisers-- Henry Jordan, Haynes Pain, Thomas Lewis 3/4/1816, Jasper, OM

JOUCE, James, decd, L/A to William Joyce 9/7/1840, Tattnall, AB

JOURDAN, Warren, decd, Samuel Tate issued L/A 10/2/1849, Paul Purry, John Davis, secs, Hall, AB

JOURDEN, Abner, decd, Benjamin L. Jourdan issued L/A 1/19/1826, Benjamin Tarver, Burrell Jordan, Sterling Towns, secs, Morgan, AB

JOURDEN, Burwell apptd gdn of Benjamin G., his own child, 2/9/1827, Morgan, GB

JOURDEN, Thomas, decd, Reuben Jourden, gdn to minor heirs: Amasa and Thomas 9/2/1833, Habersham, MIC

JOWERS, F. M., William P. Jowers, gdn, 12/1862, Webster, OD

JOWERS, James, decd, Wilson Jowers exr of LWT 3/1862, Webster, OD

JOYCE, Alexander, decd, of Baldwin Co., James Willy issued L/A 4/17/1827, William Micou, sec, Richmond, AB

JOYCE, Martha, decd, Washington Joyce, admr, 9/2/1839, Randolph

JOZEE, John, decd, James Henderson, exr, makes retn 7/4/1836, Tattnall, I&A

JUDSON, Beach, minor, chose Joseph Dorr his gdn, 6/7/1803, Camden, MIC

JUDSON, Joseph, decd, Joseph Dorr and wife, Phoebe apply to set aside LWT; request was refused, sd LWT having already been probated, 6/6/1804, Camden, MIC

JUDSON, Joseph, decd, Joseph Dorr in rt of his wife, Phoebe, was apptd admr w/LWT annexed 1/9/1805; final retn made by R. McD. Elliott and William Johnston, exrs were dismissed 1/9/1805, Camden, MIC

JUDSON, Joseph, decd, William Johnston and Richard McD. Elliott apptd admrs w/LWT annexed, 6/7/1803, Camden, MIC

JUMAN, Arthur, decd, L/A to Henry C. Faqua 2/7/1820, Laurens, AB

JURDINE, John, decd, Benjamin Amarus, William Jurdine qualified as admrs 11/9/1784, Liberty, Ests

JURDINE, Leonard, decd, Samuel Saltus and Charles Thorp qualified as admrs 10/27/1784, Liberty, Ests
JUSTICE, Dempsey, decd, Levi Justice, admr de bonis non w/LWT annexed 1/7/1840, Baldwin
JUSTIS, William, decd, Henry and Polly Justus apptd admrs 11/7/1814, James Cash, sec, Jackson, OM
KAHLDEN, Frederick William, decd, William Limbert, Merchant of Savannah, Ga., applies for admn 11/10/1801, Effingham, Misc
KAIN, William M., decd, Mrs. Eugenia Kain, gdn of orphs--Amanda, John, Patrick, William, 5/8/1828, Richmond, GB
KARR, John, decd, Thomas Davis issued L/A 1/11/1796, Samuel Jack and Collin Reid, secs, Richmond, AB
KEALL, Henry, decd, Merchant, John Keall apptd admr, 4/3/1785, Chatham, Adms
KEATING, Richard, decd, Richard T. Keating apptd exr, 10/1809, Bryan, Writs
KEATING, Richard F., decd, LWT pvd, Archibald Clark, exr, 7/10/1839, Camden, MIC
KEATING, Sarah, decd, Richard Broughton and wife, Sarah, formerly Sarah Thorp Brandford and niece of decd, 3/10/1821, Bryan, CR
KEEBLER, James, decd, LWT admitted to record 5/2/1831; Joshua Keebler, Jr., exr 5/9/1831, Effingham, MIC
KEEBLER, John, decd, Mrs. Rosanna Keebler applies for adm 10/29/1799, Effingham, Misc
KEELING, William, decd, Thomas Worthy and Leonard Keeling issued L/A 3/1/1813, Putnam, OM
KEELING, William, late of Putnam Co., John W. Compton, to make title to lot of land in 16th dist, 1/3/1814, Jasper, OM
KEELOUGH, Ebenezer, decd, John Keelough apptd admr 6/30/1784, Wilkes, MxR
KEEN, Gilbert, LWT pvd 1/1808, Oglethorpe, OM
KEENER, Jacob, decd, of Augusta, William Keener, Harbet Stallings issued L/A 2/5/1829, Eli Morgan, William Thompson, secs, Richmond, AB
KEIFFER, Joel, decd, Reuben Keiffer applies for L/A 4/23/1831, real estate to be sold 11/4/1833, Effingham, MIC
KEITH, George W., decd, Allen Keith, Jasper L. Keith, admrs, M. A. Keith, sur, 8/1/1853, Cherokee, AB
KEITH, James, orph of Samuel, decd, Allen Sperlock apptd master, James Jones, sur, 1/20/1802, Oglethorpe, MIC
KELL, John, decd, David Rees, Francis Coddington qualified exrs 12/13/1784, Liberty, Ests
KELLAM, Davis, Seth Kellam, gdn, 1/21/1845, Dooly, OD
KELLAM, Susannah, decd, David I. Bothwell, exr 1/21/1845; apprs: David Graham, Wiley Cobb, Simeon Royal; purchasers at sale: Seth Kellam, Elizabeth Fenn, Disey Pipkin, Jane Eubanks, Willis Leonard, Moses Pipkin, Jas McLain, etc., Dooly, I&A
KELLEY, William, Jr., decd, William Kelley, Sr., admr, Jordan Anderson, sur on bond 6/31/1862, Dawson, WB
KELLY, Isaac, bound to Daniel Kemp, p. 45, Screven, OM
KELLY, James, decd, Armsted Fulcher issued L/A 11/13/1820, David and Moses Kelly, secs, Richmond, AB
KELLY, John, bound to James Lambert, p. 45, bound to John Smith, p. 50, Screven, OM
KELLY, John, decd, David and Moses Kelly issued L/A 11/11/1817; 1817 purchasers at sale-D. Kelly, M. Kelly; 1826 David Kelling, acting admr, pd for defending suit of Verlinda Ward vs est, Richmond, AB
KELLY, John, decd, Elizabeth Kelly, admx, 4/19/1794, John Carson, John Gibson, surs, Warren, AB
KELLY, John, decd, Thomas Haney issued L/A 4/1/1861, Fulton

KELLY, John, minor orph of John, decd, Susannah Kelly issued L/G
3/6/1820, Thomas Everingham, sec, Richmond, GB
KELLY, Noah C., decd, William Stocks issued L/A 5/16/1825,
William B. Gregory, sec, Morgan, GB
KELLY, William, bound to James Poythress, p. 96, Screven, OM
KELOUGH, John, decd, Jane Kelough, admx, to file retns, 1802,
Jackson, OM
KELSALL, John, Mrs. Amelia Kelsall, admx 4/1785, Liberty, Ests
KELSEY, Joel, decd, John R. Wallace issued L/A 1/8/1868, Fulton
KELTON, Martha E. D., orph of Eadison, decd, Nathan N. A.
Bramlett, gdn 3/4/1850, Nathan Bramlett, sec, Hall, GB
KELTON, Robert, Sr., decd, Katharine Kelton issued temp L/A
9/1/1848; Hiram Kelton issued temp L/A 9/19/1848, Sharp Reynolds,
R. H. Waters, secs; inv 11/8/1843, Hall, AB
KELTON, Eadison, decd, Alexander Robertson issued L/A 1/2/1849,
Guilford G. Thompson, sec, Hall, AB
KEMP, Alexander, gdn acct appvd, p. 131, Screven, OM
KEMP, H. B., decd, Jehu Kemp, admr, 1855, Cobb, BB
KEMP, Hipple, decd, Rebecca Kemp applied for adm 11/19/1800, Seth
Wolsey, sur, Warren, MIC
KEMP, Mary, Sarah Kemp, gdn, p. 126, Screven, OM
KEMP, May C. Kemp, Handy Harris applied for L/G on 12/1870,
Cobb, MIC
KEMP, Solomon, admrs acct appvd, p. 179, Sarah, admx, p. 115,
116, 122, 124, Screven, OM
KEMP, William, decd, L/A to Aquilla Coney 2/6/1816, Laurens, AB
KEMPSEY, Archibald, decd, Robert Abercrombie, Joseph Howell,
surs, 7/10/1801, Matthew Hubert, James Jones, surs, Warren, AB
KENDALL, William, decd, Henry Kendall, exr of LWT, gtd leave to
sell negro, 11/6/1809, Warren, MIC
KENDALL, William, decd, L/T gtd Jeremiah Kendall and Henry
Kendall and Phillip Brantley as exrs, LWT pvd on 3/1/1802,
Warren, MIC
KENDRICK, Abel, decd, Robert Kendrick issued L/A 9/5/1853, H. H.
Beall, James P. and James M. Kendrick, secs, Hall, AB
KENDRICK, Benjamin B., minor orph of of Shildrake, decd, Martin
Hatcher apptd gdn 3/7/1820, Jasper, OM
KENDRICK, John, orph of John H., decd, Benjamin Hill apptd gdn
11/4/1822, Jasper, Om
KENDRICK, Jones apptd gdn of his minor ch: Elijah C., Elizabeth
P., Amanda L., James D. and Benjamin C., 4/26/1852, Houston, GB
KENDRICK, Jones, decd, Charles Kendrick, gdn of orphs: Parmelia
E., Benjamin C., James D., Amanda L. and Martha O., 12/4/1854,
Houston, GB
KENDRICK, Martah, orph of John H., decd, Benjamin Hill apptd gdn
11/4/1822, Jasper, OM
KENDRICK, Mary, decd, Jane Kendrick issued temp L/A 1/3/1813,
Putnam, AB
KENDRICK, Nancy apptd gdn of: Elizabeth, Sarah and Robert C. S.,
minor orphs of Shildrake, decd, 3/7/1820, Jasper, OM
KENDRICK, Rebecca, minor orph of Shildrake, decd, Martin Hatcher
apptd gdn 3/7/1820, Jasper, OM
KENDRICK, Seaborn, orph of John H., decd, Benjamin Hill apptd gdn
11/4/1822, Jasper, OM
KENDRICK, Shildrake, decd, Robert and Nancy Kendrick, admrs,
Stokely Morgan states that decd gave bond to make title to land
in 18th dist, 1/6/1817, Jasper, OM
KENDRICK, Susan, orph of Benjamin, decd, Isaac Harvey, John Gay,
gdns, 3/2/1812, Jones, GB
KENEDY, William W., decd, John B. Kenedy, admr, George R. Kenedy,
Wm Z. Corine, surs, 10/1852, 1853 retn, Fayette, AB

KENER, Michael I., decd, Rowland Stubbs, admr, 1851-1852 retns, Fayette, AB
KENNADY, Ely, decd, inv and appr 12/16/1843 by H. Hodges, admr; apprs: Sheppard Williams, John Williams, Allen Williams; land in Bulloch and Thomas Co.´s, Bulloch, Misc
KENNEBREE, Harrison, minor orph of Shadrack, decd, Hope Hull apptd gdn 6/21/1803, William Graves, sur, Oglethorpe, MIC
KENNEGREE, Littleberry, orph of Shadrack, decd, Phillimon Owen apptd gdn, Elizabeth Kennebree, William Graves, surs, 6/21/1803, Oglethorpe, MIC
KENNEBREE, Polly, minor orph of Shadrack, decd, Hope Hull apptd gdn 6/21/1803, William Graves, sur, Oglethorpe, MIC
KENNEBREE, Shadrack, decd, Elizabeth Kennebree and William Graves apptd admrs, 6/21/1803, Oglethorpe, MIC
KENNEBREW, Shadrach, decd, an acct exhibited by Natt Porter in name of Elizabeth Kennebrew, admx, 3/2/1807, Oglethorpe, OM
KENNEDY, Ann, minor orph of Benjamin, decd, Solomon Metzger apptd gdn 7/6/1829, Effingham, MIC
KENNEDY, Benjamin, decd, John Charlton, admr, 7/6/1829, Effingham, MIC
KENNEDY, Benjamin, minor orph of Benjamin, decd, Solomon Metzger apptd gdn 7/6/1829, Effingham, MIC
KENNEDY, Campbell, decd, temporary L/A issued Robert Kennedy 6/19/1811, Caleb Tate, sec, Elbert, AB
KENNEDY, Darby, decd, 2/3/1793 apprs: William Bugg, Samuel Bugg, Henry Turknett, McCarton Campbell, admr, Richmond, AN
KENNEDY, David, decd, LWT pvd 3/1/1830, wife, Ann and nephew, Ely Kennedy, exrs, Bulloch, Misc
KENNEDY, Dorothy, orph of Benjamin, decd, Benjamin C. Porter, gdn, 7/6/1829, Effingham, MIC
KENNEDY, Edward, decd, LWT exhibited 2/4/1867, Jennie Kennedy, extrx, Fulton
KENNEDY, Ely, decd, inventory and appraisement 12/16/1843 by H. Hodges, admr; land in Bulloch and Thomas Co. s, Bulloch, Misc
KENNEDY, Gideon, minor of Samuel, decd, Jesse Brown, James Marsh, gdns, 8/7/1821, Emanuel, GB
KENNEDY, James, decd, John Achord issued L/A 1/6/1817, Simon Reaves, sec, Morgan, AB
KENNEDY, James, decd, LWT exhibited 4/3/1865, Mrs. Laleton G. Kennedy, extrx, Fulton
KENNEDY, Thomas, decd, LWT and Codicil pvd 6/2/1863 by William Ezzard and W. P. Orme, L/T issued Thomas A. Kennedy, Fulton
KENNEDY, William, decd, LWT pvd 12/12/1793, bro., Fields Kennedy and Thomas Carleton, exrs, Greene, Misc
KENNERLY, Joshua, decd, appr 12/3/1801, Risdon Moore, Davis McGee, admrs; purchasers: Belitha Beaton, Mary Langston, Isaac Benson, Saml Maddox, Davis Magee; pd for Everton Kennerly, orph of decd for schooling, R. Moore, gdn, Hancock, AAAA
KENNY, Joshua, decd, LWT dtd 6/14/1801 pvd 9/2/1801, names wife, Catherine "now pregnant", son, Anderson (when 21), dau, Nanny, dau, Betsy, Hancock, AAAA
KENT, Isaac, decd, John Rountree, Henry Durden, admrs, 9/3/1833, Emanuel, AB
KENT, James, bound to Theophilus Thomas, p. 40, Screven, OM
KENT, Joseph, bound to John McWade, p. 92, Screven, OM
KERBLAY, Joseph Maria Lequinio, decd, of Edgecombe Co., South Carolina, James B. Lafitte issued temporary L/A 12/16/1812, Nicholas DeLaigle and Bernard Bignon, secs; Peter Laborde apptd permanent admr 12/1/1813, Richmond, AB
KERBY, Arthur, decd, LWT pvd 11/1838, wife, Rowena, ch: Wm, Arthur, Moab, Nancy Hagin, John, James, Robert, Mary, ordered that James Kerby sell 22-1/2 acres in Cherokee purchase as admr,

5/6/1839, Bulloch, MIC, Misc
KERBY, Hannah, orph of Arthuavid Rodden, one of legatees, Jasper, OM
KERBY, Hannah, orph of Arthur, decd, Rowena Kerby, gdn, made retn 2/3/1840, Bulloch, MIC
KERBY, Mary, orph of Arthur, decd, Rowena Kerby, gdn, made retn 2/3/1840, Bulloch, MIC
KERSHAW, Joseph, decd, William Stafford, admr, 3/1838; apprs: Calvin B. Seymour, Bryan Bedingfield, Stewart, Adms
KESLER, Elbert, orph of Valentine, decd, William Kesler, gdn, 5/4/1847, Effingham, MIC
KESLER, Ephraim, orph of Valentine, decd, Richard Zittrour gtd gdnship 5/4/1847, Effingham, MIC
KESLER, Israel, orph of Valentine, decd, John G. Kesler, gdn, 5/4/1847, Effingham, MIC
KESLER, Joseph, orph of Valentine, decd, James Rahn gtd gdnship 5/4/1847, Effingham, MIC
KESLER, Valentine, decd, LWT pvd 7/7/1845, Effingham, MIC
KETTLES, Amanda, orph, Amy Blake was apptd gdn 9/3/1838, Effingham, MIC
KETTLES, Peter M., decd, Rebecca Kettles, admx 1/2/1837, Effingham, MIC
KETTLES, Sarah, orph, Amy Blake was apptd gdn 9/3/1838, Effingham, MIC
KIDD, James, decd, James H. Kidd apptd admr 7/1/1816, Jackson, OM
KIDD, Theodore H., decd, Stephen Brown issued L/A 10/2/1854, Zacheus Hudgins, Samuel J. Parrish, secs, Hall, AB
KIDD, Webb, decd, 1808 tuition-Webb & Frances; Wm, Martin & Jno W. Kidd, exrs; 1806 div-Martin Kidd, decd, Jno W. Kidd, Wm Jennings, Jno Cleveland, Tarlton Hall, Berry Ryan, Francis Kidd, Charter Harper & Jno Greenwood's heirs, Elbert, AR
KIDD, Zachariah, decd, petition of James and John Kidd state that admr is decd and the orphans without legal representatives, asking to be apptd gdns. Thomas S. Bailey, sec, 9/1809, Oglethorpe, OM
KIEFFER, Christina, spinster, decd, Joshua Zant and Godhelf Smith as next of kin apply for adm 7/26/1797, Effingham, Misc
KIEFFER, David, decd, planter, LWT 9/14/1775 lost during British evacuation; cy obtd. Mary Appollonia-Nungezer, sister, heir, petd 6/18/1783 for L/A; caveat entd for David Kieffer, decd's bro by Proctor W. Stephens 9/12/1783, Chatham, Adms
KIERNAN, James, decd, of Edgefield Co., S. C., George Pearson issued L/A 5/14/1816, William C. Dillon, Henry Mealing, secs, 3/20/1820 Robert McCoombs, admr de bonis non, Richmond, AB
KILBURN, Isaac, decd, C. Meaders issued L/A 6/1/1863, J. M. Dean, sec, White, AB
KILE, John, decd, William Kile issued L/A 8/3/1863, Fulton
KILE, O. G., decd, Thomas Kile issued L/A 11/5/1862, Fulton
KILGORE, William, decd, Joseph Higginbotham issued temp L/A 3/3/1812, Putnam, AB
KILLEBREW, Wiggins, decd, Tully Biggs, admr, 10/17/1803, John Rushing, Wm Simmons, dismissed 4/13/1805, surs, Warren, AB
KILLGORE, Ralph, decd, dtd 6/9/1783, wife, Alender, Mill Cr. plantation, Savannah R.; ch-John, Mary Elison, Elizabeth Sutherland, Caty, Robert, Ralph; Wm Delaney, decd, prop (decd admr), be sold, 1/3rd to Mary Delaney Allison, Wilkes, MxR
KILLGORE, Samuel, minor of William, Charles Smith apptd gdn 11/4/1822, Jasper, OM
KILLGORE, Simon, minor of William, Charles Smith apptd gdn 11/4/1822, Jasper, OM
KILLINGSWORTH, Freeman, decd, Wm F. Hamrick, admr, 7/16/1855, Lee, MSC

KILLOCH, John, planter, decd, Peter Ritter, admr, and Michael Ritter, (also decd), late of sd co., admr, 4/12/1788, Chatham, Adms

KIMBELL, Lucy L., orph of Gideon, decd, John T. Kimbell, gdn, John Bryant, Thomas H. Connel, sur, 11/3/1845, Butts, GB

KIMBELL, Martha F., orph of Gideon, decd, John T. Kimbell, gdn, John Bryant, Thomas H. Connel, sur, 11/3/1845, Butts, GB

KIMBELL, Mary G., orph of Gideon, decd, John T. Kimbell, gdn, John Bryant, Thomas H. Connel, sur, 11/3/1845, Butts, GB

KIMBERLY, Isaac, decd, William J. Kimberly, admr, Charles E. and James M. Kimberly, surs, 1/1849, 1852 retn, Fayette, AB

KIMBRELL, Sarah, decd, late of Burke Co., John Kimbrell issued L/A 9/10/1828, Davis Bottom, sec, Richmond, AB

KIMSEY, Thomas M., decd, LWT dtd 1/10/1861 names wife, Emeline (Habersham Co. land), est to div betwn children and married children; son, William D., White

KINDAR, Peter, decd, Isaac Cliatt issued L/A 7/7/1788, Enoch Richardson, Samuel Hanson, secs, Richmond, AB

KINDRICK, Elizabeth, decd, John McDavid, admr, Edward Edwards, P. F. Wood, sur, 3/6/1854, Cherokee, AB

KINDRICK, Isham, decd, John McDavid issued temp L/A, Edward Edwards, sur, 1/3/1854, Cherokee, AB

KINDRICKS, Burwell, decd, John Garret and William Kindrick issued L/A 5/5/1817, Jeptha Fannin, sec, Morgan, AB

KINEBREW, Henry, decd, Jasper Kinebrew, Benjamin H. Fortson, exrs of LWT, 2/1853, L/D 1854, Fayette, AB

KING, Caroline, decd, George W. Boston applied for L/A 3/25/1847, Effingham, MIC

KING, Caroline G., George W. Boston apptd gdn 7/4/1846, Effingham, MIC

KING, Cyrus C., decd, Elisha King and Israel Palmer issued L/A, 5/4/1835, Baldwin

KING, Elisha, decd, Wm King and James Mills, temporary L/A 1/7/1812, Thomas Carter, Martin White, sec, Elbert, AB

KING, Elizabeth, minor of E. Y., decd, John King issued L/G 1/1864, Webster, OD

KING, Elizabeth G., G. W. Boston was apptd gdn 7/4/1846, Effingham, MIC

KING, E. P., decd, John Terry issued temporary L/A; applies for L/G of minors; apptd gdn of Elizabeth and E. T. King, 3/1864, Webster, OD

KING, Ephraim, decd, Shadrick Fluwellin, exr, dismissed 3/2/1799, Warren, MIC

KING, George W., decd, William Y. Hansell issued L/A, 7/14/1846, Baldwin

KING, Harry, Jr., Henry R. Sadler was apptd gdn, 1/13/1845, Camden, MIC

KING, Henry, decd, William King applies for adm 1/22/1795, Effingham, Misc

KING, James, decd, James R. McCord, admr, John W. McCord, David J. Bailey, sur, 12/5/1848, Butts, AB

KING, James G., orph of John, decd, William H. C. Mickelberry, admr, Egbert P. Daniel, sur, 1/19/1850, Butts, GB

KING, John, decd, (Justice) Jane King, William King and James King apptd admrs, 6/6/1804, Camden, MIC

KING, John, decd, LWT dtd 9/2/1835 pvd 8/1836, names wife, Nancy and ch: William P., Isham, John W., Peter, Amy Roe, Margaret, Habersham, MIC

KING, John, decd, Nancy and Curtis King applied for L/A 9/23/1796, Greene, Misc

KING, John, decd, extn gtd to James King, Jane King and William King, admrs to file retn 6/7/1808, Camden, MIC

KING, Joshua, decd, Jacob Moore, admr, gtd leave to sell perishable prop, 10/11/1811, Glynn, MIC
KING, Lewis, a man of colour, chose James Freeman as his gdn 3/7/1820, Jasper, OM
KING, Littleberry, decd, James Millen, John King, admrs, Needham Massey, John Spurlin, sur, 7/6/1812, Jones, AB
KING, Mary E., decd, LWT pvd 1/5/1852, Camden, MIC
KING, Mary Frances, orph of John, decd, William H. C. Mickelberry, admr, Egbert P. Daniel, sur, 1/19/1850, Butts, GB
KING, Mathew E., orph of Lewis, decd, Francis Flournoy, gdn, 2/10/1820, Morgan, GB
KING, Matilda, Henry R. Sadler apptd gdn, 1/13/1845, Camden, MIC
KING, Michael, decd, John King, admr de bonis non w/LWT annexed 12/24/1799, Thomas Winn, Wm Pickett, secs, Richmond, AB
KING, Robert, decd, Robert A. King issued L/A 1/7/1839, Ebenezer King, John Chambers, James R. King, secs, Hall, AB
KING, Robert C., orph of John, decd, William H. C. Mickelberry, admr, Egbert P. Daniel, sur, 1/19/1850, Butts, GB
KING, Samuel B., decd, James King, admr, Robert Mayo, sur, 9/20/1842, Butts, AB
KING, Thomas, decd, LWT pvd and wid, Mrs. Mary E. King, qualified extrx, 5/3/1828, Camden, MIC
KING, Thomas, decd, LWT pvd, William F. Kelly qualified as exr, 11/1/1819, Camden, MIC
KING, Thomas, decd, inv 10/2/1798, Greene, Misc
KING, William, decd, George W. Boston and James O. Goldwire, admrs 10/23/1834, Effingham, MIC
KING, William, decd, Letterlie? King apptd extrx, 3/19/1799, Columbia, Ests
KING, William, orph of John, decd, Josiah T. King issued L/G 11/1/1841, Washington
KINGSBURY, John, decd, William Savage issued L/A 1/8/1823, Arba Washburn, sec, Richmond, AB
KINKADE, Hugh, decd, Matthew Collers applied for L/A 12/15/1791; apprs: Christopher Clarke, Wm Walton, Wm Blake, Elbert, AB
KINKAYD, James, decd, Robert Kinkayd and William Kinsey, exrs, make retn 7/1837, Gilmer, Misc
KINMAN, Kendrick, decd, LWT issued 1/5/1841, Mary Kinman and Abel Massey, exrs, Washington
KINSEY, Archibald, decd, Col. Robert Abercrombie and Joseph Howell apply for adm, Matthew Hubert, James Jones, sur, 1/10/1801, Warren, MIC
KINSEY, Daniel, decd, Edward Kinsey, admr, 5/6/1816, Jeremiah Burkhalter, Willamm Ussery, surs, Warren, AB
KINSEY, Edward, decd, James Gray, temp admr 5/2/1825, John Fontaine, John Littleton, surs, Warren, AB
KINSEY, James, decd, David Kinsey, admr, made retn 7/25/1803, Jackson, OM
KINSEY, Martin, decd, Delilah Kinsey, admx, 1/24/1825, John W. Kinsey, Robert Black, surs, Warren, AB
KINSEY, William, decd, John W. Kinsey, admr, 2/2/1824, Abner McCormick, Wm Castleberry, surs, Warren, AB
KIRBLAY, Joseph Mary Liquino, decd, of Edgefield Co., S. C., Jane Mary Odette Kirblay, admx de bonis non 3/8/1821, Richmond, AB
KIRBY, Richard, decd, James and Carter Shepherd issued L/A 12/8/1826, John H. Davis, sec, Morgan, AB
KIRK, Laura, petition of W. J. Eubanks to be reld from gdnship, 9/30/1869; Ephraim L. Braswell apptd, Cobb, MIC
KIRK, Levi, decd, William Kirk, Jemimah Hallum, gdn of orphs, 7/7/1834, Harris
KIRK, Samantha, petition of W. J. Eubanks to be reld from gdnship, 9/30/1869; Ephraim L. Braswell apptd, Cobb, MIC

KIRKLAND, Emma, orph of John, decd, E. H. Callaway, gdn, Josiah
Drew, Simon Banks, sur, 7/7/1819, Emanuel, GB
KIRKLAND, John, decd, Simeon Banks, admr, est appraised 5/3/1819,
Emanuel, A
KIRKLAND, John, decd, Simon Banks, admr, William Purvis, John
Clifton, sur, 1/4/1819, Emanuel, AB
KIRKLAND, John, decd, inv and appr 1/4/1843 by James Elerbee,
Malachi Mercer, John Gay, John Hendricks, land in Emanuel,
Bulloch, Cherokee and Irwin Co.´s, Bulloch, Misc
KIRKLAND, John, decd, recpts from Ralph Kirkland, admr, to
William L. Perry, James Kirkland, Daniel Kirkland, Sion Kirkland,
Richard Kirkland, Coleson McCuller, John Kirkland, William Irvin,
3/7/1818, Bulloch, Misc
KIRKLAND, Kisiah, orph of John, decd, E. H. Callaway, gdn, Josiah
Drew, Simon Banks, sur, 7/7/1819, Emanuel, GB
KIRKLAND, Richard, decd, acct of sales 3/15/1789 by Isaac and
Samuel Kirkland, admrs, Effingham, Misc
KIRKLAND, Richard, decd, retn filed 3/16/1822, Bulloch, Misc
KIRKLAND, William, decd, Claiborne Hinson qualified admr
1/26/1790, Liberty, Ests
KIRKLAND, William, decd, Elizabeth Kirkland issued L/A 9/2/1806;
Wm Ship, sec for Elizabeth Kirkland, admx, asks to be relieved
4/4/1808, Jackson, OM
KIRKLIN, William, decd, Elizabeth Kirklin, admr, makes retn
5/1/1809, Jackson, OM
KIRKPATRICK, James H., decd, Thomas M. Kirkpatrick admr w/LWT
annexed 1/16/1858, L. A. Simpson, A. Connell, Jno Barrett, surs;
1/22/1859, LWT devised Margaret Ann Hoyle $2000...W. W. Cochran &
wife, Margaret Ann, formerly Hoyle, DeKalb, AB
KIRKPATRICK, Thomas, decd, Thomas A. Kirkpatrick, admr 3/1841;
apprs: Neil Robinson, Robert H. Sherman, William Stokes, James W.
Dunaway, decd owned prop in Muscogee Co., Stewart, Adms
KISON, Hazelworth W., decd, Charles Kennon and Ervin Morrow
issued L/A 1/6/1818, Francis Flournoy, sec, Morgan, AB
KITCHELL, Joseph, decd, Elizabeth Rudolph petitions ct that she
is sole legatee under his LWT and asks that Isaac Miller, exr,
show cause why he should not pay same over to her, 5/6/1811,
Camden, MIC
KITCHEN, William, Sr., decd, Benjamin Howard apptd temp admr,
8/13/1805, Warren, MIC
KITCHENS, Boze, James M. Kelly, gdn, 8/7/1854, Hall, GB
KITCHENS, E. A., James M. Kelly, gdn, 8/7/1854, Hall, GB
KITCHENS, Elizabeth, James M. Kelly, gdn, 8/7/1854, Hall, GB
KITCHENS, Jacob, decd, James Campbell, Elizabeth Kitchens apply
for L/A 10/25/1855, George McCormick, sur, Lee
KITCHENS, James W., James M. Kelly, gdn, 8/7/1854, Hall, GB
KITTLE, Peter, decd, Robert M. Williamson, etc. to div est, p.
138, Screven, OM
KITTLES, Amy, deed of gift dtd 10/10/1797 from David Porter,
planter to friend´s wife, Amy, wife of Jacob Kittles; wit: James
and Elizabeth Porter, Effingham, Misc
KITTLES, John, decd of Chatham Co., Jacob Kittles, as nearest of
kin, applies for adm, 3/12/1799, Effingham, Misc
KNAP, Justice, decd, Charley Knap applied for L/A 6/24/1798,
Greene, Misc
KNAPEN, Thomas, decd, Samuel Hale, Ralph Ketchum, Emily Knapen
issued L/A 11/2/1813, Wm Micou, John Howard, John Carmichael,
secs, adm also in S. C., Richmond, AB
KNIGHT, Bethamy, decd, 9/10/1841, apprs: J. A. Leary, Sol. B.
Wilkes, Solomon Fokes, Dooly, I&A
KNIGHT, Eli, illegitimate child, Calvery F. Knight, gdn, Samuel
Bellah, sur, 5/7/1832, Butts, GB

KNIGHT, Eli, minor, Calvary F. Knight, gdn, 1840, pd 8 mos bd for ward, 2/5/1841, Butts, ER
KNIGHT, Elizabeth, decd, Robert B. and John Knight issued L/A 5/7/1810, Putnam, AB
KNIGHT, Enoch, decd, Susan Knight issued L/A 10/13/1831, Samuel Hale, John P. King, secs; co surveyed land for decd, orig gtd Wm Bugg 1785; 1834-6 retns, board, etc. for Gazaway, Mary Margaret, Wm, Susan and Woodward Knight, Richmond, AB
KNIGHT, Jerusha, decd, Alexander Knight, admr, inv and appr by Isaac Richerson, Wm Lee, George Mikell, 1/26/1828, Bulloch, Misc
KNIGHT, Nathaniel, decd, LWT exhibited 7/11/1863, Thomas Knight, exr, Fulton
KNIGHT, Nehemiah, decd, John Knight, John Williams issued L/A 11/1/1819, Anselm Bugg, Waddel Allen, secs, Richmond, AB
KNIGHT, Peter, decd, John Ross apptd admr 1/8/1806, Camden, MIC
KNIGHT, Richard, decd, inv and appr by: Samuel Bellah, Yelventon Thaxton, Thomas Williamson, Willis Jarrell 3/12/1831, Butts, ER
KNIGHT, Sylvanus, decd, LWT pvd 7/3/1843, Lewis Knight, exr, Washington
KNIGHT, T., decd, Augustine D. Pope, admr, Ermine K. Gahagn, sur, 8/19/1829, Butts, AB
KNIGHT, Valerie, minor orph of Rufus, decd, John C. McMillan, gdn, 3/5/1867, Fulton, GB
KNIGHT, Walter T., decd, inv, apprs: Charles Bailey, Ermine Case, John Simmons, 11/18/1829, prop sold 23/?3/1829, purchasers: Hamlin Freeman, O. P. Cheatham, T. R. Barker, etc; Augustin B. Pope, admr, acct 1830, Butts, ER
KNIGHT, Walter T., decd, Augustine B. Pope, admr, Silas Eillis, sec, 11/2/1829, Butts, AB
KNOLES, Benjamin F., orph of Benjamin E., decd, Edmond Knoles, gdn, Eli Edmondson, A. McBridge, surs, 1/1851, Fayette, GB
KNOLES, James M., orph of Benjamin E., decd, Wm N. Hill, sur, 7/1852, Fayette, GB
KNOWLES, Francis, decd, Merchant, David Montaigut, admr, 12/4/1783, Chatham, Adms
KNOX, James, decd, Abraham Scott and Ann Knox issued L/A 7/25/1803; Abraham Scott, admr, makes retn: Abraham Scott and Ann Knox apptd gdns of Sally and David Luckie Knox, 7/22/1805, Jackson, OM
KNOX, John, decd, Richard Knox issued L/A 1/5/1812, Putnam, AB
KNOX, John, decd, Samuel Knox apptd admr 7/1/1816, Jackson, OM
KNOX, Joseph S., decd, Marcus A. Bell, admr w/LWT annexed 8/2/1852, Thomas Kile, sur, DeKalb, AB
KOLB, George, decd, Moses Sinquefield issued L/A 9/2/1833, Washington
KOLB, Harmon, decd, of Providence, 4/1842; apprs: Thomas House, J. G. Eckles, J. Willett; purchasers at sale: H. Boynton, O. P. Cheatham, patrick Garland, William Jordan, Mrs. Kolb, E. Kolb, William Wheelas, etc., Stewart, Adms
KOLB, Harmon, orph of Jonathan, decd, William Potts chosen gdn 7/4/1814, Jackson, OM
KOLB, James, age 12, orph son of Jonathan, decd, bond to Abraham Scott, 8/1/1814, Jackson, OM
KOLB, Jonathan, decd, LWT pvd by Ephraim Lindsey and Patrick Cook 3/2/1812; James Cash retn 1814; Rebecca Kolb, orph, chose David Witt, gdn, sd Witt apptd gdn of Polly, her sister; James Kolb, age 13, bound to Joseph McLester, to learn hatters trade, 3/1/1815, Jackson, OM
KOLB, Susannah, age 3, orph of Jonathan, decd, bound to David Witt, 8/1/1814, Jackson, OM
KOLB, Susannah, decd, James Cash apptd admr 3/1813, Jackson, OM

KRATMAN, Edward, decd, LWT pvd 5/9/1788, Samuel Elbert and John Shick, admrs, Chatham, Adms
LACKEY, Celia E., orph of William, decd, George W. Lackey, gdn, S. L. Strickland, sur, 3/7/1859, Paulding, GB
LACKEY, William, decd, William A. Reaves and Rachel Lackey issued L/A 12/3/1866, White, AB
LACY, Annains?, decd, Hart Long, admr, 8/2/1813 presents accts of real estate, Tattnall, MIC
LACY, John, decd, LWT, Jane Lacy and William Lacy, exrs, 9/13/1794, Columbia, Ests
LACY, Thomas, decd, Samuel Wilkinson, admr, David J. Bailey, sur, 9/10/1850, Butts, AB
LAIRD, John, decd, Margery Laird applied for L/A on est of her father 12/15/1789, Greene, Misc
LAKEY, William, decd, Isaac A. Haiston, admr, 9/1/1856, Azariah Doss, sur, DeKalb, AB
LALLISTER, Laurann, orph of Lawson C., decd, Mark Shipp, gdn, 5/4/1835, Hardy Leverett, sec, Lincoln, GB
LALLISTER, Polly Ann, orph of Lawson C., decd, Mark Shipp, gdn, 9/7/1835, Wm Wallace, sec, Lincoln, GB
LALLISTER, Sarah Jane M., orph of James M., decd, Elijah L. Scott, gdn, 11/6/1837, Hardy Leverett, Henry Evans, secs, Lincoln, GB
LAMAR, Jefferson J., decd, of Lumpkin, 1/1840, Thomas Lamar, Abner McGehee, exrs; apprs: L. Bryan, Willis N. Calloway, John West, Richard Kidd, John Thorntonl decd owned 127, Stewart, Adms
LAMAR, Lucius Q. C., decd, Jefferson Lamar issued L/A 11/3/1834, Baldwin
LAMAR, Samuel, decd, John O'Neill, Jr. issued L/A 3/30/1786, Richmond, AB
LAMB, Abram, illegitimate, L/G issued James Berryhill, 1830, Washington
LAMB, Bernard T., decd, LWT exhibited 11/4/1867, John Lamb, exr, Fulton
LAMB, Nathan, Mary Lamb, gdn, Isaac Lamb, David Kirkman, sur, undtd, Emanuel, GB
LAMBERT, James, admr acct appvd, p. 195, Screven, OM
LAMBERT, John, decd, Thomas Stevens qualified exr 1/12/1790, Liberty, Ests
LAMBERTOZ, Mary E. L., retn of Joseph Bell, gdn, 1/2/1837, Tattnall, I&A
LAMBETH, John, decd, John Lambeth issued temporary L/A 3/16/1816, George Adams, G. kennedy, secs; Holland McTyeire, permenant admr 9/5/1816; John Lambeth apptd gdn of Elizabeth, minor orph, Richmond, AB
LAMBRIGHT, John, decd, Joseph Law, Jr., John Lambright qualified exrs 10/26/1792, Liberty, Ests
LAMON, James, decd, John Tompkins qualified exr 6/23/1787, Liberty, Ests
LAMPKIN, Harriett, colored, 15 yrs of age, A. C. Bell to be dischgd from his bond 2/1875, Webster, OD
LANCASTER, Thomas L., decd, of Union, Thomas A. Lancaster, admr, 7/1839; apprs: Neil Roberson, John N. Dupree, J. Dunaway, Wm Porter; purchasers at sale: Augustus and Kinchen Baldwin, T. J. Barfield, Lewis G. Dupree, etc., Stewart, Adms
LANCASTER, William M., decd, L/A issued Mrs. Lancaster 12/1865 and Talitha A. Lancaster 1/1866, Webster, OD
LANCY, Elizabeth, decd, Gabriel Rainwater, admr, John Epperson, William S. Christain, sur, 6/11/1855, Cherokee, AB
LANDER, James, decd, of Richmond Co., Amasa Jackson gtd L/A 4/8/1790, Columbia, Ests

LANDERS, James, decd, Amasa Jackson issued L/A 4/8/1790, Wm Longstreet, Thomas Wagnon, secs, Richmond, AB
LANDRUM, Larkin, decd, Jane Landrum, Josiah R. Bosworth, exrs, 7/1842, 1843 retn, Fayette, AB
LANDRUM, Thomas, decd, LWT names half brother, Lawson Adams when he comes of age, Jesse and Timothy Landrum, exrs, 8/3/1814, Jasper, OM
LANDRUM, Thomas, decd, LWT pvd by Saml Holloway, L/T gtd Timothy Landrum 11/1814, Jasper, OM
LANE, Ann, decd, William Gibson, admr of James Vincent est, rendered acct showing funds for Rachel Elliott, dau of Mary Elliott, decd, one of heirs, and interest for children of Ann Lane, another heir, 1/5/1831, Camden, MIC
LANE, Catherine (Mrs.), Rule Nisi gtd last term of ct on appl of Peter Corb, Tr of Mrs. Catherine Lane, to require Wm Lane, her husb, show cause why cy of marr settlement should not be established in lieu of lost orig, 12/6/1832, Camden, MIC
LANE, Edward, decd, James Hancock, admr, James Anderson, sur, 7/6/1829, Emanuel, AB
LANE, Edward, decd, L D. Price issued temp L/A, Benjamin Sherrad, sur, 4/9/1830, Emanuel, AB
LANE, Henry, orph and minor of Richard, decd, Charles Stewart apptd gdn, George Phillips, Robert Freeman, surs, 1/1804, Oglethorpe, MIC
LANE, Joel, orph and minor of Richard, decd, Charles Stewart apptd gdn, George Phillips, Robert Freeman, surs, 1/1804, Oglethorpe, MIC
LANE, John, decd, Stephen Denmark exonerated from paying $50 to est, 1/1815, Bulloch, MIC
LANE, John, decd, est apprd and distributed betwn heirs: Richard Lane and Arrien Vickers. Stephen Denmark, gdn for Richard Lane, 2/6/1818, Bulloch, Misc
LANE, Joseph, Sr., decd, Joseph and Luther K. Lane issued L/A, 8/8/1842, Baldwin
LANE, Levin, decd, L/A to Starling Fannin 7/3/1826, Morgan, AB
LANE, Obedience, decd, James Dean issued L/A 1/8/1828, Baldwin
LANE, Quincy, orph and minor of Richard, decd, Charles Stewart apptd gdn, George Phillips, Robert Freeman, surs, 1/1804, Oglethorpe, MIC
LANE, Richard, decd, Charles Stewart exonerated from gdnship of orphs of decd, 1/1804, Oglethorpe, MIC
LANE, Richard, heir of John, decd, Allen Denmark apptd gdn 2/1/1819, Bulloch, MIC
LANE, Thomas, decd, Mrs. Mary Lane, relict, applies for adm 3/22/1793, Effingham, Misc
LANE, Thomas, decd, affidavit of Mary Hurst & Mary Crawford 3/16/1793 that they were at decd´s home 3/11/1793 when he said he had given wife, Mary and children slaves; sons: Thomas and Samuel Lane--daus: Jancey, Elizabeth; , Effingham, Misc
LANG, Isaac, decd, Willis Lang apptd admr 1/5/1830, dismissed 3/5/1838, Camden, MIC
LANG, Willis, decd, B. A. Brown, John M. King, John Tompkins, J. B. Mizell apptd to make a divison betwn heirs of est 1/6/1851, Camden, MIC
LANGIERS, William, orph, was bound to Thomas Wilson 9/1/1817, Jasper, OM
LANGLEY, Oswell, decd, Polly Langley and Elisha Lolly apptd admrs 3/4/1816, Jackson, OM
LANGLEY, Samuel, decd, James Bryan and Benjamin Langley, admrs, dismissed 5/8/1799, Effingham, Misc
LANIER, Benjamin and John, Robert Lanier, gdn, p. 64, Screven, OM

LANIER, Bird, decd, Clement Lanier, exr, retn, p. 3, Robert
Lanier, gdn acct of heirs, p. 74, Screven, OM
LANIER, Hannah, gtd leave to sell property, p. 102, Screven, OM
LANIER, John and Thomas, Valentine Hollingsworth, gdn, p. 85,
Screven, OM
LANIER, John, decd, James Young, Thomas Beesley, Sr. and William
Beesley to div est, 11/3/1817, Bulloch, MIC
LANIER, John, decd, negroes and horses divided among heirs:
Hannah, Lucey, Augustin, James, Selita and Nancy Lanier, and
William Johnson, 2/9/1818, Bulloch, Misc
LANIER, John, orph of Bird and Elizabeth Lanier, decd, Edward
Lane, gdn, John Clifton, John Lane, sur, 1/4/1819, Emanuel, GB
LANIER, Lemuel, Sherrod McCall exonerated from securityship of
gdnship, 1/5/1818, Bulloch, MIC
LANIER, Nancy, illegitimate child of Polly, be bound to Sherod
Malone, 1/3/1816, Jasper, OM
LANIER, Robert, decd, Valentine Hollingsworth, admr, p. 81, Wm
Brack, etc., apprs, p. 81, 104, Screven, OM
LANIER, Thomas, orph of Bird and Elizabeth Lanier, decd, Edward
Lane, gdn, John Clifton, John Lane, sur, Emanuel, GB
LANIER, William, decd, L/A gtd James Lanier, 7/4/1814, Jasper, OM
LANK, John, decd, Holland McTyeire issued L/A 6/25/1832, Michael
F. Boisclair, sec, Richmond, AB
LAPERRE, John, decd, Lewis Laperre, admr, dismissed 1/4/1831,
Camden, MIC
LAPINA, Matthias, decd, Mrs. Mary Lapina qualified admx
10/1/1783, Liberty, Ests
LARD, Sally, orph, bound to John Dorsey 1/11/1811; 5/3/1813
Robert Chandler states that Joseph Yates is treating orph illy
and inhumanly, Franklin, OM
LARD, Samuel, orph, bound to John Dorsey 1/11/1811; 5/3/1813
Robert Chandler states that Joseph Yates is treating orph illy
and inhumanly, Franklin, OM
LARGINS, William now in possession of Mrs. Thomas Steedman is to
be bound to Robert Humber to be taught reading, writing,
arithmetic 5/2/1814, Jasper, OM
LA ROCHE, Isaac, decd, Samuel Hale issued L/A 6/2/1825, William
Micou, sec, Richmond, AB
LARRIMORE, Ann, decd, Simeon Hall, admr, 6/4/1860, William M.
Raygen, sur, DeKalb, AB
LARY, Darby, decd, appr 4/30/1803, Lary and Hinchia Lary, admrs;
purchasers-Comfort and Lary Lary, Jer., John, Daniel and Hinchia
Lary; div betwn 7 heirs:James Willson, George Lary, Willie
Hillard, Jeremiah and Comfort Lary, Hancock, AAAA
LASETER, Jeremiah, orph of Charles, decd, retns for 1808-1811;
Jeremiah age 11 on 16th May next, Jacob Boon, gdn, Jasper, Ests
LASETER, John, orph of Charles, decd, retns for 1808-1811; John
age 9 yrs 10th of Jan next, Jacob Boon, gdn, Jasper, Ests
LASETER, John F., decd, Eliza Laseter gtd L/A for minors of decd,
3/1855, Webster, OD
LASLIE, Charles, decd, retn by John McInnes, gdn of minors of
decd, Daniel, Mary Jane and Rachel Ann, 12/1842, Randolph
LASSETER, Blake, decd, of Halifax Co., N. C., LWT pvd by Henry
Cocroft 10/8/1811, Warren, MIC
LASSETER, Elisha, James Haines, Jr., gdn, T. W. Miner, sur,
2/1854, 1854-1855 retns, Fayette, GB
LASSETER, Elizabeth, James Haines, Jr., gdn, T. W. Miner, sur,
2/1854, 1854-1855 retns, Fayette, GB
LASSETER, Jesse, decd, Andrew J. Mundy, Reuben T. Mundy, admrs,
John O. Dickson, Wm J. Russell, surs, 7/1853, 1853-1854 retns,
Fayette, AB

LASSETER, Jesse, decd, James Haines, Jr., exr of LWT, 11/1848, 1852-1854 retns, Fayette
LASSETER, John, decd, Lewis Lasseter, admr 8/7/1826, Camden, MIC
LASSETER, Lofton, James Haines, gdn, no date, Fayette, GB
LASSETER, Sophia, James Haines, gdn, James F. Johnson, sur, 4/1855, Fayette, GB
LASSETTER, Elisha, decd, L/A issued Nancy and Robert Lassetter, with Isaac McClendon and Matthew Lasseter, secs, 7/7/1814, Jasper, OM
LASTIGUE Gerard, decd, Mrs. Ann Lastigue issued L/A 7/17/1818, Daniel Tobin, George Wallace, sec, Richmond, AB
LASTIGUE, Peter, decd, Jared Lastigue issued L/A 1/6/1808, John Cashin, P. Jaillet, secs, Richmond, AB
LATHAM, George, decd, Loyd Coursey, temporary admr 8/17/1866, Fulton, AB
LATHORP, Asa, decd, LWT produced by Asa Holton and qualified as exr 1/3/1809, Camden, MIC
LATHRUM, Anthony Jackson, George Lathrum, gdn, Tyre H. Smithwick, sur, 1/8/1855, Cherokee, GB
LATHRUM, Elizabeth J., George Lathrum, gdn, Tyre H. Smithwick, sur, 1/8/1855, Cherokee, GB
LATHRUM, John, decd, George Lathrum, admr, Tyre H. Smithwick, John Lathrum, sur, 3/1/1852, Cherokee, AB
LATHRUM, Samuel W., George Lathrum, gdn, Tyre H. Smithwick, sur, 1/8/1855, Cherokee, GB
LAUGHAN, Humphries, decd, L/A gtd Joseph P. J. White 9/1832, Habersham, MIC
LAVELS, William, decd, of Augusta, merchant, Josiah Morse, Elias Haven issued L/A 12/1/1800, Hiell Chatfield, Nelson Crawford, secs, Richmond, AB
LAVENDER, John, Sr., John Lavender, Jr., admr, p. 79, Screven, OM
LAVINDER, Benjamin, decd, planter, Rebecca Lavinder, extrx, 9/7/1784, Chatham, Adms
LAW, Elijah, decd, Charles Roberts and Richard Shipp issued L/A 1/12/1824, Richmond, AB
LAW, Zachariah J., decd, Thomas B. Landrum applies for L/A 10/18/1858, Adoniah J. Landrum, sur, Lee
LAWHON, Allen, decd, James M. Fielders, admr, William W. W. Fleming, sur, undtd, abt 1860, Cherokee, AB
LAWLESS, John, decd, William Lawless issued L/A 1/13/1846, Robert Young, Allen Blake, secs, Hall, AB
LAWLIS, Betsy, orph of John, decd, James Rowsey, gdn, John Rowsey, Wm McCoy, secs, 7/6/1812, Elbert, GB
LAWLIS, Tabitha, orph of John, decd, John Rowsey, Sr., gdn, James Rowsey, George Booth, sec, 7/6/1812, Elbert, GB
LAWRENCE, Athelston D., decd, Sarah Lawrence, admx, William Piles petitioned ct to require admx to make settlement 1/5/1821, 3/4/1822 Sarah Ringgold, admx required to render acctg; George Dupree & John Harris, sur on bond of Sarah Ringgold, admx applied to be reld, she having failed to appear & give new bond, admn vested in John Burnett, Jr., Clk of Ct, in her place, 3/5/1824, Glynn, MIC
LAWRENCE, Georgiana, minor over 14, chose John Harris and John Burnett as gdn 3/5/1824, Glynn, MIC
LAWRENCE, James A. D., minor over 14, chose John Harris and John Burnett as gdn 3/5/1824, Glynn, MIC
LAWRENCE, John, decd, L. A. Jernigan issued L/A 1/9/1843, Washington
LAWRENCE, Melanchthon, decd, John P. Mann qualified exr 1789, Liberty, Ests

LAWRENCE, Sarah Salena chose James A. Lawrence her gdn; he, along
with B. B. Lamb, in rt of his wife, Georgiana Lawrence Lamb, pet
ct for div among heirs of est of A. D. Lawrence, 1/14/1828,
Glynn, MIC
LAWRENCE, William C., decd, of Augusta, merchant, William J.
Hobby and Job S. Barney issued L/A 10/18/1817, John McKinney,
Jacob Danforth, secs, Richmond, AB
LAWS, Martin, decd, apprs: David White, Jacob Mercer, John
Painter, Gilbert Barden; Joseph Laws, admr, inv 7/5/1809;
purchasers at sale: Joseph Laws, Isham Laws, Stephen Laws,
Jasper, AR
LAWSON, A. B., decd, James Lawson, gdn of orphs 6/8/1835, Harris
LAWSON, Davenport, decd, Thomas and James Lawson, admrs 12/1840;
apprs: Asberry Cowles, Langley Granberry, Wm H. Perkins;
purchasers at sale: John Causey, James Clements, James, Thomas,
Margaret, Langley & William Lawson, Stewart, Adms
LAWSON, Francis, decd, Susannah Lawson, admx, appr 6/20/1803;
purchasers at sale: Susannah and Francis Lawson, Chas. Jordan,
etc; Salley Lawson to Susan Lawson for schooling; Francis B.
Lawson to Susannah Lawson for bd, Hancock, AAAA
LAWSON, Henry, decd, 5/17/1804 inv includes Jonas, Robert and
Jonas Lawson, Jr., purchasers, Elbert, AR
LAWSON, John Sr., decd, Adam Alexander, John Lawson, Jr.
qualified exrs 1791, Liberty, Ests
LAWSON, Roger, decd, Alexander E. Lawrence issued L/A 1/9/1843,
Washington
LAWSON, William, decd, LWT pvd 10/25/1800, Jane and Francis
Lawson, exrs, wife, Jane, ch: Thomas, Montford, Dudley, David,
Francis, William, Sarah Thomas, Mary Slaughter, Jane Lawrence,
Margaret Bullock, Hancock, AAA
LAWSON, William, decd, William and Nicholas Johnson request L/D
from est 11/2/1818, Jasper, OM
LAY, David, decd, Larkin Landrum, Samuel H. Elvin, admrs, Jeptha
Landrum, sur, 1841; Jeptha Landrum, gdn of orphs, Larkin Landrum,
Josiah R. Bosworth, surs, 1/1842, Fayette, GB
LAY, James M., decd, M. A. Keith, admr, Jasper L. Keith, sur,
6/20/1852, Cherokee, AB
LEACH, Arthur, decd, Sarah Ann Leach, admx, 3/6/1854, Andrew and
T. A. Browning, surs, DeKalb, AB
LEAGO, B. L., decd, H. R. Leago issued L/A 9/3/1866, Fulton
LEANS, William M., Sampson Bell, gdn, files his retn 7/1862,
Webster, OD
LEAPTROT, Aquilla, decd, Bolen Leaptrot issued L/A 9/5/1836,
Washington
LEARS, William M., S. Bell not held responsible for 8 negroes
7/1866, Webster, OD
LEARY, John A., decd, William Hooks, Pearcy Leary, apptd admrs,
Dooly, OD
LEATHERS, Mary, William and Patsy, heirs of James Shaw, chose
Nimrod Leathers as their gdn 5/7/1827, Habersham, MIC
LEDBETTER, Joseph, decd, LWT pvd by Wiley Buckner 11/23/1823,
Jane Ledbetter, admx; to wife, Jinny and children (not named),
Pike, MIC
LEDBETTER, Lewis J., decd, James L. Heard, admr, David Hill, sur
on bond 4/2/1861, Dawson, WB
LEDBETTER, William, decd, Amanda M. Parks, gdn of orphs: Minerva
and Martha O., minors, 1/8/1866, Fulton, GB
LEE, Ambrose, decd, John Gibson gtd L/A 7/10/1794, Columbia, Ests
LEE, Archibald, decd, Robert and Levi Benson issued L/A
11/2/1819, Isaac A. Parker, secs, Morgan, AB
LEE, C. M., decd, L/A issued John J. Lee 8/1869, Webster, OD
LEE, David, decd, Mary Lee, admx, p. 84, Screven, OM

LEE, David, decd, apprs: Thomas Mills, James Mikell, Edmund Warren, 5/2/1829, Bulloch, Misc
LEE, Henry, decd, Stewart Lee, exr, 12/31/1839 pd Miles Parker, J. R. and J. W. McCord, 1838 taxes, Samuel Snoddy, John McClure, A. L. Robinson, James H. Stark, Butts, ER
LEE, James, Sr., LWT pvd by Daniel Beesley, John Waters, Sr., Malachi Denmark 9/7/1840, William and James Lee make ann retn 1/4/1841, Bulloch, MIC
LEE, James, Sr., decd, 3/20/1843 retn of William Lee Sr. and James Lee, Jr., exrs, pd heirs: James, Jr., David, William (as as gdn for Thomas) Lee, Augustus Lanier, Jesse Bird, Sharp Roberts, Mitchell Lanier, John Lee, Bulloch, Misc
LEE, James, Sr., decd, LWT pvd 9/9/1840 wife, Patience; s-i-l, Joshua Kirkland, neph, Wm Lee; apprs-Wm Groover, Allen Mikell, Isaiah Beesley, Redding Denmark 1/20/1851; 7/6/1842 Augustus Lanier recd prop left his wife, Eliza, Bulloch, Misc
LEE, James W., decd, James A. May issued L/A 11/7/1821, Daniel Meigs, Robert Thomas, sec, Richmond, AB
LEE, Jesse, decd, L/A to Jesse Lee 7/5/1845, Effingham, MIC
LEE, Jesse, Sr., decd, Thomas and Jesse Hurst applies for L/A 6/10/1845, Effingham, MIC
LEE, John, decd, LWT exhibited 8/16/1866, James E., admr w/LWT annexed 10/1/1866, Fulton, AB
LEE, John, decd, Samuel and Tabitha Stokes applied for L/A 2/6/1792, Greene, Misc
LEE, John, etc., relieved from bond, p. 58, Screven, OM
LEE, Lillis (wife of Henry), decd, Charles Wakefield, admr, John Andrews, Robert W. harkness, sur, 7/11/1842, Butts, AB
LEE, Nancy, decd, Robert W. Lee, admr, Zachariah Lawrence, sur, 4/3/1849, Butts, AB
LEE, Richard, decd, Alcy Lee applies for L/A, apptd with Thomas Rogers and William Pilcher, sur, 6/21/1803, Warren, MIC
LEE, Sampson, decd, LWT pvd 1/6/1829, L/A issued to Elias Lee, Joseph Daniel, sur, Washington, AB
LEE, Thomas, orph of James, Sr., decd, William Lee, Jr., gdn 7/6/1842, Bulloch, Misc
LEE, Thomas M., decd, Joseph Willis issued L/A 12/4/1866; John T. Abercrombe, gdn of orphs: Cassa Ann, Marion D., Thomas, Malinda, 1/11/1867, Fulton
LEE, William, decd, A. H. Daugherty, admr; pd James W. Watins, J. W. Williams, Robert Greer, J. & T. Winship, Charles Bailey, John Hall, R. C. Mays, Cornelius Slaten, 1/20/1836, Butts, ER
LEE, William, decd, Alexander H. Daugherty, admr, David Spencer, P. H. White, sur, 6/16/1834, Butts, AB
LEE, William, decd, LWT pvd by Peter W. Gautier, Thomas Traylor, Henry Stephens, L/T issued Maria Lee, 11/1814, Jasper, OM
LEE, William, decd, late of London, Freeman Walker issued temp L/A 2/27/1819, Valentine and Robert Walker, secs, Richmond, AB
LEE, Zachariah J., decd, E. P. Minor, admr w/LWT annexed, A. J. Minor, sur, 7/3/1876, Gwinnett, AB
LEFEVRE, Maria Louise, decd, Leon Deveneau qualified as exr 1/5/1804; Claud Bores apptd admr w/LWT annexed 1/9/1805, Camden, MIC
LEGGETT, John, decd, LWT pvd by Isaac Collier, 7/1809, Oglethorpe, OM
LEGRAND, S. H., decd, N. J. Reinhart, admr, Lewis W. Reinhart, sur, 12/15/1859, Cherokee, AB
LEGRAND, Terrell, decd, Stephen M. Satterfield, admr, Harrison Black, sur, 10/10/1859, Cherokee, AB
LEIGH, Anselm, decd, Sarah and Benjamin Leigh issued L/A 1/14/1794, Abemaleck Hawkins, Conrad Liverman, secs; 1799 retn, boarding 3 ch: Thomas, Agnes and Anselm, etc., Richmond, AB, AR

LEIGH, James J., decd, LWT pvd, Mrs. Mary Leigh qualified as extrx, 7/10/1839, Camden, MIC

LEIGH, James J., decd, Mary Knight, late Leigh, removed as admx w/LWT annexed; Elias Knight apptd 6/5/1842; ordered that property of decd be taken out of hands of Elias Knight, admr, & put in possession of Mary Knight (formerly Leigh), extrx named in LWT, 9/7/1846; Wm Hodges applies for temp admr 1/2/1848, Camden, MIC

LEIGH, Thomas G., decd, Benjamin Leigh issued L/A 5/3/1819, Walter Leigh, sec, Richmond, AB

LEITNER, John C., decd, late of Wilkes Co., Daniel McCormick apptd gdn of minor orphs: John C., Charles B. and Henry D., Benjamin F. Barton, sec, Richmond, GB

LEMARS, Samuel, decd, Samuel Brazel, admr 2/15/1784, Wilkes, MxR

LEMLEE, Solomon D., decd, purchasers at sale: Wm M. Corbitt, Alexander Meriwether, Thomas H. Dawson, Robert Savage, T. H. Smith, B. Purvis (not dtd), Dooly, I&A

LEON, Andrew, decd, Nancy Leon issued L/A 7/4/1808, Jackson, OM

LEONARD, James, decd, James Fox issued temp L/A 7/22/1805, John D'Antignac, Chesley Bostick, Jr., secs; 9/19/1805 George Ruddell of Kentucky apptd permanent. admr, Richmond, AB

LEONARD, James, decd, LWT pvd 1/1855 names wife, Tabitha and ch: Isaac, Solomon D., Mickey T., John W., and Jesse J., Cherokee

LEONARD, Jesse J., decd, Mary Louisa Leonard, John W. M. Cafre, admrs, 1/10/1853, Cherokee, AB

LEONARD, Thomas, minor orph of Abel, decd, Charles A. Hill, gdn, 1/10/1814, Laurens, GB

LEONARD, Wilkes F., decd, John D. Leonard issued L/A 7/7/1862, Frederick Dover, sec, Hall, AB

LEOPARD, Holland, decd, Jeptha Landrum, Sr., exr of LWT, 1851-1854 retns, Fayette

LEROY, Francis, decd, John Ajeret, admr, 1/6/1817, Camden, MIC

LESLEY, Joseph, decd, L/A Mary Lesley 7/27/1796, Columbia, Ests

LESLIE, Nancy Catharine, minor dau of Felix who is apptd gdn, Rowland W. Hudson, Stephen G. Lane, sur, 11/27/1848, Troup, GB

LESLIE, William Peter, minor son of Felix who is apptd gdn, Rowland W. Hudson, Stephen G. Lane, sec, 11/27/1848, Troup, GB

LESTER, Benjamin L., decd, L/A issued to Henrietta P. Lester 3/5/1849, Baldwin

LESTER, Daniel, decd, LWT pvd 10/4/1835 by Peter Cone, Matthew Donaldson, Benjamin Lee; wife, Mary and William Lester, exrs; ch: Ramona Kirby, Sarah Lester, William Lester, Bulloch, MIC, Misc

LESTER, Eli, decd, Robert B. Lester issued L/A 5/5/1851, Baldwin

LESTER, Emeline, orph of Napoleon A., decd, Andrew J. Osborn, gdn, Isaac Osborn, John C. Leverett, Seaborn Gann, surs, 5/2/1859, Paulding, GB

LESTER, Harrison, decd, L/A to Sarah A. Lester 1/12/1863, Fulton

LESTER, J. H., minor orph of Alexander, decd, John L. Callaway, gdn, John S. Callaway, sur, 1/10/1859, Paulding, GB

LESTER, Joseph H., orph of Alexander, decd, James M. Lard, gdn, James J. Austin, sur, 9/5/1859, Paulding, GB

LESTER, Stephen A., orph of Napoleon A., decd, Andrew J. Osborn, gdn, Isaac Osborn, John C. Leverett, Seaborn Gann, surs, 5/2/1859, Paulding, GB

LESTER, Thomas, decd, LWT pvd by Richard Hargrves and William Stokes, 7/1807, Oglethorpe, OM

LESUEUR, Drury M., decd, James Clarke, admr 3/1840; apprs: F. D. Wimberly, Henry B. Lee, John Dorsey, decd owned 40 slaves, etc., Stewart, Adms

LESURE, Solon A., orph of James, decd, Samuel Lesure, gdn, 11/5/1838, Benjamin F. Tatom, sec, Lincoln, GB

LEVERETT, Cealy, decd, Simon Smith, admr, 5/1/1854, J. T. Heney, sur, DeKalb, AB

LEVERETT, M. U., decd, L/A to Jno W. Leverett 4/1871, Webster, OD
LEVERETT, R. J., decd, L/A to P. W. Reddick 10/1862, Webster, OD
LEVERETT, William, decd, James G. M. Ball issued L/G of orphs,
with legal notice given in Sumter Republican, 6/1854, Webster, OD
LEVERETT, William T., orph of R. J., decd, P. W. Reddick issued
L/G 10/1863, Webster, OD
LEVERITT, John, decd, Anna Leveritt issued L/A 7/4/1825, John H.
Jones, Matthew Cochran, secs; John H. Jones, admr de bonis non
7/17/1826, Benjamin M. Peeples, sec, Morgan, AB
LEVINGSTON, Robert, decd, inv 11/6/1795, apprs: Peter Cartwright,
Thos. Johnson, Gilbert Greer, Greene, Misc
LEWIS, Abraham, decd, Lewis Lewis, admr, p. 109, Screven, OM
LEWIS, Abram, decd, Prudence, admx, retn, p. 1, 22, Screven, OM
LEWIS, Anthony, decd, 9/6/1843, apprs: Stephen Hurst, Abner
Tison, Elijah Wade; Nicholas Reddick, Jonathan Platt, admrs;
purchasers at sale: John B., E. and Elizbeth Lewis, Griffin
Raines, Folton Kemp, W. S. Hammell, etc., Dooly, I&A
LEWIS, Davis, decd, inv filed, Mrs. Croxon his widow; clk
authorized to sell perishables, 1/5/1819, Camden, MIC
 LEWIS, Daniel, decd, 9/16/1842, apprs: Jacob Watson, Jno J. S.
Miles, Wm B. Cone, Robt Williams, Danl Mashburn; sale 10/7/1845,
Matthew Floyd, admr; purchasers: J. R. Hooks, Jas Lightfoot, J.
B. Smith, Thos Cone, W. H. P. Floyd, Dooly, I&A
LEWIS, Francis, gentleman, decd, Christian Lewis, Neil Fannin,
admrs 4/1/1786, Chatham, Adms
LEWIS, Jacob and Mary, notice to appear, p. 54, Screven, OM
LEWIS, James M., orph of Redding R., decd, L/G issued to James M.
Warthen 3/4/1839, Washington
LEWIS, John, Jr., decd, John Lewis, Sr., admr, John Malone and
Richardson Mayo, sur, 7/3/1830, Butts, AB
LEWIS, Nathan G., decd, Reuben N. Player, gdn of orphs: Mary,
Martha G., Laurence and Susan P., 11/6/1855, Houston, GB
LEWIS, Philip, decd, L/T to Thomas and Katharine Lewis 1/1820,
Jasper, OM
LEWIS, Prudence, decd, Simon Banks, admr, Emanuel Bennett, John
Clifton, sur, 3/1/1819, Emanuel, AB
LEWIS, Prudence, orph of Abraham, decd, Simon Banks, William
Davis, William Purcis, gdns, 1/4/1819, Emanuel, GB
LEWIS, Rebecca H., decd, LWT pvd by Elizabeth McWomack, Alfred
Doolittle apptd admr 1/6/1835, Camden, MIC
LEWIS, Stephen, orph of Abraham, decd, Simon Banks, William
Davis, William Purvis, gdns, 1/4/1819, Emanuel, GB
LEWIS, William H., orph of Redding R., decd, L/G issued to James
M. Warthen 3/4/1839, William Warthen issued L/G 3/13/1843, Washington
LEWIS, Willie, decd, L/A to Mary Ann Lewis 5/6/1822, Bulloch, MIC
LEWIS, Willis, decd, inv 1822; Mary Ann Lewis, admx, apprs: Wm
Groover, Pugh Pollard, Jno Groover, Sr., 5/20/1822, Bulloch, Misc
LIEMBERGER, Christian Israel, decd, inv 7/18/1791 by Apolona
Liemberger, admx, Effingham, Misc
LIENHARDT, Elizabeth, decd, late of Philadelphia, Pa., John H.
Mecaslin issued L/A 8/14/1866, Fulton
LIGON, John, decd, William Ligon apptd gdn of minor orphs
3/7/1827: Susan and Thomas, Wm Doyle, sec, Richmond, GB
LIGON, Thomas, decd, of S. C., Charles Carter issued L/A
9/25/1828, Wm McGar, sec, Richmond, AB
LINDER, Daniel, decd, George Linder and Elizabeth Laws issued L/A
1/1/1821, Laurens, AB
LINDSEY, Moses, decd, Dennis Linsey issued L/A 7/18/1788, John
and Wm Lindsey, secs, Richmond, AB
LINDSEY, Reuben, decd, Dr. Marshall Durrett's oath as admr in rt
of wife, Nancy, 3/4/1811, Elbert, AR
LINDSEY, Sion, decd, L/A to John Lindsey 2/1/1808, Laurens, AB

LINDEBURGER, Applonia, decd, Benjamin Dasher, Jr. applies for L/A 10/4/1836, Effingham, MIC
LINEBURGER, Christopher, decd, Benjamin Dasher applies for L/A 9/1830, Effingham, MIC
LINEBURGER, David, decd, accts of Joshua Lineburger, exr, 3/3/1828; Christopher Lineburger qualified as exr 3/2/1829, Effingham, MIC
LINEBURGER, Mary C., decd, Joshua Lineburger, admr, gtd division 3/7/1831, Effingham, MIC
LINECEAN, Gideon, decd, inventory 2/18/1784, William White, James Morgan and Rezan Bowie, apprs, Wilkes, MxR
LINES, Dorcas, decd, late of Liberty Co., appr 5/12/1834 by B. A. Busby, E. J. Delegal; Sheppard Williams, Sr. and Caroline Lines, admrs, dtd Liberty Co., Bulloch, Misc
LINES, John, decd, Lazarus Mallard, exr, 2/5/1788, Liberty, Ests
LINES, Samuel J., decd, of Liberty Co., 1/12/1835 inv and appr by B. A. Busby, A. Stewart, E. J. Delegal, Bulloch, Misc
LINN, John, decd, Fergus Linn, admr, 7/18/1799, Thomas Jones, Daniel McCowan, surs, Warren, AB
LINN, John, decd, Ferguson Linn applies for adm 5/16/1799, Daniel McCowan, Thomas Jones, sur, Warren, MIC
LINZA, William, minor of Mary, decd, Royal B. Philips, gdn, Wm C. Philips and Stephen Philips, sur, 5/1/1837, Emanuel, GB
LIPSEY, Elijah, decd, Luvicy Lipsey, admx, p. 134 and 150, Screven, OM
LIPSEY, John, decd, Benjamin Lipsey issued L/A 1/6/1823, John C. Woods, Levy Lane, secs, Morgan, AB
LISHMAN, William, decd, est placed in hands of Clk to administer 6/3/1817, Camden, MIC
LITTLE, E. E., decd, L/A issued J. J., Robert and Sam Little 2/1865, Webster, OD
LITTLE, Jacob, decd, Joseph James issued L/A 1/2/1826, George Pearson, Matthew Fox, sec, Richmond, AB
LITTLE, Jacob, decd, Joseph James issued L/A 1/2/1826, John James, Wm Dassett, secs, Richmond, AB
LITTLE, James, decd, James H. Little and John Westbrook issued L/A 9/7/1807, Franklin, OM
LITTLE, James, decd, of Church Hill, Robert P. Little, admr 4/1844; apprs: David C. Sears, John Person, Green Dupriest, Lyddal Bacon, Stewart, Adms
LITTLE, Jane, William Little apptd gdn of his dau 1/2/1837, Bulloch, MIC
LITTLE, J. L., decd, L/A to S. H. Hawkins 12/1865, Webster, OD
LITTLE, Jonathan, decd, Robert Little apptd temporary admr 3/1854; Robert Little issued L/D 2/1857, Webster, OD
LITTLE, Kindrick D., James W. Tally, gdn, Jordan Williams, James L. Lovejoy, surs, 5/1854, Fayette, GB
LITTLE, Ransome, decd, LWT pvd 9/5/1836, wife, Elizabeth Little and Jacob Little, exrs, wits: J. W. Little, John J. Little, William Edwards, Harris
LITTLE, Robert, decd, J. A. Little issued L/A 1/1862, Webster, OD
LITTLE, Samuel, decd, J. L. Little issued L/A de bonis non 2/1862, Webster, OD
LITTLE, Thomas, decd, mary Little, wid, apptd admx 10/6/1784, Wilkes, MxR
LITTLE, William, admr, to show cause, p. 164, Screven, OM
LITTLEJOHN, Abraham, decd, James Glenn issued L/A 5/4/1868 w/LWT annexed, White, AB
LITTLETON, Alexander, decd, James Loyless, admr, 9/13/1819, James Cody, Jr., sur, Warren, AB
LLOYD, Edmond, decd, L/A gtd John S. Drew and Peggy Lloyd 3/1819, Margaret, wid, claims a child's pt, Jasper, OM
LLOYD, James, decd, Erasmus D. Tracy, admr, 6/4/1838, Camden, MIC

LLOYD, John, decd, L/A gtd 10/16/1793 John and Charles Lloyd;
purchasers at sale: Philip Allen, John Lloyd, William Lloyd,
Charles Lloyd, Wm Phillips, Joseph Smith, Wm Gilbert, Martin
Gilbert, John K. Robertson 12/24/1793, Greene, Misc
LLOYD, Sarah A., decd, Joseph Billups, admr, 9/18/1818 bond,
Thomas Pennington, George W. Moore, surs, Clarke, AB
LOCK, Jonathan, decd, LWT pvd, Mary Lock and John Lock qualified
exrs, 3/4/1810, Warren, MIC
LOCKETT, Warren, decd, Solomon Lockett, admr, 12/2/1823, James
Ellet, Asa Chapman, surs, Warren, AB
LOCKHART, Richard, decd, appr 11/14/1800, Mary Lockhart, Collin
Pope, Wm Rabun, admrs; recpt signed by John Benton, gdn for orphs
1/7/1811, Hancock, AAAA
LOCKHART, Samuel L., decd, LWT pvd 5/5/1834, wife, Rhoda, ch:
Sarah Johnson, wife of James, Charles Harris (age 21 on
2/4/1839), John, Anderson, Matthew, Thomas and Batt Jones
Lockhart, sons, Mary Williams, wife of Thomas, Bulloch, Misc
LOCKHART, Susan, orph of Brittian, decd, Wm Dallis, gdn,
1/5/1829, Thomas Jenning, Thomas Dallis, secs, Lincoln, GB
LOCKRIDGE, Daniel, decd, F. M. Lockridge, admr, James W. Langly,
Amon Lockridge, sur, 11/3/1873, Gwinnett, AB
LOCKWOOD, James, decd, LWT pvd, L/T issued William Lockwood and
Wm Herrin, 11/1814, Jasper, OM
LOFLEY, N. L., decd, Elisha Nowell, exr, 11/1862, Webster, OD
LOFLIN, Elizabeth, decd, orph of Elijah, decd, Wm L. Walker, gdn,
1/17/1826, John H. Walker, sec, Lincoln, GB
LOFLIN, Nancy Jane, orph of Elijah, decd, Daniel Walker, gdn,
3/7/1825, Wm L. Walker, sec, Lincoln, GB
LOFLIN, Shelton, orph, Harrison W. Hagerman, gdn, 10/6/1832, John
H. Walker, sec, Lincoln, GB
LOFTIN, Eli, decd, Osborn Durham issued L/A 5/6/1850, Sterling
Roberts, sec, Hall, AB
LOFTIN, Joseph bound to John Brown until age 21, 1/7/1822,
Jasper, OM
Loftin, Robert W., minor of James B., James B. Lofton, gdn,
6/7/1858, Fulton, GB
LOFTIN, William James, minor of John, decd, John Lofton, gdn,
John H. McDaniel, sur, 3/19/1845, Butts, GB
LOFTON, James, decd, Isaac Bailey, admr, 1/6/1835, Camden, MIC
LOFTON, James, decd, Mrs. Elizabeth Lofton apptd admx 6/4/1822,
Camden, MIC
LOFTON, James, decd, the admx of sd estate being removed from
State, and est being in danger of loss by being unrepresented,
Clk to take charge as admr de bonis non, 5/2/1831, Camden, MIC
LOGAN, Josephine, minor of Phillip D., decd, John Sasser gtd L/G
12/1854, Webster, OD
LOGAN, Lawrence, decd, Sarah A. Logan issued L/A 3/3/1851 and
12/4/1854, Amos G. Robinson, sec, Hall, AB
LOGAN, Mitchell G., minor of Phillip D., decd, John Sasser gtd
L/G 12/1854, Webster, OD
LOGAN, Patrick, decd, Sarah A. Logan issued L/A 3/3/1851 and
12/8/1854, Amos G. Robinson, Terry Couch, secs, Hall, AB
LOGAN, Phillip D., decd, Tempey Logan, admx, retn 10/1854,
Webster, OD
LOGAN, William H., orph of James, decd, David H. Logan, gdn,
11/7/1857, Dawson, WB
LOLLISTEN, Louis, decd, Henry Parnell, gdn of orphs: Polly Ann
and Louisann, 3/3/1834, Lauren and Covington Searls, secs,
Lincoln, GB
LONG, John, decd, Alex Cunningham issued L/A 11/27/1819, Abraham
Twiggs, R. H. Wilde, secs, Richmond, AB
LONG, Joseph, decd, 1810 retn includes settlement betwn Charles
Wheeler and est, a co-partnership in merchandizing, James Long,
exr, Elbert, AR

LOTT, Jesse, Sr., decd, Jesse Lott, Jr., Andrew and H. J. Lott
issued L/A 12/4/1854, H. J. Lott, Ambrose Kennedy, H. W. Blake,
secs, Hall, AB
LOUTHER, Catharine, orph of John, decd, Joseph Hagin apptd gdn in
lieu of Jeremiah Hill 4/6/1818, Bulloch, MIC
LOUTHER, John, decd, Mary Louther, admx, to sell 30 acres in
Screven Co., 2/1/1819; Sheppard Williams, Jehu Everitt, Joseph
Hagin, apprs 11/3/1817; Jeremiah Hill, gdn of heirs, Bulloch, MIC
LOUTHER, John, decd, div betwn Nancy, Sarah, Celity, Eliza, John,
Mary, Catharine and Rebecca Louther, and J. Hill, 11/17/1817,
Bulloch, Misc
LOUTHER, Rebecca, orph of John, decd, Joseph Hagin apptd gdn in
lieu of Jeremiah Hill, 4/6/1818, Bulloch, MIC
LOVE, John T., decd, Henry T. Harris issued L/A 12/2/1814, Andrew
Harrison, Wm Harris, secs, Richmond, AB
LOVEJOY, Edward, decd, Jemima and Wm Lovejoy, Jethro Mobley,
admrs 5/4/1807, Jackson, OM
LOVELESS, Bartow, decd, Abner P. Loveless, admr, Thomas M.
Johnston, sec, 3/12/1847, Cherokee, WB
LOVELESS, Levi, decd, William S. Woodward, John G. Loveless,
admrs, Levi J. Loveless, B. S. Strickland, sur, 8/4/1873,
Gwinnett, AB
LOVETT, John F., order to pay $25000, p. 30-31, 102, Screven, OM
LOVING, Sanford, decd, William M. Varnum, gdn of orphs: Mary A.
and William R., 11/3/1851, Lumpkin, GB
LOVINGOOD, Harmon, decd, 7/22/1800 inv includes 100 acres,
Franklin Co., Va., 500 acres Lincoln Co., Ky., Richland Cr., 219
acres Elbert Co., Cedar Cr.; due from Saml & Ann Lovingood for
cash recd, Moses Haynes, admr, Elbert, AR
LOW, Andrew, an alien, decd, James Miller, James McLea, Wm
Mackie, apprs 4/17/1821, Richmond
LOW, Daniel Johnson, decd, LWT dtd 3/17/1800 pvd 9/2/1801, wife,
Elizabeth, son, William; grson: Daniel Low, Hancock, AAAA
LOW, George, decd, Elizabeth Low issued L/A 9/5/1803, John
Savage, Hugh Magee, secs, 1803 retns pd tax on Columbia Co. land;
heirs---Wm Hart, Isaac Low, Miss Sarah Low and John Low,
Richmond, AB, AR
LOW, Isaac, decd, of Richmond Co., LWT, Abraham Johnston and
George Low, exrs, 1/4/1790, Columbia, Ests
LOW, Jane, decd, Maj. Phillip Low, Elizabeth Powell qualified
exrs 9/9/1783, Liberty, Ests
LOW, Phillip, decd, Mrs. Mary Low qualified admx 6/22/1786,
Liberty, Ests
LOWERY, Ann E. (Mrs.), decd, Henry L. Smith, trustee 10/1/1860,
John Wyley, sec, an antenuptial entered into betwn her and her
husband, David R. Lowery before her intermarriage with him,
Richmond, AB
LOWERY, James, minor and orph of David, decd, petitions for
Daniel W. Easley as gdn, Roderick Easley, Tarpley Flint, surs,
11/28/1796, Oglethorpe, MIC
LOWERY, Mary, minor and orph of David, decd, petitions for Daniel
W. Easley as her gdn, Roderick Easley and Tarpley Flint, surs,
11/28/1796, Oglethorpe, MIC
LOWERY, Patience, minor and orph of David, decd, petitions for
Daniel W. Easley her gdn, Roderick Easley, Tarpley Flint, surs,
11/28/1796, Oglethorpe, MIC
LOWREY, Benjamin, decd, Mary and John Lowrey and Joseph Moore
applied for L/A 10/6/1794, Greene, Misc
LOWREY, John, decd, LWT pvd 1/4/1808, LWT names wife, Ellender,
"the children"; Ellender Lowrey and James Lowrey, exrs dtd
9/13/1807, wit: David Lowrey, John Parks, William Lowrey,
Franklin, OM
LOWTHER, Joseph, decd, LWT pvd by Robert Thomas, Stephen McCall
qualified as exr 9/1849, Camden, MIC

LOYD, Edmund, decd, pet of John S. Drew and John Norwood in rt of wife, admx of est, prays to be dismissed 1/7/1822, Jasper, OM
LOYD, James, decd, LWT exhibited 7/8/1862, Robert M. Clark and Thomas F. Grubbs, exrs, Fulton
LOYD, James, decd, William J. Russell, admr de bonis non, Wm H. Blalock, T. C. Mathews, Wm N. Hill, Charles Clements, John and Mitten Loyd, surs, 3/1850, 1851-1852 retns, Fayette, AB
LOYD, Jasper, orph of James, decd, Jarrell I. Whitaker apptd gdn, John I. and Simon T. Whitaker, surs, 7/1850, 1851-1854 retn, Fayette, GB
LOYD, John, decd, Wm Few, Sr. issued L/A 1786, Ignatius Few, John Ramsey, secs, Richmond, AB
LOYD, Newton, orph of James, decd, Jarrell I. Whitaker apptd gdn, John I. and Simon T. Whitaker, surs, 7/1850, 1851-1854 retns, Fayette, GB
LOYD, Samuel, orph of James, decd, James Loyd, gdn, John Loyd, Wm Whatley, Walter J. Campbell, surs, 11/1850, 1851-1853 retns, Fayette, GB
LOYD, Sarah F., orph of James, decd, John Loyd, gdn, Sarah and James Loyd, Mary Fernander, J. L. Jones, surs, 7/1850, 1851-1854 retns, Fayette, GB
LOYD, Thomas, decd, Ann Loyd, admx, leave to sell land in 18th dist for benefit of heirs, 9/5/1814, Jasper, OM
LOYD, Thomas E., orph of James, decd, John Loyd, gdn, Sarah and James Loyd, Mary Fernander, J.L. Jones, surs, 7/1850, 1851-1854 retns, Fayette, GB
LOYD, Thomas, Jr., decd, 1811 retn, Thomas Noland pd for schooling children; boarding four children from 13 to 8 yrs, boarding two children from 3 to 4 yrs. Ann Loyd hired 4 slaves, James Love hired one,; Ann Loyd, admr, Jasper, Ests
LOYD, Thomas, Jr., decd, 1811 retn, Thomas Noland pd for schooling children; boarding four children from 13 to 8 yrs, boarding two children from 3 to 4 yrs. Ann Loyd hired 4 slaves, James Love hired one,; Ann Loyd, admr, Jasper, Ests
LUCAS, John (Major), decd, James Jackson, admr, 11/25/1789, Chatham, Adms
LUCKETT, William R., decd, Gustus Luckett, admr, 11/7/1831, Martin Griffin, James Dewberry, surs, Warren, AB
LUCKEY, John B., decd, Floyd T. McAlpin, admr, 7/7/1862, H. Hudgens, sur, DeKalb, AB
LUCKIE, William, decd, pet of Jno Wooldridge that decd during life (5/6/1796) conveyed 400 acres to Wm Brown who deeded Wooldridge 10/6/1806; ct ordered James Luckie and Hezekiah Luckie, exrs of est, give title, 7/1809, Oglethorpe, OM
LUCKIE, William F., decd, LWT pvd, L/T issued to Peggy Luckie, 3/2/1818, Jasper, OM
LULLETE, George, decd, John T. Sims, George W. B. Howard, William Heard, admrs 10/5/1835, Harris
LUMDUS, Reubin F., decd, James M. Lumdus, gdn, issued L/D 7/1861, Webster, OD
LUMPKIN, Joseph, decd, William Lumpkin, exr, states that one of witnesses to LWT of his decd father is living in Virginia and asks ct to permit Oglethorpe Co. Clk to give up LWT so that he can take it to Virginia for proving, 7/1809, Oglethorpe, OM
LUMPKIN, Polly, minor and orph of Pittman, decd, John Lester apptd gdn, 1/1804, Oglethorpe, MIC
LUNDAY, Eliza W., gdn, to show cause, p. 133, Screven, OM
LUNDAY, Frances, decd, Macklin Lunday, exr, p. 73, Screven, OM
LUNDAY, Jane, of Effingham Co., makes gift of slave her son, Theophilus Lunday and her dau, Mary E. Lunday of sd co.,3/7/1791, Effingham, Misc
LUNDAY, Robert, William Lunday, gdn, p. 83, Screven, OM
LUNDAY, Theophilus, decd, Mrs. Frances Lunday, relict and admx, applies for dismission 11/27/1801, Effingham, Misc

LUNSFORD, John, decd, J. Lunsford, exr, to divide lands among heirs 12/1873, Webster, OD
LYDD, Isaac, decd, William Cranshaw issued L/A 1/6/1816, Beany Franklin, sec, Morgan, AB
LYNCH, Michael, decd, John and James Lynch qualified as exrs of LWT 1/11/1858, Fulton
LYNCH, Jeter, decd, L/A issued James Hudgins 5/12/1824, Habersham, MIC
LYNER, Adam, decd, LWT names wife, Betsy, father, land on east bank of William Black's; Abner Franklin, Moses Wilcox exrs 7/19/1803, pvd 2/14/1804, Franklin, OM
LYNER, Henry, decd, LWT pvd 7/9/1805, names wife, Margaret; ch: Margaret, Christopher; heirs of son, Adam--Catharine, Eve and Mary, Franklin, IMW
LYON, George, decd, Johnson Lyon, admr, 2/10/1862, F. H. Gay, A. McWilliams, Thomas J. Lyon, James White, surs; James W. Crockett, admr 5/5/1862, Samuel Potts, James C. Avary, surs, DeKalb, AB
LYON, James, decd, Rebecca Lyon, Jonathan Crook issued L/A 3/24/1797, John Smith, Elijah Anderson, secs; Jonathan Crook apptd gdn of Patsy and James, minor orphs, Richmond, AB, GB
LYON, Johnson, decd, John M. Hawkins, admr, 7/7/1862, Allen Wooddall, E. R. Chamberlain, surs, DeKalb, AB
LYON, Rezin, decd, William R. Venable qualified as admr 6/1/1857, dismissed 8/6/1860, Fulton
LYON, Thomas, decd, appr 4/11/1801; purchasers at sale: Betsey Lyon, Joshua Askey, Wm Thornton, Wm Purify, Jesse Blakey, John T. Spencer, Wm Griggs, Arrington Purify, David and Wm Blakey, etc.; Wm Griggs, admr, Hancock, AAAA
LYON, Thomas A., decd, late of Newton Co., LWT presented 9/6/1858, W. W. Ruark and Martha F. Lyon, admrs, w/LWT annexed 6/6/1859, Fulton
LYON, William, decd, late of Edgefield Dist., S. C., Mary Lyon issued L/A 4/19/1814, Michael Collins, Absolom Rhodes, Jr., secs, Richmond, AB
MABRY, Adam, decd, L/A issued Samuel Hix, 3/2/1818, Jasper, OM
MABRY, Daniel, decd, L/A to Margaret Mabry 1/6/1806, Oswell Eve, Wm Bacon, secs; Margaret Mabry, now Margaret Taylor, admx, Richmond, AB
MABRY, Gray, decd, Nathan Hackney issued L/A 9/11/1826, Benjamin M. Peeples, Henry Brown, secs; James Watson, admr de bonis non 12/6/1826, Terry B. Watson, John G. Colbert, Morgan, AB
MABRY, Thomas, minor orph of Adam, decd, chose Parham Mabry for his gdn, 5/1818, Jasper, OM
MABRY, Woodford, decd, Charlotte P. Mabry issued L/A 8/3/1806, Joseph Ashton, Walter Leigh, secs, Richmond, AB
MACK, Francis, decd, Charles Mack, admr, William Daniell, John H. Daniell, sur, 5/6/1822, Emanuel, AB
MACKEY, Alexander, minor over age 14, Freeman Walker, gdn, 1/5/1826, Valentine Walker, sec; 10/7/1823 John Mackey apptd gdn of his brother, Richmond, GB
MACKEY, John, decd, Wilhemina Mackey issued L/A 7/8/1826, J. W. Hunter, H. W. Scovell, secs; 1826 retns mentions prop belonging to John and Alex Mackey, Richmond, AB
MACKIE, Peter, decd, of Augusta, William Mackie issued L/A 11/15/1811, William Ross, Adam Hutcheson, secs; 1812 recpt of Wm Ross, being all due on bro's est, Richmond, AB
MADDEN, Louisa, minor, now residing in Ireland, appraisers apptd for trust prop delivered up by Richard McD. Elliott, resigned Trustee of Madden children, 7/2/1807, Camden, MIC
MADDEN, Mary Eliza, orph of Peter, Thomas Doyle, gdn, had ward restored to him, she being in ct, over age 14, expressing dissatisfaction; admrs to pay his expenses for bringing her to America, 11/2/1805; Isaac Crews apptd gdn 4/15/1807, Camden, MIC

MADDEN, Peter, decd, Davis Lewis and R. McD. Elliott, admrs,
4/1/1805, Camden, MIC
MADDOX, Benjamin, decd, Mary and Joseph Maddox, Sephaniah Harvey,
William Anglin issued L/A 11/5/1810, Putnam, AB
MADDOX, Jacob, decd, Sally and Clayborn Maddox and Ewing Morrow
issued L/A 8/15/1796; 10/4/1796 Mrs. Sarah Maddox and said she
consented for Clayborn Maddox to join her as admr, Greene, Misc
MADDOX, John C., decd, George Lathrum, temp admr, John Lathrum,
T. H. Smithwick, sur, 1/23/1852, Cherokee, AB
MADISON, J. H., inf son of John R., decd, John McIntosh apptd gdn
1/6/1829, Camden, MIC
MADISON, J. R., decd, John H. McIntosh apptd admr w/LWT annexed
1/5/1830, Camden, MIC
MADISON, J. R., decd, LWT pvd 6/4/1822, Camden, MIC
MADISON, John H. M., orph of John R., decd, Gen. Duncan L. Clinch
apptd gdn 1/3/1836, Camden, MIC
MADISON, John R. (Captain), LWT pvd 3/3/1823, Camden, MIC
MADISON, Mariah C., decd, John H. McIntosh apptd admr, 3/3/1823,
Camden, MIC
MAFFETT, John, decd, William J. Woodwad, admr, James W. Wilson,
sur, Gwinnett, AB
MAGBEE, Rachel, decd, E. W. Lane, Labon Magbee, exrs, sold 50
acres on Tussahaw Cr., negroes to: Jesse T. Gunn, Mrs. McCord,
John Hendrick, James Apperson, Hiram Magbee, Wm H. Wyatt, Labon
Magbee, 12/8/1835, Butts, ER
MAGEE, Hugh, decd, Holland McTyeire apptd gdn of minor orph-Hugh,
Richmond, GB
MAGEE, Mary, decd, Holland McTyeire issued L/A 2/2/1822,
Richmond, AB
MAGEHEE, Nathan, decd, LWT pvd by Jesse McGehee 10/29/1803,
Jackson, OM
MAGNAN, Claudius, decd, Louis Poisson issued L/A 1/9/1812, John
D'Antignac, Anthony Labuzan, secs, Richmond, AB
MAGUIRE, John J., decd, Thomas Maguire, John H. Mecaslin, admrs,
J. H. Maguire, David Anderson, sur, 5/3/1875, Gwinnett, AB
MAHAN, Benjamin L., illegitimate son of Margaret, Robert Mahan
apptd gdn 8/7/1827, dismissed 5/4/1829, Habersham, MIC
MAHARRY, John, decd, Charity Maharry L/A 1/4/1826; 1827 retns;
heirs-Jos. P., Robt, Wm H. Malina & Cornelia & Mary Shelton
(formerly Maharry); pd Henry Merritt, rt of wf, Malvina, Wm H.
Maharry, tr for Mrs. Cornelia A. Green, Richmond, AB
MALLONE, William, orph of George, decd, Josiah Drew, gdn, James
Waller, John Chasan, sur, 7/6/1829, Emanuel, GB
MALLORY, Alzira Amanda, orph of William, decd, Elizabeth Mallory
apptd gdn, Reubin W. Mallory, Shelton W. Moore, sec, 9/4/1848,
Troup, GB
MALLORY, Jasper Newton, orph of William, decd, Elizabeth Mallory
apptd gdn, Reubin W. Mallory, Shelton W. Moore, sec, 9/4/1848,
Troup, GB
MALONE, Emily, orph of John A., decd, Martha Malone, gdn, Henry
S. Lee, Charles Wakefield, Thomas B. Burford, sur, 1/14/1845,
Butts, GB
MALONE, George, decd, ordered that list of sales made by admrs be
submitted to clk 1/7/1822, Jasper, OM
MALONE, Gilbert, orph of George, decd, Frances Malone apptd gdn
12/14/1818, Jasper, OM
MALONE, John, decd, Daniel Savage apptd gdn of minor orph: Mary
Agnes, James R. Danforth, Edmund B. Glascock, secs, Richmond, GB
MALONE, John, decd, Jr., inv, apprs: William Giles, Spencer
Maddox, Wm Vickers 4/13/1830; purchasers at sale 5/8/1830: John
Malone, Sr., Augustus Wise, Butts, ER

MALONE, John A., decd, Martha Malone and Britton Buttrill, exrs, files retn, Butts, ER
MALONE, Martha, orph of John A., decd, Martha Malone, gdn, Henry S. Lee, Charles Wakefield, Thomas B. Burford, sur, 1/14/1845, Butts, GB
MALONE, Nancy, minor dau of George, decd, Daniel McDowell apptd gdn 12/14/1818, Jasper, OM
MALONE, Peter, a mulatto boy, son of Molley, a free white woman, bound to Baynes Bridges, farmer, until 21. Peter is now said to be 12 mos old the 29th day of last April, 9/1806, Oglethorpe, OM
MALONE, Sarah, orph of John A., decd, Martha Malone, gdn, Henry S. Lee, Charles Wakefield, Thomas B. Burford, sur, 1/14/1845, Butts, GB
MALONEY, Patrick, decd, John Griffin, admr, Benjamin Pitard, sur, 8/30/1788, Chatham, Adms
MALPASS, Morris, decd, Francis Spears issued L/A 9/2/1833, Washington
MALSBY, John, decd, Marshall Malsby, Mariah Malsby, admrs, Willis H. Hughes, William H. McCarthy, sur, 7/19/1847, Bibb, AB
MAN, Josiah, decd, LWT signed 3/7/1783, wife Milley, pvd 3/17/1783, Wilkes, MxR
MANDERS, James, decd, Nancy Manders, admx, R. F. Daniel, sur, 3/6/1854, Cherokee, AB
MANGHN, Sarah E., orph of William, decd, John W. Mitchell, Julia C. B. Mitchell, Gordon Mitchell, admr, 11/2/1835, Harris
MANGUM, James, decd, S. A. Mangum issued L/A 4/5/1863, Fulton
MANGUNS, Robert C., decd, Thomas W. J. Hill, admr w/LWT annexed 7/9/1864, Fulton
MANLEY, Isaac D., decd, L/A issued Daniel Manley w/LWT annexed 3/3/1812, Franklin, OM
MANN, Daniel, decd, Darius Woodworth apptd admr 11/6/1815, Camden, MIC
MANN, Jesse, decd, Thomas Watts issued L/A 7/3/1826, William Stocks, sec, Morgan, AB
MANN, John, decd, Luke Mann for self and est vs. Wm Clark of Clark, Telfair & Co., 11/1793, Bryan, Writs
MANN, John, decd, Luke Mason, exr of LWT 7/1/1789, Chatham, Adms
MANN, John, decd, Andrew G. Semmes issued L/A 3/13/1818, John Starnes, Wm Jones, secs; 3/9/1818 Augustin Slaughter and Charles Labuzan apptd gdns of: Thomas, Emily, Mary, Martha, Sarah, Ann, William and John, minor orphs, Richmond, AB, GB
MANN, Peter, Sidney D. Mann, admr de bonis non, Reuben Wallis, sur, 5/1854, Fayette, AB
MANN, Sarah, decd, Gideon F., exr, 1/1854, Fayette, AB
MANNING, Benjamin, decd, Ambrose Manning, Solomon Manning, admrs, George W. Cook, John R. Galt, sur, 3/12/1849, Cherokee, AB
MANNING, K. G., decd, temp L/A issued James Manning 12/11/1890, Twiggs, Misc
MANNING, Mary, decd, LWT pvd 4/7/1852 by Allen Lawhon, Saml McCanless names mother, Ruth Manning; niece, Mary Antionette Timmons; bro, Ambrose Manning; neph, Ambrose Alexander Timmons; niece, Ruth Timmons; Ambrose Manning, exr, Cherokee
MANNING, Reuben H., decd, Mary Manning, admx, Arthur T. Camp, George McCollum, sec, 9/4/1848, Cherokee, AB
MANNING, William J., orphan of John P., decd, John F. Caldwell, gdn, Thomas P. Floyd, Simeon Pitts, sec, 1/10/1848, Troup, GB
MANORS, John T., John H. Hanson, gdn, 1/3/1837, Hall, GB
MANSELL, John, decd, Lemuel J. and Samuel Mansell, admrs, 7/3/1848, Cherokee, AB
MANSFIELD, Frederick, Sr., decd, John Mansfield applies for L/A 3/29/1859, Frederick Mansfield, sur, Lee

MAPP, Jeremiah, decd, 7/1812 Isaac McClendon gtd L/A; Elizabeth
Mapp took child s pt 2/1813; inventory made by William Traylor,
F. T. Traylor and John McMichael; 1812 ann retn made by Isaac
Jackson and Isaac McClendon, admrs, Jasper, Ests
MAPP, Littleton, decd, Anna Mapp issued L/A 3/19/1817, Isham L.
Farmer, sec, Morgan, AB
MAPP, William, decd, LWT dtd 5/14/1799 pvd 9/2/1799 by Elam Ward,
"to care of my father", bro., Howsin Mapp, bro., Jeremiah; exrs,
father, Littleton Mapp Sr. and Howson Mapp, Hancock, AA
MAPPIN, Thomas W., decd, James W. Mappin, admr, 6/7/1852, E.
Perryman, sur, DeKalb, AB
MARABLE, Erasmus, orph of John, decd, John Gordine, gdn 3/7/1818,
Walton Harris, Matthew Marable, surs; Lucy Marable, gdn 1/4/1819,
Clarke, GB
MARABLE, George, orph of John, decd, John Gordine, gdn 3/7/1818,
Walton Harris, Matthew Marable, sur; Lucy Marable, gdn 1/4/1819,
Clarke, GB
MARABLE, John, decd, Leander A. Erwin, Matthew and Lucy Marable,
admrs, bond 2/3/1817, John Johnson Cox, John Gerdine, surs,
Clarke, AB
MARABLE, John, decd, William Stock issued L/A 3/22/1827, Benjamin
S. Ogletree, Thomas Watts, secs, Morgan, AB
MARABLE, John, orph of John, decd, 3/2/1818 Samuel Brown, gdn,
Thomas Mitchell, James M. Burton, surs, Clarke, GB
MARBURG, Mary, decd, L/T gtd Elizabeth Bass 5/12/1820, Jasper, OM
MARBURTON, Thomas, decd, Sarah Marburton issued L/A w/LWT annexed
9/16/1817, Drewry Rogers, sec, Morgan, AB
MARBURY, Leonard, decd, George N. Lyles issued L/A 6/1/1807;
George N. Lyles, admr, asks to be dismissed 5/1/1809, Jackson, OM
MARBUT, Young J., decd, Samuel F. Alexander, admr, 7/4/1859, J.
J. Diamond, sur, DeKalb, AB
MARKS, Joseph, decd, Mary Marks, admx, 2/7/1814, Edwin Baker,
Solomon Ogden, Wm Teddlie, Ansel McKinney, surs, Warren, AB
MARKS, Polly, legatee of Martha Harvee, decd, John H. Marks apptd
gdn, 1/1804, Oglethorpe, MIC
MARLER, John, decd, Ann Marler, admr 1/4/1836, Camden, MIC
MARNOCK, Mathew, decd, a traveller in Pendleton Co., S. C.,
Robert Marnock applied for L/A 12/25/1794, Greene, Misc
MARONEY, William D., decd, T. D. Evans, admr, John T. Dickerson,
sur, 6/13/1859, Cherokee, AB
MARS, Morgan, decd, of Liberty Co., Ann Mars, admx, no date,
Bryan, CR
MARSHALL, M. H. and J. G., minors, Mary E. Marshall makes retns
as gdn, 7/1863, Webster, OD
MARSHALL, M. T., decd, Mathew T. Marshall issued L/A 6/1862,
Webster, OD
MARSHALL, Robert, decd, John Moore issued L/A 11/17/1795, Henry
Crutcher, Angus Martin, secs, Richmond, AB
MARSHALL, William, decd, LWT pvd 12/1873, Webster, OD
MARTAIN, Betty, decd, inv 10/27/1782, apprs: Ambrose Downs, John
Herinton, Wilkes, MxR
MARTAIN, George, decd, Elizabeth Martain, wid, apptd admx
10/14/1782, Wilkes, MxR
MARTAIN, George, decd, Levina issued L/A 2/5/1810, Laurens, AB
MARTIN, Aaron, orph, Almarin Dillard issued L/G 9/5/1831,
Washington
MARTIN, Bird, decd, Elizabeth Martin issued L/A 3/20/1815, Thomas
Cobb, Peter Donaldson, secs; div 3/30/1821, heirs-Smith, Eliza
Eleanor, Charles and Washington Martin; Mrs. Martin, wid,and C.
L. Acee in rt of wf, Martha, Richmond, AB
MARTIN, Charles C., decd, James Galaway qualified as exr
2/11/1806, Franklin, OM

MARTIN, Charles, decd, George J. S. Walker issued L/A 3/8/1830, George A. B. Walker, sec, Richmond, AB
MARTIN, Clement, decd, Richard Leake qualified admr 7/2/1783, dismissed 5/11/1785, Liberty, Ests
MARTIN, Clement, Jr., decd, late of Effingham Co., Mrs. Elizabeth Nowlan, wid, applies for adm 3/5/1799; William Lister Hill applies for admr de bonis non 1/8/1801, Effingham, Misc
MARTIN, Eliza, decd, of Providence, Henry Beacham, admr 1/1842; apprs: Michael Duskin, Jordan Hodges, William Bartlett, John Crocker; purchasers at sale: Harvey Bartlett, Charles, Chestnut, Samuel Etheridge, etc., Stewart, Adms
MARTIN, Elizabeth, decd, LWT pvd 7/1832 names ch: Allan V., Philip, John W., James, Wm T.; to William Torry, children of decd dau, Charlotte; grsons: George H., son of Philip, James V., John and William, sons of Allan V., Habersham, MIC
MARTIN, Elmira (Mrs.), decd, William A. Martin issued L/A 12/4/1865, Fulton
MARTIN, Geofrey, decd, John Dean, Francis Martin, admrs, Bradford Peddy, Wood Moreland, sur, 10/22/1811, Jones, AB
MARTIN, Gideon, decd, David Martin issued L/A 3/7/1841, B. Dunagan, William T. Brazel, secs, Hall, AB
MARTIN, Henry, decd, David Downie issued L/A 6/8/1808, George Adams, Geo. Smith Houston, secs; inv shows plantation in Colleton Dist., S. C.; div 1815--Mrs. Garus (wid of decd) Mary Maria, John Henry and Sarah Margaret Martin, Richmond, AB
MARTIN, Henry, decd, Lewis Linder, gdn of orphs: Mary Mariah, above 14 yrs, and Sarah Margaret, under 14 yrs, 3/6/1815, Laurens, GB
MARTIN, Henry, decd, Wesley S. Bagley issued temp L/A, Newton McDill, James E. Bagley, sur, 9/19/1855, Cherokee, AB
MARTIN, Isaac D. N., decd, L/A gtd James Lanier and Absalom Kennedy, Welcome Parks, Moses Rosser, secs, 11/4/1822, Jasper, OM
MARTIN, James C., decd, 7/1843; apprs: John Rice, J. L. B. and Michael Duskin, Stewart, Adms
MARTIN, John, decd, Eliza J. Martin, admr, E. L. Dillard, Charles Walker, sur, 3/7/1847, Bibb, AB
MARTIN, John, decd, L/A issued Elizabeth Martin, wid, 7/1/1811; Simon Terrell apptd gdn of orphs: Van Allen, Phillip, Charlotte, James Van, John Washington and William Terrell Martin 11/1/1811, Franklin, OM
MARTIN, John, decd, LWT pvd by Green W. Smith 10/4/1831, names wife, Milly, all property, "my children", Habersham, MIC
MARTIN, John, minor, Lewis Linder, gdn, 11/10/1823, Laurens, GB
MARTIN, Jonathan, Sr., decd, Jonathan Martin issued L/A 8/2/1852, William S. Barton, Jefferson Saye, John Harris, E. J. Dunagan, secs, Hall, AB
MARTIN, Margaret, orph of Thomas, decd, Bryant Daugherty, gdn, 9/6/1841, Emanuel, GB
MARTIN, Mary, orph of Thomas, decd, Bryant Daughtery, gdn, Ellington Willis, sur, 9/2/1839, Emanuel, GB
MARTIN, Mary, minor of Thomas, decd, Littleton Deakle, gdn, John Gillis, Solomon Williamson, sur, 9/3/1849, Emanuel, GB
Martin, Mary, or Peddy, Wood Moreland, sur, 10/22/1811, Jones, AB
MARTIN, Matilda Russell, bastard child, Tabitha Martin apptd gdn 11/2/1812, Barnabas Barron, sec, Jackson, OM
MARTIN, Murdock, decd, Nathaniel Smith issued L/A 1/11/1847, E. M. Johnson, sec; Katherine Martin, gdn of orphs: Griffin and Elizabeth 1/11/1847, George W. Money, Willis Martin, secs, Hall, AB, GB
MARTIN, Peter, decd, Col. William Melton, Elizabeth Martin, Jesse Standifer applied for L/A 11/4/1796; appr 3/1/1797 mentions 550 acres in Elbert Co., Greene, Misc

MARTIN, Rachael, decd, Mel M. Mathews, admr, Samuel Kislin, sur, 6/1854, Fayette, AB
MARTIN, Richard, decd, LWT pvd 5/6/1839, Green and John Martin, exrs, Washington
MARTIN, Samuel, decd, Andrew McBride, admr, Edward Conner, sur, 3/1854, Fayette, AB
MARTIN, Thomas, Margret, orph of Thomas, decd, Brian Daughtery, gdn, Ellington Willis, sur, 9/2/1839, Emanuel, GB
MARTIN, Thomas, decd, Cassa Martin, admx, James Scarborough, Ashford Jenkins, sur, 7/1/1833, Emanuel, AB
MARTIN, Thomas, decd, Green B. Ball, admr 4/1839; apprs: Howell Vaughn, Anderson Burns, James Mathews, Joseph Williams, Matthew Wright; purchasers at sale: Henry Bartlett, Jared Brunsen, Seymour Catchings, etc., Stewart, Adms
MARTIN, Thomas, decd, William Proctor, admr, appr 8/22/1833, Emanuel, A
MARTIN, William J., decd, John W. Martin, admr, David Hamilton, sur, 10/2/1871, Gwinnett, AB
MARTIN, Wright, decd, James L. Hobgood, admr de bonis non, Nathan Camp, Lewis Hobgood, surs, 1/1851, 1851, 1853 retns, Fayette, AB
MARTINLEER, George W., orph of William, decd, Richard Gordon issued L/G 9/5/1831, Washington
MASHBURN, Henry, James J. Oliver, gdn, Dooly, OD
MASHBURN, Jefferson, decd, Joseph Mashburn, Joseph Weldon, admrs, 9/14/1835, Harris
MASON, Ann (Mrs.), decd, LWT pvd 5/4/1863, Maria T. C. Mason, extrx, Fulton
MASON, Charles, decd, Alexander M. Mason, admr w/LWT annexed, James P. Phillips, sur, 6/5/1876, Gwinnett, AB
MASON, George, decd, L/A issued to John F. Mason 1/9/1843, Washington
MASON, James, decd, James A. Fowler issued temp L/A 5/6/1856, Joseph L. Jones, sur; perm L/A issued 11/10/1856, N. J. Garrison, sur, Cherokee, AB
MASON, James, decd, James Hicks issued L/A 1829, Washington
MASON, Madison, orph of James, decd, George Mason issued L/G 5/7/1832, Washington
MASON, Miles, orph of James, decd, George Mason issued L/G 5/7/1832, Washington
MASON, Morris R., orph of James, decd, George Mason issued L/G 5/7/1832, Washington
MASON, Pellina, orph of James, decd, George Mason issued L/G 5/7/1832, Washington
MASON, Sarah Ann, orph of James, decd, George Mason issued L/G 5/7/1832, Washington
MASON, William, decd, Edward Rowell issued L/A 7/16/1814, Patrick Kelly, sec, Richmond, AB
MASSAULT, Francis, decd, late of St. Marys, Merchant, M. F. D. Petit Devillers, temp admr, gtd leave to sell prop, 12/8/1806; William Gibson pvd LWT and qualified as exr 1/7/1807; F. Pelot Devillers applied for L/A w/LWT annexed in place of William Gibson, 1/3/1809, Camden, MIC
MASSEY, Artemessa, orph of Sampson, decd, George W. Massey issued L/G 1/13/1840, Washington
MASSEY, Baldwin S., orph of Sampson, decd, George W. Massey issued L/G 1/13/1840, Washington
MASSEY, Joseph, decd, John Graves qualified admr 1/24/1785, Liberty, Ests
MASSEY, Robert L., orph of Sampson, decd, George W. Massey issued L/G 1/13/1840, Washington
MATHESON, Duncan, decd, Alex. Matheson issued L/A 4/26/1813, Peter Bennock, William Ross, secs, Richmond, AB

MATHEWS, Charles, decd, temp L/A issued Timothy and Jesse Mathews 2/15/1821, Benjamin Fitzpatrick, secs; Timothy Matthews, gdn of orphs 1/6/1823: Sarah, Margaret, Jesse, Lewis Brantley, sec, Morgan, AB, GB
MATHEWS, Edmund (Rev.), decd, Allen P. Powell qualified exr of LWT 5/6/1828, Glynn, MIC
MATHEWS, Emily, orph of John, decd, Daniel Hanes issued L/G 7/23/1838, Washington
MATHEWS, Ferelia, orph of John, decd, Morris Walden issued L/G 1/11/1836, Washington
MATHEWS, Galba, decd, J. M. W. Peel, Anderson C. Mathews, admr 11/1839; apprs: James Wilson, David Cody, Sampson Bell, Joseph Wood; decd owned 20 slaves, 1405 acres, Stewart, Adms
MATHEWS, Isaac, decd, Loftin Nuthercut, William Davis, B. Johnson, gdn of orphs 1/3/1837, Harris
MATHEWS, Jesse, decd, John Emerson, gdn, 1/6/1823 of orphs: Almira and Betsey, Bennett Fitzpatrick, sec, Morgan, GB
MATHEWS, Jesse, decd, Reuben Massey issued L/A 2/14/1821, James Hill, sec, AB
MATHEWS, John, Henry J. Mathews, gdn, 1/6/1823, J. Fitzpatrick, Instant H. Gilbert, secs, Morgan, GB
MATHEWS, John, decd, LWT pvd 7/7/1834, James Gamis, John J. Long, Charles J. Jenkins, exrs, Washington
MATHEWS, John H., Samuel Kisler, gdn, Allen Reeves, no date, Fayette, AB
MATHEWS, Lodiwick, decd, Giles Mozingo issued L/A 1/14/1839, applied 9/1843 for L/D, legal notice given in Sandersville Telescope, Washington
MATHEWS, Margaret, orph of John, decd, Morris Walden issued L/G 1/11/1836, Washington
MATHEWS, Mary, orph of John, decd, Morris Walden issued L/G 1/11/1836, Washington
MATHEWS, Milly, orph of John, decd, Morris Walden issued L/G 1/11/1836, Washington
MATHEWS, Moses, decd, Methodist Minister, of Roanoke, William A. Mathews, John T. B. Turner, admrs 3/1836, Frederick D. Wimberly, sur on bond; apprs: Moses P. Willis, Drury M. Leseur, Allen Turrentine, David W. Lowe, Stewart, AB
MATHEWS, Robert C., decd, Thomas and Mary Mathews, admrs 7/1832, Fayette, AB
MATHEWS, William R., orph of John, ded, James H. Gilmore issued L/G 9/10/1843, Washington
MATHIS, Caroline, orph of John, decd, L/G issued Lewis Dupree 1/3/1832, Washington
MATHIS, Clarissa B., orph of John, decd, L/G issued Lewis Dupree 1/3/1832, Washington
MATHIS, David A., decd, Martha A. Mathis, admx, John P. Rhine, sur, 10/20/1859, Cherokee, AB
MATHIS, Elizabeth N., orph of John, decd, L/G issued Lewis Dupree 1/3/1832, Washington
MATHIS, Jarrett, orph, Joseph Mashburn, J. Weldon, gdns 12/14/1835, Harris, Gb
MATHIS, Jefferson, decd, Joseph Mashburn, Joseph Weldon, admrs, 1/14/1835, Harris, AB
MATHIS, Jeremiah, orph of Jarrett, decd, John E. Jones, gdn, Aldon Mickelberry, Robert R. Saunders, Isaac Low, John W. Williams, surs, 1/12/1836, Butts, GB
MATHIS, Jesse M., orph of Jarrett, decd, John E. Jones, gdn, Aldon Mickelberry, Robert R. Saunders, Isaac Low, John W. Williams, surs, 1/12/1836, Butts, GB
MATHIS, John, decd, L/A issued to Lewis Dupree 1829, Washington

MATHIS, Jubel, orph of Jarrett, decd, John E. Jones, gdn, Alden
Mickelberry, Robert R. Saunders, Isaac Low, John W. Williams,
surs, 1/12/1836, GB
MATHIS, Rebecca T., orph of John, decd, L/G issued Lewis Dupree
1/3/1832, Washington
MATHIS, Sarah C., orph of John, decd, L/G issued Lewis Dupree
1/3/1832, Washington
MATHIS, William R., orph of John, decd, L/G issued Lewis Dupree
1/2/1832, Washington
MATTHEWS, Arthur, decd, Edward Matthews, admr 12/2/1828, William
Castleberry, Francis Hardaway, surs, Warren, AB
MATTHEWS, James, decd, Charles Matthews, gdn of orphs--Charles,
Nancy, Caroline, Susan 7/7/1817; Reuben Massey, gdn 1/1/1821,
Morgan, GB
MATTHEWS, Jesse P., orph of Jesse, decd, Zachariah Fears, gdn,
1/9/1826, Morgan, GB
MATTHEWS, John, decd, Mary Matthews issued L/A 12/9/1787, Daniel
McNeill, Andrew Danielly, secs, Richmond, AB
MATTHEWS, J. W., decd, Mrs. Priscilla Thomas says that decd was
indebted to her for $25 for services in last illness and that he
left only his wearing apparel in her house; Sheriff directed to
sell same 6/21/1830, Camden, MIC
MATTHEWS, Morris, decd, Morton Bledsoe, admr, John Hay, James R.
McCord, surs, 8/11/1838, Butts, AB
MATTHEWS, Thomas, decd, Elizabeth A. Matthews issued L/A
9/28/1824, Benjamin F. Lyon, John N. Philpot, secs, Richmond, AB
MATTHEWS, William, decd, late of South Carolina, William Garrett
issued L/A 6/6/1803, Nicholas and Matthew Fox, secs, Richmond, AB
MATTHEWS, William A. apptd gdn of his child, William B. 2/7/1853,
Houston, GB
MATTOCKS, Michael McKenzie, decd, John Mattocks and Elijah
Mattocks qualified as exrs of LWT 1/1816, Tattnall, MIC
MATTOX, Aaron, decd, est appraised 10/7/1836 by James Underwood,
Albert Duke, Archibald Hodges, Tattnall, I&A
MATTOX, John, decd, est appraised by Henry Strickland, J. B.
Stripling, Shadrack Hancock 8/25/1836, Tattnall, I&A
MAXWELL, Ann (Mrs.), decd, John Floyd, exr, filed retn 4/12/1808,
dismissed as exr 1/3/1809, Camden, MIC
MAXWELL, James B. (Major), decd, Ann Maria, widow, admx, 1808,
Bryan, CR
McAFEE, Abram, decd, Jesse Roberts, gdn of orphs: Morgan, Mary
Ann and Abram, 5/3/1824, Morgan, GB
McAFEE, Green, decd, Joel Crawford, Joseph Beavers, Matthew Lyle,
apprs; Phebe McAfee, admx, 3/7/1814, Jasper, WAR
McAFEE, Green, decd, L/A gtd Filery McAfee, Abraham McAfee and
Jonathan Anderson, John Bohannon, James Richards, surs, 1813;
William Armstrong issued L/A 1/6/1817, Jasper, OM
McAFEE, Morgan, decd, LWT pvd 1/12/1840, L. G. Sholard, Jess
Roberts, exrs, Harris
McALLISTER, Charles C., minor orph of Henry S., decd, Mrs. Aury
Whitehead, gdn, 6/4/1860, Fulton, GB
McALLISTER, James, decd, Matthew Nelson issued L/A 11/3/1835,
Green B. Marshall, sec; 1837 retn shows E. L. Scott, gdn for
Sarah Jane McAllister, Richmond, AB
McAlPIN, James M., decd, John W. Scruggs, admr, 6/3/1861, F. M.
Allen, sur, DeKalb, AB
McALPIN, Robert, decd, Solomon and Alexander McAlpin, admrs,
9/8/1804 bond, Peter McAlpin, John Forther, surs, Clarke, AB
McARTHUR, John, decd, LWT dtd 2/1/1833, pvd 3/4/1839, names wife,
Mary and ch: John, Dunkin, Margaret McKinnon, and Alexander,
Tattnall, I&A

McBRIDE, Andrew J., minor of William, Marcelus K. McIntosh, gdn, A. C. McIntosh, sur, 6/1853, Fayette, GB
McBRIDE, Lochland S., minor of William, Marcelus K. McIntosh, gdn, A. C. McIntosh, sur, 6/1853, Fayette, GB
McCAFFERTY, John, decd, Jeremiah Morris, gdn of orphs: John and James, 9/8/1829, Benjamin Brantley, sec, Richmond, GB
McCALL, John E., decd, inv and appr by James Rawls, General Lee, John Mikell, 1/20/1827; div 6/5/1835, lots to: Sarah E. McCall, Margaret Mikell, John M. McCall, Hannah E. McCall, Bulloch, Misc
McCALL, William, decd, James W. Shine issued L/A 12/3/1810, Laurens, AB
McCALLAY, James, orph of William, decd, Susan McCallay apptd gdn, Benjamin Cleveland, sur, 3/6/1848, Troup, GB
McCALLISTER, Avalina, orph of John, decd, bound to Isaac M. D. Martin, 9/1820, Jasper, OM
McCALLISTER, Henry, orph of John, decd, bound to Isaac M. D. Martin, 9/1820, Jasper, OM
McCALLUM, James, decd, Archibald Jamieson issued L/A 8/7/1795, Richmond, AB
McCANNON, James, decd, pet of Winfield Shropshire that during decd's lifetime he executed bond of 300# for 400 acres, but failed to give title to 200 acres; ct ordered Susannah McCannon, admx, to make title, 1/18/1810, Oglethorpe, OM
McCARREL, Fanny, infant bastard child, Battle Mayfield apptd gdn 8/1/1814, Jackson, OM
McCARTNEY, John, minor and orph of James, decd, John Wallace apptd gdn, William McCree, David Killough, surs, Oglethorpe, MIC
McCARTNEY, Nancy, minor and orph of James, decd, John Wallace apptd gdn, William McCree, David Killough, surs, Oglethorpe, MIC
McCARTNEY, Nancy, orph of Daniel, decd, Johnson Clarke apptd gdn, 6/1794, Oglethorpe, MIC
McCARTNEY, Polly, minor orph of James, decd, William McCree, gdn, John Wallace and Spencer Reynolds, surs, 6/1795, Oglethorpe, MIC
McCARTIN, Francis, decd, McCarton Campbell issued L/A 1/5/1793, Dalziel Hunter, sec, Richmond, AB
McCARTY, Dennis, decd, David Martin, admr, William L. Wilson, sur, 7/30/1836; 1839 retn by admr, Butts, AB
McCASKELL, John, decd, Elizabeth McCaskell issued L/A 8/28/1818, James McLaws, William Lamkin, secs, Richmond, AB
McCAUGHMAN, Josiah, orph of Drury, decd, be bound to Thomas Ray 1/1820, Jasper, OM
McCLAIN, Ephraim, Sr., E. F. Starr apptd gdn 12/6/1858, J. L. Richardson, sec, White, GB
McCLAIN, Susannah (Mrs.), decd, Claiborn Wright apptd admr 6/4/1822, Camden, MIC
McCLANE, Daniel, decd, John Wilson of Richmond Co., planter, apptd admr 11/30/1782, Wilkes, MxR
McCLARY, Robert, decd, Thomas and James Cameron apply for L/A 11/29/1791; John Hawthorne, John Cameron, apprs, Elbert, AB
McCLEAN, James, minor orph of Lewis, decd, bound to Timothy Duck 1/7/1817, Jasper, OM
McCLEAN, William, minor orph of Lewis, decd, bound to Timothy Duck 1/7/1817, Jasper, OM
McCLENDON, Allen, decd, William F. Mapp, admr, Mary S. McClendon, William Ham, Pouncey Maxey, John Ham, John W. Phillips, sur, 12/14/1835; appraisal 12/23/1835, Wm F. Mapp, admr; 1836, plantation, Mary S. McClendon; mill, J. M. McClendon; Towaliga plantation, J. J. Mapp; 20 acres, S. W. Thaxton; Zebulon prop, Pike Co., J. Smith, George Jordan; retn of William F. Mapp, admr, 1838; pd John N. McCune, A. L. Robinson, J. A. Fellows, James H. Stark, Samuel Ridgeway, Thomas Wilson, Mary S. McClendon, Egbert P. Daniel, Samuel Snoddy (for Jeremiah P.); 1839 pd Jeptha

McClendon, Peter W. Welton, Wm Pryor, Nicholas Purifoy, Eli
Parks, John McCord, S. T. Bailey, Butts, AB, ER
McCLENDON, Daniel, idiot, retn of est, pd Nancy McClendon, John
McCord, Goodman & Andrews, John Goodman, gdn, 4/4/1840, Butts, ER
McCLENDON, Daniel, minor lunatic orph of Wiley F., decd, John
Goodman, gdn, John Hendrick, sur, 5/8/1836, Butts, GB
McCLENDON, Jeremiah P., O. H. P. McClendon, gdn, retn from
3/16/1814, Butts, ER
McCLENDON, Jeremiah P., orph of Allen, decd, Samuel Snoddy, gdn,
William Stroud, James Harkness, sur, 12/16/1837; Oliver H. P.
McClendon, gdn, William F. Map, John Goodman, sur, 7/1/1839, Butts, GB
McCLENDON, Joel, decd, Lucy McClendon, admx, John G. Cooke,
Thomas McClendon, sur, 2/11/1813, Jones, AB
McCLENDON, Joseph, orph of Allen, decd, William F. Mapp, gdn,
Isaac Low, James W. Harkness, Mary S. McClendon, Samuel Snoddy,
sur, 12/16/1837, Butts, GB
McCLENDON, Joseph F., retn of William F. Mapp, gdn, for 1838-9,
4/3/1840, Butts, ER
McCLENDON, Oliver H. P., orph of Allen, decd, William F. Mapp,
gdn, Isaac Low, James W. Harkness, Mary S. McClendon, Samuel
Snoddy, sur, 12/16/1837; retn of William F. Mapp, gdn, 1838,
Butts, GB, ER
McCLENDON, Wiley F., decd, L/A issued Allen McClendon, Jonathan
McClendon, with Isaac McClendon, Etheldred McClendon and Jesse
Loyall, surs, 9/29/1821, Jasper, QM
McCLENDON, William, retn of William F. Mapp, gdn, for 1838-9,
4/3/1840, Butts, ER
McCLENDON, William C., orph of Allen, decd, William F. Mapp, gdn,
Isaac Low, John Goodman, sur, 12/16/1837, Butts, GB
McCLEOD, John, decd, John McCleod, admr, 8/20/1785, Chatham, Adms
McCLESKEY, James J., a poor orph of co., son of Sally, decd,
Jesse Holcomb, gdn, 10/6/1854, Alexander Deal, sec, Hall, GB
McCleskey, James, decd, David H. McCleskey issued L/A 12/6/1842,
James R. and J. H. McCleskey, H. Jarrett, secs, Hall, AB
McCLESKY, David G., William H. McClesky apptd gdn, Solomon W.
Peek, sur, 6/6/1853, Cherokee, GB
McCLOUD, Mary Ann, William Finley, gdn, William Phillips, sur,
9/7/1838, Emanuel, GB
McCLUNG, J., decd, John C. Mason issued L/A 1/15/1808, Putnam, AB
McCLUNG, Reuben, an incompetent and imbecile, Samuel B. L. C.
McClung apptd gdn, James Stewart, Paulding, GB
McCLUNG, William, decd, John Carson issued L/A 7/29/1786, Richard
Bonner, James Wooten, sec, Richmond, AB
McCLURE, Robert B., decd, John A. McClure, David J. Roe, admrs,
Stephen Cantrell, Robert N. McClure, surs on bond 12/9/1859;
Robert N. McClure, Stephen Cantrell bound unto John A. McClure &
David J. Roe, admrs, 3/21/1860, condition that sd McClure & Roe
deliver to Robert N. McClure his sh of land and negroes, it being
1/5th, Dawson, WB
McCLURE, William, decd, late of Charleston, S. C., merchant,
William Muir produced LWT, it having been probated S. C.
10/14/1813, Muir, one of exrs, 12/4/1813, Camden, MIC
McCOLLUM, George W., decd, James A. Maddox, George W. Cook,
admrs, 12/6/1852, John C. Maddox, sur; Margery McCollum, admx,
Daniel H. McCollum, sur, 6/8/1857, Cherokee, AB
McCOMMON, James, minor orph of Peggy Hunter, decd, Richard Bailey
apptd gdn, Alex Gordon, Henry Bailey, surs, 6/21/1803,
Oglethorpe, MIC
McCONNAY, McCenay, or Mackenay, Ruth McConnay, wid, apptd admx
10/11/1782, Wilkes, MxR

205

McCOOMBS, Robert, decd, John McCoombs issued L/A 1/14/1833; 1834 retns pd Wm Glover, gdn of Martha Coombs; Upson Co., Sarah Bozeman gives p/a to father, Etheldred Bozeman to collect from exr of LWT of her aunt, Sarah Hunster, Richmond, AB

McCORD, Abram, decd, Robert McCord apptd gdn of orphs: James, Nancy and Polly 1802, Jackson, OM

McCORD, James A., James R. McCord made gdn of his son, John Goodman, sur, 11/17/1845, Butts, GB

McCORD, John William, James R. McCord made gdn of his son, John Goodman, sur, 11/17/1845, Butts, GB

McCORD, Mary Ann, James R. McCord made gdn of his dau, John Goodman, sur, 11/17/1845, Butts, GB

McCORD, Rutha Emeline, James R. McCord made gdn of his dau, John Goodman, sur, 11/17/1845, Butts, GB

McCORMICK, John, decd, John and Ann Read issued L/A 11/4/1784, John Germany, John Peek, secs, Richmond, AB

McCOWEN, Betsy Ann, orph of William D., decd, William McCowen, gdn, 9/16/1822, John W. McCowen, sec, Morgan, GB

McCOWEN, Daniel, decd, John Myhan issued L/A 3/4/1816, Nathan Hackney, sec; Alvan Myhand issued L/A 9/7/1817, John Gilpin, sec, Morgan, AB

McCOWEN, Jimason M., orph of Noble, decd, Joseph Harris, gdn, 7/6/1818, Morgan, GB

McCOWEN, Mayberry, orph of Noble, decd, Alexander M. Brown, gdn, 5/11/1821, Morgan, GB

McCOWEN, William D., decd, William McCowen and J. Johnston issued L/A 5/27/1821, Morgan, AB

McCOY, Charles, decd, John Burkhalter, admr, 3/1/1824, Moses McKinney, sur, Warren, AB

McCOY, Cornelius, decd, Benjamin Williams, William Youngblood, admr of orphs, 9/2/1833, Harris

McCOY, James, Sr., decd, LWT dtd 1/4/1853, pvd 9/18/1854, names wife, Elizabeth and ch: Elizabeth, John, Elijah, Cherokee

McCOY, Lewis, decd, formerly of Augusta, late of Charleston, Jane McCoy issued L/A 5/11/1818, Alex MacKenzie and James S. Walker, secs, Richmond, AB

McCRADIE, David, decd, John Bachlott, Jr. dismissed as admr 1/5/1830, Camden, MIC

McCRARY, Ezekiel, decd, William F. Sears issued L/A 3/5/1866, C. Cox, sec, White, AB

McCRARY, Mary Jane, orph of Samuel, decd, John Boroughs, gdn, 1/13/1851, R. H. McCrary, sec, Hall, GB

McCRARY, Matthew, decd, Lettice McCrary apptd admx 7/3/1809, Warren, MIC

McCREDIE, David, decd, John Bachlott apptd admr w/LWT annexed 6/7/1824, Camden, MIC

McCRERY, Matthew, decd, John McCrery, Samuel Hall, admrs, 7/1/1816, Henry Kendall, Sr., Thomas Williams, surs, Warren, AB

McCRIMSON, Duncan, decd, Chas & Geo W. McCrimson L/A 7/4/1836, Jno McArthur, sec; Chas McCrimmon, gdn of Nancy & John 8/7/1837; Danl McCrimmon, gdn of Catherine & Charity 8/7/1837; Jno Peterson, gdn of Charity 11/5/1838, Montgomery, AB, GB

McCRORY, John, LWT dtd 9/15/1800, pvd 10/6/1800 devises est to wife, Rachel and son, John, a minor, Effingham, Misc

McCULLARS, Charles, decd, L/A gtd to Malacah and Rachel Wilder 12/2/1783, Wilkes, MxR

McCULLARS, David, decd, Amy McCullars, wid, apptd admx 10/31/1782, Wilkes, MxR

McCULLEN, Samuel, decd, Margaret McMullen issued L/A 7/1/1811, Jackson, OM

McCULLER, Matthew, decd, of Lumpkin, Penelope McCuller (wid), admx 4/1843; apprs: Willard Boynton, John Talbot, L. Bryan, John West, Stewart, Adms

McCULLERS, Britton, decd, Wright R. Coleman issued L/A 7/2/1821; John Thomas, admr de bonis non 7/1/1822, Laurens, AB

McCULLERS, David, decd, Lin Lowry, gdn of orphs, (Dudley and Matthew) makes retns 3/1/1815; pet of Robert Cummins, heir, in rt of wife, Ridley, dau of sd decd for div according to LWT, 1/3/1814, Jackson, OM

McCULLERS, David, decd, William Ball, admr, 12/4/1826, John W. Kinsey, sur, Warren, AB

McCULLERS, Drury, decd, LWT pvd by John Sallis and James Smith 2/2/1807, Warren, MIC

McCULLERS, Fatha, decd, Hiram McCullers, George Carter, Samuel Newman, Willis Evans, admrs, Harris

McCULLOCK, David, decd, Levi Lowry, gdn of orphs, makes retn 1809, Jackson, OM

McCULLOCK, James, decd, Samuel McCullock issued L/A 3/16/1816, Charles McCullock, David Patterson, secs, Richmond, AB

McCULLOCK, James W., decd, E. A. Davis, admr, 1/12/1863, A. C. Fowler, M. W. Davis, surs, DeKalb, AB

McCULLOCK, John, decd, William Belisle, admr de bonis non with LWT annexed, 1/12/1863, P. F. Hoyle, Milton A. Candler, surs, DeKalb, AB

McCULLOUGH, John, decd, Samuel McCullough issued L/A 4/?9/1813, Samuel McCullough issued L/A 4/29/1813, Peter Donaldson, D. Lamkin, secs, Richmond, AB

McCUNE, Cornelius M., William A. McCune, gdn, files retn; pd Nancy McCune, John McCord, 1840, Butts, ER

McCUNE, Cornelius M., orph of Micajah F., decd, William A. McCune, gdn, James A. McCune, David Spencer, sur, 11/4/1839, Butts, GB

McCUNE, Elijah, decd, William McCune, admr, acct 1830-1840, pd James A. McCune, Anna Byars, John Higgins, Cornelius McCune, gdn of Nancy McCune, William A. McCune, admr, etc., 4/6/1840, Butts, ER

McCUNE, Micajah F., decd, William A. McCune, admr, Thomas C. Taylor, Nelson Meredith, Creed T. Wise, sur, 10/13/1838; 3/1/1841 retn by William A. McCune, admr, cash pd Jesse McClendon, R. P. Mann, T. C. and David Higgins, 3/4/1841, Butts, AB, ER

McCUNE, Thomas B., decd, L/A issued Elizabeth McCune 1/1820, Jasper, OM

McCUNE, William, decd, 1805-1807 retn against minors, James and Peggy McCune, Thomas B. McCune, gdn, Elbert, AR

McCURDY, David, decd, John McCurdy applied for L/A 10/23/1795, Elbert, AB

McCURRY, Laughlin, decd, Laughlin Johnston and John McDonald apply for L/A 1/7/1811, Angus and John McCurry, Joshua Carpenter, sec, Elbert, AR

McCUTCHEON, David M., decd, Robert B. McCutcheon, admr, William A. Williams, sur, 3/7/1853, AB

McCUTCHEON, Joseph, decd, Shadrach T. Crawford issued L/A de bonis non 3/3/1851, Robert Hamilton, sec, Hall, AB

McDANIEL, John, decd, inv 3/30/1784, James Bowie, Oran Sinkfield, Solomon Barfield, apprs, Wilkes, MxR

McDONALD, Alexander, decd, John McDonald applies for adm on est of his father 11/23/1793, Effingham, Misc

McDONALD, Barbary, decd, Zadock Blalock, admr, Wm H. Blalock, sur, 5/1852, Fayette, AB

McDONALD, Donald M., decd, Isaac E. Bower issued L/A 1/18/1845, Baldwin

McDONALD, Jeremiah, decd, Nathan Brewton, Sr. made retn 12/3/1836, Tattnall, I&A
McDONALD, Josiah, decd, George Humphries and John Bradley, admrs, to sell Jackson and Clarke Co.´s land, 1809, Jackson, OM
McDONALD, Sarah, decd, Edward L. Langmade issued L/A 9/6/1841, Washington
McDOUGALD, Alexander, orph, Kinchen Carr, gdn, to sell Lot 299, 9th Dist., 4th Sec, orig. Cherokee Co., 2/5/1836, Habersham, MIC
McDOUGALD, Daniel, Sarah, Miles E. and Alexander apply for Jonathan C. Chastain as their gdn 3/1/1830; Jonathan P. Chastain to sell their property-Lot 112, 3rd Dist., formerly Troup, now Meriwether, 1/3/1832, Habersham, MIC
McDOWELL, James, decd, Winkfield Bagwell and Martha McDowell issued L/A 5/4/1812, Franklin, OM
McDOWELL, Peter, decd, Peter Bennoch issued L/A 7/9/1821, Samuel Hale, Thomas McDowell, secs, Richmond, AB
McDOWELL, Samuel, decd, John G. Winger, admr, 12/5/1825, Jeremiah Butt, sur, Warren, AB
McDOWELL, Thomas, decd, L/A to Robert A. Reid, surviving partner of Reid & McDowell, 11/9/1825, Peter Bennoch, sec, Richmond, AB
McDOWELL, William, decd, LWT pvd by John S. Drew, Isaiah Langley and Solomon Fudge, 1/6/1823, Jasper, OM
McDUGLE, Thomas, decd, William Bateman issued L/A 1/10/1859, Fulton
McELROY, Esther, minor orph of John, decd, Wiley Sems apptd gdn, Charles McElroy, Simon Hancock, surs, 1/1805, Oglethorpe, MIC
McELROY, Harvey, minor orph of John, decd, Wiley Sems apptd gdn, Charles McElroy, Simon Hancock, surs, 1/1805, Oglethorpe, MIC
McELROY, Henry, decd, 8/15/1809 est appraised by Charles Wheeler, George Eberhart, Samuel Patten, Pelatia and James McElroy, admrs, Elbert, AR
McELROY, Samuel B., decd, Samuel McElroy, admr, 5/4/1863, John McElroy, sur, DeKalb, AB
McELROY, Thomas, decd, died without Will or known heirs, leaving trunk, watch, etc; Clk to administer est 6/4/1816, Camden, MIC
McELVIN, Cathren, orph of William, decd, Peter Strickland makes retns 1839-40, 5/8/1841, Bulloch, MIC
McELVIN, William, Sr., decd, 3/4/1839 sale of two negroes in Chatham Co., Margaret and Susan McElveen entitled to 1/7th pt o est; Wm McElveen, gdn for Margaret; Peter Strickland, gdn for Susan Catharine McElveen, Bulloch, Misc
McELWEEN, William, decd, Susannah McElween issued L/A 9/8/1826, Edmund Burnside, Andrew Bird, secs, 9/8/1826, Bryan, CR
McFADDEN, William, orph, age 15 tghe 26th inst, bound to John Oxford 1/12/1830, Habersham, MIC
McFARLAN, James M., decd, James Case, admr, Ezekiel A. Wimberland, sur, 1/12/1852, Bibb, AB
McFARLAND, Thomas to be bound as apprentice to Samuel Curtley to learn taning business, 10/5/1818, Jasper, OM
McFARLAND, Thomas to be bound to William H. Miles, John Moore, sur, 11/1814, Jasper, OM
McFARLAND, William (Dr.), decd, of Richmond Co., Margaret and Robert Shields gtd L/D 3/22/1790, Columbia, Ests
McFARLAND, William, decd, Margaret Shields and Robert Shields issued L/A 2/18/1785, Richmond, AB
McFARLIN, Peter, decd, Robert Mayo, admr, P. M. Compton, sur, 4/1/1840, Butts, AB
McFARLIN, Peter, decd, prop sold in Macon 1/5/1841; retn 8/27/1840 by admr, Robert Mays, purchasers at sale: A. Shockley, G. Tredwell, John Andrews, P. M. Compton, J. W. Watkins, J. Aycock, D. J. Bailey, A. L. Robinson, etc., Butts, ER

McFARLIN, Punch, decd, John Wilson issued L/A 9/8/1807, Thomas Cumming, sec, Richmond, AB

McFARLIN, Sarah (Mrs.), John Pottle pvd her LWT, William Gibson qualified as exr 9/5/1825, Camden, MIC

McGAHAGIN, Eliza, decd, John M. Lucas applies for L/A 1/5/1832, Effingham, MIC

McGAHAGIN, Joshua L., John M. Lucas chosen gdn 1/7/1833, Effingham, MIC

McGAHAGIN, William, decd, John M. Lucas qualified admr 7/2/1827; John Graham, exr, filed accts, dismissed as admr 7/2/1827, Effingham, MIC

McGAHAGIN, William L., John M. Lucas chosen gdn 1/7/1833, Effingham, MIC

McGAR, Leah, decd, Alexander R. White issued L/A 7/8/1858, Fulton

McGAR, Owen, decd, William McGar issued L/A 2/17/1826, James Longstreet, Edward Byrd, secs; 1830 inv mentions judgment on Leah Simons, alias Leah McGar, Richmond, A

McGEE, Elizabeth, decd, John Mattox, gdn for heirs, makes retn 11/7/1837, Tattnall, I&A

McGEE, Henry, decd, Elenor McGee, extrx, p. 167, Screven, OM

McGEE, James, decd, Levin McGee, gdn of John Wesley & Peter Williamson McGee, orphs, 3/5/1821, Aaron Clifton, sur, Clarke, GB

McGEE, Samuel, decd, W. J. H. Davis, admr, Jesse L. McGee, sur, 10/4/1875, Gwinnett, AB

McGEHEE, Samuel, decd, James N. issued L/A 5/5/1828, Baldwin

McGEHEE, Samuel, decd, William C. Humphries issued L/A 1/7/1839, Baldwin

McGHEE, Edward, decd, L/A issued John and James McGhee, 5/2/1814; Betsey McGhee, wid, chose child´s pt 7/4/1814, Jasper, OM

McGHEE, Edward, minor orph of Edward, decd, Wm Johnson and James McGhee apptd gdns 1/1816, Jasper, OM

McGHEE, James, decd, John H. McGhee, Sarah McGhee, William Whitaker, Thomas Whitehead, admrs, 7/1837, Harris

McGHEE, John, decd, Barclay McGhee issued L/A 5/4/1852, R. B. Lewis, sec, Lumpkin, AB

McGHEE, William, minor orph of Edward, decd, Wm Johnson and James McGhee apptd gdns 1/1816, Jasper, OM

McGILL, Eliza, decd, LWT was pvd by Jacob Miller 6/3/1837, Camden, MIC

McGILL, Susanna, decd, Charles Carden, admr, James Luke, Elisha Palmore, sur, 7/6/1812, Jones, AB

McGILL, T. J., decd, L/A to Mason H. Bush 12/1862, Webster, OD

McGILLIS, Randolph, decd, William Gibson, admr, 8/7/1826; Hannah McGillis, wid, requested ct to appt Gillis McDonald admr with her to admr est 1/3/1825, Camden, MIC

McGIRT, Daniel, decd, William Ashley apptd admr, replacing Mrs. Susannah McGirt, 1/8/1806; William Niblack, Isaac Lang, Donald Tompkins apptd to div est, 1/11/1813, Camden, MIC

McGOWAN, John, decd, John Broadfoot for Whatley Bradfoot issued L/A 3/6/1800, Wm Drew, Patrick McDowall, secs, Richmond, AB

McGOWIN, James, decd, Joseph McGowin, admr, p. 100 and 106, Screven, OM

McGOWIN, John, decd, Jacob McGowin, admr, p. 103, Screven, OM

McGOWIN, Sophia, bound to Mathew Rogers, p. 199, Screven, OM

McGRADY, Adaline, W. P. James makes retn 12/1865, Webster, OD

McGRADY, Edward, minor of William B., decd, William Skelton issued L/G 3/1856, Webster, OD

McGRADY, Isaac V., decd, L/G of Helena, Adeline, Martha, Mary and Arabella, minors of decd, 3/1856, Webster, OD

McGRADY, Isaac V., decd, Silas M. McGrady apptd temporary admr 3/8/1856; Benjamin Griffin issued L/A 9/1856, Webster, OD

McGRADY, Martha, W. P. Jones makes retn 12/1865, Webster, OD
McGRADY, Sarah, decd, Silas M. McCrady apptd temporary admr
9/1855, Webster, OD
McGRADY, Sarah Ann, minor of William B., decd, William Skelton
issued L/G 3/1856; Silas M. McGrady asks for leave to sell real
estate 3/1857, Webster, OD
McGRADY, W. B., decd, Martha C. McGrady issued L/G of the orphs
7/1862, Webster, OD
McGRANN, Patrick, decd, William Jackson issued L/A 11/8/1823,
Walton Knight, William Savage, secs, Richmond, AB
McGRATH, John, decd, Western B. Thomas issued L/A 2/11/1829, John
Howard, sec, Richmond, AB
McGRATH, Patrick, decd, Richard Bolan issued L/A 5/5/1814, George
Adams, John Cashin, secs, Richmond, AB
McGREGOR, James, decd, William Gibson qualified as exr of LWT
10/6/1817, Camden, MIC
McGUIRE, Abiah, decd, H. N. Byars, admr w/LWT annexed, R. G.
Byars, John E. Pettigrew, sur, 2/8/1851, Butts, AB
McGUIRE, Allegany, decd, 5/28/1804 acct of Robert Holliday for
moving sd Holliday and family from Va. to Ga. and boarding Robert
for 3 yrs, 6 mos, Elbert, AR
McGUIRE, Frederick, decd, William F. McGuire issued L/A 3/6/1854,
Adolphus E. Brooks, Thompson McGuire, secs, Hall, AB
McGUIRT, Wyatt, decd, Wm H. Blalock, admr, Jesse L. Blalock, sur,
5/1849, Fayette, AB
McGULLION, Matthew R. C., a poor orph, son of Thomas, bound to
Caleb Herndon 3/5/1832, Robert Kendrick, sec, Hall, GB
McINTOSH, Eliza (Mrs.), LWT pvd, Henry R. Sadler qualified as exr
1/3/1848, Camden, MIC
McINTOSH, George, decd, Col. William McIntosh, admr, 5/24/1784,
Chatham, Adms
McINTOSH, J. H., decd, George S. McIntosh, Henry R. Saddler,
Duncan L. Clinch and John H. McIntosh, Jr., heirs of decd,
approve retn admrs made 6/15/1848; admrs gtd leave to sell real
est, 1/2/1838, admrs gtd leave to sell real est 1/2/1838, Camden, MI
McINTOSH, John H., lately Justice of Inf Ct, decd, Mr. & Mrs.
Swinton testify he was not of sound mind when Will signed,
probate refused, LWT dtd 2/8/1836. Duncan L. Clinch & John H.
McIntosh, Jr. apptd temp admrs 6/3/1836, Camden, MIC, AB
McINTOSH, Lachlan, Jr., decd, William McIntosh, Jr., admr (son of
Lachlan) 4/4/1783, Chatham, Adms
McINTOSH, Winewood (Mrs.), decd, George Troup, Sr. qualified as
exr 6/25/1786; William McIntosh of Mallow qualified as exr
12/8/1791, Liberty, Ests
McINTYRE, John, decd, LWT dtd 12/12/1835, pvd 3/1836 names wife,
Anny (land in Murray Co.); Elijah Sisk issued L/A 3/7/1836,
Habersham, MIC
McIVER, Donald, decd, David Reid issued L/A 5/31/1810, Thomas
Cumming, John Carmichael, secs; ltr to David Reid from John
McIver of N. Y. dtd 1809 addressed "Dear Nephew"; John McIver pd
as heir of Donald in 1810, Richmond, AB
McIVER, Hannah petitioned for James Smith to be apptd her gdn,
she being over 14 yrs old; he gave bond for her; also as gdn for
Euphemia Seymour McIver and Alexander Munro McInver, minors,
10/3/1803, Liberty, MIC
McKAY, Isabella, decd, David Montaigut qualified exr 4/15/1784,
Liberty, Ests
McKAY, James, decd, Joshua Meals issued L/A 5/1808, James Walker,
John F. Love, secs, Richmond, AB
McKAY, William, decd, late of Fla., Mary Ann, admx, applied for
leave to sell 4500 acres on St. Marys River 3/11/1841, Camden,
MIC

McKEE, John, decd, L/A issued to Elizabeth McKee and Henry Parks 2/12/1803; L/A issued Elizabeth and Samuel McKee 4/12/1803, Franklin, OM

McKEE, Patsy, orph of John, decd, Henry Parks apptd gdn 1/4/1808, Franklin, OM

McKEE, Roseanna, orph of John, decd, Henry Parks apptd gdn 1/4/1808, Franklin, OM

McKEEN, Jane, minor of Van L., Hays Bowdre, gdn, 1/2/1836, Richmond, GB

McKEEN, Robert W., decd, Hays Bowdre issued L/A 11/2/1835, John H. Mann, sec, Richmond, AB

McKEITHAN, Eli, decd, of Pleasant Valley, Lemuel B. Morton, admr 2/1843; apprs: Isham Watkins, Joseph J. Dowd, Daniel Richardson; purchasers at sale: Dougle McKeithan, Bryan Bedingfield, John Blackshear, Stewart, Adms

McKEITHAN, Neil, decd, of Pleasant Valley, Lemuel B. Morton, admr 2/1843; apprs: Joseph Dowd, Isham Waters, Daniel Richardson, John Blackshear; purchasers at sale: John T. & Wm Allday, John Blackshear, John W. & Turner Bowden, Stewart, Adms

McKELLER, John, decd, Jesse Ansley issued L/A 5/6/1817, Alex. MacKenzie, Angus Martin, secs; 1319 retn pd Donald and Peter McKellar, legatees, and sd Peter as atty for Archibald and Mary McFarlin, Richmond, AB

McKENIE, James apptd gdn of Frances, Jane, Mary Ann, John G. and Harriett, orphs of John, decd, 1/7/1822, Jasper, OM

McKENLEY, Sarah, decd, L/A to James Butler 12/8/1820, Bryan, CR

McKIGNEY, Bayly, decd, Peter Puryear, gdn of Rebecca C. and William, orphs, 5/2/1825, John Puryear, Chas. Dougherty, surs, Clarke, GB

McKINLEY, Sarah, decd, James Butler, admr, 3/7/1827, Bryan, CR

McKINLEY, William, decd, John Martin applies for adm on est, Joseph McKinley, sur, 12/5/1803; James Martin apptd admr 1/2/1808; Severn Bukie or Rukie apptd admr 3/6/1809, Warren, MIC

McKINLEY, William, decd, James Martin apptd admr 1/2/1808, Warren, MIC

McKINNE, Ann B., decd, A. J. Miller issued L/A 4/23/1843; pd Joseph S. Burnett, Anthony Green, John W. Farrell, all in rt of their wives, Richmond, AB

McKINNE, Barna, decd, Ann McKinne issued L/A 5/11/1833, George W. Crawford, sec, Richmond, AB

McKINNE, John, decd, Elizabeth McKinne issued L/A 5/14/1795, William J. Hobby, sec, Richmond, AB

McKINNE, Nancy Jane, orph of Zachariah, decd, Travis McKinne, gdn, 1/21/1822, Elisha McCord and John McCord, secs, Lincoln, GB

McKINNEN, Roger, decd, Solomon Kemp and others, apprs, p. 106, Screven, OM

McKINNEY, David, decd, Constance Sophia & Jno McKinney L/A 1820; ch-Sarah, Mary Ann, Eliza; heirs-Benja Hall (Mary's gdn), Elizabeth, Ann, Saml Wigfall (wf-Sophia), Anthony Green (wf-Elizabeth); pd Mary Farrell, wf of J. W., Richmond, AB

McKINNEY, Eliza Ann, Robert McKinney, gdn, p. 22, Screven, OM

McKINNEY, Elizabeth, decd, LWT dtd 4/3/1836 pvd 3/1836 by John B. Cloudy and Bird Cannon, names friend, John Tate, Sr. (a note on Andrew Dorsey), Habersham, MIC

McKINNEY, James W., orph of William, age 15, John T. James, gdn, James M. Bledsoe, sur, 1/3/1844, Butts, GB

McKINNEY, Jane, orph of Zachariah, decd, Hardy Leverett, gdn 1/13/1834, Mark Shipp, Wm Wallace, secs, Lincoln, GB

McKINNEY, Kinchen, decd, John Burkhalter, admr, 3/1/1824, Moses McKinney, sur, Warren, AB

McKINNEY, Mary, acct appvd, p. 133, Screven, OM

McKINNEY, Mordecai, decd, of Pendleton Dist., South Carolina, LWT
dtd 1/1825 pvd 9/1828 by Franky Cox, names wife, Elizabeth,
extrx, Habersham, MIC
McKINNEY, Moses, decd, Polly McKinney offered LWT, she qualified
as extrx, 2/10/1802, Warren, MIC
McKINNEY, Robert D., leave to sell lots, p. 43, relieved from
gdnshp, p. 49, Screven, OM
McKINNEY, Roger, decd, Mary McKinney, etc., admx, p. 103,
Screven, OM
McKINNEY, Rose, etc., petitions to be relieved from bond, p. 30,
33, Screven, OM
McKINNEY, Thomas B., orph of Robert, decd, Travis McKinney apptd
gdn 9/3/1839, Wm McKinney, sec, Lincoln, GB
McKINNEY, Timothy, to pay $13.00, p. 36, Screven, OM
McKINNEY, William, decd, Sarah and Roger McKinney, admrs, p. 62,
Screven, OM
McKINNEY, William, decd, James Lambert, etc., apprs, p. 62,
Screven, OM
McKINSTRY, Alexander, decd, Elizabeth McKinstry issued L/A
1/15/1824, Job S. Barney, Thomas Crayton, secs; 1829 retn pd
Henry S. Lee in rt of wf and as gdn of the children in Conn,
recepts of Alex McKinstry and Ann, Richmond, AB
McKINSY, Allen, decd, James C. Mangham, James Piles, heirs of
decd, applied for div of est among heirs, 7/1/1816, Glynn, MIC
McKLEROY, James, decd, L/A issued Wm H. Pearson, with John M.
Pearson, Enoch Pearson, Drury Rogers, surs, 3/5/1821, Jasper, OM
McKNIGHT, Washington (Rev.), decd, John R. Thompson issued L/A
12/4/1805, Thomas Cumming, sec, Richmond, AB
McLAIN, John, decd, Peter G. Morrow and William Timmons issued
L/A 2/14/1825, Benjamin Brown, Van Leonard, secs, Morgan, AB
McLAIN, Rebecca, decd, Samuel Lines qualified admr 11/21/1789,
Liberty, Ests
McLANE, Daniel, decd, Joseph May, admr, 1/29/1783, Wilkes, MxR
McLAUGHLIN, George T., decd, Mrs. Mary A. McLaughlin issued L/A
9/10/1860, Fulton
McLAURIN, James, decd, Peter Bennoch issued L/A 4/30/1833, Samuel
Hale, Thomas McDowell, secs, Richmond, AB
McLEALAND, John, decd, Samuel Fulton, John Fulton qualified as
exrs 5/3/1783, Liberty, Ests
McLEAN, John, decd, Jane D. Tract apptd admx, gtd leave to sell
400 acres 9/7/1804, Camden, MIC
McLEAN, John, decd, Josiah McLean qualified as admr 9/13/1785,
Liberty, Ests
McLEAN, John, decd, Martha E. and Joseph M. McLean, exrs of LWT,
apptd 11/1850, 1853-1854 retns, Fayette, AB
McLEER, Joseph, decd, Michael Rudolph apptd admr, 3/12/1788,
Chatham, Adms
McLEMORE, Charles chose John S. Drew for his gdn 1/6/1823,
Jasper, OM
McLEMORE, Franklin, John Martin apptd gdn of person and property
1/1820, Jasper, OM
McLEMORE, Hosea, decd, Chesley B. McLemore, Ira T. McLemore,
admrs, George Clifton, B. C. Brinson, William Godfrey, Nathan
Barwick, Jr., 1/4/1842, Emanjel, AB
McLEMORE, James, John Martin apptd gdn of person and property
1/1820, Jasper, OM
McLEMORE, John, decd, L/A issued John Martin, John S. Drew,
Catherine, wid, claims child's pt, 3/1819, Jasper, OM
McLENDON, Dicey, orph of John, decd, William King apptd gdn
1/20/1860, John H. Kitchens, sur, Lee
McLENDON, E. B., decd, Jonathan McLendon issued L/A on est of his

wife 5/17/1854, Lee, MSC

McLENDON, Eletha Ann, orph of Jeremiah M., decd, Freeman McLendon apptd gdn, Jesse McLendon, sec, 3/7/1848, Troup, GB

McLENDON, John, orph of John, decd, William King apptd gdn 7/18/1859, Josiah McLendon, sur, Lee

McLENDON, Pethena, orph of Jeremiah M., decd, Freeman McLendon apptd gdn, Jesse McLendon, sec, 3/7/1848, Troup, GB

McLENDON, Sarah Jane, orph of John, decd, William King apptd gdn 7/18/1859, Josiah McLendon, sur, Lee

McLENDON, Silas William, orph of Jeremiah M., decd, Freeman McLendon apptd gdn, Jesse McLendon, sec, 3/7/1848, Troup, GB

McLENDON, Thomas, decd, Nicholas H. Bacon, gdn of orphs: Robert W. and Josephine M., 12/7/1863, Fulton, GB

McLENDON, William Harrison, orph of John, William King apptd gdn 5/16/1859, Lee

McLEOD, Alexander M., decd, LWT pvd 2/7/1814; Angus McLeod qualified admr 1/7/1812, Tattnall, MIC

McLEOD, Angus, decd, Thomas G. McFarland and Nancy McLeod issued L/A, John B. M. McFarland, W. L. McLeod, secs, 3/1/1830; Alexander T. McLeod, gdn to orphs: William A., Nancy and George T., 12/8/1840, Montgomery, AB, GB

McLEOD, Catharine, David Kennedy, gdn 11/6/1815, Bulloch, MIC

McLEOD, Margaret Murphey, decd, Donald McLeod issued L/A 11/1/1835, John Peterson, sec, Montgomery, GB

McLEOD, Mary Ann, orph of Turtle, decd, Stephen Findley, gdn, 1/6/1840, Tattnall, GB

McLEOD, Murdock, decd, Donald McLeod, admr, no date, Bryan, CR

McLEOD, Nancy, natural gdn for ch (orphs of Angus)-Alexander, Catharine, William, nancy and George 6/8/1836, William C. Phillips, Charles McCrimson, sec, Montgomery, GB

McLEOD, Turtle, decd, James Hancock makes retn 11/4/1839, Tattnall, I&A

McLEROY, Emily, decd, James McConnell, admr, M. B. DeVaughan, Elijah Glass, surs, 3/1855, Fayette, AB

McLEROY, Henry, decd, LWT pvd 9/4/1848, Henry McLeroy, Charles G. Hartsfield, exrs, Harris

McLEROY, Henry, decd, M. P. DeVaughan, exr, W. P. and P. H. Allen, Wm E. Tucker, surs, 2/1855, 1853-1854 retns, Fayette, AB

McLEROY, John, decd, Martha McLeroy, admx, Eli Edmondson, sur, no date, Fayette, AB

McLEROY, Mary, orph of John, decd, Andrew McBride, gdn, Eli Edmondson, sur, 11/1849, Fayette, GB

McMAHAN, John, decd, late of S. C., John R. McMahan, admr, Henry Hatcher, sur, 9/5/1831, Butts, AB

McMANNES, Thomas, decd, John McMannes issued L/A 9/23/1814, Holland McTyeire, sec, Richmond, AB

McMICHAEL, Elmira, appl of William R. Marchman, gdn for distribution of personal est of Zachariah McMichael, decd, McMICHAEL, Green L., decd, L/A issued Elijah and Elizabeth McMichael, with John McMichael, Sr. and Nicholas Johnson, surs, 1/7/1822, Jasper, OM

McMICHAEL, James, decd, L/A issued Peggy McMichael, Benjamin Irvin and John Lang, Sr., surs, 9/2/1816, Jasper, OM

McMICHAEL, John B., decd, of Bibb Co., William H. Freeman issued L/A 4/3/1866, Fulton

McMICHAEL, Levi, child of John, John McMichael, gdn, William J. McMichael, sur, 11/15/1842, Butts, GB

McMICHAEL, Levi, husband of Mary C. (formerly Mary C. Redman), John McMichael, gdn; pd James Carter, gdn of Martha, William T. C. Redman and Mrs. Mary Redman 12/9/1841, Butts, ER

which est the said William McMichael, decd, was an exr, Greene

McMICHAEL, William, decd, John McMichael, Richard Carter and James Harral in rt of his wife, Elizabeth McMichael, exr, 1/7/1822, Jasper, OM

McMICHAEL, William, decd, LWT names wife, Betsey and son, John McMichael, and Richard Carter, exrs, dtd 1/17/1809, Jasper, WAR

McMICHAEL, William, decd, pet of William McMichael prays removal of proceedings of est of Hugh Jones, decd, to Randolph Co. to which est the said William McMichael, decd, was an exr, Greene Co. 7/1810, Jasper, Ests

McMICHAEL, Zachariah, decd, L/A issued Charles McMichael and Moses Powell, Nuborne B. Powell, sur, 1/1820; admr to have leave to sell property 5/7/1821, Jasper, OM

McMILLAN, Martha, decd, William H. Jones issued L/A 12/23/1834, Richmond, AB

McMILLEN, Samuel, decd, Margaret McMillen, admx, to sell two slaves 5/6/1816, Jackson, OM

McMURPHY, Susannah (Mrs.), decd, Luke Reed issued L/A 1/3/1822, Wm. W. Holt, Abiel Camfield, secs, Richmond, AB

McMURTREY, William, decd, John Dalrymple, admr w/LWT annexed 1/11/1858, Fulton

McNAB, Robert, decd, Mary McNab apptd admx 2/20/1784, Wilkes, MxR

McNABB, James, decd, Thomas Bloodworth issued L/A 7/1/1822, William Bloodworth, sec, Morgan, AB

McNAIR, Jacob, decd, George M. Duncan, admr, Dooly, OD

McNamara, Nicholas, decd, Edmund Mathews apptd admr and gtd leave to sell perishable prop of est 10/4/1826, Glynn, MIC

McNEAL, John, decd, 2/13/1821 div by Augustus McNeal and Holland McTyeire, gdns of Parthena and Augustus, heirs, Richmond, AB

McNEALY, John, decd, Nancy McNealy issued L/A 5/5/1806, John Carter, James Hamilton, secs, Richmond, AB

McNEEL, John T., orph of Thomas, decd, Jesse Gunn, gdn, 9/16/1822, William McCowen, sec, Morgan, GB

McNEIL, Malcolm, decd, James McNeil was gtd L/A 4/30/1796, Columbia, Ests

McNEILLY, Augustus, minor orph of John, decd, Anthony Blache, gdn 3/19/1813, John D´Antignac, Holland McTyeire, sec, Richmond, GB

McNEILLY, John, decd, William McTyeire issued L/A 1/5/1811, George Pearson, sec; 3/19/1819 Anthony Blache apptd admr, Richmond, AB

McNIECE, Henry, decd, LWT was pvd by Edmond Hays, 7/1/1799, Warren, MIC

McNISH, William, decd, LWT pvd, Mrs. Ann McNish, extrx 1/6/1829, Camden, MIC

McOWEN, Elizabeth, orph of William D., decd, John W. McOwen, gdn, 12/6/1826, Wade Hemphill, Georgia Langford, secs, Morgan, GB

McQUEEN, Charles J., decd, Rachel, admx, p. 161, exr to leave to sell property, p. 124,Screven, OM

McROY, Jackson, decd, Edwin McRoy applies for L/A 5/6/1846, Effingham, MIC

McROY, John P., decd, Edwin McRoy applies for L/A 5/6/1846, Effingham, MIC

McROY, Rachael, decd, John McRoy applies for L/A 8/26/1839, Effingham, MIC

McSPARN, John, decd, Elizabeth McSparn, gdn of John and William, orphs, 12/6/1819, John Smith, Wm Mitchell, surs, Clarke, GB

McSWAIN, John, decd, Martin Dupreast issued L/A 3/22/1827, Booker Lawson, sec, Morgan, AB

McWHIRT, John, decd, George D. Case issued L/A 5/7/1838, Baldwin

McWHIRTER, Nancy, decd, George A. McWhirter, admr of late wife, 1/15/1828, Habersham, MIC

McWHORTER, Isaac, decd, Warren R. D. Moss issued temp L/A, Birdwell Hill, sur, 1/24/1851; perm L/A 5/5/1851, Cherokee, AB

McWILLIAMS, Alexander, decd, William T. Langford and Robert McWilliams issued L/A 8/13/1868, Fulton
McWILLIAMS, William, decd, Catharine McWilliams, admx, 12/1/1862, R. McWilliams, sur, DeKalb, AB
MEAD, Joseph Hays, decd, LWT exhibited 7/7/1862, Mrs. Sarah Mead, extrx, Fulton
MEAD, Samuel, decd, John Mead issued L/A 1793, Richmond, AB
MEADOWS, Margaret Anna H., orph or Abraham, decd, Robert M. Clarke issued L/G 10/1/1855, Fulton
MEADOWS, Margaret, decd, Henry D. Phillips, admr w/LWT annexed 12/1/1856, Fulton
MEALS, John, decd, Joshua Meals issued L/A 4/23/1794, Patrick Hayes, sec, Richmond, AB
MEALS, Joshua, decd, Mildred Meals issued temp L/A 3/13/1819, Thomas Glascock, Lindsey Coleman, sec; heirs-Asalph Waterman, tr for Celestia F. Combs, Henry H. Meals, Mildred J. Waterman, Rhesa Bostick, Richmond, AB
MEALS, Joshua, Sr., decd, Joshua Meals, Jr. and John Walker issued L/A 11/3/1806, Allen Nesbitt, John Campbell, secs, Richmond, AB
MEARS, Henry B., William B. Michiner, gdn, p. 134, Screven, OM
MEARS, John, decd, Delia O. Mears, admr, p. 133, Screven, OM
MEARS, Stephen, decd of Richmond Co., Abraham Jones admr 9/19/1789; Samuel Mears, sole exr (son) came to State, relinq exr power; Amasa Jackson gtd L/A 9/11/1790, Columbia, Ests
MEDLOCK, George, Clk of Ct of Ordinary of Hancock Co. recorded est proceedings which had been transferred 11/1/1813, Warren, MIC
MEDLOCK, George, decd, LWT pvd by James and George Taylor 2/9/1801; L/T issued to George Medlock, Jr. 1/2/1797, Warren, MIC
MEDLOCK, George Lafayette, minor orph of George, decd, Zachariah Phillips apptd gdn 9/1813, Jasper, OM
MEEK, Francis, decd, appr 6/29/1822, Emanuel, A
MEEKS, Benjamin, decd, Howell Meeks issued L/A 1/5/1842, Washington
MEERS, John, decd, William Meers issued L/A 1/3/1843, T. W. Henderson, James M. Tate, John Dickson, secs; Joroyal Blackwell, admr de bonis non 11/2/1846, Ausbon Seay, Thomas Barnett, secs, Hall, AB
MEERS, Sarah, decd, ThomaHughes, William H. McCarthy, sur, 7/19/1847, Bibb, AB
MEGEE, Benjamin F., decd, Marah Megee issued L/A 1/12/1863, Fulton
MEIGS, Benjamin H., decd, R. J. Meigs issued L/A 3/9/1819, Richmond, AB
MERCER, Henry, decd, Isabel Mercer issued L/A 1/4/1819, John Collins, Etheldred Tarver, sec, Richmond, AB
MERCER, Jesse, minor of William, decd, James S. McNair, gdn, Richmond, GB
MERCER, John, John S. Mauer, gdn, p. 159, Screven, OM
MERCER, Solomon, decd, David Griffin, admr, admr 10/29/1823, Emanuel, A
MERCER, William, decd, Samuel McNair, Isabel Mercer issued L/A 9/5/1814, Benjamin Dunn, Wm Bryant, secs; legatees: Francis Miller, John, Wm, Peter, Jesse, nancy and Catherine, Richmond, AB
MEREDITH, James, decd, 1810 retn of Isaac Suttles, exr, receipts of Zachariah and Nancy Faulkner, Henry and Sally Clift, Buckner and Polly Eaves, legatees, Elbert, AR
MERIWETHER, Thomas Sr., decd, Thomas Meriwether, Jr. issued L/A 12/11/1794, Richard White, John Cobb, Nicholas Meriwether, Richard White of Columbia Co., secs, Richmond, AB
MERRITT, James, decd, William A. Merritt issued L/A 7/2/1860, Edwin P. Williams, sec, White, AB

MERRITT, Nancy, orph of Benjamin, decd, Wade Hemphill, gdn, 12/6/1826, Morgan, GB
MESSER, Nathaniel S., decd, Philander O. Paris, admr, 12/3/1821, John W. A. Pettit, sur, Warren, AB
MESSER, William, decd, LWT pvd, L/T issued to William, John W. and Martha Messer, 3/2/1818, Jasper, OM
METTS, William, decd, Redding Metts, admr, appr 5/2/1820, Emanuel, A
MICHALER, John, LWT 4/22/1799-to Michl Exley, dau Catherine's husb; Jno Frickinger; Susanna Catherine, Jno Ernest Bergman's wf; Jno Exley (Michl, Catherine's son), grdau, Mary, Benj. Bechtly's wf;Benj. & Catherine Reisser, Effingham, Misc
MICKLER, David, LWT pvd, David G. Jones qualified exr 9/2/1816, Camden, MIC
MICKLER, Jacob, decd, LWT pvd, David G. Jones qualified exr, 9/2/1816, Camden, MIC
MICKLER, Jacob, minor, David G. Jones, gdn, 2/5/1816, Camden, MIC
MICKLER, Peter, decd, John Hebbard, apptd admr 11/2/1840; applied for div of personal property, refers to "the other heirs" having had notice 1/5/1842, Camden, MIC
MICKLER, William, minor over 14 yrs old, William Gibson apptd gdn 2/5/1816, Camden, MIC
MICOU, William, decd, William M. Micou issued L/A 9/1/1834, Thomas J. Wray, sec, Richmond, AB
MIDDLETON, Hugh, Jr., decd, late of S. C., Samuel Savage, Jr. of S. C. , Isaac Randolph and John Furry of Augusta issued L/A 6/25/1805, Richmond, AB
MIDDLETON, William, a free mulatto,G. P. Cohen apptd gdn 9/5/1842, Camden, MIC
MIEKEZ?, William, orph of Martin, decd, Wm Reynolds, gdn, 5/7/1832, Peter Lamar, sec, Lincoln, GB
MIKELL, Charles, decd, L/A to David Lee 3/3/1823, Bulloch, MIC
MIKELL, James, decd, inv and appr 6/5/1835 by M. Denmark, James Rawls, Thomas Knight; Margaret R. Mikell, admx, Bulloch, Misc
MIKELL, Seaborn, decd, Allen Mikell, admr to have leave to sell negro man, Ceasor, for benefit of heirs 9/2/1839, Bulloch, MIC
MILAM, Benjamin, Sr., decd, LWT pvd 3/4/1832, James G. Maull, exr, Harris
MILES, Jacob, orph of Jeremiah, decd, Green Lee, gdn, 1/6/1821, Joseph Harris, sec, Morgan, GB
MILES, Theora F., decd, George J. Miles, admr, Wm Miles, sur, 1854 retn, Fayette, AB
MILES, Thomas, decd, William Lyon issued L/A 3/9/1808, Peter Donaldson, Abraham Nash, secs, Richmond, AB
MILLEN, John, decd, L/D issued to George Millen, 10/1/1790, Chatham, Adms
MILLEN, John, planter, decd, Stephen Millen and John Millen and Mrs. Catherine Millen, admrs 4/12/1788; George Miller, admr, 6/13/1789; Sarah and George Millen, admrs, 7/24/1789, Chatham, Adms
MILLER, A. J., minor, Mrs. S. H. Miller apptd gdn 1/11/1841, Glynn, MIC
MILLER, Alexander, decd, Isaiah Parker and Garret Hudman issued L/A 1/7/1811, Putnam, AB
MILLER, Alexander, decd, John Barren and Elinor Barren, his wife, late relict of Alexander Miller, cited on L/A 9/1789 or 1799, Greene, Misc
MILLER, Catherine (Mrs.), decd, Russell Goodrich qualifies as exr 4/10/1815; James and Louisa C. Shaw, exrs, reports bal due est of $912.07, 3/1/1819, Camden, MIC
MILLER, Charles, decd, James A. Miller, admr, 2/13/1863, J. W. Miller, sur, DeKalb, AB
MILLER, Cynthia, Richard Miller, gdn, p. 35, 54, Screven, OM

MILLER, David Y., decd, Robert Baxter, admr, 7/6/1863, John Y. Flowers, sur, DeKalb, AB
MILLER, David, decd, Mary Miller qualified admx 6/16/1785, Liberty, Ests
MILLER, David, decd, late of Glynn Co., John W. Hunter issued L/A 10/1/1828, Daniel Savage, sec, Richmond, AB
MILLER, Elisha, decd, David and Joshua Miller qualified admrs 11/18/1788, Liberty, Ests
MILLER, Elizabeth, now Kenneday, John Pain and Isaac McClendon exonorated from being security for gdnship 7/3/1815, Jasper, OM
MILLER, Ephraim, decd, John Dasher applies for L/A 9/9/1847, Effingham, MIC
MILLER, Georgian, orph of George, decd, Thomas Dallas, gdn, 1/3/1831, Wm Dallas, sec, Lincoln, GB
MILLER, Hezekiah, decd, Robert M. Emerson, admr, Henry Emerson, sur, 11/18/1855, Cherokee, AB
MILLER, Isaiah, decd, Gideon Morris, admr, 3/6/1854, James S. Elliott, John Z. Flowers, surs, DeKalb, AB
MILLER, James A., decd, James R. Jackson, admr, William A. Jordan, sur, 4/1/1872, Gwinnett, AB
MILLER, James J., minor orph of James, decd, Nathan Jones made his retn on amt he recd as gdn 5/8/1841, Bulloch, Misc
MILLER, John, decd, Alex. McKenzie issued L/A 1/29/1830, Aug B. Longstreet, sec, Richmond, AB
MILLER, John, decd, Dennis Miller, Joseph Miller, gdn of orphs 1/4/1841, Harris, GB
MILLER, John, decd, Joseph Calvert applied for L/A 4/20/1792, John Frugus, Arthur Crawford, William Appleby, apprs, Elbert, AB
MILLER, John, decd, Mrs. Agnes Miller applied for L/A 12/2/1793, Greene, Misc
MILLER, John, decd, Thomas Sparks issued L/A 5/5/1843, Washington
MILLER, John B., minor, Mrs. S. H. Miller apptd gdn 1/11/1841, Glynn, MIC
MILLER, John C., decd, LWT pvd 1/11/1847, Effingham, MIC
MILLER, Joseph, decd, J. C. and Margaret Miller, admrs, William T. Lang, sur, 1/13/1815, Bibb, AB
MILLER, Joshua, decd, L/A issued to Eliza Miller 3/6/1832, Washington
MILLER, Joshua, decd, late of Glynn Co., John W. Hunter issued L/A 5/26/1828, Daniel Savage, sec, Richmond, AB
MILLER, Phineas, decd, Edmond Bacon of S. C. applies for extrx to title him 700 acres, Upton's Cr, Wilkes Co., Ga. in conformity with contract made testator 2/7/1803, 1/8/1811, Camden, MIC
MILLER, Phineas, decd, Ray Sands notified to appear before ct as agt for representatives of est to explain his acct against Araminta Dilworth est, 6/4/1805, Camden, MIC
MILLER, Phineas, decd, Russell Goodrich qualifies as exr 4/10/1815, Camden, MIC
MILLER, Phineas, decd, leave gtd Catherine Miller, extrx, to sell prop, 4/15/1807, Camden, MIC
MILLER, Samuel, decd, Mrs. Mary Miller qualified exr 7/23/1784, Liberty, Ests
MILLER, Samuel, decd, Joseph and Phereby Miller issued L/A 7/4/1830, John Miller, sec; Norman Gillis, gdn of orphs 5/2/1836, William C. Phillips, sec, Montgomery, AB, GB
MILLER, Stephen, decd, Susan apptd gdn of orphs 3/3/1834: Stephen S. and Milly A. E., minors, Daniel Kelly, sec, Richmond, GB
MILLER, William, a lunatic, Pleasant M. Glass, gdn, John Goodman, Charles W. Still, Abiah McGuire, sur, 1/14/1850, Butts, GB
MILLER, William, orph of Benjamin, decd, Garrett Williams was exhonorated as gdn, William Coursey was apptd gdn 3/5/1821, Bulloch, MIC

MILLER, William, orph of Benjamin, decd, William A. Coursey, gdn,
makes retn 5/12/1822, Bulloch, Misc
MILLER, William, orph of Benjamin, decd, received of Garrett
Williams, cattle, being prop of William, signed W. A. Coursey,
7/12/1821, Bulloch, Misc
MILLIGAN, John, decd, Polly Milligan and Owen Holliday issued L/A
11/3/1817, William Gill, sec, Morgan, AB
MILLS, Alex, decd, LWT pvd 11/1/1777, ch: Agnes Tompson,
Elizabeth Ayer, Gilbert, Alex, John, Jane, Margaret Baker,
William, Abigail, James, Sarah, Absolom, Jesse, David Alexander;
wife Alias and Wm Gent, exrs, Wilkes, MxR
MILLS, Catherine Augusta, orph of Joseph, decd, Mrs. M. E. Mills
apptd gdn 6/7/1846, Camden, MIC
MILLS, Jane, admx appvd, p. 137, Screven, OM
MILLS, Joseph, decd, Isaac Slayton, James Wainwright and Franklin
Wainwright, apprs, 6/1/1846, Camden, MIC
MILLS, Joseph, orph of Joseph, decd, Mrs. M. E. Mills apptd gdn
6/7/1846, Camden, MIC
MILLS, Joseph Sr, decd, Mrs. M. E. Mills apptd gdn of Joseph,
Sarah Ann, Margaret Jane, Samuel McClellan, Catherine Augusta,
Seaborn Foster & Mary Ann Elizabeth Mills, 6/7/1846, Camden, MIC
MILLS, Margaret Jane, orph of Joseph, decd, Mrs. M. E. Mills
apptd gdn 6/7/1846, Camden, MIC
MILLS, Margaret, John Conner apptd gdn, 4/15/1807, Camden, MIC
MILLS, Margaret, orphan, John Conner, gdn, 4/15/1807, Camden, MIC
MILLS, Mary Ann Elizabeth, orph of Joseph, decd, Mrs. M. E. Mills
apptd gdn 6/7/1846, Camden, MIC
MILLS, Obedience O., decd, David Johnson, James Thompson, admrs,
9/2/1811, Jones, AB
MILLS, Samuel McClellan, orph of Joseph, decd, Mrs. M. E. Mills
apptd gdn 6/7/1846, Camden, MIC
MILLS, Sarah Ann, orph of Joseph, decd, Mrs. M. E. Mills apptd
gdn 6/7/1846, Camden, MIC
MILLS, Seaborn Foster, orph of Joseph, decd, Mrs. M. E. Mills
apptd gdn 6/7/1846, Camden, MIC
MILLS, Stephen, decd, Jane and Thomas, admrs, p. 111, John B.
Mills relieved from bond, p. 112, Screven, OM
MILLS, Thomas, decd, Joseph Blackshear issued L/A 7/7/1817,
Laurens, AB
MILLS, Thomas, decd, Mrs. Sarah Mills, extrx of LWT 2/15/1791,
Chatham, Adms
MILLS, William, decd, Mrs. Mary Mills and Stephen Brinson apply
for adm 11/29/1791, Effingham, Misc
MILLSAP, Reuben, decd, John Williams, Parthena Millsap, admrs,
1852-53 retns, dismissed 1856, Fayette
MILLWOOD, James, decd, Letty Millwood, admx, Levin Clarke, sec,
7/5/1830, Hall, AB
MILNER, Elizabeth, orph of Pitt W., decd, Eli Edmondson, J. V.
May, surs, 5/1847, Fayette, GB
MILNER, James, decd, Cynthia Milner, admx 2/7/1784, Chatham, Adms
MILNER, Jessie, illegitimate child of Rebecca, John Foster, gdn,
11/6/1817, John Thrasher, sur, Clarke, GB
MILNER, Pitt W., decd, James F. Johnson, admr de bonis non, 1851-
1853 retns, Fayette, AB
MILNER, Pitt W., orph of Pitt W., decd, William N. Hill, gdn,
1851-1853 retns, Fayette, GB
MILNER, Susan, orph of Pitt W., decd, Eli Edmondson, J. V. May,
surs, 5/1847, 1851-1853 retns, Fayette, GB
MILNER, William L., orph of Pitt W., decd, Parker Eason, gdn, Wm
Brown, sur, 1/1848, 1851-1855 retns, Fayette, GB
MIMMS, Thomas, decd, 10/28/1840, apprs: Henry H. Ross, J. J.
Collier, Malcolm Hall, Dooly, I&A

MIMS, Franklin P., minor orph of John F., decd, Thomas F. Grubb
issued L/G 9/7/1857, Fulton
MIMS, Georgia A., minor orph of John F., decd, Thomas F. Grubb
issued L/G 9/7/1857, Fulton
MIMS, John F., decd, Mary Jane Mims and Thomas F. Grubbs, admrs,
8/4/1856, Fulton
MIMS, John F., minor orph of John F., decd, Thomas F. Grubb
issued L/G 9/7/1857, Fulton
MIMS, Marcia, orph of John F., decd, Thomas F. Grubb issued L/G
9/17/1857, Fulton
MIMS, William, minor of John F., decd, Thomas F. Grubb issued L/G
9/17/1857, Fulton
MINCHEW, Philip, decd, inv 4/20/1827 by James Hollaway, Allen
Dixon, Joshua Everett, Enoch Fagan, Bulloch, Misc
MINCY, Philip, decd, LWT pvd 6/20/1827 names wife, Elizabeth;
dau, Susan Barer; grson, John Barer; Abram Ross; Jacob Mincy,
John C. Everitt, exrs, wit: William Holland, Josiah J. Everitt,
Enoch Fagan, Bulloch, Misc
MINGLEDORFF, George, minor, Godhelf Smith, gdn, makes retn
3/24/1797, Effingham, Misc
MINGLEDORFF, Jacob, minor, Godhelf Smith, gdn, makes retn
3/24/1797, Effingham, Misc
MINIS, Philip, decd, Judith Minis, Leroy Morchams, admrs, 4/1789,
Chatham, Adms
MINUS, Elizabeth (Mrs.), apptd gdn of her ch: Sarah M., Francis
M., Elizabeth, Emily, Nancy W., and Ann A.; James M. Means,
Martin Cagle, sur, 5/3/1852, Cherokee, GB
MINUS, William, minor orph of John F., decd, Thomas F. Grubb
qualified as gdn 9/7/1857, dismissed 9/5/1859, Fulton
MINYARD, Thomas, decd, John Bell issued L/A 1/4/1842, w/LWT
annexed, Richard Banks, sec, Richmond, AB
MITCHEL, James, minor orph of John, decd, Charles Stewart apptd
gdn, Jesse Lee, Stephen Grenade, surs, 1/6/1806, Oglethorpe, MIC
MITCHEL, John, decd, Christina Mitchel and Charles Stewart apptd
admrs 1/1804, Oglethorpe, MIC
MITCHEL, John, orph of John, decd, John Collier apptd gdn,
Richard Bailey, Joseph Harrison, surs, 1/1804, Oglethorpe, MIC
MITCHEL, J. Z., decd, L/A issued W. H. Bush 12/1861, Webster, OD
MITCHEL, Robert, minor orph of John, decd, Isaac Collier apptd
gdn, John Powell, William Collier, surs, 1/1804, Oglethorpe, MIC
MITCHEL, Stith, minor orph of John, decd, Isaac Collier apptd
gdn, John Powell, William Collier, surs, 1/1804, Oglethorpe, MIC
MITCHEL, Thomas, orph of John, decd, John Collier apptd gdn,
Richard Bailey, Joseph Harrison, surs, 1/1804; ordered that
Thomas be bound and apprenticed to Joel Colley, bricklayer, James
Jones, William Brown, surs, 1/1805, Oglethorpe, MIC
MITCHELL, Abner, decd, William Berry, James Mitchell apptd temp
admrs; perm L/A gtd to Robert Rutherford 4/28/1801, 9/24/1800,
Warren, MIC
MITCHELL, Abner, decd, Robert Rutherford, admr, 2/10/1801, R.
Abercrombie, Henry Shelton, surs, Warren, MIC
MITCHELL, Daniel, decd, L/A issued to Henry Mitchell, 5/2/1814,
Jasper, OM
MITCHELL, David B., decd, Donald M. McDonald, admr 1/15/1838,
Camden, MIC
MITCHELL, David B., decd, John J. Mitchell, admr 1/13/1845,
Camden, MIC
MITCHELL, Ebenezer A., decd, of Lumpkin, harness and shoemaker,
George B. Perry, admr 1/1844; apprs: Benjamin H. Brown, John
Blackshear, Silas Ramey, Wm Smith, Stewart, Adms
MITCHELL, Henry, decd, William and Julia C. B. issued L/A
1/18/1819, Laurens, AB

219

MITCHELL, Henry, decd, L/D issued Mason H. Bush, 11/1856, Webster, OD
MITCHELL, James, decd, Lorany Mitchell, admr, William Berry, Joseph Bowen, sur, 1/4/1808, Warren, MIC
MITCHELL, James, decd, Peter Clower, admr in rt of his wife, dismissed 2/3/1812, Warren, MIC
MITCHELL, Jefferson M., orph of Jackson, decd, Henry Mitchell, gdn, F. M. Mitchell, sur, 3/6/866, Paulding, GB
MITCHELL, John, decd, LWT pvd 6/7/1841, Hiram W. Brooks, Alex McDoughal, exrs, Harris
MITCHELL, John, decd, Mrs. Christiana, wid, applied to ct to grant her guardianship in place of Charles Stewart of her child, James, 39/1808, Oglethorpe, OM
MITCHELL, Margaret S. L. C., decd, Loyd Coursey issued L/A 1/8/1863, Fulton
MITCHELL, Patrick, decd, inv, Ambrose Dollar, Cornelius Dunahoo, Edward Harper, apprs, 1/14/1808, Elbert, AR
MITCHELL, Richard, decd, LWT pvd, L/T issued Walter and Robert Mitchell, 3/2/1818; the widow, Elizabeth, is apptd extrx in place of Walter Mitchell 9/7/1818, Jasper, OM
MITCHELL, Thomas H., decd, Robert E. Mitchell, Mathew A. Mitchell, admrs, T. K. Mitchell, R. D. Winn, sur, 11/6/1876, Gwinnett, AB
MITCHELL, William A., decd, Richd C. Baldwin issued L/A 11/15/1834; 1836 retns heirs: Mary L. Norton, Saml Dutton, Saml A. Mitchell, Mary, Juliet, Leicester and Wm. Carrington, Almira Carrington, wid, Chas and Aloze Thompson, Richmond, AB
MITCHELL, William H., orph of William, decd, James E. Cook, gdn, Isham Fannin, Joshua Askew, secs, 9/5/1816, Morgan, GB
MITCHINER, William B., exr acct appvd, p. 107, Screven, OM
MIZE, James, decd, LWT pvd, L/T issued Rhoda Mize 1/5/1818, Jasper, OM
MIZE, Zachariah, decd, LWT dtd 10/9/1833, pvd 7/7/1834 names wife, Jemima and ch: Frederick, William D., Littleton, Howel, Jemima Forister, wife of Thomas, Sally Johnson, wife of James, Habersham, MIC
MIZELL, Jesse, decd, LWT pvd by James Scott, Mrs. Mary Mizell qualified as extrx 1/2/1837, Camden, MIC
MIZELL, Luke, decd, Patience Mizell, etc., extrx, p. 148, LWT pvd by George Newton, p. 147, 148, Screven, OM
MOBLEY, Levi E., decd, James Mobley, admr 5/30/1831, Effingham, MI
MOBLEY, Reuben, decd, LWT pvd 9/1844, Lennard, D. A. and J. L. Mobley, sons, exrs, Harris
MOBLEY, Silas, Elenor Mobley, gdn, p. 147, Screven, OM
MOBLEY, Thomas, decd, Elenor Mobley, admx, 116, William Mobley, etc. appraised est, p. 116, Screven, OM
MOCK, Benjamin, decd, Esther Mock, admx, p. 20, Screven, OM
MOCK, Charlotte, Andrew Mock, gdn, p. 56, George Mock, gdn, p. 93, Screven, OM
MOCK, Esther, admx, to show cause, p. 84, Screven, OM
MOCK, James, George H. Mauer, gdn, p. 173, Screven, OM
MOCK, Mary, decd, George F. Mock, admr, Dooly, OD
MOISE, Jacob, apptd gdn o f his own minor ch 5/5/1836: Sarah A., Philip A., Jefferson, Franklin, Howard and Rosalie C., John J. Cohen, sec, Richmond, GB
MOLDER, Catharine, decd, P. B. Cox, admr de bonis non, Almen Stratten, sur, 5/1850, Fayette, AB
MOLDER, Daniel, decd, retn by James Mitchell, Catharine Molder, exrs; LWT dtd 2/17/1806 names wife, Catharine, ch--Daniel, Jacob, Elizabeth, Sarah, Abraham and Lewis Molder, Mary Mitchell, Catharine Mitchell and Anne Mitchell, Franklin, OM
MOLLOY, James, decd, L/A gtd Jeremiah Molloy 1/1816, Jasper, OM

MOMAN, Pleasant, decd, Polly Moman issued L/A 3/4/1816, William W. Rose, sec, Morgan, AB

MONACK, John, decd, Mary Monack applies for L/A 4/19/1796, inv includes 250 acres on Coldwater Cr, also 190 acres; apprs: Mark Thornton, Job Teasley, Richard Tiner, Elbert, AR

MONEY, John, decd, Mary Money and Richard Moore, exrs of LWT 4/20/1796, Columbia, Ests

MONEY, Mary, decd, Samuel Brown and Joseph Miller gtd L/A 6/1/1798, Columbia, Ests

MONK, Hiram, decd, Mary Monk, wife, bequeathed all prop, 1/24/1815, Bulloch, Misc

MONTCRIEF, Benjamin, orph and minor of William, decd, Robert Harper apptd gdn, Willis Whatley, Walter Shropshire, surs, 1/1805, Oglethorpe, MIC

MONTCRIEF, Samson, orph and minor of William, decd, Robert Harper apptd gdn, Willis Whatley, Walter Shropshire, surs, 1/1805, Oglethorpe, MIC

MONTGOMERY, James, decd, Elizabeth Montgomery issued L/A, 1/1866, Webster, OD

MONTGOMERY, James, decd, Nancy Montgomery issued L/A 11/6/1848, Baldwin

MONTGOMERY, James M. C. (Major), apptd gdn of orphs: Sally and Nancy Morris 7/1/1811, Jackson, OM

MONTGOMERY, John Harford (Dr.), decd, William W. Montgomery, Richard H. Wilde issued L/A 3/11/1823; 8/24/1824 div to Mrs. Sarah C. H. Montgomery, wid, and inf child (only heirs); Wm. W. Montgomery gets share in his own rt, Richmond, AB

MONTRAY, John, decd, Cassandra Montray applied for L/T on LWT of her decd father 12/26/1797, Warren, MIC

MOON, Jacob, decd, Capt. Michael Gilbert applied for L/A 11/15/1793, Greens, Misc

MOON, James, decd, Germain T. Dortic issued L/A 7/5/1832, John P. King, sec, Richmond, AB

MOON, Jesse, bound to Archilaus Moon 5/4/1812 to be taught farming, William H. Moon, sec, Elbert, GB

MOON, Jesse, decd, Bolar Moon issued L/A 7/4/1808, Jackson, OM

MOON, Sally, bound to Sarah Moon to be taught housewifery, Archilus and Robert Moon, sec, 5/4/1812, Elbert, GB

MOON, Stephen, bound to William H. Moon to be taught farming 5/4/1812, Archilaus Moon, sec, Elbert, GB

MOON, William, decd, 2/25/1811 inv inclues 200 acres ss of Broad River, 80 acres ns sd river, slaves; legatees receipts: A. and B. Moon, William Power, Martha and John Blake, David Power, 1811, Elbert, AR

MOONEY, Christopher, decd, William C. Dillon, gdn of minor orphs: James, Richard, Sarah, George Pearson, Henry Mealing, secs, Richmond, GB

MOONEY, Elizabeth, decd, Moses Eadleman issued L/A 3/6/1820, Isaac Moore, sec, Morgan, AB

MOONEY, Isaac, decd, Isaac Mooney issued L/A 11/1/1819, John Hodge, sec, Morgan, AB

MOONEY, Thomas, decd, Thomas Smedley issued L/A 11/6/1820, Jacobus Watts, sec, Richmond, AB

MOONEY, Valentine, decd, Joseph Heard and Stephen Durden issued L.A 7/7/1817, James Hitchcock, Drewry Brewer, secs, Morgan, AB

MOORE, A., decd, Jeremiah Moore, admr, 1855, Cobb, BB

MOORE, Aaron, decd, Williau Moore, exr 12/30/1789, Chatham, Adms

MOORE, Abram, decd, Thompson Moore, temp, admr, Joseph W. Baxter, sur, 7/20/1874; Thompson Moore apptd admr, A. G. Harris, Aaron Swinney, sur, 9/7/1874 dtd at Lawrenceville, Gwinnett, AB

MOORE, Alis A., Elizabeth D. B. Moore apptd gdn, 3/10/1856, Cherokee, GB

MOORE, All. C., decd, John L. Moore issued L/A 11/8/1843, Baldwin
MOORE, Ambrose Jr., orph of Jesse, decd, Esther Morris, gdn,
4/4/1859, Paulding, GB
MOORE, Arthur, decd, Mrs. Priscilla Moore apptd admx 6/3/1837,
Camden, MIC, AB
MOORE, Arthur, Sr., decd, Arthur Moore apptd admr 1/6/1835,
Camden, MIC
MOORE, Casin, decd, LWT pvd 1/9/1843, Sarah Moore, exr,
Washington
MOORE, Catherine, orph of Robert, decd, James L. D. Harbin, gdn,
William F. Mullins, sur, 3/11/1856, Cherokee, GB
MOORE, Catherine (Mrs.), decd, wid, Mrs. Mary Eustace, extrx
1/17/1791, Chatham, Adms
MOORE, Charles, decd, LWT dtd 4/1/1799 pvd 1/16/1800, ch: Risdon,
Jonathan; grson, William Moore, son of Risdon (Greene Co. land),
Hancock, AA
MOORE, Edward, decd, inv 8/11/1799; apprs: Loyd Kelly, Drury
Cook, Reubin Jones, Hancock, AA
MOORE, Elijah, decd, Leroy W. Moore issued L/A 5/6/1833, Baldwin
MOORE, Elizabeth, dau of John Moore, Sr., chose her father as gdn
7/1806; heir of Martha Harvee, decd, John Moore, Sr. apptd gdn
1/1804, Oglethorpe, MIC
MOORE, Ephraim, decd, LWT dtd 7/16/1801, wife, Nancy, ch:
William, Neubil (to be bound as apprentice to Thomas Taylor to
learn house carpenter's trade), Tabitha, Levin, wife "now
pregnant", Hancock, AAAA
MOORE, Francis (Mayor), decd, George Handley, admr, 6/30/1789,
Chatham, Adms
MOORE, Frederick, decd, Duncan Cameron applied for L/A 3/15/1799,
Greene, Misc
MOORE, George, decd, LWT pvd 8/1/1859, Paulding
MOORE, Jacob Alexander, Elizabeth D. B. Moore, gdn, 3/10/1856,
Cherokee, GB
MOORE, James, decd, Bryant Meredith repots to ct that John W.
Jones, admr, has removed from State, 1/13/1845, Camden, MIC
MOORE, James, decd, Joseph A. Eve issued L/A 7/20/1830, Milton
Antony, Lewis D. Ford, secs, Richmond, AB
MOORE, James, decd, LWT pvd 5/17/1825; William Moore, exr, gtd
leave to sell, 2/2/1828, Glynn, MIC
MOORE, James, decd, Thomas Moore, admr, 8/4/1856, Martin Defoor,
Thomas L. Thomas, John Jones, James Davis, surs, DeKalb, AB
MOORE, James, decd, William Moore qualified as exr, 1/10/1825,
Glynn, MIC
MOORE, James C., Cullen Davis issued L/G 12/1866, Webster, OD
MOORE, James J., decd, James H. C. Maguire, admr, Thomas Maguire,
William Galloway, sur, 3/6/1876, Gwinnett, AB
MOORE, James R., Elizabeth D. B. Moore apptd gdn, 3/10/1856,
Cherokee, GB
MOORE, Jane, orph of John, decd, Richardson Woods apptd gdn
9/1/1817, Jasper, OM
MOORE, Jeremiah A., decd, Mrs. Susannah Moore, admr, applies for
leave to sell land in Bartow Co., 8/30/1869, Cobb, MIC
MOORE, John bound to William Holloway 9/1/1817, Jasper, OM
MOORE, John, decd, Celia Moore issued L/A 9/4/1815, Laurens, AB
MOORE, John, decd, Hezekiah Evans, admr, dismissed 9/5/1831,
Effingham, MIC
MOORE, John, decd, William Moore of Chatham Co. apptd admr
4/2/1793, Effingham, Misc
MOORE, John, decd, William Moore, admr, dismissed 3/25/1795,
Effingham, Misc
MOORE, John, decd, Willoby Hammock, Jacob Laughridge, exrs,
7/9/1795, Franklin, OM, EB

MOORE, John, decd, late of Edgefield Dist., S. C., William J. Wightman issued L/A 11/3/1834, James P. Stuart, Robert Philip, secs; 1834 retn shows 1000 acres Washington Co., Richmond, AB
MOORE, John, ordered that Hezekiah Evans sell pt of real est 1/7/1839, Effingham, MIC
MOORE, John, orph of John, decd, bound to William Holloway 9/1/1817, Jasper, OM
MOORE, John, Sr., decd, L/A issued James Moore, Sr. and Jr., 11/4/1816, Jasper, OM
MOORE, Joseph, decd, LWT pvd 5/1807, Oglethorpe, OM
MOORE, Margaret, dau of John Moore, Sr., chose her father as gdn 7/1806; heir of Martha Harvee, decd, John Moore, Sr. apptd gdn 1/1804, Oglethorpe, MIC
MOORE, Mary, decd, Hezekiah Evans, admr, dismissed 9/5/1831, Effingham, MIC
MOORE, Mary, ordered that Hezekiah Evans sell pt of real est 1/7/1839, Effingham, MIC
MOORE, Mary A. H. J., orph of John, decd, Jason Powell issued L/G 3/7/1831, Washington
MOORE, Michael, decd, James Moore, admr, makes retns, 10/25/1802, Jackson, OM
MOORE, Mordecai, decd, Alexander Moore, admr, 1/5/1795, James Raley, sur, dismissed 8/14/1805, Warren, AB, MIC
MOORE, Nubas?, decd, Tomlinson Flora issued L/A 3/20/1835, Baldwin
MOORE, Rebecca Ann, orph of James M., decd, Elizabeth Moore, gdn, 9/3/1849; William Hazlewood, gdn, William A. Williams, sur, 8/1/1853, Cherokee, GB
MOORE, Robert, decd, James Strain, admr, James L. O. Harbin, Benjamin F. Strain, sur, 12/10/1855, Cherokee, AB
MOORE, Robert S., decd, Rowland Moore issued temporary L/A 1/1864, Webster, OD
MOORE, Samuel, decd, Deborah Moore gtd L/A, 1802, Jackson, OM
MOORE, Samuel, decd, LWT pvd, Olive Moore and Joda Newsom qualified as exrs 12/18/1795, Warren, MIC
MOORE, Samuel L., decd, James R. Moore, admr, produces application from Stewart Co. and order to make retn, 6/1854, Webster, OD
MOORE, Sarah, decd, Jemimah Holland, Joseph A. Floyes, Samuel Huey, Fleming R. Nance, admrs, 11/7/1836, Harris
MOORE, Susan E., orph of Jonathan, decd, Andrew F. Woolley, gdn, Carey Jackson and A. Chastain, secs, 11/1/1830, Hall, GB
MOORE, Thomas, decd, Frances Moore issued L/A 7/7/1806, John Campbell, John Moore, secs, Richmond, AB
MOORE, Thomas, decd, William A. McCune, admr, Thomas J. Giles, James W. Faulkner, sur, 11/3/1845, Butts, AB
MOORE, Underhill, decd, LWT pvd 5/7/1838, Shadrack Moore, exr, Washington
MOORE, W. H., minor, retn of John T. Sharpe, gdn, 2/13/1837, Tattnall, I&A
MOORE, William, David Kennedy and John W. McLeon for self and as atty for William Moore of Glynn Co. declares they will abive by div made by Jonathan Robinson, Sheppard Williams and John Barber, 3/7/1818, Bulloch, Misc
MOORE, William, decd, Jemimah Hallman, Campbell Burton, James Huey, A. Huey, gdns of orphs 11/7/1836, Harris
MOORE, William, decd, late of Augusta, Arthur Scott issued L/A 8/3/1815, John Cashin, Benjamin Moore, secs, Richmond, AB
MOORE, William, decd, late of Barnwell Dist., S. C., John Leverman issued L/A 3/6/1824, Wm Glover, Walton Knight, secs; 1824 retn pd Sarah Moore, board for Sarah A. Moore, 202-1/2 acres Henry Co., Richmond, AB

MOORE, William, son of John, John Davenport apptd gdn, John Gresham, Sr, sur, 6/18/1800, Oglethorpe, MIC
MOORE, William Arthur, minor of Nancy, John Moore, gdn, Marian Moore, James Herington, sur, 5/6/1839, Emanuel, GB
MOORE, William B., decd, Willis Vaughan, admr de bonis non 1/14/1850, Baldwin
MOORE, William D., decd, Tomlinson Fort issued L/A 1/13/1845, Baldwin
MOORE, William H., John T. Sharp, gdn, makes retn 7/8/1836, Tattnall, I&A
MOOYER, W., decd, Abram Green, exr, 1855, pvd LWT, records appraisement, Cobb, BB
MORAN, James, decd, an alien, I. Abrahams, Escheator of Glynn Co., gtd leave to sell prop, 6/10/1818, Glynn, MIC
MORE, Elizabeth M., decd, A. F. Northcutt applies for L/A 4/6/1870, Cobb, MIC
MORE, Joseph, decd, William and Elizabeth Golson apptd admrs, Wilkes, MxR
MOREL, Georgianna chose John G. Morel as gdn 11/3/1834, Effingham, MIC
MOREL, H. W. chose John G. Morel as gdn 11/3/1834, Effingham, MIC
MORELAND, Francis, Sr., decd, appr 4/8/1797, apprs: Wm Cimbro, John Kimbrough, Greene, Misc
MORELAND, John, decd, Lucey Moreland applied for L/A 2/14/1799, Greene, Misc
MORELAND, John, decd, Rebecca Moreland, gdn of orphs: Rosetta Pirenas and Martha Jane, 1/4/1840, Gilmer, Misc
MORGAN, David, decd, Sarah Morgan and others, admrs, p. 94, John Jackson, etc., apprs, p. 99, Screven, OM
MORGAN, John, decd, James Moore, admr, gtd leave to sell slave of est, 6/14/1819, Glynn, MIC
MORGAN, John, decd, LWT pvd by John Cargile, Robert and Thomas Gaston, L/T issued Charles Morgan 7/3/1815, Jasper, OM
MORGAN, John, decd, inv 2/10/1784, Jonathan Ragan, John Fling, Walton Harris, apprs, Wilkes, MxR
MORGAN, John, minor, chose James Moore as his gdn, 1/11/1819, Glynn, MIC
MORGAN, John, decd, Elizabeth Morgan and Nathaniel Hunt, exrs, 6/6/1790, inv by John Williams, William Gough, John Mullin; list of accts against est 1/10/1798, Franklin, OM, EB
MORGAN, Luke, decd, LWT pvd 3/17/1783, wife, Mary all est for life to rear children, Wilkes, MxR
MORGAN, Milton, decd, L/A gtd James Morgan, 7/3/1815, Jasper, OM
MORGAN, Morgan, (or Magnan) decd, William Maltbie issued temp L/A 11/12/1816, Ralph Ketchum, Nathl Sturges, secs, Richmond, AB
MORGAN, Moses, decd, William C. Gill applies for L/A 1/15/1858, Henry P. Wooten, sur, Lee
MORGAN, Nathaniel, decd, John Nelson, Samuel Huey, gdn of orphs of decd, 11/21/1837, Harris
MORGAN, Robert, decd, Elizabeth Morgan issued L/A 5/7/1783, William and Habakkuk Wright, secs, Richmond, AB
MORGAN, Robert, decd, inv 1806, John Stewart, Benjamin Scott, Owen Fluker, admrs, Richmond
MORGAN, Samuel, decd, LWT dtd 2/8/1832 names ch: Samuel, Jr., John, Jonathan, Thomas, Martha Garison, Patsy Paris and Talitha Cockram, pvd 1/14/1834, Habersham, MIC
MORGAN, Thomas, decd, John Carmichael, Robert and Polly Morgan issued L/A 4/4/1808, Jackson, OM
MORGAN, William, decd, Saml Hay, Priscilla Morgan exrs LWT 5/1/1809; Geo. D. & Priscilla Lester, gdns to orphs: Priscilla, Esther & Mahaly under 14, & Wm, over 14 chose Jos. McLester; Samuel Hay, gdn of Jesse, 3/6/1815, Jackson, OM

MORGSOUM?, George W., orph of Simon, decd, John D. Pope, gdn,
4/2/1866, Fulton, GB
MORRELL, Benjamin, decd, Benjamin Joseph Morrel, admr, 5/1833,
Effingham, MIC
MORRELL, Jordan, decd, Dennis Madden issued L/A 6/20/1816, Davis
Madden, sec, Morgan, AB
MORRIS, Amey A., orph of Jesse, decd, Esther Morris, gdn,
4/4/1859, Paulding, GB
MORRIS, Benjamin, decd, Mary Morris, admx, to sell prop 1/6/1817,
inv and sale 2/15/1817; recd of Jeremiah Pittman $129.13 "in
full of all demands against estate....being my part of the estate
of John Grimes, decd, my father", signed John Grimes, 10/2/1822;
Jeremiah Pittman, admr, orphs named as: Sarah, Edward, Susan,
Mary. Signed John Grimes, 2/15/1823; inv of pers prop, div to:
Cannon R. Rodgers, Mary Morris, Jeremiah Pittman, Sarah H.
Morris, Edward Morris, signed Aaron Cone, Malachi Denmark, John
Wise, 1/25/1823; receipt of Jeremiah Pittman, admr, "$712.50 in
full of my legacy from estate", signed C. B. Rodgers, 1/25/1824,
Bulloch, MIC, Misc
MORRIS, Elizabeth, orph of George, decd, Jordan Morris, gdn,
James S. Morris, William R. Bankston, sur, 11/20/1843, GB
MORRIS, James, decd, Sally and Isaac Morris apply for L/A
7/22/1795; inv includes land on which Sherod Morris lives; John
Staples, Joseph King, Andrew Johnson, apprs, Elbert, AR
MORRIS, Jesse, decd, Alex and Ann Morris apptd admrs, John Mills,
etc., apprs, p. 125, Thomas Mills, admr, p. 128, Screven, OM
MORRIS, John, decd, Benjamin Rees, admr, 11/6/1825, Jeremiah
Burkhalter, David Sallis, surs, Warren, AB
MORRIS, John, decd, Griffith Campbell and John C. Evans issued
L/A 1/12/1824, Morgan, AB
MORRIS, John, decd, LWT proved, L/T issued Hardy Gregory and
Rebecca Morris, 11/4/1816, Jasper, OM
MORRIS, John, decd, LWT pvd by Joseph Camp and Wm Nichols
3/4/1811; Frederick Thompson, one of exrs, makes inventory
7/1/1811, Jackson, OM
MORRIS, John G., decd, M. B. W. Still, admr, 11/2/1829, Butts, AB
MORRIS, Mary Ann, age 13, orph of Moses, decd, Littleberry
Bagwell, gdn until age 18, Saml Bellah, sur, 9/3/1832, Butts, GB
MORRIS, Nancy to be bound to Mason Ezzard until age 18, 4/6/1802,
Jackson, OM
MORRIS, Nancy, decd, John Morris issued L/A 3/6/1837, Matthias
Adams, Neill McLeod, secs, Montgomery, AB
MORRIS, Richard J., decd, of Barnwell Dist, South Carolina, Allen
Moye, admr, 3/1833, rec Stewart Co. 1/13/1837, mentions John Rice
of S. C., Edward B. and James G. Morris, wid, Delilah Morris and
6 ch, 16 slaves, Stewart, Adms
MORRIS, Thomas, decd, John Stewart issued L/A 1/6/1823, C. Allen,
sec, Morgan, AB
MORRIS, Thomas, decd, Rees Morris issued L/A 9/16/1736, John
Morris, John Foster, secs, Richmond, AB
MORRIS, Thomas, decd, Samuel Morris issued L/A 1/3/1803, John
Andrews, sec, Richmond, AB
MORRIS, Thomas, decd, William Morris qualified as admr 1/26/1785,
Liberty, Ests
MORRIS, Thomas, decd, John Harvey, John Dollar qualified as admrs
4/27/1783, Liberty, Ests
MORRIS, William, decd, Nathaniel Durkee issued L/A 7/30/1799,
Noah Kelsey, sec, Richmond, AB
MORRISON, Angus, Daniel Peterson apptd gdn (natural), minor of sd
Daniel Peterson, 9/3/1838, Hugh Hughs, Neill Gillis, secs,
Montgomery, GB

MORRISON, Daniel Q., minor, John Peterson, gdn, 9/3/1838, Montomgery, GB
MORRISON, Daniel W., minor, Archibald McCrimmon, gdn, 9/3/1838, Montgomery, GB
MORRISON, Edward, decd, Susanna Davison issued temp L/A 11/5/1833, Hall
MORRISON, Francis, decd, 2/24/1803, div according to LWT: Peter and Frances Morrison, john Satterwhite, Ezra Morrison, Washington, Clary and Polly D. Morrison; decd´s heirs are heirs of Aron Higginbotham of Amherst Co., Va., Elbert, AR
MORRISON, George, LWT pvd 6/7/1824, Camden, MIC
MORRISON, Hugh, decd, of Lee Co., John Morrison issued L/A 9/30/1830, Philip H. Mantz, sec; Danile Morrison purchaser of slaves 7/5/1831, Richmond, AB
MORRISON, J. E., decd, LWT pvd 3/23/1863, John Campbell, exr, Fulton
MORRISON, Joseph, decd, John S. Higginbotham apptd gdn of minors: Clary G., Polly D., Frances; certain fees to be pd by them to Clary Higginbotham, wid of Aron, decd, Elbert, AR
MORRISON, Joseph, decd, William B. Hardeman, admr, 2/2/1857, Fulton
MORRISON, Katharine, decd, Charles McCrimmon issued L/A 7/2/1838, Montgomery, AB
MORRISON, Thomas, decd, Francis Morrison, James Morrison issued L/A 6/16/1790, L/A retd, sd property lying in Wilkes Co., Richmond, AB
MORRISON, Thomas, decd, Francis and James Morrison gtd L/A 6/16/1796, Columbia, Ests
MORRISON, William, decd, Nathaniel Ward applied for adm 12/29/1803, Michael Burkhalter, sur, Warren, MIC, AB
MORRISSY, Joseph, decd, William B. Hardman qualified as admr 2/2/1857, dismissed 8/5/1861, Fulton
MORROW, Francis, Jr., decd, Fendrick H. and William Morrow, admrs, Francis Whelchel, Daniel Madams, secs, 3/18/1834, Hall, AB
MORROW, James, decd, Lavina Morrow issued temp L/A 11/7/1850, Vincent Sears, sec; Lavina Morrow, gdn of orphs: David, Martha Ellis, Mary Ann, James and John Thomas Morrow 9/5/1853, H. E. Morrow, sec, Hall, AB, GB
MORROW, John, decd, Ewing Morrow applied for L/A 12/7/1790, Greene, Misc
MORROW, John, decd, LWT presented 8/4/1873, David W. Spence, exr, Robert R. Wood, John T. Henderson, sur, Gwinnett, AB
MORROW, Margaret (Mrs.), decd, LWT pvd 3/14/1791, s-i-l Jacob Maddox & Sarah, his wife; dau, Elizabeth Bell, Amherst Co, Va., L/T to Jacob Maddox 9/22/1791; inv 10/20/1791 listed plantation whereon decd husb, John Morrow, died, Greene, Misc
MORSE, Clemsey, decd, Ann Morse, Robert Johnson issued L/A 62/1808, Richmond, AB
MORSE, George, decd, Ann Morse and Robert Johnson issued L/A 5/11/1806, James Hamilton, John McKenzie, secs, Richmond, AB
MORSE, Jacob, decd, James Johnson issued L/A 5/31/1828, Philip H. Mantz, Willie Jones, secs, Richmond, AB
MORSE, James, decd, John Johnson issued L/A 5/31/1828, Philip H. Mantz, Willie Jones, sec, Richmond, AB
MORSE, James, decd, Lud Harris, Cleon Nally issued L/A 1/5/1816, Lewis Harris, Peter Donaldson, secs, Richmond, AB
MORSE, James, decd, Jacob and George Morse issued L/A 12/21/1795, Richmond, AB
MORSE, John, decd, Lud Harris, Cleon Nally issued L/A 1/5/1816, Lewis Harris, Peter Donaldson, secs, Richmond, AB

MORTON, Charles S., decd, LWT dtd 1/3/1804, ch: Olympia Muse
Morton, "my desire that my sd dau remain in care of Frances
Galloway & Sally his wife...."; est apprd 2/25/1806 by Henry
Smith, Elias Burgess, John Carter, 9/1805, Franklin, IMW
MORTON, Charles S., decd, inv 2/25/1806 by Henry Smith, Elias
Burgess, Jno Carter, 1/11/1806; LWT 1/3/1806-dau, Olympia Muse
Morton to remain with Francis & Sally Gallaway to raise her, etc;
250 ac to sd Francis Calloway, Franklin, OM
MORTON, Hiram, decd, Emily and William Morton, orphs, 3/6/1820,
gdn not named, Morgan, GB
MORTON, Hiram, decd, Richard Smith, gdn of orphs: Emily and Wm
11/7/1825, James Shepherd, John W. Stark, secs, Morgan, GB
MORTON, John, orph of Josiah, decd, Joseph F. Morton, gdn,
9/6/1819, Joel Morton, sur, Clarke, GB
MORTON, Margaret I., orph of Josiah, decd, William Morton, gdn,
9/6/1319, Joel Morton, sur, Clarke, GB
MORTON, Silas, gdn, acct appvd, p. 128, 195, Screven, OM
MOSALY, William, decd, James Vann apptd admr, Wilkes, MxR
MOSELEY, Benjamin, decd, Jane Moseley was gtd L/A 4/9/1794,
Columbia, Ests
MOSELEY, Henry, decd, LWT pvd by Rhoderick Harper, Benjamin
Moseley, exr, 1/7/1822, Jasper, OM
MOSELY, Alexander, decd, appr 6/17/1799, Greene, Misc
MOSES, Hiram, decd, Drury B. May, admr, Jeptha V. May, sur,
10/1852, 1852-1854 retns, Fayette, AB
MOSES, John, decd, 1821 retn by Moses Perkins, admr, payments to:
James Herndon, Samuel Moses, Williamson Mimms, Neale Moses, Amos
Young, meredith Moses, William Head, Moses Perkins, Jasper, Ests
MOSES, John, decd, inv 4/14/1810 apprs: Nehemiah Williams, Richd
Head, Garland Hardwick, Robt E. Richardson, 1810 pd Ann Moses;
1819 retn names heirs-W. Minner, Jas Horender, Neil Moses, Samuel
Moses, Meredith Moses, Wm Head, Jasper, OM
MOSES, Solomon, decd, Nancy Mercer, admx, George Deakle, Uriah
Anderson, David Griffin, sur, 10/6/1823, Emanuel, AB
MOSS, Andrew F. P., orph of Alexander, decd, Warren R. D. Moss,
gdn, Newton J. Perkins, sur, 2/12/1855, Cherokee, GB
MOSS, Gabriel, decd, LWT headed Meriwether Co., pvd 1/3/1846,
Henry E. Moss, exr, Harris
MOSS, John, decd, John Moss, gdn of William Willis, Fanny, James,
Archer and Susannah, minors, 9/1/1817, William Flippen, sur,
Clarke, GB
MOSS, John, decd, Elizabeth M. Moss, gdn of orphs: David M.,
Sarah S., Jane E. and Richard P., orphs, 3/3/1834, Mark Anthony,
Nicholas G. Barksdale, secs, Lincoln, GB
MOSS, John, decd, planter, Clammy Moss, Peter Paris issued L/A
5/20/1783, Abraham Jones, John Garrett, secs, Richmond, AB
MOSS, Sally, orph of John, decd, Mary Moss, gdn, 3/6/1820,
Benjamin Hagood, sur, Clarke, GB
MOSS, Stephen, decd, James Moss issued L/A 5/5/1819, Joshua Boon,
sec, Morgan, AB
MOSS, William, decd, John Knight, admr, Isaac Lamb, Jesse
Scarborough, sur, 3/1/1830, Emanuel, AB
MOSSES, Elizabeth, decd, retn on est for 1811 for schooling orph,
John; cash recd of Mosses Perkins and Samuel Mosses, admrs of
John Mosses, decd, Jasper, Ests
MOSSES, John, decd, orphs, William Mims, gdn, retn 1/6/1811,
Jasper, Ests
MOTE, Abel, decd, David Mote issued L/A 1/4/1820, Laurens, AB
MOTE, Hardy bound to Jesse Grizzle four years to learn
blacksmith's trade 2/6/1816, Jackson, OM
MOTE, Jethro, decd, Abel Mote issued L/A 5/3/1819; Edward Sealey,
admr de bonis non 11/6/1820, Laurens, AB

MOTT, William A., decd, William A. Mott issued L/A 5/6/1850, Baldwin
MOULDER, Daniel, decd, LWT dtd 2/17/1806 names wife, Catharine and ch: Daniel, Jacob, Elizabeth, Sarah, Abraham, Mary, Lewis, Catharine Mitchel, Anne Mitchel, dtd 2/17/1806, Franklin, IMW
MOULTRIE, Patience, admx, to show cause, p. 189, Screven, OM
MOYE, George, decd, Samuel B. Tarver issued L/A 5/25/1842, Washington
MULINAX, James D., decd, Caroline H., admx de bonis non 7/25/1863, Andrew Dorsey, sec; Champion Ferguson makes inv 9/3/1860, White
MULKEY, James, decd, Elizabeth Mulkey issued L/A 2/5/1827, Morgan, AB
MULKEY, Washington, decd, J. H. Reddick issued L/A 1/1862; Sarah Mulkey, admr de bonis non 3/1865 and gdn of Lavonia, minor, Webster, OD
MULLETT, David, decd, Jeremiah Mullett issued L/A 5/3/1830, Effingham, MIC
MULLINS, Burton, decd, Nancy Ann Mullins, John Westbrook, admrs, R. F. Daniel, William F. Mullins, sur, 10/10/1854; Newton J. Perkins, admr, William F. Mullins, Warren R. D. Moss, sur, 2/12/1855, Cherokee, AB
MULLINS, King H., decd, James M. K. Little issued L/A 3/1855, Webster, OD
MURDOCK, Allen, one of heirs of Joseph, states that Priscilla Cherry (formerly Murdock), admr and gdn, has mismanged est; Priscilla to appear and give accounting 7/4/1825, Habersham, MIC
MURDOCK, David, decd, Peter Karr, admr, LWT dtd 4/10/1788, 1/6/1789, Chatham, Adms
MURDOCK, Eliza H., orph of Joseph, chose Samuel Haden as gdn 11/6/1826, Habersham, MIC
MURDOCK, Elizabeth H., orph of Joseph, chose Samuel Haden as gdn 11/6/1826, Habersham, MIC
MURDOCK, Frances E., orph of Jeptha F., decd, Francis Kenaman, gdn, Wm Henderson, sec, 12/7/1863, White, GB
MURDOCK, Jeptha F., decd, William F. Sears, admr w/LWT annexed 11/22/1820, A. J. Comer, sec, White, AB
MURDOCK, Jeptha F. H., orph of Allen A., decd, Jeptha Freeman apptd gdn 7/1832, Habersham, MIC
MURDOCK, Joseph, decd, Jno Barton, Obadiah Hooper, secs for Priscilla Murdock, admx reld 5/1824; David C. Cherry, admr de bonis non for wf Priscilla, formerly wid 5/1825; Allen H. Murdock L/A 9/1826; Jno Boman L/A 9/1832, Habersham, MIC
MURDOCK, Judianna H., orph of Allen H., decd, Jeptha Freeman apptd gdn, 7/1832, Habersham, MIC
MURDOCK, Watson H., orph of Joseph, chose John Stanch, Jr., gdn, 11/6/1826, Habersham, MIC
MURPHEY, Charles, decd, Milton A. Candler, admr, 5/6/1861, E. Mason, sur, DeKalb, AB
MURPHEY, James, decd, Archibald Beall, Benjamin Leigh, George Weissinger, apprs, 6/1/1791, Richmond
MURPHEY, James, decd, John Murphey, admr, Andrew Murphey, Elisha Hill, Wm N. Hill, Thomas B. Gay, surs, 3/1850, 1851 retn, Fayette, AB
MURPHEY, Simon P., decd, Rebecca and Joseph H. Murphey, admrs w/LWT annexted, Thomas E. and Jeptha M. Murphey, Nathan Eason, E. M. Murphey, surs, 7/1850, 1851-1855 retns, Fayette, AB
MURPHEY, William, decd, Abbey Morrison, admx de bonis non, Edmund Murphey, sur, 12/3/1851, Bibb, AB
MURPHY, Benjamin, decd, Thomas H. Murphy, Churchill Blakeley, Felix Lasley, admrs, 7/25/1835; Thomas H. Murphy, John T. Thornton, J. W. Cato, gdns of orphs of decd, Harris, AB, GB

MURPHY, Edward, decd, Elizabeth and John Murphy, admrs 6/1/1802, John Rushin, John Wilson, surs, Warren, AB
MURPHY, Edward, decd, Elizabeth Murphy apptd admr 6/1/1802, John Rushing, John Wilson, sur, Warren, MIC, AB
MURPHY, Edward, decd, John Murphy, admr, dismissed 11/5/1810, Warren, MIC
MURPHY, Edward, decd, John Rushin and James Willson petition to be reled as sureties on bond of Elizabeth Rosser (formerly Murphy), Rule Nisi issued, 3/7/1808, Warren, MIC
MURPHY, James, decd, Mary Murphy issued L/A 4/19/1798, Absolom Rhodes, Aaron Rhodes, George Weissinger, secs, Richmond, AB
MURPHY, John, decd, Abner Vaughan dismissed from trust on est 10/3/1801, Franklin, OM
MURPHY, Martin H., orph of William, decd, under age 21, Francis Murphy apptd gdn 12/4/1798, Oglethorpe, MIC
MURPHY, Pascal H., orph of William, decd, under age 21, Francis Murphy apptd gdn, 12/4/1798, Oglethorpe, MIC
MURRAY, Daniel, decd, Richard Bolan issued L/A 5/5/1814, George Adams, John Cashin, secs, Richmond, AB
MURRAY, Daniel, decd, of Augusta, John Murray issued L/A 12/7/1818, Richard Bush, George Wallace, secs, Richmond, AB
MURRAY, Gabriel, decd, James P. Gardner issued L/A 5/23/1832, Alexander McKenzie, sec, Richmond, AB
MURRAY, James bound to Edward Sims to learn hatters trade 9/2/1811, David S. Booth, sec, Elbert, GB
MURRAY, John (Dr.), decd, Western B. Thomas issued L/A 2/11/1829, Robert Phillips, James Haynie, secs, Richmond, AB
MURRAY, William, decd, est acct appvd, p. 129, John Moore, etc., apprs, p. 124, Screven, OM
MURREN, James, decd, Joseph Cumming issued L/A 9/7/1813, Jesse Watson, Augustine Slaughter, secs, Richmond, AB
MURREN, William, decd, Goodwin Wilson issued L/A 7/1/1789; dismissed 8/15/1790, Chatham, Adms
MURREN, William, decd, Savannah Turpin apptd admx, 7/1/1789, Chatham, Adms
MURRY, John, decd, planter, Francis Lewis, of Savannah, publican admr 6/21/1783, Chatham, Adms
MUSE, George Washington chose John Fort as his gdn, 10/7/1811, Glynn, MIC
MUSSAULT, Francis, decd, Pelot DeVillers having failed to qualify as admr, William Gibson reinstated as exr 6/8/1809, Camden, MIC
MUSSELWHITE, Charles R., orph of William, decd, William W. Vann issued L/G 3/1/1841, Washington
MUSSELWHITE, James, orph of William, decd, William W. Vann issued L/G 3/1/1841, Washington
MUSSLEWHITE, Redding B., decd, Sarah L. Musslewhite issued L/A 3/4/1844, Baldwin
MUSSELWHITE, Sarah, orph of William, decd, William W. Vann issued L/G 3/1/1841, Washington
MUZU, Anderson, decd, L/A issued John E. Plunkett 1/1857, Webster, OD
MYERS, Benjamin P., decd, LWT pvd 11/3/1834, John W. Myers, exr, Harris
MYERS, Catherine, decd, William R. Venable issued L/A 3/5/1866, Fulton
MYERS, Elizabeth, a poor child, bound t William Hudnall, 7/3/1815, Jasper, OM
MYERS, Maria, orphan, Thomas Jones apptd gdn, whereupon the Clk was ordered to pay him 1/8th part of sd Myers est, 6/13/1814, Glynn, MIC
MYERS, Mary, decd, heirs asked for leave to sell negroes of est, 1/4/1814, Glynn, MIC

MYERS, Mary, orph, Thomas Jones apptd gdn, whereupon Clerk was ordered to pay him 1/8th part of Myers est, 1/13/1814, Glynn, MIC
MYERS, Michael, decd, John Lynch issued L/A 10/6/1862, Fulton
MYERS, Nicholas, decd, LWT admitted to record 11/2/1835, Effingham, MIC
MYERS, Sarah, decd, james Myers, one of heirs, complained that Isaac Abrahams, former Clk of this Ct and admr of her est, had not made acctg of est, 1/12/1824, Camden, MIC
MYHAND, John, decd, Jesse Butler issued L/A 3/3/1817; Alvan Myhand issued L/A 5/5/1817, John Gilpin, sec, Morgan, AB
MYRDON, John, decd, Willis Rhymes, admr, 3/1/1824, Micajah Rogers, sur, Warren, AB
MYRES, Margaret G., orph of Thomas, decd, Richard Brown issued L/G 3/1/1841, Washington
MYRES, Thomas, decd, Robert Whitefield issued L/A 1/5/1841, Washington
MYRICK, Goodwin, decd, Martha Myrick issued L/A 11/30/1834, Baldwin
MYRICK, John, decd, LWT pvd 11/2/1835, Elizabeth Cody, extrx: named: Ann Rinsey, Howell Myrick, William, Richard and Josiah Myrick, Mary Milford, Swanford Cady, William Cady, Harris
MYRICK, John, decd, LWT pvd, John Myrick, Jr. and Nathaniel Myrick qualified exrs 1/23/1804, Warren, MIC
MYRICK, John, Sr., decd, LWT heard testimony of witnesses, caveat was filed; Thomas Flinn apptd temp admr; case appealed to Superior Court by consent 7/7/1806, Warren, MIC
MYRICK, Owen, decd, Elizabeth Myrick applies for L/A, apptd 2/15/1804, Thomas Edmonds and Septimus Weatherby, sur, Warren, MIC, AB
MYRICK, Owen, decd, Elizabeth Myrick, admx, 2/15/1804, Thomas Edmondson, Septimus Weatherby, surs; Elizabeth Myrick, wid, to ct w/minor son, Nathaniel, says that if he lives with her to age 21, she won't make charge against him in final distr for support, 3/4/1811; agreement made betwn Elizabeth Myrick, wid and admr, and Nathaniel Myrick, son and legatee of decd 11/15/1814, Warren, AB, MIC
NAGLE, John, decd, Richard Boland issued L/A 9/9/1818, John D'Antignac, Cleon Nally, secs, Richmond, AB
NAIL, Casper, decd, Felix McKinne issued L/A 7/20/1833, George W. Crawford, sec, Richmond, AB
NAIL, Joseph, decd, Mary Nail, widow, was apptd admx 11/3/1784, Wilkes, MxR
NAISH, Jeremiah bound to Daniel Tucker to learn to farm 3/4/1811, Robert Tucker and Daniel Hudson, secs, Elbert, GB
NALL, Nathan, decd, James Nall, admr, applied for L/A 9/12/1820, Jasper, OM
NALL, Nathan, decd, inventory and appraisement by John Portwood, David Caldwell and William Walker 4/27/1812; James Nall, admr, payments to Martin Nall and John Nall; 1817 recpt to Richard Nall, Elizabeth Fealdres?, heirs, Jasper, Ests
NALLY, Cleon, decd, Mary Nally issued L/A 11/7/1822, Jacob Dill and James Lynes, secs, Richmond, AB
NANCE, Eugenia M., minor orph of H. W., decd, William R. Hill, gdn, 3/4/1867, Fulton, GB
NAPIER, James, decd, Lydia Napier issued L/A w/LWT annexed 2/10/1800, Hardy Smith issued L/A 12/1/1801; Lydia Napier and Samuel Ridgedale, admrs w/LWT annexed 2/7/1802, Solomon Newsome, Sr. and Elisha Brown, surs, Warren, MIC, AB
NAPIER, Rene, decd, recpts of legatees to John Morrison, exr, for horse, etc., left to Dorothy Napier, wife of decd, 1/11/1808, Elbert, EB

NAPPER, Drury, decd, Absalom Napper and John Buckhalter apptd temp admrs, Henry Harbuck, Jeremiah Burkhalter, sur, 11/3/1806, Warren, AB

NARRAMORE, Ransome, decd, Daniel Richardson, Samuel Dobbs, admrs, 10/7/1833, Harris

NASH, Abner, orph of William, William P. Graham, gdn, 3/4/1822, William B. Nunnally, John Gordon, surs, Clarke, GB

NASH, Clement (Captain), decd, John Peter Wagon, admr, 6/1/1784, Chatham, Adms

NASH, Susan, minor orph of Henry, decd, George Hudspeth apptd gdn 9/18/1806, Oglethorpe, OM

NASH, Thomas J., minor orph of Henry, decd, chose Samuel Patton his gdn, James Jordan, sec, 9/1806, Oglethorpe, OM, GB

NATIONS, Elizabeth, illegimate child of Hester, William Castleberry apptd gdn 1/5/1835, Hall, GB

NATIONS, Mary, illegitimate child of Hester, David Putnam apptd gdn 1/8/1835, Hall, GB

NEAL, Benjamin F., Simon T. Whitaker, gdn, John J. Whitaker, O. J. Head, surs, 6/1854, Fayette, GB

NEAL, David, decd, James Maddox, Thomas Maddox, admrs, Thomas Neal, John Hardaway, Reuben Jones, surs, no date; James Neal and Thomas Maddux apptd admrs 12/2/1811; Mrs. Joice Neal, wid, chose child's part 3/1/1813; admrs gtd leave to sell town lot in Warrenton and 100 acres where grist and saw mills are located, also 150 acres, 3/1/1813, Warren, AB, MIC

NEAL, Francis A. E., Simon T. Whitaker, gdn, John J. Whitaker, O. J. Head, surs, 6/1854, Fayette, GB

NEAL, George, Simon T. Whitaker, gdn, John J. Whitaker, O. J. Head, sur, Fayette, GB

NEAL, James, Simon T. Whitaker, gdn, John J. Whitaker, O. J. Head, sur, Fayette, GB

NEAL, James H., decd, John Neal issued L/A 11/6/1865, Fulton

NEAL, Jehu, decd, Thomas Maddox, temp admr, 3/15/1814, James Neal, sur, Warren, AB

NEAL, John, Simon T. Whitaker, gdn, John J. Whitaker, O. J. Head, sur, Fayette, GB

NEAL, John, decd, Rebecca Neal, wid, chose child's part for her share 11/7/1814, Warren, MIC

NEAL, John, decd, Thomas Maddux applied for admn 6/6/1814, Warren, MIC

NEAL, Joseph, decd, Frances Neal issued L/A 4/6/1802, Jackson, OM

NEAL, Joseph, decd, L/G to John & Julia Neal for decd's 6 ch "now of wife of Burwell Whitehead, viz-Jacob, Alexander, Kesiah, Judith, Obadiah, Tabia" 2/16/1803; clk's order in favor of Burwell Whitehead, $50 as gdn 2/14/1804, Franklin, OM

NEAL, Lemuel, decd, Benjamin Lipsey issued L/A 1/6/1823, C. R. Zachary, sec, Morgan, AB

NEAL, Pocahontas, Simon T. Whitaker, gdn, John J. Whitaker, O. J. Head, sur, Fayette, GB

NEAL, Richard, decd, LWT dtd 11/24/1851, pvd 9/1852, names wife, Mary Jane and ch: James, Richard, John Wesley, Ann Olivid and Jesse Horatio, Cherokee

NEAL, Samuel, decd, David Neal, admr, 4/11/1803, Reuben Jones, John McCormick, surs, Warren, AB

NEAL, Samuel, decd, James Neal, Jr., temp admr 8/19/1816, James Neal, sur, Warren, AB

NEAL, Samuel, decd, Patty Neal applied for L/A 3/10/1801, apptd 8/10/1801, James McCormack, sur (released); David Neal apptd admr 3/9/1803, Warren, MIC, AB

NEAL, Samuel, decd, James Neal, Jr. apptd gdn of three minor children insofar as relates to legacy left them by their late grandfather, James McCormick, decd 9/6/1814, Warren, MIC

NEAL, Sarah, decd, LWt pvd 10/3/1814, Warren, MIC
NEAL, Sarah Jane, Simon T. Whitaker, gdn, John J. Whitaker, O. J.
Head, sur, Fayette, GB
NEAL, Thomas, decd, David Neal gtd L/A 5/5/1806, Warren, MIC
NEAL, Thomas, decd, David and Samuel Neal, admrs, 2/18/1800,
James McCormick, Joseph Duckworth, surs, Warren, AB
NEAL, Thomas, decd, Sterling Gardiner, Walter Bell apply for adm
w/LWT annexed, offered for probate; proved by Shadrach Flewellin,
Solomon Slatter 1/4/1808, Warren, MIC
NEAL, Thomas, decd, David Neal and Samuel Neal apply for L/A
12/24/1799, apptd 2/11/1800, Jos. Duckworth, sur Warren, MIC, AB
NEAL, William, decd, James K. Cotton, admr w/LWT annexed, G. N.
Foote, sur, 10/10/1858, Paulding, AB
NEASE, Benjamin, George Nease applied for gdnshp 10/5/1846,
Effingham, MIC
NEAVES, Daniel, decd, John Neaves applies for L/A, Shadrick
Fluwellin, sur 8/10/1804, Warren, MIC, AB
NEEL, Caroline Fair, orph of Hezekiah, decd, Mary Neel, gdn,
3/7/1835, Emanuel, GB
NEEL, Elizabeth, orph of Hezekiah, decd, Mary Neel, gdn,
3/7/1835, Emanuel, GB
NEEL, John, orph of Daniel, decd, Moses Thomas, gdn, Nathan
Roland, sur, 5/1/1837, Emanuel, GB
NEEL, John, orph of Daniel, decd, Noah Tison, gdn, Mitchel Peak,
sur, 7/5/1836, Emanuel, GB
NEEL, Mitchel, decd, Elizabeth Neel, Wilson Rhynor, admrs,
William Rhynor, A. E. Wiggins, John A. Sumner, sur, 9/7/1840,
Emanuel, AB
NEEL, Mitchel, decd, William Rhynar and Elizabeth Neel, admrs,
appr 12/5/1839, Emanuel, A
NEEL, R., decd, appr 1824, Emanuel, A
NEEL, Reuben, decd, Mary Neel, John Neel, admrs, George Deakle,
David Kirkman, Matthew Lamb, Isaac Lamb, surs, 10/6/1823,
Emanuel, AB
NEELAND, Alexander, orph of William, decd, L/G issued William
Bates 9/2/1833, Washington
NEELAND, Elizabeth, orph of William, decd, L/G issued William
Bates 9/2/1833, Washington
NEELY, Elizabeth, orph of Thomas, decd, Julia Neely issued L/G
3/4/1833, Washington
NEELY, James J., orph of Thomas, decd, Julia Neely issued L/G
3/4/1833, Washington
NEELY, John T., orph of Thomas, decd, Julia Neely issued L/G
3/4/1833, Washington
NEELY, William, decd, Mary Neely apptd admx 1/3/1814, Camden, MIC
NEELY, William, decd, Mary, admx, says she has pd all debts of
est; that decd left four minor children and est owns eight
working negroes, asks permission to hire same out 1/6/1823,
Camden, MIC
NEESE, Andrew, decd, Frances Neese, extrx, Isaac N. Craven apptd
admr de bonis non 4/5/1858, Fulton
NELMS, J., decd, Andrew Maybank, admr vs. West Harris 6/22/1812,
Liberty, MIC
NELMS, Jesse, decd, Curtis Nelms issued L/A 9/6/1819, Laurens, AB
NELSON, Alexander, decd, 9/1834 ch-Wm, Sarah, Ruth Chappell,
Elizabeth Speers, Jno, Wm, Matilda Jamerson (decd), Geo
Robertson, Martha Ann, Jos Wilson, Joshua Jackson, Mary Jane,
Benjamin Franklin; Wm & s-i-l, Thos Chappell, exrs, Stewart, MIC
NELSON, Andrew, decd, Andrew Bush, admr, 7/5/1830, Warren, AB
NELSON, Benjamin F., decd, of Friendship, Thomas S. Chappell,
William Nelson, admrs, Samuel Passmore, George R. Nelson, Jared
Irwin, surs, Stewart, AB, Adms

232

NELSON, Harben, decd, William T. Nelson, admr, John A. Nelson, George T. Rogers, sur, 9/17/1851, Bibb, AB
NELSON, John, decd, Bozeman Adare L/A 4/22/1805; est to Bozeman Adare for use of Elinor Nelson, sister of helpless child by name of Francis Nelson, child of sd decd, ordered Elinor Nelson be allowed support for child, 3/8/1800, Jackson, OM
NELSON, Joseph Wilson, orph of Alexander, decd, Sarah Nelson and Archibald Spears, gdns, 1/1836, Larkin Reynolds, Garland Statham, Robert Hatcher, George R. Nelson, Galba Mathews, sur, Stewart, GB, Adms
NELSON, Joshua Jackson, orph of Alexander, decd, Sarah Nelson and Archibald Spears, gdns, 1/1836, Larkin Reynolds, Garland Statham, Robert Hatcher, George R. Nelson, Galba Mathews, sur, Stewart, GB, Adms
NELSON, Malcolm, decd, John Boykin applies for adm 10/27/1792, Effingham, Misc
NELSON, Martha Ann, orph of Alexander, decd, Sarah Nelson and Archibald Spears, gdns, 1/1836, Larkin Reynolds, Garland Statham, Robert Hatcher, George R. Nelson, Galba Mathews, sur, Stewart, GB, Adms
NELSON, Mary Jane, orph of Alexander, decd, Sarah Nelson and Archibald Spears, gdns, 1/1836, Larkin Reynolds, Garland Statham, Robert Hatcher, George R. Nelson, Galba Mathews, surs, Stewart, GB, Adms
NELSON, Noah, decd, Noel Nelson and Elisha Watson issued L/A 1/4/1310 and 11/10/1815, Laurens, AB
NEPHEW, Peter, decd, James Nephew qualied as admr 9/2/1788, Liberty, Ests
NEPPER, James, decd, Lydia Nepper, Samuel Ridgedell, admrs w/LWT annexed, 2/8/1802, Elisha Brown, Solomon Newsom, surs, Warren, AB
NESBIT, Eleanor L., decd, James W. Davis issued L/A 1/7/1839; 1843 div to heirs: Hugh O. K., Robert, Mary Ann W. and Thomas Nesbitt, james W. Davis, in rt of wife, Elizabeth B. Davis, Richmond, AB, AR
NESBIT, Hugh O. K., decd, LWT pvd 1855, Cobb, BB
NESBIT, Jane N., decd, Agnes A. Nesbit issued L/A 5/6/1839, Mary A. Nesbit, sec; 1843 retn lists Mary Ann Nesbit and Mrs. A. A. Nesbit, distributees, Richmond, AB
NESBIT, John, decd (son of Hugh), John W. Davis issued L/A 7/2/1838, Hugh O. K. Nesbit, sec; 1840 retn lists John W. Davis a distributee, Richmond, AB
NESBIT, John, decd, Hugh Nesbit issued L/A 10/22/1816, John Cumming, William White, secs; inv shows Agnes A. Nesbitt, admx, Richmond, AB
NESSMITH, James, Jr., lunatic, inv and appr of est by M. Denmark, William Groover, Sr., John Goodman 2/14/1845, Bulloch, Misc
NEVELL, John, carpenter, deed of gift 7/3/1790, to his children: Jacob Nevell of Great Ogeechee, Sarah Nevell, Mary Winslow, Frances Nevell, Elizabeth Nevell, Effingham, Misc
NEVES, Daniel, decd, John Neves, admr, 2/15/1804, Shadrach Flewellin, sur, Warren, AB
NEVILS, Eleanor, age 13, orph, Stephen Bowen came forward as next of kin; her minority went to Mrs. Jane Stripling 8/2/1313, Tattnall, MIC
NEWBERRY, Isaac, decd, James Hollingsworth, admr, Luke Ross, John Hollingsworth, sec, 9/24/1832, Bibb, AB
NEWDIGATE, John (Captain), decd, Mariner, died intestate, Penelope Newdigate, widow, John Lowrey, Chairmaker, admrs 3/1/1783, Chatham, Adms
NEWELL, Arnder?, decd, A. J. Davis issued L/G of minors 12/1869, Webster, OD

233

NEWMAN, Daniel, decd, James B. Newman discharged as admr 9/2/1839, Bulloch, MIC
NEWMAN, Elizabeth signed as having recd from James B. Newman, admr of est of Daniel Newman her share of est, 9/15/1837, Bulloch, Misc
NEWMAN, Samuel, decd, Richard Castleberry, William Newman, admrs, 4/11/1795, Mark Littleton, sur; admr dismissed 10/17/1800, Warren, AB, MIC
NEWSOM, David, decd, Frederick Newsom applies for L/A 1/19/1803, Warren, MIC, AB
NEWSOM, David, decd, Mary Newsom apptd admx 5/1/1809, Warren, MIC
NEWSOM, David, decd, Michael Burkhalter, admr, 7/3/1797, Sterling Gardner, Basil Wright, surs, Warren, AB
NEWSOM, David, decd, Michael Harbuck apptd temp admr 9/6/1804, Warren, MIC, AB
NEWSOM, Joeday, decd, LWT pvd 1/28/1839, Solomon Newsom, exr, Washington
NEWSOM, John, decd, Gideon Newsom, admr, 2/7/1820, Joshua Newsom, Henry Newsom, surs, Warren, AB
NEWSOM, John, decd, Frederick and Sarah Newsom apply for L/A, Michael Burkhalter, sur, 12/5/1803,Sarah Newsom, admx 2/14/1805, Michael Burkhalter, sur; Michael Burkhalter petitions to be released as surety on bond of Sarah Newsom, admx; Rule Nisi issued directing Sarah to shaw cause at next term, etc. 3/7/1808, Warren, AB, MIC
NEWSOM, John, orph of Holliday, decd, Archibald Stewart, gdn, 2/1/1819, Joseph Still, sec, Morgan, GB
NEWSOM, Joseph K., minor of Seaborn, David Curry issued L/G 1/5/1842, Washington
NEWSOM, Lorenzo D., decd, Emanuel Brown issued L/A 3/9/1840, Washington
NEWSOM, Mary M., minor of Seaborn, David Curry issued L/G 1/5/1842, Washington
NEWSOM, Nancy, decd, John Long issued L/A 3/13/1843, Washington
NEWSOM, Nathaniel, decd, Littleberry Little apptd admr 1/2/1808, Warren, MIC
NEWSOM, Peter, LWT pvd 3/3/1806, Warren, MIC
NEWSOM, Solomon, decd, Elizabeth, Frederick, Solomon & David Newsom apply L/A 2/16/1803, apptd 8/1803; Jody Newsom apptd temp admr 10/17/1803; David Newsom apptd admr, Thos Dent, Robt Moses, Sr., Wm Ursery, Jody Newsom, sur, , Warren, MIC
NEWSOM, Solomon, decd, Asa Newsom apptd admr de bonis non, succeeding David Newsom, decd admr 5/1/1809, Warren, MIC
NEWSOM, Solomon, Jr., decd, David Newsom, admr, 10/17/1803, Thomas Dent, Wm Ursery, surs, Warren, AB
NEWSOM, Temperance, minor of Seaborn, David Curry issued L/G 1/5/1842, Washington
NEWTON, Amos, decd, Mrs. Harriett Newton issued L/A 9/8/1813, George Pearson, John Garvin, secs; John Howard, gdn of minor orphs: George and William, later John Howard, Richmond, AB, GB
NEWTON, Barrett, admr, gtd leave to sell property, p. 124, Screven, OM
NEWTON, Bramblett, decd, Frances F. Juhan, admx, John C. Harris, D. J. Dewbern, William M. McGee, W. L. Vaughan, sur, 10/7/1872, Gwinnett, AB
NEWTON, James A., decd, William N. Hill, admr, Wm J. Russell, Wm H. Blalock, surs, 6/1852, 1853 retn, Fayette, AB
NEWTON, Levi, decd, James Newton applied for L/A 1/7/1796, Greene, Misc
NEWTON, Samuel, exr, to show cause, p. 185, Screven, OM

234

NIBLACK, William, decd, LWT pvd by Gillis McDonald, James Niblack qualified as exr 6/1/1829; leave to sell gtd James Niblack, exr, 1/4/1832, Camden, MIC
NICHOLS, Martha, orph, Ely Howell and William Zertman, secs for David Nichols, as gdns bond, released, 4/6/1830, Habersham, MIC
NICHOLS, Peter, Charles Coutteau, gdn, p. 67, Screven, OM
NICHOLS, Richard J., decd, George L. Denning and Thomas B. Lamar issued L/A 11/5/1849, Baldwin
NICHOLS, Solomon, decd, David Nichols was apptd gdn of orphs: James, Sarah, Andrew, Thomas, Wyly, Mary and Martha, 12/1827, Habersham, MIC
NICHOLS, William P., illegitimate child, David Nichols, gdn, 12/1827, Habersham, MIC
NICHOLS, William Pinckney, minor son of Martha, Andrew J. Nichols, gdn, 3/26/1836, Habersham, MIC
NICHOLSON, A., decd, Mrs. E. Nicholson, apptd extrx 2/1865; Jasper Nicholson, exr, 9/1867, Webster, OD
NICHOLSON, James, decd, Celia Nicholson admitted LWT 11/1864, Webster, OD
NICHOLSON, John, decd, James Gamble, admr, p. 82, 84, Screven, OM
NICKLES, Simon, decd, David Perryman issued L/A 10/2/1784, Stephen Collins, James Cobb, secs, Richmond, AB
NICKOLS, John, decd, Benjamin Neal, admr, A. Nichols, William Morgan, surs, 7/1840, 1845 retn, Fayette, AB
NICKS, Elendor, admr, leave to sell negroes, p. 21, Screven, OM
NICKS, William, acct sales of est, p. 22, Screven, OM
NICKSON, E. P., decd, Charles Clements, admr, Josiah R. Bosworth, sur, 1/1849, Fayette, AB
NICOLL, Francis Edward, LWT pvd, Miller Halloms qualified exr 1/4/1850, Camden, MIC
NIESS, George, decd, of Ebernezer, LWT dtd 2/21/1772, pvd 5/1/1792, devises to children: George Niess, Elizabeth Niess. Wife, Sibella Niess; Joseph Schubtrine, exr/gdn, Effingham, Misc
NIGHTENGALE, John C., decd, LWT probated, Russell Goodrich qualified admr w/LWT annexed 2/3/1817, Camden, MIC
NIGHTENGALE, John C., decd, Isaac Crews sd Mr. Bevan applied for pers prop proceeds under L/A gtd Wilkes Co. 9/7/1808; Randolph McGillis, late Col of Customs, St. Marys gave acct in favor of USA vs. est for $471.23 1/3/1809, Camden, MIC
NIX, Nancy, natural gdn of her ch: Susan E., William J., Bethena C., John L., Rachel M. J. and Rutha M. P. Nix, to whom there has lately come an est from Thomas Nix, 3/4/1861, Dawson, WB
NIX, Thomas, decd, Nancy Nix, Samuel Weaver, admrs, 9/5/1859, Dawson, WB
NIX, William C., decd, L/A to James Cathey 2/7/1859, White, AB
NIXON, Hamilton, decd, Ann and Edward Nixon issued L/A 1/9/1800, Benjamin Nowland, sec, Richmond, AB
NIXON, Robert, decd, John and Hamilton Nixon issued L/A 4/21/1792, James Edwards, Edmund B. Hicks, secs, Richmond, AB
NOBLES, Henry, decd, Ezekiel Bryan, admr 3/5/1838, Randolph
NOBLES, John, decd, Lewis Nobles issued L/A 12/16/1782, John Pittman, Peleg Rogers, sec, Richmond, AB
NOBLOCK, Adam, decd, Thomas Brannen, et al, apprs, p. 70, Screven, OM
NOLAND, George, decd, James Gordan issued L/A 1/6/1816, Thomas B. Noland, Rebecca Noland, secs, Morgan, AB
NOLAND, George, decd, Rebecca Noland, gdn of orphs: Avery, Polly, Thomas and Rebecca 1/6/1817, Samuel Harris, Joseph Hughey, secs, Morgan, GB
NOLEN, Mary, a lunatic, William Nolen, gdn, James Nolen, sur, 11/8/1848, Butts, GB

NOLEN, Richard, decd, Charles F. Newton, Isaac W. Newton, temp admrs, William H. C. Mickleberry, Richard Barlow, sur 11/3/1851, Butts, AB
NOLES, Mary, colored female child, age 9, bound to Thomas Bryan, 5/1830, Habersham, MIC
NORMAN, John, decd, Rebecca Norman, admx 1793, Liberty, Ests
NORMAN, Joseph, decd, Ann Norman issued L/A 11/13/1816, Samuel Hale, William McGar, secs, Richmond, AB
NORREL, Henry, idiot, G. W. F. and Sarah Norrell issued L/G 1/1867, Webster, OD
NORREL, L. S., decd, George W. and Mrs. Sarah Norrell issued temporary L/A 11/1866, Webster, OD
NORRIS, James, decd, 1804 retn, pd Robert Y. Norris, Sarah Norris for support of herself and children, Betsy Norris, legacy, James Norris, legacy, and Nathaniel Booth, Wm Dudley, exr, Elbert, AR
NORRIS, James, decd, Jane M. Norris, gdn of orphs: Susan M., Samuel J., James J., Jurelda, 10/2/1849, Walter W. Webster, sec, Hall, GB
NORRIS, James, decd, William Dudley, admr, 1810 retn, recpt of Sarah Norris for support of herself and children, Elbert, AR
NORRIS, Jesse, decd, Nancy Norris and Alexander Kemp issued L/A 1/2/1832, William C. Phillips, sec, Montgomery, AB
NORRIS, Josiah William, decd, William Norris, Jemimah Holland, admrs, 11/7/1836, Harris
NORRIS, Thomas, decd, Sarah Thomas issued L/A 3/1/1819, Edward Lane, sec; Sarah Norris L/A 7/12/1823, Nathaniel Allen, sec, Morgan, AB
NORRIS, Thomas, decd, Wm Gibson apptd admr 6/6/1804, Camden, MIC
NORRIS, William, decd, LWT pvd 5/6/1844, Benjamin Cleveland qualified as exr, Harris
NORSWORTHY, George, decd, inv produced by Salley Norsworthy, admx w/LWT annexed, div of negroes to: Salley Shivers, Frederick Norsworthy, Betsey Norsworthy, Hancock, AAAA
NORTHCUTT, Robert, decd, L/A to Vincent E. Vickers 3/5/1821, Laurens, AB
NORTON, Alice, minor dau of John, decd, bound to Jonathan Norton until age 16 (now abt age 11) 6/1802; recpt to her uncle Jonathan Norton to whom she had been bound 3/2/1807, Oglethorpe, MIC, OM
NORWOOD, John, decd, LWT pvd 7/1/1844, E. J. Norwood and dau, Espann Norwood, exrs, Harris
NOTTAGE, Thomas, decd, LWT pvd 11/5/1827, wife, Priscilla, extrx, Bulloch, Misc
NOWLAN, Ann, minor dau of George, decd, William Lister apptd gdn 2/18/1800, Effingham, Misc
NOWLAN, George, decd, Mrs. Elizabeth Nowlan, wid, applies for adm 3/5/1799, apptd 4/5/1799, Effingham, Misc
NOWLAN, George C., decd, David Gugel, exr, to sell property 5/5/1828; petitions to sell certain land drawn in land lottery by orphs 3/2/1829, Effingham, MIC
NOWLAN, George Galphin, minor son of George, decd, William Lister apptd gdn 2/18/1800, Effingham, MIC
NPWLAN, Hannah, decd, Jno Charlton apptd admr 9/20/1833, Effingham, MIC
NULSON, Nicholas, decd, of Island of Hilton Head, S. C., David Brydie Mitchell apptd admr 4/23/1790, Chatham, Adms
NUMAN, Thomas, decd, LWT pvd 8/20/1790, Mary Numan, extrx, Columbia, Ests
NUNES, Moses, decd, Samuel Nunes, Jonas Nunes, George Galphin qualified as exrs LWT dtd 10/14/1785, 1/23/1790, Chatham, Adms
NUNEZ, Daniel, Benjamin Stripling, gdn, 4/23/1807, Tattnall, MIC
NUNN, Elizabeth, orph of James, decd, James R. Nunn, gdn, David Edenfield, Jr., James Edenfield, sur, 5/7/1838, Emanuel, GB

NUNN, Hiram, orph of James, decd, James R. Nunn, gdn, David Edenfield, Jr., James Edenfield, sur, 5/7/1838, Emanuel, GB
NUNN, Joshua, orph of James, decd, James R. Nunn, gdn, David Edenfield, Jr., James Edenfield, sur, 5/7/1838, Emanuel, GB
NUNNELLE, William, decd, Benjamin F. Nunnelle, John Hubbard, gdn for orphs, 7/5/1835, Harris
NUTT, James, decd, Jane Nutt issued L/A 5/1/1826, Andrew Nutt, John Shackleford,ecs, Morgan, AB
NUTT, John, decd, James and Martha Nutt issued L/A 3/15/1823, John Barkley, sec, Morgan, AB
NUTT, John, orph of John, decd, Benjamin Brown, gdn, 2/5/1827, Morgan, GB
OAKES, Jesse, decd, Davis E. Suton issued L/A 12/16/1863, Mary Turner, sec, White, AB
OATES, John, decd, planter, Mrs. Tamer Waters, extrx of LWT 6/17/1789, Chatham, Adms
OATTS, Nathaniel, decd, LWT dtd 1/25/1794, pvd 2/15/1794, bequeaths to bro., Godlif Oatts; to wife, Christianah Elizabeth Oatts, wit: Solomon Gnann and Godlif Oatt, Effingham, MIsc
O'BRIEN, James, decd, William O'Brien issued L/A 3/4/1850, Baldwin
O'BRIEN, William, Sr., decd, William O'Brien, Jr. to make retn 5/5/1788, Chatham, Adms
O'BRYAN, William, Mrs. Henrietta O'Bryan, admr, 12/17/1788, Chatham, Adms
O'BRYAN, William, the elder, decd, Joseph Clay, admr, 11/13/1788, Chatham, Adms
ODELL, Thomas, decd, William E. Willson and John Evans issued L/A 1/2/1837, Hall
ODEN, Thomas, decd, Wilson Oden produced copy from McIntosh Co. showing him admr of est, requests transfer of est to this co. 6/7/1841, admr dismissed 1/1846, Camden, MIC
ODLE, Andrew, orph of Thomas, decd, John Stringer, gdn, James Law, sec, 9/7/1840, Hall, GB
ODLE, John H., orph of Thomas, decd, E. M. Johnson, gdn, John Stringer, John Evans, secs, 9/17/1850, Hall, GB
ODLE, Mary, orph of Thomas, decd, E. M. Johnson, gdn, John Stringer, John Evans, secs, 11/2/1840, Hall, GB
ODLE, Thomas, decd, John Evans issued L/A 3/2/1840, John Lesley, sec, Richmond, AB
ODOM, H. J., decd, A. J. Swords, admr, E. L. Braswell, sur, 3/2/1874, Gwinnett, AB
OFFUTT, Nathaniel, decd, LWT pvd 11/4/1839, Jabez Jones apptd exr, Washington
OGDEN, Alexander, decd, LWT pvd, Darius Couch qualified as admr w/LWT annexed 1/5/1820, Camden, MIC
OGILBY, John, decd, Richard Ogilby applied for L/A 9/1809, Oglethorpe, OM
OGLBY, Anne, decd, Robert M. Brown, admr w/LWT annexed 9/5/1853, Reuben Haynes, W. E. Oglby, William Ezzard and J. A. Reeve, surs, DeKalb, AB
OGLESBEE, Elizabeth bound to Patience Mobley, p. 118, Screven, OM
OGLESBEE, Mary Ann bound to Patience Mobley, p. 118, Screven, OM
OGLESBY, Alden, decd, John Oglesby, admr, Seaborn Oglesby, James Oglesby and John Shearwood, surs, 9/3/1849, Emanuel, AB
OGLETREE, John, decd, Benjamin L. Ogletree and Joseph Ogletree issued L/a 1/6/1817; Benjamin S. Ogletree, gdn of orphs: Edward and Nancy 5/5/1817, Joseph Scott, sec, Morgan, GB
O'HARA, Thomas, decd, Alexander Cunningham issued L/A 6/17/1815, Richard H. Wilde, sec, Richmond, AB

O'KEEFE, C. T., decd, William Jennings issued L/A 10/7/1867; Cyrus H. Tugles, admr, 5/7/1866, Fulton
O'KELLY, Thomas C., decd, F. S. O'Kelly issued L/A 7/6/1863, C. Meaders, sec, White, AB
OLCOTT, James S., decd, Daniel Reinshart applied for L/A 10/8/1847, Effingham, MIC
OLIFF, Mary, orph of John, decd, Joannah apptd gdn 7/7/1817, Bulloch, MIC
OLIFF, Susannah, orph of John, decd, Joannah apptd gdn 7/7/1817, Bulloch, MIC
OLIPHANT, James, decd, George Gordon of Laurens, S. C. issued L/A 4/13/1798, Seaborn Jones of Richmond Co., sec, Richmond, AB
OLIVE, A., decd, Joseph Embry and James Olive pet ct to authorize William H. Crawford to adjust and settle all accts, 3/2/1807, Oglethorpe, OM
OLIVE, Betsey, minor orph of Anthony, decd, Joseph Embrey was apptd gdn, William M. Stokes, Hendon Olive, surs, 6/1802, Oglethorpe, MIC
OLIVE, Elizabeth, minor of Anthony, decd, James Olive apptd gdn, William Clift, John Olive, John Holmes, surs, 1/6/1806, Oglethorpe, MIC
OLIVE, James, minor of Anthony, decd, Thomas Hendon apptd gdn, Andrew Bell, John Gresham, Jr., surs, 6/18/1800; Joseph Embry apptd gdn, William M. Stokes, Hendon Olive, surs, 6/1802, Oglethorpe, MIC
OLIVE, John, minor orph of Anthony, decd, Joseph Embrey, gdn, William M. Stokes, Hendon Olive, surs, 6/1802, Oglethorpe, MIC
OLIVE, Kiddy, minor orph of Anthony, decd, Joseph Embrey, gdn, William M. Stokes, Hendon Olive, surs, 6/1802, Oglethorpe, MIC
OLIVE, Nancy, minor orph of Anthony, decd, Joseph Embrey apptd gdn, William M. Stokes, Hendon Olive, surs, 6/1802; James Olive apptd gdn, William Clift, John Olive, John Holmes, surs, 7/1806, Oglethorpe, MIC
OLIVE, Sarah (Sally), minor orph of Anthony, decd, Joseph Embrey apptd gdn, William M. Stokes, Hendon Olive, surs, 6/1802; James Olive apptd gdn 1/6/1806, William Clift, John Olive, John Holmes, surs, Oglethorpe, MIC
OLIVER, Benjamin, Sr., decd, Sarah Oliver and Thomas Friend pvd LWT, they qualified as exrs 7/3/1809, Warren, MIC
OLIVER, Dorcas, Elijah Oliver, gdn, p. 22, Screven, OM
OLIVER, Elijah, decd, Civility Oliver, admr, p. 110, Screven, OM
OLIVER, Hannah, Thomas Oliver, gdn, p. 23, Screven, OM
OLIVER, Jacob, William Oliver, gdn, p. 23, Screven, OM
OLIVER, James and McD., petition to be relieved from bond, p. 27, 32, Screven, OM
OLIVER, James, decd, LWT refused record, p. 159, Thomas W. Oliver, admr, p. 159, Jacob Oliver, etc. div est, p. 116, Screven, OM
OLIVER, Jane, decd, Elias Wood issued L/A 3/5/1863, Fulton
OLIVER, John, exr, to sell personal property, p. 24, Screven, OM
OLIVER, Joseph, decd, James H. martin apptd gdn of orphs: James M. and Joseph 9/5/1836, Randolph
OLIVER, Moses, Thomas Oliver, gdn, p. 22, Screven, OM
OLIVER, Peter, decd, Benjamin Oliver, Jr. applied for adm 5/2/1808, John Oliver, sur; James Oliver apptd admr with Benjamin Oliver, Jr. 7/3/1809, Warren, MIC
OLIVER, Samuel C., decd, John G. Felton, admr, Arthur T. Camp, Lawson Fields, sur, 1/8/1855, Cherokee, AB
OLIVER, Solomon, decd, app; pd: John Oliver, Hubert Reynolds, Peter McFarlin, Saml Hawkins, John Cook; legatees: Henry Pitt, John Oliver, Elizabeth Oliver, Charles Oliver, Joseph Venting, Hancock, AAAA

OLIVER, William, Elijah Oliver, gdn, p. 23, Screven, OM
OLIVER, William, decd, Thomas Oliver and Charles Tait apptd gdns
of orphs: Maria, Matilda and Mary Ann Oliver, 9/2/1811, George
Cook, sec, Elbert, GB
OLIVER, William, decd, William W. Oliver, admr, p. 130, Screven, OM
OLLIFF, John, decd, memo of notes delivered by Catherine Jackson
to Joannah Olliff due est 12/14/1815, Bulloch, Misc
OLLIFF, John, decd, ordered that Joannah Oliff receive $600
7/1/1816, Bulloch, MIC
O'NAIL, Aaron, decd, Edward W. Onail, admr, Josiah Crane, sur
3/1/1841, Butts, AB
O'NEAL, Axiom, decd, Ruth O'Neal applied for L/A 11/22/1793,
Greene, Misc
O'NEAL, Axiom, decd, Greene Co. est filed 5/12/1800, 1797 vous-
Jno McCullock (schooling), M. Hammer, Jas Thweatt, Boreland
Mitchell, Geo Hargraves, Isaac Moreland (schooling), Jno White,
Nathan & Edmund O'Neal, etc., Hancock, AAAA
O'NEAL, Elizabeth, to dau., Honor Chew, both of Wilkes Co., all
goods and chattels now in my possession, 3/13/1779, Wilkes, MxR
O'NEAL, James, decd, John McCoy issued L/A 11/1/1824, Morgan, AB
O'NEAL, Nancy, decd, E. M. Poulhou issued L/A 10/5/1863, Fulton
O'NEAL, William, decd, Hogan Wadsworth, gdn for orphs: William,
Benjamin P. and Mary E., 5/1/1837, Hardy Leverett and Wiley G.
Tatom, secs, Lincoln, GB
O'NEIL, John, decd, Osborne O. Martin issued L/A 9/5/1836,
Washington
ORME, J. C., decd, LWT exhibited 1/14/1861, William P. Orme, exr,
Fulton
ORR, J., decd, D. W. and A. L. Orr, admrs, 1/29/1857, Cobb, BB
ORR, James, decd, LWT pvd 5/6/1816, Jackson, OM
ORR, John, decd, Lydia and Hugh Orr issued L/A 5/3/1841,
Washington
ORR, Noble, decd, Hamilton Goss, admr, 5/4/1812, George
Hargraves, sur, Warren, AB
ORR, Penelope, decd, William Orr issued L/A 3/1/1841, Washington
ORRICK, James, decd, Celia Orrick and John Greer issued L/A
7/3/1319, Putnam, AB
ORTEUS, Henry, decd, Elizabeth Orteus apptd admx, 4/20/1778,
Chatham, Adms
OSBORN, Benjamin, decd, John Shackleford, gdn of orphs: Mary and
Loving 1/9/1826, T. Bryant, Nathaniel Allen, secs, Morgan, GB
OSBORNE, George, decd, Daniel Coleman and Susannah Coleman issued
L/A 8/16/1783, Levi Lancaster, Joseph Ray, secs, Richmond, AB
OSBORNE, Henry, late of Richmond Co., decd, Richard Pearis and
Catherine, his wife, were apptd admrs de bonis non 1/8/1806,
Camden, MIC
OSBORNE, John, decd, Job Pray, Joseph Foster, Francis Watlington
apptd admrs, 5/17/1785, Chatham, Adms
OSBORNE, Mariah F., decd, partitioners apptd to div est 4/8/1829,
Camden, MIC
OSBURN, William, decd, Gay Upchurch, John M. Osburn, exrs, Jethro
H. Barnes, John L. Dodd, surs, 5/1838, 1848 retn, Fayette, AB
OSGOOD, Thomas, decd, Thomas Sheppard qualified as exr 9/10/1787,
Liberty, Ests
O'STEEN, Solomon, ct ordered $15 be pd overseer of the Poor for
use of family, 6/2/1818, Camden, MIC
OSWALD, Joseph, decd, Thomas Oswald qualified as exr 4/5/1786,
Liberty, Ests
OSWALD, Thomas, decd, Ann Oswald, Lachlan McIntosh qualified as
admrs 5/20/1791, Liberty, Ests
OUTER, Nathan, decd, William R. Venable, Clk, Superior Ct, issued
L/A 9/3/1866, Fulton

OUTLAW, Edward, decd, Young P. Outlaw, admr, 10/3/1845; apprs: Benjamin Culpepper, Thos. Bembry, Charles H. Higdon, Edward O. Sheffield; purchasers at sale: Keziah, Young P. and Edmond Outlaw, Jesse Gilbert, Thos. W. Ellis, etc., Dooly, I&A

OUTLAW, Edward Jordan, orph of Meshack, decd, L/G issued Morgan Outlaw 1830, Washington

OUTLAW, Elizabeth, orph of Meshack, decd, L/G issued Morgan Outlaw 1830, Washington

OUTLAW, Harriett, orph of Meshack, decd, L/G issued Morgan Outlaw 1830, Washington

OUTLAW, John Linwood, orph of Meshack, decd, L/G issued Morgan Outlaw 1830, Washington

OUTLAW, Meshack, decd, Morgan Outlaw issued L/A 1830, Washington

OUTLAW, Morgan Anderson, orph of Meshack, decd, L/G issued Morgan Outlaw 1830, Washington

OUTLAW, Nancy, decd, L/A to Morgan Outlaw 3/5/1838, Washington

OUTLAW, Polina, Hezekiah Outlaw, gdn, Dooly, OD

OUTLAW, Solomon, Hezekiah Outlaw, gdn, Dooly, OD

OVERBY, A. C., minor orph of Basil H., decd, Earley W. Thrasher, gdn, 10/1/1860, Fulton, GB

OVERBY, Barton, minor orph of Basil H., decd, Earley W. Thrasher, gdn, 10/1/1860, Fulton, GB

OVERBY, Basil H., decd, exr renounced appointment; Madison L. Lenoir of Gwinnett Co., apptd admr 2/6/1860; Joseph Winship, admr de bonis non 8/5/1861, Fulton

OVERBY, Earle, minor orph of Basil H., decd, Earley W. Thrasher, gdn, 10/1/1860, Fulton, GB

OVERBY, Elizabeth S., orph of Basil H., decd, Nathaniel J. Harrison, gdn, Mrs. E. S. Overby, sec, 2/4/1861, Fulton, GB

OVERBY, Hugh, minor orph of Basil H., decd, Nathaniel J. Harrison, gdn, Mrs. E. S. Overby, sec, 2/4/1861, Fulton, GB

OVERBY, Mary F., minor orph of Basil H., decd, Earley W. Thrasher, gdn, 10/1/1860, Fulton, GB

OVERBY, Nicholas, minor orph of Basil H., decd, Earley W. Thrasher, gdn, 10/1/1860, Fulton, GB

OVERSTREET, Daniel, decd, Martha Overstreet, admx, appraisal 4/3/1826, Emanuel, A

OVERSTREET, David, decd, Martha Overstreet, admx, John R. Daniels, John Scott, sur, 7/6/1826, Emanuel, AB

OVERSTREET, Henry, orph of James, decd, John Overstreet, gdn, Thomas M. Jenkins, N. T. Hotton, sec, 12/6/1834, Emanuel, GB

OVERSTREET, James, orph of James, decd, John Overstreet, gdn, Thomas M. Jenkins, N. T. Hotton, sur, 12/6/1834, Emanuel, GB

OVERSTREET, Martha, orph of James, decd, John Overstreet, gdn, Thomas M. Jenkins, N. T. Hotton, sur, 12/6/1834, Emanuel, GB

OWEN, Augustin, decd, Catherine Owen issued L/A 1/6/1817, Faulkner Heard, Francis Flourney, secs; Catherine, gdn of orphs: Catherine, Eliza, Jonathan, Augustus, Hearty & Baby, 11/2/1818, Morgan, GB

OWEN, Jacob, minor orph of Augustin, decd, Wm Graves apptd gdn, John Gresham, Cuthbert Collier, surs, 6/18/1805, Oglethorpe, MIC

OWEN, Thomas, decd, L/A issused to Dr. Thomas Owen 3/30/1797, Greene, Misc

OWEN, William, decd, John Clark, gdn to orphs 1/12/1852: Marian and Jane, Hall, GB

OWENS, Augusta, decd, Robert H. Elliott gdn of orphs: Augustus, Jonathan, Shirley, Baxter 12/23/1825, Wm Tinsley, sec, Morgan, GB

OWENS, Ephraim, decd, Mary Owens issued L/A 2/8/1785, John Moore, Ephraim Owen, secs, Richmond, AB

OWENS, Leroy, minor and orph of Micajah, H. Durden, gdn of prop, James Waters, Martin Rich, Josiah Drew, Jr., surs, 9/7/1818, Emanuel, GB

OWENS, Louisa, orph, Vincent Lockhart, gdn, 9/2/1833, Covington
Searls, sec, Lincoln, GB
OWENS, Martha, gdn of: Martha A., Sarah E., Matilda C., Lucinda
C., and Robert M., William Owens, sur, 1/1854, Fayette, GB
OWENS, Stewart, decd, L/A to Woodford Owens, 1/5/1819, Jasper, OM
OZBURN, George, decd, Daniel and Susannah Coleman, apptd admrs
2/28/1783, Wilkes, MxR
OZBURN, William K., decd, Haywood Ozburn, admr, Henry Rentfrow,
sur, 3/1854, Fayette, AB
PACE, Barnabas, David Crawford, gdn, files retn 1805, pd Wm Pace,
etc. for clothing, Richmind, GR
PACE, Dreadzil, Sr., decd, William Pace issued L/A 8/30/1796,
Drury Pace, sec, Richmond, AB
PACE, Dredzel of St. Paul's Parish, sells to Dredzel Pace, Jr.,
son of Charles Pace, four head of horses 9/7/1770, Wilkes, MxR
PACE, Dredzel, Indian Trader, decd, Silas Pace apptd admr*
9/15/1777, Wilkes, MxR
PACE, Dredzel, minor child of Charles of Richmond Co., decd, asks
that Barnabas Pace of Wilkes Co. be apptd his gdn 7/21/1778,
Wilkes, MxR
PACE, Ella, minor orph of Richard, decd, P. N. Randall, gdn,
4/2/1866, Fulton, GB
PACE, Francis A., orph of Hardy, decd, Mary Ann Thompson, gdn,
Edward W. Onail, sur, 1/11/1847, Butts, GB
PACE, Julia A., orph of Hardy, decd, Mary Ann Thompson, gdn,
Edward W. Onail, sur, 1/11/1847, Butts, GB
PACE, Knowel, decd, LWT pvd 3/3/1783, to Leroy, son of Barnabas
Pace; Barnabas Pace and Henry Ware, Sr., exrs, Wilkes, MxR
PACE, Mary T., orph of Hardy, decd, Mary Ann Thompson, gdn,
Edward W. O'Nail, sur, 1/11/1847, Butts, GB
PACE, Thomas, decd, Dredzel and Drury pace issued L/A 10/25/1794,
Jesse Rice, sec, Richmond, AB
PACE, William, decd, Martha Patton, admx, James Thompson, William
Cumming, sur, 1/11/1830, Bibb, AB
PACE, William, decd, Mary Pace issued L/A 8/26/1790, John Smith,
Saml Langston, secs, Richmond, AB
PACE, William, decd, of Richmond Co., Mary Pace gtd L/A
8/20/1790, Columbia, Ests
PACE, William A., orph of Hardy, decd, Mary Ann Thompson, gdn,
Edward W. O'Neal, sur, 1/11/1847, Butts, GB
PADEN, Moses W., decd, John M. Delaney, admr, William Carmichael,
sur, 11/3/1851, Cherokee, AB
PADGET, Elijah, decd, Elisha Padget, admr, appr, 6/29/1816,
Emanuel, A
PADGET, Silia, decd, Sion Kirkland, admr, appraisal 2/2/1815,
Emanuel, A
PADGETT, Elijah, decd, Susan, admr, made retn 3/27/1836,
Tattnall, I&A
PADGETT, Martha Ann Lamenda, Susan Padgett, gdn of her
illegtimate child, 11/2/1840, Tattnall, GB
PAGE, Joseph H. issued L/G 11/1/1841 for his minor children:
Solomon, Mary E., Nancy and George S., Washington
PAGE, Solomon, decd, Elizabeth Page issued L/A 11/10/1834,
Washington
PAGE, Thomas, orph of Thomas, decd, retn by S. D. Brown, gdn,
5/5/1834, his having recd 40 acres in the Cherokee Purchase,
Bulloch, Misc
PAGE, William, decd, Mrs. Ann Matilda King qualified as extrx of
LWT of her father, 2/5/1827, Glynn, MIC
PAGET, Elizabeth, orph of Elizabeth, decd, Asa Humphries, gdn,
Reuben Thompson, sur, 9/2/1822, Emanuel, GB

PAGET, Grace, orph of Elizabeth, decd, Asa Humphries, gdn, Reuben Thompson, sur, 9/2/1822, Emanuel, GB

PAGET, Silas, decd, Samuel Williams, admr, David Johnson, sur, 6/2/1815, Emanuel, AB

PAGNEUL, Raimond, decd, (commonly called Toulsuse), Francis Duc (or Due) issued L/A 1/5/1814, B. Bonyer, Francis Saincrie, secs, Richmond, AB

PAIN, Samuel of St. Pauls Parish, to Johnray, inf son of James, trader, 7 hd cattle, 6/21/1775, Wilkes, MxR

PAINE, Orris, decd, Charles I. Paine issued L/A 1/10/1834, Baldwin

PAINTER, Richard, insane, William Belcher, gdn, 9/6/1819, Wm Parramore, sec, Laurens, GB

PALMER, Benjamin, natural gdn of: Etheldred J., 1828-1840 retns for schooling in powellton, studying medicine, in Charleston and Philadelphia, exp money to Alabama, Richmond, GR

PALMER, Henry, decd, Henry Lester, admr, A. G. Bulloch, sur, 1/11/1858, Paulding, AB

PALMER, John, deed of gift 7/30/1799, to Miss Elizabeth Mikell, conveying slave, household goods, wit: Mary Ravot and Christian Truetlin, Camden, MIC

PALMER, John, deed of gift to Miss Elizabeth Mikell 7/30/1799, conveying slave, hsehold goods, Effingham, Misc

PALMER, Martin, decd, F. M. Scarlett, exr, directed to div $448.73 recd from Major Hunter, US Paymaster, and to pay same out in accordance with LWT of decd, 3/3/1828, Glynn, MIC

PALMER, Martin, decd, Francis M. Scarlett, exr, gtd leave to sell, 1/5/1825, Glynn, MIC

PALMER, Sally, decd, Matthew Gaston, admr, Samuel Nutt, sur, 9/5/1831, Butts, AB

PALMER, William, decd, Willis Palmer issued L/A 1/2/1832, Isaac Palmer, Silas Fitzgerald, secs; 1845 recpts from John Thompson for wife's pt, Alfred Palmer for himself and Mary, being last eir of decd, Richmond, AB, AR

PALMORE, John of Wilkes Co. to John Heard, all my bounty land for minute service which I was to have as refugee and soldier at siege of Augusta, 11/17/1782, Wilkes, MxR

PALMOUR, Aaron V., decd, Nancy R. Palmour issued L/A 5/7/1860, William A. Merritt, sec, White, AB

PALMERINE, Peter, decd, Sarah Gadden, wid, admx apptd 6/5/1785, Chatham, Adms

PAMORE, Martha and Frederick D., minors of Elisha Palmer who deserted them, Frederick Daniel apptd gdn, 6/26/1824, James A. Campbell, sec, Pike, MIC

PANTON, James, decd, Littleberry Bush issued L/A 9/6/1824, Richard Bush, Holland McTyeire, sec; 1829 div to heirs-James Alexander and William Panton, Littleberry Bush, Richmond, AB, AR

PARADISE, Mary Jane, orph of James, decd, William Paradise issued L/G 5/7/1832; Mary Paradise issued L/G 3/4/1833, Washington

PARDIE, Leveret, decd, Martin Grannis issued L/A 6/12/1827, William Shannon, J. W. Whitcock, secs, Richmond, AB

PARDUE, Agrippa, decd, James Riddle issued temp L/A 5/4/1814, David Donaldson, Burton Rucker, secs, Richmond, AB

PARDUE, Morris, decd, Seth Bishop issued L/A de bonis non 3/7/1820, Daniel Meigs, John M. Turner, secs, Richmond, AB

PARHAM, Elizabeth, decd, John C. Turner, Samuel Pitts, admrs, 12/22/1817, Wm H. Blount, Henry Dewberry, surs, Warren, AB

PARHAM, Erathus E. made gdn of his minor ch: Mary Frances and John Duncan, 8/6/1855, Houston, GB

PARHAM, Fanny, orph of Matthew, decd, John Wilson apptd gdn 1/1819, Jasper, OM

PARHAM, James, decd, Edmond Parham, admr, 4/5/1817, Robert Bonner, sur, Warren, AB

PARHAM, John, decd, Elizabeth Parham and Samuel Pitts apply for admn 9/2/1811, apptd 11/4/1811, John Turner, Hardy Pitts, surs; Mrs. Elizabeth Parham, wid, came into ct and chose her pt of est, taking 1/3 of real estate and child´s pt of pers prop 12/2/1811; Turner Persons, Shadrach Flewellin, Archelaus Flewellin, William Blount, John Myrick apptd partitioners to div est 12/2/1811, recd and appvd the report of partitioners to div est, 2/3/1812, Warren, AB, MIC

PARHAM, Lewis, decd, Fanny Parham, Nathaniel Parham, admrs, 11/2/1829, David Mims, Hartwell Heath, surs, Warren, AB

PARHAM, Matthew, orph over 14 yrs old of John, decd, chose John C. Turner gdn 12/2/1811, Warren, MIC

PARHAM, Polly, orph of Matthew, decd, John Wilson apptd gdn 1/1819; retn 4/23/1920, Jasper, Ests, OM

PARHAM, Rebecca, orph over 14 yrs old of John, decd, chose John C. Turner gdn 12/2/1811, Warren, MIC

PARHAM, Tamsy, minor, retn by John Nelson, the gdn, 4/23/1820, Jasper, Ests

PARIS, Elias, decd, James B. Conley, Joseph Ragsdale, admrs, Garrett Gray, sur, 7/5/1858, Paulding, AB

PARIS, Gresham, minor orph of Elias, decd, James B. Colley, gdn, 11/20/1858, Paulding, GB

PARIS, James, decd, William Bugg issued L/A, Samuel Bugg, William F. Booker, secs, not dtd, Richmond, AB

PARIS, James, minor orph of Elias, decd, Joseph Ragsdale, gdn, James B. Colley, sur, 11/1/1858, Paulding, GB

PARIS, James N. J., orph of Nathaniel, decd, Sarah L. Paris, gdn, 4/4/1859, Paulding, GB

PARIS, Jane, decd, Jesse Dooly, admr, to sell real estate 11/7/1836, Habersham, MIC

PARIS, John, minor orph of Elias, decd, James B. Colley, gdn, 11/20/1858, Paulding, GB

PARIS, Kezia, decd, Sherwood Bugg issued L/A 9/21/1785, Abraham Jones, Daniel Wollecon, sec, Richmond, AB

PARIS, Mary Jane, minor orph of Elias, decd, Joseph Ragsdale, gdn, James B. Colley, sur, 11/1/1858, Paulding, GB

PARIS, Nathaniel J., decd, Sarah L. paris, admx, Duncan Bohanon, R. A. Turner, sur, 7/5/1858, Paulding, AB

PARIS, Peter, decd, Kezia Paris issued L/A 5/27/1785, James Fox, Sherwood Bugg, secs, Richmond, AB

PARIS, Sarah Ann, orph of Nathaniel, decd, Sarah L. Paris, gdn, 4/4/1859, Paulding, GB

PARIS, William A., orph of Nathaniel, decd, Sarah L. Paris, gdn, 4/4/1859, Paulding, GB

PARK, Garrett W., decd, Russell Jones and John Espy issued L/A 3/7/1814, Jackson, OM

PARK, James, decd, Sally, Garrett W. and John Park issued L/A 10/29/1803, Jackson, OM

PARK, Joseph, decd, Isaiah Park issued L/A 10/18/1826, John L. Park, Edward Gallin, secs, Morgan, AB

PARK, Robert, decd, LWT pvd 10/25/1802; Garrett W. Parks, admr, 4/22/1805, Jackson, OM

PARKER, Ann, decd, LWT, James Parker, exr 7/8/1787, Chatham, Adms

PARKER, Caroline, illegitimate child of Elizabeth, David Curry issued L/G 3/5/1838, Washington

PARKER, Dudley P., Thomas Cross apptd gdn, 3/2/1829, removed 3/7/1836, Habersham, MIC

PARKER, F. C., decd, ct ordered to set aside support for widow 12/1867, Webster, OD

PARKER, George, Thomas Cross apptd gdn, 3/2/1829, Habersham, MIC
PARKER, George, decd, Richard H. Wilde issued L/A 12/10/1814, Thomas Cumming, sec, Richmond, AB
PARKER, Isaiah, decd, John W. Scruggs, admr w/LWT annexed 9/2/1861, E. J. Bailey, George K. Hamilton, surs, DeKalb, AB
PARKER, Jacob, decd, LWT pvd 7/11/1791, wife, Mary, ch: William, Jacob, Mary; temp L/A gtd William Lanier 5/25/1793, Greene, Misc
PARKER, James, decd, Martha Parker, extrx 1/1839; apprs: William H. Brown, James Turner, Joseph Glenn and James W. Dunaway, Stewart, Adms
PARKER, James, decd, Mary Parker, Solomon Thompson apply for adm, John Matthews, Amos Parsons, sur, 1/13/1803, dismissed 7/4/1808, Warren, MIC, AB
PARKER, John, decd, LWT pvd, William Gibson qualified as exr 9/3/1827, Camden, MIC
PARKER, John D., decd, Posey P. Brooks issued L/A 1/15/1824, H. H. Goss, F. Fitzpatrick, secs, Morgan, AB
PARKER, Matthew W., decd, Sally Parker issued L/A 5/2/1814, Jackson, OM
PARKER, Moses, Sr., decd, Mrs. Susannah Parker and Moses Parker applied for L/A 1/2/1799, Moses Parker, Jr. dying before the citation was printed on 2/19/1799, Susannah Parker and James Taylor applied for L/A, Greene, Misc
PARKER, Samuel, decd, LWT pvd, Mary Parker qualified as extrx 1/5/1807, Warren, MIC
PARKER, Samuel, decd, extrx gtd leave to sell 257 acres Warren Co. 3/1/1813, Warren, MIC
PARKER, Stephen, decd, James Alford Parker applied for L/A 3/17/1788, Greene, Misc
PARKER, William, decd, Robert Parker applies for admn 1/25/1803, granted, admr, 2/15/1804, James Matthews, Solomon Thompson, surs, Warren, AB, MIC
PARKES, John, decd, Posey P. Brooks, Joseph Fitzpatrick and Hezekiah F. Goss issued L/A 1/15/1824, Morgan, AB
PARKINS, Job, decd, Charles Stringer and Josiah Stringer issued L/A 2/10/1809, George King, Simon Stringer, secs, Laurens, AB
PARKS, Amanda M., decd, LWT exhibited, Mary J. Parks, admx, 3/21/1868, Fulton, AB
PARKS, Erastus, decd, late of Camden Co., Samuel Hale issued L/A 2/10/1828, Benjamin Hall, sec, Richmond, AB
PARKS, James, decd, Sarah and Garrett W. Parks, admrs, ask to sell 250 acres on Cabin Cr for benefit of heirs 1/6/1807, Jackson, OM
PARKS, John B., decd, L/A gtd Welcome Parks, with Charles Cargile, Isaac McClendon, secs, 3/6/181; Mary Parks chose child's pt 9/5/1814, Jasper, OM
PARKS, John H., decd, Talitha C. Parks, admx, 5/2/1853, John Blackwell, M. W. McCravey, surs, DeKalb, AB
PARKS, Joseph, decd, Douglas Watson, sec for Richard Parks in adm of est, asks ct to relieve him of his suretyship, for he thinks himself in danger of being injured by sd admr, 7/1809, Oglethorpe, OM
PARKS, Joseph, decd, Richard Parks, admr; Douglas Watson & James Parks, sureties, stated that "in their opinion there is great probability of their suffering damage by the said administrator, and pray relief....", 5/1808, Oglethorpe, OM
PARKS, Laban, decd, Mary Parks issued L/A 11/27/1793, Abemeleck Hawkins, sec, Richmond, AB
PARKS, Mary Henrietta, orph of James G., decd, Hezekiah Dyer, gdn, 11/7/1836, Habersham, MIC
PARKS, Wilson apptd gdn for Samuel C., Sophia, and Clarke D., rphs and minors of John B. Parks, decd, 9/1821, Jasper, OM

PARLAND, Adam, minor orph of John, decd, F. M. Scarlett apptd gdn 1/14/1839, Glynn, MIC
PARLAND, Frances Ann, minor orph of John, decd, F. M. Scarlett apptd gdn 1/14/1839, Glynn, MIC
PARLAND, Jane, minor orph of John, decd, F. M. Scarlett apptd gdn 1/14/1839, Glynn, MIC
PARLEY, Judeama, orph of J. W., decd, John A. Fain, gdn, 6/1/1863, Fulton, GB
PARLEY, M. A. (Mrs.), decd, J. J. Irvin issued L/A 4/7/1863, Fulton
PARMAN, John, decd, LWT, Andrew and John McCullough of Savannah, Merchants, apptd admrs, 3/1/1790, Chatham, Adms
PARNELL, Jeremiah, decd, Charles Thompson, Patsey Parnell issued L/A 1/12/1824, Morgan, AB
PARR, Harriet, orph of David, decd, John N. Calhoun issued L/G 1/13/1840, Washington
PARR, John C., decd, William L. Parr, admr, 11/3/1823 bond, Robert Orr, sur, Clarke, AB
PARR, Lemuel W., orph of David, decd, John N. Calhoun issued L/G 1/13/1840, Washington
PARRISH, Absalom, "recd of James Williams in full for money he recd from Jacob Mincey ..s my gdn 12/30/1818", Bulloch, Misc
PARRISH, Edward, decd, Lydia Parrish apptd admx 3/13/1837, Effingham, MIC
PARRISH, Harris, age 9 of 12/22nd next, bound to Philander O. Parrish to learn carriage-makers trade until age 21, 7/4/1814, Warren, MIC
PARRISH, Henry, decd, planter, LWT names wife, Mary Ann; children: Mary, Josiah, Jerusha, Hezekiah, Ezekiel, Henry, Joel, Ansel, Absolom and Morning pvd 6/28/1800, Bulloch, Misc
PARRISH, John, decd, Gerard Camp, admr w/LWT annexed, 9/1/1823, Benjamin Sandeford, Benjamin Hurt, surs, Warren, AB
PARRO, George W. bound to Alexander Walden, Jr., shoe and bootmaker, 5/1816, Jasper, OM
PARROTT, Nathaniel, decd, Lander Thrash issued L/A 5/2/1814, Putnam, AB
PARROTT, Thomas, decd, Daniel Parrott produced p/a to him from William Fish and James Parrott authorizing him to receive their share of estate; Martin Palmer, admr, ordered to pay over, 1/4/1814, Glynn, MIC
PARTRIDGE, William H., decd, George W. Massey issued L/A 5/23/1843, Washington
PASCHAL, Samuel, decd, 1813 retns names ch-Nancy, Mahala, Fereby, Samuel, Matilda, Betsey, Jas Madison; 1819 retn pays heirs; John Leverett, Allen Tucker, Richard Holt, Benjamin Reason, admr rt of wf, Elizabeth, Jasper, Ests
PASCHAL, Samuel, decd, est apprd 5/15/1812 by Richd Carter, Saml Mays, Royal Clay; sold by Burrel Green, Elizabeth Paschal, admr, Jasper, Ests
PASCHALL, Samuel, decd, Burrell Greene, admr, has leave to sell negroes 1/7/1817; Elizabeth Paschall recd interest on est for maintenance of heirs, 11/1814, Jasper, OM
PASCOE, John, decd, LWT dtd 11/25/1852, pvd 1/1853 names bro., Samuel, sister, Catharine; John Moore, exr; Solomon D. Leonard, admr, Isaac Darter, James Leonard, Henry Strickland, 9/5/1853, Cherokee, AB
PASS, William, decd, Mourning Pass and Anthony Holloway issued L/A 4/4/1812, Putnam, AB
PATCH, Joseph, decd, inv of est 12/25/1791, Camden, MIC
PATE, Drury, decd, Joseph Leonard, admr, 9/3/1827, Stith Hardaway, Benjamin Thompson, surs, Warren, AB

PATE, Redding, decd, LWT pvd 1/7/1839, Silas Floyd, Green B. Burney, Elizabeth Pate, exrs, Washington
PATE, Willis A., minor child of Herod, Harvey Pate, gdn, 1845 retn, Fayette, GB
PATRICK, James, decd, LWT pvd by James King and William Hitchcock, L/T gtd Wm Armor, 5/1816, Jasper, OM
PATRICK, John C., decd, L/A gtd Joseph Heard and Ollive Patrick, with Vallentine Mooney, sec, 7/3/1815, Jasper, OM
PATRICK, Joseph, decd, Jeremiah Sharks, gdn of orphs: Jeremiah B., Ezekiel, Joshua C., 5/3/1824, Roderick Leonard, sec, Morgan, GB
PATRICK, William, decd, Thomas Watts issued L/A 3/15/1826, Joseph Morrow, sec, Morgan, AB
PATTEN, Malony B., decd, Robert S. Patton, admr, Robert B. Lewis, Thomas Bomer, secs, 6/7/1852, Lumpkin, AB
PATTEN, Samuel, decd, 8/15/1810 inv, apprs: Jonathan Cooper, Archelaus Moon, Charles Wheeler, Elbert, GB
PATTERSON, Amsy Jane, James P. Patterson, gdn, 2/1836, Stewart, L/G, Adms
PATTERSON, Charles, decd, Elizabeth Patterson, admx, Charles McCardle, Thomas Towson, sec, 1/10/1831, Bibb, AB
PATTERSON, Charles, decd, Thomas Victory, admr, James H. Stoddard, George Wood, sec, 1/9/1832, Bibb, AB
PATTERSON, Elizabeth Perkins, James P. Patterson, gdn, 2/1836, Stewart, L/G, Adms
PATTERSON, George R. D., decd, Alfred Barksdale issued L/A 5/25/1841, Washington
PATTERSON, Harriet Elizabeth, Maria Patterson gtd guardianship 3/3/1830, Effingham, MIC
PATTERSON, John, decd, late of St. Marys, William Cook apptd admr 1/5/1804; sd admr applied est contrary to law, and admitted he illegally transferred $2800 bond for no valuable consideration, removedd as admr 3/17/1806, Camden, MIC
PATTERSON, John, decd, Ann Patterson, wid, and Francis Young apptd admrs 6/9/1802, Camden, MIC
PATTERSON, John, decd, Lewis Levi apptd in rt of wife as admr 6/7/1803, Camden, MIC
PATTERSON, John (Colonel), decd, William Cook, admr, makes his retn 1/8/1805, Camden, MIC
PATTERSON, John R., decd, Jared Irwin, Mary Patterson, admrs 1832, Stewart, Adms
PATTERSON, William, decd, Maria Patterson applies for L/D 1/5/1829, Effingham, MIC
PATTERSON, William, decd, petition of Mrs. Ann Holmes, mother of Arthur and Josiah, orphs for Wm Barnett to be apptd gdn 3/3/1806, Jackson, OM
PATTERSON, William B., decd, James P. Patterson, admr, 4/1841; apprs: Robert Etheridge, Brady M. Smith, William Nelson, William D. Fitch; purchasers at sale: Lydia Patterson (wid), Hampton Allen, Wiley Ammons, Wright Andrews, Stewart, Adms
PATTILLO, David, decd, John V. Pattillo, gdn of orphs: Rebecca, Swinnie?, and Sarah 9/7/1818, Samuel Pattillo, sec, Morgan, GB
PATTILLO, Patillo, orph of David, decd, James Pattillo, gdn, 1/6/1820, John R. Pattillo, sec, Morgan, GB
PATTILLO, Sarah, orph of David, decd, James Pattillo, gdn, 1/6/1820, John R. Pattillo, sec, Morgan, GB
PATTON, Jacob, decd, Jane Patton, wid, apptd admx 9/9/1783, Wilkes, MxR
PAUL, Phillip, decd, Francis Brown issued L/A 6/14/1794, Henry Crutcher, sec, Richmond, AB
PAULETT, David, decd, Harry Paulett and James Ligon, admrs, 1/24/1819 bond, George W. Moore, sur, Clarke, AB

PAVERY, Catharine, decd, LWT pvd 1/10/1848, Effingham, MIC
PAXTON, Samuel, decd, 8/22/1809 inv, apprs: Richardson Hunt,
Benjamin Higginbotham, Thomas Smith, Elbert, AR
PAYNE, Barnabas, decd, Nathaniel Wilder issued L/A 1/10/1798,
William McTyeire, sec, Richmond, AB
PAYNE, Champness, decd, L/A gtd Mary Payne 7/9/1805; inv by
Dudley Jones, Asa Allen, Benjamin Baker 8/2/1805, Franklin, IMW
PAYNE, Champness, decd, inv of est appraised by Dudley Jones, Asa
Allen, Benjamin Baker 7/9/1805, Franklin, OM
PAYNE, Cleveland, decd, L/A issued Zebadiah Payne 5/2/1808;
Zebadiah Payne, admr, to sell 80 acres gtd Thomas Payne on Broad
River 3/3/1812; accts of est-Kenneth McKinney pd is pt of debt
due from heirs of Thomas Payne for horse sold John Burks to
heirs, Franklin, OM
PAYNE, Daniel, decd, LWT pvd 3/3/1807 by John McCartha, Ann Payne
qualified as extrx, Tattnall, MIC
PAYNE, Daniel, decd, Samuel Payne, bro of decd, apptd admr
12/26/1781, inv 1/18/1782, Isaac perry, Wm Ayers, Nicholas Ware,
apprs, Wilkes, MxR
PAYNE, James, decd, H. W. McDaniel and Elizabeth Payne issued L/A
1/10/1859, Fulton
PAYNE, John, decd, pers est sold public sale 10/15/1804, mostly
to Nancy Payne; notes due Payne 2/12/1806 turned in by
Paynedexter Payne; judgment vs est obtd by Hugh Patrick; debts
include costs of children's school, 5/4/1807, Franklin, OM
PAYNE, John, decd, inv; due est from Obadiah and Moses Ayers by
note dtd 11/27/1803 $100, etc; ordered that Ann and Paynedexter
Payne receive L/A on est upon giving bond 2/12/1803, Franklin, OM
PAYNE, John, decd, ct ordered adm, est to give title to land
given by decd prior to his death to Charles Payne, 2/12/1805,
Franklin, IMW
PAYNE, John, decd, pet of Charles Payne shows that decd gave his
bond in lifetime to make titles to certain l and and died without
performing sd bond, 8/3/1804, Franklin, OM
PAYNE, Miley, orph of Champness, Mary Payne, gdn, 7/9/1805,
Franklin, IMW
PAYNE, Rutha, heir and relict of Cleveland Payne, decd, Kenith
McKinzie gtd L/G 7/6/1812, Franklin, OM
PAYNE, Sarah (formerly Carlton), decd, Thomas Payne, admr in rt
of wife, asking to sell 192 1/2 acres on Middle Fork of Broad
River, 1/4/1813, Franklin, OM
PAYNE, Thomas, Jr., decd, to bros: Nathaniel, Cleveland, Moses,
Champness, Shrewsbury, Zebadiah & Payndexter Payne, land on sou
fork of Broad River (150 acres orig gtd William Payne); sister
Ruth Payne; mother Yannaky Payne, Franklin, OM
PEABODY, Francis, decd, Thomas G. McFarland issued L/A 3/4/1833,
Duncan McArthur, sec, Montgomery, AB
PEACOCK, Arthur, decd, Allen Belsher issued L/A 5/3/1814,
Laurens, AB
PEACOCK, Hannah, minor, John R. Daniell, gdn, Jeremiah Drew, John
McConner, sur, 9/1/1823, Emanuel, GB
PEACOCK, James, decd, William Peacock qualified as admr
1/18/1791, Liberty, Ests
PEACOCK, John, orph of Michael, decd, John R. Daniell, gdn,
William Daniell, Lavinnah Drew, surs, 9/1/1823, Emanuel, GB
PEACOCK, Leoda C., minor daughter of James T., John F. Fain apptd
gdn 6/1/1863, Fulton, GB
PEACOCK, Thomas J., minor orph of Lewis, decd, Mrs. Avey Peacock
qualified as gdn, dismissed 10/3/1859, Fulton
PEAK, Candace, illegitimate child of Judith, David Peek apptd
gdn; ordered that Jacob Lindsay, the reputed father, pay sd gdn
$20 a yr for 4 yrs, 4/6/1802, Jackson, OM

PEAN, Charles J., decd, Lemuel Pean issued L/A 2/2/1863, Fulton
PEANEAS, John, decd, inv 10/3/1784, apprs: Jacob Bankston, Loyd
Kelly, H. Morgan, Wilkes, MxR
PEARCE, James choses Wm Hamilton as gdn 9/1829, Habersham, MIC
PEARCE, William A., Stephen W. Pearce, gdn, Dooly, OD
PEARCE, Willis, decd, Susannah Pearce issued L/A 5/6/1816,
Jackson, OM
PEARRE, Cassandra, minor orph of Major James, decd, William P.
Dearmond, gdn, 5/31/1819, Richmond, GB
PEARRE, Humphrey G., decd, late of Columbia Co., L/A to John C.
Talbert 7/171823, John Coombs, W. P. Dearmond, secs, Richmond, AB
PEARRE, James, decd, LWT pvd 12/29/1797, Massee and Nathaniel
Pearre, exrs, Columbia, Ests
PEARSON, Benjamin, decd, LWT pvd 3/27/1836 names wife, Sarah,
gave 1/2 of his possession to the poor school of Bulloch Co.,
James Hendrix, Wiley Hendrix, exrs, Bulloch, Misc
PEARSON, George, decd, Lucy M. Pearson, Jno H. Mann L/A 5/6/1818;
pd Jno H. Mann, gdn/Mary H. & Arabella, Benja. Yarnold (wife,
Lucy M., wid of decd); 1823 div-Mrs. Mary H. Jones, Arabella L.
Pearson, Mrs. Lucy M. Yarnold, Richmond, AB, AR
PEARSON, Hiram, illegitimate child of Leona, L/G issued David
Williams 3/3/1834, Washington
PEARSON, Thomas R., decd, Sterling J. Elder, admr, Jesse L.
Blalock, James F. Johnson, Wm H. Blalock, surs, 1851-1854 retns,
Fayette, AB
PEARY, Thomas, decd, L/D gtd James Culbreath, admr 4/16/1796,
Columbia, Ests
PEATUS, John bound to Abner Durham 11/1/1819, Jasper, OM
PEAVY, James, orph of Abram, decd, Samuel Walker apptd gdn, Silas
Baker, Hugh B. T. Montgomery, Louisa Walker, sur, 11/27/1848,
Troup, GB
PEAVY, Mary Emily, orph of Abram, decd, Samuel Walker apptd gdn,
Silas Baker, Hugh B. T. Montgomery, Louisa Walker, sur,
11/27/1848, Troup, GB
PEEBLES, Mary, decd, John Moore, admr, 7/3/1832, Thomas P. F.
Threewits, James Harris, surs, Warren, AB
PEEK, John, decd, Henry and Leonard M. Peek issued L/A 11/2/1812,
Putnam, AB
PEEL, James H., decd, Forrester Little, John Peel, admrs; apprs:
Jonas Griffin, Robert Beaty, John M. W. Peel, G. J. Stapleton, J.
D. Stapleton; purchasers at sale: M. M. Bush, John Cheatham, Job
Glovenor, Reubin Hay, Stewart, Adms
PEEL, Mary, minor of Thomas F., decd, George R. Gathard issued
L/G 9/1856, dismissed 2/1857, Webster, OD
PEEL, Mary, minor orph of Thomas F., decd, John D. Stapleton
issued L/G 3/1857, Webster, OD
PEEL, Thomas F., decd, John A. Stapleton issued L/D 1/1857,
Webster, OD
PEEL, Thomas T., decd, John D. Stapleton issued L/A 4/1856,
Webster, OD
PEEPLES, Albert L., orph of John, decd, Benjamin M. Peeples, gdn,
7/19/1826, Henry Brown, Paschal M. Watts, secs, Morgan, GB
PEEPLES, Burwell, decd, memo of sale of pt of prop 8/10/1799, all
items bt by Rebekah Peeples; 3/2/1799 Mrs. Rebekah Peeples and
David Peeples gtd L/A, Greene, Misc
PEEPLES, David, decd, inv 1/6/1796, apprs: Davis Gresham, Thomas
Watts, certified by Elizabeth, Nathan and David Peeples, exrs,
Greene, Misc
PEEPLES, David R., orph of John, decd, Benjamin M. Peeples, gdn,
7/19/1826, Henry Brown, Paschal M. Watts, secs, Morgan, GB
PEEPLES, Dudley, decd, Wm F. Buckhannon & Matilda Peeples issued
L/A 9/16/1824, Jesse Roberts, Arden Evans, secs, Morgan, AB

PEEPLES, James D., orph of Dudley, decd, Remembrance Chamberlain, gdn, 11/7/1825, William Johnston, Morgan, GB
PEEPLES, John, decd, Benjamin Peeples issued L/A 11/3/1823, Morgan, AB
PEEPLES, Julia, orph of Dudley, decd, William F. Buckhannon, gdn, 12/23/1825, Reuben Mann, sec, Morgan, GB
PEEPLES, Nathan, decd, Frances and Joseph Peeples and John Browning applied for L/A 10/16/1797, Greene, Misc
PELATEER?, Basil, decd, silversmith, late of St. Marys, Louis Dufour apptd temp admr, leave gtd to sell perishable prop, 1/6/1823, Camden, MIC
PELLERY, Benjamin, orph, bound to Daniel McDowell 1/7/1817, Jasper, OM
PELLETIER, Robert, decd, Martin Grannis issued L/A 6/12/1827, William Shannon, J. W. Whitcock, secs, Richmond, AB
PEMBERTON, Allen, James Ponder relived from bond, p. 14, 38, Screven, OM
PEMBERTON, Elizabeth, admx, gives notice to show cause, p. 9, Screven, OM
PENCE, Charles, decd, of Richmond Co., Frederick Kimbal gtd L/A 12/9/1790, Columbia, Ests
PENDER, David R., decd, John D. Stapleton, admr, 4/1843; apprs: James Griffin, James G. Peel, Cullen Roberts, purchasers at sale: John Pender, A. Prim, Hugh Montgomery, J. W. and J. M. McGrady, E. E. Little, William L. Clark, Stewart, Adms
PENDLETON, Edmund, decd, Eidson Davis Pendleton apptd admr 2/15/1791, Chatham, Adms
PENDLETON, Solomon, decd, LWT dtd 2/3/1787 pvd 4/14/1787; petition of Daniel Pendleton, Robert Montford and Richard Wylly, exrs, 8/17/1787, Chatham, Adms
PENDRY, R. F., decd, Mary Pendry, extrx, 1/1865, Webster, OD
PENNY, Jesse, decd, of Augusta, Milly Penny issued L/A 4/25/1801, Edmund B. Jenkins, sec, Richmond, AB
PENNY, Malachi, decd, LWT pvd 9/4/1838, John W. Penny, James G. Thompson, exrs, Harris
PEOPLES, Delilah, William Simpson applied for John Bailey be apptd gdn 2/7/1827, Camden, MIC
PEOPLES, Isham, William Simpson applied for John Bailey be apptd gdn 2/7/1827, Camden, MIC
PEOPLES, Rebecca, decd, John Bennett, admr, L. J. Jeffers, sur, 11/15/1849, Bibb, AB
PERDIEU, Morris (or Maurice), decd, Ann Perdieu and Shadrack Rozer issued L/A 8/15/1795, John Perry, sec, Richmond, AB
PERKINS, Berry C., decd, Joseph Walker, admr, 10/6/1862, Reuben Perkins, sur, DeKalb, AB
PERKINS, Constantine, decd, late of Morgan Co., Sally Perkins and David Boring apptd gdns of orphs: Zeno and Malissa 9/2/1816, Jackson, OM
PERKINS, Eliza Janes, orph, Thomas J. Stell, gdn, 1834, Stewart, L/G, Adms
PERKINS, John, was bound out to Thomas M. Livingston 4/1856, Webster, OD
PERKINS, Joshua, decd, Nancy Perkins issued L/A 7/6/1818, Laurens, AB
PERKINS, Peter, decd, LWT pvd by Solomon Thompson, L/T issued to John Baker and John Torrence, exrs, 2/16/1803, Warren, MIC
PERKINS, Robert, decd, Wm Perkins, gdn of orphs: Wm R. and John C., 5/7/1827, Caleb Cook, Burnell Russell, secs, Morgan, GB
PERKINS, Sarah, decd, Jethro Darden, Sr., admr, 11/1/1819, Sampson Wilder, sur, Warren, AB
PERKINS, Thomas, decd, Jonathan Shaw qualified as admr 7/11/1783, Liberty, Ests

PERNELL, Henrietta R., dau of Henry who is apptd gdn 3/3/1834, Peter A. Lauren, Covington Searls, secs; Mark Shipp, gdn 11/3/1838, M. Wallace, sec, Lincoln, GB

PERRIN, Jacob Jean, decd, Joseph Hutchinson issued L/A 10/19/1812, James S. Walker, William Bowie, sec; 4/21/1813 Seaborn Jones issued L/A, John McKinne, Felix McKinne, secs, Richmond, AB

PERRIN, James, decd, A. C. Atkinson, admr, gtd leave to sell land in 15th dist, 7/1813, Jasper, OM

PERRITT, John, decd, Agnes Perritt issued L/A 9/1/1783, Samuel Baldwin, John Moore, secs, Richmond, AB

PERRY, Amelia E., decd, of Lumpkin, Mathew Wright, admr; apprs: Hollis Boynton, Erasmus T. Beall, Henry Beacham, Stewart, Adms

PERRY, Caroline, illegitimate child of Mary A., Lewis Knight issued L/G 1/13/1840, Washington

PERRY, Georgeann, orph of James, decd, Hamilton H. Sharpe, gdn, 1/5/1841, Tattnall, GB

PERRY, Isaac, decd, Agnes Perry, orph, 3/7/1836, Harris

PERRY, James, decd, Hamilton H. Sharpe issued L/A 5/4/1840; inv 5/5/1840, apprs: Joshua Dasher, John Mosley, Hugh G. Partin, Tattnall, AB, I&A

PERRY, James, decd, Hamilton W. Sharp issued L/A 1/13/1840, Tattnall, AB

PERRY, James, orph of James, decd, Hamilton W. Sharpe, gdn, 1/5/1841, Tattnall, GB

PERRY, John, decd, John P. Wynne issued L/A 1/2/1815, Laurens, AB

PERRY, John, decd, John Rayburn, admr, John H. Lowe, sur, 7/21/1847, Bibb, AB

PERRY, John, decd, late of Augusta, James Cravey issued L/A 4/12/1802, Conrad Liverman, sec, Richmond, AB

PERRY, Joseph, decd, Andrew Odom, admr, 1/26/1846; apprs: Daniel Smith, John H Eubanks, John Hodges; purchasers at sale: Andrew Odom, Richard Watson, Eli Fenn, Henry Turner, Jesse Watson, Dooly, I&A

PERRY, Thomas, decd, L/D gtd to James Culbreath 4/16/1796, Columbia, Ests

PERRY, W. B., decd, L. F. and Joseph T. Perry, exrd, 9/1865, Webster, OD

PERRY, W. N., decd, LWT pvd by M. Matthews 12/1871, Webster, OD

PERRYMAN, Anthony Major, minor and relict of David, decd, under age 14, David Perryman apptd gdn 9/5/1808, Franklin, OM

PERRYMAN, Montford, decd, Daniel Perryman apptd temp admr 1/4/1806, Warren, MIC

PERSA, Manuel, native of Spain, Lewis Bandy and Greene Talbot, gdns, 1/10/1817, Isham F. Fannin, sec, Morgan, GB

PERSONS, Henry, decd, Grigsby E. Thomas, admr, 1/6/1823, Jeremiah Butt, Arthur Moncrief, surs, Warren, AB

PERSONS, Josiah, decd, Thomas and Rachel Persons, admrs, 5/4/1807, Turner Persons, Wormsley Rose, surs, Warren, AB

PERSONS, Turner, decd, Amos J. Persons, admr, 12/1/1827, Henry Lockhart, G. W. Persons, Samuel Pitts, Nicholas W. Persons, James Flewellen, surs, Warren, AB

PETITE, Solomon, a freeman of colour, Jeremiah Pearson apptd gdn 5/1817, Jasper, OM

PETTEE, Thomas W., decd, Henry Pettee, admr, 4/6/1844; apprs: Thomas B. Donally, Daniel McLeod, Samuel P. Bond; purchasers at sale: Henry Pettee, A. R. Pettee, Dooly, I&A

PETTIGREW, John, decd, John N. Wood qualified as admr 9/26/1785, Liberty, Ests

PFLIEGER, John, decd, Emanuel Zeigler and David Zeigler apply for admn 8/1/1796, apptd 8/27/1796, Camden, MIC

PHARR, Francis, decd, Jonathan Pharr issued L/A 10/29/1803, Jackson, OM
PHARR, Hezekiah W., decd, Samuel T. Pharr apptd admr, 12/1/1855, Cobb, BB
PHARR, Joseph W., decd, LWT dtd 11/1/1858, pvd 1/4/1859 names wife, Mary Ann, Cherokee
PHELAN, John, decd, Thomas Duffy issued L/A 9/26/1832, Robert Philips, sec, Richmond, AB
PHILBRICK, Paul, decd, Martha Philbrick, admx, Elam Alexander, sur, 2/2/1848, Bibb, AB
PHILIPS, Charles, decd, LWT pvd 1/1/1837, Ann Philips, Henry Moffett, Reuben P. Crews, exrs, Harris
PHILIPS, Henry, decd, Hardy Philips issued L/A 1/1/1821, Jesse Mathews, sec, Morgan, AB
PHILIPS, John, decd, William Philips, son of decd, apptd admr 1781, Wilkes, MxR
PHILIPS, Nathan, decd, LWT pvd 3/6/1837, Wiley Philips, J. H. Terry, exrs; John L. Lewis, Pearce A. Lewis, gdn of orphs 12/12/1836, Harris
PHILLIPS, Bartholomew, decd, Thomas Dorough, gdn of orphs: Polly and Smith, 4/23/1817, Benjamin Phillips, sec, Morgan, GB
PHILLIPS, Bartholomew, decd, Uriah E. Ammons, gdn of orphs: Cynthy and Polly 1/10/1825, William Barton, sec, Morgan, GB
PHILLIPS, Benjamin, Louisa Miles bound two children to, p. 10, Screven, OM
PHILLIPS, Benjamin F., Hiram B. Phillips, gdn, 2/5/1836, Habersham, MIC
PHILLIPS, David, decd, John Phillips, Sr., admr, William Phillips, James Douglas, sur, 3/2/1840; sale of property 10/6/1840, Butts, AB, ER
PHILLIPS, David R., decd, David P. Phillips, temp admr, James P. Phillips, sur, 11/29/1873; J. P. Phillips, David P. Phillips, admrs, W. L. McDaniel, sur, 2/2/1874, file inv, Gwinnett, AB
PHILLIPS, Dicey, decd, Burrell Phillips issued L/A 9/8/1820, Laurens, AB
PHILLIPS, Ephraim, decd, Robert Hodges issued L/A 9/12/1821, Laurens, AB
PHILLIPS, Isaac, decd, L/A gtd Jenny Phillips 1/1813, Jasper, OM
PHILLIPS, Isaac, decd, appraisers: Thomas Ramsey, Edmond Chapman, James Simmons, Z. Phillips, Thomas Hayns 8/7/1807, Jasper, WAR
PHILLIPS, John, decd, Hezekiah Beall issued L/A 10/28/1784, Nathaniel Beall, L. Berry Bostick, secs, Richmond, AB
PHILLIPS, John, illegitimate child, Dawson Phillips apptd gdn 1/1820, Jasper, OM
PHILLIPS, Joseph, decd, Susanna Phillips issued L/A 2/3/1818, Laurens, AB
PHILLIPS, Levi, decd, Asa Shaw issued L/A 9/25/1804, John Turman, Angus Martin, secs, Richmond, AB
PHILLIPS, Mary Ann, orph of Henry J. B., decd, Seaborn A. Johnson apptd gdn, Robert D. A. Tharp, John B. Phillips, surs 5/15/1848, Troup, GB
PHILLIPS, Matthew, decd, William Wa. Carlisle issued L/A 3/1/1824, Edmond Carlisle, sec, Morgan, AB
PHILLIPS, Reuben, decd, Robert White, admr, James Brownlee, William Phillips, surs, 11/5/1844, Butts, AB
PHILLIPS, Ryal N., decd, Joseph Phillips, admr, D. McLeod, sur, 3/6/1843, Butts, AB
PHILLIPS, Samuel, decd, James Hitchcock issued L/A 7/1/1822, Ezekiel Strickland, sec, Morgan, AB
PHILLIPS, Susan Ann Elizabeth, orph of Henry J. B., decd, Seaborn A. Johnson apptd gdn, Robert D. A. Tharp, John B. Phillips, surs, 5/15/1848, Troup, GB

PHILLIPS, Thomas, decd, John Bates, admr, W. F. Mullins, sur, 9/12/1848, Troup, GB
PHILLIPS, Thomas, decd, Wiley G. Brady apptd admr with Joseph and John Phillips, sons of decd, 11/4/1811, Warren, MIC
PHILLIPS, Thomas, decd, Willy Giles Brady, Joseph and John Phillips, admrs, 11/4/1811, Cullen Lewis Brady, sur, Warren, AB
PHILLIPS, Thomas J., orph of Henry J. B., decd, Hardy Phillips apptd gdn, Stephen W. Beasley, Larkin Floyd, surs, 5/15/1848; John B. Phillips apptd gdn 5/7/1849, Rufus M. Johnson, Cephus R. Johnson, sur, Troup, GB
PHILLIPS, William H., orph of Henry J. B., decd, Hardy Phillips apptd gdn, Stephen W. Beasley, Larkin Floyd, surs, 5/15/1858; Rufus M. Johnson apptd gdn 5/7/1849, John B. Phillips, Cephus E. Johnson, surs, Troup, GB
PHILLIPS, Zachariah, decd, John W. Burney apptd admr 1/7/1822, Jasper, OM
PHINIZY, Ferdinand, decd, Jacob, Mary H., John Phinizy issued L/A 10/30/1818; pd John Egan (wife, Mary H., decd´s widow), Thomas A. Bones (wife, Eliza), Jacob Phinizy, gdn of John F. and Benjamin (Marco´s Phinizy´s children), John Phinizy, gdn of Ferdinand V. Burdell, Richmond, AB, AR
PHIPPS, Joseph, decd, Milly Philips, gdn for orphs: Nusell G. and Amanda 1/3/1831, Mark Golding, sec, Lincoln, GB
PICKARD, Robert, decd, appraisal 7/10/1802, Jonathan Davis, admr, purchaser at sale: Micajah Pickard, Hancock, AAAA
PICKERING, John, decd, John M. Wade, etc. to divide estate, p. 21, Screven, OM
PICKERING, Mary, John Oliver, gdn, p. 74, Screven, OM
PICKET, John, decd, LWT pvd by Joseph Williams, 11/4/1822, Jasper, OM
PICKETT, Mary, decd, L/A gtd Jeptha B. Pickett 4/1856, dismissed 3/19/1857, Webster, OD
PICKETT, Muse P., decd, L/A issued Benjamin F. Harrell 1/1875, Webster, OD
PICKETT, Priscilla, decd, LWT pvd 11/1/1824; heirs--Sarah, Wiley, Rebecca and James Rogers; grch---Martha Ann Spain, Elizabeth Sims, Rebecca Sims; Samuel Sims, exr, Pike, MIC
PICKINS, Robert, decd, Jonah Weakley issued L/A 3/5/1838, Washington
PICKREN, Charles and Jane, orphs, John Oliver, gdn, p. 177 and 185, Screven, OM
PICKREN, E. E., decd, William W. Oliver dismissed as admr, p. 180, Screven, OM
PICKREN, Elijah, orph, John Oliver, gdn, p. 70, Screven, OM
PICKREN, Elijah E., decd, Seaborn Goodall, admr, p. 180, Elvis Pickron, admx and others, p. 133, Screven, OM
PIERCE, Fanny, James and Nancy, orphs, Caleb Griffith and William Disheroon to be discharged as secs, John Butler, gdn, 9/1824, Habersham, MIC
PIERCE, Jane, decd, L/A to Jesse Dooly 1/12/1836, Habersham, MIC
PIERCE, John, decd, Merchant at Augusta, Robert Hamilton of Wilkes Co. and James Hamilton of Richmond Co., Ga., issued L/A 1/15/1805, James Pearre, Angus Martin, secs, Richmond, AB
PIERCE, Lovett, decd, Leah and Everett Pierce, admrs, 1839; purchasers at sale--Leah Pierce, Everett Pierce, Abner Perry, Hardy Howard, Allan Moye, Randolph
PIKE, Lewis, decd, Mary Pike and Hezekiah Linccm? issued L/A 10/4/1808, Putnam, AB
PILES, Eliza Ann, minor, John Piles, trustee, gtd leave to sell real estate 11/7/1825, Glynn, MIC
PILES, Sarah Frances, minor, John Piles, trustee, gtd leave to sell real estate 11/7/1825, Glynn, MIC

PILGRIM, Lucinda C., orph, Zachariah Cross, gdn, William Worley, sur, 3/10/1856, Cherokee, GB
PINKARD, John, orph of James N., decd, John L. Callaway, gdn, 10/10/1859, Paulding, GB
PINKARD, Noah, orph of James N., decd, John L. Callaway, gdn, 10/10/1859, Paulding, GB
PINKARD, Peter J., orph of James N., decd, John L. Callaway, gdn, 10/10/1859, Paulding, GB
PINKSTON, Shadrack, decd, David Pinkston, admr, 7/1841; appraisers: John and William West, James Garrett, James M. Granberry, Stewart, Adms
PINSON, Elizabeth, orph of Grandison, decd, Alexander Williams, gdn, George W. Brooks, sur, 11/11/1859, Cherokee, GB
PINSON, James, decd, inventory and appraisement 5/17/1810, appraisers: Jeremiah Willingham, Gilbert Shaw, Elijah Gibson; 1811 retn; Mary and Margaret Pinson, orphs on 1812 retn, Arthur C. Atkinson, gdn; Lewis J. Dupree, gdn of orphs--Amy, Joseph, Susanna and James (latter under age 14) 5/4/1812; Jane Pinson recd $30 for boarding the girls in 1812; town lot in Monticello, Ga. sold 10/25/1814, purchasers, Lewis Deupree, at request of Henry Koon, an heir; 1815 retn shows Mary Pinson, dau of James, Jasper, Ests, OM
PINSON, Levy, orph of Grandison, decd, Alexander Williams, gdn, George W. Brooks, sur 11/11/1859, Cherokee, GB
PINSON, Mary bound to Lewis McKee 3/4/1816, Jasper, OM
PINSON, Thomas Rhoden, decd, John Kelly apptd temporary admr 3/6/1805, Warren, MIC
PINSON, Winney, decd, Thomas Jones applies for L/A w/LWT annexed 10/20/1798; caveat filed 12/4/1798 by John Kelly, Benjamin Mitchell, Solomon Newsom, surs, Warren, MIC
PINSON, Winnie, decd, Thomas Jones, admr 2/3/1799, Benjamin Mitchell, Solomon Newsom, surs, Warren, MIC
PINYAN, Stokes, decd, wife, Nancy; Polly Barker, wife of Jeremiah; Sally; William; Jacob; Nancy Sluder, wife of William; Ellerson; Rebecca Brown, wife of Andrew; Thomas; Elizabeth Brown, wife of William; Jeptha; Dovey Rouse, wife of Nanan; Peggy (all children named), LWT dtd 1357 Lumpkin Co., Dawson, WB
PIPKIN, Jesse, decd, Asa Pipkin issued L/A 8/7/1809, Laurens, AB
PIRKLE, Jacob, decd, Robert and Nathaniel Pirkle issued L/A 8/6/1855, H. W. Blake, sec, Hall, AB
PITCHFORD, Lewis, decd, Andrew Dorsey issued temporary L/A 12/28/1862; Rebecca Pitchford issued L/A 2/1/1864, Andrew Dorsey, sec, White, AB
PITT, John W., decd, Mary Pitt issued L/A 7/10/1834, Baldwin
PITTMAN, Jeremiah acknowledged receipt of three slaves from John Grimes 12/26/1828, Bulloch, Misc
PITTMAN, John, decd, of Savannah, Ga., Merchant, James Greenbold apptd admr 9/20/1790, Chatham, Adms
PITTMAN, Phillip, decd, Etheldred and Benjamin Pittman, admrs, 7/23/1838, Randolph, AB
PITTS, Elizabeth, minor orph of Noel, decd, late of North Carolina, Nicholas Williams apptd gdn, Sterling Gardner, sur, 10/8/1811, Warren, MIC
PITTS, Hardy G., decd, John J. Pitts applied for L/A 7/5/1841, Effingham, MIC
PITTS, Jack, minor orph of Noel, decd, late of North Carolina, Nicholas Williams apptd gdn, Sterling Gardner, sur, 10/8/1811, Warren, MIC
PITTS, Nancy Williams, minor orph of Noel, decd, late of North Carolina, Nicholas Williams apptd gdn, Sterling Gardner, sur, 10/8/1811, Morgan, MIC

PITTS, Nester, minor orph of Noel, decd, late of North Carolina, Nicholas Williams apptd gdn, Sterling Gardner, sur, 10/8/1811, Warren, MIC

PITTS, Nicholas Williams, orph over age of 14 yrs, son of Noel, decd, late of North Carolina, Nicholas Williams apptd gdn, Sterling Gardner, sur, 10/8/1811, Warren, MIC

PITTS, Noel, decd, Nicholas Williams apptd admr 1/2/1808; Mrs. Martha Pitts came into court and made choice of child's part of estate 2/3/1812, Warren, MIC

PITTS, Solomon, minor orph of Noel, decd, late of North Carolina, Nicholas Williams apptd gdn, Sterling Gardner, sur, 10/8/1811, Warren, MIC

PLASTER, Daniel S., orph of Edwin, decd, Benjamin F. Plaster, gdn, 11/7/1859, Fulton, GB

PLASTER, Edwin, decd, Edward Hayes and B. F. Plaster issued L/A 2/7/1859, Fulton

PLASTER, Sarah, orph of Edwin, decd, Benjamin F. P'aster, gdn, 11/7/1859, Fulton, GB

PLATT, James, bound to M. M. Potter, p. 115; bound to Wyley Wright, p. 62, Screven, OM

PLATT, James, decd, Mary Platt, admx, p. 43, Screven, OM

PLATT, James W. and William, Ephraim Hunter and others divide estate, p. 174, Screven, OM

PLATT, Mary, Ephraim Hunter, admr, p. 105, 199, Screven, OM

PLATT, William, James Poythress, gdn, p. 157; released as gdn, p. 196, Screven, OM

PLATT, William, John Hannings, gdn, p. 82, Screven, OM

PLEDGER, John W., decd, Council Rentfrow, admr, Elijah Glass, sur, 5/1852, Fayette, AB

POOLE, Adam, decd, Thomas M. Poole and Allen J. Poole qualified as exrs of LWT 7/2/1855, dismissed 5/1859, Fulton

POOLE, Baxter, decd, Anne W. Sturgess issued L/A 2/20/1809, Richmond, AB

POOLE, Thomas M., decd, Mahulda S. Poole, Jno S. Wilson, admrs 3/2/1857; 10/8/1860 Crawford S. Poole, gdn of orphs-Mary S., Jno J. L., Thos A. and William F., minors, 10/1/1866, Mahulda O., admx, has married Edgar Garlick & Crandall L. Poole apptd admr, Fulton, GB

POPE, Eliza, orph of James, decd, Stephen W. Brown, gdn, 1/8/1855, Houston, GB

POPE, Henry, decd, LWT pvd 7/1807, Oglethorpe, OM

POPE, Henry, decd, on petition of Miles Hill, one of exrs, ct ordered Robert Pope apptd gdn of Clara, Benjamin and Henry J. Pope, minors and orphans of Henry, 1/1810, Oglethorpe, OM

POPE, James, decd, Ezekiel Wimberly, gdn of orphs: Smith and Jennett 1/8/1855, Houston, GB

POPE, Jesse, decd, Wilson Pope, Benjamin Pierce, admrs, 7/1841; apprs: Daniel Richardson, Lemuel B. Horton, John Crocker, Stewart, Adms

POPE, Jonathan, decd, Fleet Pope issued L/A 9/8/1820, Laurens, AB

POPHAM, John, decd, LWT pvd 1/7/1828 names ch: Elijah, Betsy, Sisk, Patsy, Crawford, John, Nancy Odom; wife, Ann (Muscogee Co. land), Gabriel Sisk, exr, Habersham, MIC

PORCH, Thomas, decd, Peter W. Walton issued L/A 9/16/1822, H. Walton, sec, Morgan, AB

PORCHER, Peter, decd, of S. C., planter, LWT pvd, Jane Porcher, James Moore apptd exrs 5/8/1789, Chatham, Adms

PORTER, Albert S., Christian Treutlen apptd gdn 1/5/1835, Effingham, MIC

PORTER, James, decd, Matthew Resier offered security to become admr 9/3/1827; John Charlton, admr, 11/1/1827; issued citation on appl of Wm King for adm of est, 10/6/1828, Bulloch, MIC

PORTER, James binds himself (Indemnity Bond) 8/19/1799 to abide agreement made with wife, Elizabeth--prop owned by them divided betwn them...at her death to go to her five ch: William, Thomas, James, Elizabeth, Ann Harriett, Effingham, Misc
PORTER, Mary Ann, Archibald Wilkins apptd gdn 1/5/1835, Effingham, MIC
PORTER, Noble, decd, Joseph W. Guilford, admr, 3/6/1837, Randolph
PORTER, Richard, decd, Henry Lockhart, admr, 8/10/1830, Arthur Moncrief, sur, Warren, AB
PORTER, Sarah of Eggingham Co., deed of gift from Samuel Bostick to his dau, 50 acres, 3/7/1799, Effingham, Misc
PORTER, Susannah, retn of Harmon Crum, her gdn, for her est recd from her father, William Porter, 6/30/1795, Effingham, Misc
PORTER, Thomas D., accts of Benjamin C. Porter, gdn of heirs 9/7/1829, Effingham, MIC
PORTER, William, decd, Mrs. Rachel Porter, relict, applies for admn 1/22/1802, Effingham, Misc
PORTER, William G., decd, William King, admr 1/4/1830; Archibald Wilkins, Jr., admr 1/5/1835, Effingham, MIC
PORTER, William, Sr, decd, inv 5/23/1791, Effingham, Misc
POSEY, Samuel, decd, Rebecca Posey, admx, 11/7/1808, Warren, MIC
POSSON, Louis (Dr.), decd, Jane Ann Poisson issued L/A 1/25/1816 w/LWT annexed, B. Bonyer, L. Barie, secs, Richmond, AB
POULSON, Jonathan, orph abt age 13, bound to Thomas Castleberry, 1808, Jackson, OM
POULSON, Mark, orph abt age 11 (bro of Jonathan), bound to William Shipp, 1808, later bound to Samuel Watson (age 13) 5/1/1809, Jackson, OM
POUNCEY, Anthony, decd, L/A gtd Sarah Pouncey 1/1/1821; inv and appraisement 1/10/1821, Bulloch, Misc, MIC
POUNDS, Richard, decd, Mary Pounds, gdn of Catherine, Elizabeth and Mary, orphs, 9/6/1819, Newman Pounds, sur, Clarke, GB
POWELL, Charity, decd, George Dukes petitioned for adm with non-cupative LWT annexed 1/4/1808, Warren, MIC
POWELL, James, decd, 1/29/1844, Ambrose Powell, admr; apprs: Norvell Truluck, George W. Knowles, Eliab Jones, Celia (wid), Charles, Ambrose, Mary Powell, Jefferson Westberry, John I. Culpepper, Council Clarke, Ichabod Davis, Dooly, I&A
POWELL, Joseph, decd, Mary and Jacob Powell, admrs, 7/1835, Mason H. Bush, Leonidas W. Hill, James Hillard, sur, Stewart, AB, Adms
POWELL, Josiah, decd, Keronhappuck Powell, admx 6/26/1792, Liberty, Ests
POWELL, Lewis, John Zeigler, gdn, p. 199, Screven, OM
POWELL, Lindy, orph of Nathan, decd, William Hamilton, gdn, 3/1/1819, Jesse Thomas, Henry Williams, secs, Morgan, GB
POWELL, Moses, decd, LWT pvd, L/T gtd John Heard, George Powell 1/7/1822, Jasper, OM
POWELL, Nathan M., decd, William Hamilton and Elizabeth Powell issued L/A 9/1/1817, Stephen Hackney, sec, Morgan, AB
POWELL, Polley, minor orph of Edward, chose William Collier her gdn, John Arnold, William Smith, sur, Oglethorpe, OM, GB
POWELL, Rebecca, minor orph of Edward, decd, William Collin apptd gdn, John Arnold, William Smith, sur, Oglethorpe, OM, GB
POWELL, Sydney, orph of Nathan, decd, Hary S. Williams, gdn, 9/16/1824, John Vason, Morgan, GB
POWELL, William, decd, William A. Smith, temp admr, George H. Jones, sur, 10/10/1871; apptd perm admr 1/1/1872, Gwinnett, AB
POWELL, Wade H., decd, Mary A. C. Powell, admx, Dooly, OD
POWELL, William, decd, LWT pvd 5/6/1833, Sarah Powell, exr, Washington

POWELL, William, decd, apprs: Johnson Strong, John Armstrong, Jesse Tucker 10/3/1808, Susannah Powell, admx; heirs: Susanna, John, Nancy, Zacheus, Allen, Thomas, 11/17/1812, Jasper, WAR
POWELL, Zachariah, decd, Wm McDowell and John White, admrs, have leave to sell negro woman and her child; L/A gtd Wm McDowell and John White, 7/1813, Jasper, OM
POWER, Josiah, decd, A. H. Power issued temporary L/A 5/10/1858, Samuel Power, sur, DeKalb, AB
POWER, Michael, decd, Mariner, Owen Owens, merchant, apptd admr 12/3/1784, Chatham, Adms
POWERS, Jeptha, decd, Ann Powers issued L/A 9/13/1796, William McTyeire, Jeremiah Wood, secs, Richmond, AB
POWERS, John, decd, LWT pvd 11/5/1832, Effingham, MIC
POWERS, Lydia, decd, LWT pvd by Robert Bourquin 9/4/1837, Effingham, MIC
POWERS, Thomas F. G., Nicholas F. Powers, gdn, George Powers, sur, 3/1853, Fayette, GB
POWERS, Timothy S., decd, William Lyon issued L/A 11/25/1804, James Collins, sec, Richmond, AB
POWLEDGE, David, decd, George Powledge applies for adm 8/1/1829, Effingham, MIC
POWSER, James, decd, Alex Hendry Sr. and others div est, p. 112, Screven, OM
POYNER, George, decd, L/A to William Wiley 9/2/1816, Jackson, OM
POYTHRESS, Cleton, decd, Hope Brannon, exr, p. 145, Robert M. Williamson, etc. appraise est, p. 145, Screven, OM
POYTHRESS, Meredith, admr, L/D, p. 98, Screven, OM
PRAT, John, decd, inv 1774, Edmond Cartledge, John Pitman, Moses Marshall, apprs, Richmond
PRATER, Daniel, decd, Elizabeth Danielly issued L/A 12/2/1788, James Danielly, James Watters, secs, Richmond, AB
PRATER, Edward, decd, Sarah Prater issued L/A 9/6/1791, Willoughby Barton, John Bosler, secs, Richmond, AB
PRATHER, John, decd, Haysmon Jay, admr 11/20/1788, Chatham, Adms
PRATHER, John, decd, Roderick Leonard issued L/A 12/6/1826, Morgan, AB
PRATHER, Sarah E., minor of Elias, late of Wilkes Co., decd, Samuel Cowles, Toliver Jones, gdns, 12/10/1838, Harris
PRATHER, Thomas W., decd, E. I. Prather, Taliaferro Wells, John W. Mays, gdn of orphs 9/4/1837, Harris
PRATT, H. S. apptd natural gdn of his children: Israel C., John W. and Isabell J. Pratt, minors, 6/3/1837, Camden, MIC
PRATT, H. S., decd, late of Alabama, A. J. Bessant apptd admr 1/4/1841; dismissed; directed to pay bal of $1583.15 to Isabella A. Pratt, the admx in Alabama, 1/13/1845, heirs request ct to authorize A. J. Bessant, admr, to purchase from S. C. King, White Oak Plantation on St. Marys River & 118 slaves, admr having made contract with King for prop 12/23/1842, 1/3/1843; John Bessant apptd admr de bonis non 3/2/1845; gtd leave to sell house and lot in St. Marys 9/7/1846, Camden, MIC
PRATT, John, decd, Mary Pratt, admx, gtd leave to sell perishable prop, 6/4/1822, Camden, MIC
PRATT, John, decd, carpenter, Martha Pratt issued L/A 9/28/1782, James Martin, Robert Bonner, secs, Richmond, AB
PRATT, H. S., decd, Camden, MIC
PRAY, John, decd, John G. Maxwell and George M. Waters, exrs, 5/10/1820, Bryan, Writs
PRESKETT, Martha, Sarah Preskett, gdn, p. 142, Screven, OM
PRESNEL, John, son of Jacob, Jeremiah Presnel, gdn, 5/1/1837, Randolph
PRESTON, Gilliam, Elisha J. Preston, James Preston, admrs, Francis Douglass, Thomas Moore, sur, 5/28/1832, Butts, AB

PRESTON, Gilliam, decd, James Preston, admr, James H. Stark, sur, 3/5/1832, Butts, AB
PRESTON, Gilliam H., orph of Gilliam, decd, John F. Preston, gdn, Dawson McKleroy, John M. Mayo, sur, 1/1/1844, Butts, GB
PRESTON, Henry, decd, planter, Chesley Bostick issued L/A 8/20/1784, Robert Middleton, Horatio Marbury, planters, secs, Richmond, AB
PRESTON, Thomas J., orph of Gilliam, decd, John F. Preston, gdn, Dawson McKleroy, John M. Mayo, sur, 1/1/1844, Butts, GB
PREWETT, Samuel apptd gdn of Phillip, Patsy, Tilman and Zachariah Prewett, 5/4/1807, Franklin, OM
PREWITT, Japheth, decd, est retd by Samuel Prewitt May term 1812, pd Charles Toney for boarding four of the orphans of decd, Franklin, OM
PREWITT, Joseph, decd, Samuel Prewitt issued L/A 2/12/1805, Franklin, OM
PRICE, Ann, Robert Higdon, gdn, John Wiggins, Jesse Scarborough, sur, 6/7/1830, Emanuel, GB
PRICE, Edward, decd, late of Philadelphia, now Ft. Wilkinson, Creek Nation, LWT pvd 9/2/1799 to Sarah, Susannah Baker's dau of Phila, my natural ch & male ch of Rachel, dau of Thos Giles, late of sd co. named ? , King of the Cussetah, Hancock, AA
PRICE, Elizabeth, decd, Thomas B. Burford, admr w/LWT annexed, James H. Stark, sur, 11/1/1847, Butts, AB
PRICE, Elvih, minor orph of John, decd, John Adams, gdn, 5/4/1812, Laurens, GB
PRICE, Ephraim, decd, Stephen W. Price, admr, James M. Bledsoe, sur, 1/12/1846, Butts, AB
PRICE, George, illegitimate, Jesse Wiggins, admr, Henry Durden, sur, 3/4/1833, Emanuel, GB
PRICE, Jesse, decd, Mary Price, admx, John R. Daniell, Francis Collins, sur, 5/6/1826, appraisal 6/15/1826, Emanuel, A
PRICE, John, decd, Jonathan Sawyer and John G. Underwood issued L/A 11/5/1811, Laurens, AB
PRICE, Joseph, decd, Rosanna and Joseph Price applied for L/A 12/9/1794, Greene, Misc
PRICE, Martha, minor of William H., C. R. Hardy issued L/G 11/1864, Webster, OD
PRICE, Matilda, orph, James Jordan, gdn, 3/1836, Samuel Williams, Thomas P. Helton, sur, Stewart, AB, Adms
PRICE, Miles, decd, Frederick Clem issued L/A 7/4/1792, James Mitchell, James Richards, secs, Richmond, AB
PRICE, Patrick, Josiah Scutchens, gdn, L. C. Price, sur, 6/7/1830, Emanuel, GB
PRICE, Phillip, Josiah Scutchens, gdn, L. C. Price, sur, 6/7/1830, Emanuel, GB
PRICE, Roxanna, James Waller, Rufus Knight, gdns, 3/7/1832, Emanuel, GB
PRICE, William, decd, Gary Grant, admr 5/3/1790, Chatham, Adms
PRICE, William, decd, John S. Raiford, admr, appr 6/12/1830, Emanuel, A
PRICE, William, decd, Lorenzo D. Price, admr, Josiah Scutchens, sur, 6/7/1830, Emanuel, AB
PRICE, William, decd, Robert Higdon, admr, James Hottten, sur, 6/7/1830, Emanuel, AB
PRICE, William, decd, Stephen Swain, admr, appraisal 10/1818, Emanuel, A
PRICE, William, decd, Thomas P. Helton, admr, 8/1838; apprs: Robert S. Rabb, Reuben Weathersby, James Patterson, Stewart, Adms
PRICE, William, illegitimate, Jesse Wiggins, admr, Henry Durden, sur, 3/4/1833, Emanuel, GB

PRICE, William H., decd, L/A issued R. T. Price 7/1862; L/A issued A. Nicholson 1/1863; L/A issued J. H. Carter 3/1865, Webster, OD
PRICHARD, Joshua, decd, George W. Prichard applies for L/A 12/6/1869, Cobb, MIC
PRICKETT, George, decd, LWT bequests to eldest son, Israel; dau, Ann Knight, sons: George, John, Josiah, Jacob and Joel Prickett; daus: Sarah Williamson, Mary Young, Elizabeth Weems; wife, Mary Prickett, 9/12/1803, Franklin, OM
PRICKETT, Jesse H., orph of Jesse H., Harriett A. Prickett, gdn, Mary Eidson, Wiley Curry, sur, 5/5/1851, Butts, GB
PRICKETT, Mary E., orph of Jesse H., Harriett A. Prickett, gdn, Mary Eidson, Wiley Curry, sur, 5/5/1851, Butts, GB
PRIDE, William, decd, appr 2/8/1802, William Reese, admr; purchasers at sale: Balaam Wallace, Duke Hamilton, Thos Carroll, Jno Stone, Henry Mitchell, Jno Hamilton, Robt Pollard, Wm Reese, Edmund Abercrombie, etc., Hancock, AAAA
PRIDGEN, Susy Ann, Amelia Pridgen, gdn, 7/7/1817, Bulloch, MIC
PRIEST, John C., decd, William C. Sargent, admr, John McCoy, sur, 1/8/1855, Cherokee, AB
PRIMROSE, Edward, decd, Edward Burch issued L/A 10/15/1808, Chesley Bostwick, William McTyeire, secs, Richmond, AB
PRINCE, George, decd, LWT pvd 5/7/1838, Rebecca Prince, extrx, Washington
PRINCE, William, decd, Thomas P. Helton, admr, 8/1838; apprs: Robert S. Rabb, Reuben Weathersby, James P. Patterson, Stewart, Adms
PRINGLE, Mrs., David Crum applies for his dau & issue, says her health renders her unable to support them; that her husband has absconded. Ct apptd David Crum gdn for Mary, Samuel W. & James J. Pringle, her children, 6/7/1824, Camden, MIC
PRIOR, Haden L., orph of John, decd, Asa Prior, gdn, 3/15/1823, Samuel Harris, sec, Morgan, GB
PRITCHARD, James H., decd, Robert Pritchard qualified as exr 12/17/1825, Glynn, MIC
PRITCHARD, Richard, decd, John B. Pritchard, one of heirs, applies for his part of est, 7/1/1316, Glynn, MIC
PROCTOR, Richard, decd, LWT pvd 9/6/1813, Camden, MIC
PROPER, Ann Matilda, orph of I. N., decd, Solomon Zipperer apptd gdn 7/6/1829, Effingham, MIC
PROPER, Caroline, orph of I. N., decd, Solomon Zipperer apptd gdn 7/6/1829, Effingham, MIC
PROPER, William, orph of I. H., decd, Solomon Zipperer apptd gdn 7/6/1829, Effingham, MIC
PROSSER, Jesse, decd, John Prosser issued L/A 11/21/1831, Baldwin
PROSSER, Oty, decd, LWT pvd 7/22/1839, Thomas and William Prosser, exrs, Washington
PROSSER, William, decd, John O. and Eliza L. Prosser issued L/A 5/5/1848, Baldwin
PRUDEN, Joseph J., decd, L/A issued Nancy Pruden 11/4/1833, Washington
PRUETT, Japheth, decd, inv appraised by Joakim Hudson, William Ash, Henry Parks, 3/29/1805, Franklin, IMW
PRUETT, Joseph, decd, L/A issued to Samuel Pruett, 2/12/1805, Franklin, IMW
PRUETT, Samuel apptd gdn of: Philip, Poley, Tilmon and Zachariah Pruett 5/4/1807, Franklin, IMW
PRUETT, S. D., Jacob Meadows apptd gdn, 1855, Cobb, B
PRUETT, William C., Jacob Meadows apptd gdn, 1855, Cobb, BB
PRUETT, William G., decd, J. H. Pruett, temp admr, Reuben Thornton, James W. Yarber, sur, 11/6/1876; J. A. Pruett, admr, Reuben Thornton, R. L. Marbet, sur, 12/9/1876, Gwinnett, AB

PRUITT, Hardin apptd gdn of his own minor children who are entitled to legacy left them by their grandfather, James McCormick, decd, 9/6/1811, Warren, MIC

PRUITT, Levi, decd, Elizabeth Pruitt and Byrd Pruitt apptd temp admrs, Isaiah Tucker, Joel Neal, Harden Pruitt, sur, 1/7/1805, apptd permanent admrs 3/4/1805, Isaiah Tucker, Hardin Pruitt, surs, Warren, AB, MIC

Pruitt, Levi, decd, Elizabeth and Bird Pruitt, admrs, 3/4/1805, Isaiah Tucker, Hardin Pruitt, surs, Warren, AB

PRUITT, Levi, decd, Isaiah Tucker, sur on bond of Byrd Pruitt and Elizabeth Pruitt, admrs, having been relieved as bondsman, admrs cited to give new bond, 5/4/1807, Warren, MIC

PRYOR, John, decd, overseer, Mrs. Delphia Pryor apptd admx 5/19/1790, Chatham, Adms

PUCKETT, Edmund, decd, 10/1841, apprs: James Miller, Moses Ramsey, Elbert Lewis, James L. Williams, Stewart, Adms

PUGH, Anna, decd, Sampson O. Pugh, admr, B. L. Edwards, sur, 3/7/1853, Cherokee, AB

PUGH, Frances, decd, Richard H. Thomas, admr, Josiah Everitt, sur, 12/9/1818; Richard H. Thomas, admr, James Waters, Sibran Johnson, William Martain, sur, 1/6/1819, Emanuel, AB

PUGH, Francis, decd, Eli Whiddon, admr, appraisal 2/13/1819, Emanuel, A

PUGH, Jeremiah, free person of colour, Joseph B. Bond apptd gdn 3/7/1831, Hall, GB

PUGH, John, decd, Francis A. Pugh, William Chamlee, Jr., admrs, Charles M. Scott, William Wayne, sur, 3/18/1853, Cherokee, AB

PUGH, John, orph of John, decd, Nancy Pugh, gdn, Francis Pugh, William Chamlee, sur, 2/8/1858, Cherokee, GB

PUGH, John Henry, orph of John, decd, Nancy Pugh, gdn, Nathan Wheeler, John W. Henson, sur, 8/1/1853, Cherokee, GB

PUGH, Willis, free person of colour, Joseph B. Bond apptd gdn 3/7/1831, Hall, GB

PULLIAM, Adeline, illegitimate child of Elizabeth, Adley Hulsey, Jr., gdn, Adley Hulsey, Sr., sec, 7/6/1829, Hall, GB

PULLIAM, John, decd, James Pulliam issued L/A 7/16/1792, William Bellamy, John Furey, secs, Richmond, AB

PULLIN, Micajah, decd, Augustine Edwards, admrs, 1805 retn, Wilkes, Retns

PULSELF, Freeman, decd, Lewis Bachlott apptd admr 1/5/1824, Camden, MIC

PURCEL, Archibald, an alien, Isaac Herbert issued L/A 4/17/1824, Richmond, AB

PUREY, John L., decd, John Hall issued L/A 7/5/1819, John Williams, James Hitchcock, secs, Morgan, AB

PURKINS, Alexander J., illegitimate child bound to Jesse Ponder for 14 yrs, 7/13/1830, Habersha, MIC

PURKINS, Mary Ann, age 2, illegitimate, bound to John Crow until age 18, 9/1829, Habersham, MIC

PURNAL, James, decd, Solomon Purnal, admr, 2/1840; apprs: James Stafford, Joseph King, J. Jarrell, John Sims, George M. Champion, Samuel Purdy; purchasers at sale: R. Applewhite, Abe Burk, N. A. Purafoy, etc., Stewart, Adms

PURNALL, Jonathan, decd, James Garrard and Rebecca Purnall issued L/A 1/3/1832, Hall

PURVIS, James, decd, William Purvis, admr,to sell real est, 1836, Bulloch, MIC

PURVIS, John, decd, Mary and John N. Purvis apply for L/A 8/22/1854, Webster, OD

PURVIS, Mary, decd, T. P. Everett issued L/A 12/1861, Webster, OD

PURVIS, Pharr, Jeptha Purvis, gdn, Bird L. Newton, sur, 9/7/1840, Emanuel, GB

PURVIS, Sarah, minor, over age of 14 yrs, selected James Purvis for her gdn 6/8/1818, Glynn, MIC
PURVIS, William, decd, Lewis Beacham, admr, appraisal 11/22/1837, Emanuel, A
PURYEAR, Benjamin M., decd, Daniel Meigs issued L/A 2/13/1826, George Hill and A. G. Raiford, secs, Richmond, AB
PURYEAR, Peter, decd, John Puryear and William Dougherty, admrs, 1/1/1827 bond, Charles Dougherty, sur, Clarke, AB
PUTNAM, Wilson, decd, David Putnam, admr, Thomas Putnam, sec, 1/4/1830, Hall, AB
QUARTERMAN, Elijah, decd, John Quarterman and James Wilson qualified as exrs 2/16/1786, Liberty, Ests
QUARTERMAN, John, decd, Thomas Sumner and James E. Wilson qualified as admrs 3/11/1791, Liberty, Ests
QUARTERMAN, Rebecca, decd, Samuel Jones qualified as exr 2/4/1793, Liberty, Ests
QUARTERMAN, Robert, decd, W. Quarterman, Sr., Elizabeth Quarterman and William Baker, admrs, 3/15/1787, Liberty, Ests
QUARTERMAN, Thomas, decd, Rebecca and Joseph Quarterman qualified as exrs 7/12/1791, Liberty, Ests
QUARTERMAN, Thomas, Jr., decd, John Norman, Renchie and Joseph Quarterman qualified admrs 3/3/1789, Liberty, Ests
QUILLIAN, Fletcher A., decd, LWT dtd 11/21/1864, names wife, Malissa and "my children", Osborne P. Quillian, exr, White, AB
QUILLING, John, decd, William Baker qualified as admr 6/17/1788, Liberty, Ests
RACHELS, William, decd, Zadoc Rachels issued L/A 11/6/1836, Washington
RADFORD, Reuben Westly, orph of Reuben, decd, John Radford, gdn, 5/12/1821, William Radford, sec, Morgan, GB
RADFORD, Silas, orph of Henry, decd, Reubin Radford, gdn, 3/4/1817, David Meriwether, sur, Clarke, GB
RAE, James, decd, Ann Rae issued L/A 7/22/1789, 6/8/1795, Mrs. Ann Rae, now Mrs. Cobbinson, issued L/A, John Cobbison, William Hayes, George Conn, secs, Richmond, AB
RAE, James, decd, of Richmond Co., Ann Rae gtd L/A 7/22/1789, Columbia, Ests
RAGLAND, Charles F., decd, John G. Myers, admr, Thomas A. Brown, sur, 8/7/1847, Bibb, AB
RAGLAND, Irby, decd, Hudson Ragland qualified exr 1/5/1804, Camden, MIC
RAGLAND, John R., decd, 1807 retn, recpt of Jay Garvis to Mrs. Franky Ragland for legacy of Sally Ragland, dau of John R., now his wife, dtd Petersburg, 12/15/1804, Wm Oliver, acting exr in place of Mrs. Frances Ragland 1808, Elbert, AR
RAGLIN, David, decd, LWT pvd 11/5/1810, Warren, MIC
RAGSDALE, Catton, decd, William Carmichael, admr, Amos Braselton, sur, 3/4/1850, Cherokee, AB
RAGSDALE, Catton B., orph of Catton, decd, William Carmichael, gdn, James Tippen, sur, 11/3/1851, Cherokee, GB
RAGSDALE, Elijah, decd, LWT pvd 7/7/1858, Sanders W. Ragsdale, exr, Paulding
RAGSDALE, Ira A., decd, Susan Ragsdale, admr, Larkin A. Ragsdale, sec, 9/4/1848, Cherokee, AB
RAGSDALE, Martin, orph of Catton, decd, William Carmichael, gdn, James Tippen, sur, 11/3/1851, Cherokee, GB
RAGSDALE, Mary, orph of Catton, decd, William Carmichael, gdn, James Tippen, sur, 11/3/1851, Cherokee, GB
RAGSDALE, Richard, decd, LWT names Susannah (wife of 57 yrs) dtd 12/23/1847, children: Larkin A., Ira, Carleton B., Mary M. Lesson, Elizabeth M. Roach, Martha C. Williams, Malissa C. Dudley, Susannah Philips, Cherokee, WB

RAGSDALE, Richard, orph of Catton, decd, William Carmichael, gdn, James Tippen, sur, 11/3/1851, Cherokee, GB
RAHN, Alexander, minor heir of Matthew, decd, Jacob Gnann, Jr. apptd gdn 5/4/1829, Effingham, MIC
RAHN, Ann Eveline, orph of Emanuel, decd, Jacob Gnann, Jr. apptd gdn 7/7/1828, Effingham, MIC
RAHN, Charlotte Caroline, orph of Emanuel, decd, Jacob Gnann, Jr. apptd gdn 7/7/1828, Effingham, MIC
RAHN, Eliza, minor heir of Matthew, decd, Jacob Gnann, Jr. apptd gdn 5/4/1829, Effingham, MIC
RAHN, Emanuel, decd, Jacob Gnann, admr asked to be dismissed from adm 7/7/1828, Effingham, MIC
RAHN, Frederick, decd, Cletus applies for L/A 7/30/1833, Effingham, MIC
RAHN, Israel, minor heir of Matthew, decd, Jacob Gnann, Jr. apptd gdn 5/4/1829, Effingham, MIC
RAHN, Jonathan, decd, LWT admitted to record 9/2/1840; William Rahn and John Wilson apply for adm 3/1841, Effingham, MIC
RAHN, Joshua, minor heir of Matthew, decd, Jacob Gnann, Jr. apptd gdn 5/4/1829, Effingham, MIC
RAHN, Maria Christian, orph of Emanuel, decd, chose Jacob Gnann, Jr. as her gdn 7/71/1828, Effingham, MIC
RAHN, Martha, decd, Joshua and Israel, minor heirs, chose Jacob Gnann, Jr. as their gdn, 7/7/1834, Effingham, MIC
RAHN, Matthew, decd, the accts of John Rahn, exr 3/3/1828, Effingham, MIC
RAHN, Salomi, orph of Emanuel, decd, Jacob Gnann, Jr. apptd gdn 7/7/1828, Effingham, MIC
RAHN, Susannah, orph of Emanuel, decd, Jacog Gnann, Jr. apptd gdn 7/7/1828, Effingham, MIC
RAHN, Susan S. chose Christopher R. Reiser for her gdn 5/3/1841, Effingham, MIC
RAHN, William Obadiah, orph of Emanuel, decd, Jacob Gnann, Jr. apptd gdn 7/7/1828, Effingham, MIC
RAIFORD, Morris, decd, LWT pvd 3/6/1837, Matthew Raiford, Camel Raiford, wife, Patience Raiford, exrs, Harris
RAIN, Cornelius, decd, LWT pvd, John Lee qualified as exr 1/6/1829; John Lee made final retn and dismissed, balance on hand of $14.84 turned over to Clk for benefit of heirs, all of whom are minors 1/4/1832; Joseph Howell apptd admr w/LWT annexed 6/4/1832; Cornelius Rains apptd admr de bonis non 1/7/1840, Camden, MIC
RAIN, Cornelius apptd gdn of his sisters, Margaret and Sarah Rain 1/2/1838, Camden, MIC
RAIN, Giles Y., decd, William Raines issued L/A 6/5/1799, Shadrach Rozar and Hill Chatfield, secs, Richmond, AB
RAINS, Joseph, decd, planter, died intestate, John Francis Courvoisie apptd admr 3/1/1783, Chatham, Adms
RAINEY, Alexander, decd, Owen Owens, admr 4/5/1791, Chatham, Adms
RAINEY, Birdine, orph of John, decd, T. G. Ross, gdn, James Ross, sur, 1/3/1852, Cherokee, GB
RAINEY, David, decd, Susanna Scudders issued L/A 17_5, Robert Dixon and Thomas Key, secs, Richmond, AB
RAINEY, James, orph of John, decd, T. G. Ross, gdn, G. W. Rainey, sur, 11/3/1851, Cherokee, GB
RAINEY, John, decd, LWT dtd 5/1/1845 pvd 7/15/1851 names wife, Sarah, and eight sons--Oliver, George, John, Thomas, William R., Martin, James and Borden; daughters--N. Caroline, Julutta, Amanda and Parsati?; George W. Rainey, exr, Cherokee
RAINS, Caldwalder, decd, L/A to John G. Rains 1/16/1833, Baldwin

RAINS, Cornelius, decd, Joseph Howell, admr, ordered to show new bond 7/1/1833; Joseph Howell, temporary admr, reports that he is abt to remove from co. and asks to be allowed to surrender est property to Isaac Bailey 1/7/1834, Camden, MIC
RAKESTRAW, Rachael, decd, William W. Bagwell, admr, Nicholas Spearn, sur, 5/14/1854, Cherokee, AB
RAKESTRAW, William, decd, E. H. Rakestraw, admr, applies to sell real estate 11/1/1869, Cobb, MIC
RAMEY, Elizabeth, child of Ann Ramey (now Pounds), 11/4/1816, Benjamin Williams, sur, Clarke, GB
RAMEY, Henry, decd, John L. Pennington, admr, to sell real estate 1/7/1817, Jasper, OM
RAMSEY, Alexander, decd, of Randolph Co., Ga. LWT names sisters and brothers--Mary, Margaret, Elizabeth, Henry Givens and James Harvey Ramsey. To Alexander´s other brothers: John, George, Thomas Ramsey; Henry G. Ramsey, brother, sole exr; inventory 1812; LWT pvd by Mathew Lemkin and Elizabeth Duncan; Henry Ramsey, exr, 11/1812, Jasper, OM
RAMSEY, Allen, decd, William Harrell, gdn for orphs: William P., Julia and Josephine 3/4/1833, William Curry and Robert Searls, secs, Lincoln, GB
RAMSEY, Catey, Bozeman Adare states that sd Catey has had several illegitimate children, among them, a child of Robert Adare, decd, who acknowledged him in life; sd Bozeman, gdn, for orphs education 4/22/1805, Jackson, OM
RAMSEY, Henry, decd, Jesse Mitchell wants title to Oglethorpe Co. land which decd and William Ramsey, Sr. gave bond to in 1802, sd Henry has since died, John Pennington & Elizabeth Ramsey, admrs, Elizabeth has since married Adair Pool 5/1/1809, Jackson, OM
RAMSEY, Henry, decd, late of Jackson Co., Ga., L/A gtd John Pennington 7/7/1814, Jasper, OM
RAMSEY, James, decd, LWT dtd 1/17/1855 pvd 1/9/1860, mentions decd son´s ch, daughter, Rachel P. Keith and her husband, Jasper L. Keith, Cherokee
RAMSEY, Sally Ann, minor orph of Henry, decd, Isaac Pennington apptd gdn 11/1814, John L. Pennington, sur, Jasper, OM
RAMY, Jacob made gdn of his ch--George, Harriett, Carey H. and William 2/1/1833, Hall, GB
RANDALL, Charles, decd, Jacob P. Strozier applies for L/A 6/21/1859, Mary Ann Randall and Priscilla Woolbright, surs, Lee
RANDLE, Lockington, decd, William Randle issued L/A 11/3/1822, Henry H. Cook, sec, Morgan, AB
RANDOLPH, George F., decd, William McGar issued L/A 4/4/1829, James L. Coleman, sec, Richmond, AB
RANDSOM, Archibald, decd, Andrew Nutt issued L/A 3/18/1822, Reuben Masser, David McIntosh, secs, Morgan, AB
RASBERRY, Benjamin, decd, David Love, gdn of orphs: Benjamin and Green 3/4/1816, John Dawson, sec, Morgan, GB
RATCLIFF, James, decd, on application of John Graham, one of heirs, division ordered of estate 1/8/1827, Glynn, MIC
RATCLIFF, Lewis, decd, Mary Ratcliff, admx, 1/8/1806, Camden, MIC
RATCLIFF, Richard, decd, James Ratcliff, admr, made annual retn 7/1/1816, Glynn, MIC
RATLIFF, John, decd, John Bond, admr, Hinsy Peeples and James Ryles, secs, 11/5/1832, Hall, AB
RATTEREE, John, Alexander Ratteree qualified as gdn 4/2/1860, Fulton
RAVOT, Abraham, decd, LWT pvd 5/25/1796, owns lot in Purysburgh, South Carolina; wife, Mary; ch--Henrietta Porter, Marguerite Mary Ravot; daus-in-law, Mary Mikell and Elizabeth Mikell; exrs, wife, Mary and David Hugienin of South Carolina, Effingham, Misc

RAWDON, Abner, decd, L/A to David Rawson 9/29/1821, Jasper, OM
RAWLINS, Fleming, decd, William C. Barksdale issued L/A
11/22/1803, John Milner, sec, Richmond, AB
RAWLS, Cyrenus F., decd, Andrew Ford, admr, A. A. Dyer, sur,
10/31/1872, Gwinnett, AB
RAWLS, Jane E. F., orph of Jones, decd, Allen Rawls apptd gdn
9/2/1822, Bulloch, MIC
RAWLS, John, decd, LWT named Allen Denmark, ch--Allen, James and
John Rawls, Harriet Brown; grch-- John Sherrod Rawls and William
Henry Rawls, heirs of Thomas Rawls, decd; apptd son-in-law,
Morgan Brown and sons, Allen and James, exrs, 2/4/1823, inventory
and appraisement by Edward Warren, Peter Cone, Sheppard Williams,
Aaron Everitt, Alexander Knight, 4/25/1823, Bulloch, Misc
RAWLS, John S., orph of Thomas, decd, retn of sale of two
negroes, 21 cattle; Wayne Co. land sold to William Stafford;
Allen Rawls, gdn, 8/2/1836, Bulloch, Misc
RAWLS, John S., orph of Thomas, decd, Sarah Rawls apptd gdn
11/3/1823, Bulloch, MIC
RAWLS, John Sr., decd, inventory of property sold at public sale,
divided into five equal shares; John, Allen, James, John L. and
William H. Rawls, Morgan Brown, 12/4/1823; "recd of Morgan Brown,
Allen Rawls and James Rawls, exrs of LWT...in full for legacy to
John S. and William H. Rawls, heirs of Thomas Rawls, decd by LWT
of John Rawls." signed Sarah Rawls, admr, 9/12/1826, Bulloch, Misc
RAWLS, Silas, decd, Elizabeth Rawls and William Rawls, admrs
2/2/1818, appraisal, Emanuel, A, AB
RAWLS, Silas, minor orph of Silas, Sr., William Hines apptd gdn,
8/3/1818, Emanuel, GB
RAWLS, Thomas, decd, Sarah and Allen Rawls issued L/A 7/1/1822,
Bulloch, MIC
RAWLS, Thomas, decd, inventory and appraisement by Sherrod
McCall, S. Wilson, Jehu Everitt, 8/1/1822, Bulloch, Misc
RAWLS, Thomas, decd, Sarah Wilson and Allen Rawls, admrs, Monroe
and Wayne Co. lands, estate divided betwn heirs 12/20/1826;
William, John, Jane and Sarah Rawls, by Joseph Hagin, S. Wilson,
John Mikel, James Rawls, William Lee, Bulloch, Misc
RAWLS, William H., minor orph of Thomas, decd, Sarah Rawls apptd
gdn 11/3/1823; 1838 retn, sale of 21 head of cattle, Wayne Co.
land sold to William Stafford, Allen Rawls, gdn, 8/2/1836; recd
legacy 9/10/1842, Bulloch, Misc
RAY, George Washington, minor, bound to William Ansley until 21
yrs old 11/4/1811, Warren, MIC, GB
RAY, Jane is apptd gdn of: Nancy and Solomon Ray, orphs of
Solomon 1/7/1822, Jasper, OM
RAY, John, decd, inventory by William George, Benjamin Jones,
John Tankesley (not dtd); 5/9/1784 Joseph Ray issued L/A, Thomas
Bush, Waters Dunn, secs, Richmond, AB
RAY, John, minor orph of Solomon, to be bound to John Loyal
7/3/1820, Jasper, OM
RAY, Major W., orph, Josiah T. Melton apptd gdn, Benjamin
Sheppard, Dunston Traylor, secs, 9/4/1848, Troup, GB
RAY, Solomon, decd, Joseph Beavers, William Broom, Joel Crawford
to appraise est 8/9/1813; Jane Ray, extrx, Jasper, Ests
RAY, Solomon, decd, L/A gtd Jane Ray, George Ray, with John
Moore, sur, 7/1813; rule nisi, Tench Farmer, in rt of wife
formerly Jane Ray, admx, 1/1820, Jasper, OM
RAY, Wiley, decd, Wiley White, George White, James White, admrs,
Harris
RAY, William, decd, Coleman L. Ray, admr, Elsy B. Thornton, Dory
Taylor, sur, 11/7/1836, Butts, AB
RAY, William, decd, William G. Ray, Coleman L. Ray, admrs, Dory
Taylor, George L. Thompson, sur, 11/17/1836, Butts, AB

RAY, William, decd, William G. Ray, admr, retns 1839-1840, Cherokee Co. land sold, pd: Elizabeth Ray, W. H. Miller, Aaron O'Nail, D. H. Ellis, W. H. Ray, R. Y. Ray, J. L. Ray, and S. S. Scott; 1840-1841 retns, pd heirs: H. Youngblood, S. S. Scott, R. Y. Ray, Aaron O'Nail, W. H. Ray, W. H. Miller, Elizabeth Ray, Daniel H. Ellis, J. L. Ray and C. L. Ray; court case in Henry Co., Ga. 1839, Butts, ER
RAYSE, Linny, a minor, Silas Burkholts apptd gdn 9/7/1812, Warren, MIC
REAGAN, William M., decd, Augustus L. Pitts, admr, 9/1/1861, Joseph Pitts and Laban Sturgess, surs, DeKalb, AB
REAUX, Mary, decd, John B. Guidron issued L/A 7/9/1828, Alexander Cunningham, sec; 1828 retn pd school books for Catherine Kinsley, heir, Richmond, AB, AR
REAVES, Benjamin, decd, inventory 7/1801 by C. Ingram, J. Lane, and R. Williamson, apprs, Franklin, OM
REAVES, Crene, James G. Davis, gdn, 1/20/1837, Harris, GB
REAVES, Richard, James G. Davis, gdn, 1/20/1837, Harris, GB
REAVES, William, James G. Davis, gdn, 1/20/1837, Harris, GB
RED, Thomas Davis, decd, L/A issued Hannah and Robert H. Davis 5/1816, Jasper, OM
REDDICK, James, minor orph of Peter, decd, late of Burke Co., Ga. 3/7/1831, Samuel Clarke, gdn, Ulric B. Clarke, sec, Richmond, GB
REDDICK, J. H., decd, L/A issued P. W. Reddick and Mary Reddick, Webster, OD
REDDICK, John, Charles Courteau, gdn, p. 67, Screven, OM
REDDICK, Nicholas bound to Fulton Kemp, p. 65, Screven, OM
REDDICK, Peter, order to be bound out until age 21, p. 21, 33; Charles Courteau, gdn, p. 67; William Smith, gdn, p. 84, to sell land, p. 122, 194, Screven, OM
REDDING, Ann, minor orph of James, decd, Mary Beach, gdn, 1/21/1818, Thomas Quisenberry, and Sylvester Porter, secs, Richmond, GB
REDDING, Ann M., orph of James, decd, Charles Beach, gdn, 3/19/1808, Richmond, GB
REDDOCK, William, Sr., appraisal 11/8/1798, purchasers at sale: Mary, William, John, Alexander & David Reddock, etc., Hancock, AA
REDING, Rehum, decd, L/A to Jasper Hester 11/5/1821, Laurens, AB
REDMAN, Elizabeth, a lunatic, James Carter, gdn, James R. McCord, sur, 1/23/1837, Butts, GB
REDMAN, Martha, orph of William, decd, James Carter, gdn, James R. McCord, William G. McMichael, surs, 2/1/1841, Butts, GB
REDMAN, Mary, decd, James Carter, admr, acct of hiring seven negroes, 2/4/1841, Butts, ER
REDMAN, Mary C., orph of William, decd, James Carter, gdn, James R. McCord, sur, 5/6/1839, Butts, AB
REDMAN, William, decd, Benjamin Redman issued L/A 6/18/1793, Richmond, AB
REDMAN, William, decd, James Carter, Mary Redman, admrs, Smith Boling, William J. Stephens, surs, 10/14/1831; pd: Hugh B. Stewart, tuition for Mary Redman, orph; Mary Redman for boarding Mary, Martha & William, orphs; Mary Redman for taking care of Elizabeth Redman, mother of decd, 1/11/1836, 1840 retn pd Mary Redman, J. R. and J. W. McCord, John W. Williams, James M. Fielder, 2/4/1841; order to divide estate 1/11/1841; Mary Redman (wid), James Carter, gdn for Mary C., Martha and Wm T. C. Redman (heirs), waive notice, Butts, ER
REDMAN, William T. C., orph of William, decd, James Carter, gdn, James R. McCord, William G. McMichael, sur, 2/1/1841, Butts, GB
REDWINE, Jacob, decd, Azariah Mims issued L/A 9/3/1866, Fulton

REECE, Alexander bound as apprentice to William Brown, Riding Chair maker, to learn the trade, Isham Rainey, sec, 4/6/1807, Oglethorpe, OM, GB
REECE, Julian, decd, Jesse H. Smith and Robert Rogers issued L/A 1/12/1824, Morgan, AB
REED, Andrew, son of Alexander, chose his father as his gdn for purpose of making titles to land to Nathaniel McClurg and Thomas Jones, 5/1808, Oglethorpe, GB
REED, Joseph, decd, Thomas Reed issued L/A, not dtd, abt 1809, Putnam, AB
REED, Robert, decd, Susannah Reed and Thomas Kimbrough, Sr. issued L/A 4/4/1814, Putnam, AB
REED, William, Sr., decd, William Reed, Jr., exr, retns 1/5/1841 and 1/4/1842, Gilmer, Misc
REEGAN, John, decd, Catherine Reegan gtd L/A 10/16/1798, Columbia, Ests
REES, Talbot S., decd, Zephaniah Franklin, admr, 1/2/1830, William Hurt, sur, Warren, AB
REESE, Edmond, decd, David Mims, admr, 7/4/1831, Spivey Fuller, Felix D. Franklin, sur, Warren, AB
REEVE, James, decd, John Y. Flowers, admr, 1/10/1859, DeKalb, AB
REEVE, Thomas, decd, John Reeve issued L/A 12/8/1787, Wm Hoge, Thomas Jones, secs, Richmond, AB
REEVES, D. A., decd, Wyatt L. Reeves, admr, Thomas Henderson, sur, 1/1848, 1850 retn, Fayette, AB
REEVES, Green B., decd, George L. Thompson, admr, Joseph Wilson, Dory Taylor, sur, 11/17/1836; 1836 retn pd Nancy A. Reeves, taxes 1838-1839, John McCord; ann retn, 8/30/1841; pd John Eidson, Stephen Bailey, John McCord, Peyton H. White, Samuel Snoddy, Travy G. Bledsoe, Nancy A. Reeves, 5/1/1839 retn, Butts, AB, ER
REEVES, Jesse, decd, LWT pvd by David Reeves, Malachi Reeves, L/T issued Jonathan Reeves, 1/1816, Jasper, OM
REEVES, Martha A., gdn of: Martha W., William F., Henry C., Amos W., Robert H., Sarah Ann, Allen Reeves, sur, 1854, Fayette, GB
REEVES, Mary Ann, orph of Dempsey A., decd, Wm Reeves, sur, 11/1849, 1851-1852, Fayette, AB
REEVES, William, decd, Allen Reeves, admr, James H. Williams, O. J. Head, 5/1851, Fayette, AB
REID, Alexander, decd, LWT pvd by Larry Ricks, John Thompson, Isaiah Phipps, L/T to John and Joseph Reed, 1/4/1814, Jasper, OM
REID, Andrew, decd, Mrs. Elizabeth Reid, George Reid and Rev. Daniel Thatcher applied for L/A 8/8/1791, Greene, MiscBooker Lawson, sec, Morgan, AB
REID, David, decd, John Cumming and Eliza Reid issued L/A 7/5/1814, Richard Tubman, sec; 1815 retn, tuition for Mary, Robert and David; 11/9/1825, Robert A. Reid, gdn for minor orphs: David, Mary E. and Harriett O., Richmond, AB, GB
REID, George, decd, John L. Summerour apptd admr, Effort Seay, Henry Wikle, surs, 7/5/1858, Dawson, AB
REID, Hiram, orph of Asa, decd, 10/7/1834, Harris
REID, Mary, illegitimate orph of Isabella, decd, John E. Odell, gdn, 11/5/1855, Ralph S. Laws, sec, Hall, GB
REID, Nancy, decd, L/A issued Samuel Reed, Martin Stanley 3/4/1816, Martin Stanley, Thomas Carter, surs, Jasper, OM
REID, William bound to John Mitchell 1/8/1855, Cherokee, GB
REID, William C., decd, Nancy Reid and William A. Stringer issued L/A 11/7/1853, Richard Wilson, Y. G. Floyd, secs, Hall, AB
REISER, David, decd, John Israel Reiser applies for L/A 3/12/1832, Effingham, MIC
REISSER, Lunexer, decd, Amy Blake objects to Albert G. Porter on his applying for admn 5/1/1843, Effingham, MIC

REISSER, Nathaniel, decd, David Reisser applies for admn 2/10/1800, Effingham, MIC

REMSON, David, orph of Harnetten?, decd, William Curry, gdn, 10/6/1829, Charles Jennings, Peter Larm, secs, Lincoln, GB

RENFROE, Delilah, orph of Peter, decd, L/G issued Thomas Sparks, 1829, Washington

RENFROE, Enoch, Sr., decd, John Rushin and Enoch Renfroe, Jr. gtd L/T on LWT 10/17/1803, Warren, MIC

RENFROE, Margaret, orph of Peter, decd, L/G issued Thomas Sparks, 1829, Washington

RENFROE, Nathaniel, orph of Peter, decd, L/G issued Thomas Sparks, 1829, Washington

RENFROE, William, decd, LWT pvd 5/2/1831, Nathan and James Renfroe, exrs, Washington

RESPESS, Churchwell, decd, L/A gtd George Powell and John Heard, Joel Bailey, William Gill, surs, 1/7/1822; Nancy, wife, chose child´s pt of estate 7/1/1822; inventory and appraisement by James Smith, William R. Russell, John Martin 1/19/1822; Nancy Respass recd $250 1/1824 for support of minors--Mary Ann, Narcissa, Sarah, Richard and Martha; John Heard and George Powell, admrs, Jasper, Ests, OM

RESPESS, John, decd, LWT dtd 3/1/1800 names nephew, Thomas Respess; brother, Richard; niece, Polley Respess Lockey; niece, Polley Lockey; Thomas Respess; wife, Nancy, Hancock, AAA

REYNOLDS, Aaron, son of Caty James, petitions for Thomas Reynolds be apptd her gdn, William Strawther, sur, 6/1795, Oglethorpe, MIC

REYNOLDS, Amanda, Sharp S. Reynolds, gdn, 3/5/1855, Hiram Kelton, sec, Hall, GB

REYNOLDS, Andrew J., Sharp S. Reynolds, gdn, 3/5/1855, Hiram Kelton, sec, Hall, GB

REYNOLDS, Anna Eliza, orph of John M., decd, John J. Allen, gdn, 9/5/1853, Houston, GB

REYNOLDS, Arminda, Sharp S. Reynolds, gdn, 3/5/1855, Hiram Kelton, sec, Hall, GB

REYNOLDS, Bartemas, decd, Jonathan Martin issued temporary L/A 11/24/1854, Lewis Jones, William P. Red, secs; permanent L/A to Sharp S. Reynolds and Jonathan Martin 2/5/1855, Lewis Jones, N. R. Wright, secs, Hall, AB

REYNOLDS, C. H., decd, Jonathan Martin issued L/A 9/4/1854, Baylos and Pickens T. Reynolds, Benjamin Bryan, secs, Hall, AB

REYNOLDS, Eliza A., orph of Elijah H., decd, William P. Reynolds apptd gdn 7/2/1860, Dawson, GB

REYNOLDS, James W., decd, E. P. Bond apptd temporary admr 6/5/1861, Dawson, WB

REYNOLDS, John B., Sharp S. Reynolds, gdn, 3/5/1855, Hiram Kelton, sec, Hall, GB

REYNOLDS, Joseph, heirs of to choose gdn, p.33, Richard Wayne, etc., divides estate, p. 25, James Bevil, p. 5, Screven, OM

REYNOLDS, Josiah, decd, Spencer Reynolds, Stafford Gibson, gdn of orphs 11/6/1837, Harris, GB

REYNOLDS, Lurania E., orph of Elijah H., decd, William P. Reynolds apptd gdn 7/27/1860, Dawson, WB

REYNOLDS, Margarett S., orph of Elijah H., decd, William P. Reynolds apptd gdn 7/27/1860, Dawson, WB

REYNOLDS, Mary C., decd, Henry Haws, admr, 8/1837; apprs: Cullen Roberts, Richmond Statham and Garland Statham, Benjamin Hill, Stewart, Adms

REYNOLDS, Moses, son of Caty James, petitions for Thomas Reynolds to be apptd gdn, William Strawther, sur, 6/1795, Oglethorpe, MIC

REYNOLDS, Ransom P., decd, William P. Reynolds apptd admr 9/5/1859, William L. Reynolds, G. B. Hudlow, A. Beam, surs, Dawson, WB

REYNOLDS, William E., orph of Elijah H., decd, William P. Reynolds apptd gdn 7/2/1860, Dawson, WB

RHODES, Aaron, decd, L/A to Absolom Rhodes 12/20/1805, John Rhodes, Frizzell McTyeire, secs; purchasers at sale: Mrs. Nancy Rhodes, Lavina and William Rhodes, Sampson Lamkin, Richmond, AB

RHODES, Absolom, Jr., decd, Sarah Rhodes issued L/A 10/30/1819; purchasers at sale: A. Rhodes, Sarah and Levi Rhodes; 1821 bt corn, etc. from Absolom Rhodes, Sr., Richmond, AB, AR

RHODES, Jabez R., decd, L/A issued to Thomas W. Wilkinson 11/2/1863, Fulton

RHODES, James, decd, Josiah Draper, admr, 1/6/1835 sold 150 acres; Nancy Rhodes to James Draper, gdn of orphs, cash pd Nancy Rhodes 3/6/1839, Butts, ER

RHODES, James M., decd, Josiah Draper, admr, Calvary F. Knight, sur, 1/18/1834, Butts, AB

RHODES, John, decd, Kindred Bobo, gdn for minor orphs---Hiram Bobo Rhodes, Hiram Rhodes, Panela Rhodes, Susannah Matilda Rhodes and Minima Murphy Rhodes 1/6/1812, Richmond, GB

RHODES, John, decd, Mary Rhodes issued L/A 1/6/1808, Absolom Rhodes, John Willcox, secs, Richmond, AB

RHODES, John, decd, appraisement of estate, Elisha Garnett, admr; apprrs: Aaron Cone, Alexander Knight, Thomas Knight, James Rawls 2/12/1825; sale of personal property 1/18/1826, Bulloch, Misc

RHODES, John F., orph of John Y., decd, Nancy A. Rhodes, gdn, Andrew J. Norten, sur, 1/10/1856, Paulding, GB

RHODES, Josiah, orph of James M., decd, James Draper, gdn, Thomas H. Connell, sur, 7/20/1836; James Draper, gdn, Elijah Draper, John Draper, William Green, surs, 3/4/1839, Butts, GB

RHODES, Sarah, minor orph of John, decd, Absolom Rhodes, gdn, 1/7/1812, William Rhodes, sec, Richmond, GB

RHODES, William, decd, 7/1838 retn, sold Samuel Bellah, John Urquehart, Eli Cooper 4/14/1829, lot to James Rhodes; 1/7/1829 retn pd legatees---James, Harriet, Nancy, William, Benjamin and Josiah Rhodes; Samuel Bellah, admr, retn 1835, pd John Urquehart for clothing for Nancy Rhodes, one of heirs; John Singleton, in right of his wife, Nancy J. Rhodes, now Singleton 1/14/1836, Butts, ER

RHODES, William M., orph of James M., decd, James Draper, gdn, Thomas H. Connell, sur, 7/20/1836; James Draper, gdn, Elijah Draper, John Draper, William Green, surs, 3/4/1839, Butts, GB

RHYMES, John, decd, Celia Rhymes, admx w/LWT annexed 4/3/1809, Putnam, AB

RICHARDSON, Enoch, decd, L/A to Mary Richardson, Isaac Pennington, Milligan Patrick, surs, 5/1/1815, Jasper, OM

RICHARDSON, Enoch, decd, Sarah Richardson, admx, ordered that 108 acres in Jasper Co. and 100 acres in Elbert Co., etc. be divided between the heirs 1/3/1815, Jasper, OM

RICHARDSON, Isaac, decd, inv and appraisement 1/6/1844 by James Cone, James Lastinger, John Brown, Bulloch, Misc

RICHARDSON, Robert D., decd, Enoch G. Brown, A. Miles, Eli Clark, gdn of orphs 7/1/1839, Harris, GB

RICHARDSON, Schuyler, decd, Thomas Sandwich issued L/A 1/6/1808, George F. Randolph, George Smith Houston, secs, Richmond, AB

RICHARDSON, Thomas of the ceded lands of Ga., LWT pvd 9/15/1777, wife, Barbary and Jacob McClendon, Sr., exrs, Wilkes, MxR

RICHARDSON, William, decd, sons: Abraham and Isaac, exrs of LWT 12/16/1817, Bulloch, Misc

RICHER, Joseph, decd, Nicholas Delaigle issued L/A 12/29/1818, Joseph Bignon, Henry Zinn, secs, Richmond, AB

RICKETSON, Jesse, decd, Thomas P. F. Threewitts, admr, 5/4/1835, Henry Lockhart, Thomas Gibson, surs, Warren, AB

RIDLING, John M., decd, J. M. Lord, admr, 9/2/1861, Joseph Stewart, W. J. Ridling, J. U. Ridling, G. M. Ridling, surs, DeKalb, AB
RIERDON, Francis I., Jeremiah Rierdon, gdn, Dooly, OD
RIESSER, Benjamin, decd, Jonathan Bechtly applied for admn 7/20/1801, Effingham, Misc
RIESSER, Israel, decd, LWT dtd 12/15/1801 pvd 1/2/1802; exrs, William Kennedy, Christopher Gugel, and son, Matthew Riesser. Wit: David Riesser, Jesse Bell, exrs qualified 1/5/1802, Effingham, Misc
RIEVES, John and H., James Scott, gdn, p. 75, Screven, OM
RIEVES, John and Richard, Robert M. Williamson, gdn, p. 72, Screven, OM
RIEVES, Richard W., Robt M. Williamson, gdn, p. 114, Screven, OM
RIEVES, Thomas, decd, Catharine Rieves, admx, p. 5, Screven, OM
RIGGINS, Samuel, decd, David Appling and Martha Riggins issued L/A 5/3/1819, Laurens, AB
RIGHT, James, decd, Daniel Blackstock, admr w/LWT annexed, 5/6/1833, Hall
RIGHT, Nancy (now Nancy Battlesby), orph and minor of Francis Right, chose Thomas W. Scott as her gdn, 7/1806, Oglethorpe, MIC
RIGHT, Obadiah, decd, Hannah Right and John Right gtd L/A 2/16/1803, Franklin, OM
RILAND, James, decd, 5/1843; apprs: Charley D. Woodard, Samuel Haddan, William Sallis, James G. Peel, Stewart, Adms
RILEY, William, decd, Marvin Riley, admr, Warren Riley, sur, 9/9/1851, Bibb, AB
ROACH, John, decd, Anthoret Roach and John Collier issued L/A 8/6/1810, Laurens, AB
ROACH, Richard, orph of John, decd, Josiah Horn, gdn, 2/4/1818, Laurens, AB
ROAN, Tunstall, decd, LWT, planter, dtd 2/25/1800, pvd 6/1/1801 by Ajonadab Read and John Wilson, names wife, Milley, ch: James, George and Nancy, Hancock, AAAA
ROARK, John A., decd, Jones W. Roark issued L/A 11/5/1855, William Sitton, sec, Hall, AB
ROARK, William W., decd, Washington L. Goldsmith issued L/A 9/5/1867, Fulton
ROBARTS, Abraham J., decd, John Bailley apptd admr 6/5/1832, Camden, MIC
ROBARTS, John, decd, John Robarts, et all (in S. C.), qualified exr 3/1791, Liberty, Ests
ROBB, Wild, decd, petition of Perin Turner for gdnship of orphs 1/1869, Cobb, MIC
ROBBINS, A. S., decd, A. Z. Mims, admr 1/11/1864; James E. Ramsey apptd gdn of minor orphs: Louisa, Cordelia, Robert P. 11/5/1866, Fulton, GB
ROBBINS, George, admr, gtd leave to sell property, p. 132, Screven, OM
ROBBINS, Plenny, decd, Wm O. Robbins, temporary L/A 3/17/1812; L/A gtd 5/4/1812 Isabella Robins, Elbert, AB
ROBERSON, David Sr., decd, John Wilson, admr, makes retns 1805; 1803 cetn of Fitz M. Hunt, admr shows support for Andrew Robeson, idiot son, etc., Richmond, AR
ROBERT, B. F., Francis W. Robert, gdn, 1855, Cobb, BB
ROBERTS, Edmond, decd, Wm T. Roberts, admr, p. 15, Screven, OM
ROBERTS, Elisha, decd, Willis Roberts, admr w/LWT annexed, 3/2/1835, Elisha P. Bolton, Moses Johnson, Larkin B. Roberts, surs, Warren, AB
ROBERTS, Elizabeth and Mary, Samuel J. Bryan, gdn, p. 113, Screven, OM
ROBERTS, Elizabeth, James Ponder apptd gdn 9/2/1816, Bulloch, MIC

ROBERTS, Griffin A., Hugh Porter, gdn, H. F. Underwood, sur,
5/1854, Fayette, GB
ROBERTS, Henry P., decd, 11/8/1844, apprs: W. R. Manning, Burwell
Shiver, Wade Crozier, William McNeese, Dooly, I&A
ROBERTS, Jacob, decd, 9/4/1841, apprs: Thomas Marshall, E. V.
Munroe, Wm McNeese; cattle & horses in possession of: Martin,
Jane, William and Henry Roberts, Dooly, I&A
ROBERTS, James, decd, Amelia Roberts, admx, p. 91, Screven, OM
ROBERTS, James, decd, Robert M. Williamson, etc., appraises est,
p. 92, Screven, OM
ROBERTS, James L., Hugh Porter, gdn, H. F. Underwood, sur,
5/1854, Fayette, GB
ROBERTS, J. C., decd, temporary L/A issued W. J. Roberts 11/1867;
William J. Roberts issued L/A 10/1869, Webster, OD
ROBERTS, Jesse, admr in rt of his wife and Robert Reddick, prays
to be dismissed from admn of est of Greene McAfee 9/2/1816,
Jasper, OM
ROBERTS, John, Samuel Bryan, gdn, p. 44, Screven, OM
ROBERTS, John, decd, Henry Parrish to receive $24 from est,
1/1/1821, Bulloch, MIC
ROBERTS, John, decd, James Roberts issued temp L/A 6/28/1814,
Putnam, AB
ROBERTS, John, decd, Theophilus Thomas and others div est, p. 44,
Screven, OM
ROBERTS, John R., Nathaniel Roberts, gdn, p. 107, Screven, OM
ROBERTS, Jonah, Priscilla Roberts, gdn, p. 12, Screven, OM
ROBERTS, Jonah, William Roberts, gdn, retn, p. 5, Screven, OM
ROBERTS, Lewis E. H. G., Hugh Porter, gdn, H. F. Underwood, sur,
5/1854, Fayette, GB
ROBERTS, Mark, decd, Joel W. Hightower, admr, 11/16/1846; apprs:
Abner Tison, John E. Dykes, Wiley Cobb, J. J. Collier; purchasers
at sale: A. G. Roberts, Susan Hightower, James Salter, Irwin
Brown, Hardy Morgan, A. D. Higdon, Dooly, I&A
ROBERTS, Mary, Jeremiah Farmer, gdn, p. 44, Screven, OM
ROBERTS, Mary, William Roberts, gdn, p. 67, Emily Roberts, gdn,
p. 101, Screven, OM
ROBERTS, Mary A., choses child's pt, p. 107, Screven, OM
ROBERTS, Mary A. P., Hugh Porter, gdn, H. F. Underwood, sur,
5/1854, Fayette, GB
ROBERTS, Patience, orph of Thomas, decd, James Ponder apptd gdn
5/1/1820, Bulloch, MIC
ROBERTS, Ransom J., gdn acct appvd, p. 191, Screven, OM
ROBERTS, Samson, decd, Hugh Porter, admr, Eli Edmondson, sur,
12/1853, 1854 retn, Fayette, AB
ROBERTS, Sarah T., Hugh Porter, gdn, H. F. Underwood, sur,
5/1854, Fayette, GB
ROBERTS, Thomas, decd, statement by dividers of est that Elizar
Roberts had recd cattle, signed John Wise, Malachi Denmark Jehu
Everitt, 5/25/1820, Bulloch, Misc
ROBERTS, William, decd, Henry Pettee, admr, Dooly, OD
ROBERTS, William, decd, Mary Ann Roberts, admx, p. 93, John
Green, etc. divides est, p. 113, Screven, OM
ROBERTS, William H., Hugh Porter, gdn, H. F. Underwood, sur,
5/1854, Fayette, GB
ROBERTS, Willis, decd, Joseph Willis, admr 9/7/1863; H. C.
Roberts, gdn of orphs: H. L., A. J., Hepsey A., Margaret C. and
George C. and John M., minors, 10/5/1863, Fulton, GB
ROBERTSON, Amos G., Jr. made gdn of his children: Elizabeth C.,
Amos and James M., William Robertson, sec, 9/17/1850, Hall, GB
ROBERTSON, Benjamin, decd, John Robertson, admr, William Ferrel,
Cuthbert Ferrel, Kinchen Curl, sur, 2/3/1313, Jones, GB

ROBERTSON, Elizabeth states she has been delivered of a boy child by the name of Terrell Robertson and prays that her father, Frederick Brazel be apptd gdn 3/1/1813, Franklin, OM

ROBERTSON, Ferdinand, bastard child of Jenne, Richard Cox, gdn, 5/2/1814, Thomas Moore, Daniel Ramey, surs, Clarke, GB

ROBERTSON, John, decd, LWT dtd 5/5/1849, pvd 4/1855 by wife, Elizabeth, Cherokee

ROBERTSON, John, decd, Hiram Reid and Samuel Pitts, gdn of orphs 3/4/1833, Harris, GB

ROBERTSON, Louisa Jane, minor of Mildred who is made gdn 4/5/1819, James M. Burton, Thomas Robertson, surs, Clarke, GB

ROBERTSON, Thomas, minor, Jane Robertson, gdn, Wm Starn, sur, Clarke, GB

ROBERTSON, William, decd, L/T issued exrs 10/11/1803; LWT dtd 3/23/1803 names wife, Geen, ch: Elizabeth, Margret, Sarah, Rebekah, Rhoda, William and Samuel, Franklin, OM

ROBERTSON, William, decd, Robert B. Washington issued L/A 9/1/1828, Baldwin

ROBEY, Marcus, decd, John N. Robey, admr, Francis Douglas, sur, 7/8/1828, Butts, AB

ROBEY, Robert, decd, Timothy Robey, admr, to have leave to sell real est, 1/7/1822, Jasper, OM

ROBINSON, Andrew, orph of John, decd, Samuel P. Robinson apptd gdn 3/2/1818, Jasper, OM

ROBINSON, Andrew J., orph of William, decd, Rebecca Robinson apptd gdn 12/5/1859, Dawson, WB

ROBINSON, Elizabeth, decd, LWT dtd 5/17/1820, pvd 3/1821, names father, Frederick Brazill, gdn of son, Ferrel Robinson, minor, Jasper, Retns

ROBINSON, Elizabeth, decd, LWT pvd, L/T issued Frederick Bazel, 2/5/1821, Jasper, OM

ROBINSON, Henry C., decd, A. C. Wyly issued L/A 5/4/1863, Fulton

ROBINSON, Isham, decd, William C. Parker and Royal Willard issued L/A 7/7/1817, Stephen White, sec, Morgan, AB

ROBINSON, James, decd, Sarah Robinson issued L/A 1/2/1815, Laurens, AB

ROBINSON, Jane B., decd, James M. Smith, exr, dismissed, 1/5/1852, Camden, MIC

ROBINSON, J. B., Mrs., decd, James Barnard, exr, dismissed 1/3/1848; J. M. Smith, exr named in LWT of decd qualified as exr 6/4/1849, Camden, MIC

ROBINSON, John, decd, LWT pvd, L/T gtd Lydia and John Robinson, Jr., 1/7/1817, Jasper, OM

ROBINSON, John B., orph of William, decd, Rebecca Robinson apptd gdn 12/5/1859, Dawson, WB

ROBINSON, Jonathan, decd, of Burke Co., Elizabeth Robinson issued L/A 7/7/1812, Peter Donaldson, Shadrack Rozer, secs, Richmond, AB

ROBINSON, Joseph C., decd, LWT exhibited 4/1/1869, Charles T. Campbell, exr, Fulton

ROBINSON, Littleberry, decd, Milus C. Nisbet issued L/A w/LWT annexed 11/5/1821, Morgan, AB

ROBINSON, Mary, orph of John, decd, Samuel P. Robinson apptd gdn 3/2/1818, Jasper, OM

ROBINSON, Sarah E., orph of William, decd, Rebecca Robinson apptd gdn 12/5/1859, Dawson, WB

ROBINSON, Thomas, decd, inv 5/5/1823 pd boarding for Thomas Robinson to J. Gibson for one yr, Jasper, Retns

ROBINSON, William, decd, William Martain issued L/A 9/5/1851, Alsey B. Barker, sec, Lumpkin, AB

ROBINSON, William T., orph of William, decd, Rebecca Robinson apptd gdn 12/5/1859, Dawson, WB

ROBINSON, Willis, decd, Allen Robinson issued temp L/A 11/2/1812, Putnam, AB
ROBISON, Ann E., minor of Lewellin M., L/G issued Samuel Robison 1/8/1838, Washington
ROBISON, Greene R., minor of Lewellin M., L/G issued Samuel Robison 1/8/1838, Washington
ROBISON, John S., decd, blacksmith, Sarah D. Robison, admx, 3/1836, James Griffin, sur on bond; apprs: Neil Robison, William Porter, Thomas C. Curry; purchasers at sale: J. H. Armstrong, Jesse Cliatt, Littleton Collins, Stewart, Adms
ROBISON, Robert A., minor of Lewellin M., L/G issued Samuel Robison 1/8/1838, Washington
ROBISON, Samuel Williamson, minor son of Will Robison, L/G issued 3/4/1833, Washington
ROCHE, David, decd, an alien, jeweler, apprs apptd 2/16/1819, Richmond
ROCKMORE, James, decd, Elizabeth Rockmore applies for adm, with LWT annexed, David Robertson, William Ussery, sur, 8/9/1803, Warren, MIC, AB
RODDEN, Abner, decd, David Rodden, admr, retn 2/14/1823, Jasper, Retns
RODDEN, James, orph of Abner, decd, David Rodden apptd gdn 1/7/1822, David Rodden, one of legatees, Jasper, OM
RODGERS, Paul T., orph of John, decd, James H. Rodgers apptd gdn 1/6/1823, Jasper, OM
RODGERS, Sarah, illegitimate of Nancy, Thomas Quales, gdn, James Floyd, sec, 5/7/1832, Hall, GB
ROE, James, decd, 11/16/1841, apprs: Charles H. Higdon, Peyton Mimms, Henry Pettee; purchasers at sale: John Baker, M. G. Brady, Thomas H. Dawson, Isabella Sanford, James Quinn, Edward Rowell, Caleb W. Harvey, Dooly, I&A
ROGERS, Benjamin, decd, Drewry Rogers issued L/A 11/3/1817, E. Winn, Morgan, AB
ROGERS, Benjamin, decd, Unity Rogers issued L/A 2/1/1808, Jackson, OM
ROGERS, Celia, decd, William May issued L/A 3/1/1841, Washington
ROGERS, David, orph of Thomas, decd, chose Thomas Hyde and James M. C. Montgomery his gdn 3/2/1812, Jackson, OM
ROGERS, Drury, decd, LWT pvd by Wm Bowden and Jarrel W. Crenshaw, L/T gtd Delilah Rogers and Turner Hunt, Jr., 1/6/1823, Jasper, OM
ROGERS, Fanny, decd, L/A to Drewry Rogers 1/5/1818 Richmond, AB
ROGERS, George, orph of John, decd, chose Robert Wilson, gdn, 9/3/1810, Jackson, OM
ROGERS, James, decd, minor, bound to Joshua Standford until 21 yrs old to learn shoemaker's trade; sd minor to be age 11 next Feb, 9/6/1813, Warren, MIC
ROGERS, John, decd, Thomas E. and John C. Rogers issued L/A 9/6/1819, Jasper, OM
ROGERS, John, decd, James and Nancy Thurmand (his wife, formerly wife of decd), mother of three children-Milly, George and Zilla, obtain gdnshp 7/9/1806, Jackson, OM
ROGERS, John, decd, Mary Rogers and John Parker gtd L/A 2/4/1799, Columbia, Ests
ROGERS, John, orph of John, decd, James Rogers, gdn, makes retns 3/4/1811, Jackson, OM
ROGERS, John, decd, Nancy Rogers applied for L/A 7/28/1795; apprs: John Mackey, Jonathan Lear, John H. Johnston; purchasers at sale: James, Thomas, Nancy, Benjamin and Mary Rogers; James Rogers, admr, Elbert, AR
ROGERS, Lebeus, decd, Martha Rogers produced LWT, she qualified as extrx 5/5/1812, Camden, MIC

ROGERS, Meshack, decd, Wiley F. and Hezekiel Rogers, Sr. issued L/A 3/3/1845, Baldwin

ROGERS, Reuben, Sr., decd, John Rogers, admr, 5/4/1829, Henry Hight, Willis Darden, sur, Warren, AB

ROGERS, Simeon G., Glin Simeon, gdn, 1809 retn, Elbert, GR

ROGERS, Susannah M., Glin Simeon, gdn, 1809 retn, Elbert, GR

ROGERS, Thomas, decd, Daniel Johnson (in rt of wife, Martha) and Peleg Rogers makes retns 4/4/1808; David Rogers and James M. C. Montgomery apptd gdns for orphs: Polly and John Henderson Rogers, 3/6/1815, Jackson, OM

ROGERS, Thomas Stanfer, orph of Thomas, decd, upon motion of Mr. Hanson that wish of decd that his bro., Peleg Rogers see that orph is taught science, etc; Walton Harris to take him until age 21, 1/2/1809, Jackson, OM

ROGERS, William, decd, 1807-1808 retns, Mary Rogers, admx, 1811 retn signed by Mrs. Mary Bragg, admx, Elbert, AR

ROLLINS, John W., minor son of Williamson, decd, Martha Rollins, gdn, G. H. Spinks, sur, 4/5/1858, Paulding, GB

ROLLINS, Lucy A., orph of Williamson, decd, Martha Rollins, gdn, G. H. Spinks, sur, 4/5/1858, Paulding, GB

ROLLINS, Margaret J., orph of Williamson, decd, Martha Rollins, gdn, G. H. Spinks, sur, 4/5/1858, Paulding, GB

ROLLINS, Mary A., orph of Williamson, decd, Martha Rollins, gdn, G. H. Spinks, sur, 4/5/1858, Paulding, GB

ROLLINS, Nancy E., orph of Williamson, decd, Martha Rollins, gdn, G. H. Spinks, sur, 4/5/1858, Paulding, GB

ROLLINS, Richard, Elizabeth Rollins, gdn of her minor son, 1/10/1853, Houston, GB

ROLLINS, Robert J., orph of Williamson, decd, Martha Rollins, gdn, G. H. Spinks, sur, 4/5/1858, Paulding, GB

RONEY, Daniel D., decd, Thomas N. Perkinson, Washington Drummond, James McConnel, admrs, 1/5/1858, Cherokee, AB

ROPER, Lewis W., decd, late of Stewart Co., George S. Roper petitions to move adm of est to Webster Co., 1/1869, Webster, OD

ROQUEMORE, James, decd, Elizabeth Roquemore, admx, 2/14/1804, David Robertson, sur, Warren, AB

ROSE, Hugh F. (Dr.), decd, James B. Boyer, admr, 1/1843; apprs: William Nelson, Joseph Sessions, John Talbot; purchasers at sale: John F. Alday, Elias Bell, Loverd Bryan, Isaac Dennard, Lewis Douglass, Lydia M. Rose, etc., Stewart, Adms

ROSE, Stephen, decd, Hardy Pitts, admr, 12/4/1815, James Neal, sur, Warren, AB

ROSE, William, decd, Sarah & Edmond Rose apply for adm 12/4/1800, apptd 2/9/1801, Shadrick Fluwellin, sur, Warren, MIC, AB

ROSELOUPE, Lawrence, decd, Lewis Bachlott apptd admr 1/1/1821, Camden, MIC

ROSS, Cornelius A., decd, Joseph H. Watts, James B. Henderson, William I. Henderson, admrs, 5/6/1839, Harris

ROSS, Donald, decd, LWT, Leonard D. Cecil, exr, 2/26/1791, Chatham, Adms

ROSS, John (Dr.), decd, late Justice of Inferior Ct, his LWT pvd, John Atkinson qualified as exr 9/13/1815, Camden, MIC

ROSS, John, decd, John Hudson vs. admrs of sd decd 4/11/1816, Bryan, MSC

ROSSER, Isaac, decd, Elijah Rosser, admr, Henry Anderson, Reuben Cook, secs, 10/17/1861, Fulton, AB

ROSSER, James, decd, Louisa Rosser, admr, 3/3/1806, John and Fanny Whittington, Warren, AB

ROSSIGNOL, Lewis, decd, Paul Rossignol issued L/A 3/10/1830, James Rossignol, Charles A. Crawford, secs, Richmond, AB

ROUGHTON, Eli P., minor child of Enoch, L/G issued Enoch Roughton 1/9/1843, Washington
ROUNTREE, Cader, decd, Francis Rountree and Robert Applewhite issued L/A 8/27/1821, Aron Strother, Johnston Ferguson, secs, Morgan, AB
ROUNTREE, Jesse, late of Edgefield Co., S. C., Thomas S. Oliver issued L/A 2/21/1817, John C. Holcombe, Isaac LaRoche, secs, Richmond, AB
ROUNTREE, Lupinu, petitions for 1/3rd of est, p. 178, Screven, OM
ROUNTREE, Roba, decd, Joshua Hanes, Elizabeth Rountree, admrs, James and Elijah Hanes, admrs, 7/1829, 1843 retn, Fayette
ROUNTREE, William, decd, John W. Rountree apptd admr, p. 163, Screven, OM
ROURK, William W., Sr., John McMartin, gdn of orphs William L., Samuel and Isadora, 10/1/1866, Fulton, GB
ROUSE, James R., decd, Berry M. Williams applies for L/A 4/25/1859, Jonathan David, Kittrell J. Warren, sur, Lee
ROUSSEAU, John, decd, LWT pvd 11/7/1796 by exrs, William and Ignatius Few, Columbia, Ests
ROUSSET, Peter, decd, a French citizen, Claudius Magnan, William Verdery, Abram Jones, Andrew Jones and Lewis Harris apptd to search bags and trunks--gold, French crowns, etc. was sent to French Consulate for North Carolina, South Carolina, and Ga., 8/11/1799, Richmond
ROUX, John, decd, carpenter, Israel Geer, admr dismissed 6/3/1833, Camden, MIC
ROWELL, Howell, decd, L/A to Edward Rowell 7/4/1786, Richmond, AB
ROWELL, Oliver H., decd, John T. Rowell, admr, Dooly, OD
ROWLAND, Benjamin, decd, Willis Palmer issued L/A 1/14/1833, James Palmer, Samuel Tarver, secs, Richmond, AB
ROWLAND, William, decd, Sarah & Merit Rowland issued L/A 1/6/1808, Nathl Palmer, Cullors Bedingfield, secs; 1808 div to heirs: Jeptha, Merit, James, Barbary, Benjamin, William and Harriett Rowland, Eleazer Anderson, Richmond, AB, AR
ROY, James, decd, an alien, carpenter, apprs apptd 11/17/1818, Richmond
ROYAL, Hardy, decd, Moses Pipkins, Jno C. Ryals, admrs, Dooly, OD
ROYAL, Jus. B. H. M., bound to Wm Lambert, p. 100, Screven, OM
ROYALS, Alfred, decd, 1/17/1840; purchasers at sale: John C., Simon and William Royal, William C. Spivey, John Tulley, John Hammond, John C. Sheffield, David I. Bothwell, James Harrell, Seth Kellam, Moses Pipkin and Enoch Shiver, Dooly, I&A
ROYALS, Hardy D., decd, Sarah Royals, admx 1/17/1840, Dooly, OD
ROYALS, Hardy D., decd, 2/17/1843, apprs: Benjamin Culpepper, Edward Outlaw, John Cox; purchasers at sale: Harmon H. Parker, Thomas B. Donally, W. H. Andrews, Nathan Bowen, Henry Rouse, Jesse Burkett, David Graham, etc, Dooly, I&A
ROYALS, Hardy, Jr., decd, 1/26/1843, appraisers: Benjamin Culpepper, Wiley Cobb, John Varnadore; John C. Royal, Moses Pipkin, admrs; purchasers at sale: Mrs. Royal, Raiford Royal, James C. Royal, John Champion, James Broxton and Wilson McLemore, Dooly, I&A
ROYALS, Henry, was bound to Archibald T. O. Bryan, p. 125, Screven, OM
ROYSTON, Robertson, orph of Robert, decd, William Clark, gdn, 11/4/1815, Edward Paine, Samuel Jackson, sur
RUCKER, Ammon, decd, Nancy Rucker issued L/A, John Rucker, John Jones, Jr., secs, 1/6/1812, Elbert, AB
RUCKER, Gideon Pope, orph of William, decd, a poor child, was bound and apprenticed to Wiley Hill, farmer, until 21 yrs old, which boy is now 10 yrs old on the 31st of Jan, 9/1806, Oglethorpe, OM, GB

RUD, Henry, decd, James Blasingame issued L/A 9/11/1818, Michael
Clower, sec, Morgan, AB
RUDDY, Alexander B., decd, John Walker issued L/A 10/18/1826, A.
Means, E. A. Nisbet, secs, Morgan, AB
RUDISILL, Levi, decd, LWT dtd 3/22/1859 pvd 2/15/1860, names
Margaret S., Jonas E., Sarah S. Wgly, Catherine M. Dyer and
Ephraim J. Rudisill, Cherokee
RUDOLPH, John T., decd, Emily Rudolph apptd admx 4/2/1844, gtd
leave to sell town lot 27 in town of St. Mary's 6/1845, Camden, MIC
RUDULPH, Michael, decd, Elizabeth Rudulph, admx, gtd leave to
sell 6/7/1830; also leave to sell lot of land #86, 15th Dist,
Cass Co., Ga. 1/1846, Camden, MIC
RUFF, Rachel and Jack, minor persons of colour, bound to David
Mims. Rachel to be age 12 next Feb., Jack to be age 10 next
April, Warren, MIC, GB
RUFFIN, Robert R., decd, Harriet P. Ruffin, gdn of Albert G. and
William R., minor orphs, 6/7/1832, Richmond, GB
RUMPH, J. G. S., John Clow, gdn, 1855, Cobb, BB
RUMPLE, Eugene, orph of Jacob, decd, Lewis Rumple, gdn, 3/7/1853,
Houston, GB
RUSH, Joseph, Jr., decd, of Savannah, Ga., LWT and Codicil dtd
11/14/1794 was pvd, Peter Donworth qualified as exr; caveat filed
for Robert Cumming and Edward Barraugh by Samuel Stirk 1/26/1785,
Chatham, Adms
RUSK, Darrel, decd, James R. Rusk, admr, 7/3/1848, Cherokee, AB
RUSSEL, David, decd, L/A issued John R. and Aaron Russel 9/1821,
Jasper, OM
RUSSELL, Alexander and Robert, decd, William Shannon issued L/A
6/20/1827, Martin Grannis, Charles Urquhart, secs, Richmond, AB
RUSSELL, Henry R., decd, George W. Hardee and Caroline C. H.
Russell apptd admrs 1/1846, Camden, MIC
RUSSELL, Henry R., decd, admrs of est authorized to sell Yellow
Bluff plantation in Camden Co, 6/1/1846, Camden, MIC
RUSSELL, James, decd, Angus Martin and Silas Bronson issued L/A
9/12/1825, Richmond, AB
RUSSELL, James A., Sr., decd, L/A to James A. Russell, Jr.
9/4/1843, Baldwin
RUSSELL, Jane, decd, A. S. Morris issued temporary L/A 9/7/1854,
O. S. Morriss, G. B. Alford, J. R. Bunt, Thomas Barnes, B. F.
Chapman, surs, DeKalb, AB
RUSSELL, Jane, wid, decd, of Savannah, James Habersham and
William Stephens, exrs of LWT, 7/14/1790, Chatham, Adms
RUSSELL, John, decd, Thomas Knapen issued L/A 7/6/1808, Anderson
Watkins, Ralph Ketchum, secs, of W. J. Eubanks to be reld from
gdnship, 9/30/1869; Ephraim L. Braswell apptd, Cobb, MIC
RUSSELL, John, decd, exrs and heirs of decd petitioned for div of
est, 1/11/1819, Glynn, MIC
RUSSELL, John, decd, Mary and James H. Russell, exrs, gtd leave
to sell real est of decd in East Fla., 6/11/1821, Glynn, MIC
RUSSELL, Keziah, decd, Geo. A. Walker, admr, 1831 pd Mrs. Nancy
E. Demarest for board, etc. for Mary E. & Benjamin B. (their
aunt), another aunt-Mrs. Catherine R. Anghlsey, Richmond, GR
RUSSELL, Sanford, orph of William, decd, George W. Bray apptd
gdn, David B. Hunter, James Hunter, secs, 3/5/1849, Troup, GB
RUSSELL, Simeon, decd, William Jackson issued L/A 5/19/1824,
Robert Jones, sec, Richmond, AB
RUSSELL, Thomas C., decd, of Augusta, Ga., Simeon Russell issued
L/A 12/9/1819, William Jackson, L. H. Marks, secs, Richmond, AB
RUSSELL, William, decd, Andrew J. Sheffer, admr, R. D. Winn, sur,
11/3/1873, Gwinnett, AB
RUTAKER, J. N., decd, L/A to Mason H. Bush 9/1861, Webster, OD
RUTHERFORD, Annie L., Aaron Smith, gdn, p. 41, Screven, OM

RUTHERFORD, Daniel, decd, Samuel Jackson, admr, 5/4/1806, John McGlamery, sur, Warren, AB

RUTHERFORD, J., decd, Isaac Rutherford, admr, 1855, Cobb, BB

RUTHERFORD, James H., decd, Benjamin B. Norris, admr, p. 84, John M. Wade, etc., divides est, p. 41, Screven, OM

RUTHERFORD, Samuel, decd, Samuel Jackson apptd temporary admr, John McGlamery, sur, 1/31/1806, Warren, MIC, AB

RUTHERFORD, Samuel, decd, extrx gtd leave to sell 50 acres 9/6/1813, Warren, MIC

RUTLEDGE, John, decd, Richard Stewart, gdn of Samuel and Alvah, orphs, 10/3/1814, Ezekiel Stanley, sur, Clarke, GB

RUTLEDGE, John, decd, Samuel Rutledge, gdn of John S. and Richard, orphs, 11/4/1821, Elam Ward, sur, Clarke, GB

RUTLEDGE, John, decd, W. S. Wiley, admr, James W. Rutledge, sur, 11/4/1872; William S. Wley, admr, John D. Wiley, D. B. Oliver, A. J. Webb, surs, 5/1/1876, Gwinnett, AB

RYAL, Elizabeth, decd, recpt from David Williams, admr; Sarah Rawls took share of father's estate, Elizabeth Ryals, admx; Sherrod McCall, Jr. recd Massey Rayl's share; Samuel Lanier, gdn, recd Rebecca and Zachariah Ryal's share 7/11/1816, Bulloch, Misc

RYAL, James, decd, James F. Johnson, admr de bonis non, Jeptha Landrum, sur, 1/1847, Fayette, AB

RYALL, Elizabeth, decd, sale of property 9/15/1815; David Williams dismissed as admr 12/7/1818, Bulloch, MIC

RYALL, Rebecca, orph of Samuel, decd, Allen Rawls apptd gdn 7/1/1822, Bulloch, MIC

RYALL, Samuel, decd, David Williams for Elizabeth Ryall, decd, allowed $50 against estate 4/1/1816, Bulloch, MIC

RYALL, Zacheus, orph of Samuel, decd, Allen Rawls apptd gdn 7/1/1822, Bulloch, MIC

RYALS, Charles, decd, Christianna Ryals and John R. Morgan, admrs, 9/9/1836, Effingham, MIC

RYALS, Christian, decd, LWT admitted to record 5/1/1843, Effingham, MIC

RYALS, Dennis, decd, Daniel Murphy issued L/A 1/10/1859, dismissed, Robert Jones, sec, Richmond, AB

RYALS, Edmund, decd, Emma Croom issued L/A 7/7/1834, Washington

RYALS, Mary M., John R. Morgan apptd gdn 5/1/1843, Effingham, MIC

RYALS, Mary Mercy, Christianna Ryals apptd gdn, 1/2/1837, Effingham, MIC

RYAN, Dennis, decd, Daniel Murphy issued L/A 1/10/1859, dismissed 11/5/1860, Fulton

RYAN, Laurence D., decd, Joseph Wright and Chloe Ryan, admrs, dismissed 11/7/1811, Warren, MIC

RYAN, Nathan, decd, Mrs. Elizabeth Ryan applied for L/A 12/16/1796, Greene, Misc

RYAN, Warris? (Dr.), decd, Joseph Wright and Chloe Wright apptd admrs, Basil Wright, sur, 3/7/1808, Warren, MIC, AB

RYLEE, Mary, orph of Elizabeth, Lavenia Rylee apptd gdn, 3/5/1855, Y. J. Rylee, sec, Hall, GB

RYONS, Michael, decd, Lewis Gerdine issued L/A 6/7/1799, Samuel Bugg, sec, Richmond, AB

SABIN, Resolved, decd, L/A issued to Elijah W. Hane, 9/1821, Jasper, OM

SADDER, Thomas S., decd, James G. Cotton, Thomas M. Buford and Smith Cotton, admrs, 7/6/1840, Harris, AB

SADDLER, Caroline, minor orph of Bartlett, decd, Polley and Eliza Ann Peel, Robert and Pinckney Collier, William H. Miles, Moses Smith, William Weldor, Charles Webb and John Moore to give evidence as to treatment of sd orph in care of Alexander Dale, 5/1816, Jasper, OM

SADDLER, Mary (Mrs.), LWT pvd 1/3/1848, Camden, MIC

SAFFOLD, Reuben, note for $100 to prove that slave in possession of Col. Gresham is his, 2/3/1781, Wilkes, MxR
SAFFOLD, Reuben T., decd, late of Savannah, Isham H. Saffold issued L/A 5/10/1820, Bryan, Writs
SAIL, Anthony, decd, Cornelius Sail applied for L/A 4/5/1796, Elbert, AB
SALE, Cornelius, decd, 9/2/1808 inv, Wm Thompson, John Paxton, Enos Tait, jr., apprs; Dudley and Joseph Sale, admrs, Elbert, AR
SALLENS, Robert, decd, Richard and Mary Esther Cooper qualified admrs 1/11/1793, Liberty, Ests
SALLETT, Robert, decd, Simon Fraser, Jonathan Bacon, Nathan Taylor qualified exrs 2/21/1791, Liberty, Misc
SALLINS, Peter, Jr., decd, John Foster, John Way, Joseph Way, Sr. qualified admrs 7/2/1788, Liberty, Ests
SALLIS, John, decd, LWT of David and John Sallis, admrs, 11/6/1815, James Neal, Isaac Burson, Washington Hardaway, surs, Warren, AB
SALLIS, Joseph, minor, Galby Matthews, gdn, 5/5/1817, David Sallis, sur, Warren, GB
SAMPLER, W., decd, Fraser and Sampler, admrs, 1855, Cobb, BB
SAMPSON, Martha A., Oliff Bradshaw, gdn, Dooly, OD
SAMSON, Archibald, decd, L/A issued Elizabeth Samson 7/7/1814, Jasper, OM
SAMSON, Franklin B., Clifford Woodruff apptd gdn 9/1/1817, Jasper, OM
SAMSON, Glenn H., Clifford Woodruff, gdn, 9/1/1817, Jasper, OM
SAMSON, James, decd, apprs: David Peeples, Nathan Peeples, Joseph Carmichael, 2/15/1794, Greene, Misc
SAMSON, Mary A. L., Clifford Woodruff, gdn, 9/1/1817, Jasper, OM
SAMSON, Matilda Maria, Clifford Woodruff apptd gdn 9/1/1817, Jasper, OM
SAMSON, Richard, decd, LWT pvd, L/T issued Lewis McLean and Jary Smith, 9/2/1816, Jasper, OM
SAMSON, Tilpha Calvert, orph dau of Archibald, age 14, chose Clifford Woodruff as her gdn 9/1/1817, Jasper, OM
SAMUEL, Thomas, decd, Benjamin Bentley, gdn of orphs: Eliza, Mary, etc., 7/1/1839, Jeremiah Grisham, sec, Lincoln, GB
SAMUELS, Thomas, decd, inv dtd 10/1/1792, Effingham, Misc
SAMPLER, W., decd, Fraser and Sampler, admrs, 1855, Cobb, BB
SAMPSON, Martha A., Oliff Bradshaw, gdn, Dooly, OD
SAMSON, Archibald, decd, L/A issued Elizabeth Samson 7/7/1814, Jasper, OM
SAMSON, Franklin B., Clifford Woodruff apptd gdn 9/1/1817, Jasper, OM
SAMSON, Glenn H., Clifford Woodruff, gdn, 9/1/1817, Jasper, OM
SAMSON, James, decd, apprs: David Peeples, Nathan Peeples, Joseph Carmichael, 2/15/1794, Greene, Misc
SAMSON, Mary A. L., Clifford Woodruff, gdn, 9/1/1817, Jasper, OM
SAMSON, Matilda Maria, Clifford Woodruff apptd gdn 9/1/1817, Jasper, OM
SAMSON, Richard, decd, LWT pvd, L/T issued Lewis McLean and Jary Smith, 9/2/1816, Jasper, OM
SAMSON, Tilpha Calvert, orph dau of Archibald, age 14, chose Clifford Woodruff as her gdn 9/1/1817, Jasper, OM
SAMUEL, Thomas, decd, Benjamin Bentley, gdn of orphs: Eliza, Mary, etc., 7/1/1839, Jeremiah Grisham, sec, Lincoln, GB
SAMUELS, Thomas, gdn of his ch: Sarah, Martha, William, Henry and Elizabeth, minors, 3/6/1837, Benjamin Graves, sec, Lincoln, GB
SANCHEZ, Mary, decd, Samuel Clark, admr, 11/1/1813, Camden, MIC
SANDERLIN, Joseph, minor orph of Robert, decd, George A. P. Whitfield, gdn, 4/4/1825, James Primrose, John Willcox, Jr., secs, Richmond, GB

SANDERS, Brittain, minor and orph of Hardy, decd, William Sanders apptd gdn 6/28/1798, Oglethorpe, MIC
SANDERS, Christopher, decd, William Fitzpatrick applied for L/A 4/1/1793, Greene, Misc
SANDERS, Drusell M., decd, Elias Beall, admr de bonis non w/LWT annexed, Jeremiah Beall, Edward E. Sanders, Thomas N. Beall, Elias Beall, sur, 5/3/1847, Bibb, AB
SANDERS, Elizabeth, minor and orph of Hardy, decd, William Sanders apptd gdn 6/28/1798, Oglethorpe, MIC
SANDERS, Ephriam, decd, Nancy Sanders gtd L/A 2/24/1797, Columbia, Ests
SANDERS, James, decd, L/A to Jno G. Westmoreland 8/9/1867, Fulton
SANDERS, Jesse, decd, Jonathan D. Chastain, gdn of orphs: Henry T., John L., Daniel M. and William N., 9/4/1837, Gilmer, Misc
SANDERS, Jonathan, minor and orph of Hardy, decd, William Sanders apptd gdn 6/28/1798, Oglethorpe, MIC
SANDERS, Keziah, decd, LWT pvd, L/T issued John Martin and Thomas Broddus 1/5/1818, Jasper, OM
SANDERS, Lydia, Henry Ross, gdn, Dooly, OD
SANDERS, Mary, decd, Lovel Smith issued L/A 3/27/1843, Washington
SANDERS, Polly, minor and orph of Hardy, decd, William Sanders apptd gdn 6/28/1798, Oglethorpe, MIC
SANDERS, Priscilla, decd, LWT pvd by Nicholas Meriwether and George Gilmer; Clement Glenn, exr, 5/1808, Oglethorpe, OM
SANDERS, Thomas, decd, H. H. Ross, admr (who married the widow and was gdn of minor children), 7/26/1845; apprs: Thomas Musselwhite, Echols Hightower, Thomas Cobb; purchasers at sale: John Sanders, Henry H. Ross, Dooly, I&A
SANDERS, Thomas, decd, Henry A. Ross, admr, Dooly, OD
SANDERS, Thomas, Jr., decd, Thomas Sanders, Sr. issued L/A 5/28/1814, Putnam, AB
SANDERS, Thomas M., decd, William R. Simpson, admr, Mariah Sanders, John T. Simpson, William A. Sanders, sur, 9/7/1874, Gwinnett, AB
SANDIFORD, John, decd, Mary and John Sandiford qualified admrs 2/10/1784, Liberty, Ests
SANDIFORD, John, Jr., decd, James Wood qualified exr 3/8/1785, Liberty, Ests
SARTON, George W., decd, James Roberts issued L/A 11/20/1854, Robert Young, E. M. Johnson, secs, Hall, AB
SASSER, Britton, decd, inv 1/10/1824; John Sasser, son, sd he resides in Ala & that there is another heir besides himself 12/20/1824; Lemuel Owens sd decd claimed John for his son, also had two other ch-Joseph and Jerusha, Pike, MIC
SASSER, Michael J., orph of Lewis M., decd, from Pulaski Co., Joseph Tooke, gdn, 1825, tuit pd to Daniel Mathison and Grantham for 1830, Stewart, Adms
SATERFIELD, Curtis, decd, Jasper L. Keith, admr, M. Anderson Keith, sur, 3/7/1853, Cherokee, AB
SAULES, Chesley, decd, Cullen Saules, Thomas H. Key, Benton Byrd, Raiford Royal, etc.; Henry Pettee, admr, Dooly, I&A
SAULS, Abram, decd, inventory 3/30/1836, apprs: Ezekiel Clifton, William Clifton, Wade W. Coleman, Elander N. Smith, Tattnall, I&A
SAUNDERS, Elizabeth, decd, L/A issued to Burwell Saunders 5/7/1832, Washington
SAUNDERS, Jacob, decd, Thomas J. Saunders, admr, Nancy Saunders, sur, 7/20/1846; pd George T. Bartlett, in rt of wife, Virginia L. Bartlett, formerly Virginia L. Saunders, her legacy, 7/31/1847, Butts, AB, ER
SAUNDERS, James M., decd, L/A issued to Sarah Saunders 1/1868, Webster, OD

SAUNDERS, Jesse, decd, Yancy, Lewis and James Saunders issued L/A 11/6/1809. Putnam, AB
SAUNDERS, John, decd, Nancy Saunders, admx, Thomas J. Saunders, Simon H. Saunders, Alexander Saunders, surs, 2/5/18444, Butts, AB
SAUNDERS, L. C., decd, J. M. Saunders issued L/A 3/1862; W. H. Chappell issued L/A w/LWT annexed 8/1862, Webster, OD
SAUNDERS, L. L., Nancy Saunders, gdn, Thomas Saunders, admr of est of Jacob Saunders; recd of Thomas J. Saunders, admr of Jacob, legacy for L. L. Saunder 7/31/1847, Butts, ER
SAUNDERS, Lucian Lafayette, orph of John, decd, Nancy Saunders, gdn, S. H. Saunders, Thomas J. Saunders and William Saunders, surs, 7/7/1845, Butts, AB
SAUNDERS, Marry Arthur, decd, Elizabeth Saunders apptd admx 1/7/1822, Jasper, OM
SAUNDERS, S. W., decd, Nancy T. Saunders qualified as extrx 9/1865, Webster, OD
SAUNDERS, Virginia, orph of John, decd, Nancy Saunders, gdn, S. H. Saunders, Thomas J. Saunders and Alexander Saunders, surs, 7/7/1845, Butts, GB
SAURIS, Antoine, decd, james M. Lindsey and Rachel Sauris, admrs, gtd leave to sell estate prope*rty 8/5/1806, Camden, MIC
SAURIS, Rachel applied for Archibald Clarke to be apptd gdn of her infant ch--Rachel, Sally, Judith and Antoine, 4/14/1807, Camden, MIC
SAUSOM, James, decd, LWT pvd 1/14/1794, ch--Polly, Francis, Nancy, Jackey, James, William, Thomas; wife, Patsy, Greene, Misc
SAUSOM, John, decd, in the continental service of last war, Troops of Virginia, William Sausom applied for L/A 1/25/1793, Greene, Misc
SAVAGE, Caesar A., decd, Frances M. T. Savage, extrx, William Newsom, exr, 7/5/1855, Lee, MSC
SAVAGE, Charles, decd, L/A to Michael Bloomfield 7/5/1865, Fulton
SAVAGE, Robert, decd, 1/21/1842, apprs: Thomas H. Key, Mark Roberts, Richard Bowen; purchasers at sale: Mary and James Savage, J. G. Oliver, Daniel McLeod, Thomas H. Key, Benton Byrd, Raiford Royal, etc.; Henry Pettee, admr, Dooly, I&A
SAVAGE, Thomas, decd, late of Charleston, S. C., LWT, John Wereat, exr, 9/20/1786, Chatham, Adms
SAVAGE, William B., minor orph of John, decd, Elizabeth Savage, gdn, 3/5/1823, Daniel Savage, sec, Richmond, GB
SAVELS, William, decd, inv merchant, 10/27/1800 by Josiah Morse, Elias Havens, William Mitchell, Richmond
SAVIDGE, Robert (Capt.), decd, Amey Savidge issued L/A 8/30/1789, John Foster, Cornelius Whittington, secs, Richmond, AB
SAVIDGE, Robert, decd, of Richmond Co., Anney or Amey Savidge gtd L/A 8/13/1799, Columbia, Ests
SAWYER, Charles, decd, Jeremiah Warren, admr, Thomas Sawyer, William Sawyer, sur, 6/8/1857, Cherokee, AB
SAX, Daniel, decd, Margaret Sax, admx, Philip Hillyer, admrs, 4/16/1789, Chatham, Adms
SAYE, James, Sr., decd, John Saye issued L/A 3/4/1851, R. H. Waters, David Martin, secs, Hall, AB
SCALES, Thomas, decd, 1797 purchasers-Ann Scales, Sr. (later Thompson, wid-admx), Ann Jr., Elizabeth Scales, Moses Sr. and Jr., Stephen, Thomas and William Haynes; orphs--Thomas b. 5/4/1789, Benjamin b. 6/1/1792, Elijah b. 5/25/1796, Nathaniel b. 12/18/1799, Elbert, AR
SCARBER, Theophilus, Absolom Parrish, gdn, retd by exrs of sd orph of Burke Co., Ga., no date, Bulloch, Misc
SCARBOROUGH, Elias, decd, L/A to David Scarborough 1/1/1822, Laurens, AB

SCARBOROUGH, Frances A., orph of Enos, decd, Martin D. Sanders, gdn, 12/21/1857, Hamilton Hatcher, John R. Reeves, sur, Lee, GB
SCARBOROUGH, Jesse, decd, William C. Gill applies for L/A 2/18/1859, William C. Gill, sur, Lee
SCARBOROUGH, Thomas, dismissed as admr, p. 49, Screven, OM
SCARTH, Jonathan, decd, Elizabeth Scarth, John Osgood, James McCulloch qualified exrs 1/17/1789, Liberty, Ests
SCHENAULT (CHENAULT?), Abram, decd, John B. Sutton, gdn of orphs: George S., John N. and Dromous? 11/6/1837, Nicholas G. Barksdale, John McLane, secs, Lincoln, GB
SCHERMERHORN, Peter, decd, Gideon C. Bevill and Clem Powers issued L/A 8/6/1846, Effingham, MIC
SCHIFF, Maurice, decd, of Barnwell Dist., S. C., L/A to John Cashin no date, James Edwards, David McKinney, secs, Richmond, AB
SCHNEIDER, Frederick John, decd, Barnett Schneider gtd L/A 12/3/1796, Columbia, Ests
SCHWEIGHOFFER, Abiel, decd, LWT dtd 12/8/1801 pvd 1/2/1802, names ch: Abial (others not named); wife, Margaret, Effingham, Misc
SCONYERS, Emily, orph of Cassandra, Thursday Sconyers, gdn, John Sconyers, William Phillips, sur, 1/2/1844, Emanuel, GB
SCONYERS, July Ann, orph of Cassandra, Thursday Sconyers, gdn, John Sconyers, William Phillips, sur, 1/2/1844, Emanuel, GB
SCONYERS, Sarah, orph of Cassandra, Thursday Sconyers, gdn, John Sconyers, William Phillips, surs, 1/2/1844, Emanuel, GB
SCONYERS, Yella, orph of Cassandra, Thursday Sconyers, gdn, John Sconyers, William Phillips, surs, 1/2/1844, Emanuel, GB
SCOTT, Abraham, minor age of 14, chose Jonas H. Holland as his gdn, with George W. Holland and William H. Cargile, secs, 1/7/1822, Jasper, OM
SCOTT, Andrew, minor, Charles M. Scott, gdn, James Jordan, David H. Bird, secs, 11/6/1848, Cherokee, GB
SCOTT, Catharine (Mrs.), decd, William F. Scott issued L/A 5/5/1845, Baldwin
SCOTT, Charles M., decd, Drusilla Scott, temporary admr, John Scott, sur, 5/6/1856, Cherokee, AB
SCOTT, James, decd, 1/11/1808 inventory, James Ware, Edward Ware, Elisha Johnston, apprs, Elbert, AR
SCOTT, James, Sr., admr, leave to sell lands, p. 53, Screven, OM
SCOTT, John, decd, Mary Scott, admx, John R. Daniell, Jordan Flanders, sur, 3/7/1836, appraisal 3/17/1836, Emanuel, A, AB
SCOTT, Josiah, caveat sustained, p. 136, Screven, OM
SCOTT, Mary, decd, LWT 9/5/1848, names sister: Jane Woods, brother: Allen S. Woods; Andrew T. Scott, son of Charles M. Scott, brothers and sisters of my decd husband and my brothers and sisters, Cherokee, B
SCOTT, Miles, decd, William H. Flowers, admr, E. M. Pool, sur, no date, Fayette, AB
SCOTT, Thomas W., decd, L/A issued to Martha Scott 6/1/1812, Putnam, AB
SCOTT, William (Colonel), decd, lately a member of this court, Elihu Atwater apptd admr 12/7/1816, files retn, bal due him of $1507.97 6/4/1822; admr dismissed 1/6/1823, Camden, MIC
SCOTT, William E., decd, L/A to Lemuel P. Hargrove 3/2/1816, Laurens, AB
SCOTT, William F., decd, Thomas N. Beall and William H. Scott issued L/A 1/11/1845, Baldwin
SCREWS, James, decd, Beverly Evans, exr, LWT names wife, Nancy and ch--Mary Evans, Enoch Screws, Elizabeth Thomas, Sally Webb, pvd 1/10/1839; pd taxes 1839, John T. Wells for a legacy, 2/8/1841, Butts, ER
SCRIMSGER, John, decd, Charles Scrimsger qualified as admr 1/22/1789, Liberty, Ests

SCRUGGS, Groll, decd, M. Sunday applies for L/D 3/3/1828, Effingham, MIC
SCRUGGS, James, idiot, William Hurst, gdn, 1828 retn, Butts, ER
SEABORN, Margaret, decd, Joseph Bachlott, Coroner, Camden Co., filed acct against est for $66.25; bal on hand ($30.43) ordered pd by Sheriff to William Sinclair, Charleston, South Carolina, for benefit of Mary Ann, minor daughter, 1/6/1818, Camden, MIC
SEABORN, Thomas G., decd, John Bailey, Sheriff, presented accts of Elizabeth Bailey, Zachariah Motes, William H. Williams and himself vs. est of decd, having been murdered by his wife and she having been executed in Oct last, 12/5/1817, Camden, MIC
SEABREES, Luther, decd, David Edmund Dillon, admr, 2/23/1791, Chatham, Adms
SEAGO, Alfred H., minor, Lucinda Seago, gdn, James Haly, sur, 7/2/1849, Cherokee, GB
SEAGO, Benjamin W., decd, LWT dtd 4/23/1857, pvd 6/1857 names wife, Sarah and sons: Eli M. and B. M. Seago, Cherokee
SEAGO, Lewis B., minor, Lucinda Seago, gdn, James Haly, sur, 7/2/1849, Cherokee, GB
SEAGO, Luther K., minor, Lucinda Seago, gdn, James Haly, sur, 7/2/1849, Cherokee, GB
SEAGO, Posey W., minor, Lucinda Seago, gdn, James Haly, sur, 7/2/1849, Cherokee, GB
SEAGO, Thomas P., minor, Lucinda Seago, gdn, James Haly, sur, 7/2/1849, Cherokee, GB
SEAGO, Tilman R., minor, Lucinda Seago, gdn, James Haly, sur, 7/2/1849, Cherokee, GB
SEAGROVES, Ann (Mrs.), decd, LWT produced by Archibald Smith, pvd by Henry Bacon, 4/2/1832, Camden, MIC
SEAL, Joseph W., a lunatic, Presley N. Seal, gdn, 11/7/1836, Nicholas B. Banks, sec, Lincoln, GB
SEAL, Robert, orph of Robert, decd, Presley N. Seal, gdn, 11/7/1836, Nicholas G. Banks, sec, Lincoln, GB
SEALS, Anthony, decd, LWT, John I. Rowe, exr, Harris
SEARCY, Aaron, decd, L/A to Benjamin R. Searcy 11/4/1839, Baldwin
SEARCY, George, decd, L/A to Benjamin R. Searcy 3/7/1842, Baldwin
SEARS, Vincent, decd, Mary and William F. Sears issued L/A 5/7/1855, G. W. Johnson, F. M. Strickland, secs, Hall, AB
SEARS, Vincent T., decd, Lucretia E. Sears issued L/A 4/1/1867, John M. Odell, sec, White, AB
SEAVOUS, John, decd, L/A to Wm C. Seavous 1/14/1856, Hall, AB
SEAY, Dempsey, decd, Ransom, Effort, Lorenda Seay and Caroline Goss testify they were present 7/28/1862 at decd's residence at his death when he named his wife, Caroline and bro., Ramon Seay, and cousin, Effort Seay, 7/29/1862, Dawson, WB
SECKINGER, Gotthief, decd, Cletus Rahn applied for L/A 9/24/1846, Effingham, MIC
SECKINGER, Ishu, decd, W. W. Wilson apptd gdn of orph child 5/5/1845, Effingham, MIC
SECKINGER, J., decd, ordered that Clk take possession of prop and act as admr 5/4/1829, Effingham, MIC
SECKINGER, John Samuel, decd, John Charlton, admr, applies for leave to sell real est 7/6/1840; ordered that clk take possession of est 11/4/1839, Effingham, MIC
SEEDS, Samuel, decd, blacksmith, Edward Davies, admr, 10/16/1784, Chatham, Adms
SELL, Thomas, decd, Mary Sell, admx, 1/2/1804, Isaac Davis, Jeremiah Burkhalter, surs, Warren, AB
SELLERS, Brown F., decd, Aaron Whelchel issued L/A 11/5/1855, John Whelchel, sec, Hall, AB
SELLERS, John, decd, Ishmael Dunn, Martha W. Sellers, admrs, 1/1847, 1851-1853 retns, Fayette, AB

SELLERS, Judith, decd, Minor W. Brown issued L/A 9/3/1851, John
E. Brown, sec, Hall, AB
SELLERS, Louisa, orph of John, decd, Ishmael Dunn, gdn, Chris C.
Bowen, sur, 5/1849, 1850 retn, Fayette, GB
SELLERS, Samuel, decd, LWT dtd 8/29/1794, pvd 5/11/1799, devises
to children: John, Samuel, Penelope, Effingham, Misc
SELLICK, Gershom, decd, Frederick Selleck and Luke Reed issued
L/A 7/14/1823, Salina Manton, John and Thomas Greene, secs; land
in Hancock, Twiggs, Early and Greene Co.'s, Richmond, AB
SELLS, Thomas, decd, Martha Sells applies for adm, Isaac Davis,
Jeremiah Burkhalter, sur, 8/9/1803, Warren, MIC
SENN, Uriah, decd, M. N. Leverett and P. W. Reddick apptd exrs
8/1863, Webster, OD
SENNEY, E. B., decd, Sampson Bell, admr, 5/1857, Webster, OD
SEPHAUS?, F. A. (Mrs.), decd, Adolphus A. Underwood issued L/A
10/7/1862, Fulton
SESSIONS, Charles, decd, LWT dtd 10/10/1832, pvd 7/1832 by
William B. Sessions names sons-in-law, John Martin and John
Robinson; ch: Polly and R. Benson, Habersham, MIC
SESSIONS, Charles Benson, James Allen, apptd gdn, 9/1832,
Habersham, MIC
SESSIONS, Jeremiah M., decd, temp L/A issued Sally E. Sessions
8/7/1860, White, AB
SESSIONS, Joseph, decd, Ezekiel Perry, admr, 1834, Stewart, Adms
SESSIONS, Sherrod, decd, LWT pvd 6/7/1839, John J. Long, Silas
Floyd, exrs; John McCullers apptd admr de bonis non w/LWT
annexed, exrs having been dismissed 11/14/1842, Washington
SEUTELL, Nancy, decd, LWT exhibited, L. F. Heflin, exr, Fulton
SEWELL, Thomas, decd, George G. Bowman, Susannah J. Sewell,
admrs, Noah Pinkle, sur, 12/1/1873, Gwinnett, AB
SEXTON, Nancy, Polly Sexton apptd gdn 1/1820, Jasper, OM
beth M., minor, Lucinda Seago, gdn, James Haly, sur, 7/2/1849,
Cherokee, GB
SHADWICK, Thomas, decd, William McTyeire, Thomas McDade, apprs,
make inventory 8/9/1806, Richmond
SHAFFER, Nicholas, decd, David Downie issued temp L/A 4/3/1816,
George Adam, Richard Bush, secs; 12/4/1817 Harrison Bury issued
L/A, George Pearson, Thomas Pye, secs, Richmond, AB
SHANNON, John C., minor, Dudley M. Hughes, gdn, 11/24/1873,
Charles S. Hill apptd gdn ad litem, Twiggs, Misc
SHANNON, Patrick, decd, John Fletcher issued L/A 12/8/1817 and
gdn of orphs: Evans and Polley, 3/4/1916, Morgan, GB
SHANNON, Semion D., minor, Dudley M. Hughes, gdn, 11/24/1873,
Charles S. Hill apptd gdn ad litem, Twiggs, Misc
SHARLOCK, John, decd, Peter Jaillet issued L/A 2/3/1806, Henry
Tate, Thomas Lowry, secs, Richmond, AB
SHARP, John, Sr., decd, L/A to John Sharp 8/4/1806, Tattnall, MIC
SHARP, Mary B., orph of James, decd, of Jasper Co., Savannah
Jinkins, gdn, Samuel Brown, sur, 3/5/1832, Butts, GB
SHARP, William, decd, 8/6/1801 inv includes slave, 170 acres;
Watt Nunnelee, R. Middleton, Samuel McGehee, apprs, 4/7/1803
sale, Lucrecy Sharp, main purchaser, Elbert, AR
SHARP, William, decd, Nathan Johnson apptd admr 10/2/1815; Henry
Sharp, admr, makes retns 3/6/1816; Avilla Sharp, wid, takes her
dower, 3/6/1816, Jackson, OM
SHAVE, Mary, decd, John Elliott, admr, 10/26/1784, Liberty, Ests
SHAW, C. L., decd, William J. Blake, admr, William Collins, sur,
5/6/1850, Bibb, AB
SHAW, George, decd, of Pleasant Valley, John Blackshear, admr
3/1838; apprs: Isham Watkins, L. B. Morton; purchasers at sale:
Mary Shaw, P. L. Gunnels, Needham Harrell, Hewey M. Jenkins,
James Paul, Whittington Wiggins, etc., Stewart, Adms

SHAW, George, minor son of Josiah, chose Edward Jones his gdn to take into possession and preserve for his use that part of est fallen to him by his brother, James Shaw, decd, 3/2/1807, Oglethorpe, OM

SHAW, James, decd, Edward Jones, Josias W. Shaw gtd L/A, Josias W. Shaw, Jr., sec, 9/1806, Oglethorpe, OM

SHAW, James, decd, LWT pvd, Louisa C. Shaw qualified admx 4/3/1820, Camden, MIC

SHAW, James, decd, Charles Baker issued L/A 1/1825, 1/23/1826 William Gordon objects to same as he is nearest relative of decd, L/A gtd sd Gordon, Habersham, MIC

SHAW, John H., decd, John A. and Elizabeth Shaw issued L/A 7/2/1821, Edward Butler, sec, Morgan, AB

SHAW, Joseph B., decd, Richard M. D. Elliott apptd admr 1/4/1803, Camden, MIC

SHAW, Labon L. D., decd, Absalom Montgomery issued L/A 3/22/1827, B. S. Ogletree, Thomas Watts, secs, Morgan, AB

SHAW, Louisa C. (Mrs.), decd, Phineas Miller Nightengale produced her LWT, pvd by Ray Sands; sd P. M. Nightengale and Henry R. Saddler qualified as exrs 5/2/1831, Camden, MIC

SHAW, William, decd, 10/11/1809, Peggy (Margaret) Shaw, Reubin Hill, Spencer Reynolds, admrs bond, Joseph Brown, Edward Bond, surs, Clarke, AB

SHEARER, Alexander, decd, Andrew McCredie issued L/A 8/21/1789, Thomas Cumming, Edward Rowell, secs, Richmond, AB

SHEARMAN, Edward, decd, LWT pvd by Josiah Gates; Susan Hopkins qualified admx, 6/4/1827, Camden, MIC

SHEARMAN, Elizabeth (Mrs.), decd, LWT pvd 11/6/1815, Camden, MIC

SHEARMAN, Nancy, decd, Elisha F. Kirkey issued L/A 7/1856, Webster, OD

SHEERHOUSE, Emanuel, decd, LWT pvd 11/7/1846, Effingham, MIC

SHEERHOUSE, Godlieff, Emanuel Sheerhouse qualified as exr 4/1833, Effingham, MIC

SHEERHOUSE, James, decd, inv dtd 10/1/1792, Effingham, Misc

SHEFFEY, Daniel, decd, John Lynch, admr, 11/5/1855, dischgd 11/2/1857, Fulton

SHEFFEY, Michael M., decd, John Lynch, admr, 7/7/1856; dischgd 11/2/1857, Fulton

SHEFFIELD, Randall, decd, Bryant Sheffield, admr, adm of est recd by certified cy from Wayne Co. and ordered filed (transferred to Camden Co.), 1/6/1825, Camden, MIC

SHEHEE, Allafair, decd, LWT pvd 9/5/1842, Francis T. Tennille, exr, Washington

SHEILEY, John, decd, Andrew Gnann applies as greatest creditor of est 11/20/1793; LWT dtd 9/30/1793 devised 50 acres where he lived; 200 acres on Three-Runs; town lot in Ebenezer to wife, Mary; L/T issued Mary 2/4/1794, Effingham, Misc

SHEILEY, John, decd, Andrew N. Simpson, admr, 2/1840; apprs: John W. F. Lowery, P. F. Sapp, Shadrack Pinkston, James M. Granberry; purchasers at sale: D. L., James, & L. P. Rice, C. N., Tom Peter & John N. Simpson, Stewart, Adms

SHELNUT, Andrew, decd, John Shelnut, admr, John Ward, sur, 7/1850, Fayette, AB

SHELTON, William B., decd, James E. Griggs issued L/A 6/1/1863, William P. Nichols, sec, White, AB

SHEPHERD, Albert H. (Dr.), decd, James M. Smyth, Anne E. Shepherd, admrs, 9/1837; apprs: John T. B. Turner, Wiley Bullard, Isaac Smith, James M. Miller, Stewart, Adms

SHEPHERD, William, decd, Mary Shepherd qualified admx 3/26/1790, Liberty, Misc

SHEPPARD, Benjamin, gdn, additional bond, p. 138 and 150, Screven, OM

SHEPPARD, B. F., decd, J. J. Sheppard files retns 4/1862, Webster, OD
SHEPPARD, Cassandra, John Burnett, gdn 5/6/1822, Bulloch, MIC
SHEPPARD, Charles, decd, LWT pvd 5/1/1843 by Elizabeth Sheppard, admx, Washington
SHEPPARD, Elizabeth, decd, Thomas Sheppard, Elizabeth Sandiford qualified exrs 3/8/1785, Liberty, Ests
SHEPPARD, John B., et., leave to sell real estate, p. 147, Screven, OM
SHEPPARD, John Baptist, decd, William Sheppard, admr, applies for dismission 1/10/1801, Effingham, Misc
SHEPPARD, Joseph, decd, Joseph Sheppard qualified as exr, 3/3/1818, Bulloch, MIC
SHEPPARD, Thomas, decd, William Baker, Sr., Frances Shepphard qualified exrs 1/10/1793, Liberty, Ests
SHERIFF, John, minor of Hinchy B., decd, J. J. Burt, John Hockenhull, Sr., gdns, 5/2/1859, Dawson, WB
SHERIFF, K. B., decd, Malinda Sheriff issued L/A, Thomas Sheriff, sec, 4/3/1852, Lumpkin, AB
SHERIFF, Sarah, minor of Hinchy B., decd, J. J. Burt, John Hockenhull, Sr., gdns, 5/2/1859, Dawson, WB
SHERMAN, Ann, decd, Benjamin Head applied for L/A 3/17/1795, Elbert, AB
SHEROD, Beneta, minor of Benjamin, decd, William Sherod, gdn, John Sherod, Benjamin Sherod, Joseph Dunn, sur, 1/16/1843, Emanuel, GB
SHEROD, Susan, minor of Benjamin, decd, William Sherod, gdn, John Sherod, Benjamin Sherod, Joseph Dunn, sur, 1/16/1843, Emanuel, GB
SHERRAUS, John, Sr., Godhelf Sherraus, admr, applies for dismission 7/20/1801, Effingham, Misc
SHERRELL, Reuben, decd, David Sherrell apptd admr 12/9/1784, Wilkes, MxR
SHERRILL, William, decd, James Robinson issued L/A 3/1/1786, William Hogg, Samuel Johnson, secs, Richmond, AB
SHERROD, Benjamin, decd, Thomas Drew, admr, appr 8/6/1836, Emanuel, A
SHERWOOD, George, decd, Nancy Sherwood and Samuel J. Parrish issued L/A 5/6/1850, S. J. Parrish, Elias Miller, Samuel C. Fraser, secs, Hall, AB
SHIELDS, Lewis Thomas, minor, bound out to Asa Lathorp until age 21, David G. Jones apptd gdn 6/7/1808, Camden, MIC
SHIELDS, Patrick, decd, Jane, Thos, Jas Shields L/A 5/4/1807; 8 shs, w/one to Thos Thurmond 5/4/1812; George, Polly, Nancy, John, Betsy, Patsy, orphs, ask grfather Joseph Shields & uncle James Shields be apptd gdns 7/1/1811, Jackson, OM
SHIELDS, Thomas, decd, LWT pvd, L/T issued Jemima Shields and Williams Shields 11/3/1817, Jasper, OM
SHINHOLSTER, Mary, decd, William J. Shinholster issued L/A 10/1856, to sell real estate 12/1856,Webster, OD
SHIPLEY, George, Martha Shipley apptd gdn 7/8/1801, Franklin, OM
SHIPLEY, John, decd, LWT pvd 12/3/1788 by Moses McCrea, names wife, Martha, ch: William, George, Nancy, Naomi, Elizabeth and Polly; exrs, Robert and Nathaniel Shipley failed to report to ct 7/8/1801, Franklin, OM
SHIPLEY, Polly, Martha Shipley apptd gdn 7/8/1801, Franklin, OM
SHIPP, Benjamin, decd, purchasers at sale: James Perry, David Shipp, John Spear, Jesse Ashlock, Wm Hardwick, Daniel Mitchell, Robt Knight, Chas Sturdivant, Wm Stith, Jr., Benjamin Colding, Hancock, AA
SHIPP, Thomas apptd gdn of his ch: Mary Ann, Jane Louisa, Adaline and Lucinda 11/5/1832, Thomas Shipp, Harry Evans, Wm Gray, sec; 3/3/1834 Henry Evans apptd, , Lincoln, GB

SHIRLING, Bryant W., decd, James M. Tullis issued L/A 9/1862, revoked 12/1868, Webster, OD

SHIRLING, Isham, decd, carpenter & blacksmith, William B. Shirling, exr, 2/1837; apprs: William Porter, Christopher S. Baldwin; purchasers at sale: James, Jacob and John Cravey, Neil Culpepper, Columbus Evans, Stewart, Adms

SHIRLING, Isham W., decd, Peyton Reynolds, 11/1836; apprs: James Webb, Jacob Cravey, John R. Bartee; purchasers at sale: Gideon Croxton, Charles & Larkin Gunn, Philip Mathison, John Jr. & Sr., Wm B., John A. & Mary Shirling, Stewart, Adms

SHIRLING, John A., decd, William B. Shirling, James Webb, admrs, 10/1838; apprs: John and Jacob Cravey, Philip Mathison; notes due from: John A. and Isham Shirling, James Givens, Charles Gunn, Neal Culpepper, etc., Stewart, Adms

SHIVERS, Jonas, decd, James Shivers, admr, 1/2/1827, Edwin Baker, James Flewellin, Samuel Pitt, Joseph Roberts, Warren, AB

SHOCKLEY, James, decd, L/A gtd Aquila and Richard Shockley 3/1813, Franklin, OM

SHOCKLEY, Thomas, through age and infirmity abt to squander his property, Gideon Shockley apptd his gdn 5/3/1813, Jackson, OM

SHORT, Reuben apptd gdn of James, Francis, William and Jesse, minor orphs of William Short 1/1821, Jasper, OM

SHORT, William, decd, Joel Moody apptd admr 1/1820, Jasper, OM

SHORTELL, Patrick, decd, John Ennis, admr, Thomas Haney, sec, 10/7/1861, Fulton, AB

SHORTER, Rachel, decd, Jesse Mixon applies for adm of est of Rachel Shorter & Co., 11/11/1793, apptd admr 12/27/1793, Effingham, Misc

SHRIMP, William, decd, Jonathan Seckinger applies for L/D 7/2/1827, Effingham, MIC

SHUBTREIN, Goblieb, minor, Jonathan Seckinger apptd gdn 2/18/1800, Effingham, Misc

SHUBTREIN, Hannah, minor, Jonathan Seckinger apptd gdn 2/18/1800, Effingham, MIsc

SHUBTRINE, Israel, decd, John Shubtrine issued L/A 2/15/1838, Effingham, MIC

SHUFFIELD, Austin, decd, sale of articles attached to est, certified by Allen Denmark, 3/6/1821; recd of Sarah Geiger, admx of est, in full my proportionate pt of est, signed, Reddick Thomas, 3/26/1825; recd of Sarah Geiger 1000 acres in full of all demands as heir of est of my father, signed Simeon Shuffield, 1/15/1830, Bulloch, Misc

SHUFFIELD, Barnaby, decd, inv and appr by John Knight, Thomas Jackson, John Hix, Elizabeth Shuffield, a purchaser, 1/12/1811, Jasper, Ests

SHUFFIELD, Simeon, decd, James Hagin, admr, to pay Isaac Richardson $100 to relinquish liability to heirs of decd, 9/2/1839, Bulloch, MIC

SHUFFIELD, Simeon, orph of Austin, decd, Sarah Geiger apptd gdn 1/1/1821, Bulloch, MIC

SHUFFIELD, William, orph of Austin, decd, Sarah Geiger apptd gdn 1/1/1821, Bulloch, MIC

SHUFFIELD, Zachariah, decd, Jacob Shuffield issued L/A 5/7/1827, Joseph Heard, James Hitchcock, secs, Morgan, AB

SHULTZ, Daniel, decd, John Charlton issued L/A 3/2/1842, Effingham, MIC

SHUMAN, Henry, minor of James, decd, Clem Powers apptd gdn 1/4/1830, Effingham, MIC

SHUMAN, James, decd, accts of George H. Shuman, exr 9/3/1827, Effingham, MIC

SHUMAN, Martin, decd, George Henry Shuman applies for adm on est of his decd father 1/21/1800, Effingham, Misc

SHUMAN, Martin, decd, LWT dtd 10/4/1793 pvd 12/1/1800, names ch: John, Martin, George Henry, Jonathan and James Martin, Elizabeth Womack, Effingham, Misc

SIFFLEY (OR SIFFLE), Lewis, decd, William McTyeire and George Weissinger issued L/A 12/17/1797, John Turman, John McManus, secs; 1811 retn pd widow and Henry Siffley, Richmond, AB, AR

SIKES, Delia, minor orph of William, decd, Solomon Sikes, gdn, 5/14/1817, David Patterson, Henry Sikes, secs, Richmond, GB

SIKES, Edward, decd, Catherine Sikes, gdn of orphs: Catherine, Samuel, Rebecca and Isaac 9/13/1828, Jacob Sikes and Alexander Bird, secs, Bryan, CR

SILBERT, Michael, decd, of Augusta, Ga., Mary Silbert, Andrew J. Dill issued L/A 12/16/1817; 1828 division to Mary Ann, Sarah Ann & John M. Silbert, & Nathan Leeds & wife (heirs), Richmond, AB

SILL, John, decd, Benjamin Williams and James McCorkel gtd L/A 5/9/1791, Columbia, Ests

SILLEVANT, Thomas, decd, Daniel Sillevant qualified admr 5/26/1793, Liberty, Ests

SILVA, Silvester, decd, LWT pvd by A. J. Bessant, the wid qualified as admx 6/7/1842, Camden, MIC

SILVA, Sylvester, decd, John Makin, admr, 11/4/1850, Camden, MIC

SIMMES, Susan (Mrs.), decd, L/A to George D. Case 1/2/1843, Baldwin

SIMMONS, Adam, decd, Adam Simmons, Jr., admr, Nathan Johnson, Andrew Mickleroy, sec, 3/1808, dismissed 9/1809, Oglethorpe, OM, AB

SIMMONS, Brice, decd, Mrs. Margery Simmons issued L/A 7/3/1820, inv and appraisement by Aaron Everett, John Matthews, Samuel Slater 12/4/1820, Bulloch, MIC, Misc

SIMMONS, Charles, decd, David Cockram issued L/A 3/26/1788, Robert Bonner, James Dannelly, secs, Richmond, AB

SIMMONS, Charles, decd, L/A to Polly Simons 3/7/1814, Putnam, AB

SIMMONS, Edward, decd, Richard L. Simmons issued L/A 11/7/1853, John S. Simmons, John E. Redwine, secs, Hall, AB

SIMMONS, Jasper, Haskell Simmons apptd gdn 1/4/1841, Bulloch, MIC

SIMMONS, John, decd, Mary Ann Simmons, gdn for orphs: John, Stern and Mary Ann 11/4/1833, Jared E. Grove and Stern Simmons, secs, Lincoln, GB

SIMMONS, John W., decd, L/A issued Martha G. Simmons 3/1863, Webster, OD

SIMMONS, Joshua, decd, Andrew Polk applied for L/A, Greene, Misc

SIMMONS, Matthew, Cyrus H. Yarborough apptd gdn, 11/7/1853, Houston, GB

SIMMONS, Rebecca, Cyrus H. Yarborough apptd gdn, 11/7/1853, Houston, GB

SIMMONS, William, decd, James M. Simmons apptd admr 1/1855; John R. Simmons apptd gdn 3/1856 of minors: Reuben H., Martha E., William M. and Sarah Y., Webster, OD

SIMMONS, William, decd, LWT pvd by Rawleigh Crawford 5/1808, Oglethorpe, OM

SIMONS, Robert W., decd, William B. Brightwell, admr, Milledge S. Durham, William P. Harden, secs, 6/25/1862, Fulton, AB

SIMONTON, Jean, Theophilus Simonton apptd gdn, D. Holmes, sur, Clarke, GB

SIMONTON, Theophilus, decd, Rebecca Simonton, gdn of Samuel, Elizabeth and Theophilus 9/3/1821, James Robison, T. Moore, surs, Clarke, GB

SIMPSON, Charles D., minor of Arpha Simpson who is apptd gdn, William Dent, sur, 1/19/1802, Oglethorpe, MIC

SIMPSON, James T., decd, Miles B. Simpson issued L/A 9/3/1855, J. D. Hudgins, sec, Hall, AB

SIMPSON, William L., decd, Charles N. Simpson, admr, 2/1840; apprs: John W. F. Lowery, P. F. Sapp, Shadrack Pinkston, James M. Granberry; purchasers at sale: D. L., James and L. P. Rice, C. N., Tom Peter and John N. Simpson, Stewart, Adms

SIMPSON, Winfred, decd, Daniel Nunez and David Montaigut, exrs of LWT 1/4/1787, Chatham, Adms

SIMS, Frederick, decd, Benjamin Sims issued L/A 12/29/1795, Ambrose Gordon, John MacIntosh, secs, Richmond, AB

SIMS, Jacob, decd, Mrs. Conrad issued L/A 3/18/1786, Francis Willis, Joseph Anthony, secs, Richmond, AB

SIMS, Little B., Samuel Whitehead apptd admr, 5/1808, Oglethorpe, OM, AB

SINCLAIR, Barbary, Robert C. Sinclair, admr, Dooly, OD

SINGLETON, Francis C., orph of Murdock M., decd, John W. Edwards, gdn, 12/8/1852, Houston, GB

SINGLETON, John, decd, L/A gtd to Benjamin Waits, 5/2/1814, Jasper, OM

SINQUEFIELD, Moses, decd, LWT pvd 3/6/1832, Moses Sinquefield, exr, Washington

SINQUEFIELD, Zachariah, decd, Holland McTyeire issued L/A 10/19/1824, Absolom Rhodes, Littleberry Bush, secs, Richmond, AB

SIZEMORE, Henry, orph of William, decd, Thomas Duke apptd gdn 6/4/1794, dismissed 6/1802, Oglethorpe, MIC

SIZEMORE, Isom, decd, Stephen Williams issued L/A 8/12/1839, Benjamin Brewton, sec, Tattnall, AB

SIZEMORE, William, decd, inv 5/1/1784, apprs: Abner Legett, Zobar Duke, William Duke, Wilkes, MxR

SKAGGS, Henry, decd, Charles Skaggs issued temp L/A 3/26/1814, Putnam, AB

SKAGGS, William, decd, Mary and Charles Skaggs issued L/A 1/11/1813, Putnam, AB

SKIDMORE, Samuel, decd, Samuel Skidmore, gdn of orphs: Jett T., Crosby L. and Sally P., 9/7/1821, Morgan, GB

SKINNER, John H., decd, Beverley Purkenson applied for adm 5/6/1816, Jackson, OM

SKINNER, Martha, wife of Seaborn, late Martha Ann Hall. William Kennedy, gdn in acct w/Seaborn, 1830 retns, collecting money from John Greiner of Philadelphia, Richmond

SKINNER, Noah S., orph of James G., decd, Richard Harp, gdn, Nathan C. Williamson, sur, 9/5/1842, Butts, GB

SKINNER, William, decd, Livingston Skinner, gdn of minor orphs: Caroline and Seaborn 11/15/1820, William Skinner, Josiah Brunson, secs, Richmond, GB

SKIPWITH, Peyton (honorable), member of Inf Ct, decd, Mrs. C. L. Skipwith produced his LWT, she qualified as extrx 4/3/1809, Camden, MIC

SKRINE, Sarah M., decd, Quintelann Skrine issued L/A 1/8/1838, Washington

SLADE, Joseph, decd, Mary Slade issued L/A 4/14/1794, George Graves, John McKinne, secs, Richmond, AB

SLADE, William, decd, William Slade, admr, 1/13/1847: apprs: John C. Ross, Jeremiah Slade, James Lewis; purchasers at sale: wid, Catherine, William, K., Jeremiah, & E. Slade, N. Futrell, J. C. Sutton, R. B. Rutland, etc., Dooly, I&A

SLADE, William, Sr., decd, William Slade, Jr., Dooly, OD

SLAGGS, James, idiot, William Hurst, gdn, 1828 retn, Butts, ER

SLAPPEY, Henry, decd, LWT pvd by Ann Slappey 5/7/1821, Jasper, OM

SLAPPEY, Henry, decd, died intestate, John C. and Ann Slappey apptd exrs, 9/1820, Jasper, OM

SLAPPEY, Jacob, decd, John W. Compton, admr, Joel Crawford, atty for Margaret Slappey....Wm W. Kennon, Stokely Morgan, Hiram Glazier, Joseph Beavis, Henry Walker apptd to make div 7/3/1815, Jasper, OM

SLAPPY, Jacob, decd, John W. Compton, admr, William Hitchcock, James O. K. Garrett, George Cabiness, John R. Gregory, sur, 3/1/1813, Jones, AB

SLATER, Clem, minor orph of William, decd, Barber Cone made retn 1841, Bulloch, MIC
SLATER, Georgeann, minor orph of William, decd, Barber Cone made retn 1841, Bulloch, MIC
SLATER, John G., minor orph of William, decd, Barber Cone made retn 1841, Bulloch, MIC
SLATER, Sena, orph of William, decd, Patrick Lanier made retn for 1839 as gdn, 2/3/1840, Bulloch, MIC
SLATER, William, decd, 8/4/1840 div of est by Barber Cone, admr, lots drawn by heirs: R. J. Brantly, Lina Slater (sister), J. S. Lyons, John, Mary and Clera Slater, Barber Cone, Bulloch, Misc
SLATER, William, decd, Mary Slater, admx, inv and appr by Peter Cone, Asa Cox, William Burnsed, Nathan Jones 11/20/1834; retn for 1834 of admx, by Margaret Hagin, gdn, 5/3/1835, Bulloch, Misc
SLATER, William, decd, ordered that Barber Cone sell bal of stock of cattle of est 5/6/1839, Bulloch, MIC
SLATLER, Solomon, decd, Nancy Slatler, admx, John Gibson, Abner E. Slatler, sur, 10/16/1812, Jones, AB
SLATON, Charles W. G., orph of Cornelius, decd, John H. Thompson, gdn, William Andrews, James Boughan, sur, 11/2/1846, Butts, GB
SLATON, Cornelius, decd, James R. McCord, John W. McCord, admrs, James H. Stark, John Andrews, sur, 1/13/1845, Butts, AB
SLATON, Henry W., orph of Cornelius, decd, Thomas M. Harkness, gdn, William S. Harkness, sur, 1/11/1847; to receive his distributive share, Butts, GB
SLATON, Mandain, orph of Cornelius, decd, James Boughton, gdn, John H. Thompson, John Hall, sur, 11/28/1846; Rufus W. McCune, gdn, James A. McCune, sur, 11/19/1849, Butts, GB
SLATON, Oliver H., orph of Cornelius, decd, James R. Lyons, gdn, John E. B. Lyons, sur, 11/2/1846, Butts, GB
SLATON, Samuel J., orph of Cornelius, decd, William B. Nutt, gdn, Samuel Nutt, sur, 9/7/1846; William B. Nutt, gdn, to recieve his distributive share of est 3/6/1847, Thomas M. Harkness, sur, James R. and John W. McCord, admrs, Butts, GB
SLATON, William G., orph of Cornelius, John H. Thompson gdn for his distr of est, James Boughton, sur, James R. McCord, John W. McCord, sur, 1/20/1847, Butts, GB
SLATTER, James, decd, John Slatter, admr, 3/7/1808, Warren, MIC
SLATTER, James F., decd, Emma Bails issued L/A 11/4/1839, Baldwin
SLAUGHTER, Ezekiel, decd, LWT pvd 8/21/1792, ch: Mary Worsham, John, Salley Robbarts, Bettey Jones, Judea Gill, Samuel, Susannah Hawkins, Patty Gill, Reuben, Ann; grch: Ezekiel Slaughter, Ezekiel Gill, Ezekiel Hawkins, Greene, Misc
SLAUGHTER, Frances apptd gdn of Lydia, Henry P., Frances, William Thomas and Isaac, all the children of Henry, decd, 1/7/1822, Jasper, OM
SLAUGHTER, Henry, decd, L/A gtd Fanny Slaughter, with Jonah Burgess, Christopher Deadwilder and Nicholas Johnson, secs, 11/2/1818, Jasper, OM
SLAUGHTER, John, decd, appr 6/17/1788, Greene, Misc
SLAY, William, decd, Lewis Thomas, admr de bonis non 12/6/1852, Noah Slay, John Simpson, surs, DeKalb, AB
SLAYTON, Isaac, decd, Charles J. Patterson applied for adm, but withdrew his application; ct apptd Henry R. Fort, admr, 5/7/1849, Camden, MIC
SLEDGE, John, decd, LWT dtd 4/14/1798, names ch: Nathaniel, Hartwell, John, Jane Jackson, Rebecca Southall, Shirley, Martha, pvd 10/1798, Hancock, AA
SLEDGE, Nathaniel, decd, appr 10/29/1802; purchasers at sale: widow Sledge, John Sledge, Isham Let, Peyton Sledge, Chappell Sledge, Nancy Sledge, Elisha Whatley, etc.; Mrs. Sledge, Henry Harris, Benjamin Chappell, admrs, Hancock, AAAA

SLIGH (or SLEIGH), Harriet, Henry Harden apptd gdn 3/4/1805, Bryan, MIC

SLIGH (or SLEIGH), Samuel, decd, Mrs. Mary Sligh or Sleigh petitions for gdnshp of her children, Mary and Samuel, 9/5/1803, Bryan, MIC

SLITERNE, Peter, decd, Mrs. Eleanor Sliterne, admx, 7/30/1789, Chatham, Adms

SLOCUM, Fitch J., decd, Duncan M. Millan issued L/A 1/9/1830, Hartwell R. Mitchell, sec; Norman McRae issued L/A 7/4/1831, Malcom Currie, sec, Montgomery, AB

SLOCUM, Seth, decd, Samuel Slocum, admr, 2/2/1795, Orandatus Watson, sur, dismissed 6/9/1795, Warren, AB, MIC

SLONE, James, orph, bound to Allen Denmark for 8 yrs, 11/3/1821, Bulloch, MIC

SLONE, John, orph of Samuel, decd, be bound to James Denmark for 12 yrs, 11/3/1821, Bulloch, MIC

SLONE, Richard, orph of Samuel, decd, be bound to Malachi Denmark for 4 yrs, Bulloch, MIC

SLONE, Samuel, decd, Allen Denmark, admr, to sell pers est 11/3/1821, Bulloch, MIC

SMALL, Robert C., decd, Martha C. Small, admx, John D. Stell, Robert McCatchen, surs, 1/1848, 1849, 1852-1853, Fayette, AB

SMALL, W. J., decd, LWT pvd 2/5/1867, Mary Ann Small, extrx, Fulton

SMALLPEACE, Wiley S., minor orph and illegitimate child of Amos, James M. Tapley, gdn, Lewis Davis, Richard Sumner, sur, 1/4/1842, Emanuel, GB

SMALLWOOD, Elisha, age 3 yrs, orph of William, decd, 5/2/1836 bound to John D. Floyd for 3 yrs, Fulton, GB

SMALLWOOD, Isaac, decd, Benjamin and Frances Smallwood qualified admrs 8/7/1792, Liberty, Ests

SMALLWOOD, Mack, decd, Samuel H. Elenen, admr, D. D. Denham, Littleton Stokes, Janot Handley, surs, 9/1851, Fayette, AB

SMART, Francis B., decd, Eliza Smart, relict, and John Hill issued L/A 9/6/1319, Jasper, OM

SMITH, Aaron, admr, leave to sell property, p. 53, Screven, OM

SMITH, Abraham, decd, William D. Lane and Winny Smith issued L/A 1/2/1809, Putnam, AB

SMITH, Abram, decd, LWT pvd by Isaac Rosser and Jesse George, L/T issued to Sarah Smith 5/1/1815, Jasper, OM

SMITH, Alexander, decd, Davis Smith issued L/A 7/3/1820, John Thomas, Lewis Sanders, secs, Laurens, AB

SMITH, Alexander, decd, William W. Mathews, exr of LWT, 1852, Fayette, AB

SMITH, Amanda E., illegitimate girl child of Robert Higdon, sd Robert Higdon, gdn, Daniel E. Rich, sur, 9/4/1837, Emanuel, GB

SMITH, Archibald, Sr., decd, LW dtd 2/22/1799, ch: Jehu, Archibald, Nancy Thompson, Judith Sharp, Salley, George W.; wife, Mary, pvd 3/9/1799, Hancock, AA

SMITH, Ashabel, decd, James W. Chastain, admr w/LWT annexed 1/1845, Gilmer, Misc

SMITH, Barbara Ann, William Hayes, gdn, 3/22/1827, Charter Campbell and Van Leonard, secs, Morgan, GB

SMITH, Barett, decd, John Langford, millwright, apptd admr 1/15/1784, Wilkes, AB

SMITH, Bartley M., decd, William Ezzard, Sr., admr, Joseph Thompson, sec, 11/4/1861, Fulton, AB

SMITH, Benjamin, decd, Alexander H. McDonald applies for L/A 5/10/1838, Effingham, MIC

SMITH, Benjamin, decd, LWT pvd 5/6/1844, wife, Dedams Smith and James M. Smith, exrs

SMITH, Benjamin, decd, William Smith apptd admr 9/18/1783, Wilkes, MxR
SMITH, Benjamin, Sr., decd, Edward and Benjamin Smith, Jr., admrs, 3/1843; apprs: Randolph Pearson, Bryan Gause, Samuel Johnston, Allen Bates, Stewart, Adms
SMITH, Bennett, decd, L/A issued Jesse Butts 3/6/1837, Washington
SMITH, Calvin, orph of William, decd, James Baker, gdn, 10/16/1837, Randolph
SMITH, Charles, decd, William Smith issued L/A 5/17/1788, Nathan Fowler, Edmund Nugent, secs, Richmond, AB
SMITH, Charles A., decd, 6/1842, apprs: Anderson Watson, Robert S. Wimberly, Anderson Robinson, Stewart, Adms
SMITH, Cullen, minor orph of Nathan, Elias G. Longham apptd gdn 11/3/1817, Jasper, OM
SMITH, Daniel, decd, Mary Smith issued L/A 12/2/1784, Samuel Blair, Thomas Jones, secs, Richmond, AB
SMITH, Edward, decd, James W. Meredith issued L/A 8/9/1822, John Marshall, David Smith, secs, Richmond, AB
SMITH, Enoch, decd, Henry Weaver and John Prather, exrs of LWT 1/1845, Gilmer, Misc
SMITH, Ezekiel, decd, Kenneth McLennon issued L/A 10/6/1839, John Morrison, sec, Montgomery, AB
SNUTG, James, decd, LWT pvd by Wm Ellington and Wm Hancock 3/1813, John and James Smith, exrs, Jackson, OM
SMITH, James H., orph of Coleman, decd, Richard Thornton, gdn, 3/6/1843, Randolph
SMITH, James P., orph of John, decd, Charles Smith, gdn, 3/15/1823, Benjamin Brown, W. S. Stokes, secs, Morgan, GB
SMITH, Jane P. John, decd, Charles Smith, gdn of Jane P., orph 7/1/1816, Richard A. Blount, gdn of Nancy, John, Mary and Burwell, Richmond, GB
SMITH, Joel, decd, Henry Smith issued L/A 5/4/1812, Lewis Maddox, sec, Laurens, AB
SMITH, John, decd, Daniel Ford´s retn in pt of as sale on 3/1/1823, 6/7/1824, Habersham, MIC
SMITH, John, decd, George W. and Elizabeth Smith issued L/A 7/5/1813, Putnam, AB
SMITH, John, decd, Jacob Smith issued L/A, undtd, William Foster, Jacob Johnson, secs, Richmond, AB
SMITH, John, decd, Joseph Shores issued L/A 1/8/1821, William D. Algins, James Brantley, secs, 1/8/1821, Laurens, AB
SMITH, John A., bound to Eden C. Smith 10/16/1837, Randolph
SMITH, Joseph, decd, Benajah Smith issued L/A 11/7/1825, Jesse Mullins, sec, Morgan, AB
SMITH, Josiah, decd, John Smith issued L/A 11/4/1822, Matthew Smith, Fleeet Pope, secs, Laurens, AB
SMITH, Lursey, orph of Isham, decd, Coleby Wheeler, gdn, 11/1831, Habersham, MIC
SMITH, Martha M., William Hays, gdn 3/22/1827, Charter Campbell and Van Leonard, secs, Morgan, GB
SMITH, Matthew, decd, Ezekiel Smith issued L/A 3/2/1818, Lewis Maddox, sec, Laurens, AB
SMITH, Nehemiah, decd, John, James and Alexander McHargus issued L/A 3/3/1806, Jackson, OM
SMITH, Samuel, decd, John Smith issued L/A 12/2/1784, Samuel Blair, sec, Richmond, AB
SMITH, Simon, decd, Benjamin T. Dowdy, admr makes retn 1/1/1836 (the heirs oF Rebecca Strickland mentioned), Tattnall, I&A
SMITH, Thomas, decd, Alton Pemberton and Susan M. Smith, admrs of decd of Chatham Co. vs. Mary Torrence, 1811, Bryan, Writs
SMITH, William, gdn, to sell land, p. 132, Screven, OM

SMITH, William, orph of John, decd, Thomas Elliot, gdn, 7/3/1820, Benjamin Brown, sec, Morgan, GB
SMITH, William Munroe, William Hayes, gdn 3/22/1827, Charter Campbell and Van Leonard, secs, Morgan, GB
SMITHERS, George, decd, Eliza B. Martin issued L/A 3/8/1823, William C. Dillon, sec, Richmond, AB
SNEED, Samuel, decd, Rebecca Sneed issued L/A 7/3/1826, George Brodnax, Robert Allen, secs, Pike, MIC
SNELGRAVES, Requel?, decd, motion of Margaret to have a poor orph child, Clarissa Phebe, age 13, bound to William B. Sack, until age 18, Habersham, MIC
SNELGROVE, D. D., decd, William Snelgrove, admr, 10/16/1837, Randolph
SNELLGROVE, Benjamin, decd, Catharine Snellgrove issued L/A 7/5/1819, Laurens, AB
SNIDER, Frederick, decd, William Longstreet issued L/A 1/22/1788, William Freeman, Daniel Longstreet, secs, Richmond, AB
SNOW, Henry, decd, LWT pvd by John C. Watkins, Joel and Jane Jetton 7/1/1811, Jackson, OM
SNOW, Moses, decd, Battle Mayfield, admr, 2/6/1816, Jackson, OM
SOLOMON, Owen Fort, decd, William Solomon issued L/A 2/6/1860, Fulton
SOWELL, Josiah, decd, Wm Sowell, admr, p. 55, Screven, OM
SPALDING, Isham, decd, LWT pvd, Mrs. Lucy Spalding qualified as extrx 3/16/1824, Camden, MIC
SPALDING, Isham, decd, Lucy Spalding, extrx, rendered her report appvd by Jane E. Spalding "now of age" 6/4/1827, Camden, MIC
SPALDING, Lucy (Mrs.), LWT pvd by Ray Sands; Robert Stafford qualified as exr 1/2/1837; exr gtd leave to sell 200 acres on St. Marys River, 40 shs of stock in Marine & Fire Ins Bank of Savannah, 1 sh in U. S. Bank, 6/3/1837, Camden, MIC
SPANN, Caroline, J. T. Stapleton issued L/G 1/1866, Webster, OD
SPANN, Francis, decd, Eleanor Spann applied for adm, John Bruton, Wyatt Bonner, sur, 9/7/1807, Warren, MIC, AB
SPANN, George C., W. H. Bush issued L/G 1/1866; P. H. Spann issued L/G 3/1868, Webster, OD
SPANN, Henry, decd, William L. Clarke issued L/A 8/1862; Mrs. L. Clarke commissioned to set apart allowance for wid and children of decd 12/1862, Webster, OD
SPANN, J. N., minor of John R., L/G gtd Sarah A. Spann 3/1865, Webster, OD
SPANN, John R., decd, James G. M. Bell, admr w/LWT admitted to record, 11/1864, Webster, OD
SPANN, Laura, minor of Henry, decd, W. L. Clarke issued L/G 1/1866, Webster, OD
SPANN, Sarah Jane, minor of Henry, decd, W. L. Clarke issued L/G 1/1866, Webster, OD
SPANN, Silas H., decd, Hiliam J. Lott, gdn of minor ch: Mary A. and William A. 12/3/1855, Ambrose Kennedy, sec, Hall, GB
SPARKS, James, decd, Jeremiah and Ann Sparks issued L/A 5/2/1808, Franklin, OM
SPARKS, John, decd, LWT pvd 7/6/1840, wife, Elizabeth and son, Wilkinson Sparks, exrs, Harris
SPARKS, Morgan, orph of Benjamin, decd, William Harrison issued L/G 3/3/1834, Washington
SPEAK, Margarette T., illegitimate, William Blalock, gdn, John Saunders, sur, 1/5/1834, Butts, GB
SPEARS, Abraham, decd, Waters Dunn, admr, inv 2/17/1783 by apprs: Charley Bostick, James Harris, Robert Jones, Richmond
SPEARS, John L. W., decd, William Johnson, gdn of orphs: Martha E., Henry and Mary E., 1/1/1841, Randolph

SPEARS, Joseph G., decd, retn by Eli Conger for orphs and minors, pd John Tarpley, schooling for 1826-1830, Butts, ER
SPEARS, Moses, decd, L/A to Francis Kirby 7/5/1824, Morgan, AB
SPEARS, William, decd, Alexander Spears, John Thomas, Richard, Ruth and Wade Spears issued L/A 5/6/1816, Laurens, AB
SPEARS, William, decd, Rebecca Spears, gdn of orphs: William, Elizabeth and Rebecca 5/6/1816, Laurens, GB
SPEER, Elizabeth B., orph of Charles, decd, Jane Speer apptd gdn 3/1819, Jasper, OM
SPEIGHTS, Mary C., minor orph of Thomas, decd, late of Burke Co., John A. Barnes, gdn, 5/13/1819, Barna McKinne, Milledge Galphin, secs, Richmond, GB
SPEIR, William, decd, div of est gtd 3/7/1831, Effingham, MIC
SPENCE, Bluford, decd, William Hilliard, admr, 4/1837; apprs: William Hilliard, Isaac Smith, Asa Joiner, Wiley Hilliard; purchasers at sale: James and Liston Spence, Miles Smith, Samuel Middleton, etc., Stewart, Adms
SPENCE, Joseph, orph of Tharp, decd, Bluford Spence, David Stringer, Henry Drugen, gdns, 9/3/1821, Emanuel, GB
SPENCE, Leaston, orph of Tharp, decd, Bluford Spence, David Stringer, Henry Durden, gdns, 9/3/1821, Emanuel, GB
SPENCE, William, decd, W. B. Richardson applies for L/A 4/19/1858, Samuel Lindsey, William King, sur, Lee
SPENCER, David, decd, James W. Harkness, admr (in rt of his wife, Jane Spencer), John B. Harkness, sur, 7/3/1848, Butts, AB
SPENCER, David, decd, Jane Spencer, admr, Abel A. Lemon, Abraham Lemon, sur, 9/6/1847, Butts, AB
SPENCER, George Basil, decd, Mrs. Elizabeth Spencer, Joseph William Spencer and William Henry Spencer, exrs, 4/3/1791, Chatham, Adms
SPENCER, Paul, decd, John Simmons, gdn of Edward T. L. and Mary E., orphs, 9/4/1820, John Williams, Jesse C. Paulett, surs, Clarke, GB
SPENCER, Rosina, decd (formerly Rosina Postell), LWT pvd 7/19/1800 bequeathed whole est to her husband; William Holzendorf applies for adm 6/14/1800; John Spencer caveats the appoointment 6/23/1800, at same time offering her LWT for probate, Effingham,
SPENCER, Sarah, decd, Samuel Spencer qualified exr 8/16/1790, Liberty, Ests
SPENCER, Thomas A., orph of David, James W. Harkness, gdn, James Harkness, sur, 9/4/1848, Butts, AB
SPIERS, Hezekiah, decd, Abraham Ayers, gdn for orphs: Polly and Rhoda 5/7/1821, John Crawford, Elisha McCord, secs, Lincoln, GB
SPIERS, Mary Ann, orph of Hezekiah, decd, James McCorkle, gdn, 5/3/1823, James McCord, Thomas Farrow, secs, Lincoln, GB
SPIKES, Josiah, decd, Mrs. Mary Spikes applied for L/A 10/10/1792, Greene, Misc
SPIKES, Martha, orph, Shadrack Turner, gdn, 3/5/1832, George W. Dallas, sec, Lincoln, GB
SPIKES, Patsy, orph of Fanny, decd, John Hardy, gdn 3/7/1831, Shadrack Turner, sec, Lincoln, GB
SPONEGAL, Albert, decd, late of Alabama, H. J. Sprayberry issued L/A 11/7/1865, Fulton
SPRADLEY, Charles, decd, Allen Spradley, admr, Dooly, OD
SPRADLEY, James E., decd, Henry M. Christmas, admr, Dooly, OD
SPRIGGS, Catherine, decd, John Bessant, apptd admr 1/3/1837, dismissed 1/5/1852, Camden, MIC
SPRINGFIELD, Mary, orph of Aaron, decd, John S. Springfield, gdn, 12/12/1830, Butts, GB
SPRINGS, Mary, orph of Jacob, decd, John Chapman, gdn, O. Dillard, sur, 1/7/1822, Emanuel, GB

SPRY, Royal, decd, Gideon Dowse qualified as exr 10/16/1786, Liberty, Ests
SPULLOCK, Drury, decd, Peter Williamson, apptd admr 9/2/1812, Richard Cox, Joseph Brown, surs, Clarke, AB
SPULLOCK, James, decd, James Spullock, gdn of Comfort and Winnifred, orphs, 11/7/1814, Owen Spullock and Peter Williamson, surs, Clarke, GB
SPULLOCK, Sallie, orph of James, decd, Owen Spullock, gdn, 11/7/1814, James Spullock, Peter Williamson, surs, Clarke, GB
SPURLOCK, Comfort, minor, Owen Spurlock, gdn, 9/6/1813, George W. Moore, Peter Williamson, surs, Clarke, GB
SPURLOCK, Fanney, James Brooks, gdn, relieved from making retns, 1/6/1806, Oglethorpe, MIC
SPURLOCK, James, minor, Owen Spurlock, gdn, 9/6/1813, George W. Moore, Peter Williamson, surs, Clarke, GB
SPURLOCK, Robert, decd, planter, Mary Spurlock issued L/A 8/7/1783, John O'Neal, John Cone, secs, Richmond, AB
SPURLOCK, William, decd, William Cone issued L/A 1/31/1794, John Cone, sec, Richmond, AB
SPURLOCK, William W., decd, Levi Glass issued L/A 5/5/1816, Laurens, AB
STACEY, John, Sr., decd, John and James Stacey qualified as admrs 2/22/1792, Liberty, Ests
STACY, William, decd, James Stacy qualified admr 2/22/1792, Liberty, Ests
STAFFORD, Robert, decd, LWT pvd, John Stafford qualified as exr 1/5/1818, Camden, MIC
STAFFORD, Theodore, decd, Edward Rowell issued L/A 1/29/1805, Richmond, AB
STAFFORD, Thomas, decd, Lucy Spalding, extrx and Isham Spalding, her husband, gtd extn to file their retn, 6/7/1808, Camden, MIC
STAFFORD, Thomas, decd, Robert Stafford, Susannah Hawkins and John Tompkins in rt of his wife, Mary, as heirs, filed petition asking for distribution of est, slaves and horses 1/4/1820, Camden, MIC
STAFFORD, William, decd, John Tison applies for LWT to be pvd 2/18/1800, Effingham, Misc
STAFFORD, William, decd, on testimony, non-cupative Will was pvd 7/21/1800 and L/A w/LWT annexed to John Tison, Effingham, Misc
STAFFORD, William, decd, affidavit of John Tison, Jr. 6/25/1799 that he heard decd before he died say he meant to leave his prop to his sister, Mrs. Elizabeth Tison, his bro-in-law, John Tison, to have his property at his death, Effingham, Misc
STALLINGS, Ann L., decd, of Columbia Co., Isabella Clarke, Jno Mann L/A 9/7/1812; div ests of Capt. Ezekiel & Mrs. A. L. Stallings, wid to-Isabella Clarke, Jno H. Mann (rt of wf), Jno Gindrat (rt of wf), Charlotte & Henrietta, Richmond, AB
STALLINGS, Ezekiel, decd, of Columbia Co., Isabella Clarke and John H. Mann issued L/A 1/24/1812, Peter Donaldson, George Walton, secs, Richmond, AB
STALLINGS, Frederick, decd, Hannah Marcus and James Stallings issued L/A 12/7/1784, Richmond, AB
STALLINGS, James, decd, LWT pvd 1/1808, Oglethorpe, OM
STALLINGS, John (Dr.), decd, temporary L/A issued William Stallings, Webster, OD
STAMPS, Timothy, decd, James Stamps, exr of LWT, makes retns 10/25/1802 and 10/29/1803, Jackson, OM
STANALAND, Susannah, decd, verbal LWT made during last illness names four sisters and sister-in-law, Nancy Stanaland; also John Rimes, Jr, Aaron Daniel; Susannah d. 9/18/1819, signed Dempsey Stanaland, Richard T. Stanaland, Bulloch, Misc

STANCELL, Baron D., E. C. Stancell applies for L/G 10/5/1869,
Cobb, MIC
STANCELL, Calvin L., E. C. Stancell applies for L/G 10/5/1869,
Cobb, MIC
STANCELL, James N., E. C. Stancell applies for L/G 10/5/1869,
Cobb, MIC
STANCELL, Nancy J., E. C. Stancell applies for L/G 10/5/1869,
Cobb, MIC
STANDARD, William, son of John, William Turner, gdn, 1/21/1822,
Lincoln, GB
STANDFORD, Keziah, orph of Thomas, decd, David Standford apptd
gdn 1/17/1841, Randolph
STANDFORD, Robert, LWT pvd 10/15/1805, Warren, MIC
STANDFORD, Robert, decd, John Bayne, exr of LWT, gtd L/D
1/5/1807, Warren, MIC
STANDFORD, William, decd, Elisha Burton, admr, 7/6/1835, Hugh
Montgomery, sur, Warren, AB
STANDLEY, James, decd, of Columbia Co., LWT pvd 1/6/1795,
everything left to aunt, Ann Wall, L/A gtd her with Thomas Howard
and Martin Mallorn as witnessed, Columbia, Ests
STANDLY, Robert, decd, est appraised 11/30/1835 by Benjamin and
James B. Stripling and Elhanan McCall, retn filed 7/4/1836,
Tattnall, I&A
STANDRIDGE, Isaiah, decd, James M. Dean issued L/A 6/1/1863, C.
Meaders, sec, White, AB
STANFORD, Jesse, decd, Reuben Stanford, admr w/LWT annexed
7/11/1828, Wm B. Harris, Richard S. Lazenby, surs, Warren, AB
STANFORD, John, decd, Francis Jones, admr, 7/5/1827 acct with
heirs of est, Bulloch, Misc
STANHOPE, John, decd, Sarah Davenport, wid, admx, 10/2/1785,
Chatham, Adms
STANHOPE, Nathan, decd, Sarah Davenport of Savannah, wid, admx
11/7/17ckett in rt of wife, Patsy, Franklin, OM
STANLEY, Ader, wid, gtd L/A 5/20/1784, Wilkes, MxR
STANLEY, John, decd, John Hefner and William T. Popham issued L/A
9/9/1833; William T. Popham, gdn of minor heirs-William and Jane
9/2/1833, Habersham, MIC
STANLEY, William, decd, John and Charlotte Sutherland issued L/A
4/13/1786, Henry Allison, Matthew Miller, secs, Richmond, AB
STANSEL, William, decd, LWT presented 2/7/1814, Tattnall, MIC
STANTON, John J., decd, William R. Venable issued L/A 5/12/1868,
Fulton
STARK, Ebenezer, decd, on or before 4/11/1816, Bryan, MSC
STARK, James H., one of distributees of est of Samuel C. Stark
assigned one negro by John Simmons, Ermine Case, Abel L. Robinson
2/1/1830, Butts, ER
STARK, James H., orph of James C., decd, James H. Stark, gdn,
Charles Bailey, sec, 6/10/1833, Butts, GB
STARK, Phoeba L., orph of Phillip, decd, John W. Stark, gdn
9/15/1825, James Evans, Thomas M. Stark, secs, Morgan, GB
STARK, Rosannah, one of distributees of est of Samuel C. Stark
assigned one negro by John Simmons, Ermine Case, Abel L. Robinson
2/1/1830, Butts, ER
STARK, Samuel C., decd, James H. Stark, admr, Charles Bailey, A.
L. Robinson, surs, 10/8/1829; pd Ezekiel Trible for his share in
rt of wife; pd Wm Jones, L. B. Eubanks, Joseph R. Hicks, William
Harmon, Alexander Lemon, A. L. Robinson 2/1/1830, Daniel Osburn
for repairs on house 7/24/1835, Butts, AB, ER
STARK, Samuel, one of distributees of est of Samuel C. Stark
assigned one negro by John Simmons, Ermine Case, Abel L. Robinson
2/1/1830, Butts, ER

STARLING, Francis, decd, LWT pvd, John Bailey qualified as exr 6/3/1828, Camden, MIC
STARNES, Daniel, decd, Harriet E. Starnes issued L/A 7/18/1815, Simeon Russel, Peter Donaldson, secs; 9/23/1815 Harriet E. Starnes and Simeon Russel apptd gdns of-Ebenezer, Rebecca Camilla and Augusta Mary Starnes, minor orphs, Richmond, AB
STARNES, Elizabeth, decd, LWT pvd by James B. Broughton and George W. Babcock, Aaron and David Starnes, exrs 1/7/1822, Jasper, OM
STARNES, George P., decd, Comfort Starnes, admx, H. A. Madden, sur, 11/1/1858; Richard Carver, admr de bonis non, "one, Comfort Starnes, admx, has since intermarried with William Brown", 3/7/1859, Paulding, Ab
STARNES, James, illegitimate of Tempy, Nicholas Delafield apptd gdn 3/1/1831, Hall, GB
STARNES, William P., minor of William, William Starnes, gdn 10/19/1818, Samuel Jackson, sur, Clarke, GB
STARR, E. F., made natural gdn of his ch: Martha S., Mary Hannah, Henry, minors, E. P. Williams, sec, 10/20/1866, White, GB
STARRETT, William, decd, Mrs. Appy Starrett applied for admx, but later asked court to appt Henry R. Saddler in her place 6/7/1831, Camden, MIC
STATHAM, Eliza, idiot, Charles McCoy, gdn 1/8/1855, Houston, GB
STATHAM, Harriet, Robert Griffin, gdn, to hire out negroes 1/1863, Webster, OD
STATHAM, M. C., M. G. Statham issued L/G 1/1864, Webster, OD
STATHAM, Meredith, orph of Gordon, decd, John J. Speers issued L/G 12/1856, Webster, OD
STATHAM, Richmond, decd, Benjamin Griffin produced LWT 6/1854, Webster, OD
STATHAM, Susan, Robert Griffin, gdn, to hire out negroes 1/1863, Webster, OD
STATON, John, decd, Wm Hall and Isaac Kirksey applied for relief as securities for Elijah Payne, admr 3/3/1806, Tattnall, MIC
STATON, Mary, decd, Jacob Pettyjohn issued L/A w/LWT annexed 1/2/1809, Jackson, OM
STATON, Polly, orph of Mary, decd, chose her brother, Fleming Staton as gdn 5/6/1816, Jackson, OM
STAUNTON, William, decd, late of New York, Mariner, LWT pvd, Martha Staunton qualified as extrx 11/6/1815, Camden, MIC
STEEDMAN, John, decd, L/A gtd Polly Steedman with Harrison Lumkin, sec, 1/5/1818, Jasper, OM
STEEN, Benton, decd, Solomon Long, Samuel Parsons, admr, applies for leave to sell real estate 7/5/1819, Jasper, OM
STEEN, James, minor orph of Benton, decd, Samuel Parsons apptd gdn 3/5/1821, Jasper, OM
STEEN, Susannah, minor orph of Benton, decd, Samuel Parsons apptd gdn 3/5/1821, Jasper, OM
STEGALL, Francis M., decd, Charles H. Elyen, admr, C. F. Wood, sec, 10/8/1861, Fulton, AB
STELL, James J., decd, R. Manson Stell, admr, John B. Stell, T. D. King, surs, 7/1850, 1851-1852 retns, Fayette, AB
STEPHENS, Arolis M., Sharp S. Reynolds, gdn, 3/5/1855, Hall, GB
STEPHENS, Daniel, decd, Larkin Stephens, John Stephens, admrs, Eli M. Seago, James Fowler, surs, 10/4/1852, Cherokee, AB
STEPHENS, Elizabeth, decd, L/A issued A. H. Adams 11/1866, Webster, OD
STEPHENS, Henry, decd, L/A gtd James S. Weeks, James E. Brown and Jane Stephens 1/7/1822, Jasper, OM
STEPHENS, Isaac, decd, Pleasant Ray, admr, Dooly, OD
STEPHENS, Jackey, Harrell Dickens, gdn, Dooly, OD

STEPHENS, James, decd, Colson Crowns, gdn for minors, makes his retn 12/31/1835, Tattnall, I&A
STEPHENS, James, decd, LWT pvd by George and Stephen Stephens, John Rivers and Thomas Stephens, exrs, 3/6/1814, Jasper, OM
STEPHENS, James, decd, retn for 1/1/1839-4/22/1839, Samuel, Micajah, Elizabeth and Matthew named as minor heirs in gdns retn of Charles Blount 5/4/1840, Tattnall, I&A
STEPHENS, John F., decd, David Stephens, gdn of Young, John, William and Thomas, orphs, 11/4/1824, Josiah Daniell, sur, Clarke, GB
STEPHENS, Joseph H., decd, Archibald Clarke apptd admr 7/5/1813, Camden, MIC
STEPHENS, Richard, decd, James Stephens, admr, Dooly, over 14, chose his mother, Mrs. Sarah Stewart as gdn 6/7/1830, Camden, MIC
STEPHENS, William, decd, Isaac Daniels and Robert Johnson, admrs, Dooly, OD
STEPHENS, Winefred, Harrell Dickens, gdn, Dooly, OD
STEPHENSON, Daniel, decd, John Conn issued L/A 9/2/1850, Baldwin
STEPHENSON, John, decd, 7/1834, heirs-wife, Lucy and children: Washington Irving, William B., Ann Amelia, wife and friend, Calvin B. Seymour, exrs, Stewart, MIC
STEPHENSON, John, decd, LWT pvd 6/30/1794, wife, Hannah, children: Thomas, William, Mary, Elizabeth, Joseph; iv, pt of est disposed of in N. C. 9/1794, Greene, Misc
STEPHENSON, John, decd, inv 1835 (10 pages long), mercantile stock, etc., Stewart, Adms
STEPHENSON, Joseph A., decd, Martha Stephenson, admx, 10/1/1860, Moses R. Stephenson, William M. Stephenson, Singleton james, Needham Whitney, Thomas Gardner, secs, DeKalb, AB
STEPP, William, decd, Hugh Montgomery issued L/A 1/29/1852, James H. Worley and Jesse Hanley, secs, Lumpkin, AB
STEURMAN, Henry, decd, Isaac Benedix of Chatham Co. and Ananias Cooper Riohmond Co. issued L/A 8/15/1798, two tracts in Franklin Co. of 500 acres, Richmond, AB
STEVENS, Aquilla, decd, Ross Stevens, admr 9/10/1821, Benjamin Wynne, Benjamin Hurt, surs, Warren, AB
STEVENS, Owen B., decd, Ross Stevens, admr 9/10/1821, Benjamin Wynne, Benjamin Hurt, surs, Warren, AB
STEVENSON, Elizabeth, retn of Woodson Robers, gdn, 9/1812, Franklin, OM
STEVENSON, Morre, retn of Woodson Roberts, gdn dtd 9/1812, Franklin, OM
STEVENSON, Polly, heir of William, decd, John Sandidge apptd gdn 3/7/1808, Franklin, OM
STEVENSON, Polly, heir of William, decd, now Polly Hardin, receipt given by Sandling Hardin to Woodson Roberts, gdn, 9/1812, Franklin, OM
STEVENSON, Rebecca "has since married David Ballinger", retn of Woodson Roberts, gdn 9/1812, Franklin, OM
STEVENSON, Rebecca, heir of William, decd, John Sandidge apptd gdn 3/7/1808, Franklin, OM
STEVENSON, William, decd, exrs of the est request bonds of Malachi Jones be entered in records (est filed Bk A, P. 1), Franklin, IMW
STEWART, Alexander, decd, Jonathan Shaw qualified as admr 7/1783, Liberty, Ests
STEWART, Edward, decd, L/A to James Knight 1/12/1824, Morgan, AB
STEWART, George, decd, Sarah Stewart apptd admx 11/6/1815, Camden, MIC
STEWART, Henry, decd, John Varnadoe, admr, 12/8/1843; purchasers at sale: James Carlisle, James Peacock, J. S. Russell, Wilson McLemore, John Hammond, Daniel Higdon, D. J. Bothwell, Dooly, I&A

STEWART, James, decd, Josiah Bacon, James Stewart qualified as
exrs 10/31/1785, Liberty, Ests
STEWART, James, orph of James, decd, Joshua McConnell, gdn,
1/1/1856, Cherokee, GB
STEWART, James, over age 14, chose his mother, Mrs. Sarah Stewart
as his gdn 6/7/1830, Camden, MIC
STEWART, James M., decd, William Thompson and his wife, Susan,
admrs, 10/1809, Bryan, Writs
STEWART, Jesse, decd, David Downie issued temp L/A 4/3/1816,
George Adam, Richard Bush, sec; 12/4/1817 Harrison Bury issued
L/A, George Pearson, Thomas Pye, sec, Richmond, AB
STEWART, John (Capt), decd, Capt. William Walker, vendue master,
sold and appraised est, 100 acres in Richmond Co., 1/8/1784,
Wilkes, MxR
STEWART, John, decd, Hugh Nesbitt issued L/A 1/3/1801, James
Walker, sec, 1816 retn pd Eleazer Cumming and Shadrack Suttles
(latter, heir at law), Richmond, AB
STEWART, Mary, decd, John W. Walde issued L/A 11/9/1826, Richard
H. Wilde, sec, Richmond, AB
STEWART, Matthew, decd, late of Camden Co., apprs apptd to div
est 1/8/1806, Camden, MIC
STEWART, Nathaniel, decd, LWT pvd 11/5/1832, Samuel Robinson,
Lewis Dupree, sur, Washington
STEWART, Robert, decd, John Simmons, admc, 9/9/1783, Wilkes, MxR
STEWART, Samuel, decd, Jane Stewart, admx, John Harmon, Nathaniel
Gammage, John Dean, surs, 2/3/1813, Jones, AB
STEWART, Sarah, orph of John, decd, Jane Picket, gdn 5/5/1834,
William Reynolds, Ezekiel Lamar, secs, Lincoln, GB
STEWART, Thomas, decd, Hannah Stewart issued L/A 11/8/1826,
Joshua Danforth, Thomas J. Dasher, secs, Richmond, AB
STEWART, Thomas, LWT dtd 2/2/1852 pvd 1/1853 names wife, Rachael,
Cherokee
STEWART, Wiley, orph of James, decd, James R. Rusk, gdn, Joshua
McConnell, sur, 1/14/1856, Cherokee, GB
STEWART, William, decd, Roland Bivins, admr, James W. Bivins,
sur, 9/7/1847, Bibb, AB
STEWART, William, decd, attorney, Joseph Woodruff, admr,
10/3/1783, Chatham, Adms
STICK, Benjamin, decd, David Montaigut of Savannah, attorney, for
Samuel Stick to administer estate 7/6/1787, Chatham, Adms
STILES, Benjamin, decd, Samuel and Joseph Stiles, exrs of LWT
11/17/1789, Chatham, Adms
STILL, M. Robert, decd, Wyatt Heflin, gdn of orphs: Thomas,
Martha, John D. and Robert M. Still 1/6/1817, Simon Reaves,
Thomas B. Malone, secs, Richmond, GB
STINER, David and Christian, decd, Samuel Kraus and Mrs. Margaret
Stiner, relict of David, apply for adm of ests 9/19/1794,
Effingham, Misc
STINSON, Michael, decd, William Castleberry, admr 8/24/1835,
Peter Ussrey, William H. Brickley, surs, Warren, AB
STIRK, John, decd, Thomas Polhill applies for admr de bonis non
2/16/1802, Effingham, Misc
STITH, Holly, late of Coweta Co., decd, John Hall, admr, David J.
Bailey, sur, 5/23/1835, Butts, AB
STITH, Millie, decd, John Hobson, admr w/LWT annexed 2/4/1811,
(and w/LWT of William Stith annexed) Solomon Lockett, Timothy
Matthews, surs, Warren, AB
STITH, William, decd, Milly Stith petitioned court for L/T on LWT
pvd by John Stith, Hartwell Jones and John Henery 6/4/1808,
Warren, MIC
STITH, William, Sr., decd, William Stith, Jr., admr, 4/29/1799,
Warren, MIC

STOCKMAN, John, decd, Mrs. Rosanna Stockman and Mr. Christian Shubtrine apply for admx 12/17/1796, Effingham, Misc
STOCKS, Isaac, decd, apprs: Davis Gresham, John Cook, O. Porter, 4/15/1796, Greene, Misc
STOCKTON, Andrew H., decd, L/A to B. F. Bomar 6/6/1859, Fulton
STODGILL, Joel, decd, Martitia Stodgill and Calbe Oliver apply for L/A 9/14/1795; inv includes slaves, Francis Satterwhite, Peter Stubbs, James Carter, Benjamin Fortson, apprs, Elbert, AR
STOKES, A. H., decd, E. P. Watkins issued L/A 1/9/1860, Fulton
STOKES, Ann, decd, L/A to Wm Stokes 7/12/1829, Washington
STOKES, Archibald Y., decd, L/A to Young Stokes 12/4/1821, Simeon Walker, sec, Morgan, AB
STOKES, Drury Jackson, orph of Drury, decd, L/G issued James Jones, 1829, Washington
STOKES, Georgiana, orph of Drury, decd, L/G to James Jones 1829, Washington
STOKES, Georgianna, orph of Drury, David Robison issued L/G 7/5/1842; Allen Smith issued L/G 5/25/1842, Washington
STOKES, John C., orph of Richard H., decd, Richard H. Stokes, gdn, 9/24/1830, Peter Lamar, Wm W. Stokes, secs, Lincoln, GB
STOKES, John R., orph f William, decd, John Hardin issued L/G 11/14/1836, Washington
STOKES, Matthew T., decd, Sally Stokes, gdn of orphs: Mary Elizabeth and Sarah M., 9/1/1823, A. Hearnsberger and Stephen Hearnsberger, secs, Lincoln, GB
STOKES, Nancy, decd, L/A to Almarin Dillard 3/6/1832, Washington
STOKES, Nancy, orph of William, decd, John Hardin, gdn, 11/14/1836, Washington
STOKES, Richard H., decd, Nicholas G. Barksdale, gdn of orphs: Richard S. and John C. 1/1/1829, Acmstead T. Stokes, Thomas L. Walton, secs, Lincoln, GB
STOKES, William, decd, inv 2/14/1797 includes slaves and 600 acres on Beaverdame Creek, 30 acres on Oconee River, Elbert, AR
STOKES, William A., orph of William A., decd, Micajah T. Anthony, gdn, 3/2/1829, Nicholas G. Barksdale, John Moss, secs; 3/3/1834, Nicholas G. Barksdale, gdn, Lincoln, GB
STONE, Mary, wld, decd, Wm Stone, admr 11/18/1822, Joseph Hill, Henry Heath, surs, Warren, AB
STONE, Micajah, decd, Mary Stone, admx 2/14/1805, Robert Jenkins, Jeremiah Bell, surs, Warren, AB
STONE, Micajah, decd, Wm Stone, admr de bonis non 11/18/1832, Joseph Hill, Henry Heath, surs, Warren, AB
STONE, Rolling, ordered that poor child be bound to David Kennedy for 6 yrs 5/5/1821, Bulloch, MIC
STONE, Samuel, decd, inv and appraisement by Christopher F. Bunce, Joseph Knight, Abraham Richards, Alexander Knight 9/10/1821, Bulloch, Misc
STONE, Sarah Ann, Jenk E. Young, gdn, Dooly, OD
STORER, Thomas, decd, Robt Allen, Matthew Clark, admrs, 9/20/1790, Chatham, Adms
STORIE, James, decd, John Storie of Savannah, tailor, admr 12/16/1786, Chatham, Adms
STORY, Mahala, orph of Asa, bound to Levi Stanford until age 16, she now being 7 yrs old on the 7th of this month, 11/1/1813, Warren, MIC, GB
STORY, Richard, decd, Rachel Wells issued L/A 10/2/1784, David Parryman, Stephen Collins, secs, Richmond, AB
STOTESBURY, John, apptd gdn of his minor ch: Arthur, John, Peter, Henry, James and George 6/3/1833, Camden, MIC
STOUT, Jehu, decd, Phillip Low, admr, 3/9/1785, Liberty, Ests
STOVALL, George, James Christian, gdn, 1806, Elbert, GR

STOVALL, Linas, decd, Stephen Stovall, gdn for orphs: Mary, Matilda and Thomas 11/2/1835, Thomas Florence, Joshua Daniel, secs, Lincoln, GB
STOVALL, Stephen, gdn for his orphs: Anderson J., Stephen B., Jane E., children by his decd wife, Jane Jennings Stovall 1/4/1833, Charles Jennings, sec, Lincoln, GB
STOVER, John, decd, Jacob Stover, admr, A. Allison, Elijah McCoy, surs, 4/4/1853, Cherokee, AB
STOW, Abraham, decd, Eaton Hanes, gdn of orphs: William Columbus, George W., Mary J., Nancy P., Andrew J. & Abraham F.; Mary Stow, John Clark, Wm Sitton, secs; Mary Stow, gdn, 3/4/1851, Hall, GB
STOWER, Willy, illegitimate child, John Stoner, gdn 11/1830, Habersham, MIC
STOY, Frederick, decd, of Augusta, Abiel Camfield and Wm Micoy issued L/A 1/14/1822, John Howard, Benjamin Hall, secs; 1823 retn, receipts from Abigail Stoy for herself and minors and Henry W. Stoy, one of heirs, Richmond, AB
STRAWTHER (or STROTHER), Samuel, orph of Francis, decd, Thomas R. Strawther, gdn 11/4/1839, David Campbell, John G. Strawther, secs, Lincoln, GB
STREET, Samuel, decd, Samuel Street issued L/A 5/3/1813; admr makes retn 1/6/1817, Jackson, OM
STRENGTH, Lemuel, a poor child abt 11 yrs old bound to John Chafin until he becomes of age 1/7/1822, Jasper, OM
STRIBLING, Anthony, decd, Francis Stribling, gdn of orphs: Martha, Mitchell, Patrick and Dennis 1/1/1838, Simpson Stribling, sec, Lincoln, GB
STRICKLAND, Henry, decd, Walton Harris, counsel for admrs of estate, prays gdn be apptd for: Clement, Isaac and Nancy; Wilson Strickland apptd gdn of Clement and Isaac, Hardy Strickland apptd gdn to Nancy 3/2/1812, Jackson, OM
STRICKLAND, Irvin, decd, F. M. Strickland issued L/A 7/6/1851, Hiram Liles, sec, Hall, AB
STRICKLAND, Jacob, decd, planter, pvd 8/3/1804 names wife, Priscilla; ch: Faithee (her daus, Priscilla and Elizabeth Myers), Tamer, Isaac, Priscilla, Mary, Sarah, Elizabeth, Henry, Wilson, & Sarah, dtd 4/4/1804, Franklin, IMW
STRICKLAND, Jacob, decd, Samuel Parrish and wife, Elizabeth, apply for admn 5/12/1798, Effingham, Misc
STRICKLAND, John M., orph, Bathsheba Strickland, gdn 7/8/1828, R. H. I. Holley apptd gdn 1/1829, Butts, GB, ER
STRICKLAND, John Milledge, illegitimate child, William Stroud apptd gdn 11/1/1819, Jasper, OM
STRICKLAND, Kinchen, decd, A. J. Mundy, admr, Jesse Ward, Reuben Wallis, surs, 3/1848, 1852 retn, Fayette, AB
STRICKLAND, Lewis, decd, inv 9/13/1838, James Smith, G. Moore, S. P. Smith, apprs, Tattnall, I&A
STRICKLAND, Martha E., orph of Irvin, Martha Strickland, gdn, 10/4/1852, Hall, GB
STRICKLAND, Odessa, minor orph of James A., decd, Anderson M. Parker, gdn, 3/5/1860, ernon S. Grier, Butts, ER
STRICKLAND, Rebecca's minor heirs mentioned in retn of Penelope Archer, gdn for Labinah and Mary Ann Archer, orphs of John, 4/27/1836, Tattnall, I&A
STRINGER, Marah, minor, John Stringer, gdn, 5/4/1840, Brice McEver, sec, Hall, GB
STRINGER, William, minor, John Stringer, gdn, 5/4/1840, Brice McEver, sec, Hall, GB
STRINGFELLOW, Henry, decd, Wm Cooper, admr, land sold in S. C. to Bennett Stringfellow 1835; purchasers at sale: Gideon Croxton, Kennedy Dennard, John Sims, Green Ball, James Bates, Lee Blackmon, Nathan Clifton, etc., Stewart, Adms

STRINGFIELD, J. B., decd, John McKinne issued L/A 3/12/1816, James Gardner, Gilbert Longstreet, secs, Richmond, AB
STROBAKER, Mary, Robert M. Williamson, gdn, p. 101, Screven, OM
STROBBAR, Alexander and Laurina chose Henry J. Strobber as gdn 5/6/1844, Effingham, MIC
STROBBAR, John D., decd, Henry J. Strobbar applies for L/A 1/23/1844, Effingham, MIC
STRODDAR, Shadrack, decd, Lettice Stroddar, admx 9/14/1816, Wm Goyne, sur, Warren, AB
STROM, G. W., decd, Elizabeth Strom, admx 7/16/1874, Webster, OD
STROMON, Charles, Henry L. Kelly, gdn, petitions to remove gdnship from Stewart Co. to Webster Co. 4/1869, Webster, OD
STROMON, Marietta, Henry L. Kelly, gdn, petitions to remove gdnship from Stewart Co. to Webster Co. 4/1869, Webster, OD
STRONG, Elijah, decd, bond of Rebecca Strong, Lewis Pope, Burwell Pope, all of Oglethorpe Co. as admrs 11/20/1795, Franklin, OM
STRONG, Isham, decd, Jacob Lindsey, admr, makes retns 10/25/1802, Jackson, OM
STRONG, Penina, orph of Elijah, decd, John K. Binford, gdn, 9/5/1814, Wm Ogilvie, John Ector, surs, Clarke, GB
STRONG, William, decd, Jack F. Cook, gdn of Elijah Munford, George Jackson, John, Madison and Harriet Strong, orphs, 11/1/1813, Thomas Moore, Joseph Brown, surs, Clarke, GB
STROTHER, Francis, decd, John G. Strother, gdn of orphs: Thomas A., George S. and Chaply 3/2/1829, Jeremiah G. Griffin, John B. Hamock, secs, Lincoln, GB
STROTHER, John G. and Lucinda T., orphs of Francis, John C. Jordan, gdn, 1/4/1825, James Lockhart, Travis McKinney, secs, Lincoln, GB
STROTHER, William, decd, Susannah Strother, admx 4/20/1795, David Kelly, suc, Warren, AB
STROTHER, William, orph of Francis, decd, Thomas halliday, gdn, 11/3/1820, Wm O'Neal, sec, Lincoln, GB
STROUD, Edward, decd, David McKinney issued L/.A 1/6/1808, George Smith Houston, sec, Richmond, AB
STROUD, Isham, decd, Wm Moss apptd admr 10/29/1792, Garrard Walthall, Wm Alston, apprs, Elbert, AR
STROUD, James and John, minors of Thomas, decd, Robt Higdon, gdn, Stephen Swain, sur, 1/14/1837, Emanuel, GB
STROUD, Mark, decd, LWT 6/7/1798, wife, Martha, ch: Wm, Levi, Eli, Mary, Sarah, Alban, Orien, Tillatha; exrs, Jonathan Melton, Isaac Crow, pvd by George Norsworthy 11/5/1798, Hancock, AA
STROUD, Thomas, decd, Sarah Stroud, wid, apptd admx 9/1/1783, Wilkes, MxR
STROUD, Thomas, minor of Thomas, decd, Robt Higdon, gdn, Stephen Swain, sur, 1/3/1837, Emanuel, GB
STROUD, William, decd, Barsheba Stroud, admx, Robt C. Mays, Robt W. Harkness, Henry S. Mays, surs, 1/14/1840; appraisal 2/1/1842, 630 acres, apprs: Richard Shepard, T. L. Grimmet, Algernon S. Grier, Butts, AB, ER
STROZIER, John, decd, Peter Strozier, Valentine Thrasher, Abram Evans issued L/A 9/16/1824, Morgan, AB
STUART, (or STEWART) Samuel, decd, L/A to Hardy Howard 11/4/1816; admr asks that slave be sold 1/7/1817, Jackson, OM
STUART, James, decd, Eli McConnell, admr, 10/9/1854, Cherokee, AB
STUBBLEFIELD, Peter, decd, of Columbia Co., LWT pvd 11/8/1794, Evans Long, Maj. Nicholas Long, Thomas Haynes, John Graves and William Walton, exrs, Columbia, Ests
STUBBS, Alston F., decd, John M. Griswald, admr, Samuel Griswald, suR, 1/15/1850, Bibb, AB
STUBBS, Elenor, orph of George, decd, James Stubbs apptd gdn 1/3/1837, Randolph

STUBBS, George, decd, William Stubbs, admr, 1/7/1840, Randolph
STUBBS, Sarah, decd, Simon L. Whitaker, Dennis Stubbs, admrs, Oliver J. Head, John O. Dickson, John D. Stell, surs, 11/1851, 1852-1854, Fayette, AB
STUBBS, William, decd, Rowland Stubbs, admr de bonis non, R. K. Holliday, sur, 5/1852, Fayette, AB
STUCKEY, John, Sr., decd, John Stuckey issued L/A 7/3/1815, Jeptha Daniel, Jonathan Lyon, sec; 1818 Hester Stuckey apptd admx, Richmond, AB
STUCKEY, Lewis, decd, L/A to Mary Stuckey 1/4/1819, Laurens, AB
STUCKEY, William, decd, Sarah Stuckey issued L/A 3/6/1821, Thomas H. Jones, Armstead Fulcher, secs, Richmond, AB
STUDSTILL, Hustus, decd, Thomas Studstill, admr, 1/4/1803, Camden, MIC
STUDSTILL, Hustus, decd, ordered heirs of E. L., Sr., decd, Waynesborough, Samuel Sturges, Sr. issued L/A 11/7/1826, John Whitehead, Samuel Dowse, secs, Richmond, AB
STURGIS, Henry, decd, Allen H. Curry, gdn for orphs: Polly and Mariah 7/1/1833, Lincoln, GB
SUARIS, Antoine, decd, Rachel Suaris, James M. Lindsey and Charles Stahl apptd admrs 1/5/1804, Camden, MIC
SUGS, Aben, son of Lucinda, age 12 on Jan 12th last, bound to Thomas Bowen for 9 yrs., 5/7/1858, Isaac Bowen, sec, White, GB
SULLEY, David, decd, Asa C. Shackleford, gdn of orphs: Sarah Ann and Allen Brewer Sulley 1/1/1838, Randolph
SULLIVAN, Margaret, minor over age 14, James Smylie, Jr., gdn, 2/5/1818, Liberty, MIC
SULLIVAN, Mark, decd, Richard E. Story, gdn of orphs-Sylvanus, Susannah, Silas, Mary Jane, Abel, Elvira, 2/13/1854, Houston, GB
SULLIVAN, Samuel, decd, Thomas Sullivan issued L/A 8/10/1786, Owen and Mark Sullivan, secs, Richmond, AB
SULLIVAN, Samuel, decd, Ulysses and Mary Ann Sullivan apply for L/A 2/15/1853, Henry P. Wooten, William C. Gill; Ulysses Sullivan applies for L/A 4/19/1859, Lee
SULLIVAN, Thomas Clubb, minor over age 14, James Smylie, Jr., gdn, 2/5/1818, Liberty, MIC, GB
SULLIVAN, William, minor orph of John, decd, Elizabeth Miller apptd gdn 9/5/1814, Jasper, OM
SUMMERALL, Henry, decd, Charles Wakefield prays admrs will give him title to land in Oglethorpe Co. 10/29/1803, Jasper, OM
SUMMERALL, Jesse, decd, inv dtd 6/22/1792, Effingham, Misc
SUMMERGILL, Thomas, decd, William M. Arnold, admr, A. N. Robinson, sur, 12/2/1872, Cherokee, AB
SUMMERLIN, Elizabeth, decd, inv 10/18/1838, apprs: M. Collins, Frederick Noland, H. Cobb, Tattnall, I&A
SUMMERLIN, Hardy, decd, 1/5/1844 Garrett Williams and Jacob Summerlin testify that they heard death wishes 12/9/1843 when he named wife, Penelope, and children: James, Berryann A. and Eliza Summerlin, heirs, Bulloch, Misc
SUMMERLIN, Sarah, decd, James H. Amason, admr, Warren Amason, sur, 7/23/1849, Bibb, AB
SUMMERLIN, Thomas, decd, James Ramie and Joseph Summerlin issued L/A 12/22/1823; Polly, gdn of orphs-James J., Anna, Gilley, Mary Ann and William, 12/22/1823, Morgan, AB, GB
SUMMERS, Emily Juhan, minor, John Amason, gdn, 1830, Washington
SUMMERS, J. M., gdn for William and Sallie Y., makes retns 7/1862, Webster, OD
SUMMONS, William, decd, 3/3/1856 ordered that James Glass, Micajah Picket, William Averet, James H. Averet and James C. Kindreck distribute estate to heirs, Webster, OD
SUMNER, Edward, decd, Thomas Sumner, Peter Winn qualified admrs 1/18/1790, Liberty, Ests

300

SUMNER, Elizabeth, decd, Peter Winn qualified admr 1/25/1793, Liberty, Ests
SUMNER, Job, decd, Jesse Sumner, admr, 5/14/1790, Chatham, Adms
SUMNER, Joseph, decd, John C. Sumner, admr, appraisal of estate 2/20/1828, Emanuel, A
SUMNER, Joseph, Mary, Richard and Ruth, minors of Richard, Richard and Elizabeth C. Sumner, gdns, 11/5/1821, Emanuel, GB
SUMNER, Thomas, decd, Peter Winn, James Wilson, exrs, 1792, Liberty, Ests
SUMTER, Maria Flanagan (formerly Waddell) now of insane mind, Nicholas Waddell, gdn, John Messer, James Adkins, Birdwell Hill, surs, 5/5/1851, Cherokee, GB
SUNDERLAND, James, decd, A. C. Ernest, admr, Daniel F. Clark, sur, 7/4/1848, Bibb, AB
SURRENCY, John W., orph of James, decd, Elizabeth Surrency's retn as gdn 11/2/1840, Tattnall, I&A
SUTT, Benjamin, decd, Benjamin Sutt, gdn of orphs-Benjamin, James, Henry, George and Elizabeth, minors, 7/1/1839, Lincoln, GB
SUTTLES, Micajah, embecile, Joseph Willis, gdn, 7/5/1860; Joseph Willis, admr w/LWT annexed 11/5/1860, Fulton, GB
SUTTON, Henry, bound to David S. M. McCravy 3/6/1816, Jackson, OM
SUTTON, Lydia and Martha, Lane Sutton, gdn, Dooly, OD
SUTTON, Roseanna and Leon, decd, L/A to S. Loving 8/18/1808, Tattnall, MIC
SUTTON, Theodore, decd, Jane Sutton, admx, 11/2/1846; apprs, Joseph Sutton, Benjamin Grantham, A. M. Dorsett, Nathan Futrell, Silas Powell, Eli Varnedoe, John Bodiford, Jr., Dooly, I&A
SUTTON, William, decd, Alsay Sutton and James McClusky applied for L/A 6/18/1791; sale by exr, James Sutton 11/2/1799, 1800 retn, board and keep for Sally, Joel and George Sutton, expenses to Oglethorpe Co., Elbert, AB
SWANSON, William, ct ordered adm on real estate with John M. Sims, Joseph Baughan, admrs, John Hubbard, Beverly Daniel, sec, 7/1809, Oglethorpe, OM
SWANSON, William, decd, James and John Swanson vs. est; ct ordered the LWT as regards real estate be void, but that personal property be admitted for probate, 1/1809, Oglethorpe, OM
SWIFT, John, Sr., decd, Benjamin Stripling, Jesse Embree & Allan Johnson, Jr. to settle estate to heirs 3/3/1807, Tattnall, MIC
SWIFT, William A., orph of William, decd, John D. Swift, gdn, 9/15/1825, James Grimes, sec, Morgan, GB
SWILLY, John, decd, Morgan Brown, admr, 11/14/1836, Washington
SWINNEY, E. B., decd, S. Bell makes retn 7/1863, Webster, OD
SWINNEY, John M., orph, Elizabeth Swinney, gdn, makes retn 5/7/1838, Tattnall, I&A
SWINNEY, John, decd, appraisal 3/3/1800; recpts-Jeremiah Moore, Ransom Swinney, Jas Bishop, Jeremiah Moore gdn for Dudley Swinney, Rosey Swinney gdn for Wilson Swinney, Jno Freeman, Jesse Baker, Jno Shackelford, J. Dudley Swinney, Hancock, AA
SWINT, John, decd, LWT dtd 1/12/1801 pvd 3/28/1801, wife, Elizabeth, ch-John (when 21), Edmond, Frederick, James, William, Joseph, Samuel, Hancock, AAAA
SYKES, Benjamin, decd, William Sykes issued L/A 5/17/1816, James Sykes, Reuben Walker, Abraham Walker, secs, Richmond, AB
SYKES, James, decd, Josiah Sykes, John J. Harper, admrs, 9/14/1835, Harris
SYKES, Joseph, decd, of Richmond Co., Ga., Charles Jackson gtd L/A 9/13/1790, Columbia, Ests
SYKES, Joseph, decd, of Savannah, Ga., 7/1795 inventory by William Wallace, George Barnes, Amasa Jackson, Richmond
SYKES, William, decd, Savannah Merchant, Joseph Sykes, admr, 12/30/1786, Chatham, Adms

SYMONDS, Benjamin, decd, John Peter Canget, admr, 5/21/1786,
Chatham, Adms
TALLY, Abraham, decd, Sally Tally issued L/A 9/3/1804, Elijah
Walker and John Lambeth, secs, Richmond, AB
TALLY, Elisha, decd, Thomas Tally issued L/A 1/1/1821, Jesse
Moreley, James Turner, secs; Elizabeth Tally, gdn of orphs:
Obediah and John 5/17/1821, Richard Copeland, sec, Morgan, AB, GB
TAMNERS, John, decd, John Chasen apptd gdn of heirs of, Chesnut
Summer, William Douglas, surs, 11/24/1827, Hancock, GB
TANNER, Fleming P., under age 14, Andrew A. Barnes apptd gdn, his
mother, Celia Barnes, wife of A. A. Barnes, consenting thereto
1/5/1830, Camden, MIC, GB
TANNER, John M. D., decd, Charles Tanner, admr, A. L. Robinson,
sec, 1/18/1830, Butts, AB
TANNER, Simon A., age 15, Andrew A. Barnes apptd gdn, his mother,
Celia Barnes, wife of A. A. Barnes, consenting thereto 1/5/1830,
Camden, MIC, GB
TANNER, Zilpha, under age 14, Andrew A. Barnes apptd gdn, her
mother, Celia Barnes, wife of A. A. Barnes, consenting thereto,
1/5/1830, Camden, MIC, GB
TARBOROUGH, William, decd, Alsay Sutton and James McClusky
applied for L/A 6/18/1791; sale by exr, James Sutten 11/2/1799,
1800 retn, board and keep for Sally, Joel and George Sutten,
expenses to Oglethorpe Co., Elbert, AB
TAYLOR, Elijah, decd, Moses Brian issued L/A 3/7/1842, William H.
and Mary Taylor, secs, Hall, AB
TAYLOR, Elizabeth, orph of William J., decd, Lucy Taylor, gdn,
3/10/1859, Paulding, GB
TAYLOR, Francis, decd, Wade White, admr, 11/7/1825 bond, H. W.
Scoville, sur, Clarke, AB
TAYLOR, George, decd, LWT dtd 4/1/1863 (dim), White
TAYLOR, James, decd, James Crane, admr, 7/17/1835, Effingham, MIC
TAYLOR, James, minor son of John L., decd, acctg recd and appvd
by George G. Fleming, gdn, 1/4/1847, Camden, MIC
TAYLOR, James C., orph of William J., decd, Lucy Taylor, gdn,
3/10/1859, Paulding, GB
TAYLOR, Jane, decd, John Benby, exr, applied for Zachariah Motes
as gdn of orphs of James Wilson, decd, 2/7/1827, Camden, MIC
TAYLOR, Jane, decd, LWT pvd, John Bailay, Jr. qualified as exr
5/6/1820, Camden, MIC
TAYLOR, Jane, minor dau of John L., decd, acctg recd and appvd by
George G. Fleming, gdn, 1/4/1847, Camden, MIC
TAYLOR, Jared, Deasant Ray, admr, 10/17/1845; apprs: James S.
Bealle, Folton K. Lewis, John Ross; purchasers at sale: Elender
Stephens, Norvell Stephens, Chadwell Culpepper, Thomas H. Dawson,
John C. Sutton, Dooly, I&A
THACKER, Margaret, decd, William Sitton issued L/A 7/3/1854,
William D. Pittman, sec, Hall, AB
THACKER, Mary, orph of James, decd, Joseph Greer issued L/G,
Jonathan Martin, sec, 6/4/1851, Hall, GB
THACKER, William, decd, Hiram A. Thacker issued L/A 10/2/1849, S.
G. Furr, sec, Hall, AB
THARP, C. A., decd, LWT dtd 10/1/1868 names wife, Elizabeth and
ch: Frances, ch of Benjamin, Joseph and David, Simeon Jefferson,
dau, Leaner Horn, Sonezer Passmore, Marthy Ann Jones, Elizabeth
Jessup, Frances and Emaline Nash. Twiggs, Misc
THARP, Elizabeth, decd, 1/24/1873 retn of Simeon Tharp, one of
exrs, Twiggs, Misc
THARP, Nancy, decd, LWT names ch: Thomas S., Ida E. Patterson
(decd), and heir of decd son, W. D., and G. W. Tharp, 10/5/1900,
Twiggs, Misc

THARP, S. A. (Reverand), decd, buyers at sale 12/4/1872-Jefferson, Bird and G. W. Tharp, Bob Solomon, Allen Deshage, J. A. Burkett, heirs: Jefferson Tharpe, Thomas H. Jones, E. A. Marsh, H. D. Horn, Fannie Tharp, Twiggs, Misc

THAXTON, Charles A., orph of Charles C., decd, Yelventon Thaxton, gdn, Samuel W. Thaxton, Jarret Weaver, sur, 1/3/1837, Butts, GB

THAXTON, Charles G., minor of Charles G., decd, Gideon Mathis, gdn, inv, notes due by Yelventon and Wiley Thaxton, Nelson Cofield, Thomas Beardin, 1/1/1831, Butts, ER

THAXTON, John P., decd, LWT pvd 7/11/1833, Harris

THIGPEN, Green, illegitimate of Celia, Robert Whitefield issued L/G, 1829 and 7/2/1838, Washington

THIGPEN, Travis, decd, John D. Gillis, admr, William Thigpen, sur, 5/5/1849, Emanuel, AB

THOMAS, Absolom, of St. George Parish to Sabra Perkins of St. Paul's Parish, slave, 1/3/1781, Wilkes, MxR

THOMAS, Allen, decd, Mrs. Allen Thomas dismissed as admx 1/5/1842, Camden, MIC

THOMAS, Allen, decd, Priscilla Thomas produced LWT and qualified as extrx; pvd by John Bailey 1/3/1826, Camden, MIC

THOMAS, Ann B., Mrs., LWT pvd by James Barnard; Hugh Brown qualified exr, 11/13/1837, Camden, MIC

THOMAS, Ann B., decd, Hugh Brown, co-exr with W. B. Thomas, complained that W. B. Thomas is insolvent and failed to make retns 6/7/1842, Camden, MIC

THOMAS, Benjamin, decd, Matthias Adams and Clement T. Morely issued L/A 1/4/1830, William C. Phillips, Wiley Adams, secs, Montgomery, AB

THOMAS, Catherine, free person of colour, M. M. Patton, gdn, 6/1/1863, White, GB

THOMAS, Clary, Darious Echols apptd gdn 7/1833, Habersham, MIC

THOMAS, David, decd, Mary Thomas issued L/A 1/10/1832 and 7/10/1834, Baldwin

THOMAS, George, decd, Milton Anthony issued temp L/A 5/29/1820, Elisha Searl, John Marshall, secs, Richmond, AB

THOMAS, George W. apptd gdn for his minor brothers, Joseph, Robert and David, orphs of late, Joseph Thomas, 6/21/1830, Camden, MIC, GB

THOMAS, Green B., decd, L/A to John G. Thomas 9/2/1833, Baldwin

THOMAS, Hannah, decd, Darius Echols, gdn of minors, to sell Lot 68, 10th Dist., Carroll Co. and 231, 13th Dist., Muscogee Co., drawn by illegitimate children, 5/5/1834, Habersham, MIC

THOMAS, Hugh, decd, Nancy Thomas, Eli Whidden issued L/A 7/3/1820, Laurens, AB

THOMAS, James, decd, Azariah Mims issued L/A 7/2/1866, Fulton

THOMAS, James, decd, Basil Lamar and Morris Kelley issued L/A 6/2/1806, Tattnall, MIC

THOMAS, James, decd, Boanum, admr, 7/1/1833, Thomas Haynes, Stephen Thomas, secs, Hall, AB

THOMAS, James, decd, Hugh Brown petitioned to be relieved as bondsman for William B. Thomas 7/10/1839, Camden, MIC

THOMAS, James, decd, John S. Thomas issued L/A 9/20/1833, Baldwin

THOMAS, James, decd, William B. Thomas and Mrs. Ann B. Thomas, wid, apptd admrs 3/6/1836, Camden, MIC

THOMAS, James M., inf child of Ann B. Thomas, wid; W. B. Thomas, one of her exrs and gdn of child, filed complaint against Hugh Brown, co-exr and gdn, alleging Brown made unjust charges in his retns 3/4/1859, Camden, MIC

THOMAS, Joel, decd, William Thomas and John Newman apptd admrs 9/2/1793; inv includes 100 acres on Savannah river, 200 acres in Franklin Co., br of Hudson River; apprs: Moses Haynes, John Ross, Thomas Scales, Elbert, AR

THOMAS, John, decd, Frederick Daniel applies for adm 4/20/1799,
gtd 7/18/1799, William Mims, sur, 4/20/1799, Warren, MIC, AB
THOMAS, John, decd, Frederick Daniel, admr, 7/18/1799, William
Mims, sur, Warren, AB
THOMAS, John, decd, Jonathan Thomas applied for adm of his bro.,
6/13/1814, Glynn, MIC, AB
THOMAS, Joseph, decd, LWT pvd, George W. Thomas, Jane W. Thomas
and John Tompkins qualified as exrs 6/1/1829; exr, directed to
pay widow, Jane W. Thomas, $225.48 out of est funds for the
shares of herself and infant, Martha E. Thomas, 1/4/1832; George
W. Thomas, exr, reports he has on hand considerable amt of money
of est; authorized to invest it in bank stock, 6/2/1835; exr gtd
leave to sell ten lots, town of Jefferson 10/10/1836, Camden, MIC
THOMAS, Joseph, decd, Mrs. Jane W. Thomas, wid, applied for her
sh of est w/George W. Thomas & John Tompkins, exrs, objecting;
1/4/1831, div to: Mrs. Jane W. Thomas, wid; Martha E., her dau;
Joseph, Jr.; Robert; David Thomas, Camden, MIC
THOMAS, Madison, a minor W. B. Brown apptd gdn 1/5/1852, Camden,
MIC, GB
THOMAS, Martha E., infant dau of Jane W. Thomas who was apptd gdn
1/6/1836, Camden, MI
THOMAS, Martin, Darious Echols apptd gdn 7/1833, Habersham, MIC
THOMAS, Philip, decd, Edward Lord Thomas and Elizabeth C. Thomas
applied for L/A 7/9/1805, Franklin, IMW
THOMAS, Phillip, decd, Edward Lloyd Thomas and Elizabeth C.
Thomas apply for L/A 1/5/1807, Franklin, OM
THOMAS, Ralph, decd, Abiel Camfield issued L/A 12/14/1822, John
Howard, Solomon Kneeland, John McCormich, Samuel Hale, Augustin
Slaughter, apprs, Richmond, AB
THOMAS, Sarah, free person of colour, M. M. Patton, gdn,
6/1/1863, White, GB
THOMAS, Sopha, free person of colour, M. M. Patton, gdn,
6/1/1863, White, GB
THOMAS, Stewart, decd, Bell or Bill Thompson, admr, 9/14/1832,
Samuel Newman, Daniel Dennis, surs, Warren, AB
THOMAS, Theophilus, decd, Lucy Thomas, admx, p. 79, Screven, OM
THOMAS, Thomas, free person of colour, M. M. Patton, gdn,
6/1/1863, White, GB
THOMAS, Thomas L., decd, Mrs. Elizabeth Thomas apptd admr, John
C. Peek, William H. C. Cowan, John W. Terry, secs, 6/2/1862,
Fulton, AB
THOMAS, Wiley, decd, Isaac Humphries and Rebecca Thomas issued
L/A 5/6/1816, Andrew Maddox, James Caldwell, secs, Morgan, AB
THOMAS, Wiley, decd, Rebecca Thomas, gdn of orphs: Catherine,
Anderson, Merril, Wiley, Sims, Betsy, Jordan and Green Thomas,
1/11/1819; Charles Thompson, gdn, 1/7/1822, Morgan, GB
THOMAS, William, decd, Christina Thomas issued L/A 3/2/1812,
Jackson, OM
THOMAS, William, decd, Hardy Pitts, admr, 9/6/1824, Elijah Jones,
Robert Palmer, sucs, Warren, AB
THOMAS, Wyly, Darious Echols apptd gdn 7/1833, Habersham, MIC
THOMASON, John, decd, Zimri and Harmon Thomason issued L/A
11/2/1846, Young, H. D. and I. A. Thomason, secs, Hall, AB
THOMASON, Richard, decd, 2/1843, apprs: Jordan Hodges, William
Stokes, Jesse Cliatt; purchasers at sale: G. Barfield, Isaac
Cliatt, James M. Duncan, Elk Hooks, Jane Thomason (wid), J. M.
Whitaker, etc., Stewart, Adms
THOMPSON, Alexander, decd, 1808 retn, James and Alexander
Thompson, exrs; legatees receipts: William Langford, Sary
Robinson, Elbert, AR
THOMPSON, Berry E., Phereby Thompson, gdn, William Thompson, sur,
7/7/1829, Emanuel, GB

THOMPSON, Bryan, decd, Dorothy Thompson, admx, p. 100, 119, Screven, OM
THOMPSON, Buckner, decd, James Lanier issued L/A 1/6/1816, John Sparks, sec, Morgan, AB
THOMPSON, Burkett D., decd, Thomas J. Wray issued L/A 5/29/1839, Augustin Slaughter, Joel Catlin, secs, Richmond, AB
THOMPSON, Charles I., decd, LWT to ch: Henry C., Andrew J., William W., pvd Lumpkin Co. by Andrew J. Thompson, James Cantrell, Elias P. Bond, Andrew J. Logan 10/5/1857, Dawson, WB
THOMPSON, David, decd, leave to sell 230 acres of land gtd admrs 5/4/1812, Warren, MIC
THOMPSON, David, minor orph of James, decd, Matthew Thompson apptd gdn, Robert Thompson, Benjamin Hodnett, surs, 1/6/1806, Oglethorpe, MIC
THOMPSON, Drury, Jr., decd, 3/11/1809 appr of est by Samuel Watkins, Willis Thompson, Asa Thompson, Wm Brewer, Elbert, AR
THOMPSON, Elender, orph of Philemon, decd, Samuel Hester, gdn 5/4/1811, John Foster, sur, Clarke, GB
THOMPSON, Elizabeth, orph of George, decd, Clemenchus R. Zachary, gdn 1/10/1825, Benjamin Brown, Thomas Wilkerson, secs, Morgan, GB
THOMPSON, Elmira E., orph of Asa, decd, John Goodman, gdn, John W. McCork, sec, 3/5/1838, Butts, GB
THOMPSON, Elmiry E., minor, John Goodman, gdn, acct 6/4/1839, Butts, ER
THOMPSON, George, decd, William Gill, gdn of orphs: William G. and Elizabeth P., 7/7/1817, Jeremiah Davis, sec, Morgan, GB
THOMPSON, Hannah, minor orph of John, decd, Robert Thompson was apptd gdn, William Lasley, George Paschal, surs, 6/18/1805, Oglethorpe, MIC
THOMPSON, Hannah, orph of John, decd, chose Wm Stewart her gdn, James Swanson, Edward McGehee, secs, 1/1808, Oglethorpe, OM, GB
THOMPSON, Henry, decd, LWT pvd, L/T issued Hannah Thompson and John McMichael, 9/1/1817, Jasper, OM
THOMPSON, Isham, decd, John Thompson applied for L/A 3/26/1796; caveat 4/3/1796 by Elizabeth W. Thompson, inv includes slaves, Elbert, AR
THOMPSON, Isham, decd, appraisal 3/3/1800, Edmond Corley, admr; apprs: James Lucas, John Burch, Jerard Burch, Hancock, AA
THOMPSON, James, son of Allen, Jesse Barintine, gdn, James F. Johnson, sur, 5/1850, Fayette, GB
THOMPSON, James B., decd, LWT pvd 7/4/1814; H. B. Thompson apptd admr w/LWT annexed 10/3/1814, Warren, MIC
THOMPSON, James B., decd, Henry B. Thompson, admr w/LWT annexed, 10/3/1816, Chappel Heath, Joseph M. Semmes, surs, Warren, AB
THOMPSON, James C., minor, John Goodman, gdn, acct 6/4/1839, Butts, ER
THOMPSON, James C., orph of Asa, decd, John Goodman, gdn, John W. McCork, sec, 3/5/1838, Butts, GB
THOMPSON, John N., minor, John Goodman, gdn, acct 1838, Butts, ER
THOMPSON, John N., orph of Asa, decd, John Goodman, gdn, John W. McCork, sec, 3/5/1838, Butts, GB
THOMPSON, John, decd, Agnes Thompson, Thomas Hall, James Akins applied for L/A 11/6/1797, Greene, Misc
THOMPSON, John, decd, Nathaniel Thompson, admr, 1/6/1817, James Neal, Sr. Peyton Baker, surs, Warren, AB
THOMPSON, Joseph, minor orph of John, decd, Robert Thompson, gdn, Wm Lasley, George Paschal, surs, 6/18/1805, Oglethorpe, MIC
THOMPSON, Joseph, decd, William Thompson, Benjamin Morris, exrs, 9/3/1855, Fulton
THOMPSON, Keziah, Robert L. Burnet, gdn, having absconded from the State, Jane Gorman apptd gdn in his place 6/9/1809, Camden, MIC, GB

305

THOMPSON, Leuena, orph of Henry, decd, John E. Jones, gdn, Robert
C. Mays, sur, 9/7/1835, Butts, GB
THOMPSON, Littleberry, William C. Phillips, gdn, 8/7/1837,
Patrick Phillips, Phereba Thompson, secs, Montgomery, GB
THOMPSON, Lizzie, minor orph of Dr. Charles Thompson, Joseph
Thompson, gdn, 2/5/1867, Fulton, GB
THOMPSON, Lucy, Mrs., decd, LWT pvd, Alexander Thompson, exr,
2/7/1814, Warren, MIC
THOMPSON, Mariah Louisa, orph of Jeremiah, decd, William Parks,
gdn, 2/17/1834, Lincoln, GB
THOMPSON, Martha, Wm B. Fuller, gdn, M. M. Tidwell, John O.
Dickson, John L. Holliday, surs, 1854, Fayette, GB
THOMPSON, Mary, Wm B. Fuller, gdn, M. M. Tidwell, John O.
Dickson, John L. Holliday, surs, 1854, Fayette, GB
THOMPSON, Mary, minor dau of James, decd, Samuel Bellogh apptd
gdn 8/1802; failed to furnish bond, dismissed 6/24/1803,
Oglethorpe, MIC
THOMPSON, Moses, decd, Hannah Thompson, Moses Thompson, admrs,
12/1/1827, Giles Smith, Jonathan Huff, surs, Warren, AB
THOMPSON, Oliver, decd, Samuel Watkins, Robert and Jesse Thompson
apptd admrs 2/22/1792, inv includes a negro in Va.; Wm Thompson,
Sr., Wm Chisholm, Robert Easter, apprs, Elbert, AR
THOMPSON, Peter, decd, Clement Wilkins gtd L/A 10/3/1801,
Franklin, OM
THOMPSON, Peter, decd, James Seagrave apptd admr 6/7/1808,
Camden, MIC, AB
THOMPSON, Peter, decd, R. J. Snelling, admr, later, Thomas P.
Helton, 5/1835, Stewart, Adms
THOMPSON, Robert, decd, Robert Thompson, Jr. apptd admr 7/3/1810,
Warren, MIC, AB
THOMPSON, Robert, minor orph of Thomas, decd, John R. Wallace,
gdn, 7/7/1868, Fulton, GB
THOMPSON, Samuel, decd, S. J. Ramsey, admr, 1855, Cobb, BB
THOMPSON, Samuel B., decd, Jason J. Thompson, W. C. Osborn, admrs
12/21/1835, Harris
THOMPSON, Thomas, decd, L/A to George Edwards 4/1/1867, Fulton
THOMPSON, Wiley, orph, receipt of his gdn, Middleton Woods, for
money from George Woods, admr of Isham Thompson, decd, 2/19/1800,
Elbert, AR
THOMPSON, William, Mathew Jones, gdn, Wm J. Russell, sur, 1854,
Fayette, GB
THOMPSON, William, decd, Andrew Thompson issued L/A 5/7/1839,
Guilford G. Thompson, W. P. Reed, secs, Hall, AB
THOMPSON, William, decd, Catharine Thompson issued L/A 11/5/1790,
James Ingram, George Graves, sec, Richmond, AB
THOMPSON, William, decd, Susannah Jane Thompson issued L/A
10/7/1832, Palmer Goulding, Donald Fraser, secs, Bryan, CR
THOMPSON, William, decd, late of London, Alexander Mein apptd
admr, 6/9/1802, Camden, MIC
THOMPSON, William, decd, of Richmond Co., Catherine Thompson gtd
L/A 12/3/1790, Columbia, Ests
THOMPSON, William H., decd, John R. Warner issued L/A 1/5/1818,
Thomas Turner, sec, Morgan, AB
THOMSON, Ichabod, decd, William Wilkins issued L/A 5/2/1814,
Putnam, AB
THOMSON, James, decd, Merchant, William Thomson, Merchant, of
Savannah, admr 5/1/1785, Chatham, Adms
THOMSON, Pheriba, natural gdn to Berry C., her illegitimate child
6/8/1836, William C. and Patrick Phillips, Montgomery, GB
THORN, David, decd, Wm Sheppard, Sr., admr, p. 80, Screven, OM
THORNTON, Elizabeth, minor orph of Noel, decd, Richd Thornton,
gdn, Patton Wise, John Thornton, surs, 1/1805, Oglethorpe, MIC

THORNTON, Henry, decd, John Duncan, Richard Hingson, gdn of orphs 7/1/1833, Harris
THORNTON, John Willey, minor orph of Noel, decd, Richd Thornton, gdn, Patton Wise, John Thornton, surs, 1/1805, Oglethorpe, MIC
THORNTON, Jonah, decd, Wilkerson Jamison, admx, John J. Fard, Madison Jamison, sur, 7/9/1855, Cherokee, AB
THORNTON, Levicy (formerly Levicy Hammock), decd, Thomas Thornton, William Thornton, admrs 1/5/1835, Harris
THORNTON, Owen, minor orph of Noel, decd, Richard Thornton apptd gdn, Patton Wise, John Thornton, surs, 1/1805, Oglethorpe, MIC
THORTNON, Patsey, minor orph of Noel, decd, Richard Thornton, gdn, Patton Wise, John Thornton, surs, 1/1805, Oglethorpe, MIC
THORNTON, Richard, decd, LWT pvd 1/1808, Oglethorpe, OM
THORNTON, Sarah, LWT pvd 12/23/1844, William Thornton, Asa Chester, admrs, Harris
THORNTON, Thomas Johnson, minor orph of Noel, decd, Richard Thornton apptd gdn, Patton Wise, John Thornton, surs, 1/1805, Oglethorpe, MIC
THORNTON, William, decd, LWT pvd 7/2/1849, John T. Thornton, Shadrack Rowe, exrs, Harris
THORNTON, William, deed of gift to his son, John, a minor, 9/22/1797, Effingham, Misc
THRASHER, Benjamin, decd, Robert Walton and Reuben Payne gtd L/T 3/1802, Franklin, OM
THRASHER, Harbart, orph of Cloud, decd, Willitha C. Thrasher, gdn 5/6/1816, Wm Clark, Wm Fears, surs, Clarke, GB
THRASHER, Joseph A., decd, L/A to John J. Thrasher 11/2/1857, Fulton
THRASHER, Martha, orph of Isaac, decd, Talitha C. Thrasher, gdn, 11/4/1816, Clarke, GB
THRASHER, Pinkney, orph of Isaac, decd, Talitha C. Thrasher, gdn, 11/4/1816, Wm Clark, sur, Clarke, GB
THRASHER, Robert, decd, John Bryan, exr, to advertise sale of 210 acres where Thrasher lived for benefit of heirs and creditors 11/1/1811, Franklin, OM
THRASHER, Robert, decd, LWT dtd 1/5/1797 pvd 2/4/1797 names wife, Elizabeth; acct of Warren Philpott includes schooling for Betey Thrasher, dau of decd, 12/26/1799, also for keeping Elizabeth, dau of decd, 5 yrs, Franklin, OM
THRASHER, Sally, orph of Robert, late of Franklin Co., chose Capt. James Blair her gdn 9/2/1811, Franklin, OM
THREADCRAFT, George, decd, of South Carolina, Lachlan McIntosh, Sr. and George Threadcraft apptd admrs 10/9/1789, Chatham, Adms
THREEWITS, Joel, decd, William Cocks and Sally Threewits apply for admn, Thomas Cocks and Turner Persons, surs, 7/18/1797, Warren, MIC, AB
THRIFT, Robert J., decd, Jacob S. West issued L/A 1/8/1818, Washington
THROOP, Cary, decd, Thomas King issued L/A 5/6/1822, Laurens, AB
THURMAN, Samuel, decd, LWT exhibited 1/29/1837, George Carter, Hardy Crawford and James Huff, exrs, Harris
THURMAN, William, decd, Benjamin Thurman, admr, Wesley and William Hudson, secs, 5/6/1862, Fulton, AB
THURMAN, William, decd, James and Philip Thurman, admrs, bond 11/12/1810, Edward Bond, sur, Clarke, AB
THURMON, James M., orph of Benjamin, decd, Polly Thurmond, gdn, 12/7/1818, George Rochfort, sur, Clarke, GB
THURMOND, Benjamin, decd, Micajah Thurmond, gdn of: James M. and John B., orphs, 11/6/1817, Polly Thurmond and George Rockfort, surs, Clarke, GB
THURMOND, James, decd, inventory produced 9/3/1810, Jackson, OM

THURMOND, W. R. P., decd, Mrs. Narcissa P. Thurman apptd gdn of orphs: Sarah P., Mary Ann E., Charles R. and W. W., 2/2/1863, Fulton, GB

TIBBITTS, Moses, decd, John L. Anderson issued L/A 9/16/1822, Daniel S. Roman, sec; 1832 retn pd William Coffin, only heir of est, Richmond, AB

TICKNER, George C., decd, Mathew E. Williams applies for L/A 11/1/1852, Jesse M. Davis, John W. Jordan, sur, Lee

TIDWELL, David, decd, Clementus R. Zachry, gdn of orphs: Patsy, Mary Ann, Thomas and Nancy 5/1/1820, Thomas Wilkinson, Abner Jordan, secs, Morgan, GB

TIDWELL, W. J., decd, M. E. Tidwell, admr, H. Ritch, sur, 3/5/1866, Paulding, AB

TIGNER, Freeborn G., orph of Phillip, decd, John Foster, gdn, 10/4/1819, Hope H. Tigner, sur, Clarke, GB

TIGNER, Philip, Jr., orph of Phillip, decd, Edmund Elder, gdn, 10/4/1819, David Elder, sur, Clarke, GB

TIGNER, Urbin C., orph of Phillip, decd, William L. Franbrough, gdn, 10/4/1819, Wm Fambrough, sur, Clarke, GB

TIGNER, Young F., orph of Phillip, decd, Hope H. Tigner, gdn, 10/4/1819, John Foster, sur, Clarke, GB

TILGHMAN, Aaron, decd, Nathl Cocke, James Pearre, C. W. Simmons, apprs 7/30/1785, Richmond

TILLERY, Jeffery, illeg child of Margaret Tillery, Andrew Tenent, gdn, Amos Edmonds, sur, 9/5/1842, Butts, GB

TILLET, Samuel, decd, John Johnson, admr, 9/23/1783, Wilkes, MxR

TILLETT, George, decd, John Tillett, admr, 8/3/1835, Camden, MIC

TILLINGHAST, Daniel, decd, George Foster qualified as admr 9/14/1790, Liberty, Ests

TILLMAN, Daniel, decd, William J. Tillman applies for L/A 10/4/1853, Jonathan Tillman, Ashley Phillips, Jonathan Davis, Samuel Lindsey, Joel E. Hunter, sur, Lee

TILLMAN, Martha, decd, John Maroney, admr w/LWT annexed, John M. Chambers, sec, 3/13/1849; nephew, William Dixon Maroney; nieces-Mary Ann and Eliza Maroney naamed; Berry G. Tillman, exr, LWT dtd 3/20/1833, pvd 8/1848, Cherokee, AB

TILLOT, Giles, Jr., L/A gtd Wm Cunningham, planter, caveator on sd est 3/1784, Wilkes, MxR

TILLY, Stephen, decd, Ebenezer Tilly, admr, 10/6/1862, Samuel House, sur, DeKalb, AB

TILLY, Burgess, decd, Stephen and Nancy Tilly issued L/A 7/1829; John D. Chastain pets that decd in life gave his bond to him for Lot 46, 10th Dist., TGroup Co.; Stephen and Nancy Tilly, admrs, to make title, 5/1830, Habersham, MIC

TIMMONS, John, decd, William Myers, Macha Timmons qualified admrs 12/1787, Liberty, Ests

TINER, Elijah, decd, gift deed from John Wilson, Jr., shoemaker to Ephraim Tiner, son of Elijah, 10/3/1791, Effingham, Misc

TINSLEY, David, decd, John Tinsley & Jas Leatherlin L/A 5/4/1801, George Collins, John Rivers, sec; purchasers at sale: John and William Tinsley, Alex Wilson, Jas Leatherlin, Willoughby Barton, Benjamin Nowland, Jno Hatcher, Richmond, AB

TINSLEY, James, minor orph of John, decd, David Tinsley, gdn, 7/3/1837, John and Vincent Tinsley, secs, Richmond, GB

TINSLEY, Mariah, orph of Samuel, decd, Samuel Tinsley, gdn, Ralph Lemaster, John Nichols, secs, Hall, GB

TIPPEN, Dennis, Wiley Potty, gdn, John Gibbs, sur, 5/10/1858, Cherokee, GB

TIPPEN, Dennis, decd, Newton A. Tippen, admr, Lee Barrow, sur, 4/7/1858; N. A. Tippen, admr, D. J. Tippen, sur, 5/10/1858, Cherokee, AB

TIPPEN, D. S., decd, John W. Grantham, admr, Joseph Chastain, J.
R. Grantham, sur, 2/11/1859, Cherokee, AB
TIPPEN, John L., decd, LWT dtd 10/7/1857, pvd 11/1857, names ch:
Parthenia A. Kemp, Elizabeth M. Wills, Eliza M. Elliott, Martha
M. Hardburgen, Amanda C., William W., Cherokee
TIPPEN, Thompson, decd, LWT dtd 10/17/1857, pvd 3/1859, names
wife, Jane W., Cherokee
TIPPEN, Elizabeth, decd, John L. Tippin, admr, Thomas J. Perkins,
sur, 6/12/1854, Cherokee, AB
TIPPEN, George, decd, James Tippin, admr, William Tippin, sur,
1/24/1854; George W. Tippin, admr, 3/10/1856, Cherokee, AB
TIPPIN, James, decd, Sarah B. Tippin, admx, William Tippin, sur,
3/10/1856, Cherokee, AB
TIPPIN, Mary, decd, James Tippin, admr, Robert W. Trout, sur,
5/8/1854, Cherokee, AB
TISMORE, David, minor, Micajah Phillips, gdn, 3/3/1834,
Montgomery, GB
TISON, Aaron, decd, Martha Tison, admx, gtd leave to sell slaves
10/17/1825, Camden, MIC
TISON, Aaron, decd, of South Carolina, Isaac Bailey apptd admr;
Mrs. Martha Tison filed her caveat which was sustained and she
was apptd admx 11/4/1822, Camden, MIC
TMSEL?, Nehemiah, decd, James Wood qualified as admr 3/3/1791,
Liberty, Ests
TISON, John, decd, George W. Boston applies for adm 1/13/1835,
Effingham, MIC
TOBBERT, John, decd, Elizabeth Tobbert, wid, admx, Wilkes, MxR
TODD, David, Sr., decd, Joshua Todd issued L/A 5/3/1802, John
Ashley, sec, Richmond, AB
TODD, Hardy, decd, Elizabeth Todd and Job Todd apply for adm
w/LWT annexed 2/19/1802, Warren, MIC
TODD, Lewis, decd, Aaron English, admr, 12/5/1825, Matthew
English, John English, surs, Warren, AB
TODD, Richard C., decd, Martha Todd apptd gdn of orphs: James H.,
Richard F. and John C., 12/1/1856, Fulton
TODD, Richard C., decd, Martha Todd, admx w/LWT annexed,
3/1/1852, W. T. Ivy, M. J. Ivy, surs, DeKalb, AB
TODD, William made retn as gdn for his children 9/1/1822-
12/31/1836, Tattnall, I&A
TOLLOS, Stephen, decd, LWT admitted to record 7/5/1841,
Effingham, MIC
TOMAY, John, decd, James D. Cogan issued L/A 1/10/1814, John
D'Antignac, Thomas Quisenberry, secs, Richmond, AB
TOMBERLIN, Jackson, minor, John D. Terrell, gdn, 1/5/1841, A. W.
Bell, sec, Hall, GB
TOMLIN, Isaac H., decd, Edward Hagin, admr, H. N. Hagin, sur,
3/5/1866, Paulding, AB
TOMLIN, Rachel, decd, Edward Hagin, admr, H. N. Hagin, sur,
3/5/1866, Paulding, AB
TOMLINSON, A. H., decd, L. H. Tomlinson, admr, 7/4/1853, Joseph
A. Reeve, sur, DeKalb, AB
TOMLINSON, David Y., decd, L/A to E. M. Taliaferro 10/1/1860,
Fulton
TOMLINSON, Ephraim M., decd, Ed. M. Taliaferro, admr, Benjamin
Thurmond, A. J. Hutchins, secs, 4/1/1861, Fulton, AB
TOMLINSON, John, decd, John Glen issued L/A 5/14/1863, Fulton
TOMLINSON, Leonard H., decd, David Y. Tomlinson apptd gdn of
minor orphs 3/2/1857: Leonard P., Sarah P. and Nancy H., Fulton
TOMLINSON, Leonard H., decd, late of Fayette Co., David Y.
Tomlinson and Allen J. Poole qualified as exrs of LWT 11/6/1854,
dismissed 5/3/1859, Fulton

TOMLINSON, L. H., decd, George C. Lovincy, gdn of minor orphs:
Sarah R., Nancy H., Leonard P., 9/3/1860, Fulton, GB
TOMLINSON, Margaret C., minor orph of Leonard H., decd, D. Y.
Tomlinson apptd gdn 1/11/1858, Fulton
TOMLINSON, Mary, minor orph of John, decd, Mary A. Tomlinson,
gdn, 8/3/1863, Fulton, GB
TOMPKINS, John, apptd natural gdn of his children: Lucy, John and
Robert, minors, 1/3/1836, Camden, MIC, GB
TOMPKINS, John, decd, William Johnston and wife apptd admrs,
6/9/1802, Camden, MIC
TOMPKINS, John, Sr., decd, John Tompkins apptd admr 6/2/1835,
dismissed 11/13/1837, Camden, MIC
TOMPKINS, Louisa, decd, William B. Thomas apptd admr; also gdn of
Lawrence, Amanda, Ray and Euphemia, her minor children 7/25/1850,
Camden, MIC
TOMPKINS, Robert and John; petition of John Tompkins, gdn, for
div to be made between them of prop inherited by sd minors from
their mother, Mary Tompkins, decd, 1/4/1841, Camden, MIC
TOMPKINS, Samuel, decd, L/A issued to John Y. Tompkins 1/25/1843,
Washington
TONDEE, Peter, decd, carpenter, Elisha Elon, bricklayer, admr
w/LWT annexed 10/29/1785, Chatham, Adms
TOOMBS, William, decd, James Ware applied for L/A 7/15/1796,
Greene, Misc
TOOSING, John P., decd, Henry Grovenstein, exr, applies for
dismission 1/28/1828, Effingham, MIC
TOOTTE, John, decd, Nancy Tootte and Robert C. Surrency issued
L/A 11/2/1840, Tattnall, AB
TORBET, Francis, decd, Elizabeth Torbet, Joseph Caldwell, admrs,
acct w/Ordinary of Fairfield District, South Carolina, cash recd
to 1830; heirs--Elizabeth, widow, Sarah McCrory Torbet, Robert
W., Rosannah S., Hugh S. & Frances J. Torbet 1/1/1835, Butts, ER
TORBET, Francis J., orph of Francis, decd, David Smith, gdn,
Robert W. Smith, sur. 7/6/1835, Butts, GB
TORBET, Hugh S., orph of Francis, decd, David Smith, gdn, Robert
W. Smith, sur, 7/6/1835, Butts, GB
TORBET, Robert W., orph of Francis, decd, David Smith, gdn,
Robert W. Smith, sur, 7/6/1835, Butts, GB
TORBET, Rosanna S., orph of Francis, decd, David Smith, gdn,
Robert W. Smith, sur, 7/6/1835, Butts, GB
TORBET, Sarah M., orph of Francis, decd, David Smith, gdn, Robert
W. Smith, sur, 7/6/1835, Butts, GB
TORRAS, Joshua, decd, James W. Abernathy qualified as exr
4/6/1857, dismissed 10/5/1858, Fulton
TORRENCE, William, decd, Polly Torrence apptd admx 3/6/1809,
Warren, MIC, AB
TOUCHTON, Annis apptd gdn of her minor ch---Rebecca, Luthena,
Catherine, Christopher David, 1/11/1819, Glynn, MIC, GB
TOUCHTON, Daniel, decd, Ann Touchton, extrx, petitions ct to
require Martha Waters, admx of Thomas Waters of Washington to
deliver her all of the estate´s assets 1/5/1821, Glynn, MIC
TOULOUSE, Raimond Pajenuel, decd, 10/25/1813 appraisement,
Richmond
TOWERS, Benjamin, decd, John Love apptd admr 1785, Chatham, Adms
TOWNS, David H., minor orph of Bartlett, decd, Marlin Towns apptd
gdn 11/1812, Jasper, OM
TOWNS, Joel, decd, L/A gtd Carter B. Harrison 5/1816, Isaac
McClendon, Howell Tatum, surs, Jasper, OM
TOWNS, John, decd, Aylse and Joel Towns issued L/A 3/8/1788,
Isaac Sampson, James Ryan, secs, Richmond, AB

TOWNS, William, minor orph of Joel, decd, Ann Towns apptd gdn
7/1816, Carter B. Harrison, John G. Towns, surs; Howell Tatum,
Sr., Howell Tatum, Jr., Joel Tatum apptd to divide property to
heirs, Jasper, OM
TOWNSEND, Joshua, decd, James N. Abernathy, admr 4/7/1857, Fulton
TOWNSEND, Thomas, decd, Abraham Jones issued L/A 2/27/1796,
Anselm Bugg, sec, Richmond, AB
TRAMMEL, James Jared, orph of Jared, decd, under age 14, James
Spier, gdn, 5/2/1814, Laurens, GB
TRAMMEL, Jared, decd, Charles A. Hill issued L/A 9/6/1813; Elijah
Blackshear, gdn of orphs: Nancy and Sally 4/26/1814, Laurens, GB
TRAMMELL, Daniel, decd, Fannie Trammell, gdn of James Madison,
Polly & Jeremiah, orphs, 1/2/1815, Richard Boyd, sur, Clarke, GB
TRAMMELL, John, decd, Caswell G. Trammell issued L/A 10/24/1870,
W. W. Leak, sec, White, AB
TRAMMELL, Thomas, decd, LWT pvd 11/1/1823 names wife, Mary and
ch: Nancy Stroud, Milky Stroud, Drakeford Lee Trammell, Farr
Harris Trammell and John Trammell, Pike, MIC
TRAVIS, Elizabeth, Frances & Mary ask for James Waters as gdn,
James Briggs, Jno Todd, James Waters, sur, 1/28/1811, Emanuel, GB
TRAVIS, John, decd, Amos Travis, admr, 12/1/1817, Simeon Travis,
Lawrence Kitchens, surs, Warren, AB
TRAVIS, Biel, decd, Dixon Tillman, exr, makes retns 3/7/1814,
Jackson, OM
TRAVIS, Elizabeth applies for James Waters to be her gdn, James
Briggs, John Todd and James Waters, surs, 1/28/1811, Emanuel, GB
TRAVIS, Francis applies for James Waters to be her gdn, James
Briggs, John Todd and James Waters, surs, 1/28/1811, Emanuel, GB
TRAVIS, Mary applies for James Waters to be her gdn, James
Briggs, John Todd and James Waters, surs, 1/28/1811, Emanuel, GB
TRAVIS, John, decd, Amos Travis, admr, 12/1/1817, Simeon Travis,
Lawrence Kitchens, surs, Warren, AB
TRAVIS, William, decd, LWT pvd, Amos Travis qualified as exr
8/14/1805, Warren, MIC
TRAYLOR, Champion, decd, LWT pvd, L/T issued Avarilla Traylor
3/3/1817, Jasper, OM
TRAYLOR, Frances, orph of William, decd, James Brooks apptd gdn
6/1794, Oglethorpe, MIC
TRAYLOR, Martha, orph of Wiley, decd, Charles Freeman apptd gdn,
Jarrel Beasley, William P. Beasley, surs, 7/2/1849, Troup, GB
TRAYLOR, Milly, orph of William, decd, James Brooks apptd gdn
6/1794, Oglethorpe, MIC
TRAYLOR, Thomas, decd, LWT pvd, Betsey W. Traylor qualified as
extrx, 9/1/1817, Jasper, OM
TRAYWICK, James, decd, James Rushing issued L/A 11/1/1841,
Washington
TRAYWICK, Moses, decd, Jane Traywick issued L/A 1/8/1830,
Washington
TREANOR, Nicholas D., decd, L/A to John Treanor 3/6/1843, Baldwin
TREEMAN, William, decd, LWT pvd, L/T issued Polly Freeman and
Josiah Freeman 1/7/1817, Jasper, OM
TRENT, John, decd, Sophia Trent applies for admn 5/16/1799, apptd
7/18/1799, Warren, AB, MIC
TREUTLEN, Joseph C., decd, John Charlton applies for admn
1/3/1828, Effingham, MIC
TREUTLIN, Christian of Effingham Co., Ga., planter, deed of gift
conveys back to his brother, John, now of Orangeburg District,
South Carolina, all property given him 10/1792, to protect
himself against a lawsuit abt to be filed against him, 2/23/1801;
Levi Dyon applies for L/D 1/3/1828, Effingham, MIC
Effingham, Misc

TREUTLIN, John Adam, planter, gift deed to brother, Christian, planter, 10/20/1792, conveys his entire estate, Effingham, Misc
TRICE, James K., decd, Ezekiel Trice issued L/A 3/7/1838, Baldwin
TRIMBLE, James K., decd, LWT exhibited 8/12/1863, John Y. Flowers and M. J. Trimble, exrs, Fulton
TRIMBLE, William J., minor orph of James F., decd, Calhoun Ramsey, gdn, 3/10/1866, Fulton, GB
TRIPLETT, Daniel, minor orph of Francis, decd, Rachel Calhoun, gdn, 11/3/1806, Lewis Lee, sec, Richmond, GB
TRIPLETT, Francis, minor orph of Francis, decd, Major C. Collins, gdn, 11/3/1806, Lewis Lee, sec, Richmond, GB
TRIPP, William apptd gdn of his ch: Henry W., James, Sarah and Reuben, 1/7/1817, Jasper, OM
TRIPPE, Henry, decd, LWT pvd 8/12/1790, wife, Sarah, ch--William, Robert, Henry, Betsey, Anna, Henry, James, names Philip Pritchet; brother, John Trippe and David Dixon, exrs, Greene, Misc
TROTMAN, Marshal, orph of Cullen, decd, L/G issued Jasper Powell 3/7/1831, Washington
TROTMAN, Winnifred, orph of Cullen, decd, L/G issued Jasper Powell 3/7/1831, Washington
TROTTER, Robert B., decd, LWT dtd 8/4/1850 names wife, Delilah (dim); Margaret E. Trotter, gdn of orphs, James A. and Susan D., 2/5/1866, White, GB
TROUP, George, decd, Mrs. Catharine Troup, admx, 4/15/1789, Chatham, Adms
TROUT, Nathaniel, decd, Dixon Tillman, exr, makes retn 3/7/1814, Jackson, OM
TRUETT, Riley, decd, L/A to Boneta Truett 1/7/1822, Jasper, OM
TRULUCK, John W., decd, 9/14/1842; apprs: W. Beverly, N. Patrick, C. A. Yawn; mentions Lot 313, 9th Dist, Baker Co.; purchasers at sale: Elizabeth, N. B., John, N. R., Jason, and William L. Truluck, etc., N. R. T. Truluck, admr, Dooly, I&A
TRUETLEN, Christian, decd, Levi Dlyon, applies for L/D 1/3/1828, Effingham, MIC
TREUTT, Riley, decd, L/A to Boneta Truett 1/7/1822, Jasper, OM
TRUMAN, Samuel, decd, Mary Truman, A. B. Griffin, Foster Freeman, admrs 3/2/1840, Harris
TUCKER, Andrew, decd, Joseph Hull, admr, 1/8/1839, Camden, MIC
TUCKER, Arthur, minor, chose his bro., Isaac Tucker, as gdn, 1/7/1834, Camden, MIC
TUCKER, Benjamin, decd, Samuel Higginbotham dismissed as exr 7/4/1825, Glynn, MIC
TUCKER, David, decd, John Bachlott apptd admr 1/6/1823, Camden, MIC, AB
TUCKER, David, decd, John Bachlott, Jr. dismissed as admr 1/5/1830, Camden, MIC
TUCKER, Gabriel, decd, Isaac Tucker, admr, filed petition for filed petition for dismission 1/7/1834, MIC, AB
TUCKER, Germain, decd, Frances H. Tucker and William B. Hundley, admrs, 12/22/1821, Philander Parris, henry Gibson of Columbia Co., surs, Warren, AB
TUCKER, Hanford (or Harper), decd, Mary Tucker issued L/A 7/7/1851, Baldwin
TUCKER, Henry C., decd, Lewis Metts issued L/A 1/7/1834, Washington
TUCKER, Isaiah, decd, Churchill Gibson, admr w/LWT annexed, 12/13/1821, Asa Chapman, John Fontaine, surs, Warren, AB
TUCKER, Sarah, decd, Laban Taylor vs. John S. Taylor, petition to set aside LWT; John S. Taylor required to post bond for forthcoming of 5 negroes, 3/6/1835, Camden, MIC
TUCKER, Thomas, decd, LWT pvd L/T issued William and Thomas Tucker, 11/5/1821, Jasper, OM

TUCKER, Thomas, decd, Samuel Goodbread apptd admr 1/5/1836, Camden, MIC
TUCKER, Thomas, decd, Samuel Goodbread, admr, having departed this life without completing admn, his security, Thomas Goodbread, requested to turn over assets on hand to Clk, 1/1/1841, Camden, MIC
TUCKER, Willis, decd, Abner Underwood, admr, Joseph Underwood, sur, 10/23/1856, Cherokee, AB
TUGGLE, Eliza E., orph of John, decd, John Cain, Sr., gdn, 12/6/1852, Hall, GB
TUGGLE, James, decd, John W. Tuggle, admr, W. H. Tuggle, Woodward Tuggle, Elisha Chamblee, H. W. Blake, sur, 3/3/1873, dtd at Lawrenceville, Gwinnett, AB
TUGGLE, John, decd, William L. Tuggle issued L/A 11/4/1850, Benjamin F. Porter, sec, Hall, AB
TUGGLE, Nancy, minor orph of Ludowick, decd, Thomas Tuggle appd gdn, Elias Henes, Jeremiah Baxter, surs, 1/1805, Oglethorpe, MIC
TULL, Francis M., orph of Arthur, decd, William S. Swift, gdn, 1/9/1854, Houston, GB
TULLIS, G., decd, Penelopy Tullis makes retn 6/1862, Webster, OD
TULLOS, Patience, accts of William Speir, admr, examined 3/2/1829, Effingham, MIC
TULLOS, Temple, accts of William Speir, admr, examined 3/2/1829, Effingham, MIC
TURK, Theodosius, decd, Green B. Buchanan issued L/A 3/5/1832, Baldwin
TURLEY, Patrick, decd, Hugh Ward, admr, 3/5/1832, Ignatius Semmes, Thomas Turley, Henry Hare, surs, Warren, AB
TURMAN, George, decd, inv 10/3/1806, apprs: James Hatcher, Henry G. Walker, Thomas Turman, Elbert, GB
TURMAN, John, decd, Jonathan Vasser issued L/A 12/13/1810, Holland McTyeire, Lud Harris, secs, Richmond, AB
TURMAN, Matilda bound to Martin Turman to learn housewifery, James Morrison, sec, 3/4/1811, Elbert, GB
TURMAN, Prudence, Martin Turman files retn as her gdn 1811, Elbert, GB
TURMAN, Robert, decd, Caty Turman, admx, ordered to make titles of land to William Hatcher, signed by decd 1802, 2/17/1808, Wm Hatcher, admrs bond 6/10/1811, Caleb Tait, sec, Elbert, AB
TURNELL, Thomas F., decd, LWT dtd 9/17/1851 pvd 1/1852 names wife, Esther, Cherokee
TURNER, Abisha, decd, inventory of property, appraisers: Michael Young, Elisha Bowen, 3/28/1824, Bulloch, Misc
TURNER, A. G., decd, David W. Lowe, admr, 1/1841; apprs: Thomas J. Stell, James Thornton, Silas Ramsey; purchashers at sale: Lewis Dupree, Junius Jordan, Pinkston Lingo, Isaac, James and Sinantha Turner, Stewart, Adms
TURNER, Arthur 2/27/1830 recd of Jesse Turner, gdn of minor heirs of Abisha Turner, decd, $487.12; minors named as Arthur, James and John Turner, Bulloch, Misc
TURNER, Carry, orph of Butler, abt 9 yrs old, bound to William Bradford 11/7/1808, Jackson, OM
TURNER, Emily, orph of James, decd, William Jennings, gdn, James Jones, sur, 1/1853, 1853-1854 retns, Fayette, GB
TURNER, Green B., Sr., natural gdn of his minor ch: Green B., Jr., John F., Martha A., Richard M. and James M. to whom legacy was given by LWT of Solomon Hopkins, their grfather, Thomas N. Turner, George R. Turner, surs, 12/5/1859, Paulding, GB
TURNER, Henry chose Robert Piles as his gdn 1/14/1828, Glynn, MIC, GB
TURNER, James, decd, Elijah Glass, admr, John Murphey, Wm N. Hill, surs, 1/1851, 1851-1854 retns, Fayette, AB

TURNER, James J., minor of John, decd, James A. Cantrell, gdn, David Moore and James Rutherford, secs, 8/2/1852, Lumpkin, GB
TURNER, James M., minor orph of Green B., decd, Margaret Turner, gdn, T. Newton Turner, J. F. Turner, surs, 3/6/1866, Paulding, GB
TURNER, John, Elizabeth Turner petitions for John Turner, exr, to gd for negroes belonging to estate 1/11/1819, Glynn, MIC
TURNER, John, decd, James Turner, admr, 10/6/1827, Kendall McTyeire, Abram Grierson, surs, Warren, AB
TURNER, John C., decd, E. A. Turner, admr, 9/1/1862, Jacob Chupp, Levi Stidham, surs, DeKalb, AB
TURNER, Joseph, decd, Singleton Holt, Robert and Isaac Moreland issued L/A 3/1/1813, Putnam, AB
TURNER, Martin, decd, late of Greene Co., Sally Turner, gdn of Thomas and Elizabeth Martin Turner, orphs, makes retn 7/1/1811, Elbert, GR
TURNER, Mary E., William Rose of Savannah, Merchant, petitioned for guardianship of, 2/7/1826, Camden, MIC, LG
TURNER, Milledge, minor over age 14 of Abraham, decd, Mason H. Bush gtd L/G 4/1855, Webster, OD
TURNER, Nathan, orph of James, decd, Elijah Glass, gdn, 7/1852, Fayette, GBN
TURNER, Reuben, decd, Henry P. Turner, admr, John Turner, James Hollingsworth, sur, 3/5/1832, Bibb, AB
TURNER, Richard M., minor orph of Green B., decd, Margaret Turner, gdn, T. Newton Turner, J. F. Turner, sur, Amanda, James Tutte applies for adm 5/16/1836, Effingham, MIC
TURNER, Sally, abt 11 yrs old, bound to John McConnell 5/3/1813, Jackson, OM
TURNER, Sally, orph of Butler, decd, to be bound to David Witt, she being abt 4 yrs old, 11/7/1808, Jackson, OM
TURNER, Sampson, orph of James, decd, Elijah Glass, gdn, 7/1852, Fayette, GB
TURNER, Stephen, decd, L/A to John Turner 1/18/1819, Laurens, AB
TURNER, William, decd, James Gould, exr, gtd leave to sell perishable property 6/12/1820, Glynn, MIC
TURNER, Zachariah, orph of James, decd, Elijah Glass, gdn, 7/1852, Fayette, GB
TURPIN, Thomas, decd, Horatio Turpin and John Stewart issued L/A 11/2/1812, Putnam, AB
TURPIN, William Henry, decd, minor John of Henrico Co., Virginia, decd, Thomas J. Wray gdn, 11/8/1806 John Carter, sec, Richmond, GB
TUTLE, Fereby, decd, L/A to Ludwick Mathis 7/7/1834, Washington
TUTT, Benjamin, decd, of South Carolina, William Tutt issued L/A 9/6/1830, Eli Morgan and John Danforth, secs, Richmond, AB
TUTTE, Caroline Amanda, James Tutte applies for admn 5/16/1836, Effingham, MIC
TUTTLE, Joseph, decd, Luther Roll issued L/A 1828, E. B. Crane, sec, Richmond, AB
TYLER, J. B., decd, David Majen issued L/A 12/1869, Webster, OD
TYLER, William, LWT produced, L/T issued Nelson B. Tyler 5/1855, Webster, OD
TYLER, William, decd, John Willson issued L/A 7/7/1807, James Murren, sec, Richmond, AB
TYSON, Henry, minor orph of Eason, decd, Gilbert M. Stokes apptd gdn 3/21/1859, William and Isaac Tyson, sur, Lee
TYSON, Samuel, minor orph of Eason, decd, Gilbert M. Stokes apptd gdn 3/21/1859, William and Isaac Tyson, sur, Lee
e and Wm L. Truluck, etc., N. R. Truluck, admr, Dooly, I&A
UDALL, Lucy, John & Robert Tompkins seek div betwn Lucy & 2 bros 6/4/1838; to John & Robt Tompkins; Cyrus & Lucy Ann Udall recpt 12/20/1838 to John Tompkins, gdn, "being all money due fr grmother Lucy Spalding's est 12/14/1838, Camden, MIC

UMPHREY, Richard, orph of William, decd, James Jones, sur, 5/1850, Fayette, GB
UMPHREY, Thomas, orph of William, decd, James Jones, sur, 5/1850, Fayette, GB
UMPHRIES, Uriah, decd, Simon Lane, admr, bond 2/3/1817, Jonathan and Joseph Lane, surs, Clarke, AB
UNDERWOOD, Elijah made gdn of his ch: A., Adolphus F., Dicy, Ann Ellen, Enos W., and John A.; Lemuel Cook, sur, 11/7/1853, Cherokee, GB
UNDERWOOD, Jehu, decd, Fernando Underwood apptd admr, he being an heir, 6/3/1833, Camden, MIC
UNDERWOOD, John G., decd, John J. Underwood issued L/A 3/5/1821, Laurens, AB
UNDERWOOD, Wiley L., orph of William, decd, Lucy P. Underwood, gdn, 1/4/1841, Tattnall, GB
UPSHAW, Adkins, decd, 1800 retn by James Patten, admr, Elbert, AR
UPTON, John, decd, Elizabeth Upton issued L/A 6/5/1783, Rhesa Howard, Isaac Perry, secs, Richmond, AB
URQUHART, William, decd, Andrew J. Miller issued L/A 5/7/1838, James U. Jackson, William E. Jackson, secs, Richmond, AB
USSERY, Elizabeth, decd, John Ussery, admr w/LWT annexed 3/5/1821, Laurens, AB
UTT, James, decd, Jonathan Riles issued temporary L/A 6/23/1815, Charles McCulloch, Thomas Glascock, secs, Richmond, AB
VAN LANDINGHAM, George, decd, John Van Landingham issued L/A 5/4/1818, Reuben Luckett, sec, Morgan, AB
VAN VOLKINGBURG, Catherine (Mrs., decd, John G. Park issued L/A 5/6/1844, Baldwin
VANCE, James, decd, John Vance applies for L/A, Milby McGee, sur, 12/6/1798, inv. & appr filed 4/10/1799, Warren, AB, MIC
VANDEGRIFF, John, decd, L/A issued Sarah Vandegriff 10/1/1860, W. B. West, E. A. Vandegriff, secs, dismissed 8/2/1864, White, AB
VANDYKE, Peter, decd, Rachel Vandyke qualified as admx 2/2/1789, Liberty, Ests
VANN, Henry, decd, LWT pvd 7/3/1837, Sarah Vann, extrx, Washington
VANN, James, decd, David Files and Joseph Davis issued L/A 7/3/1809, Jackson, OM
VANN, James, decd, late of Cherokee Nation, David Files, admr 1/22/1810 bond, Roderick Easley, sur, Clarke, AB
VANN, Samuel, decd, James Vann issued L/A 3/2/1840, Washington
VANN, William M., decd, Allen Dennis apptd gdn of: Caroline, Augusta, Ann, Emily, Lucretia and Eliza Jane Vann, John Hogg, Hiram Howard, sur, 11/27/1848, Troup, GB
VANZANT, Abel, decd, of Augusta, Louisa B. Vanzant and Charles Beach issued L/A 10/4/1815, John Cashin, Thomas Quisenberry, sec, Richmond, AB
VANZANT, Allen, a free person of color, Vandy J. Brown apptd gdn 1/3/1843, Camden, MIC
VARDIMAN, John, decd, Thomas Vardiman issued L/A 5/2/1814, Putnam, AB
VARDIMAN, William, decd, L/A issued Rachel Vardiman and Elijah Phillips 11/4/1816, Jasper, OM
VARNER, Reuben, decd, William Varner and Allen Jones issued L/A 3/7/1814, Putnam, AB
VASSER, Jonathan, decd, Elizabeth Vasser, admx, p. 105, 117, Screven, OM
VAUGHAN, Benjamin, decd, LWT pvd 5/4/1807, names wife, Martha, and sons, Benjamin and Abner, "and rest of my lawful born children to have equal part", Samuel Winngham, Martha Vaughan, exrs dtd 8/25/1806, Franklin, OM

VAUGHAN, George, decd, Benjamin Vaughan, exr, 1/11/1831, Habersham, MIC

VAUGHAN, Highemsial?, decd, Joseph B. White, admr, makes retn 1/1833, Habersham, MIC

VAUGHN, Alexander, decd, Jane Vaughn applied for LA, Samuel Alexander, sur, 2/16/1797, Warren, MIC, AB

VAUGHN, Benjamin, decd, LWT pvd 5/4/1807, Samuel Winningham, exr, names wife, Martha and ch: Abner and Benjamin, dtd 8/5/1806, Franklin, IMW

VAUGHN, Ephraim, decd, James Cathell applied for L/A 1/22/1791, Greene, Misc

VAUGHN, James, decd, Nancy Vaughn issued L/A 1/5/1830, William Churchill, Thomas Ogg, secs, Richmond, AB

VAUGHN, James J., decd, Charles Holcombe issued L/A 5/22/1867, Fulton

VAWL, Matthew, decd, Lewis Williams was gtd L/A 7/6/1807, Franklin, IMW

VEAL, Synthia, idiot child of Nathan, Reuben Billington issued L/G 7/6/1840, Washington

VEAL, William, illegitimate minor, Robert Whitfield issued L/G 9/2/1833, Washington

VEAZEY, George W., orph of Timothy, decd, John Johnson, gdn, 12/6/1826, Wade Hemphill, George Langford, secs, Morgan, GB

VEAZEY, Isaac, orph of Ezekiel, decd, John Veazey, gdn, 1/15/1826, Jesse Fitzpatrick, John Cunningham, John Johnson, secs, Morgan, GB

VEAZEY, James, decd, LWT dtd 10/14/1788, wife, Elizabeth, ch: William, Zebulon, Ezekiel, John, Jesse, Mary Tapperly, Francina McClelland, Greene, Misc

VEAZY, Ezekiel C., decd, John Veazy issued L/A 11/3/1823, C. Campbell, sec, Morgan, AB

VENABLE, Frances, Robert Venable apptd gdn of 10/29/1803, Jackson, OM

VENRICK, Thomas, decd, Christopher Fletcher issued L/A 1/9/1822, B. B. Mitchell, Jeremiah Luther, secs, Richmond, AB

VERDIN, John, decd, Winnifred Verdin and John Verdin presented LWT for probate; they qualified as exrs 9/5/1808, Warren, MIC

VERNON, Rochella, decd, James F. Johnson, admr, John L. Holliday, sur, 7/1849, 1851-1852, Fayette, AB

VEST, George, decd, inv 3/28/1799, Mary Vest, Samuel Barron, admrs, acct of stock made use of for orphs, 1799, Hancock, AA

VICKERS, Darling, decd, LWT pvd 7/3/1848, Campbell Burton, exr, Harris

VICKERS, Elijah, decd, LWT pvd 7/27/1832, John Lawhon, exr, Washington

VICKERS, Howard, orph of William, decd, Creed T. Wise, gdn, Witt C. Wise, Francis M. Wise, sur, 11/28/1846, Butts, GB

VICKERS, Jacob, orph of William, decd, Creed T. Wise, gdn, Witt C. Wise, Francis M. Wise, sur, 11/28/1846, Butts, GB

VICKERS, Prudence, orph of William, decd, Creed T. Wise, gdn, Witt C. Wise, Francis M. Wise, sur, 11/28/1846, Butts, AB

VICKERS, Rosanna, orph of William, decd, Creed T. Wise, gdn, Witt C. Wise, Francis M. Wise, sur, 11/28/1846, Butts, GB

VICKERS, Samuel, practitioner of physic, decd, James Geoghegan and John Love, practitioner of physic, apptd admrs 11/19/1785, Chatham, Adms

VICKERS, William, decd, Creed T. Wise, admr, Witt C. Wise, Francis M. Wise, sur, 10/1/1837, retn 1839-1840, Butts, AB, ER

VICKERS, Witt, orph of William, decd, Creed T. Wise, gdn, Witt C. Wise, Francis M. Wise, sur, 11/28/1846, Butts, GB

VICKS, William, decd, Elenor Vicks, admx, p. 17, Screven, OM

VINCENT, Allen, decd, Margaret Vincent issued L/A 9/29/1818, Alexander Cunningham, Robert V. Marys, secs; 1818 retn, funeral of Austin Vincent, decd, son of Allen, decd, Richmond, AB
VINCENT, Edward A., decd, Dr. Ezekiel N. Calhoun apptd admr 1/12/1857, Fulton
VINCENT, James, decd, Thomas King apptd gdn of James and Pollie, minor heirs 1/5/1804; Thomas King and Archibald Clarke, admrs, make their retn 4/12/1808, Camden, MIC
VINCENT, James, decd, of Camden Co., Lewis Gibson issued L/A 8/7/1832, John Sharp, John M. Cooper, secs, Richmond, AB
VINCENT, James (Capt.), John Wood, atty for John Sharp, John M. Cooper, Fleming T. Colbert, heirs, want slaves sold to divide est, it appearing William Gibson represents Rachel Elliott, only other alive heir, petition gtd 11/2/1825, Camden, MIC
VINCENT, James (Capt.) M. H. Hibbard apptd temp admr of est, gtd leave to sell the sloop "Eagle as prop likely to deteriorate 9/5/1825, William Gibson applied for adm of est, John Sharp, one of heirs, consenting thereto, 10/21/1825, Camden, MIC, AB
VINCENT, Mary, decd, Wade H. Giles, admr w/LWT annexed, William A. McCune, sur, 11/4/1839, Butts, AB
VINCENT, Mary, decd, LWT pvd 9/6/1839 ch: Henry, Nathaniel, Sally Giles (two sons not named); Wade H. Giles, admr, legacy to: Nathaniel, Powel P., Thomas, & Henry Vincent; 3/14/1840 apprs: Jas G. Mayo, Stewart Lee, Saml McLin, Butts, ER
VINEYARD, Ishmael, decd, 9/10/1799 inventory, William Fuges, Edward Ware and Allen Leeper, apprs, Elbert, AR
VINEYARD, Jane, decd, John McCurdy, Samuel Groves, admrs; heirs-- John Vineyard, representative of George and James Vineyard, Ephraim Beasley, heir-representative of David and Joseph Vineyard, John McCurdy, representative of William Stephens and Matthew Blackwell, 2/27/1807, Elbert, AR
VINING, Jeptha (Reverand), decd, Dixon Perryman and James Douglas apply for admn; James Douglas apptd admr, Harmon Perryman and Joseph Vining, secs, 11/17/1797, Warren, MIC
VINSON, Elisha, decd, Hugh F. Rose, Elizabeth Rose, admrs, 3/1837; apprs: William D. Fitch, James Parrott, Isaac Dennard; purchasers at sale: Joel Miller, Henry Grantham, Levin Glison, E. Vinson, etc., Stewart, Adms
VINSON, William L., orph of James, decd, Jonath Vinson, gdn, 9/4/1854, Houston, GB
VIOLETT, Ashford, decd, George Hennessey issued L/A 1/22/1796, Anselm Hicks, David Crawford, secs, Richmond, AB
VODAN, Bradock, decd, Thomas Burton applies for L/A 10/4/1791, William Hatcher and Evan Ragland, apprs, Elbert, AB
WADDLE, Nicholas, decd, Benjamin Hill, admr, Robert J. Cowart, sur, 9/5/1853, Cherokee, AB
WADE, Edward, decd, LWT pvd 11/4/1790, wife, Mary, ch--David Wade Edward Wade, Mary Burford, Lucey Nolin, Grissel Bennett, Thomas Wade, Chloe Easley, Peyton Wade and Ann Williams; decd daughter, Christian Dalton's heirs, Greene, Misc
WADE, James H., admr, relieved from bond, p. 143, 170, 176, Screven, OM
WADE, John M., decd, LWT pvd 3/1/1841, James H. Wade, exr, dismissed, Alfred Barksdale apptd admr de bonis non w/LWT annexed, 11/14/1842, Washington
WADE, Nathaniel relieved from bond, p. 143, Screven, OM
WADE, Peyton O. gtd leave to sell property, p. 172, Screven, OM
WADE, W. H., admr, leave to sell property, p. 153, Screven, OM
WADE, W. H., decd, L. P. Wade and S. W. Parker issued L/A 3/1862; Mrs. L. P. Wade issued L/A 5/1862; L. B. Wade to sell property of decd, Webster, OD

WADE, William H., decd, Mrs. L. P. Wade issued L/A 5/1862, Webster, OD
WADE, William H., relieved as gdn, p. 112, Screven, OM
WADKINS, Joseph, decd, John Nickols issued L/A 1/2/1836, Hall
WADSOLE, William, decd, George Baillie apptd admr 6/3/1814, Glynn, MIC, AB
WADSWORTH, Hogan, orph of William, decd, James Wadsworth, gdn, 11/5/1821, Thomas Wadsworth, gdn, 1/12/1823, John H. Little, sec, Lincoln, GB
WADSWORTH, Thomas, decd, Sarah Wadsworth and Benjamin Watts issued L/A 5/5/1806, Jackson, OM
WADSWORTH, Thomas, decd, William and Sally, orphs, chose their bro., John, gdn; ct appts John and Thomas Wadsworth, gdns of James and Seaborn under age 14, 5/3/1813, Jackson, OM
WAGES, Thomas W., decd, John J. Wages, admr, G. W. Etheridge, sur, 1/4/1875, Gwinnett, AB
WAGGONER, George, decd, G. B. Waggoner apptd admr with LWT annexed 11/1/1813, Warren, MIC, AB
WAGGONER, George, decd, LWT pvd 9/2/1811, Warren, MIC
WAGGONER, George, decd, Mrs. Elizabeth Waggoner apptd extrx; she is too infirm to come to ct, 8/12/1812, Warren, MIC
WAGGONER, Henry, decd, Aaron Lipham, James Waggoner, George Waggoner apply for temp admr, William Waggoner, Solomon Slatter, sur, 10/22/1803, Warren, MIC
WAGGONER, Henry, decd, Mary James, George Waggoner, Aaron Lippham, admrs, 12/4/1803, William Lipham, Solomon Slatter, surs, Warren, AB
WAGGONER, James, decd, Mary Waggoner, David W. Waggoner, George R. Waggoner apptd temp admrs, George Waggoner, William Waggoner, sur, 1/8/1805, Warren, MIC, AB
WAGGONER, James, decd, surviving admrs of est were cited to show cause why William Waggoner should not be released on surety on their bond, 2/7/1814, Warren, MIC
WAGGONER, James, orph of Henry, decd, William McFarlin apptd gdn 5/4/1812, Warren, MIC, GB
WAGGONER, James, orph of Henry, decd, over age 14, chose William McFarland his gdn succeeding Wyatt Bonner, his decd gdn, 5/4/1812, Warren, MIC
WAGGONER, Jincy, age over 14 yrs, orph of Henry, decd, chose William McFarlin her gdn 3/2/1812, Warren, MIC
WAGGONER, John Michael, decd, appraisal 1/1/1799, Capt. Joseph White applied for L/A 9/20/1798, Greene, Misc
WAGGONMAN, Susannah, decd, LWT pvd 11/18/1803, Caleb Johnson, exr, names James Briant and Caleb Johnson, Clarke, AB
WAITES, John, decd, LWT dtd 10/17/1808, (pvd in Randolph Co.) Putnam Co., Planter, names ch: Mary Singleton, Samuel, Nancy Ryker, Sarah, John, James, Patience, Hester & Hannah, Jasper, WAR
WAITS, John, decd, James Waits, admr, gtd dismission 11/3/1817, Jasper, OM
WAITS, John P., decd, John P. Waits, gdn of orphs: Mary F., Julia C., minors, Fulton, GB
WALDBURGER, John Jacob, decd of S. C., planter, LWT apptd Cornelius Dupont, exr; John Joachim Zubley and Henry Lewis Bourquin, exrs, having departed, the LWT has never been probated 1/7/1786, Chatham, Adms
WALDHOUR, John, decd, Israel T. Waldhour applies for L/A 5/6/1830, Effingham, MIC
WALDROUPE, Thomas, decd, James Waldroupe issued temp L/A 3/7/1814, Putnam, AB
WALEA, James, decd, Eliza Walea, admx, appraisal 10/16/1835, Emanuel, A

WALEA, James, decd, Nathaniel Stateham, atty for Leaster Spence, lawful husband of Deley Spence, formerly Deley Walea, have recd of Eliza Walea, exr, $500 of legacy left Deley Spence 3/3/1837, Emanuel, A

WALKER, Charles, decd, late of West Florida, LWT dtd 12/26/1779; Joel Walker, his nephew, one of exrs and sole legatees, gtd L/A 11/7/1783, Chatham, Adms

WALKER, Charles R., decd, S. L. Strickland issued L/A 2/1/1858, Paulding

WALKER, Davis E., decd, William G. Walker, Austin M. McKee, Virgil K. Walker, admrs, 9/4/1838, Harris

WALKER, Felix F., decd, Louisa Walker was apptd gdn of minor orphs: Margaret S., Martha W., Louisa E. and Henry F., 7/6/1863, Fulton, GB

WALKER, George, decd, Matthew Talbot, Robert, Freeman and Elizabeth Walker issued L/A 2/25/1805, Richmond, AB

WALKER, George, minor orph of George, decd, George M. Walker, gdn, 9/3/1821, Absolom Rhodes, William Lamkin, secs, Richmond, GB

WALKER, Henry, decd, LWT pvd by William Willis and James McDonald 1/6/1807, Jackson, OM

WALKER, Henry, decd, L/A gtd John W. Burney with Sylvanus Walker, Zachariah Philips, secs, Jasper, OM

WALKER, Isaiah C., decd, Nancy Walker, gdn for orphs: John and Joseph Walker 11/5/1838, James Howell, John T. Hughley, secs, Lincoln, GB

WALKER, Isaiah, decd, Nancy Walker, gdn of orphs: John H. and Joseph, 11/1/1830, Joseph and James C. Walker, secs, Lincoln, GB

WALKER, James, decd, Elizabeth Walker, Louis C. Cantelou L/A 11/7/1816; 12/2/1822 Elizabeth Cumming, formerly Walker, requests dower & sh to son, James M.; 1824 div-James M. Walker, gdn of Joshua, Wm, Margaret & Cornelia, Richmond, AB, AR

WALKER, James, decd, Rebecca Walker, admx, 7/3/1828, Butts, AB

WALKER, James, decd, inv sold 2/18/1829 public sale; purchasers: Clayton M. Coody, James Ransom, Rebecca Cobb; Rebecca Cobb, admx, pd H. W. Knolls, John Towns, C. M. Coody, Ransom R. Cobb, 1/13/1830, Butts, ER

WALKER, James S., decd, Joseph Hutchinson issued L/A 4/14/1825, Alex. McKenzie, Peter Bennock, secs, Richmond, AB

WALKER, Joel, decd, A. Persons and Littleberry Walker apply for admn, Nicholas Williams, Richard Heath, Amos Persons, sec, 2/11/1800, Warren, MIC, AB

WALKER, Joel, decd, Holly Walker, Amos Persons, admrs, 4/20/1800, Richard Heath, Nicholas Williams, surs, Warren, AB

WALKER, John, decd, Mary Walker and William Mitchell issuyed L/A 11/20/1786, James Hamilton, Wm Stevens, secs, Richmond, AB

WALKER, Joseph, decd, Harriett Walker issued L/A 8/21/1863, Fulton

WALKER, Nancy, decd, James Walker, John A. Walker, W. D. Hartsfield, admrs, Harris

WALKER, Reuben, decd, Martha Walker L/A 11/6/1820; 1/6/1836 heirs-Alex C. Walker, Edwd Rhodes Carswell, Martha R. Walker, Mrs. Martha J. Walker; 3/8/1825 Abraham Walker, gdn of-Alex. Curran, Martha Rebecca, Mary Celestia, Richmond, AB, GB

WALKER, Sanders, decd, William Lumpkin, Houng Stokes, exrs, wid. still living 9/1806, Oglethorpe, OM, AB

WALKER, Savannah, decd, LWT exhibited 3/7/1864, James N. Calhoun, exr, Fulton

WALKER, Thomas, decd, 4/13/1813 div to heirs: Mary Walker, wid, Margaret, Elijah, Rachel, Rebecca, Reuben, Abraham, John, Benjamin and William Walker, Richmond

WALKER, Thomas G. Walker, decd, Elizabeth Walker, admx, p. 131, Peyton L. Wade, and others, appraise est, p. 131, Screven, OM

WALKER, William, decd of Baker Co., John N. Dicy, admr 11/30/1790, Chatham, Adms
WALKER, William, decd, Simeon Walker issued L/A 10/4/1819, Lancelot Johnston, sec, Morgan, AB
WALL, George, orph of William B., decd, Van Leonard, gdn, 6/5/1821, Roderick Leonard, sec, Morgan, GB
WALL, James H., gdn for Mary V. and Jane, 8/7/1854, Houston, GB
WALLACE, Bonnell S., L/G issued M. O. Cox 6/1866, Webster, OD
WALLACE, Catherine, decd, Cargile J. Wallace issued L/A 3/1856, Webster, OD
WALLACE, Cyrus H., decd, l/A to John R. Wallace 3/4/1861, Fulton
WALLACE, James, decd, Sophia Wallace, gdn of orphs: Jesse H., Thomas H., Sarah Ann, Elizabeth, Louisa and John 11/5/1832, Thomas S. Shipp, sec, Lincoln, GB
WALLACE, James M., decd, Thompson Bell, admr, issued L/D 1/1861, Webster, OD
WALLACE, James W., decd, of Bedford Co., Tennessee, John R. Wallace apptd admr 7/6/1857, Fulton
WALLACE, John, decd, Benjamin Wallace issued L/A 11/18/1817, Joseph Leverett, sec, Morgan, AB
WALLACE, John, Benjamin Wallace apptd gdn of orphs: Mary Ann, Martha Frances, 11/1/1825, Morgan, GB
WALLACE, John, decd, Samuel Belcher, gdn of orphs: Mary and Martha 7/7/1823, James Mitchell, sec, Morgan, GB
WALLACE, John, decd, of Hilton head, South Carolina, Thomas Mitchell of Savannah, Ga., admr 11/12/1789, Chatham, Adms sell 239 acres in Richmond Co.,
WALLACE, Joseph, decd, Joseph Willis issued L/A 1/3/1866, Fulton
WALLACE, Joseph, lunatic, William R. Venable, Clk, Superior Ct, apptd gdn 3/5/1863; William L. Wallace apptd gdn 1/13/1862, Fulton, GB
WALLACE, Oliver, decd, LWT pvd 2/28/1802, wife, Ann, ch: Hannah and Jean; wife and son, John Wallace, exrs, Clarke, AB
WALLACE, Richard, decd, L. B. Redding, admr, 9/1856, Webster, OD
WALLACE, William, decd, Alexander Wallace issued L/A 11/10/1865, Fulton
WALLACE, William B., decd, J. M. Holbrook issued L/A 1/12/1863, Fulton
WALLACE, William L., decd, John M. Holbrook qualified as admr 1/1863, dismissed 1/7/1867, Fulton
WALLER, Charles, decd, acct of sales 6/5/1801; purchasers: Rachel, Joseph, Stephen and William Waller, etc.; appraisal 4/11/1801, Joseph Waller, admr, Hancock, AAAA
WALLER, John, decd, appraisal 6/7/1798, Nathan Melvin, exr, Hancock, AA
WALLIN, George, decd, Margaret Payne issued L/A 3/14/1814, George Pearson, Elisha Owen, secs, Richmond, AB
WALLIS, Mortimer, decd, Sarah Ann Wallis, admx, Oliver H. Prince, William L. Norman, Washington Poe, surs, 9/24/1832, Bibb, AB
WALLIS, Nicholas, decd, Reuben Wallis, temporary admr, S. W. Davis, sur, 9/8/1874, inventory filed 10/5/1874, Gwinnett, AB
WALRAVEN, Andrew J., decd, L/A to Wesley Hudson 6/4/1860, Fulton
WALRAVEN, John, decd, Elizabeth Walraven, admx 11/10/1856; recd of Eli Dodgen, admr de bonis non, in full of acct 12/31/1856, Cobb, BB
WALSBY, Adam, decd, James Kendrick was apptd admr 11/6/1815, Camden, MIC
WALTER, George W. bound to John H. Russell for 16 yrs to age 20, 11/1830, habersham, MIC
WALTERS, Robert, decd, LWT dtd 11/2/1793 names ch--William, Robert, Elijah, Peter, Samuel, Moses, Betsey, Susannah, Hannah and Mary; John and Robert Walters, exrs, 10/9/1794, Franklin, OM

WALTHALL, Adelaid, decd, Benjamin F. Bowar qualified as admr 9/4/1854, Fulton
WALTHALL, Gerrard, Sr., decd, 1805 retns of William Allen, admr dtd 8/1/1807, Gerrard Walthall, Jr., debtor, 1807-8 retns, Thomas B. Creagh vs. Gerrard Walthall, Sr., decd, 1808; boarding two minors, William and Singleton Walthall, Elbert, AR
WALTON, Benton, decd, Thomas W. Murray, gdn for orphs---Thomas, jesse B., Salina, Susan, Elizabeth and Mary Evaline 11/3/1823, David Murray, sec, Lincoln, GB
WALTON, Bryant, decd, Elias Allison, admr, late gdn of Simon and Elizabeth Walton 7/1/1839, Randolph
WALTON, Elizabeth, orph of William, decd, Stephen Swain, Reuben Neel, gdns, 9/2/1822, Emanuel, GB
WALTON, Fanny, wife of Sewell, decd, William Jones, gdn, 5/2/1825, Thomas J. Murray, sec, Lincoln, GB
WALTON, George (Honorable), decd, Dorothy Walton issued L/A 6/1/1804, Robert and Anderson Watkins, secs, Richmond, AB
WALTON, Jemima, Nathaniel Walton, gdn, 3/7/1831, Emanuel, GB
WALTON, Jesse, decd, LWT dtd 6/13/1788 names wife, Mary, sons--- George (not of age) and Walker; Mary Walton, Larkin Cleveland, William Walker Walton and Jesse Bond, exrs bond 8/10/1790; inventory mentions judgment for Charles King in North Carolina, Franklin, OM
WALTON, John, decd, Charles Carter issued L/A 2/1/1828, Daniel Savage, sec, Richmond, AB
WALTON, John, decd, of South Carolina, Aaron Brown issued L/A 1/2/1831, Hall
WALTON, John, gdn for his son, Jesse, 4/1/1825, Marshal Covington, sec, Lincoln, GB
WALTON, Mary, decd, LWT names ch---Mary Carter, William Walker Walton (and his son, Jesse), Killis Walton, George Walton, Rachel; mentioned legacy left by Henry Mullins of Virginia 11/8/1800; on motion of council for Robert Walton, son, ordered temporary L/A be gtd, Franklin, IMW
WALTON, Mary E., orph of Benton, decd, Jesse B. Walton, gdn, 9/7/1835, James McLane, Thomas J. Walton, secs, Lincoln, GB
WALTON, Mary F., formerly Mary F. Jones (orph of Mason Jones, decd), wife of Wiley H. Walton, minor, Harriet E. Walton apptd gdn, 1/6/1840, Richard T. Walton, W. W. Stokes, secs, Lincoln, GB
WALTON, Noah, decd, John Moss, gdn for orphs: William D., Harriet A., Wiley N. and John H. Walton 1/1/1838, Joshua Daniel, sec, Lincoln, GB
WALTON, Overton, decd, Samuel B. Walton, gdn of orphs: Simon and Elizabeth, 7/1/1839, Randolph, GB
WALTON, Pleasant, decd, John Walton, gdn of orphs: Marian, William, Jency, Pleasant, 12/6/1824, Joel Lockhart, William Quinn, secs, Lincoln, GB
WALTON, Robert, Nathaniel Walton, gdn, 3/7/1831, Emanuel, GB
WALTON, Robert, decd, Thomas Glascock, Zachariah Williams issued L/A 1/3/1801; pd Elisha's board and JohN Walton for William and Robert; 1804 Thomas Glascock, gdn of Thomas; Robert Watkins, gdn of George; Edward Rowell, gdn of Eliza; Robert and Augustus, sons, Richmond, AB, GB
WALTON, Thomas Camber, decd, Anderson Watkins issued L/A 10/3/1804, Jacob Danforth, Thomas Glascock, secs, Richmond, AB
WALTON, William, decd, Richard Bray, gdn for orphs: John and Sophia, 1/12/1824, James E. Todd, William M. Larkin, secs, Lincoln, GB
WAMBLE, Allen B., orph of Egberton, decd, John Walker issued L/G 1/7/1834, Washington
WARD, Edward, believed to be idiot occasioned by fever, Mrs. Mary Crews applies for aid, allowed $40 per year 1/5/1825, Camden, MIC

WARD, Elias, decd, William Allen issued L/A 4/24/1795, Benjamin Nowland, sec, Richmond, AB
WARD, Elisha, decd, William A. Smith, admr, Dooly, OD
WARD, Elisha, decd, Elizabeth Ward, admx, 1/22/1844; appraisers: Lewis Simmons, David T. Ward, John J. Stevens, Robert Ward; purchasers at sale: Elizabeth, David T. and Robert Ward, John Gambell, Henry Askew, Alfred Dorsett, etc., Dooly, I&A
WARD, George, decd, John L. Holliday and Mildred Ward, admrs, Robert Holliday, Eli Edmondson, surs, 7/1849, 1851-1853 retns, Fayette, AB
WARD, Joseph, decd, L/A to John Williams 3/3/1817, Laurens, AB
WARD, Patrick, decd, Arthur Scott issued L/A 4/20/1814, Thomas Duley, Benjamin Moore, secs, Richmond, AB
WARD, Peter Zachary, chose Thomas Watson as his gdn 1/3/1814, Jackson, OM
WARD, Polly chose Thomas Watson as her gen 1/3/1814, Jackson, OM
WARD, Thomas, decd, John Lovejoy, exr, in rt of his wife, gives notice to Georgia Journal to sell 239 acres in Richmond Co., 8/1/1814, Jackson, OM
WARD, Thomas, decd, Mary Ward issued L/A 5/4/1801, Thomas Watson, James McManus, secs, Richmond, AB
WARD, Thomas, orph, Thomas Watson, gdn, 1814, Jackson, OM
WARD, William, decd, John Peter Ward apptd admr 11/20/1790, Chatham, Adms
WARD, William W., decd, James L. Waters issued L/A w/LWT annexed 3/7/1855, William Barnwell, James Rylee, secs, Hall, AB
WARDLAW, William, decd, John R. Wardlaw, A. Dunnagan, S. M. Wardlaw, admrs, Harris
WARDROBE, William, decd, George Baillie, admr, makes title to 769 acres on St. Simons Island to Thomas Young of Savannah in compliance with contract dtd 6/6/1812 betwn decd and Young, 7/1/1816, Glynn, MIC
WARE, James, decd, James Ware, gdn of orphs: Mary Jane, Ann Eliza, James and Wesley 3/5/838, Nicholas Ware, sec, Lincoln, GB
WARE, John, decd, inv of property 8/10/1795, Franklin, OM
WARE, Joseph, decd, 1/5/1819 div of slaves-Robert and Polly Ware, heirs; land divided between 7 heirs, Richmond
WARNER, Mary, decd, Pleasant H. Key issued L/A 5/4/1850, Baldwin
WARNOCK, Mathew, decd, of South Carolina, John Warnock applied for L/A 3/16/1798, Greene, Misc
WARREN, Bray, decd, L/A issued Joseph Warren with John Martin and John G. Towns as surs, 5/3/1819, Jasper, OM
WARREN, Elias, orph of Joseph, decd, under age 15, John Warren as next of kin apptd gdn 3/3/1806, Liberty, MIC, GB
WARREN, Farabee, decd, J. H. Carter was issued L/A 12/1872, Webster, OD
WARREN, John, orph of Joseph, decd, over age of 14, John Warren as next of kin apptd gdn 3/3/1806, Liberty, MIC, GB
WARREN, John Z., orph of John, decd, Daniel Kennedy, gdn, James Scarborough, Nathaniel Walton, sur, 9/2/1833, Emanuel, GB
WARREN, Josiah, orph of Josiah, decd, Mary Warren, gdn, John Youmans, sur, 1/4/1836, Emanuel, GB
WARREN, Malinda Ann issued L/G for David W. Warren and Elias Warren 9/1872, Webster, OD
WARREN, Mary, John Bryan, gdn, p. 61, Screven, OM
WARREN, Mary, orph of Josiah, decd, Mary Warren, gdn, John Youmans, sur, 1/4/1836, Emanuel, GB
WARREN, Reuben, decd, John Thomas Warren, admr 1/1836, Moses Ramsey, James Warren, S. B. Strickland, J. A. Dasher, surs on bond; apprs: E. T. Shepherd, J. S. Dasher, Dempsey Hall, Thomas Brinsfield; purchaser at sale: James T. Warren, Stewart, Adms

WARREN, Robert, decd, George W. Harrison, gdn of orphs: James H.
M. and Luther C. A., 7/3/1838, Randolph, GB
WARREN, Sarah, orph of Joseph, decd, over age 14, John Warren as
next of kin apptd gdn 3/3/1806, Liberty, MIC, GB
WARREN, Sarah, orph of Josiah, decd, Mary Warren, gdn, John
Youmans, sur, 1/4/1836, Emanuel, GB
WARREN, Solomon, orph of Joseph, decd, under age 15, John Warren
as next of kin apptd gdn 3/3/1806, Liberty, MIC, GB
WARREN, Synthy, orph of Josiah, decd, Mary Warren, gdn, John
Youmans, sur, 1/4/1836, Emanuel, GB
WARREN, Thomas, decd, William Blair, etc. to divide estate, p.
60, Screven, OM
WARREN, W., decd, L/A issued to Stephen E. Warren 6/1872,
Webster, OD
WADSDEN, Chloe, decd, John Willfox issued L/A 5/7/1827, James
Primrose, Henry Byrd, secs, Richmond, AB
WASHINGTON, William, decd, LWT names ch---John, Ephraim, Mary and
Sarah Washington, Hancock, AA
WATERMAN, Flavius, decd, James Hanney having failed to give bond
to admr the estate, Elihu Atwater apptd admr in his place, he
being atty for the heirs 7/2/1811, Camden, MIC
WATERS, Clement, decd, LWT dtd 8/30/1835 pvd by Benjamin C. Wyly,
Obadiah and William Waters, exrs, named wife, Rachel and ch--
Martha, Mary Ann, Habersham, MIC
WATERS, Isaac, decd, John Watters made annual retn as gdn of
heirs 1839, 3/2/1840, Bulloch, Misc
WATERS, Isaac, decd, appraisal 5/16/1828 by Edward Warren, David
Kennedy, Colson Groover; John Waters, admr; heirs---William,
Sarah, Thomas, James and Lucretia Waters, John Waters', gdn,
11/1/1830; George W. Rhodes for his wife, Sarah´s share,
8/7/1833, Bulloch, Misc
WATERS, James, decd, Elijah Waters, admr w/LWT annexed, Josiah
Drew, Thomas Drew, Henry Durden, surs, 7/6/1835, Emanuel, GB
WATERS, Matthew, decd, Nat Bedingfield, admr, 10/11/1789 list of
debtors; Sherwood Wise, Joshua Lea, Thomas Stroud, Richard Tiner,
William Sidwell, Randle Griffin, Wilkes, MxR
WATKINS, Robert, decd, Elizabeth M. and Anderson Watkins issued
L/A 11/22/1805; 1812 division to four of children and heirs---
Thomas, Robert, George, Claiborn Anderson and John Robert
Watkins, Richmond, AB, GR
WATKINS, Thomas, decd, Robert Watkins and Mary Hatcher, gns of
orphs 5/3/1824---Martha, Robert A., J. Thomas and V. Walker
Watkins; 5/26/1828, Mary Hatcher, gdn of orphs, Robert Arrington,
Martha, Isaac, Thomas and Walker Watkins, Richmond, GB
WATKINS, William, decd, inventory of estate 7/3/1802; L/A issued
Joseph Terrell 11/9/1801, Franklin, OM
WATSON, Anderson, decd, 7/1842 apprs: Henry B. Lee, John
Robinson, Thomas House, A. Robinson, Stewart, Adms
WATSON, Ansel, decd, John B. and Sarah Watson issued L/A
11/6/1854, David G. Watson, John Bruce, secs, Hall, AB
WATSON, David, decd, Alexander Bright issued L/A 9/15/1828, John
Morrison, sec, Richmond, AB
WATSON, Elijah J., order for cancellation of note, p. 77,
Screven, OM
WATSON, Elizabeth, orph of Thomas, decd, John Grishim, gdn,
William Grisham, Joseph E. Brown, surs, 11/1/1852, Cherokee, GB
WATSON, George W., decd, Isaiah F. B. Scrimskim apptd admr
12/1854, Webster, OD
WATSON, John, decd, Major Watson issued L/A 10/4/1819, Joshua
Sego, Robert Allen, secs; 1825 division to heirs--Mrs. Sarah
Watson, Martha (Patsy), Mary Ann, Elizabeth, William and Ellinor,
Richmond, AB, AR

WATSON, John, decd, John Hambleton and Mark Rogers, exrs of LWT 1/1808, Oglethorpe, OM
WATSON, Joseph G., orph of Thomas, decd, John Grisham, gdn, William Grisham, Joseph E. Brown, surs, 11/1/1852; James R. Brown, Joel L. Galt, gdns 7/12/1858, Cherokee, GB
WATSON, Lawrence, decd, Elizabeth Watson apptd admx 11/5/1784, Chatham, Adms
WATSON, Lewis, decd, David P. Fossett, admr, 11/1837; apprs: Henry W. Spears, A. Prim, Cullen Roberts, Jones Griffin; purchasers at sale: James Ashley, James Barber, Jacob Carter, Lewis Cowart, A. Dyass, F. D. Dyass, Thomas Dyass, Stewart, Adms
WATSON, Nancy E., orph of Thomas, decd, James R. Brown, Joel L. Galt, gdns, 7/12/1858, Cherokee, GB
WATSON, Peter, decd, Reuben Walker issued L/A 4/4/1815, Isaac Low, Smith Jones, secs, Richmond, AB
WATSON, Thomas, decd, Joseph and Peggy McCormack issued L/A 11/15/1783, Thomas Watson, sec, Richmond, AB
WATSON, Thomas, decd, William Watson, admr, 3/1847; 1850 retn, Fayette, AB
WATSON, William, decd, John Baker qualified admr 2/14/1791, Liberty, Ests
WATTERS, Collins, decd, Stacey Watters, admx, William Right, sec, 1/8/1833, Hall, AB
WATTS, Elizabeth J., orph of Richard, decd, Thomas Watts, gdn, 1/6/1820, Richard Whatley, sec, Morgan, GB
WATTS, Jubal, orph of Jubal, decd, late of Green Co., Ga., James R. McCord, gdn, John W. McCord, James H. Stark, John Goodman, John Andrews, surs, 7/5/1841, 1841 retn by gdn, Butts, GB, ER
WATTS, Jubal, decd, C. N. Daniel, exr, Butts, ER
WATTS, Littleberry, decd, Pleasant Watts and John Bailey issued L/A 5/4/1818, John Bailey, Jubel Watts, Reuben Lockett, secs; Pleasant Watts, gdn of orphs---Mahaly Ann and Emily 5/3/1819, Morgan, AB, GB
WATTS, Margaret G., orph of Richard, Ludwell Watts, gdn, 7/10/1821, Richard Whatley, sec, Morgan, GB
WATTS, Nancy M., orph of Littleberry, decd, Elisha Hunter, gdn, 5/3/1819, Joshua Askew, Martin P. Sparks, secs, Morgan, GB
WATTS, Nancy S., orph of Richard, decd, Thomas Watts, gdn, 1/6/1823, Joshua Askew, Martin P. Sparks, secs, Morgan, GB
WATTS, Paschal W., orph of Littleberry, decd, Elisha Hunter, gdn, 5/3/1819, Joshua Askew, Martin P. Sparks, secs, Morgan, GB
WATTS, Sarah, orph of Jubal, decd, late of Greene Co., Ga., James R. McCord, gdn, John W. McCord, James H. Stark, John Goodman, John Andrews, surs, 7/5/1841, 1841 retn by gdn, Butts, GB, ER
WATTS, Thomas, decd, appraisers: O. Porter, I. Browning, William Browning, 12/22/1797, Greene, Misc
WAY, Ann, decd, Joseph Winn, Mary Jones qualified as admrs 8/5/1790; Joseph Way, Sr. qualified as exr 10/1792, Liberty, Ests
WAY, Edward, decd, Joseph Way, Sr. qualified as admr 3/7/1786, Liberty, Ests
WAY, John, decd, John Bacon, admr, gtd leave to sell 220 acres in Liberty Co., 1/25/1813, Liberty, MIC
WAY, John, Sr., decd, Jemima and William Way qualified as admrs 3/2/1789, Liberty, Ests
WAY, Joseph, decd, of Liberty Co., Ga., L/A to William Rountree 5/22/1829, Robert Maharry, Benjamin F. Buel, secs, Richmond, AB
WAY, William, Jr., decd, john and Hannah Way qualified as admrs 3/7/1791; Hannah Way, now Cole, qualified as admx 1/24/1792, Liberty, Ests
WAYNE, Thomas, decd, William Gibson, admr, rendered his acct with Robert G. Shaw, admr of same est in Boston, Massachusetts 6/3/1823, Camden, MIC

WEAKS, Edward, decd, Francis Weaks applied for temporary L/A
12/1827; Juda M., widow, sd she wanted admn along with Jeremiah
Cleveland; John Weaver to be reld as security of Jeremiah
Cleveland and Juda H. Weaks, admrs, 7/13/1830, Habersham, MIC
WEATHERBY, George, decd, Septimus Weatherby applied for admn,
John Myrick, G. Smith, surs, 11/2/1807, Warren, MIC, AB
WEATHERBY, George, decd, admrs gtd leave to sell real estate
2/3/1812, Warren, MIC
WEATHERBY, Owen, decd, inventory 2/10/1813 by Peter W. Gautier,
Hiram Lazier, John Donaldson, David Smith; 1814 by Sarah
Weatherby, admx, and Richard Holmes, admr, Jasper, Ests
WEATHERS, Pleasant R., late of Alabama, decd, William S. Rockwell
issued L/A 7/5/1847, Baldwin
WEATHERSBY, Elizabeth, minor orph of Owen H., decd, Edward
Lovejoy aptd gdn 5/12/1820, Jasper, OM
WEATHERSBY, James, minor orph of Owen H., decd, Edward Lovejoy
apptd gdn 5/12/1820, Jasper, OM
WEATHERSBY, Owen, decd, L/A gtd to Sarah Weathersby 2/1813,
Jasper, OM
WEAVER, John, decd, Stephen Weaver issued L/A 10/4/1797, Jonathan
Weaver, sec, Martin and Hennery Moore and John Lambeth,
appraisers, Richmond, AB
WEAVER, Marion Lafayette, orph of Hiram, decd, John R. M. Neel,
gdn, 1/8/1838, Randolph, GB
WEBB, Benjamin, Jr., decd, Benjamin Webb, Sr., admr, 9/24/1842;
apprs: Ambrose Whittle, James Rackley, james S. odom; purchasers
at sale: Benjamin Webb, Sr., William maddox, Y. H. Daniels,
Dooly, I&A
WEBB, Calvin, decd, H. W. McDaniel issued L/A 2/7/1859, Fulton
WEBB, Eli, orph of Giles, decd, L/G issued Richard Wartus
3/4/1839, Washington
WEBB, Giles, orph of Giles, decd, L/G issued to Holland Webb
1829; Hamilton Smith issued L/G 11/4/1839; William A. Webb issued
L/G 1/2/1842, Washington
WEBB, Henry, decd, Jesse Mixon, admr, applies for dismission
12/23/1794, Effingham, Misc
WEBB, James, decd, L/T issued 5/29/1797 to John Powers and Curtis
Loper on LWT; LWT dtd 5/8/1797 pvd 5/29/1797 names: brother,
Jesse Webb, when age 21; sisters: Lydia, Elizabeth, Sarah, Martha
and Jane, Effingham, Misc
WEBB, John, orph of Thomas, decd, Isaac Webb apptd gdn with John
Hill, sec, 1/7/1822, Jasper, OM
WEBB, Mary, a poor child, bound to Lawrence Hill, Frances
McLendon, sec, 7/7/1814, Jasper, OM
WEBB, Matilda, decd, Floyd T. McAlpin, admr, 4/7/1863, james
Pierce, sur, DeKalb, AB
WEBB, Richard, decd, inventory 3/3/1780; purchasers: George
Barber, John Clark, Jerry Cloud, Daniel Butler, David Thirman,
James Smith, Mistress Webb, Capt. Nail, Ford Butler, Thomas
Johnson, William Barnett; Matthew More apptd admr 12/25/1779,
Wilkes, MxR
WEBB, W. C., Simeon Brawner, Young T. Standify, Solomon Harper,
gdns, 9/4/1837, Harris, GB
WEBSTER, William, decd, Charles Bostick issued L/A 1/1/1785,
James McNeill, Henry Allison, secs, Richmond, AB
WEED, Jacob, decd, of Camden Co., Ga., Sarah Weed issued L/A
6/1/1792, Thomas Carr, James Fox, secs, Richmond, AB
WEEKES, John, decd, George Stovall and Joseph Cooper issued L/A
2/5/1810, Putnam, AB
WEIR, Priscilla J., daughter of Samuel, decd, Sampson D.
Bridgeman of Ware Co., Ga. apptd trustee for his wife, 3/3/1836,
Clarke, LP

WEITMAN, Hannah, decd, LWT admitted to record 7/4/1846; recd from Christian Wisenbaker, extrx, 1/3rd share of est, signed R. E. Zittrour and James Rahn, 6/25/1847, Effingham, MIC
WEITMAN, John Lewis, Naomi Weitman, gdn 7/6/1840, Effingham, MIC
WEITMAN, Matthew, decd, ordered that Naomi Weitman sell real estate 11/6/1837, Effingham, MIC
WEITMAN, Solomon, decd, James Rahn applies for L/A 9/15/1837; Margaret Weitman makes choice of child's pt of est 7/3/1838, Effingham, MIC
WELCH, N. N., decd, John L. Harris, admr, 5/2/1853, A. Puckett, sur, DeKalb, AB
WELDON, Joseph, decd, Michael Griffin issued L/A 4/30/1784, John Germany, John Hammacks, secs, Richmond, AB
WELDON, Joseph, decd, Sally and Robert Weldon, Thomas McLeroy, admrs, 5/5/1838, Harris, AB
WELLBORN, Cornelius B., orph of Oliver H. P., decd, Charity Wellborn, gdn, 2/5/1855, Houston, GB
WELLS, David H., decd, L. G. Wells issued L/A 10/2/1865, Fulton
WELLS, John S., decd, L/A to John T. Carter 12//1862, White, AB
WELLS, Joseph, decd, William Jeans Baker qualified as admr 7/1785, Liberty, Ests
WELLS, Littleberry, decd, Archibald Watts and John Beasley issued L/A 1/26/1818, Morgan, AB
WELLS, Lucy May, minor orph of Jackson, decd, Mary Mary Buckner, gdn, 2/5/1866, Fulton, GB
WELLS, Mary, decd, David Rees, Jonathan Shaw qualified as admrs 5/8/1793, Liberty, Ests
WELLS, Mary A., decd, Robert B. Wells, S. L. Hill, William Hartsfield, adms, Harris, AB
WELLS, Thomas, decd, Laban T. Freeman, gdn of Joseph, Thomas and Mary, orphs, 1/3/1825, Nicholas Sheats, sur, Clarke, GB
WELLS, William W., orph of William M., decd, Edward W. Munday, gdn, 7/16/1857, Fulton
WENDERWEEDLE, Henry, decd, Jane Wenderweedle, admx, 9/1836; apprs: John Ware, Davenport Lawson, William Wenderweedle, W. A. May; purchasers at sale: Asbury Cowles, Elijah Garrett, Davenport Lawson, Washington Nix, etc., Stewart, Adms
WERTCH, John Gasper, decd, Hergen Herson apptd admr 3/2/1792, Effingham, Misc
WESENER, Thomas, decd, l/A gtd John Donaldson 3/1819, Jasper, OM
WEST, Enoch, decd, H. W. B. West and Jemima M. West issued L/A 11/7/1859, Levi Jackson H. J. Hill, secs, White, AB
WEST, John, decd, John and Elinor Nelson issued L/A 10/3/1783, William Candler, Isaac Jackson, secs, Richmond, AB
WEST, John, decd, William H. West issued L/A 9/19/1848, Elizabeth West, George W. Ogle, Jeptha B. Harrington, Ira Gaines, secs, Hall, AB
WEST, William, decd, Solomon Burford applied for L/A 2/28/1797; recd 5/16/1797 of Ellis West $300 for all claims or demands against sd Ellis West or his heirs and est of decd, signed Tyre Clements, Greene, Misc
WEST, William H., decd, Maria L. West was issued L/A 12/5/1864, Hall, AB
WESTBROOK, Moses, decd, Gainey Joseph and James Westbrook, admrs, apptd 1834; John D. Stell, J. Lamberth, surs, 11/1834; 1839 retn, Fayette, AB
WESTBROOK, Richard N., lunatic, William C. Spier, gdn, 8/7/1854, Houston, GB
WESTER, Ann, orph of Richard, decd, Ezra New issued L/G 12/3/1838, Washington
WESTER, Axsey, orph of Richard, decd, Ezra New issued L/G 12/3/1838, Washington

WESTER, Elias, orph of Elias, decd, bound to Leon Thrash 8/18/1808, Tattnall, MIC
WESTER, Elias, orph of Richard, decd, Daniel Johnson, gdn 7/6/1840, Montgomery, GB
WESTER, Elizabeth, orph of Elias, decd, bound to Leon Thrash 8/18/1808, Tattnall, MIC
WESTER, Hardey, decd, LWT pvd, Fannie Wester and Sampson Ivey qualified as exrs 5/10/1795, Warren, MIC
WESTER, Henry, orph of Elias, decd, bound to Leon Thrash 8/18/1808, Tattnall, MIC
WESTER, Nancy, orph of Richard, decd, Richmond Bedgood issued L/G 3/5/1838; Josiah T. King issued L/G 12/3/1838, Washington
WESTER, Richard, decd, inventory 10/1836; apprs: William Mann, George Grady, Thomas Grace; retns name Samuel S., Elias, Henry, John, Nancy, Elizabeth, Zilpha, Lucy Ann and Arcy Ann Wester; Alexandria Johnson, gdn of orphs 1/1/1838 (Henry, Elizabeth and Zilpha), John Morris, Samuel McAllister, secs, Montgomery, GB
WESTER, Sarah, orph of Elias, decd, bound to Leon Thrash 8/18/1808, Tattnall, MIC
WESTMORELAND, Elizabeth, decd, L/A gtd to Robert Westmoreland 3/1826, Reuben Westmoreland and Daniel Dawkins, secs, Pike, MIC
WESTMORELAND, John, decd, Calvin L. Westmoreland and Thomas C. Mathews, admrs, John A. Smith and James H. Westmoreland, secs, 11/1848; 1851 retn, Fayette, AB
WETHERBY, Gideon, decd, Joseph Herigan, admr, 3/8/1837, Randolph
WETHERFORD, Charles, decd, LWT pvd 1814, Jasper, OM
WHALEY, Caleb A., decd, J. A. Hayden issued L/A 2/2/1863, Fulton
WHALEY, John, decd, P. H. Allen, admr, Jesse Ward, sur, 1847 retn, Fayette, AB
WHALEY, William, decd, LWT pvd 9/8/1795, wife, Hannah, son, Eli; wit: Nathaniel Whaley, Wm Phillips, Greene, Misc
WHATLEY, Orman, decd, Charles Pate and Sarah Whatley issued L/A 11/8/1817, Morgan, AB
WHATLEY, Walton, decd, Archibald Whatley, exr dismissed 9/1806, Oglethorpe, OM
WHATLEY, William R., decd, Clary Whatley, gdn of orphs: Mary W., Nancy Simon, Elizabeth and William, 3/15/1823, Morgan, GB
WHATLEY, William R., decd, Michael Whatley and Ludwick Alford issued L/A 1/5/1818, Joshua Askew, sec, Morgan, AB
WHATLEY, Willis, L/G gtd Greene Whatley 11/4/1816, Jasper, OM
WHATLEY, Willis, decd, LWT dtd 5/1/1788 pvd 1/6/1800, Michael Whatley, exr, wife, Catheron, children: Willis, Shirley, Greene, Ornan, Gennit, Nancy; bro., Michael, exr, Greene Co. land, Hancock, AA
WHATLEY, Willis, minor orph of Willis, decd, Abner Bartlett apptd gdn, with Wm McDowell, John McLemore, secs, 9/1813, Jasper, OM
WHEALY, William, decd, Elizabeth Whealy gtd L/A 2/26/1788, Greene, Misc
WHEELER, Isaac, decd, LWT pvd, Henry Saddler qualified as exr 12/4/1813, Camden, MIC
WHEELER, Isaiah, decd, Mrs. Delilah Wheeler issued L/A 11/5/1844; James Seareer?, admr de bonis non 1/10/1848, Baldwin
WHEELER, James H., decd, Alexander Fitzpatrick issued L/A 3/3/1824, Bennett Fitzpatrick, sec, Morgan, AB
WHEELER, James Troup, minor heir of Martha, Hezekiah Rogers issued L/G 8/15/1843, Washington
WHEELER, Richard, Nancy Wheeler, gdn, 10/26/1844, Dooly, OD
WHEELER, William, decd, John Garman issued L/A 7/1833, Hall
WHEELER, William, decd, Nancy Wheeler, temp admx, 10/26/1844; purchasers at sale: Nancy and Josiah Wheeler, William Newman, J. F. Harvard, Richard Clewis, Daniel Rowland, Dooly, I&A

WHEELER, William, decd, LWT pvd 9/7/1812 names youngest bros-
Freeman & Richard; exr, John Echols; Mary Wheeler gtd L/A
9/6/1813; debts due from Lucy Wheeler, Robert Williams, Mary,
William and Elizabeth Wheeler 10/27/1809, Franklin, OM
WHEET, William, decd, Polly (or Patty) Wheet, wid, apptd admx
4/16/1782, Wilkes, MxR
WHELCHEL, Nancy, decd, Francis Whelchel, admr, R. F. Daniel, sur,
2/6/1854, Cherokee, AB
WHIDDON, Ely, orph of Dempsey, decd, John Barwick issued L/G
11/4/1833, Washington
WHIDDON, Jane, orph of Dempsey, decd, John Barwick issued L/G
11/4/1833, Washington
WHIDDON, Mary, orph of Dempsey, decd, John Barwick issued L/G
11/4/1833, Washington
WHIDDON, Rhoda Ann, orph of Dempsey, decd, John Barwick issued
L/G 11/4/1833, Washington
WHIDDON, Susannah, orph of Dempsey, decd, John Barwick issued L/G
11/4/1833, Washington
WHIDDON, William, decd, Eli Whiddon, admr, Ephraim Hunington,
Sampson Diland, sur, 1/4/1819, appraisal 2/13/1819, Emanuel, A, AE
WHINNEY, Joseph, decd, Elenor Whinney issued temp L/A 3/16/1814,
Putnam, AB
WHITAKER, Edwin, decd, James C. Whitaker gtd L/A 3/4/1844,
Baldwin
WHITAKER, Isaac, decd, inv appaised 2/16/1805 by Joseph Terrell,
Thomas Covington, Epps Chatham, 2/12/1805, Franklin, IMW
WHITAKER, Isaac, decd, L/A issued William Williamson 2/12/1805,
Franklin, OM
WHITAKER, Joseph J., decd, LWT pvd 12/10/1838, Henry Whitaker,
exr, Harris
WHITAKER, Mary, decd, Henry Whitaker, exr´s bond, Harris
WHITAKER, Samuel, decd, Polly Whitaker and William Graves issued
L/A 2/12/1805, Franklin, OM
WHITAKER, William, decd, 9/1842, apprs: Thomas C. Curry, Michael
Duskin, Daniel Bartlett, land owned in Columbia Co.; purchasers
at sale: Charlotte Clark, Isaac Cliatt, J. J. Jacob N., John M.
J., Nancy and V. Whitaker, Stewart, Adms
WHITE, Amelia, decd, William Jackson issued L/A 4/4/1825,
Benjamin F. Verdery, sec, Richmond, AB
WHITE, Asa, legatee of Daniel, decd, Jesse Fortson, gdn, 1809-
1810 retns, Elbert, GR
WHITE, Daniel, decd, Wm Davis, exr, 1809 retns pd Martin White,
gdn of John White, minor; 1810 retn pd P. Christian, gdn of Eppy
White, minor, Elbert, GR
WHITE, James, decd, Robert and Joseph White gtd L/A 3/7/1797,
Columbia, Ests
WHITE, James, decd, Samuel White applied for L/A 9/2/1844,
Effingham, MIC
WHITE, James T., decd, Elizabeth and William White, admrs,
1/1836; apprs: John A. Burks, William Porter, C. S. Baldwin;
purchasers at sale: Joshua Willet, James Givens, Henry Clem,
etc., Stewart, Adms
WHITE, John, decd, William Gordon, admr, 2/9/1788, Chatham, Adms
WHITE, John G., decd, Samuel Adams, admr, 1/1836; Samuel
Passmore, Samuel Johnston, surs on bond; apprs: Wesley Vinson,
Daniel & John Richardson, Henry Sarr, John Lansford, Robert
Gawley; purchasers at sale: Wm H. McGee, Stewart, Adms
WHITE, John Robert, decd, Thomas Few was gtd L/A 6/21/1797,
Columbia, Ests
WHITE, Joseph, decd, L/A gtd Thomas White, with Wm Johnson, James
Bullard, secs, 5/1816; Avarilla B. White, admx, takes child´s pt
of est 11/4/1816, Jasper, OM

WHITE, Joseph, decd, Robert White, admr, 5/6/1815, Aaron Denton, John Hamilton, surs, Warren, AB
WHITE, Joseph, decd, Thomas M. Dennis, admr, 1833, Stewart, Adms
WHITE, Mary, decd, LWT pvd 7/5/1841, Henry White, exr, Harris
WHITE, Moses, decd, Pleasant White, admr, 1803 retns, apprs: Harry Muckleroy, Enoch Pearson, Tyree Landers, Elbert, AR
WHITE, R. H., decd, A. J. White, admr, John D. White, John Garland, sur 2/14/1848, Bibb, AB
WHITE, Robert, decd, John Andrews apptd admr, Joseph C. Little, sur 5/5/1851, Butts, AB
WHITE, Sally, insane, Joseph Ratchford apptd gdn, 11/2/1812, Jackson, OM
WHITE, Samuel, decd, LWT 12/21/1810 names ch: William, Ruthey, Jiney and Mary, wife, Ann, Jasper, Ests
WHITE, Thomas, decd, Samuel Boyd apptd admr, Ezekiel Hudnal having caveated the appointment 4/3/1809, Camden, MIC
WHITE, Thomas G., gdn of children by his present wife, Olive S. White, 9/2/1839, Harris
WHITE, William, decd, Mary Ann B. White, Hugh Nesbitt L/A 12/2/1822; 1824 div wid & ch-Mrs. Mary Ann B. White, Robt F. Poe, rt of wf, Eliza P., Wm Longstreet, rt of wf, Mary Ann Olivia, Geo. O'Keefe, Anna Eve & Eleanor Nesbitt, Richmond, AB
WHITE, William, decd, Jethro Darden, Sr., admr, 3/23/1818, James Vaughan, sur, Warren, AB
WHITE, William, decd, John English, Sarah White, admrs, Randall Duckworth, Jacob Watson, sur, 5/4/1812, Jones, AB
WHITE, William, Sr., decd, William White applies for adm 2/15/1803, Jacob Burkhalter, William Matthews, sur, L/A gtd 7/6/1807, Warren, MIC, AB
WHITE, Zachariah, decd, John Charlton applies for L/A 3/12/1838, Effingham, MIC
WHITEACKER, John, decd, Edward and Martha Burch issued L/A 7/24/1783, John Smith, Nathaniel Beall, secs, Richmond, AB
WHITEHEAD, John, decd, Thomas Whitehead, Sr. issued temp L/A 3/17/1814, Putnam, AB
WHITFIELD, Richard, decd, late of Lincoln Co., Samuel Neilson was issued L/A on 9/4/1814, George Adams, John Cashin, secs, Richmond, AB
WHITMAN, William, decd, 1812 retn by Elizabeth Whitman, admx, Elbert, AR
WHITMIRE, Mary, decd, Benjamin F. Porter issued L/A 1/7/1840, R. Sandford, sec, Hall, AB
WHITMIRE, Stephen, decd, John Whitmire, admr w/LWT annexed, Hall
WHITSETT, James, decd, Thomas Whitsett applies for L/A 6/4/1853, Benjamin Green, sur, Lee
WHITSETT, John, decd, Benjamin Green applies for L/A 4/5/1852, Thomas Whitsett, sur, Lee
WHITTEN, James, decd, James Whitten, John Davenport, gdn of orphs, 3/4/1839, Harris
WHITTENDELL, James, decd, planter, Mary Whittendell apptd admx 4/4/1783, Chatham, Adms
WHITTICAR, Samuel, decd, L/A gtd to Polly Whitticar 8/3/1804, Franklin, IMW
WHITTLE, John, decd, William Barwick issued L/A 9/5/1836, Washington
WHITTON, John, decd, William Fambrough, admr, 10/17/1825 bond, Gilbert Robertson, sur, Clarke, AB
WHITTON, William, orph of William, decd, William Garner, gdn, 7/5/1824, Presley Garner, sur, Clarke, GB
WHITWORTH, Jacob, decd, LWT pvd, Samuel Whitworth exr 3/2/1812, Jackson, OM

WICKER, Keziah, decd, LWT pvd 5/2/1831, John Wicker and J. Warthen, exrs, Washington
WICKER, Linny, orph of William, decd, L/G issued Benjamin Wicker 9/7/1835, Washington
WICKER, Susannah, orph of William, decd, L/G issued Benjamin Wicker 9/7/1835, Washington
WICKER, Thomas, decd, Dennis Joseph issued L/A 1/20/1824; 1828 retn pd John, William, Benjamin and James Wicker. John Mills and wife, Robert Worthy and wife, Thomas Underwood and wife, John Beasley and wife, D. W. Crawford and wife, Monroe Co., Ga. land, Richmond, AB
WICKER, William, decd, L/A issued to Richard Warthen 9/12/1829, Washington
WIDINGTON, Robert, decd, Charity and Zeno Widington issued L/A 9/14/1812, Putnam, AB
WIGGANS, William, decd, James Wiggans, admr, est appraised, Emanuel, A
WIGGINS, Abraham, minor of Jesse, Benjamin Land, gdn, John C. hargraves, Timothy Matthews, surs, 9/5/1808, Warren, MIC, AB
WIGGINS, Belinda, minor of Jesse, Benjamin Lane, gdn, John C. Lane and Abraham L. Kirk, surs, 1/18/1849, Emanuel, GB
WIGGINS, Edmund, decd, Mary Wiggins exr of LWT 2/10/1790, Chatham, Adms
WIGGINS, Francis, minor of Jesse, Benjamin Lane, gdn, John C. Lane, Abraham L. Kirk, sur, 1/18/1849, Emanuel, GB
WIGGINS, Grace, minor of Jesse, Benjamin Lane, gdn, John C. Lane, Abraham L. Kirk, sur, 1/18/1849, Emanuel, GB
WIGGINS, Grady, John Wiggins apptd gdn, Henry Durden, Jesse Scarborough, sur, 9/6/1830, Emanuel, GB
WIGGINS, John R., decd, James A. Wiggins gtd L/A 7/7/1834, Baldwin
WIGGINS, Michael, minor of Jesse, Benjamin Lane, gdn, John C. Lane, Abraham L. Kirk, sur, 1/18/1849, Emanuel, GB
WIGGINS, Peter, decd, Rebecca Wiggins, Reuben May, admrs, 5/6/1822, Joel Neal, Peter May, surs, Warren, AB
WIGGINS, Salita, minor of Jesse, Benjamin Lane, gdn, John C. Lane, Abraham L. Kirk, sur, 1/18/1849, Emanuel, GB
WIGGINS, William, James Wiggins apptd gdn, John R. Daniell, sur, 9/5/1827, Emanuel, GB
WIGGINS, William, decd, James Wiggins apptd admr, Owen Fountain, William B. Nabb, sur, 9/7/1829, Emanuel, AB
WIGINS, Dicy, orph of Richard L., John McCullers issued L/G 1/9/1843, Washington
WIGINS, Edmund, orph of Richard L., John McCullers issued L/G 1/9/1843, Washington
WIGINS, Richard L., decd, John McCullers issued L/A 11/7/1842, Washington
WIGINS, William, decd, Eli Fenn issued L/A 1/5/1842, Washington
WIGINS, William, orph of Richard L., John McCullers issued L/G 1/9/1843, Washington
WILDER, William, decd, LWT pvd 4/19/1784, Wilkes, MxR
WILDER, William, decd, formerly of Wilkes Co., Sampson Wilder, admr de bonis non, 9/24/1822, Moses Alexander, sur, Warren, AB
WILERFORD, Wilson A., orph of Wilson P., decd, Charles W. Wilerford, gdn, Daniel D. Denham, sur, 1/1851, Fayette, AB
WILEY, Alexander, decd, William Lesly applied for L/A 5/25/1799, Greene, Misc
WILEY, George W., orph of John T., decd, John McCoy, gdn, Elijah McCoy, sur, 5/12/1856, Cherokee, GB
WILEY, John J., decd, Allen Woodall, admr, 6/1/1857, W. Wood, sur, DeKalb, AB

WILEY, Nicholas, orph and minor of Peter, decd, bound as apprentice to Henry Davis, carpenter, 1/1806, Oglethorpe, MIC

WILFS, James, decd, Burket Retnfrow, admr, R. Rentfrow, sur, 7/1844, Fayette, GB

WILHOIT, Adam, decd, 12/8/1801 Adam Gaar s recpt-he recd his father's pt of est /s/Michael & George Wilhoit, James Brown & Abraham Gaar. "each legatee to Adam Gaar for riding to Madison Court House, Va. and selling above estate", Elbert, AR

WILKERSON, Thomas, decd, David G. Hardwick issued L/A 7/3/1826, John Sidwell, sec, AB

WILKES, Benjamin, decd, L/A gtd Sarah, Moses and Aaron Wilkes, 3/1808, Oglethorpe, OM

WILKINS, Hill, minor son of Zachariah, Daniel P. Monroe and James L. Baird, gdns, 12/14/1858, Dawson, WB

WILKINS, John, decd, 7/1/1809 inventory, Thomas Wilkins, admr, Elbert, AR

WILKINS, John, decd, Micajah Williamson apptd admr 9/18/1783, Wilkes, MxR

WILKINS, John, decd, Paul Hambleton Wilkins apptd admr 12/24/1789, Chatham, Adms

WILKINS, Jonathan, decd, George Threadcraft requests for adm 5/1/1784, apptd admr 9/4/1784, Chatham, Adms

WILKINS, Thomas W., decd, Drury Pace, admr, 6/1/1863, DeKalb, AB

WILKINSON, Allen, decd, John Spears, Thomas Hickson, Richard Mitchell, admrs, 5/22/1834, Harris

WILKINSON, Ann G., orph of Young, decd, Charles Kinman, gdn, 9/7/1818, Morgan, GB

WILKINSON, Duncan, decd, Alexander Wilkinson, Thomas Hickson, admrs, 1/12/1835, Harris

WILKINSON, Hazelwood, decd, David Sidwell issued L/A 3/4/1816, John Sidwell, Thomas Davis, secs; Charles Kinnon and Erwin Morgan issued L/A 3/10/1818, Morgan, AB

WILKINSON, Young, decd, Lucy Wilkinson issued L/A 3/4/1816, Thomas and James Head, secs; Lucy Wilkinson, gdn of orph: Ann G., 3/18/1816, William Gill, sec, Morgan, AB

WILKISON, Lemuel, decd, Joseph Dobson, gdn of orphs: Elizabeth and Samuel 11/1828, Habersham, MIC

WILKISON, Mary's illegitimate child, Joseph Dobson, gdn, applies for leave to sell 150 acres, 9th Dist., Carroll Co., 5/2/1831, Habersham, MIC

WILLBANKS, Hezekiah, gdn of his ch: Nancy Jane, Mary Ann E., William H., Martha Ann, Margarett Ann, Francis P., Armina K., John Lewis and George W.; Mackey A. Keith, sur, 11/11/1859, Cherokee

WILLCOX, James W., decd, John Willcox, Jr. issued L/A 8/5/1829, Martin Willcox, sec, Richmond, AB

WILLCOX, John, Sr., decd, Martha and John Willcox, Jr. issued L/A 11/16/1829, Martin Willvox, Robert Thomas, secs; heirs: Martha Willcox, isaac Downs and wife, Betsy, Sarah and Wm Whitehead, Richmond, AB

WILLCOX, William W., decd, John Willcox, Sr. and Martin Willcox issued L/A 3/6/1822, Christopher Fletcher, B. B. Mitchell, secs, Richmond, AB

WILLFORD, Harvey, decd, Elliott Honeywell issued L/A 1/20/1824, Thomas Quisenberry, David Smith, secs, Richmond, AB

WILLIAMS, A. B., decd, James H. Williams, admr, 5/1852, 1851-1854 retns; Thomas Mathews, gdn of orphs, 11/1847, John and C. E. Westmoreland, surs, Fayette, AB, GB

WILLIAMS, Asa, orph of Thomas, decd, Elizabeth Williams, gdn, 9/2/1844, Emanuel, GB

WILLIAMS, Benjamin, decd, John Barber and Benjamin Moore issued L/A 9/7/1818, Thomas Barton, sec, Morgan, AB

WILLIAMS, Benjamin, decd, John C. Evans, gdn of orphs: Elizer, Charles and Aaron 3/6/1820, James Mitchel, Simeon Walker, secs, Morgan, GB
WILLIAMS, Berrian, decd, of Lee Co., John Richardson, admr 2/1833; apprs: Axiom Webb, David Richardson, R. F. Ford, John Crocker, John Coleman; purchasers at sale: G. G. & Robt J. Ford, James Little, Daniel & John Richardson, Stewart, Adms
WILLIAMS, Calistia, orph of Avington B., decd, William R. Moseley, gdn, James M. Bledsoe, Penelope Williams, sur, 5/7/1849, Butts, GB
WILLIAMS, Cerephia, orph of Avington B., decd, William R. Mosely, apptd gdn, James M. Bledsoe, Penelope Williams, sur, 5/7/1849, Butts, GB
WILLIAMS, Charles, decd, Susanna Williams, wid, apptd admx 11/6/1782, Wilkes, MxR
WILLIAMS, Christian, decd, L/A to Henry Williams 7/1/1811, Putnam, AB
WILLIAMS, Christopher, decd, LWT pvd 1/5/1801-ch-Joseph, Wm, Margaret, Elizabeth, Easter, Rachel Barnheard, Sarah, Mary, Bethenia; exrs, wife, Margaret Williams (later Thrower), Robt Clark; recpts-John Kindrick for Mary, wife, Hancock, AAA
WILLIAMS, David, orph of Garrett, Sr., Garrett Williams apptd gdn 7/5/1819, Bulloch, MIC
WILLIAMS, Eli, decd, L/A to Drury Mitchell 7/3/1813, Putnam, AB
WILLIAMS, Elizabeth (now Preston), John Bessant dismissed gdn 6/3/1850, Camden, MIC
WILLIAMS, Elizabeth, minor dau of William H., decd, A. J. Bessant apptd gdn 1/6/1835, Camden, MIC
WILLIAMS, Elizabeth, minor orph of Morgan, decd, chose Jonathan Wilborn, gdn, John Bailey, sec, 4/6/1807, Oglethorpe, OM, GB
WILLIAMS, Elizabeth L., orph of Avington B., decd, William R. Moseley, gdn, James M. Bledsoe, Penelope Williams, sur, 5/7/1849, Butts, GB
WILLIAMS, Elizabeth, orph of Benjamin, decd, Sarah Moore and William W. Moore, gdns, Levi Reynolds, William W. Moore, secs, 5/2/1820, Morgan, GB
WILLIAMS, Elizer, Benjamin, decd, John C. Evans, gdn of orhs: Elizer, Charles, Aaron, 3/6/1820, James Mitchel, Simon Walker, secs, Morgan, GB
WILLIAMS, Felix, orph, bound to James Colbert 5/1816, Jasper, OM
WILLIAMS, Frances, orph of Thomas, decd, Elizabeth Williams, gdn, 9/2/1844, Emanuel, GB
WILLIAMS, Frances, orph, ordered that Samuel Slater, Sheriff, take into his possession the child, 9/1/1823, Bulloch, MIC
WILLIAMS, Frederick Harrison, (orph of Frederick, LWT, Wilkes Co.) Harrison Musgrove apptd gdn, Samuel Thornton and Thomas Nelms, surs, 6/4/1794, Oglethorpe, MIC
WILLIAMS, Garrett, decd, sale bill of property, 1/11/1820, Bulloch, Misc
WILLIAMS, Henry, Sr., decd, Wingfield Cosby, admr, 1/29/1821, Frederick B. Heath, Richard Dozier, surs, Warren, AB
WILLIAMS, Hunter, decd, John Wiggins, Sr., admr, John Wiggins, Jr., sur, 9/6/1841, Emanuel, AB
WILLIAMS, James, LWT dtd 3/8/1816 named wife, Betsey and four youngest children: Polly, Sally, Sampson, Griffin and Ezekiel; oldest child, Nancy. exrs, friends, Henry Parrish & wife, Bulloch, Misc
WILLIAMS, James, decd, James Hudgins, Ruth Williams issued L/A 9/2/1833, Habersham, MIC
WILLIAMS, James, decd, John Matthews, James Lee, James Hollaway, Frederick Lanier, William Blann apptd to divide prop according to LW' 1/1/1821, Bulloch, MIC

WILLIAMS, James, decd, John S. Harmon issued L/A 7/3/1854, John Clark, sec, Hall, AB
WILLIAMS, James, decd, L/A issued Elizabeth Williams, 1/1825, Habersham, MIC
WILLIAMS, James, decd, Ruth Williams and James Hudgins issued L/A 5/1/1835, Habersham, MIC
WILLIAMS, James, decd, sale of land belonging to est 3/16/1822, Bulloch, Misc
WILLIAMS, Jane, decd, Duke Skipper apptd admr with LWT annexed; John Pierce caveated to appointment but did not appear (caveat dismissed), 8/4/1827, Camden, MIC
WILLIAMS, Jane, decd, LWT was pvd by Charles Homer 8/7/1826, Camden, MIC
WILLIAMS, Jesse, Jr., orph of Jesse, decd, Abraham Williams, gdn, 3/1836, John Russel, Marmaduke Gresham, surs on bond, Stewart, L/G, Adms
WILLIAMS, Jesse L., decd, P. F. Hoyle issued temporary L/A 11/5/1853, DeKalb, AB
WILLIAMS, John, decd, Mary Williams, admx, 3/2/1835, Shadrack Bradshaw, Woodson Bradshaw, surs, Warren, AB
WILLIAMS, John, decd, Joseph and James Williams issued L/A 11/6/1820, Ewing Morrow, Burwell Russell, secs, Morgan, AB
WILLIAMS, John, decd, William Seward issued L/A 2/7/1820, Laurens, AB
WILLIAMS, John A., orph of William M., decd, George D. Felarn issued L/G 3/1857, gdn makes retns 76/1863, Webster, OD
WILLIAMS, John G., orph of Garrett, Sr., Garrett Williams apptd gdn 7/5/1819, Bulloch, MIC
WILLIAMS, Jonathan, orph of Avington B., decd, William R. Moseley, gdn, James M. Bledsoe, Penelope Williams, sur, 5/7/1849, Butts, GB
WILLIAMS, Joseph, decd, 4/4/1807 inv, Matt J. Williams, admr; George Wynne, admr, in rt of his wife, 1809 retns, Elbert, AR
WILLIAMS, Joseph, decd, Burnell Russell and Ann Williams issued L/A 11/7/1825, Morgan, AB
WILLIAMS, Loeny, motion of James Hudgins and Benjamin Chastain, secs for Rebecca Williams that they are unwilling to stand for gdnshp 5/2/1831, Habersham, MIC
WILLIAMS, Louisa, orph, Rebecca Williams, gdn, 5/4/1829, Habersham, MIC
WILLIAMS, Marcus L., orph of Avington B., decd, William R. Moseley, gdn, James M. Bledsoe, Penelope Williams, sur, 5/9/1849, Butts, GB
WILLIAMS, Martha T., orph of Nathan, decd, Elizabeth Williams, gdn, Lemuel Atkinson, sur, 11/17/1836, Butts, GB
WILLIAMS, Mary, decd, William Tison, admr, 3/2/1846; apprs: Abner Holliday, S. C. Lippett, Littleton Chambless; purchasers at sale: Samuel Williams, R. G. Ford, L. M. Perkins, Washington Brown, Dooly, I&A
WILLIAMS, Mary Ann, orph of Nathan, decd, Elizabeth Williams, gdn, Lemuel Atkinson, sur, 11/17/1836, Butts, GB
WILLIAMS, Miles, decd, John B. Williams issued L/A 5/6/1822, Robert Brown, sec, Morgan, AB
WILLIAMS, Moses, orph of John, decd, Bennett Massey issued L/G 11/5/1832, Washington
WILLIAMS, Nathan, decd, LWT pvd 4/2/1836-wife, Elizabeth & ch: Peter, Lydia Carter, Agnes R. Evans, Clinton A., Thurzy H., Roland, Nancy O., James M., William, Martha T., Mary Ann; son, Nathan H., and nephew, Stephen W. Price, exrs, Butts, ER
WILLIAMS, Nathaniel, decd, Charloes Logue apptd admr, Nowell Robertson, sur, 3/7/1808, Bulloch, Misc

WILLIAMS, Peggy, (orph of Frederick, LWT, Wilkes Co.) Harrison Musgrove apptd gdn, Samuel Thornton and Thomas Nelms, surs, 6/4/1794, Oglethorpe, MIC
WILLIAMS, Philip, decd, Rachel Williams applies for L/A 7/4/1796, Elbert, AB
WILLIAMS, Polly, dau of Isaac, abandoned by both father and mother, bound to Wiley Ross 3/7/1808, Jackson, OM
WILLIAMS, Robert, decd, Christina Williams, admx, 3/11/1844; apprs: Elijah Bush, Thomas Cone, Caleb Fullington, Elisha Collins, Elisha Wade; purchasers at sale: Christina, David & Wm Williams, C. B. Ackrdige, F. K. Lewis, etc, Dooly, I&A
WILLIAMS, Samuel was apptd gdn of: Rowland, Deborah M., Robert and Sarah Williams, in lieu of Dilly Williams, 12/7/1818, Bulloch, MIC
WILLIAMS, Samuel, decd, 11/26/1843, Jesse Gilbert, admr; apprs: John M. Bottoms, James W. Fisher, Seth Kellam, Elisha Woodward, Alexander Meriwether, Dooly, I&A
WILLIAMS, Samuel, decd, Dilly Williams and John Williams issued L/A 1/6/1817, Bulloch, MIC
WILLIAMS, Samuel, decd, Loverd Bryan, Willard Boynton, Tomlinson Fort, Elijah E. Crocker, admrs, 3/1839; apprs: John Rushing, John West, John Talbot; decd owned 1700, 900 acres, 61 slaves, Stewart, Adms
WILLIAMS, Samuel, decd, division, heirs named: Delila, John, William, Samuel, Dilly, Rowlin, Deborah, Sarah and Robert Williams, Dolly Sweat, 2/7/1818, Bulloch, Misc
WILLIAMS, Samuel, decd, sale of two negroes belonging to est, 2/5/1818; inv. 2/15/1817, apprs: Joshua Hodges, Jus. Dell, Joseph Hodges; sale of pers est 3/13/1817, John Williams, admr, Dilly Williams, admx, Bulloch, Misc
WILLIAMS, Seth, decd, William B. Williams, exr, LWT pvd 7/5/1827, names wife, Betsey; sons: William, Carrel, Godfrey, Anson; son-in-law, Jarvis J. Frier, Bulloch, Misc
WILLIAMS, Stephen, decd, Reuben K. Williams, admr, 7/16/1855, Lee, MSC
WILLIAMS, Thomas, decd, Robert Hixdon, Jr., admr, W. R. Smith, Duncan McLeod, sur, 3/6/1843, Emanuel, AB
WILLIAMS, Thomas J., idiot, son of John H., sd John H., gdn, James H. Williams, sur, 11/1849, 1853 retn, Fayette, GB
WILLIAMS, William, decd, John Smith, William Dobbins, Margery Williams, admrs, bond 1/13/1811, Wm Jones, Greenberry Reynolds, surs, Clarke, AB
WILLIAMS, William H., decd, Ann Jane Williams produced LWT, pvd by Archibald Clark, she qualified as extrx, 1/3/1826, Camden, MIC
WILLIAMS, William H., decd, Mrs. Ann Jane Honiker (former wid of decd), extrx, submitted her retn, 1/7/1834, Camden, MIC
WILLIAMS, William H., orph of Avington B., decd, William R. Moseley, gdn, James M. Bledsoe, Penelope Williams, sur, 5/7/1849, Butts, GB
WILLIAMS, William Henry, minor, appeared with his mother, Mrs. Elizabeth Williams, and chose William Gibson his gdn, 5/7/1811, Camden, MIC
WILLIAMS, William M., N. H. Williams, gdn, 12/31/1837 acct, 1/29/1839, Butts, ER
WILLIAMS, William M., decd, Robert M. Williams issued L/A 4/6/1863, Fulton
WILLIAMS, William M., decd, N. H. Williams, exr, 2/20/1837 pd Marcuas E. Carter in rt of wife, a legacy; John Sanders, C. A. Williams, A. R. Evans, Marcus E. Carter, J. W. Falkner, Butts, ER
WILLIAMS, William M., orph of Nathan, decd, Nathan H. Williams, gdn, Stephen W. Price, sur, 11/17/1836, Butts, GB

WILLIAMS, Wilson, decd, Mrs. Elizabeth Williams extrx, filed
retn, 4/14/1807;Mrs. Elizabeth Williams gtd use of est property
on condition that she maintain and school minor children of decd,
free of any charge to est, 4/12/1808, Camden, MIC
WILLIAMSON, Anday, decd, LWT pvd 9/1812, names wife, Ruth and ch:
Anday, Mary, John, Elizabeth, James, Nancy, Franklin, OM
WILLIAMSON, Charles (Dr.), decd, Anna C. Williamson gtd L/A,
Seaborn Jones, Seaborn Grantland, sur 1/12/1829, James S. Calhoun
gtd L/A 12/10/1831, Baldwin
WILLIAMSON, Elizabeth (Mrs.), decd, Dr. Whipple Aldrich apptd
admr with LWT annexed, was cited to show cause why he had not
given bond; Noble A. Hardee apptd admr in his place, 8/7/1826,
Camden, MIC
WILLIAMSON, Isaac, decd, Nathan Williams qualified as exr of LWT
7/1/1822, Jasper, OM
WILLIAMSON, Isaac, decd, Stokely Morgan qualified as exr
11/4/1822, Jasper, OM
WILLIAMSON, James G., decd, Allen Williamson apptd admr, 1855,
Cobb, BB
WILLIAMSON, John, decd, report of Robert Williamson, gdn of John
12/25/1811, Franklin, OM
WILLIAMSON, John, orph of Peter, decd, Robert Williamson apptd
gdn 7/9/1805, Franklin, IMW
WILLIAMSON, John G. came into ct and chose Samuel H. Everet his
gdn 7/6/1812, Franklin, OM
WILLIAMSON, John T., decd, Anthony Holloway, Thomas Peavy,
William Wilkinson, admrs, Harris
WILLIAMSON, Malachi, decd, LWT pvd 1/13/1840, Sarah Williamson
and John Register, exrs, Washington
WILLIAMSON, Micajah, decd, George W. Moore prays that Wm W.
Williamson, admr, be required to make retns, 1809, Jackson, OM
WILLIAMSON, Peter, decd, planter, LWT pvd 7/17/1798-wife,
Elizabeth & ch: Robert, Richard, Elizabeth, wife of Richard
Allen, Patsey, wife of Josiah Prickett, Jennett Hamby, Mary, wife
of Wm Haily, Fanny, Nancy, Sally, Peter, John, Franklin, OM
WILLIAMSON, Peter Griffin, son of Peter, decd, Edmond Hendly
apptd gdn, 7/9/1805, Franklin, IMW
WILLIAMSON, Sally, minor dau of Peter, decd, Richard Allen apptd
gdn 8/3/1804, Franklin, IMW
WILLIAMSON, Thomas, decd, L/A gtd Alexander Williamson 5/3/1813,
Franklin, OM
WILLIAMSON, Thomas F., decd, Mrs. H. C. Williamson, J. H. Nash,
admrs, 7/6/1863, T. E. Nash, sur, DeKalb, AB
WILLIAMSON, William, decd, Joseph Terrell, surety for Sarah
Williamson, admx 1/7/1811, Franklin, OM
WILLIAMSON, William, decd, L/A issued Sarah Williamson 1/5/1807,
Franklin, OM
WILLIAMSON, William, decd, Sarah Williamson gtd L/A 7/9/1805; inv
by John, A. and Thomas Williamson, apprs; Sarah Williamson, admx
1/6/1807, Franklin, IMW
WILLIAMSON, William, decd, est reports that Sally Williamson recd
$60 for boarding three orph children of decd 12/28/1810,
Franklin, OM
WILLIAMSON, Zorababel, decd, L/A gtd Greene and William
Williamson, 11/4/1816, Jasper, OM
WILLINGHAM, Isaiah Erwin, son of Nancy, bound as apprentice to
Joshua Tillery, Sr., farmer, Isaac Collier, sur, Oglethorpe, MIC
WILLINGHAM, Mary, orph of Isaac, decd, John H. Walker, gdn,
1/12/1824, James Curry, sec, Lincoln, GB
WILLINGHAM, William, decd, Nancy Willingham, Isaac Willingham and
Eli Garrett, exrs of LWT 1/20/1798, Columbia, Ests

WILLIS, Furney, decd, William Curry and Jesse Dykes applies for
L/A 9/4/1833, Effingham, MIC
WILLIS, James, Sr., decd, Nowell Robertson apptd admr, James
Willis, George Granbury, sur, 3/7/1808, Warren, MIC, AB
WILLIS, Joseph, decd, LWT pvd 5/4/1812, names wife, Peggy, and
ch: Elizabeth, Lucinda, Charity, Partheny, William, Franklin, OM
WILLIS, Robert L., Sr., Allen Frazer gdn of: Litttlebury K.,
Arthur F., Robert L., Oliver N. P. and Elizabeth A., 7/5/1830,
James H. Frazer and Peter Lamar, secs, Lincoln, GB
WILLIS, Seyntha, orph of Isaiah, decd, Martin Wills, gdn,
9/1/1821, Thomas C. and Jesse Russell, secs, Lincoln, GB
WILLIS, William, decd, Mary Willis was issued L/A 5/1/1809,
Franklin, OM
WILLS, Jackson W. W., orph of James, decd, John B. McCollum, gdn,
Daniel H. Bird, sur, 11/5/1849, Cherokee, GB
WILLS, Ziponia Jane, orph of James, decd, John B. McCollum, gdn,
DanieL H. Bird, sur, 11/5/1849, Cherokee, GB
WILLSON, James, decd, James H. Stark, John W. McCord, admrs, John
Hall, sur, 12/18/1839, Butts, AB
WILLSON, William H., orph of William, decd, Lucinda Willson, gdn,
Benjamin Dowdy, sur, 11/12/1855, Cherokee, GB
WILLSON, William P., decd, Josiah F. Reeves, gdn of orphs,
7/1836, 1842 retn, Fayette, GB
WILSON, Abigail, William Wilson apptd gdn 1/6/1812; recd of gdn
in rt of Mary Wilson now Mary Poe, sum of $81 as husband of said
Mary, signed Samuel Poe, 2/10/1812, Franklin, OM
WILSON, Allen, minor orph of Andrew, decd, Dudley Reeves apptd
gdn 11/3/1817, Jasper, OM
WILSON, Andrew, minor orph of Andrew, decd, Dudley Reeves apptd
gdn 11/3/1817, Jasper, OM
WILSON, Ann, decd, Elishu Wilson gtd leave to sell real est
11/4/1833; Luke Wilson enters caveat against Elishu Wilson
obtaining dismission 11/20/1835, Effingham, MIC
WILSON, Arthur C., decd, Asa Whitby issued L/A 11/5/1855, Elisha
Chamlee, sec, Hall, AB
WILSON, Benjamin, Merchant, decd, Thomas Johnson, planter, apptd
admr 5/28/1785, Chatham, Adms
WILSON, Benjamin, decd, Elias Mims, gdn of orphs: Joseph, John,
Judah and Giles, 1/8/1855, Houston, GB
WILSON, Daniel, decd, Noah Calhoun issued L/A 7/7/1834,
Ludwick Matthews issued L/A 3/3/1836, Washington
WILSON, Elias, decd, Milly Ann Wilson applies for L/A 3/2/1832,
Effingham, MIC
WILSON, Eliza, orph of Daniel, decd, Ludwick Matthews issued L/G
11/9/1835; L/G issued Lott Walker 3/2/1840, Washington
WILSON, Elizabeth, decd, Howell Hines applies for adm 7/31/1832,
Effingham, MIC
WILSON, Elizabeth, orph of John, decd, Jabez Jones issued L/G
7/7/1834, Washington
WILSON, Gabriel, decd, accts of Elishu Wilson, gdn of orphs
3/2/1829, Effingham, MIC
WILSON, Guilford B., decd, William Holbrook and John M. Holbrook
issued L/A 10/7/1861, Fulton
WILSON, Hugh, decd, Henry Hustice and Mary Wilson, wid, apptd
admrs, Wilkes, MxR
WILSON, James, decd, 1840 retn, heirs: John Phillips, John R.
Wilson, A. J. Wilson, James H. Stark, gdn for James Wilson,
minor, James H. Stark and John W. McCord, admrs, 1/19/1841,
Butts, ER
WILSON, James, decd, John Benby, exr of Jane Taylor, applied for
Zachariah Motes to be apptd gdn of orphs of James Wilson,
2/7/1827, Camden, MIC

WILSON, James, decd, LWT was admitted to record 11/4/1833, Effingham, MIC

WILSON, James, decd, distribution of est: John R. Wilson, Eliza Ann Phillips, wife of John, Andrew J. Wilson, James H. Stark, gdn for James Wilson, 1/21/1840, Butts, ER

WILSON, James, decd, of Church Hill, James A. Harris, admr, 12/1840; apprs: Ira Allen, James Webb, Philip Mathison, Robert Burks, Stewart, Adms

WILSON, James, orph of James, decd, James H. Stark, gdn, Stephen Bailey, sur, 11/14/1840, Butts, GB

WILSON, James D., decd, Charles Collins, admr, Robert Collins and Jeremiah D. Mann, surs, 6/7/1832, Bibb, AB

WILSON, Jeremiah, decd, Henry Wilson, admr, 1/5/1829, Elias Wilson and Joseph Leonard, surs, Warren, AB

WILSON, Jesse, decd, L/A issued to William Wilson 7/28/1832, Effingham, MIC

WILSON, John, decd, 1808 retn of Barnabas Pace, exr, pd Benjamin Wilson by order of referee certain devts, Elbert, AR

WILSON, John, decd, James Wilson, admr, makes retns, 7/25/1803, Jackson, OM

WILSON, John, decd, James and Benjamin Wilson, admrs, 4/30/1789, Chatham, Adms

WILSON, John, decd, Joseph Leonard, admr, 9/1/1823, Henry Wilson and David Cody, surs, Warren, AB

WILSON, John, decd, P. W. Gunnells was issued L/A 12/1862, Webster, OD

WILSON, John, minor orph of Andrew, decd, Dudley Reeves apptd gdn 11/3/1817, Jasper, OM

WILSON, John B., decd, Henry J. Wilson applied for L/A 8/21/1843, Effingham, MIC

WILSON, John M., decd, Henry Wilson, admr, 2/14/1827, Henry Wilson, Joseph Leonard, surs, Warren, AB

WILSON, Joseph, decd, LWT pvd 9/22/1841, names wife, Sally, ch: William H. Wilson, Christian Foster; appr shows Henry Co. land, Butts, ER

WILSON, Joseph, decd, LWT pvd by Obadiah Echols, Allen Kelly, Burton Kelly, L/T issued Sarah Wilson, 11/4/1822, Jasper, OM

WILSON, J. W., decd, Thomas M. White apptd gdn of minor orphs: Hugh A., James C. and Jane, 1/13/1862, Fulton, GB

WILSON, Kesiah E., John Wilson chosen as gdn 11/4/1833, Effingham, MIC

WILSON, Leighton, decd, Robert Hazlehurst, Jr., James Hamilton Cooper, exrs of LWT, 1/5/1824, dismissed 9/3/1827, Glynn, MIC

WILSON, Littleberry, decd, Elisha and Francis S. Wilson, gdn of: Joseph, Eliza, Julian and Thomas, minor orphs, late of Abbeville District, South Carolina, 7/19/1825, Richmond, GB

WILSON, Martin and Parmelia, wife, free persons of colour, Tilman Carter, gdn, 9/7/1846, Hall, GB

WILSON, Mary, William Wilson apptd gdn 8/3/1804, Franklin, IMW

WILSON, Mary, orph of John, decd, Jabez Jones issued L/G 7/7/1834, Washington

WILSON, Mary, orph of John, decd, William Wilson gdn 7/9/1805, Franklin, OM

WILSON, Mary, recd from William Wilson, gdn, $10 for prosecuting suit in favor of him as gdn vs Barnabas Pace in Elbert Co. for legacy due Mary Wilson, 12/29/1811, Franklin, OM

WILSON, Mary Ann, decd, LWT pvd, L/T issued 11/2/1818 John, Leonard and Larkin Wilson, Jasper, OM

WILSON, Nancy, orph of Daniel, decd, Ludwick Matthew issued L/G 11/9/1835; L/G issued Lott Walker 3/2/1840, Washington

WILSON, Peggy, a poor woman; ordered that Thomas W. Craven be allowed $1.00 per wk for her maintenance, 9/1824, Habersham, MIC

WILSON, Polley Ann, minor orph of Andrew, decd, Dudley Reeves apptd gdn 11/3/1817, Jasper, OM

WILSON, Polly, retn of receipts made by William Wilson, gdn "now Polly Poe" 7/29/1812; receipt from Samuel Holbrook that he recd from William Wilson, now husband of Hannah Wilson 12/19/1811, Franklin, OM

WILSON, Rebecca, minor orph of Andrew, decd, Dudley Reeves apptd gdn 11/3/1817, Jasper, OM

WILSON, Robert, decd, LWT dtd 10/12/1798 names wife, Susannah, ch: James, Robert, Betsey, and wife now pregnant, pvd 12/4/1798, Hancock, AA

WILSON, Samuel, decd, Henry Dutton and Andrew Wilson, admrs, issued L/D 1/3/1842; Elizabeth Wilson recd from admrs her sh of est 1/8/1842, Bulloch, MIC, Misc

WILSON, Samuel, decd, appr 1/19/1803, accts of Peter Gordon, Samuel Wilson, John Wilson, Robert Buckhanan, exrs, Hancock, AAAA

WILSON, Samuel, minor orph of Andrew, decd, Dudley Reeves apptd gdn 11/3/1817, Jasper, OM

WILSON, Sarah, orph of John, decd, Jabez Jones issued L/G 7/7/1834, Washington

WILSON, T. C. (Dr.), decd, John G. Westmoreland issued L/A 10/1865, Fulton

WILSON, Thomas, decd, Martha Wilson apptd admx 11/28/1788, Chatham, Adms

WILSON, Thomas S., decd, John H. Wilson issued L/A 8/7/1854, A. S. Wilson, sec, Hall, AB

WILSON, Washington made gdn of Nancy and John, his minor children, John L. Holliday, sur, 7/1852, 1852 retn, Fayette, GB

WILSON, William, decd, Joel Bridge, exr vs. Lake Mann, 1819, Bryan, Writs

WILSON, William, decd, John G. Neidlinger, exr, sales acct 6/1/1793, Effingham, Misc

WILSON, William, decd, Newton J. Perkins, sur, 6/12/1854, Cherokee, AB

WILSON, William, minor orph of Andrew, decd, Dudley Reeves apptd gdn 11/3/1817, Jasper, OM

WILSON, William, the ct dismissed case of John Rollin seeking payment for four months' keeping of William Wilson, one of the list of co. pensioners, 9/7/1812, Warren, MIC

WILY, Thomas, decd, William Wiley was gtd L/A 10/22/1798, Columbia, Ests

WINDSOR, Jesse, gdn of his own children: Margaret M., Jemima C., Mary E. and Lucinda 9/6/1847, James J. McCleskey, sec, Hall, GB

WINDSOR, Silas, decd, M. H. Bush issued L/A 3/1864, Webster, OD

WINDSOR, William T., minor of Silas, decd, J. S. McJunkin, gdn 3/1864; John S. McJunkin issued citation 1/1864, Webster, OD

WINFIELD, William F., decd, Thomas Moore was issued L/A 4/2/1860, William Winfield apptd gdn of minor orphs: Green J., Cleatus J., Martha L. and William, 12/3/1860, Fulton, GB

WINGATE, Isaac, decd, Mary Wingate issued L/A 4/1802, Holland McTyeire, Hiell Chatfield, secs, Richmond, AB

WINGSELLS, Benjamin, decd, Charles Wingsells of Skidway Island, planter, and Mary Wingsells of Little Ogeechee, apptd admrs 1/13/1787, Chatham, Adms

WINN, Benjamin B., decd, Thomas Baker, admr, gtd leave to sell real est, 1/6/1817, Liberty, MIC

WINN, Elisha, decd, R. D. Winn, admr de bonis non w/LWT, Sam J. Winn, sur, 10/10/1873, Gwinnett, AB

WINN, Lydia, decd, Benjamin Andrew qualified as exr 3/5/1784, Liberty, Ests

WINN, Richard, decd, William T. Winn and Richard W. P. Winn issued L/A 7/5/1847, W. S. Williams, Robert Young, secs, Hall, AB

WINSHIP, Caroline G. (Mrs.), LWT exhibited 7/2/1860, Seaton G. Day, exr, Fulton
WINSLOW, Charles, decd, Amos Bruton, admr, James L. Saulsbury, sur, 5/13/1847, Bibb, AB
WINTER, Frederick, decd, L/A to Jeremiah Winters 6/22/1825; purchasers at sale: Elizabeth, James & Jeremiah Winters, Richmond, AB
WINTER, Sabry, a free woman of colour, chose William Cook as her gdn 1/7/1817, Jasper, OM
WINZER, Anderson, decd, John C. Plunkett issued L/A 4/1856, Webster, OD
WISE, Barney, decd, est appraised by Johnson Strong, H. Walker, William Phillips, 1809 Retn by Patson Wise, admr, Jasper, WAR
WISE, Isaiah, minor, Elizabeth Wise apptd gdn of her son 5/7/1821, Jasper, OM
WISE, Isaiah, decd, 1840 retn by Riley Wise, admr; pd Rosey Wise legacy, 2/10/1841, Butts, ER
WISE, Isaiah, decd, Riley Wise, admr, David J. Bailey, sur, 2/9/1836, Butts, AB
WISE, Isaiah, decd, inv and appr, 12/30/1833; apprs: David Higgins, Robert Mayfield, Lewis Bennett, Hugh H. Heard, Butts, ER
WISE, Jacob, decd, John Cashin issued L/A 11/17/1817, David McKinney, Alexis Tardy, secs, Richmond, AB
WISE, Jacob, decd, pd 1838 taxes, John Wise, pt legacy, retn by Witt C. Wise, exr, 1839, pd Isham Anderson, Simon H. Sanders, High Wise, John McCord, C. C. O., 30 acres in Early Co. sold, 3/30/1840, Butts, ER
WISE, James, decd, inv and appr by John Burnsed, Carter Huse, Allen Elerbee 4/30/1835, sale of est 7/4/1835, Bulloch, Misc
WISE, Jared, son of Zilpha (now Zilpha Goodman), Aaron Everitt to take into possession all prop of child, 9/3/1821, Bulloch, MIC
WISE, Joel, decd, of Jasper Co., Parham Lindsey, admr, Riley Wise, Isaiah Wise, sur, 12/4/1833, Butts, AB
WISE, Joel, decd, prop sold in town of Jackson 1/1835 by Parham Lindsey, admr; retn 1/14/1836 pd Dr. Patton Wise, Anderson & Mary Dudley, Baldwin & Shortery, James Betts, W. Phillips, M. Whitfield, Thomas Blair, John Saunders, Butts, ER
WISE, John, decd, Mrs. Rachel Wise divides property to heirs 11/4/1839; Jas Young, Charnick Selph, Jas Cone partition in Chatham Co-lots drawn by-Mrs. Rachel Wise, Aaron Cone, Basil, Mary, Sarah, Bridger & Henry Wise 11/11/1839, Bulloch, MIC, Misc
WISE, John, decd, Morgan Brewer gtd L/A 3/21/1842, Baldwin
WISE, John, orph of Riley, decd, Benjamin F. Wilson apptd gdn, Benjamin H. Cameron, Hugh P. T. Montgomery, sur, 3/20/1848, Troup, GB
WISE , John, orph of John, decd, Jabez Jones issued L/G 7/7/1834, Washington
WISE, John, decd, Mrs. Rachel Wise divides property to heirs 11/4/1839; James Young, Charmick Selph, James Cone partition in Chatham Co., Ga., lots drawn by Mrs. Rachel Wise, Aaron Cone, Basil Wise, Mary Wise, Sarah Wise, Bridger Wise and Henry Wise 11/11/1839, Bulloch, MIC, Misc
WISE, John, Jr., decd, of Edgefield Co., S. C., John Carter issued L/A, Charles Carter, sec, undtd, Richmond, AB
WISE, Mary, orph of Riley, decd, Benjamin F. Wilson apptd gdn, Benjamin H. Cameron, Hugh P. T. Montgomery, sur, 3/20/1848, Troup, GB
WISE, Patton, decd, LWT 1/31/1812, names wife, Elizabeth; minors: Riley and Isaiah (gdn, Parham Lindsey), accts in Creek Nation listed, lawsuits, etc., Jasper, Ests

WISE, Robert, orph of Riley, decd, Benjamin F. Wilson apptd gdn, Benjamin H. Cameron and Hugh P. T. Montgomery, surs, 3/2/1848, Troup, GB

WISE, Rosana, orph of Riley, decd, Benjamin F. Wilson apptd gdn, Benjamin H. Cameron, Hugh P. T. Montgomery, surs, 3/2/1848, Troup, GB

WISE, Walter J., orph of Wiley, decd, Benjamin F. Wilson apptd gdn, Benjamin H. Cameron, Hugh P. T. Montgomery, surs, 3/2/1848, Troup, GB

WISE, William, decd, LWT pvd 7/1/1816; wife, Margaret; son-in-law, Solomon Groover; ch--Henry Wise, Viny Denmark, Susannah Denmark, Rebecca Jones, Zilpha Allman, John Wise, Jincey Denmark, Preston Wise and Jared Wise 5/13/1816, Bulloch, Misc

WISE, William R., orph of Riley, decd, Benjamin F. Wilson apptd gdn, Benjamin H. Cameron and Hugh P. T. Montgomery, surs, 3/20/1848, Troup, GB

WISENBAKER, Jacob, decd, John Wisenbacker apptd admr in place of Mr. Christian Truetlin, who declined to serve any longer 4/27/1798, Effingham, Misc

WISENBAKER, John, decd, John Wisenbaker apptd gdn of minor heirs 11/1/1830; Christian Wisenbaker gtd leave to sell negroes and make division of est 11/1/1830, Effingham, MIC

WISENBAKER, John, decd, accts of Christian Wisenbaker, admr 3/3/1828, Effingham, MIC

WITCHER, D. H., decd, Mrs. Flora M. Witcher was issued L/A 9/17/1857, Fulton

WITHERINGTON, William apptd gdn of his ch: James, John H., Daniel P. and Francis E., 1/8/1855, Houston, GB

WITHERS, Mary, decd, John Coughlove issued L/A 2/17/1868, Fulton

WITHERSPOON, William, alias William Spoons, Turner H. Tripps issued L/A 9/1832, Habersham, MIC

WITTICK, Ernest C., decd, Joyse H. Wittick issued L/A 5/2/1825, Morgan, AB

WITTICK, Lucius L., gdn of Louis Lovick Wittick, Caroline Levira Wittick and Harriett Caroline Wittick, 12/7/1826, Morgan, GB

WOFFORD, James, decd, LWT dtd 7/17/1795 Franklin Co., "to my dear father and mother, all estate"; bros and sisters: Benjamin, Nathaniel, Mary Weatherspoon, Nancy Bright, Charlotte Baker, Sary Gillespie, pvd 7/1824, Habersham, MIC

WOFFORD, James, decd, payments made by Benjamin Wofford to creditors of est, retn from 8/26/1796 to 11/7/1797, Franklin, OM

WOFFORD, William H., decd, Nancy Wofford, extrx of LWT pvd 9/3/1827; LWT names wife, Nancy and ch: Martha L., Mary S., William T. (25 acres for use of my father and mother) dtd 5/12/1826, Habersham, MIC

WOLF, John, decd, E. H. Callaway and Thomas Clifton, admrs, 3/9/1821, appr, Emanuel, A

WOLLY, Bazzel, decd, L/A issued James M. Whorten 11/1868; 12/7/1867 David E. Ponder, largest creditor, claimed right to L/A, as next of kin, Webster, OD

WOLLY, John, decd, John Wolly issued L/G of minors 10/1869, Webster, OD

WOMACK, Abraham, decd, exrs retns 2/23/1799; notes: Sherwood Womack, Francis Coleman; heirs: David Womack, Wm Stone, Clemt. Glenn, Francis Coleman, 2/27/1799, Hancock, AA

WOMACK, Alfred Jackson, William A. Prevatt chosen as gdn 3/7/1831, Effingham, MIC

WOMACK, Frederick, Obadiah Edwards apptd gdn 11/4/1839, Effingham, MIC

WOMACK, Frederick, decd, LWT admitted to record 3/2/1835; Thomas Womack, bro of Frederick, objects to probate of LWT 3/23/1835, Effingham, MIC

WOMACK, James, decd, Burket D. Thompson issued L/A 11/15/1827,
William Savage, sec, Richmond, AB
WOMACK, Thomas, decd, James Young= made retn 1839 as admr,
3/2/1840, Bulloch, MIC
WOMACK, Valeria, minor and heir of William H., decd, chose
Charles Tondee as her gdn 9/1/1828, Effingham, MIC
WOMACK, William, decd, Frederick Womack applies for L/A
11/15/1830, Effingham, MIC
WOMACK, William, decd, W. W. Black applied for adm 6/1/1834,
Effingham, MIC
WOMACK, William C., decd, William A. Prevatt chosen as gdn
5/2/1831, Effingham, MIC
WOMACK, William H., decd, William A. Prevatt and Sarah Prevatt,
admrs, gtd leave to sell land on Louisville Rd 9/7/1829; admx to
sell two negroes, Jacob and Ceras, 9/3/1827, Effingham, MIC
WOMBLE, Allen, decd, H. W. Jernigan, Isabel Womble, exrs, 1833;
apprs: Samuel B. Harwell, Charles C. Simpson, Robert Edwards,
Nathan F. R. Holiway; R. and A. Womble mentioned, Stewart, Adms
WOOD, Cyrus, decd, James and Hannah Woods applied for L/A
5/1/1794, Greene, Misc
WOOD, Daniel, decd, Thomas G. Holmes issued L/A 6/25/1800, Samuel
Hammond, Jacob Morse, secs, Richmond, AB
WOOD, Drucella J., orph of Jared, decd, Elizabeth N. Wood issued
L/G 9/5/1842, Washington
WOOD, Edward, decd, James Wood qualified as admr 9/2/1784,
Liberty, Ests
WOOD, Elisha, decd, William Ball and James S. Calhoun gtd L/A
1/8/1827, Baldwin
WOOD, Etheldred, decd, James R. McCleskey and Green Wood issued
L/A 3/4/1811, Jackson, OM
WOOD, Frances S., orph of Jared, decd, Elizabeth N. Wood issued
L/G 9/5/1842, Washington
WOOD, George A., orph of Jared, decd, Elizabeth N. Wood issued
L/G 9/5/1842, Washington
WOOD, Hezekiah, decd, David Crawford issued L/A, George Henessey,
sec, Richmond, AB
WOOD, Isaac, decd, Daniel Wallecon issued L/A 3/26/1789, William
Beale, William Stith, secs, Richmond, AB
WOOD, J., decd, William Stancell, admr, 1855, Cobb, BB
WOOD, James, decd, (Capt.), James Pearre, Jr. issued L/A
5/20/1788, James Pearre, Sr., Wm Gardner, secs, Richmond, AB
WOOD, James, decd, Charlotte Wood, admx, Edward L. Strobecker,
sur, 2/13/1847, Bibb, AB
WOOD, James R., minor of Mrs. Mary J. Wood, orph of M. J., decd,
H. M. Hammett applies for L/G 3/3/1870, Cobb, MIC
WOOD, Jared, decd, Benjamin and Robert Wood apptd admrs w/LWT
annexed 9/12/1842, Washington
WOOD, Jared H., orph f Jared, decd, Elizabeth N. Wood issued L/G
9/5/1842, Washington
WOOD, John, decd, 11/9/1801 inventory, Levin Wales, Samuel
Pullen, George Eberhart, apprs; purchasers at sale: Susannah
Wood, wid, Bennett Wood, Sr., James Wood, Penuel Wood, Agrippe
Wood, Elbert, AR
WOOD, John, decd, Horace S. Pratt, Lilah Wood and Jane F. Pratt
qualified exrs of LWT 6/1/1829, Camden, MIC
WOOD, Joseph, decd, Jacob Wood qualified as exr 11/2/1791,
Liberty, Ests
WOOD, Laura A., minor of Mrs. Mary J. Wood, orph of M. J., decd,
H. M. Hammett applies for L/G 3/3/1870, Cobb, MIC
WOOD, Lelah, decd, B. E. Hand apptd admr 10/10/1836, Camden, MIC
WOOD, Maggie E., minor of Mrs. Mary J. Wood, orph of M. J., decd,
H. M. Hammett applies for L/G 3/3/1870, Cobb, MIC

WOOD, Maria L., minor of Mrs. Mary J. Wood, orph of M. J., decd,
H. M. Hammett applies for L/G 3/3/1870, Cobb, MIC
WOOD, Mary H., minor of Mrs. Mary J. Wood, orph of M. J., decd,
H. M. Hammett applies for L/G 3/3/1870, Cobb, MIC
WOOD, Miesel, decd, LWT pvd 3/2/1835, Jared Wood, exr, Washington
WOOD, Nancy E. E., orph of Jared, Elizabeth N. Wood issued L/G
9/5/1842, Washington
WOOD, Miesel G., orph of Jared, decd, Elizabeth N. Wood issued
L/G 9/5/1842, Washington
WOOD, Richard, decd, Tabithy Wood issued L/A 12/1/1817, Joseph
Lain, sec, Morgan, AB
WOOD, William, decd, Joseph Wood, admr, 3/1/1824, Harris Wood,
Mary Wood, Thomas Jones, surs, Warren, AB
WOOD, William, decd, William Wood gdn to his ch: John H.,
Lucinda, Nancy, William and Eli, minors, 1/7/1839, Anthony
Samuel, sec, Lincoln, GB
WOODALL, Isaac, decd, Robert W. Trapp gtd L/A 9/3/1849, Baldwin
WOODARD, Clark R., decd, Dr. Benjamin F. Bomar issued L/A
7/5/1858, Fulton
WOODARD, Francis, decd, Benjamin S. Woodward apptd temp admr,
Harmon Perryman, sur, 9/1/1806, Warren, MIC, AB
WOODBURY, Joseph F., decd, Joseph F. Woodbury issued L/G of
orphs: Josephine, Francis and William Albert Woodbury, 2/1/1858,
Fulton
WOODLAND, Margaret, decd, William Bailey of Fla., agt for heirs,
withdraws objections to dismissal of Isaac Bailey, admr of Jacob
Worley; property turned over to John Worley, heir of decd, upon
paying 5% value of est, 1/8/1834, Camden, MIC
WOODLIFF, Milly, decd, George Woodliff and James Law, admrs,
Wittey E. Wood, Elijah Hallman, secs, 9/3/1831, Hall, AB
WOODRUFF, Clifford, decd, Samuel Bellah, admr, Henry Jester, sur,
1/11/1843, Butts, AB
WOODRUFF, Fielding, decd, James Langley issued L/A 7/16/1807,
James Scott, sec, Richmond, AB
WOODS, Andrew, decd, Robert and Ann Woods and James Ewing, admrs,
ordered to make titles of land to Joel Miller, signed by decd in
1804, Elbert, AR
WOODS, John, decd, James Wood, admr, 1807 retn includes boarding
and clothing two children, heirs of est; 1808 retn pd Archelaus
Moon for boarding Elizabeth and Sarah Woods, orphs, Elbert, AR
WOODS, Middleton, decd, heirs--Robt Woods, Sr & Jr; Wm Burwell,
gdn/Bailey M. Woods (Hugh's orph); Joel Shrewsbury, gdn/Josiah W.
& Robt N. Dickerson & Jno Clay for wf Elizabeth (Jno Dickenson's
heirs), all of Franklin Co Va; Francis Hill for wife; Samuel
Hairston, gdn of heirs of John Woods; Hugh Martin in rtof wife;
Josiah Woods; William Woods, Elbert, AR
WOODS, Thomas, decd, Amos Anderson, admr, makes retn 3/7/1836,
Tattnall, I&A
WOODS, Wilks, decd, Joseph Thompson, admr, 1/10/1853, R. M.
Brown, sur, DeKalb, AB
WOODS, William, decd, Alson Worley apptd admr, Daniel H. Bird,
Nehemiah J. Garrison, sur, 9/14/1857, Cherokee, AB
WOODSON, Jonathan, decd, Benjamin and Judah Nicholson issued L/A
10/27/1784, David Harris, Levi Lancaster, secs, Richmond, AB
WOODSON, Mills, decd, Henry Canaday apptd admr, William Parker,
Joseph McCullarson, sur, 5/2/1825, Emanuel, AB
WOODWARD, Aaron, Sr., decd, William J. Woodward, admr, Abner
Jester, John Andrews, James R. McComb, Walter S. Andrews, Nathan
F. Camp, John B. Carmichael, sur, 7/7/1851, Butts, AB
WOODWARD, Francis, decd, Benjamin S. Woodward, admr, 11/3/1806,
Harmon Perryman, sur, Warren, AB

WOODWARD, Francis, decd, Benjamin T. Woodward, admr, 3/23/1818, Isham Woodward, Wm Jackson, surs, Warren, AB

WOODWARD, John, decd, Elizabeth E. Woodward, gdn of orphs: Charles G., William E., Martha Jane and Laura S., 12/6/1853, Houston, GB

WOODMANd, Mills, decd, H. Cannaday, admr, appr 6/10/1825, Emanuel, A

WOODWARD, Thomas, decd, LWT dtd 3/16/1800 names ch: Thomas (not 21), wife, Mary and her bro, John Howard, exrs, Franklin, MIC

WOOLF, Clem, Jimmy Woolf was qualified as gdn 1/6/1840, Effingham, MIC

WOOLF, George, decd, John Woolf was gtd L/A 11/19/1827, Effingham, MIC

WOOLF, Irvin, minor son of George, decd, chose John Woolf as his gdn 1/7/1828, Effingham, MIC

WOOLF, John, Jimmy Woolf was qualified as gdn 1/6/1840, Effingham, MIC

WOOLF, John, decd, Jenny Woolf apptd gdn of minor heirs 11/4/1839, Effingham, MIC

WOOLF, Marcia, Jimmy Woolf was qualified as gdn 1/6/1840, Effingham, MIC

WOOLF, Mary, Jimmy Woolf was qualified as gdn 1/6/1840, Effingham, MIC

WOOLF, Milly, Jimmy Woolf was qualified as gdn 1/6/1840, Effingham, MIC

WOOLF, Rebecca, Jimmy Woolf was qualified as gdn 1/6/1840, Effingham, MIC

WOOLF, Robert Thomas, Jimmy Woolf qualified as gdn 1/6/1840, Effingham, MIC

WOOLRIDGE, William, decd, Thomas Woolridge issued L/A 6/6/1814, Putnam, AB

WOOLRIDGE, William, decd, 1811 retn of Gibson Woolridge, exr, recpts: Barnett Jeter, gdn/Thos W. Davis, his sh 2/24/1810 & from Thos Woolridge to Alexander Nobles, slippers, etc. for Sarah & Absolom Davis, gdn/heirs of Jos. T. Davis, Elbert, AR

WOOTEN, Addison, minor son of James, decd, Jones Jones, gdn in 1834, Jesse Wooten, exr, 9/11/1835; pd 9/3/1835 George W. Varner for tuition, Butts, ER

WOOTEN, Addison, orph of James, decd, John Jones apptd gdn, Humphrey Gilmore, Robert W. Harkness, Henry Jackson, sur, 9/8/1832, Butts, GB

WOOTEN, Francis, decd, Anne Wooten apptd admx, LWT annexed 11/2/1829, Butts, AB

WOOTEN, James, decd, John Jones, Humphrey Gilmore, admrs with LWT annexed, Robert W. Harkness, Henry Jackson, surs, 7/8/1832, Butts, AB

WOOTEN, James, decd, John Jones, admr, 1834 Retn pd J. M. McClendon, G. L. and J. P. Smith, 3/8/1836; pd Sanford & Martin, Nicholas A. Peurifoy, A. F. Thompson, James B. Hogan, Thomas Hogan, Allen McClendon, retn dtd 5/23/1836, Butts, ER

WOOTEN, James, decd, James pvd 8/3/1828 by Farewell Jones, Bartholomew Hill, James Ransom; inv and appr 1/12/1830; apprs: P. Payne, R. Nolen, William Gilmore, Butts, ER

WOOTEN, James, minor son of James, decd, John Jones, gdn in 1834, Jesse Wooten, exr, 9/5/1835, Butts, ER

WOOTEN, James, orph of James, decd, John Jones apptd gdn, Humphrey Gilmore, Robert W. Harkness, Henry Jackson, surs, 9/8/1832, Butts, GB

WOOTEN, L. M., orph of James, decd, John Jones apptd gdn, Humphrey Gilmore, Robert W. Harkness, Henry Jackson, surs, 9/8/1832, Butts, GB

WOOTEN, Sarah, decd, James Wooten, admr, 2/9/1844; apprs: Alexander Meriwether, David T. Ward, James Broxton; purchasers at sale: J. S. Russell, Seth Kellam, E. Faircloth, Dicey Pipkin, Bennett Purvis, Stephen Simmon, Dooly, I&A

WOOTEN, Seaborn L., minor orph of James, decd, John Jones, gdn, Humphrey Gilmore, Robert W. Harkness, Henry Jackson, sur, 9/8/1832; John Jones, gdn, for 1834, 9/5/1835; 1835 retn pd John Bostick for tuition, Butts, GB,ER

WOOTEN, Simeon, minor of James, decd, John Jones, gdn in 1834, Jesse Wooten, exr, 9/5/1835; retn 5/23/1836 pd John Bostick for tuition, Butts, ER

WOOTEN, Simeon, orph of James, decd, John Jones apptd gdn, Humphrey Gilmore, Robert W. Harkness, Henry Jackson, sur, 9/8/1832, Butts, GB

WOOTEN, Thomas, decd, Hester Stuckey issued L/A 7/18/1826, Lewis Harris, Joshua Jones, sec, Richmond, AB

WOOTON, Betsey, a mulatto child, be bound to Nancy Kindrake until she is age 21, 7/1818, Jasper, OM

WOOTON, William B., decd, Lucinda Wootton, gdn of orphs, Jesse Ward, A. McBride, surs, 7/1841, 1851-1854 retns, Fayette, GB

WOOTTEN, Nathan, decd, Stephen Lawrence applies for admn, Joseph Carter, sur, 2/23/1803, Warren, MIC, AB

WOOTTEN, Nathan, decd, Stephen Lawrence, admr, 4/11/1803, Joseph Carter, sur, Warren, AB

WORKMAN, John, decd, inv retd by John Gatewood, Christopher Baker, Charls Ingram 8/7/1805, Franklin, IMW

WORKMAN, Jonathan, decd, L/A issued Charles Workman 2/12/1805; inv of est 3/9/1805 by James McDowell, Obadiah Kendrick, Elias Wileman, appraisers, 7/9/1805, Franklin, OM

WORLEY, Jacob, decd, Isaac Bailey apptd permanent admr 1/4/1832; sd admr applied for dismission, but heirs of Margaret Woodland, decd, objecting, application refused 1/7/1834, Camden, MIC

WORLEY, James, orph of Obadiah, decd, bound to Marmaduke Vickery 1/12/1830, Habersham, MIC

WORLEY, Jane, orph of Obadiah, decd, bound to Bird Cannon 1/12/1830, Habersham, MIC

WORLEY, Obadiah, decd, Pleasant Worley issued L/A 3/1/1830, Habersham, MIC

WORLEY, Silas, orph of Obadiah, decd, bound to John Stephens 1/12/1830, Habersham, MIC

WORLEY, Obediah, decd, John Morgan, Thomas Turner, Timothy Disharoon, John H. Brock, Roling B. Spears apptd apprs 3/1/1830; John Morgan, gdn for orphs: William B. W. and Alfred, 1/1833, Habersham, MIC

WORSHAM, Edward, decd, appr 4/7/1801; purchasers at sale: Reuben Slaughter, Saml Butler, John C. Mason, Buckner Duke, Wm Lawson, Joseph Higinbotham, Taylor Nelson, Hancock, AAAA

WRAY, Samuel, decd, Needham and Ingram Wray issued L/A 1/4/1814, Putnam, AB

WRAY, Solomon, decd, Jane Wray chose a child's part 1/3/1814, Jasper, OM

WREN, James, orph of William, decd, Nathaniel Holton, gdn, Daniel Kennedy, sur, 9/2/1833, Emanuel, GB

WREN, Mary, orph of William, decd, Nathaniel Holton, gdn, Daniel Kennedy, sur, 9/2/1833, Emanuel, GB

WRIGHT, Abadeah, decd, summons for admn of est ordered 5/4/1807, Franklin, IMW

WRIGHT, Albert, decd, Abednego Wright exr of LWT 9/4/1798, Columbia, Ests

WRIGHT, Ambrose, decd, Phillip Hornby apptd admr 7/9/1784, Chatham, Adms

WRIGHT, Amos, decd, LWT pvd 1/7/1811, Warren, MIC

WRIGHT, Amos, decd, Rachel Wright, admx, Joseph and Amos Wright, Jr., admrs, w/LWT annexed 4/3/1815, Reddick Bass, Chappell Heath, surs, Warren, AB

WRIGHT, Asa, orph of Francis, decd, bound as apprentice to Henry Smith to learn trade, Randolph Jones, sec, 1/1808, Oglethorpe, OM, GB

WRIGHT, Caswell, orph of Isaiah, decd, bound out to Daniel Hutchinson for four yrs to learn blacksmith trade, 5/2/1814, Warren, MIC

WRIGHT, Cornelius McCarty, orph of John, decd, chose Alsey Wright his gdn 3/2/1812, Jackson, OM

WRIGHT, David, decd, of Monroe Co., 1/1830, heirs: wife, Martha L., young children not named; Allen Turrentine, exr, Stewart, MIC

WRIGHT, Delilah, orph of Francis, decd, Henry Wright, gdn, Gabriel Jones, sec, 4/6/1807, Oglethorpe, OM, GB

WRIGHT, Drusilla, decd, Joseph Wright, admr, 2/12/1833, Henry Hight, Solomon Wilder, surs, Warren, AB

WRIGHT, Eve, decd, William W. Seals, admr, 6/4/1827, Camden, MIC

WRIGHT, Eve, wid, decd, William Mickler petitioned to be apptd gdn of Eve, insane. Witnesses: M. H. Hibbard, Elihu Atwater, Martha Tison, 1/6/1825, Camden, MIC

WRIGHT, Frances, retn of business transacted by William Wright, gdn, 10/24/1844, Bulloch, Misc

WRIGHT, Frances Ann, decd, William Hays, Joseph Fitzpatrick, gdn of minors 1/7/1837, Harris

WRIGHT, Francis, decd, upon motion of Lucy Williford, formerly Wright, that after death of her husband she sd she would take dower in real est, 3/1808, Oglethorpe, OM

WRIGHT, F. N., decd, James W. Brown, admr, 3/2/1863, William D. Brown, Eli Clay, surs, DeKalb, AB

WRIGHT, Habukkuk, decd, Susannah Wright apptd admx 1/8/1805, bondsmen applied to be relieved of admx's bond same, sd admx having failed to give new bonds, 4/13/1808, Camden, MIC

WRIGHT, Hellena, orph of William, decd, Archelaus Flewellin apptd gdn 12/2/1811, Warren, MIC, GB

WRIGHT, Isaac, decd, Ezekiel Ralston issued L/A 2/1/1808, Jackson, OM

WRIGHT, James Blue chose George Abbot and James Moore, gdns, 10/30/1815, Glynn, MIC

WRIGHT, James Nickels, decd, Eve Wright apptd admx de bonis non with LWT annexed 1/5/1804, Camden, MIC

WRIGHT, Jesse, decd, Lewis Wright, Joseph Wright petition for admn, Amos Wright, sur, 1/4/1808, Warren, MIC, AB

WRIGHT, John, decd, Joseph Davis, exr, makes retns 3/2/1812; Martha, orph, requests her mother, Alsey Wright, be apptd gdn 5/3/1813, also apptd gdn of: Cassandra and James Carr Wight, Jackson, OM

WRIGHT, John, decd, Joseph and Amos Wright, admrs, 9/21/1818, John Fontaine, sur, Warren, AB

WRIGHT, John, retn of business transacted by William Wright, gdn 10/24/1844, Bulloch, Misc

WRIGHT, Joseph, decd, Gurden Abell issued L/A 8/26/1823, James and William Harper, secs, Richmond, AB

WRIGHT, Joseph, decd, Isaiah Tucker, Daniel Culpepper, Sterling Gardner, Nicholas Flewellin and Henry Hight apptd partitioners to div est and turn over to Joseph Wright, his pt or moeity of 2/3rds of pers prop, 2/3/1812, Warren, MIC

WRIGHT, Katharine, James H. Johnson received of John Jones, gdn, legacy from est of William Wright 8/15/1844, Bulloch, Misc

WRIGHT, Lewis, decd, Solomon Lockett, Nancy Wright, admrs, 4/3/1815, Chappell Heath, Jacob Darden, surs, Warren, AB

WRIGHT, Marshall J., decd, William Wright, admr, 12/1/1862, John N. Pate, sur, DeKalb, AB
WRIGHT, Mary, decd, wid, James Gunn, planter, apptd admr 12/30/1784, Chatham, Adms
WRIGHT, Melton, orph of Isaiah, decd, bound to William A. Fuller 3 yrs to learn trade of blacksmith, 5/2/1814, Warren, MIC
WRIGHT, Milley, orph of Francis, decd, Gabriel Jones, gdn, Mason Jones, Henry Wright, sur, 4/6/1807, Oglethorpe, OM, GB
WRIGHT, Nancy, orph of William, decd, Archelaus Flewellin apptd gdn 12/2/1811, Warren, MIC
WRIGHT, Obadiah, decd, Clk ordered to issue a process against John Wright, admr 5/4/1807; Thomas Wright, sec for John Wright and Daniel Beall, in rt of wife, admrs of est, ask Thomas be excused 3/3/1812, Franklin, OM
WRIGHT, Obadiah, decd, inventory made by William Cawthon, Robert Watters, John Carter, (abt 1803) not dtd, Franklin, MIC
WRIGHT, Pleasant, decd, Meredith Wright, gdn for orphs: Nathan, David and Nancy 11/6/1837, Joshua Daniel, sec, Lincoln, GB
WRIGHT, Polly, insane, Nathan Wright, gdn 9/5/1835, Meredith Wright, sec, Lincoln, GB
WRIGHT, Rebecca, decd, LWT pvd 6/11/1818, George Abbot and James Moore, exrs, gtd leave to sell personal property, Glynn, MIC
WRIGHT, Richard, decd, David Wright issued L/A 3/3/1817, William Wright, sec, Morgan, AB
WRIGHT, Richard S., decd, R. M. Brown, admr, 2/5/1855, DeKalb, AB
WRIGHT, Sally, orph of William, decd, Archelaus Flewellin apptd gdn 12/2/1811, Warren, MIC, GB
WRIGHT, Samuel and Rebecca, decd, James B. Wright and Mrs. Mary Abbott apptd admrs 5/6/1828, Glynn, MIC
WRIGHT, Samuel chose George Abbot and James Moore, gdns, 10/30/1815, Glynn, MIC
WRIGHT, Samuel, decd, Asa Wright applied for adm 11/9/1800, apptd 6/8/1801, Johnston Wright, Blake Pearcy, sur, 11/9/1800, Warren, MIC, AB
WRIGHT, Shadrach, decd, (Capt), Nancy Wright and Abednego Wright issued L/A 10/1/1782, Zach Fenn, Wm Where, secs, Richmond, AB
WRIGHT, Thomas, decd, Samuel Wright apptd admr 1/4/1803, Camden, MIC, AB
WRIGHT, Unity, decd, of Richmond Co., (Will filed Richmond Co.) Charley Schultz, exr, 6/25/1788, Columbia, Ests
WRIGHT, William, decd, Archelaus Flewellin, Elizabeth Wright, admrs, 1/2/1809, Warren, MIC, AB
WRIGHT, William, decd, Archelaus Flewellin, admr, gtd leave to sell 320 acres on Rocky Comfort Creek, 11/7/1814, Warren, MIC
WRIGHT, William, decd, Elisha Hurt, Turner Persons, Radford Butt, Shadrach Flewellin and John C. Turner apptd partitioners to div est among heirs 12/2/1811, Warren, MIC
WRIGHT, William, decd, Henry Lane issued L/A 3/4/1822, C. Campbell, sec, Morgan, AB
WRIGHT, William, decd, LWT pvd 7/3/1839 refers to wife and several ch: Elizabeth, john and Fanny; son, William; son-in-law, Ely Futch, son, Winfield, exr, Bulloch, Misc
WRIGHT, William, decd, William Wright, Jr., acct of vouchers 9/21/1798, Hancock, AA
WRIGHT, William G., decd, Henry Lane issued L/A 5/6/1822, Ewing Morrow, sec, Morgan, AB
WRIGHT, William M., decd, Jesse C. Cobb, admr, William G. Beasley, sur, 10/30/1847, Bibb, AB
WRIGHT, William, Sr., decd, LWT pvd by James and Barber Cone 5/6/1839; Richard A. Lane, admr, made retn for 1839, 2/3/1840, Bulloch, MIC

WRIGHT, William, Sr., Richard A. Lane, exr, pays heirs-Sarah & Nancy Wright, Eli Futch, Henry M. Burnside, N. J. Dugger, John Jones & as gdn of Winfield, Wm Wright, gdn of Frances, Wm Wright, Jr. & as gdn of John, 9/10/1844, Bulloch, Misc
WRIGHT, Willis, orph of Francis, decd, Gabriel Jones, gdn, Mason Jones, Henry Wright, sur, 4/6/1807, Oglethorpe, OM, Gb
WRIGHT, Winnifred, orph of William, decd, Archelaus Flewellin apptd gdn 12/2/1811, Warren, MIC, GB
WRIGLEY, Hardyee, decd, Carolyn Wrigley, admx, T. C. Plant, sur, 12/13/1848, Bibb, AB
WYCHE, Henry, decd, Albert Wyche, Reuben Mobley, William P. Buford, admrs, 3/4/1839, Harris
WYCHE, Robert D., orph of Bartholomew, Hartwell B. Green, gdn, 9/16/1824, Thomas B. Green, William Davenport, secs, Morgan, GB
WYLER, John, decd, Thomas Simmons, admr, N. B. Beard, sur, 10/23/1847, Bibb, AB
WYLLY, Margaret, decd, St. Simons Isl, LWT pvd 11/11/1850; ch: Alexander Wm & Caroline Georgia, wf of J. Hamilton Couper; sd Couper tr for daus, Margaret, Matilda; Harriet Louisa, tr for dau, Frances Ann, wid of Dr. Wm Fraser, Glynn, MIC
WYLLY, Naomi, decd, T. R. Wylly applied for L/A 3/6/1848, Effingham, MIC
WYLLY, Thomas, Sr., his LWT was admitted to record 7/4/1846, Effingham, MIC
WYNN, John, decd, Sarah Nibb Wynn and Benjamin Wynn apply for L/A, William Roberson, sur, 7/28/1797, Warren, MIC, AB
WYNNE, Robert, decd, Clement Wynne qualified as exr 2/3/1812, Warren, MIC
YARBOROUGH, Nancy, Luke Mizel, allowed $12 for keeping her, p. 24, Screven, OM
YARBROUGH, Burrel, decd, appr 4/25/1803, Richard Fretwell, admr; purchasers at sale: Richard Fretwell, Lewis Underwood, Ephraim Rose, Hancock, AAAA
YARBROUGH, James, decd, Groves Yarbrough issued L/A 1/3/1813, Franklin, OM
YARBROUGH, James, decd, LWT pvd 1/6/1840; Robert H. Dixon, William Yarbrough, Absolom Bidell, Roland Mahone, admrs, Harris
YARBROUGH, Joel S., minor orph of Wade L., decd, James Collins, gdn, 1/9/1860, Fulton, GB
YATES, John T., decd, Samuel Jones and James Summers, exrs, 9/4/1837, Gilmer, Misc
YEARWOOD, Andrew J., decd, E. M. Compton, B. B. Little, sur, 9/5/1859, Paulding, AB
YERNOTT?, James, decd, David Payne was issued L/A 1/3/1813, Franklin, OM
YORK, James, gdn of his minor children 5/4/1835, Peter Lamar, Wm H. Norman, secs; Nelson B. York, gdn of: Lathina, Terrell, Ann, Mary, Frances, Sam and Florantine, orphs, 11/7/1835, Lincoln, GB
YOUMAN, Irene, illegitimate girl child of Sarah, John Youman apptd gdn, John North, Joseph Tifton, sur, 7/5/1835, Emanuel, GB
YOUNG, Elizabeth, orph of Richard, decd, Allen Blake, gdn 3/6/1848, Robert Sr. and Jr., secs, Hall, GB
YOUNG, Irena, orph of Richard, decd, Matthew Long, gdn, 7/7/1845, John Orr, Elisha Chamblee, secs, hall, GB
YOUNG, James, decd, Christopher Young, admr, Horatio Tatum, Adam Thompson, surs on bond, 3/5/1860, Dawson, WB
YOUNG, James A., decd, William P. McKeen issued L/A 1/4/1821, Robert McKeen, Nathaniel Truesdell, secs, Richmond, AB
YOUNG, James H., decd, Mary Young, admx w/LWT annexed, Thomas Moore, William T. Cobb, surs, DeKalb, AB
YOUNG, John, admr, to sell property, p. 57, Screven, OM

YOUNG, John, decd, Mrs. Margaret Young issued L/A 9/17/1857, Elbert, AB
YOUNG, John D., decd, Jesse Crawford was apptd admr 6/7/1824, Camden, MIC
YOUNG, Joshua wishes John Rivers, his gdn to be discharged, 1/1820, Jasper, OM
YOUNG, Mary Ann Irena, orph of Richard, decd, Lucinda Young, gdn, 1/14/1850, Elisha Chamblee, Ambrose Kennedy, secs, Hall, GB
YOUNG, Matthew T., orph of Richard, decd, Allen Blake, gdn 3/6/1848, Robert Young Jr. and Sr., secs, Hall, GB
YOUNG, Richard, decd, Robert Young, Sr., gdn of Robert C., Matthew T., Elizabeth and Emily, orphs, 5/5/1845, Robert Young Jr., Allen Blake, secs, Hall, GB
YOUNG, Samuel, minor orph of Robert, decd, Thomas Glascock, gdn, 9/4/1837, E. B. Glascock, sec, Richmond, GB
YOUNG, Sarah, James Young, gdn, p. 43, Screven, OM
YOUNGBLOOD, Ovan H., decd, Mary Youngblood issued L/A 11/7/1825, W. H. Norton, sec, Morgan, AB
ZACHARY, Bartholomew, decd, John Thurmond asks that admrs give good titles to Greene Co. land, 10/25/1802, Jackson, OM
ZACHRY, Daniel H., decd, James and Precey Zachry issued L/A 4/4/1814, Putnam, AB
ZACHRY, James, decd, of Richmond Co., LWT dtd 1/20/1789, Mary Zachry named extrx, Columbia, Ests
ZACHRY, Peter, decd, LWT pvd 2/1/1798, Mary Zachry, Thomas Walson and Thomas Ward apptd exrs, Columbia, Ests
ZANT, Joshua, decd, Mrs. Catherina Zant, relict, applies for adm 11/20/1801, Effingham, Misc
ZEIGLER, Emanuel, decd, Lewis Weitman and David Zeigler apply for leave to sell real est 1/7/1831; Christian I. Heidt and Christine, his wife, caveats appl of admrs for dismission 7/17/1829, Effingham, MIC
ZEIGLER, John George, decd, LWT dtd 3/21/1792, pvd 7/18/1796, leaves son, Emanuel Zeigler, 50 acres where he lives; to son, David Zeigler, 200 acres; wife, Anna Catherina, extrx; wit: J. G. Neidlinger, Mrs. Hannah Neidlinger, Effingha, Misc
ZEIGLER, Lucas, decd, John Waldham, admr, p. 14, Screven, OM
ZELLERS, Jacob, decd, Solomon Zellers, gdn of orphs: Catharine, Sarah and Peter, 1/21/1822, Solomon Zellers and John Guice, secs, Lincoln, GB
ZETTLER, Daniel, decd, retn of Hannah Zettler (now Mrs. Neidlinger), admx 12/14/1793. "Pd for making coffin 4/4/1784", etc., Effingham, Misc
ZETTLER, Gideon and Joseph Rahn apptd gdns of Mary, Catherine and Nathaniel Zettler, to take charge of legacy left them by decd grfather, Martin Sisson, 7/20/1801, Effingham, Misc, GB
ZILHNOW, Barnes, decd, John Guice, gdn for Jeremiah, Jonas, Nancy and Delia Guice, grandchildren of decd, 4/27/1824, Peter Gullatt, sec, Lincoln, GB
ZIMMERMAN, John Paul Godfrey, decd, Robert Sturges issued L/A 7/1/1798, Saml Scott, Wm Longstreet, Conrad Liverman, secs, Richmond, AB
ZINN, Valentine, decd, Nancy Zinn issued L/A 5/30/1827, Wm McGar, N. W. Butler, secs, Richmond, AB
ZIPPERER, Ann M., Hardy G. Pitts applies for L/A 3/30/1839, Effingham, MIC
ZIPPERER, Gideon, decd, Emanuel and Solomon Zipperer apply for adm 10/27/1827, Effingham, MIC
ZIPPERER, Jacob, orph of Gideon, decd, George Powledge apptd gdn 9/7/1829, Effingham, MIC
ZIPPERER, James, decd, Zachariah Zipperer applies for L/A 2/4/1843, Effingham, MIC

ZIPPERER, Jonathan, decd, Emanuel Zipperer applies for L/A 3/4/1834, Effingham, MIC
ZIPPERER, Solomon, orph of Gideon, decd, George Powledge apptd gdn 9/7/1829, Effingham, MIC
ZIPPERER, Sophia, orph of Gideon, decd, George Powledge apptd gdn 9/7/1829, Effingham, MIC
ZITTROUR, David, minor of William, chose father, William, as gdn 3/6/1848, Effingham, MIC
ZITTROUR, Edward, decd, Johannah Zittrour applies for L/A 12/19/1837, Effingham, MIC
ZITTROUR, Gotthief I., decd, LWT ordered recorded 5/5/1845; Edwin and Richard Zipperer have leave to sell real est 1/12/1846, Effingham, MIC
ZITTROUR, Mary Catherine, decd, David Zittrour applies for adm 7/2/1827, Bulloch, MIC
ZONDON, Mary, decd, wid, Elisha Elon of Savannah, bricklayer, petitions to be dismissed as admr 10/19/1785, Chatham, Adms
ZUBER, Mary, decd, Benjamin Smith issued L/A 9/14/1820, William Weaver, sec, Morgan, AB

Ansley, Abel 9
  Jesse 211
  Joseph 9, 125
  Ruth (Mrs.) 25
  Samuel 9
  Thomas 9
  William 9, 263
Anthony, John D. F. 10
  Joseph 35, 286
  Joseph C. 10
  Mark 10, 227
  Micajah T. 91, 298
  Milton 303
  Rosa R. 10
  Uler E. N. 10
Antony, Milton 122, 222
Apperson, James 197
Appleby, James 10
  William 217
Appleton, Sarah Jane 10
Applewhite, Elisha 76
  Elizabeth 10
  F. B. 45
  G. W. 10
  James J. 10
  Jesse 10
  John 10
  R. 259
  Robert 10, 121, 273
  Robert (Jr.) 10
  Thomas B. 114
Appling, Cornelia Ann 10
  David 268
  E. D. 10
  Edmund J. 10
  Henrietta A. J. 10
  Jane W. (Mrs.) 10
  Jno 14
  John 10
  Judith (Mrs.) 35
  M. P. 9
  Martha R. 10
  Mary 10
  Otho A. 10
  Penelope 10
  Rebecca M. 10
  Thomas K. 10
  Walter A. 10, 35
  Walter A. (Jr.) 10
  William 10
  William A. 10
  Wm 10
Appollonia Nungezer,
  Mary 179
Archer, Elizabeth Ann 20
  Harvey 20
  James 57, 65
  James K. 10
  John 298
  Labinah 298
  Labinch? 10
  Mary Ann 10
  Mary Ann (Mrs.) 298
  Penelope 10
Area, Florence 105
Arendall, John L. 10
Arline, Phereby 10
Armer, William 10
Armor, Wm 10
Armour, John 11, 137
  William 11
Armstrong, Ann (Mrs.) 11
  Dock 17
  J. H. 271
  James 11, 105
  Jesse 11
  Jesse B. 11
  John 11, 256

Armstrong (cont.)
  Martha 98
  Mary 11
  Nancy 11
  Sarah (Widow) 7, 11
  Sherman 11
  Susannah 11
  Thomas 11
  William 11, 203
Arnett, Catharine 11
  Peter 11
  Robert 11, 33
  William 11
Arnold, Charles W. 65
  John 255
  Moses 11
  Stephen 11
  Stephen (Jr.) 11
  William M. 300
Arnow, George J. 11
Arrington, (?) (Mrs.) 11
  Elizabeth 11
  Henry 11
  Robert 323
Asbury, R. R. 72
  Rufus R. R. 2
Ash, Geo Adam 11
  Hannah 11
  Hannah (Mrs.) 11
  Matthias 11
  William 258
Ashbocker, Geo Adam 11
Ashfield, Frederic 11
Ashford, Alexander W. 11
Ashley, James 324
  John 309
  Ludowick 12
  William 11, 42, 209
Ashlock, Jesse 283
Ashton, Joseph 196
Ashurst, John 102
Askew, Henry 322
  Joshua 220, 324, 327
Askey, Joshua 196
Atchison, Winnifred 12
Atkins, Asa 35
  J. H. 12
  James M. 12
  Jeremiah 12
  Sarah E. 12
Atkinson, A. C. 250
  Agrippa 93, 172
  Alexander 12, 48
  Andrew 73
  Arthur C. 253
  Cornelius 207
  E. 12
  Edmund 12, 53
  Elizabeth (Mrs.) 12
  John 12, 272
  Joseph H. 12
  Lemuel 333
  Mary Ann 110
  Mary B. 12
  Nathan 85
  Sarah 12
  Sophronia 12
  Susannah 12
  Thomas P. 12
  Washington G. 12, 92
  Winniford A. 12
Atkisson, Cornelius 12
Atwater, Elihu 3, 141,
  172, 279, 323, 345
Atwell, James 12
  John 12
  Redden 12

Atwell (cont.)
  Reuben 12
Atwood, A. G. 84
  W. H. 84
Auberry, Thomas 58
  William 58
Aubrey, Martha 12
Audulf, Henry 95
Austin, Davis 108
  James J. 190
  John C. 13, 115
  Lucinda 13
  Mary Ann (Mrs.) 13
  N. H. 13, 151
  T. F. 13
  Thomas F. 13
  William A. 13
Autrey, Alex 104
Avary, James C. 196
Avera, James A. 13
  Thomas 96
Averall, Harriet L. 13
Averat, Archibald 13
  Benjamin 13
  David (Jr.) 13
  John 13
  John (Jr.) 13
  Wm (Jr.) 13
Averell, Alfred 13
  Clara 13
  George 13
  Harriett 13
  Thomas 13
Averet, William 300
Averett, Christopher C.
  6
  Mathew 24
Avery, Elizabeth (Mrs.)
  48
  James 48
  James C. 40
  Jas 48
  Mary B. (Widow) 13
Avret, Nancy 13
Awtrey, Orlando 13
Aycock, Agnes 13
  Benjamin 13
  J. 208
  James 13
  Jesse 13
  John 13
  Juda 13
  Milton 13
  Richard 13
  Sherod 13
  Tabitha 13
  William 13
  Wm 13
Ayer, Elizabeth 218
Ayers, Abraham 291
  John 13
  Moses 247
  Obadiah 247
  Wm 247
Babcock, George W. 294
Bachlott, Alexander 14
  John 129, 312
  John (Jr.) 206, 312
  Joseph 280
  Lewis 14, 69, 259, 272
  Mary 14
Backley, Christian 14
  Hannah Margaret 14
  Jonathan 14
  Josiah 14
  Louisa M. K. (Mrs.) 14
  Mary 14
Bacon, Agnes 14

Banks (cont.)
    Simeon 182
    Simon 163, 182, 191
    Wm 73
Bankston, Abner 20
    Andrew 20
    Elijah 162
    Elizabeth 19
    Henry 19, 20, 66
    Hiram 20
    Jacob 20, 248
    James 162
    John 19
    Judy 19
    Lawrence 20
    Mary 19
    Nancy 19
    Peggy 19
    Priscilla (Widow) 20
    Sarah 19, 20
    Thomas 13
    William R. 19, 225
Barantine, Jesse 20
Barber, C. C. 20
    E. A. (Mrs.) 20
    G. 20
    George 325
    Green W. 20
    Greensby W. 20
    Holden 20
    James 9, 324
    John 223, 331
    Julia K. 20
    Mary T. (Mrs.) 20
    Matthew T. 7
    Penelope (Mrs.) 20
    Presley 20
    Robert 20
    S. A. 20
    Sarah (Mrs.) 20
    Sarah J. 20
    W. L. 20
    William 20
    William John W. 20
Barclay, Elizabeth 20
Barden, C. Arthur 20
    Gilbert 188
    Mary 1
    William 105
Barer, John 219
    Susan (Mrs.) 219
Barfield, Abi 20
    Coleman 20
    D. D. 20
    Frederick 20
    G. 304
    G. W. 20
    Guily 20
    Jemima (Mrs.) 20
    Jesse 20
    Lloyd 20
    Martha (Mrs.) 20
    Milly 20
    S. C. 20
    Samson 20
    Solomon 20, 207
    T. G. 18
    T. J. 184
Barge, Abraham 21
    Hannah 21
Barie, L. 255
Barintine, Jesse 305
Barker, Alsey B. 270
    Jeremiah 253
    Polly (Mrs.) 253
    T. R. 183
Barkley, Jane 21
    John 21, 237

Barkley (cont.)
    R. J. D. 21
    William 164
Barksdale, Alfred 246,
    317
    Elizabeth (Mrs.) 113
    Joseph 113
    Mary 21
    Mary (Mrs.) 21
    Nicholas G. 227, 279,
        297, 298
    Samuel 21
    William C. 263
Barlow, John 21, 101
    Mary (Mrs.) 21
    Richard 19, 20, 21,
        236
Barmore, Sarah A. 21
Barnady, Margaret 21
Barnard, Annie Lizzie 21
    Charles D. 21
    Daniel 14
    Frances E. (Mrs.) 21
    James 270, 303
    John 21
    Marrie 21
    Nathl L. 21
    Timothy J. 21
Barnes, A. A. 302
    Absalom 21, 22
    Absolom 49
    Andrew A. 302
    Celia (Mrs.) 302
    Davis 22
    Elijah 22
    George 22, 75, 301
    Gillod 22
    H. A. 21
    Isaac 22
    J. J. 22
    James 22, 102, 107
    Jethro H. 239
    John 22, 84
    John A. 291
    John W. 22
    Leander 22
    Leonard 22
    Mary Ann (Mrs.) 133
    Nathan 21, 22
    Permelia 22
    Priscilla 22
    Ransom 22, 57
    Thomas 22, 274
    William 37
    William L. 22
    Wm 158
Barnet, Mary (Mrs.) 22
    Samuel 22
Barnett, Eleanor 22
    Elizabeth 22
    John 22
    John F. 46
    Joroyal 22
    Leonard 22
    Nancy 22
    Nathan 22
    Sally (Mrs.) 118
    Samuel 22, 23, 94
    Thomas 215
    Thomas (Sr.) 72
    William 22, 23, 325
    William (Sr.) 72
    Wm 246
    Wm H. 23
    Wm J. 22
    Zilla 23
Barney, Job S. 100, 101,
    188, 212

Barney (cont.)
    Lyman 101
Barnheard, Rachel (Mrs.)
    332
Barnwell, Mary (Widow)
    52
    Sarah (Mrs.) 52
    William 23, 322
Baron, Nancy 75
Barr, James 17, 115
Barraugh, Edward 274
Barren, Elinor (Mrs.)
    216
    John 216
Barrett, A. M. 23, 87
    Anna M. D. 24
    Annie 23
    Benjamin 23
    D. A. 23
    Delilah 23
    Dora (Widow) 23
    Edward B. 24
    Elizabeth 23
    Erasmus 23
    Harriet 23
    Harriett 23
    Isaac 23, 118
    James L. P. 24
    James M. 23
    Jane A. H. 24
    Jno 182
    John 23
    John H. 23
    John J. 24, 25
    Juda (Widow) 23
    Keziah 23
    Kezziah 23
    Lewis 23
    Martha 24
    Mary (Mrs.) 23
    Mary L. 24
    Milley 23
    Nancy 23
    Nancy Parmelia 23
    Nathan C. 23
    Ninian 23
    Ninion 23
    Ninion (Jr.) 23
    Pamela 23
    Parmelia 23
    Patsy 23
    Poley 23
    Polly 23
    Robert 23
    Thomas 58
    Thos 18
    W. W. 23
    William L. P. 24
Barringer, John L. 24
Barrington, Celia
    (Widow) 24
    M. 24
Barron, Amanda E. 24
    Barnabas 200
    Henry 24, 166
    Jane 24
    John 24
    Joseph 24
    Margaret E. 24
    S. 61
    Sally 61
    Samuel 316
    Sarah A. 24
    Smith 24
    Susan 24
    William J. 24
    Wm 24
Barrow, Cullin 24, 145

Box (cont.)
Lemonx 61
Michael 131
Boyd, Andrew 42
Clancy O. 42
Drakeford Lee 311
Farr Harris 311
Hugh M. 42
John 42, 311
John B. 84
Levina 42
Mary (Mrs.) 311
Mary A. 42
Milky 311
Nancy 42, 311
Richard 311
Sabrey 42
Samuel 329
Susannah 42
William 42, 60
Wm 33
Boyer, James B. 175, 272
Boyet, Sabra 42
Boykin, Francis E. 24
John 233
John T. 42
Lodwick 42
Sarah 42
Boyle, Peter 2
Boynton, F. H. 127
H. 183
Hollis 18, 84, 250
Willard 334
William 207
Williard 127
Bozeman, Etheldred 206
Sarah 206
Bracewell, Burwell W.
141
James 43
Richard 67
Brack, Eleazer 153
Wm 145, 186
Bradberry, Rutha (Mrs.)
43
Braden, A. Q. 43
Bradfoot, Whatley 209
Bradford, Anne L. 43
Jno 13
Mary 43
V. 43
William 43, 313
Bradley, James C. 74
John 208
Bradshaw, Oliff 276
Shadrack 333
Woodson 333
Bradwell, Thomas 90
Brady, A. J. 129
Cullen Lewis 252
James 78
John 159
M. G. 271
Wiley G. 252
Willy Giles 252
Wylie Jiles 165
Bragg, Elijah 173
Mary (Mrs.) 272
William 66
Brailsford, Samuel 43
Bramlett, Nathan 177
Nathan N. A. 177
Bramon, Elizabeth 43
Susan 43
Branch, William 43
Brand, William 43
Brandford, Sarah Thorp
176

Brandly, R. J. 287
Branham, Henry 162
Brannen, Alexander 6
Nancy 151, 162
Thomas 171, 235
William 6, 24
Brannon, Hope 256
John 67
Brantley, Benjamin 204
James 289
John 43
Lewis 47, 74, 202
Phillip 119, 177
Zachariah 96
Braselton, Amos 260
Braston, David 24
Braswell, E. L. 237
Ephraim L. 181, 274
W. H. 36
Brawner, Elizabeth
(Mrs.) 43
John A. 43
Simeon 325
Brawton, Mary (Widow) 43
Williby 43
Bray, Benjamin B. 43
Dora 43
Elizabeth 151
George W. 274
John 145
Martha 43
Nancy 43
Richard 96, 151, 321
Sarah 43
Brazdal, Mary 43
Brazeal, Nancy 43
Willis 43
Brazel, Frederick 270
Samuel 190
Wiley 113
William T. 200
Brazell, Wiley 44
Brazelton, Elizabeth 44
John A. 44
Brazill, Frederick 270
Breedlove, John H. 44
Breton, Mary E. (Widow)
44
Brewer, Alfred 63
Burwell 44
Drewry 221
Edmond 44
Elisha 44
Horatio G. 44
Hundley 125
James (Sr.) 44
John 44, 45
John (Jr.) 44
Morgan 339
Sally 45
Sarah (Widow) 44
Thomas H. 122
William 44, 45
Wm 305
Wm B. 44
Wm. H. 44
Brewster, Jno 128
John 45
Louisa 45
Patrick 128
Patrick H. 45
Susan (Mrs.) 128
Brewton, Benjamin 10,
76, 286
Emanuel 145
Nathan (Sr.) 10, 208
Brian, Moses 302
Briant, James 318

Brickley, William H. 296
Bridge, Joel 338
Bridgeman, Ann 45
Sampson D. 325
Bridger, William F. 167
Bridges, Bayns 45
Ben. 24
Benjamin 19
Berry T. 45
James 45
Jesse 45
Jonathan 45, 129
Jonathan F. 129
Merrel 129
Merrell 45
Merril 129
Nancy 45
Nathaniel 45
Sarah 45
Susannah 45
Wiseman 45
Bridwell, Harriet 45
Martin 45
Sarah 62
Briers, Elizabeth 45
Henry H. 45
Briggs, James 311
Bright, Alexander 323
Nancy (Mrs.) 340
Brightwell, John 45
Samuel 33
William B. 285
Brincefield, Mary 45
Brinkley, J. F. 45
Brinsfield, Thomas 322
Brinson, B. C. 212
Daniel 99
Noah 45
Stephen 218
Brintle, H. G. 68, 69
Brisco, Elizabeth L. 46
Mary V. 46
Philip 46
Briscoe, John 46
Mary (Mrs.) 123
Britt, John 101
M. M. 17
Sabra J. 46
William Lawson 46
Brittain, George (Jr.)
137, 138
Britton, Emanuel 46
George 46
James 46
Jane 46
John 46
Mary (Mrs.) 46
Sanford 46
Broach, Avirilla 46
Charles 46
James 46
Jonas 141
Broadfoot, John 209
Brock, Geo 46
Hannah 46
Isaac 46
James 46
John 42, 46
John H. 344
Rebecca 46
Rebecca (Mrs.) 46
Reuben 46
Thomas 91, 100
Thos 46
Walker 46
Brockman, Elizabeth J.
46
Francis A. 46

Brockman (cont.)
James 46
James P. 46
Mary Ann S. 46
Ruthy Ann 46
Broddus, Thomas 277
Brodnax, George 290
Brogdon, G. G. 46
J. H. 49
Joseph H. 46
Bronson, Silas 274
Brook, Elizabeth 46, 80
Peter 46
Brooks, Aaron 47
Adolphus E. 210
Ann 47
Betsy 46
Charles 47
Charles A. 47
Dafner? 47
Elizabeth 47
Frances Louisa 46
George W. 253
Hiram W. 220
Isaac 147
James 47, 60, 292, 311
Job 47
Joel 47
John 46, 47
John P. 47
Lucy 46
Lultany G. 47
Lydia (Mrs.) 47
M. L. (Mrs.) 47
Martha Ann 46
Mary L. 46
Mary Virginia 46
Mathew 99
Moses 47
Nancy 46
Patsey 46
Polley 46
Posey P. 47, 244
Providence 47
Robert 61
Roger 47
Rosannah 47
Samuel 127
Stephen 33, 47
Wiley B. 46
William 47
William C. 47
Broom, William 263
Broughton, Annanias 47
Belitha 47
Charles 47
James 287
James B. 294
Nancy 47
Richard 176
Sarah (Mrs.) 176
William 47
Brown, A. E. 49
Aaron 49, 321
Abraham 49
Absolom 49
Alexander D. 117
Alexander M. 206
Allen 97, 263
Amanda 49
Andrew 253
Ann (Mrs.) 48
Ann Matilda 47
B. A. 185
B. D. 162
Bartlet 42
Benjamin 49, 113, 212,
237, 289, 290, 305

Brown (cont.)
Benjamin H. 219
Betsey 48
Betsy 48, 49
Betsy Ann 49
Butler 47
Catharine 48
Caty 49
Caty (Mrs.) 49
Clarissa 47
David 48, 49
E. J. 49
Edward 48
Edwin P. 48
Elijah 48, 49
Elisha 230, 233
Elizabeth 47, 48, 128
Elizabeth (Mrs.) 253
Emanuel 49, 234
Enoch G. 267
Frances 28, 47
Francis 246
Geo W. 48
George 48
George W. 48
Harriet (Mrs.) 263
Henry 47, 100, 196,
248
Hiram 49
Hugh 48, 303
Irwin 100, 269
Isaac 104, 155
J. B. 33
James 48, 49, 69, 120,
153, 170, 263, 331
James B. 65
James Denmark 47
James E. 294
James R. 324
James W. 345
Jas 112
Jesse 48, 142, 178
Jno 10
Jno C. 48
John 10, 47, 48, 52,
95, 119, 130, 193,
267
John E. 47, 71, 281
John R. 82
John S. 48
Joseph 5, 6, 47, 88,
97, 282, 292, 299
Joseph E. 323, 324
Julia K. (Mrs.) 20
Little Berry 47, 49
Lorenzo 49
Louise N. 47
Lucy (Mrs.) 118
Luddie 47, 50
Ludie 49
M. A. E. 48
M. L. 49
M. W. 93
Martha (Mrs.) 49
Martha A. 49
Mary 48, 97
Mary D. 49
Milley 49
Minor W. 281
Mitchell 48
Morgan 119, 263, 301
Moses 49
Nancy 119
Nathan 169
Pearson 132
Peggy 49
Peter 49
Polley 48

Brown (cont.)
Polly 47, 49
R. E. 48
R. M. 7, 19, 90, 174,
342, 346
R. S. 46
Rebecca (Mrs.) 253
Richard 230
Robert 16, 48, 49, 333
Robert A. 49
Robert M. 158, 237
Robert W. 58, 130
Robt 48
Roland 79
S. 124
S. D. 241
Saml W. 48
Samuel 48, 49, 199,
221, 281
Sarah 48
Sarah (Mrs.) 48
Sarah M. 48
Stephen 49, 179
Stephen W. 254
Sterling E. 49
Susan (Widow) 49
Thomas 48, 113, 116
Thomas A. 260
Thomas C. 49
Uriah T. 48
Vandy J. 315
W. B. 304
W. E. 49
W. G. 47
W. L. 48
W. S. 21, 22
Washington 333
William 22, 39, 97,
112, 130, 163, 164,
165, 219, 265, 294
William D. 345
William F. 49
William H. 117, 244
William L. 47
William S. 47
William W. 120
Wm 195, 218
Brownfield, Sarah 50
Browning, Andrew 188
Bunnie 50
Frances (Mrs.) 110
Francis 50
George 110
I. 324
James A. 50
John 249
Josiah 50
Lucy Ann 50
Marcellus D. 50
Margaret (Mrs.) 50
Nancy (Mrs.) 50
T. A. 109, 188
William 324
Wm 20, 50, 74
Brownlee, James 251
Broxton, James 273, 344
Bruan, William 51
Bruce, John 50, 323
William W. 40
Bruckner, J. O. 50
Brumby, Alice B. 50
Annie 50
Campbell W. 50
Hardman 50
Mary 50
Mary B. 50
McPherson W. 50
Wallis 50

Farr (cont.)
James B. 102
Lucy C. 102
Mary E. 102
Thomas J. 102
Farra, George Y. 158
Farrar, Henry H. 102
Nancy 102
Peter 10
Farrell, J. W. 211
John W. 211
Mary (Mrs.) 211
Farrow, Penny 103
Thomas 291
Faulkner, James W. 223
Nancy (Mrs.) 215
Zachariah 215
Favor, John 11
Matthew 102
Faw, E. 34
Fawley, Gates F. 142
Fealdres?, Elizabeth 230
Fears, Ann (Widow) 103
Wm 307
Zachariah 203
Fechter, Dionus 75
Fee, Elizabeth 103
George 103, 163
John 103
William 103
Felarn, George D. 333
Felder, G. D. 103
Sarah 103
Fellows, J. A. 204
Felps, Elizabeth 103
Felton, John G. 238
L. R. 171
Richard 103
Fendall, Sarah M. 103
Fendrix, Thomas 98
Fenley, Frances H. 103
John 103
John R. 103
Lucretia (Mrs.) 103
Mary Eliza 103
Nancy E. 103
Nathan L. 103
William W. 103
Fenn, Eli 250, 330
Elizabeth 103, 176
Mary 103, 139
Thomas A. 103
Travis 103
Zach 346
Fennell, Ruth 103
Ferenton, Rebecca
(Widow) 103
Ferguson, Alfred W. 103
Champion 228
Champion (Mrs.) 91
Isaac 73
Johnson 123
Johnston 273
Lewis H. 123
Rachael 103
Saml 40
Sarah 103
William 91
William H. (Sr.) 103,
104
Wm 91
Wright 46
Fernander, Mary 195
Ferrel, Cuthbert 269
William 269
Ferrell, John 80
Martin 104
Ferrington, Amanda 163

Ferrington (cont.)
Mandy 104
Nancy 104, 163
Few, B. 100
Benjamin 100, 104
Ignatius 55, 99, 104,
195, 273
Ignatius (Cpt.) 100
James 172
James (Jr.) 172
Mary 104
Thomas 328
William 157, 273
Wm (Sr.) 195
Field, Elias 104
Elijah M. 104
James H. 104
William G. 104
Fielder, George 155
James M. 2, 91, 264
John 104
Obediah M. B. 104
Terrell 104
Fielders, James M. 187
Fields, Ann (Mrs.) 104
Anna (Mrs.) 104
Cogburn 62
James H. 104
James M. 108
John H. 104
Lawson 62, 134, 238
Obedience (Mrs.) 104
Sythy 62
William G. 104
Files, David 315
Fillingim, James 68
Finch, Allen 145
Charles 104
Susannah 104
Fincher, Mary 104
Micajah 90, 91
Findley, Asa 104
Jos. H. 152
Joseph 104
Matilda (Mrs.) 104
Stephen 18, 104, 212
Finley, William 205
Finn, John 10
Finney, Jince McConel 7
Fish, George W. 105
Sarah 105
William 245
Fisher, James W. 334
Fitch, Eli 347
William D. 246, 317
Fitts, Newton M. 105
Fitzgerald, Ambrose 27
David 105
John 17, 24, 53
Michael 120
Phillip 105, 158
Silas 242
Fitzpatrick, A. 144
Alexander 116, 327
Benjamin 105, 202
Bennet 327
Bennett 202
Celia 105
Elizabeth 105
F. 244
J. 202
Jesse 316
Joseph 105, 244, 345
P. 116, 122
Phillip 105
William 277
Fitzsimmonds, Sally
(Mrs.) 105

Fitzsimmons, Henry 105
Flack, Priscilla 96
Priscilla (Mrs.) 96
Flanders, Jordan 77, 279
Fleming, Daniel H. 105
Emily 106
Emily E. 106
F. F. 38
Ferdinand 105
Francis F. 27, 105,
128
George G. 302
James 105, 106
John 38
John C. 105
John F. 106
M. M. 162
Martha 106
Nancy J. 105
Newton 106
R. A. 105
Susan 106
Thomas P. 103
William 31, 105, 106
William W. W. 187
Flemming, Royal 87
Flenniken, David 106
John 106
Samuel 106
William 106
Fletcher, C. J. 162
Christopher 316, 331
James 46
John 19, 281
John A. 83
John W. 19
L. 106
Richard 132
Richard B. 132
Winniford A. (Mrs.) 12
Flewellen, Alexander 25
Amos J. 106
Elizabeth 106
James 250
John 106
Nicholas W. 106
Flewellin, Alexander 25
Archelaus 243, 345,
346, 347
James 106, 284
Nicholas 345
Shadrach 232, 233,
243, 346
Thomas 106
Fling, John 224
Flinn, John I. 106
Thomas 230
Flint, Tarpley 194
Flippen, William 227
Flirshel, Joseph 106
Flora, Tomlinson 223
Florence, (?) (Mrs.) 106
A. J. 106
Angeline 106
B. P. 106
Lavina 106
Sophronia 106
Thomas 57, 110, 299
Zachariah 163
Flourney, Francis 240
Flournoy, Francis 181,
182
Gibson 106
John B. 106
William 1, 106
Flowers, Adaline 106
Catherine 106
Eliza 106

378

Hunter (cont.)
Priscilla W. (Mrs.)
161
Robert W. 161
Samuel S. 161
Hurst, Jesse 189
Mary 185
Stephen 191
Thomas 189
William 280, 286
Hurt, Benjamin 3, 245,
295
Elisha 346
William 96, 265
Wm 106, 167
Huse, Carter 339
Huskey, Mary 7
Huson, T. R. 134
Hustice, Henry 336
John 129
Hutchen, David Ees 91
Hutchens, Phalba (Mrs.)
100
Hutcheon, Adam 48
Hutcherson, Moses 135
Robert 85
Thomas 85, 161
Hutcheson, Adam 85, 196
Thomas 131
Hutchins, A. J. 309
Matilda 100
Thomas 100
Thos 36
Hutchinson, Adam 56
Daniel 17, 345
James G. 100
Joseph 121, 319
Nathaniel 61
Samuel B. 46
Thomas 36
William 38
Hutchison, Joseph 250
Thomas 85
Hutson, Frances H.
(Mrs.) 37
James M. 15
Hyde, Thomas 32, 271
Ingram, C. 264
Charls 344
James 306
Irvin, Benjamin 174, 212
J. J. 245
John 18
William 182
Irvine, John 16
Irwin, Davis 124
Jared 232, 246
Isom, William M. 162
Iverson, Margaret 162
Ivey, Anny 162
Elizabeth 162
H. P. 148
H. T. 162
Jeremiah 162
Levy 162
Mahala 162
Sampson 327
William 162
William F. 162
Ivie, Benjamin 162
John 162
Sally 162
Winifred (Mrs.) 162
Ivy, M. J. 309
Sampson 155
W. T. 309
Jack, Amanda Melvina 162
Elizabeth 162

Jack (cont.)
Evalina 162
James W. 162
Jane H. 162
John McCormick 162
Samuel 16, 94, 157,
176
William Dysert 162
Jackson, Amasa 184, 185,
215, 301
Asa M. 35
Barrett 145
Betsey 162
Betsey (Mrs.) 162
Carey 223
Catharine 162, 173
Catherine 168, 239
Charity 162
Charles 104, 112, 301
Charles G. 343
Daniel M. 162
David 162
Drewry W. 68
Drury 30
Edmund 162
Elizabeth 163
Elizabeth E. 343
Emanuel 103
Enoch 162
H. W. 73
Harris C. 79
Hartwell (Sr.) 68
Hellman 68
Henry 162, 343, 344
Isaac 199, 326
James 58, 126, 162,
195
James R. 217
James U. 315
Jane (Mrs.) 287
John 91, 96, 138, 162,
224
Joseph 93, 122
Laura S. 343
Levi 326
Lewis 74, 128
Littleberry 25
Littleton 162
Martha Jane 343
Mary 2, 162
Mary (Mrs.) 94
Micajah 94
Nancy 162
Peggy (Mrs.) 78
Sam 162
Samuel 162, 273, 275,
294
Samuel W. 67
Stephen 162
Thomas 53, 284
Wilkin 2
William 73, 102, 118,
210, 315, 328
William E. 7, 315, 343
William P. 113
William R. 102
Wm 109, 343
Jacksons, Judith Adams 2
Jacobs, Elizabeth C. 163
Jaillet, P. 187
Peter 105, 281
Jamerson, David 163
Matilda (Mrs.) 232
James, (?) (Maj.) 248
Caty 266
D. L. 282
Enoch 104, 163
John 192

James (cont.)
John T. 211
Joseph 192
Mary 318
Nancy A. 163
Singleton 295
W. P. 209
W. T. 115
Jameson, Sarah (Mrs.)
163
Jamieson, Archibald 204
Jamison, Madison 307
Wilkerson 307
Wm 67
Jane, Martha 224
Janes, Hilliard 154
Jangsletter, John 23
Jarnett, Hannah 163
Jarral, Willis 9
Jarrard, Jeremiah 54
Jarratt, Archibald 163
H. 31, 95
Mattie P. (Mrs.) 74
William 163
Jarrell, J. 259
Mattie Parr Dotson
(Mrs.) 74
Polly 163
William 9
Willis 79, 183
Jarrett, A. 132
H. 48, 205
James J. 162
Mary 163
Milley 163
Nathaniel 163
Patsy 163
Jay, Haysmon 256
Isaac M. 112
Jeffers, Edward G. 163
Henley S. 163
L. J. 249
Mary 163
Jeffries, Henry F. 163
Nancy 163
Jenkins, (?) 82
A. C. 164
Arthur 80
Ashford 201
Charity 164
Charles C. 163, 164
Charles D. 69
Charles J. 202
David 69, 164
Drewey 154
Drury 164
Edmund B. 161, 249
Elizabeth 163, 164
Esther 164
Francis 89
George Washington 6
Henry 163, 164
Henry M. 164
Hewey M. 281
Jesse 164
John 163, 164
Leroy 124
Lucretia 164
Martha 164
Mary 164
Mary (Widow) 164
Payton R. 6
Robert 164, 298
Royal 101
Sampson 164
Sampson (Jr.) 164
Samuel 164
Sterling 89

Jenkins (cont.)
Sterling G. 165
Thomas M. 163, 164, 166, 240
William 6, 163, 164
William C. 164
Jenning, Thomas 193
Jennings, Charles 114, 141, 165, 266, 299
Creed M. 23, 25
Henry 26, 54, 76, 78
James 38, 102, 140, 165
James J. 54
Miles 165
Nancy 165
Prudence 165
Richard 165
Robert 165
Robert H. 130
Sarah F. 165
Thomas 130
Thomas J. 165
William 238, 313
Wm 179
Jerman, Nancy 165
Jernigan, Elizabeth (Mrs.) 165
H. W. 341
Henry W. 112, 152
L. A. 187
William 165
Jessu, Elizabeth (Mrs.) 302
Jester, Abner 165, 342
Benjamin 165
Henry 165, 342
Mary 165
Nancy 165
Rosanna (Mrs.) 165
Sarah 165
Jeter, Barnett 343
Buck 135
Thomas 165
Wiley 57, 100, 165
Wm 114
Jett, Elizabeth (Mrs.) 164
James B. 102
R. B. 102
Richard B. 165
Jetton, Jane (Mrs.) 290
Joel 290
Jewell, James 165
Jane 165
Lucy Ann 160
Jinkins, Francis 165
James 165
Savannah 281
William 165
Jinks, Gale 166
Gales 166
Isaac 166
John 92
Jinnings, Allen 166
Jonathan 166
Miles 166
Solomon 166
William 166
Wm (Sr.) 166
John, Mordecai 70
Johns, Almy 166
Bartlett 9
Charles C. 166
Enoch 163, 164, 166
Griffeth 166
Jacob 166
Jeremiah 166

Johns (cont.)
Levi 166
Malinda 166
Mary 166
Susanna 6
Johnson, Abner 168
Alexandria 327
Allan (Jr.) 301
Allen E. 167, 168, 169
Andrew 225
Angus 103
Arnold 168
B. 202
Benjamin 167
Bennett S. 153
Burwell 168
Caleb 318
Catherine 169
Cephus R. 252
Charles 167, 168
Charles B. 108
Daniel 272, 327
David 218, 242
Delila (Mrs.) 169
Dorcas 169
E. M. 17, 93, 94, 200, 237, 277
Edmond 168
Elizabeth 169
Eudenia 168
G. W. 280
Harriett (Mrs.) 167
Harris 167
Hiram 168
J. A. 46
J. H. 22
Jacob 289
James 168, 169, 193, 220, 226
James (Jr.) 167
James (Sr.) 167
James C. 128
James F. 27, 127, 187, 218, 248, 275, 305, 316
James H. 345
James R. 168
James W. 109
Jasper 168
Jiley J. 70
John 167, 168, 169, 226, 308, 316
John Calvin 3
Joseph 146, 167, 169
Littleton 59, 168
M. J. (Mrs.) 167
Martha 167
Martha (Mrs.) 272
Martha J. 169
Mary Ann 168
Mary J. 169
Miles W. 70
Minor 169
Moses 108, 268
Nancy 169
Nathan 156, 169, 281, 285
Nathan Z. 169
Nicholas 169, 188, 212, 287
Patty 169
Pickins 168
Pleasant 168
Polly O. 169
Randolph 169
Rebeccah (Mrs.) 168
Richard 168
Richard (Jr.) 169

Johnson (cont.)
Robert 77, 167, 168, 226, 295
Rowland 167
Rufus M. 252
Ruthy (Widow) 169
Sally (Mrs.) 220
Samuel 57, 283
Sarah (Mrs.) 193
Seaborn A. 156, 167, 168, 251
Sibran 259
Sylvester 78
Thomas 119, 167, 325, 336
Thos. 191
Vinson 167
William 30, 32, 70, 80, 119, 159, 167, 168, 169, 186, 188, 290
William J. 109
Willis A. 169
Wm 167, 209, 328
Johnston, Abraham 194
Adam 90
Alexander 144
Chandler 170
Elisha 279
Equincy 170
Henry 169
Hiram 170
J. 206
J. M. 104
James 169, 170
James H. 170
Jamuel 328
John 11, 170
John H. 271
Joseph 16
Lancelot 113, 320
Laughlin 207
Lindsay 170
Littleton 169, 170
Marshall 170
Mary Ann 169
Posey 170
Rebekah 170
Richard 170
Rowan 169
Samuel 93, 170, 289
Seborn 169
Susan (Mrs.) 169
Susannah 169
Terrell 169
Thomas M. 194
Verlinda 169
Vincent 105
Vincent P. 64
William 14, 113, 170, 175, 249, 310
William H. 169, 170
William J. 170
Wm 80
Joiner, Asa 291
Jolly, William 170
Jones, (?) (Widow) 167
Abraham 12, 109, 118, 215, 227, 243, 311
Abrahham 73
Abram 273
Adam 17, 138, 149, 150
Allen 66, 83, 173, 315
Ambrose 9
Andrew 273
Ann 171
Ann (Mrs.) 66
Anthony 171, 174

Jones (cont.)
Arthur 171, 173
Augustus S. 174
B. O. 127
Barnabas 171, 174
Bassel 171
Benjamin 70, 167, 174, 263
Berry 171, 172, 173
Betsey 172
Betsey (Mrs.) 173
Bettey (Mrs.) 287
Bradford 92, 171
Briant 171
Bridger 171, 173
Buckner 171
C. T. 173
Charles 50
Charles A. 171, 174
Chauncy 173
Clara 172
David G. 115, 174, 216, 283
Drury 173
Dudley 116, 247
E. 173
Edward 282
Eliab 171, 255
Elijah 27, 74, 109, 304
Elijah E. 86
Elisha 174
Elizabeth 86, 172, 173
Fanny 174
Fanny (Mrs.) 170
Farewell 343
Francis 171, 172, 173, 293
Gabriel 345, 346, 347
George 81, 172
George H. 255
H. P. 171, 174
Hannah 170
Harley 172, 173
Harriet 173
Harris 174
Harrison 173
Hartwell 296
Henley 27
Henry 135, 171, 172, 173
Henry (Jr.) 170, 174
Hugh 213
Hugh (Sr.) 174
J. E. 173
J. L. 195
Jabez 237, 336, 337, 338, 339
James 20, 161, 163, 164, 171, 172, 173, 176, 177, 181, 219, 297, 313, 315
James J. 174
James M. 174
James O. 148
Jesse 173
John 115, 170, 172, 173, 174, 222, 343, 344, 345, 347
John (Jr.) 273
John E. 202, 203, 306
John H. 191
John W. 222
Jones 343
Joseph 172, 174
Joseph L. 173, 201
Joshua 174, 344
Josiah 171

Jones (cont.)
Levicy 171, 174
Lewis 134, 266
Lucy Matilda 171
Lydia 172
Lydia (Mrs.) 172
Malachi 295
Martha 172, 174
Marthy Ann (Mrs.) 302
Mary 172, 174, 324
Mary (Widow) 174
Mary D. (Mrs.) 174
Mary F. 321
Mary H. 171
Mary H. (Mrs.) 248
Mason 173, 174, 321, 346, 347
Mathew 306
Matthew 173
Medium 174
Michael 173
Moses 162, 170, 173
Nancy 171, 172, 174
Nathan 171, 217, 287
Nathaniel 171
Nicholas H. 142
Phalba (Mrs.) 100
Polley 172
Polly 172
Priscilla (Mrs.) 17
Rachel (Mrs.) 171, 172
Randolph 345
Rebecah 171
Rebecca 115
Rebecca (Mrs.) 340
Rebecca J. 174
Reuben 231
Reubin 222
Richard 174
Richard H. 174
Robert 59, 73, 172, 173, 174, 274, 275, 290
Russel 162
Russell 116, 243
Sally 174
Samuel 109, 172, 173, 174, 260, 347
Sarah 174
Sarah A. 174
Sarah M. (Mrs.) 173
Sarah R. 128
Seaborn 66, 68, 170, 172, 174, 238, 335
Seaborn A. H. 164
Sinar 174
Smith 324
Stanby 172
Standley 5
T. M. 127, 159
Thomas 83, 122, 139, 171, 172, 173, 174, 192, 229, 230, 253, 265, 289, 342
Thomas H. 300, 303
Thomas L. 173
Tignal 171
Toliver 63, 127, 170, 256
Tolliver 173
W. P. 210
William 1, 75, 76, 100, 172, 174, 321
William E. 92, 173
William H. 213
William J. 174
Willie 226
Willis 134

Jones (cont.)
Wm 128, 198, 293, 334
Wm B. 173
Jordan, Abner 308
Britton 175
Burrell 175
Chas. 188
Francis (Widow) 175
George 204
George W. 175
Henry 175
Isham 175
James 69, 231, 257, 279
John A. 113
John C. 299
John W. 308
Jorden 175
Josiah 47
Junius 313
Lizia 175
Reuben 175
William 183
William A. 113, 217
Joseph, Dennis 330
Gainey 326
Josey, Malachi 147
Wilson 147
Jourdan, Benjamin L. 175
John W. 72
Jourden, Amasa 175
Benjamin G. 175
Reuben 175
Thomas 175
Jowers, James 2
William P. 175
Wilson 175
Joyce, Washington 175
William 175
Juhan, Frances F. 234
J. A. 131, 154
Julian A. 154
N. S. 131
Nathaniel S. 154
Juie, John 159
Jurdine, William 175
Juskey, Elizabeth 7
Justice, Bivin 26
Levi 176
Thomas 26, 135
Justus, Henry 176
Polly 176
Kain, Amanda 176
Eugenia (Mrs.) 176
John 176
Patrick 176
William 176
Karr, Peter 228
Keall, Henry 51
John 176
Kean, William H. 117
Keating, Richard T. 176
Keebler, Joshua (Jr.) 176
Rosanna (Mrs.) 176
Keeling, Leonard 176
Keelough, John 176
Keen, John 163, 164
Keener, William 176
Keiffer, Ephraim 100
Reuben 176
Keith, Allen 68, 176
Jasper L. 29, 68, 71, 72, 114, 131, 159, 162, 176, 188, 262, 277
M. A. 72, 176, 188
M. Anderson 277

399

McCleskey, D. M. 80
David H. 205
J. H. 205
James J. 338
James R. 205, 341
Jas J. 93
Jas M. 93
Sally 205
McClesky, William D. 205
McCloud, Danl 84
McClung, Samuel B. L. C. 205
McClure, John 189
John A. 205
Robert N. 205
McClurg, Nathaniel 265
McClusky, James 301, 302
McCollough, Charley 42
McCollum, Daniel A. 96
Daniel H. 205
George 198
John B. 336
Margery 205
McComb, James R. 342
McConnay, Ruth (Widow) 205
McConnel, Elizabeth (Mrs.) 80
James 272
Joshua 80
McConnell, Eli 90, 133, 299
Henry B. 133
James 90, 212
John 90, 314
Joseph 29
Joshua 296
Manuel 92
P. W. 87
Samuel M. W. 45
Telford 87
McConner, John 247
McCoombs, John 206
Robert 57, 113, 179
McCord, (?) (Mrs.) 197
Elisha 211, 291
J. R. 65, 189, 264
J. W. 189, 264
James 38, 206, 291
James R. 7, 9, 19, 68, 74, 89, 180, 203, 206, 264, 287, 324
John 89, 205, 207, 211, 265, 339
John W. 19, 68, 180, 287, 324, 336
Nancy 206
Polly 206
Robert 206
McCork, John W. 305
McCorkel, James 285
McCorkle, James 291
McCormack, H. L. 54
James 231
Jas 77
Joseph 324
Peggy (Mrs.) 324
McCormich, John 304
McCormick, Abner 181
Daniel 190
George 182
James 231, 232, 259
John 231
Joseph 60
McCowan, Daniel 192
McCowen, Duncan 139
Fenlow 46
John W. 206

McCowen (cont.)
Noble 206
William 206, 213
William D. 206
McCoy, Abi (Mrs.) 20
Charles 294
Elijah 206, 299, 330
Elizabeth 206
Elizabeth (Mrs.) 206
James 147
James (Jr.) 68
Jane 206
John 147, 206, 239, 258, 330
Neilly 25
Thomas 14, 101
Wm 187
McCracking, Sarah (Mrs.) 82
McCrady, Silas M. 210
McCrary, J. W. 58
John 27
Lettice 206
R. H. 206
Samuel 206
McCravey, M. W. 244
McCravy, David S. M. 301
McCrea, Moses 283
McCredie, Andrew 282
McCree, Benjamin 22
William 204
McCrery, John 206
McCrimmon, Archibald 226
Charles 226
Danl 206
McCrimson, Catherine 206
Charity 206
Charles 212
Chas 206
Geo W. 206
John 206
Nancy 206
McCrory, John 206
Rachel (Mrs.) 206
McCullars, Amy (Widow) 206
Malacah 206
Rachel Wilder 206
McCullarson, Joseph 342
McCuller, Coleson 182
Dicey (Mrs.) 75
Penelope (Widow) 207
Saml 75
McCullers, Dilcy (Mrs.) 75
Dudley 207
Hiram 207
John 281, 330
Matthew 207
Ridley (Mrs.) 207
McCulloch, Charles 315
James 279
Jas 31
McCullock, Charles 207
Jno 239
Samuel 207
McCullough, Andrew 245
John 245
Samuel 207
McCune, Elizabeth 207
James 207
James A. 104, 138, 166, 207, 287
John N. 204
Micajah F. 207
Nancy 207
Peggy 207
Rufus 16, 138

McCune (cont.)
Rufus W. 287
Thomas B. 207
William 207
William A. 207, 223, 317
McCurdy, David 59
George R. 118
John 207, 317
McCurry, Angus 207
John 207
McCutchen, Samuel K. 23
William 133
William W. 133
McCutcheon, Robert B. 207
McDade, John (Jr.) 6
Thomas 281
McDaniel, Edmund 29
H. W. 247, 325
Henry W. 83
James 174
John 123
John H. 165, 193
Martin R. 29
Mary (Widow) 104
W. L. 251
William 24
McDavid, John 180
McDill, Newton 200
McDonald, Alexander 2
Alexander H. 288
Anner 2
Charles 110
Charles James 2
Charles M. (Jr.) 110
Donald M. 219
Elizabeth 2
Ella D. 110
Gillis 209, 235
James 124, 319
John 60, 207
M. S. (Mrs.) 56
Mary (Mrs.) 2
McDougald, Alexander 208
Miles E. 208
Sarah 208
McDoughal, Alex 220
McDowall, Patrick 209
McDowell, (?) 208
Daniel 198, 249
James 152, 344
John 174
Martha 208
Thomas 208, 212
William 40
Wm 256, 327
McElhaney, William 133
McElroy, Charles 208
John 208
Pelatia 208
Samuel 208
McElveen, Margaret 208
Susan 208
Susan Catharine 208
Wm 208
McElvey, George R. 84
McElvin, Margaret 208
Susan Catharine 208
William 208
McElween, Susannah 208
McEny, John 127
McEver, Brice 298
McEwen, A. D. 52
Alexander 137, 138
McFall, James W. 48
McFarland, Edward 105
John B. M. 212

Morse (cont.)
  Josiah 187, 278
Morton, Betsey (Widow)
    87
  E. L. 36
  Emily 227
  Joel 227
  John 46
  Joseph F. 23, 227
  Josiah 227
  L. B. 281
  Lemuel B. 211
  Olympia Muse 227
  William 227
  Wm 227
Moseley, Benjamin 227
  Jane 227
  Jesse 173
  John E. 22
  William R. 332, 333,
    334
Mosely, Elisha 45
  William R. 332
Moses, Ann 227
  John 115
  Meredith 227
  Neale 227
  Neil 227
  Robert 78
  Robt (Sr.) 234
  Samuel 227
Mosley, John 250
  Peter 47
  Sally Brown 47
Moss, Alexander 227
  Archer 227
  Clammy 227
  David M. 227
  Elizabeth M. 227
  Fanny 227
  Felix 46
  Henry E. 227
  James 227
  Jane E. 227
  John 227, 298, 321
  Mary 227
  R. D. 213
  Richard P. 227
  Sarah S. 227
  Susannah 227
  Warren R. D. 227, 228
  William Willis 227
  Wm 299
Mosses, John 227
  Samuel 227
Mote, Abel 227
  David 227
Motes, Zachariah 121,
    280, 302, 336
Mothershed, Isaac L. 109
Mott, Hiram 126
  William A. 228
Moulder, Abraham 228
  Ann Mitchel 228
  Catharine (Mrs.) 228
  Catharine Mitchel 228
  Daniel 228
  Elizabeth 228
  Jacob 228
  Lewis 228
  Mary 228
  Sarah 228
Moye, Allan 252
  Allen 225
Mozingo, Giles 202
Muckleroy, Harry 329
Muir, William 205
Mulinax, Caroline H. 228

Mulkey, Elizabeth 228
  Lavonia 228
  Sarah 228
Mullett, Jeremiah 228
Mullin, John 224
Mullins, Henry 321
  Jesse 289
  Matthew 289
  Nancy Ann 228
  W. F. 252
  William F. 96, 222,
    228
Mumford, Robert 133
Munday, Almyra 105
  Andrew J. 172
  Edward W. 326
Mundy, A. J. 298
  Andrew J. 186
  Reuben T. 186
Munro, Milla (Mrs.) 155
Munroe, E. V. 269
  Neill 146
Murdock, Allen A. 228
  Allen H. 228
  Jeptha F. 228
  Joseph 228
  Priscilla 228
  Priscilla (Mrs.) 228
  Wm P. 83
Muren, James 314
Murphey, Andrew 228
  C. 2
  E. M. 228
  Edmund 228
  Jeptha M. 228
  John 228, 313
  Joseph H. 228
  Rebecca (Mrs.) 228
  Thomas E. 228
Murphy, Daniel 275
  Elizabeth 229
  Francis 229
  James 143
  John 60, 70, 111, 229
  Lemuel M. 141
  Martha (Mrs.) 48
  Mary 229
  Nicholas 156
  Paschal 141
  Peggy (Mrs.) 66
  Peter 116
  Thomas H. 228
  William 229
  Williamm 48
Murrah, Thomas 101
Murray, Alex R. 22
  John 11, 22, 121, 229
  Thomas J. 321
  Thomas W. 321
Murren, James 22
Musgrove, Harrison 332,
    334
Musselwhite, Thomas 277
  William 229
Musslewhite, Sarah L.
    229
Myers, Elizabeth 298
  Hannah N. 68
  James 230
  John G. 260
  John W. 229
  Priscilla 298
  William 308
Myhan, John 206
Myhand, Alvan 206, 230
Myres, Thomas 230
Myrick, Elizabeth 230
  Howell 230

Myrick (cont.)
  John 142, 243, 325
  John (Jr.) 230
  Josiah 230
  Martha 230
  Nathaniel 230
  Richard 230
  William 230
Nabb, William B. 330
  William D. 126
Nabors, William 58
Nail, (?) (Cpt.) 325
  Mary (Widow) 230
Nall, James 104, 230
  John 104, 230
  Martin 230
  Richard 230
Nally, Cleon 226, 230
  Mary 230
Nance, Fleming R. 223
Nancy, H. W. 230
Nap, Charity 139
  James 139
  Patsey 139
Napier, Dorothy (Mrs.)
    230
  John 54
  Lydia 230
  Thomas 13, 73
Napper, Absalom 231
Narramore, Eli W. 1
Nash, Abraham 216
  Emaline (Mrs.) 302
  Frances (Mrs.) 302
  Henry 231
  J. H. 335
  T. E. 335
  William 231
Nations, Hester 231
  Martha J. 80
Neal, Alexander 231
  Ann Olivid 231
  Benjamin 235
  David 231, 232
  Frances 231
  Jacob 231
  James 134, 231, 272,
    276
  James (Jr.) 231
  James (Sr.) 108, 305
  Jesse Horatio 231
  Joel 259, 330
  John 96, 231
  John Wesley 231
  Joice (Mrs.) 231
  Judith 231
  Julia (Mrs.) 231
  Kesiah 231
  Mary Jane (Mrs.) 231
  Obadiah 231
  Patty 231
  Rebecca (Widow) 231
  Richard 231
  Samuel 232
  Tabia 231
  Thomas 231
Nease, Frederick I. 53
  George 232
Neaves, John 232
Neel, Daniel 232
  Elizabeth 232
  Hezekiah 232
  John 232
  John C. 126
  John R. M. 325
  Mary 232
  Mitchel 131
  Reuben 321

Pate (cont.)
  Sterling J. 143
Patrick, Churchwell 171
  Ezekiel 246
  Hugh 247
  Jeremiah B. 246
  John 157
  Joshua C. 246
  Middleton 155
  Milligan 267
  N. 312
  Ollive 246
  William 49
Patten, James 315
  Samuel 208
Patterson, Ann (Widow)
    246
  Arthur 246
  Charles J. 287
  David 207, 285
  Elizabeth 246
  Ida E. (Mrs.) 302
  James 257
  James P. 246, 258
  John 79
  Josiah 246
  Lydia (Widow) 246
  Maria 246
  Mary 246
  N. J. (Jr.) 152
  Sally (Mrs.) 52
Pattillo, David 246
  James 246
  John R. 246
  John V. 246
  Rebecca 246
  Samuel 246
  Sarah 246
  Swinnie? 246
Patton, Jane (Widow) 246
  M. M. 303, 304
  Martha 241
  Robert S. 246
  Samuel 56, 166, 231
Paul, James 281
Paulett, Harry 246
  Jesse C. 291
Paxton, John 276
Payne, Ann 247
  Benjamin 30
  Champness 247
  Charles 247
  Cleveland 247
  David 347
  Elijah 294
  Elizabeth 247
  Isaac B. 46, 138
  Margaret 320
  Mary 247
  Moses 247
  Nancy 247
  Nathaniel 247
  P. 343
  Payndexter 247
  Paynedexter 247
  Reuben 307
  Ruth 247
  Samuel 138, 247
  Samuel (Jr.) 138
  Shrewsberry 48
  Shrewsbury 247
  Thomas 247
  William 247
  Yannaky (Mrs.) 247
  Zabadiah 247
Peacock, Asa P. 45
  Avey (Mrs.) 247
  James 295

Peacock (cont.)
  James T. 247
  John (Jr.) 31
  Lewis 114, 247
  Michael 247
  William 247
  Peak, Judith 247
  Mitchel 232
  Peake, John 9
  Pean, Lemuel 248
  Pearce, Elijah 114
    Stephen W. 248
    Susannah 248
  Pearcy, Blake 346
    John L. 119
  Pearis, Catherine (Mrs.)
      239
    Richard 239
  Pearley, Jarrel 102
  Pearman, Samuel 49
  Pearre, Eli 149, 150
    James 82, 139, 252,
      308
    James (Jr.) 341
    James (Maj.) 248
    James (Sr.) 341
    John O. 82
    Massee 248
    Nathaniel 248
    Nathl 82
  Pearson, Arabella 248
    Enoch 212, 329
    George 107, 113, 120,
      179, 192, 221, 234,
      281, 296, 320
    Jeremiah 77, 250
    John M. 103, 165, 212
    Leona 248
    Lucy M. 248
    Mary H. 248
    Randolph 289
    Sarah (Mrs.) 248
    William H. 42
    Wm H. 212
  Peason, Arabella L. 248
  Peavy, Aabram 248
    Thomas 335
  Peddy, Bradford 200
    Henry 148, 149, 150
    Henry (Jr.) 148
    William 119
  Pedsian, Samuel 24
  Peek, David 247
    John 206
    John C. 94, 304
    Julius 23
    Leonard M. 165, 248
    Solomon W. 205
  Peel, Eliza Ann 275
    J. M. W. 202
    James G. 249, 268
    John 248
    John M. W. 248
    Polley 275
    Thomas F. 248
  Peeples, Benjamin 249
    Benjamin M. 100, 191,
      196, 248
    David 248, 276
    Dudley 249
    Elizabeth 248
    Frances 249
    Hinsy 262
    John 248
    Joseph 249
    Matilda 248
    Nathan 248, 276
    Rebekah 248

Peeples (cont.)
  Rebekah (Mrs.) 248
  Pegg, Samuel G. 88
  Pemberton, Alton 289
    Hatton H. 171
    Mary H. (Mrs.) 171
  Pender, John 249
  Pendleton, Daniel 249
    Eidson Davis 249
    Nathl 108
  Pendry, Mary 249
  Penn, Thomas H. 130
    William 85
  Pennell, Jonathan 135
  Penney, Isaac M. 59
  Pennington, Isaac 267
    John 67, 262
    John L. 262
    Thomas 193
    Thos. 27
  Penny, John W. 249
    Milly 249
  Perdieu, Ann 249
  Perin, Nathaniel 101
  Perkins, James 45
    John C. 249
    L. M. 333
    Malissa 249
    Moses 53, 227
    Mosses 227
    Nancy 249
    Newton J. 227, 228,
      338
    Reuben 249
    Sabra 303
    Sally 249
    Sarah 128
    Thomas J. 309
    W. 80
    Wm 249
    Wm H. 188
    Wm R. 249
    Zeno 249
  Perkinson, John D. 47
    Thomas D. 1
    Thomas N. 272
    Wm 1
  Perkle, Elijah 82
    Jacob 82
  Pernell, Henry 250
  Perritt, Agnes 147, 250
  Perry, Abner 252
    Agnes 250
    Ezekiel 281
    George B. 219
    H. J. 59
    Isaac 247, 315
    James 250, 283
    John 175, 249
    John G. 135
    Joseph T. 250
    L. F. 250
    Mary A. 250
    Susannah (Mrs.) 155
    William L. 182
    Willis 17
  Perryman, Daniel 250
    David 235, 250, 298
    Dixon 317
    E. 199
    Harmon 317, 342
  Person, John 192
  Persons, A. 319
    Amos 319
    Amos J. 250
    G. W. 250
    Nicholas 250
    Rachel (Mrs.) 250

409

417

431

www.ingramcontent.com/pod-product-compliance
Lightning Source LLC
Chambersburg PA
CBHW050557270326
41926CB00012B/2090